OLD
TESTAMENT
EXPLORER

ALSO BY EUGENE H. MERRILL

An Historical Survey of the Old Testament

Deuteronomy

1 and 2 Chronicles

Haggai, Zechariah, Malachi

Kingdom of Priests: A History of Old Testament Israel

*Qumran and Predestination: A Theological Study
of the Thanksgiving Hymns*

ALSO BY CHARLES H. DYER

Essays in Honor of J. Dwight Pentecost (editor)

Integrity of Heart, Skillfulness of Hands (coeditor)

The Christian Traveler's Guide to the Holy Land (coauthor)

The Power of Personal Integrity

The Rise of Babylon

World News and Bible Prophecy

SWINDOLL
LEADERSHIP
LIBRARY

OLD TESTAMENT EXPLORER

Discovering the Essence, Background, and Meaning of Every Book in the Old Testament

CHARLES DYER & GENE MERRILL

CHARLES R. SWINDOLL, *General Editor*

ROY B. ZUCK, *Managing Editor*

WORD PUBLISHING
NASHVILLE
A Thomas Nelson Company

THE OLD TESTAMENT EXPLORER
Swindoll Leadership Library

Published in association with Dallas Theological Seminary (DTS):
General Editor: Charles R. Swindoll
Managing Editor: Roy B. Zuck
The theological opinions expressed by the authors are not necessarily the official
position of Dallas Theological Seminary.

Library of Congress Cataloging in Publication Data:

Dyer, Charles H. 1952–
The Old Testament explorer : discovering the essence, background, and meaning of
every book in the Old Testament / by Charles Dyer & Gene Merrill.
p.   cm.—(Swindoll Leadership Library)
Includes index.

ISBN 0-8499-1447-7
1. Bible. O.T.—Commentaries. I. Merrill, Gene. II. Title. III. Series

BS1151.2.D94   2000   00-058653
221'.7–dc21   CIP

Printed in the United States of America
01 02 03 04 05 06 BVG 9 8 7 6 5 4 3 2 1

CONTENTS

Foreword VII

Preface IX

Acknowledgments XI

Genesis: In the Beginning: Foundations of Our Faith 1

Exodus: Deliverance to Covenant Privilege 39

Leviticus: Handbook on Holiness 71

Numbers: Pilgrimage to Covenant Possession 95

Deuteronomy: Covenant Faith Reaffirmed 127

Joshua: Conquest: The Ideal versus the Real 159

Judges: Anarchy versus Divine Sovereignty 179

Ruth: God's Surprising Grace 197

1 Samuel: The Movement toward Monarchy 203

2 Samuel: The Davidic Promise and Prospects 225

1 Kings: The Slippery Slope to National Ruin 245

2 Kings: Destruction and Deportation 269

1 Chronicles: Israel's History from a Global Perspective 293

2 Chronicles: The House of David: An Uncertain Future 315

Ezra–Nehemiah: Building a New Community of Faith 341

Esther: Help from a Hidden Source 365

Job: Resting in the Mystery of God 375

Psalms: Human Response to Divine Presence 403

Proverbs: Practical Guide to Peaceful Living 481

Ecclesiastes: The Man in the Street 503

The Song of Solomon: An Earthly Model of Heavenly Love............. 511

Introduction to the Prophets 517

Isaiah: Judgment and Deliverance from the Holy One of Israel 523

Jeremiah: God's Judgment on Judah's Sin 589

Lamentations: The Sorrow of Sin 645

Ezekiel: The Glory of the Lord 657

Daniel: God's Kingdom and the Times of the Gentiles 699

Hosea: God's Love for His Adulterous Wife 721

Joel: The Coming Day of the Lord... 737

Amos: Prepare to Meet Your God 745

Obadiah: God's Judgment on the Pride of Edom 765

Jonah: God's Concern for the Gentiles 771

Micah: A Just God Requires a Just People 779

Nahum: God's Destruction of Nineveh...................................... 795

Habakkuk: A Life of Trust in Troubling Times 803

Zephaniah: The "Day of the Lord" for Jerusalem 807

Haggai: Rebuilding God's House 813

Zechariah: The Lord Remembers 819

Malachi: God's Messenger 833

Bibliography.. 843

FOREWORD

*I*n our "plastic age" quality workmanship seems to have drifted out of style. Today items are mass produced and shipped into and out of the country. Assembly lines and automated robotics manufacturing has replaced detailed handcrafted items. Do you, like me, smile and enjoy the moment when you see an original piece of work which has the mark of the skilled craftsman written all over it?

Show me the fruit of a laborer who strives diligently to do his or her best, and I'll show you a store with no lack of customers. Does it take time? Absolutely. But what really worthwhile activity doesn't? How long does it take to make a Nike Air-Jordan basketball show? About two days. How long does it take to make a Michael Jordan? Over two decades. Are there lots of Jordan shoes? Yes. In fact I'm told they are bestsellers. Are there lots of Michael Jordans? Last time I checked there was only one.

Precision craftsment need good tools. And in this book you have a sharp, multipurpose tool created by two experts. Drs. Gene Merrill and Charles Dyer have put together a volume that will be of great help to you in your study of the Old Testament. Merrill and Dyer don't take scholarship lightly, and it shows. We've all seen brief overviews of both the Old and New Testaments. No doubt, they are helpful if you're in a hurry. But those of us who are mining at deeper levels need a stronger drill bit with a sharper, precision point. *The Old Testament Explorer* will take you deeper.

The subtitle alone should alert the serious Bible student of things to come: *Discovering the Essence, Background, and Meaning of Every Book in the Old Testament.* No portion of the Old Testament is taken lightly or overlooked. Areas of archaeology, theology, authorship, and meaning are all probed.

Both of these professors are classroom teachers. In other words, their material has been hammered out on the anvil of numerous question-and-answer sessions from serious inquirers. Also they both love the land of Israel and are frequent travelers to the land they love and write about. Both have been on archaeological digs and have led tours to the Holy Land. Thus what they offer is firsthand information, the best kind. And Merrill and Dyer are convinced that the Scriptures are God-breathed and inerrant.

The volume you're holding is a unique effort of scholarship shaped by two expert craftsmen who have spent many years finely honing their gifts and cultivating their skills. This is no quick-read paperback. *The Old Testament Explorer* will be used by pastors, lay leaders, educators, students, and others. I believe that you will soon discover the quality I have come to expect and admire from these two faithful stewards.

My prayer for you is that your service for the Lord will rise to the same standard these two men have modeled and that your efforts will be done for the same purpose, to bring glory to God.

—CHARLES R. SWINDOLL
General Editor

PREFACE

*M*arco Polo
Christopher Columbus
Ferdinand Magellan
Lewis and Clark
Edmund Hillary

What do these men have in common?

Each one was an explorer!

Whether crossing the wastelands of central Asia, sailing around the world, climbing over the Rocky Mountains to the Pacific Ocean, or scaling the world's highest mountain, each of these adventurers was driven by the urge to discover, to explore something he had never seen before.

Studying the Scriptures can be an exhilarating adventure too. Exploring, discovering, traversing, analyzing, and probing—that's the essence not only of famous world explorers of previous years, but also of pondering the Bible.

Marco Polo, Columbus, and Lewis and Clark may have often puzzled over their surroundings. Where were they? What was the significance of what they saw? How unique were the marvels they discovered?

Similarly in Bible study we are often perplexed by what we read in God's Word. What does this phrase mean? How does this group of verses fit the verses around it? How does this chapter relate to the flow of the book? What is the uniqueness of this Bible book in relationship to other Bible books?

These are some of the questions *The Old Testament Explorer* seeks to answer for you. Whether you are preparing a Sunday school lesson, putting together a sermon for Sunday morning, or reading the Bible devotionally for your own soul's edification, the *Explorer* can help guide you as you study the Old Testament.

Not a detailed word-by-word commentary, nor a concise Bible hand-book, the *Explorer* discusses each paragraph of each Old Testament book, showing how each human author, guided by the Holy Spirit, developed a single purpose in his book point by point. The introductory pages on each Bible book include material on the author, date, purpose, theological emphases and/or special characteristics, and an outline. Along the way biblical principles and points of application are highlighted, helping you see how the Scriptures relate to life.

A bibliography at the end of the volume lists books recommended for further study in each Old Testament book.

Eugene H. Merrill and Charles H. Dyer are experienced expositors of the Bible, with emphasis on the Old Testament. Dr. Merrill wrote the *Explorer* material on Genesis through Song of Solomon, and Dr. Dyer wrote on Isaiah through Malachi.

Like a compass to a hunter or a map to a traveler, may this volume help guide you as you explore the Scriptures, God's inerrant—and richly relevant—Word.

—ROY B. ZUCK
Managing Editor

ACKNOWLEDGMENTS

Eugene H. Merrill

I find particular delight in contributing to a series bearing the name Swindoll because that name conjures up immediate association with such traits as creativity, practicality, and integrity. I trust that my part in this endeavor will model those hallmarks of the Swindoll style.

With customary thoroughness and dedication to detail, my editor, Roy B. Zuck, has assisted me in making my work much better than it otherwise would have been. His editing has added much to the readability of the finished product.

To have coauthored this volume with Charles Dyer has brought its own challenge to move beyond the mediocre because Dr. Dyer sets a high standard. I am delighted to have my name linked with his in this manner.

As always, my wife, Janet, has put up with my frequent neglect of other duties because of my preoccupation with a project such as this whose full dimensions are not always initially clarified. I am grateful for her forbearance and support.

Charles H. Dyer

I am deeply grateful to Dr. Charles R. Swindoll for the privilege of participating in this project and for the years we have labored together in the president's office at Dallas Seminary.

I also extend heartfelt thanks to Dr. Roy B. Zuck for his editorial expertise and for his friendship. He edits with his pen held in the iron fist of a disciplined taskmaster and covered with the velvet glove of a humble servant of Jesus Christ.

I thank God for the support of my wife, Kathy, and for our children, Ben and Becky. They are God's precious gift to me and I deeply love them all.

I dedicate my portion of this book to my brother-in-law, Dr. Doug Lyon, who shares my dedication to Christ, my commitment to the Word of God, and my passion for sharing that Word with others.

GENESIS

In the Beginning: Foundations of Our Faith

AUTHOR

*T*HE BOOK OF GENESIS recounts events centuries before Moses' birth and never directly asserts Mosaic authorship. On what basis, then, can the ancient tradition that Moses wrote the book be sustained? Four answers may be given.

First, the fact that the last event of the book, namely, Joseph's death and burial, took place at least 275 years before Moses arrived on the scene (around 1525 B.C.) is no impediment to Moses' authorship of Genesis, for historians almost always write of persons and movements that long preceded them. Moses, too, did this, we believe, in dependence on oral and written sources available to him. The great events of ancient times would certainly have been recalled, recited, and transmitted orally from one generation to the next. Moses would have had access to this rich legacy. As for documents, many conservative scholars believe that the term "generations" found at a number of critical junctures in Genesis (2:4; 5:1; 6:9; 10:1; 11:10, 27; 25:12, 19; 36:1, 9; 37:2), refers to documents, that is, written texts preserved from earlier times. Since such records are commonly attested to in the ancient Near Eastern world, one can hardly make a case against their use in Israel.

Second, the fact that Genesis does not specifically state that Moses wrote the book is of no serious consequence, for it was common in ancient times for works to be composed anonymously. Also many of the Old Testament writings besides Genesis are without internal clues as to authorship. For example, 1 and 2 Kings, composed by Jeremiah according to Talmudic tradition, contain no hint as to the identity of the person who wrote them.

Third, the close connection between Genesis and Exodus, whose authorship is attributed to Moses (Exod. 15:1; 17:14; 24:4; 34:27), leads to the conclusion of common authorship. For example, the Hebrew name of Exodus is *we'ēlleh*, "now these." The fact that the book begins with a conjunction suggests it is the continuation of a previous work, namely, Genesis. Moreover, Exodus 1:1–7 recapitulates the account of Jacob's sons given in Genesis 46:8–27, thereby providing a literary/thematic bridge.

Fourth, the testimony of the New Testament is unambiguous on the matter of the authorship of Genesis. Jesus spoke of Moses implicitly and explicitly as its composer (Matt. 19:3–12; John 7:22–23) and so did the apostles and their Jewish antagonists (Acts 15:1). These witnesses alone should be sufficient in settling the matter in favor of Moses as the inspired penman of the book of beginnings.

UNITY

The unity of the Book of Genesis is related to the question of its authorship and dating. The same spirit of rationalism that denies the Mosaic authorship of Genesis views the book as a collection of documents attributed to unknown sources designated as Elohistic (E), Jahwistic (J), Priestly (P), and Deuteronomistic (D). In its present form this source-critical approach dates the book to the postexilic period (about 450 B.C.), though it concedes that the "J material" may in part be as early as Solomon's time (950 B.C.).

The basis for such an understanding of Genesis (and the Pentateuch as a whole) are (a) the use of different divine names (Elohim and Jahweh/Yahweh) in different sections; (b) the occurrence of alleged contradictions or, at least, duplications from one part to the next; and (c) evidence of religious development within the book. According to Julius Wellhausen and other proponents of the theory, religion develops from primitive forms such as animism and after many stages comes to expression in pure monotheism. In ancient Israel this must have followed a trajectory of family worship at private altars that was polytheistic in nature; through an increasingly monotheistic, more corporate and highly ethical standard under the prophets; and then a descent to a national, institutional worship headed by priests who drained the faith of its vitality and inner spirituality. Having adopted this model, the early critics adjusted the Pentateuch to it. This effectively removed Moses as author, demanded a late date for the Pentateuch's final form, and destroyed its unity. However, the only way this view can be sustained is by uncritically accepting a set of assumptions that are being increasingly eroded by decades of archaeological, historical, and literary research.

DATE

On the assumption that Moses wrote Genesis, the date of its final composition cannot be later than 1406 B.C., the date of his death. This date follows from the fact that Moses died forty years after the Exodus (Deut. 29:5; see also 31:2; 34:7), which in turn occurred 480 years before Solomon began constructing the temple in 967–966 B.C. (1 Kings 6:1). Moses most likely had access to records that he used in compiling the book and drew also on oral tradition, all under the direction of the Holy Spirit, who assured the absolute inerrancy of the process and the result.

ADDRESSEES

Just before he died, Moses assembled all Israel in the plains of Moab, just east of Jericho, where he delivered his farewell address (Deut. 1:1). That address certainly consisted of the contents of Deuteronomy, the covenant renewal text he had just composed, and it may well have included the rest of the Pentateuch as well. Initially Genesis was intended not to be a treatise on beginnings for the benefit of all humankind but a composition appropriate to Israel on the eve of her conquest of the land of promise. Eventually, of course, its purpose broadened to encompass the church as well, for the Hebrew Scriptures became the first part of the Christian Bible. Genesis, then, is for both Jews and Gentiles in the whole body of Jesus Christ.

PURPOSE

The title "Genesis" already suggests its purpose, that is, to declare the source, nature, and reason for the beginning of all things. Though it is important to emphasize that the Bible, including Genesis, is scientifically and historically accurate when it intends to speak in these categories, its purpose is not to serve as a handbook on geology, biology, or any other of the natural sciences. That is, it is not designed to describe the "how" of creation so much as the "why." It is fundamentally a theological work, not a book preoccupied with the phenomenological world. This is true of its historical nature as well. The Bible speaks of historical facts, but it does so with theological objectives in view. Thus it fails to trace the mainstream events of secular history but rather focuses on so-called sacred history, that is, history as a record of God's redemptive purposes. For Genesis this means a narration of God's relationship to individuals (the patriarchs) and not, as a rule, to the nations of the earth.

Also, Genesis was composed to provide answers to pre-Conquest Israel's most pressing questions: Who are we? Where did we originate? Where are we headed? What is God's purpose for us in history and in the ages to come? The rest of the Bible relates in one way or another to these and other questions.

THEOLOGICAL EMPHASES

The purpose of Genesis is related but not identical to its theology, for the theological message transcends the interests of Israel alone. Genesis provides reasons for Israel's existence, but it does more. It explains the universal human condition—sin—that calls for a solution. It also draws attention to Israel as a promised people who would become the human channel of divine redemptive grace.

The nation Israel originated in Abraham to whom the covenant promises of salvation were first made. He and all who descended from him were charged with the task of modeling the kingdom purposes of the Lord and also bearing a witness throughout their historical experience to the message of reconciliation by which the whole fallen world could come to faith and live again. God the Creator is thus God the Redeemer. What

He began in perfection He will accomplish to new perfection through Abraham's Seed, that One known in the New Testament as Jesus Christ.

OUTLINE

I. Primeval History (chapters 1–11)
   A. The Creation of the Cosmos (1:1–2:3)
   B. The Creation of Man and the Fall (2:4–3:24)
   C. The Two Lines of Human Descent (chapters 4–5)
   D. The Great Flood (6:1–9:17)
   E. The Descendants of Noah (9:18–10:32)
   F. Babel and Its Resolution (11:1–26)
II. The Account of Abraham (11:27–25:11)
   A. Abraham and the Covenant Promise (11:27–18:15)
   B. Abraham the Intercessor (18:16–19:38)
   C. Sarah's Testings and Triumph (20:1–21:21)
   D. Abraham's Testings and Triumph (21:22–25:11)
III. The Account of Isaac (25:12–27:45)
IV. The Account of Jacob (27:46–37:1)
   A. The Blessing of Jacob in Aram (27:46–31:55)
   B. Jacob in Canaan (32:1–37:1)
V. The Account of Joseph (37:2–50:26)
   A. Joseph's Exile to Egypt (37:2–38:30)
   B. Joseph's Fall and Rise (chapters 39–41)
   C. Joseph's Reunion with His Family (chapters 42–45)
   D. The Descent of Israel to Egypt (chapters 46–50)

I. PRIMEVAL HISTORY (CHAPTERS 1–11)

The era covered by these chapters is sometimes called the "prepatriarchal age" because it precedes the narratives of Abraham, Isaac, and Jacob. In line with the fluctuating focus of the Book of Genesis, however, it might be better to think in terms of an account cast in more universal terms at the beginning, narrowing in the middle to a series of biographical sketches, and then broadening (at least by anticipation) to a national dimension.

Chapters 1–11 explain to Israel—and to us—why all things exist, how they became corrupted by human sin, and what God intended to do by way of remedy.

A. The Creation of the Cosmos (1:1–2:3)

As noted in the introduction, two of the criteria that source critics enlist in demonstrating the "documentary hypothesis" are different divine names in different sections and repetitions or doublets between sections. The creation accounts have been favorite "proofs" of the hypothesis, for the narrative in Genesis 1:1–2:3 employs one name (Elohim) and the narrative in 2:4–25 employs another (Yahweh). The fact that there are two versions has led some to conclude that an editor (or redactor) joined two originally independent creation traditions that were so different as to preclude their being integrated into one. Such criticism, however, is insensitive to theological and other considerations that readily explain such features.

Creation on day one (1:1–5). The third word in the Hebrew Bible is Elohim, the name of God throughout the account of the creation of the cosmos. The name derives from a word meaning "power" and thus speaks of God primarily as the omnipotent one. Elohim is the subject of a verb (*bārā'*) that has only God as subject and here means to create *ex nihilo* ("from nothing"). Nothing existed, and then God made the heavens and earth (that is, all matter), followed by the creation of light (1:3).

Creation on day two (1:6–8). As on the first day, God had only to speak and things came into being. Having divided light from darkness on day one, here He divided the waters below from the waters above, that is, the waters of the earth from the clouds and other moisture above. The space between is the atmosphere, usually translated "firmament" (from the Hebrew word meaning "hammered out"), and identified here as the heavens or skies.

Creation on day three (1:9–13). The division this time was between the earthly waters and dry land (1:9). From the soil thus exposed God brought forth vegetation, all of it clearly defined by species or kind.

Creation on day four (1:14–19). Once more creation involved division, this time between day and night. God created the moon and stars for the night and the sun for the day. Their purpose was to reflect the light of creation, so they were actually "lightholders" and not lights. Moreover, they would be the means by which time—hours, days, months, and years—could be measured (1:14).

Creation on day five (1:20–23). Aquatic and aerial creatures now appear to fill the waters and skies, which had been brought into existence on day two. Again, each is set apart from the others by species differentiation, a point worth noting as a fatal flaw to the notion that the Bible accommodates macroevolution.

Creation on day six (1:24–31). At last all remaining life forms—including humankind—appear. Special attention is directed to the creation of man (*'ādām,* "mankind") for of him only is it said that he was created as the image and likeness of God (1:26). This speaks not so much of resemblance to God, even spiritually and psychologically, but of relationship. People are created *as* (not *in*) the image of God so that they can have dominion over all things as God's surrogates (1:26–28; see also Ps. 8). Man and animal alike may eat vegetation and thus "rule over" it (Gen. 1:29–30), but man rules also over animals as God's image. Man's centrality is underscored by the divine verdict that "it was very good" (1:31). Of the previous days of creation God had said merely that "it was good" (1:4, 10, 12, 18, 21, 25).

> The description of God's creative works as "good" means not only that they were untainted by sin and the Fall but also that they have intrinsic aesthetic worth. God delights in beauty—in the "fine" arts—and has given human beings the capacity to be creative, responsive, and appreciative.

No creation on day seven (2:1–3). The six days of creation gave way to the climactic seventh day on which God ceased His creative work and "rested." The resting of God suggests not that He became inactive or indifferent but only that His work had reached a perfect fullness to which nothing could or should be added. The seventh day from thenceforth would be set apart as a time to celebrate and commemorate God's grace and goodness in bringing everything into existence (1:3; see also Exod. 20:8–11).

Many scholars have noted a thematic pattern in the creation days, one that results in day seven as the capstone of all else. Some have also suggested that the arrangement of the days may be rhetorical as well as chronological, as the accompanying chart shows.

Day 7—The Sabbath Rest

Day 3—Dry land	Day 6—Animals and man
Day 2—Water and sky	Day 5—Fish and birds
Day 1—Light	Day 4—Light Holders

B. *The Creation of Man and the Fall (2:4–3:24)*

If the former narrative of creation can be labeled the "cosmic account," this should be considered the "anthropological account," because humankind, not the heavens and the earth, is now central. What Genesis 1:26–31 said about humanity's creation in general, this passage describes in particulars and in terms of a remarkable divine-human encounter. This explains the use of the name Yahweh throughout (eleven times in twenty-two verses), for that is the covenant name whereby the Lord relates to people, especially His elect. The main theme of the passage is the centrality of the human race to the creation purposes of God.

Man's formation (2:4–17). The narrative begins with an introduction that marks it off as a new unit. It then summarizes the condition of the world before man's creation as one in which there was no agriculture or even rainfall, for there was no one to tend the fields. What was needed was a creature empowered and mandated to do this as God's steward (1:28), so the Lord God (the covenant Maker), like a potter, took the ground (Hebrew, *'ădāmâ,*) and from it formed a man (*'ădām*). The anthropomorphic imagery of a potter is augmented by the declaration that God breathed into the man's body the breath of life and man became a living being. Especially noteworthy is the fact that man did not *get* a soul but he *became* one, that is, he became a person. In addition, the divine inbreathing distinguishes humankind from the animals, for they too are called "living beings" (2:19).

In anticipation of their subsequent significance Moses referred to two major features of the garden: the tree of life and the tree of the knowledge of good and evil. Though everything else in the garden was suitable for human consumption, the latter was strictly prohibited (2:16–17). As for the more precise location of the garden, the narrator, having drawn attention to the absence of rain in the pre-Flood world (2:5–6), pointed out that man's earliest environment was irrigated by rivers. Two of them, the Hiddekel or Tigris and the Euphrates, are well-known, but the other two can no longer be identified. They were branches of one great river that flowed from Eden into the garden (2:10). With all things beautifully and perfectly prepared, the Lord placed Adam in the garden to "dress" (literally, "watch over") and "keep" (literally, "work") it.

Man's incompleteness (2:18–25). A reiterated theme so far in the creation account is that "it was good." Now, however, the Lord God said that "it is not good" for Adam, the male of the human species, to be alone. Having already created all other beings (thus the sense of the verb sequence in verse 19a) and having brought them to Adam for his consideration, the Lord allowed man to exercise his dominion over them by assigning them names. As Adam did so, he observed that he was one of a kind—no other creature matched or corresponded to him.

What man needed to make him whole was female, that to which he inversely corresponded, just as he had seen in the animal world. Creation was still incomplete, then, so the Lord made woman from man's side and brought her to him for his assessment. Adam first acknowledged that they were the same in many respects ("my bones" and "my flesh") but also different. The differences are reflected in the Hebrew name puns. She will be called "woman" (*'iššâ,*) because she came from "man" (*'îš*). Technically Hebrew *'iššâ,* derives from the masculine noun (*'ĕnôš*) (also "man"), but to sustain the idea of complementariness here Moses employed a pseudoetymology.

On the basis of this understanding of the origin of the human genders, marriage is described here as "leaving" and "cleaving." The man must henceforth leave his parents and join his wife so that they can be one flesh as they were before the act of her creation. Nothing is more precious to a man than his own being, and therefore, as a part of his very being, his wife is equally precious (2:24; see also Eph. 5:28–29).

The narrative ends with the proleptic note that though the first couple were naked they were not ashamed (Gen. 2:25). This literary "teaser" invites the reader to go on to discover why this was so.

The perfection of creation and all things in it soon gave way to the ravages of sin, the effects of which still testify to its ruinous nature. How sin originated is left a mystery in the Bible (but see Isa. 14:12–20 and Ezek. 28:1–19 for hints at Satan's fall), for the present narrative already presupposes its existence before the temptation of Adam and Eve. What matters most is that man and woman sinned, came under a curse for doing so, but nonetheless were given a ray of hope that sin could be forgiven and fellowship with God could be restored.

The temptation and fall (3:1–8). The connection between Adam and Eve's innocence and their impending guilt is underscored by the pun of their nakedness (*'ărummîm;* 2:25) and the serpent's subtlety (*'ārûm;* 3:1). The talking serpent, unidentified here, was, as later revelation shows, Satan or the devil (see also Rev. 12:9; 20:2). The contest here is one of sovereignty. Who will be Lord—God or man? Implicitly underlying the whole scene is Satan's own ambition for ruling the earth.

The serpent attacked the woman and not the man because of the issue of authority roles and relationships. If the woman could overthrow the headship of the man, perhaps the man would overthrow the headship of God! God's headship was symbolized at this point in His restrictions as to what man could eat—anything but the tree of the knowledge of good and evil (Gen. 3:3; see also 2:17). This formula—"good and evil"—probably means knowledge of everything, especially in the moral realm. To be wise in this way is to be equal to God (3:5).

Satan's tactic was not to advocate rebellion openly but to raise questions about God's intentions (3:1) and motives (3:5). Man was created as God's image, Satan well knew, but not as His equal. Satan's ploy was to suggest that God was "nervous" about His role as Sovereign and was fearful that Adam and Eve would challenge that sovereignty by eating what they thought was the secret to "God-ness."

Sadly, Eve capitulated and induced her husband to sin as well, thus undermining their relationship. Adam's sin in turn was an act of insurrection against his God, one that tore asunder the covenant connection between the Lord and His creation. As a result the man and woman did come to a "knowledge of good and evil." They knew they were naked both physically and spiritually, and in their shame they attempted to hide from the omniscient One (3:7–8).

The curse and its remedy (3:9–21). The narrator described God's search for and eventual conversation with Adam and Eve. When confronted about how they knew they were naked—an implicit acknowledgment of their violation of the restriction about the trees in the garden—they began to justify their behavior by blaming others. Adam said he ate because Eve induced him, and Eve in turn blamed the serpent (3:12–13).

Turning to the serpent, the Lord consigned him (it) to the ignominy of forever crawling on its belly, a symbol of its lowly subordination in contrast to its attempted regal loftiness. Moreover, the seed [singular] of the woman would one day finish off the serpent by crushing it underfoot, while he [the seed] would be bruised in the process (3:14–15). This is a magnificent prediction of the atoning work of Jesus whereby He died for our sins (was bruised; see also Isa. 53:5) and arose from the dead (crushed the evil one; see also Rom. 16:20; 1 Cor. 15:20–28).

Meanwhile, woman must endure painful childbirth and onerous subjection to husbands who now are fallen and insensitive, and man must struggle to eke out subsistence from the dust of the ground only to return to it again in death (3:16–19; see also 2:7). Though work itself is noble—in fact, it is central to the creation mandate (2:15)—the Fall has brought on the earth a curse that forces people to labor against the handicaps of nonproductive soil choked with noxious weeds.

Despite all this, God's grace would enable human life to go on. Adam was so confident of this that he named his wife Eve ("life"), for she would be the channel through which the race would continue (3:20). And the Lord himself affirmed this hope by symbolically pointing to a means of atonement. In the first recorded act of death the Lord slew an animal, took its skin, and with it covered the nakedness of Adam and Eve. This covering anticipated a fundamental truth about the vicarious shedding of blood: It covers (thus the Hebrew word *kāpar*, "to atone") a person's guilt so that God can call him righteous.

Man's exile from the garden (3:22–24). Meanwhile sin had exacted a tragic toll. Man had come to know the full range of ethical knowledge by experience, indeed, but in doing so had forfeited the life and immortality that would have been his had he not sinned.

Now, to prevent the moral anomaly of enjoying God's very life while yet in his fallen state, Adam and Eve were expelled from the garden lest they take of the tree of life. Never again could they enjoy the access to the Holy One for which they had been created; the Lord stationed cherubim at the entrance of the garden to keep it off limits. These angelic beings represent the very presence of the Lord Himself (Exod. 25:18–22; Ezek. 10:1–22).

C. The Two Lines of Human Descent (chapters 4–5)

Sin severely crippled the creation purposes of God, but it could not destroy them altogether. Adam recognized that his wife would still be the mother of all living beings (3:20), and in due course the couple produced descendants who, because of the corrupting inroads of sin, divided into two lines, the ungodly and the righteous. From the latter came Noah, who would represent a long line of faithful ones through whom God's redemptive promises would come to pass.

The first division of the human race (4:1–15). At last Eve gave birth to a son, whose name Cain suggests that she may have believed that he was the seed God had promised (the Hebrew noun *qayin*, "smith," sounds like the verb *qāneh*, "to get"). This was not to be, however, for he turned out to be a murderer, slaying his brother Abel in a jealous rage. The reason, it seems, is that the Lord had accepted Abel's animal sacrifice but had rejected Cain's offering of grain (4:3–5). Actually, it was not the nature of the offering that was at issue but the attitude of the respective worshipers—Abel offered in faith but wicked Cain did not (Heb. 11:4; see also 1 John 3:12).

Cain was expelled from the Lord's presence (Gen. 4:14) to a life of being a nomad. The ground that had soaked up his brother's blood would yield no crops to him, so he was destined to wander as a landless fugitive. Even so, he would know God's gracious provision, for the Lord "set a sign" of protection over Cain to identify him as one to whom no harm of vengeance should come.

The genealogy of Cain (4:16–24). Cain's immediate destination was a land east of Eden called Nod ("homelessness"). There his wife (obviously a sister) gave birth to a son named Enoch, a son after whom Cain named a city that he built. The line of descent through Enoch culminated in Lamech, the seventh generation from Adam on the Cainite side. Lamech was a bigamist, whose wives produced three sons, all viewed as founders of various arts and sciences. Thus, though Cain was consigned to nomadism, his descendants quickly became urbanized.

The implicit rebellion of the Cainite line is explicitly revealed in Lamech's boastful taunt-song (4:23–24). Ignoring God's gracious protection of his ancestor Cain, Lamech vowed to take vengeance into his own hands should the need arise. He would take to himself a sovereignty that belonged only to God.

The genealogy of Seth (4:25–5:32). After Abel's brutal murder and Cain's ostracism, the Lord raised up a substitute (Seth in Hebrew means a "substitute") son to take Abel's place and, as it turned out, to be the founder of the chosen line. Seth, born in Adam's 130th year (5:3), was the image and likeness of his father, just as Adam was the image and likeness of God Himself (1:27). Though humankind was now fallen in sin, God's creation purpose of reigning through the human race was still in effect, especially through those related to Him by faith.

From Adam to Noah inclusively there were ten generations. Among these the most notable was Enoch, the seventh in line (5:18–24). He stands in contrast to the seventh in the line of Cain, Lamech, whose arrogance epitomizes human independence of God. Unlike Lamech, Enoch "walked with God" and did so with such wholeheartedness that God took him to heaven before he died (5:24). Instead of the monotonous refrain "and he died" (5:5, 8, 11, 14, 17, 20, 27, 31), there is the simple but glorious testimony that Enoch "was not, for God took him."

By way of further contrast with Cainite Lamech is Sethite Lamech, the ninth in the line (5:25–31). This Lamech was a humble man of faith who saw in the birth of his son Noah a word of promise. He was named Noah (Hebrew for "rest") because he would bring comfort to the human race. Noah himself had three sons—Shem, Ham, and Japheth—as though to fill out and complete the fractured hopes of Adam and Eve, who also had three sons, one of whom murdered another.

D. The Great Flood (6:1–9:17)

The righteous line of Seth as well as the ungodly one of Cain eventually degenerated into a universal culture whose wickedness was so great that God had no option but to eliminate the human race (with the exception of only eight people). One man and his immediate family stood apart from all this, however, and as his father Lamech had predicted, Noah became God's means of bringing comfort to the earth by surviving the judgment by a worldwide flood and providing the nucleus of a new human race.

Human wickedness and divine grace (6:1–12). In due course humanity became so depraved as to permit intercourse between angels ("sons of God," 6:2; see also Job 1:6; 2:1; 38:7) and humans. The result was a mongrel people known as the Nephilim (Gen. 6:4), a people that survived as a fearsome giant race down to Moses' own time (Num. 13:33). The biological implications of this are unclear (see 2 Pet. 2:4; Jude 6), but the intention of the text is unmistakable. Man's incorrigible and unrelenting depravity left no remedy but full and final judgment (Gen. 6:7).

> *Noah is testimony to the fact that God has always chosen His own as an act of pure grace, and that eternal salvation is because of His initiative.*

Noah, however, found grace (Hebrew, *ḥēn*, "favor") with the Lord; that is, out of all humanity he became the object of divine choice for a holy mission (6:8). The description of Noah as a righteous and upright man who walked with God (6:9; compare 5:24) does not suggest that these characteristics qualified him for divine election, for such choice is always by grace. This way of presenting Noah is to show how his character and lifestyle contrasted sharply with all others of his corrupt generation.

Preparation for the Flood (6:13–22). One hundred and twenty years after God's warning of judgment (6:3), he commanded Noah to build an ark in which all animal species along with Noah and his immediate family could find refuge. Noah's special role now became apparent—he would be a "second Adam" with whom God would carry out the original covenant mandate.

The rising of the Flood waters (7:1–24). With two of every kind of "unclean" animal (implicit in 6:19–20; see also 7:8–9) Noah took seven of every "clean" animal (7:2–3), the purpose of the latter being, of course, for sacrificial usage (8:20). Seven days after God (not Noah) sealed up the ark (7:16), the rains began to fall, perhaps for the first time in human experience (7:10; see also 2:6). For forty days they continued, accompanied by the eruption of subterranean seas (7:11–12) that together caused the oceans to rise until they covered the highest mountain by fifteen cubits (about twenty-two feet; 7:20).

The debate about a local (that is, Mesopotamian) flood as opposed to a universal (that is, worldwide) one would seem to be easily resolved by sheer physical law alone, to say nothing of the clear intent of the passage. Water seeks its own level, so if "all the high mountains" were covered (7:19), the whole earth was under water to that extent. Moreover, the insistence on the use of "all" ("all mountains," 7:19; "all flesh," 7:21; "all in whose nostrils," 7:22; "all that was on the dry land," 7:22; and so forth) can lead to no other view than a universal deluge, modern scientific opinion notwithstanding.

The abatement of the Flood waters (8:1–19). After 150 days (7:24) the rains and rising waters desisted and the water began to recede until, in the seventh month, the ark rested on the "mountains of Ararat" (8:4; not necessarily Mount Ararat) in what is now north-central Turkey. After determining that the waters had indeed dried up and that the earth was suitable for human habitation, Noah and his family emerged from the ark after being confined there for over a year (8:13; see also 8:10–11). The Lord commanded them to come forth and, with the animals, to carry out the creation mandate to "be fruitful and multiply" (8:17; see also 1:26–28).

The renewal of the covenant (8:20–9:17). As an act of gratitude and also of anticipated covenant renewal, Noah sacrificed a burnt offering to the Lord, one that pleased Him and prompted Him to pledge never again to destroy the earth by a flood (8:20–22). More positively, He reiterated the original Adamic covenant but with significant modifications necessitated by the Fall and the judgment of the Flood (9:1, 7; see 1:28). Mankind could now eat meat, since animal death was part of the curse (9:3; see 3:21). However, blood must be avoided for it was a metaphor for life itself, a thing so sacred that only God could "receive" it by its being poured out on the altar or the ground (9:4; see Lev. 17:10–16). As for human blood (or life), it was particularly sacrosanct because man was made (in) the very image of God (Gen. 9:6; see 1:26–27). Therefore, if one took another's life in murder, he must pay with his own, for to kill God's image is to be murderous toward God Himself (9:5–6).

The use of the term "My covenant" in Genesis 6:18 (the first occurrence of the word "covenant" in the Old Testament) implied an already existing one, namely, the covenant with Adam. The term occurs again here (9:9) to reinforce the idea that the Lord was beginning again with Noah. To show His commitment to Noah and his descendants that He would never again destroy the human race by a flood (8:21–22), the Lord set a rainbow in the sky as a token. Just as rain had been a means of curse, now it would be a source of blessing (9:13–17).

E. The Descendants of Noah (9:18–10:32)

Just as the human race began (or was designed to begin) with three sons of Adam, its "re-beginning" featured three sons of Noah—Shem, Ham, and Japheth. Shem, though probably not the eldest son (9:18; 10:21), is usually listed first because his descendants would issue into the messianic line of Abraham (9:26). In line with Noah's curse and blessing of his sons (9:25–27), the so-called Table of Nations (10:2–31) provides a picture of the role of the Shemites, a line culminating in Abraham. The descendants of Shem appear last in this case as a climactic finale.

The descendants of Japheth (10:1–5). The name Japheth usually occurs last in the lists of Noah's sons (5:32; 6:10; 7:13; 9:18; 1 Chron. 1:4) because he was least prominent in the outworking of God's redemptive plan. But his descendants appear first in the Table of Nations because its purpose was to feature Shem as the covenant people by placing the Shemites as the culmination of the scheme. Those names of Japhethites that can be identified with various nations put beyond doubt that they are basically Eurasian. The reference to their linguistic diversity (Gen. 10:5; see also 10:20, 31) shows that the table as a whole reflects the results of the dispersion of the nations following Babel. In other words, 11:1–9 actually precedes chapter 10 chronologically.

The descendants of Ham (10:6–20). These nations settled primarily in North Africa, certain Mediterranean islands such as Caphtor (that is, Crete, 10:14), and along the eastern Mediterranean coast (Canaan, 10:6; Sidon, 10:15). Others, however, lived in south Arabia, from whence some of them—notably Nimrod—moved on to central Mesopotamia to establish major city-states such as Babel, Akkad, and Nineveh (10:7–11). Clearly one cannot view each of the three sons of Noah as a progenitor of a particular race because many of the peoples listed as Hamites are usually considered Semitic in language and culture, especially the Phoenicians, Canaanites, Babylonians, and Assyrians. The prominence of the Hamites in the table is because of Israel's close association with both Egypt (Mizraim, 10:6) and Canaan (10:6, 15–19).

The descendants of Shem (10:21–32). There are two listings of the Shem genealogy, one here and the other following the story of the Tower of Babel (11:10–32). This enveloping structure is designed to highlight the rebellion of humankind at Babel, which reveals all the more the need for human redemption through the Shemites. That function of the Shemites is hinted at by the reference to Eber as a descendant of Shem (10:21, 24–25), for Eber (*ʿēber*) is the patronym of the word "Hebrew" (*ʿibrî*). That is, the Hebrews, through Abraham, were Eberite Semites. The nations associated with Shem are mainly to be found in Mesopotamia (Asshur, 10:22) and Arabia (Sheba, 10:28). It is quite apparent that Japhethites, Hamites, and Shemites settled among one another and often spoke languages in common.

F. Babel and Its Resolution (11:1–26)

The pervasive and irremedial corruption of the human race had resulted in a universal flood that destroyed all but Noah, his three sons, and their wives. But human pride and independence of God had not been eradicated, and the time came when that spirit manifested itself in the building of a tower at Babel, a symbol of man's determination to disobey God's mandate to "fill the earth" (1:28). Once more judgment had to fall, this time in the dispersion of humanity to the ends of the earth. But just as God had selected Noah to perpetuate His creation purposes beyond the Flood, so He selected Abraham to be the ancestor of a line that would eventually provide a means of human redemption.

The tower of Babel (11:1–9). About halfway between the time of Noah and Abraham, the earth was "divided" (10:25; 11:16), the most likely cause of that division being God's dispersion of the human race following the confusion of languages (11:7–8). A place in the plain of Shinar (central Mesopotamia) had become the focal point of civilization, and at that place wicked men began to erect a tower (known as a *ziggurat* in ancient Near Eastern writings) to celebrate their own fame and to resist the purpose of God in filling and dominating the whole earth (11:4). As He had in Noah's time, God "came down" and overturned these evil plans, terminating the construction and, by introducing incomprehensible speech dialects, scattering the human race. Thereafter the place was called Babel (from the Akkadian word *bāb-ilī*, "gate of the gods") for God had "confused" (Hebrew, *bālal*, a pun on *bābel*) their speech (11:9).

The full genealogy of Shem (11:10–26). A partial Shem genealogy tracing the descent of Eber's brother Joktan (10:25) preceded the Babel narrative (10:21–31), and now one centering on Eber followed that narrative. Eber, as noted (10:21), was the patronym of the Hebrew people. This explains his prominence in both Shem genealogies (10:21, 24–25; 11:14–17; 1 Chron. 1:18–19, 25). With ever-narrowing focus, the spotlight turns to Terah, then to his three sons, and then to Abram alone (Gen. 11:24–32). The purpose of this longer register, then, is to create a bridge between Shem and Abram, between the Semites (a later form of the word "Shemites") in general and the Hebrews, between the Noahic Covenant and the Abrahamic Covenant.

II. THE ACCOUNT OF ABRAHAM (11:27–25:11)

The seed of the woman (Gen. 3:15), having been transmitted through Noah, Shem, and Eber, would now be entrusted to Abraham and his descendants, culminating in Jesus Christ (Matt. 1:1–17; Luke 3:23–38). The formal vehicle by which this seed-promise would be conveyed and which would testify to God's faithfulness to bring it about would be a series of covenants binding Him to a chosen people. That people, later known as Israel, found their source in Abram (Abraham), a man selected by the Lord for this high and holy purpose.

A. *Abraham and the Covenant Promise (11:27–18:15)*

The call and leading of Abraham (11:27–13:18). Abram (his "precovenant" name; see 17:5) was born to a Semitic family living in the great Sumerian city-state of Ur in lower Mesopotamia (modern Kuwait). Though he was a worshiper of Nannar, the moon god (Josh. 24:2), the Lord called Abram from that place, and, together with his father and other family members, he settled in Haran, another center of moon worship hundreds of miles farther north near the Euphrates River (Gen. 11:27–32).

After his father's death, Abram, following by faith the Lord's leading (Heb. 11:8–10), traveled to Canaan. The Lord had said (the intent of Gen. 12:1) that if Abram obeyed the call to go, God would make of his descendants a great people through whom He would bless all nations (12:1–3). While this is not the Abrahamic Covenant, it does establish the basis on which the covenant would be made, and it outlines the major benefits that would accrue from it.

Arriving first at Shechem, where he built a shrine celebrating God's appearance to him there, Abram went on to a place near Bethel and eventually toward the Negev (or south, 12:9), the southern desert. Because of a famine there, he went to Egypt, the "breadbasket" of the ancient world, where, to save his own skin, he passed his wife Sarai (later Sarah) off as his sister (12:13). He feared Pharaoh would take her into his harem—which indeed he did (12:15)—and only when God revealed the truth to the king was the matter resolved to everyone's satisfaction. In fact, the Lord blessed Abram through Pharaoh despite Abram's deceptive ways (12:16, 20).

After his return to Canaan it became apparent that Abram's family and livestock were so numerous that he and his nephew Lot could no longer live together. Showing an incredible deference and generosity, Abram allowed Lot his pick of the land and agreed to take what was left. True to his greedy impulses, Lot chose the lush farmlands of the Dead Sea plains, leaving Abram with the harsh climates and soils of the hill country. However, the narrative that speaks of Lot's apparently sensible choice closes with the ominous note that the people of Sodom were exceedingly wicked before the Lord.

In contrast to this is the Lord's affirmation of Abram's self-abnegation. All the land he could see in all directions, everywhere he placed the sole of his foot, would someday belong to him and his descendants.

A testimony to Abram's sovereignty (chapter 14). The Lord had said that all the land on which he trod would be his (13:17). The verb "to trod" suggests dominion. The narrative in chapter 14 provides an example of this exercise of authority on Abram's part.

A coalition of kings from the East made a raid on Sodom and the other cities of the plain, resulting in the capture of prisoners and plunder including Lot. Stirred to anger by this assault on a loved one—even one as worldly and selfish as his nephew—Abram formed an alliance of his own and marched against the marauders, who had fled to the north. He overtook and defeated them and then brought back to Canaan the persons and goods that had been spirited away.

The main point of the narrative, however, is Abram's encounter with a priest named Melchizedek, who was also ruler of a place called Salem (that is, Jerusalem; Ps. 76:2). This mysterious figure, a prototype of Jesus Himself (Heb. 7:1–3, 11–17), spoke of God as El Elyon, "God Most High" (Gen. 14:18). This is an epithet descriptive of God's universal sovereignty. When Melchizedek blessed Abram, then, the blessing was an assertion that Abram's defeat of the eastern kings was an affirmation of Abram's own sovereignty as a servant of the Lord (14:19–20). His refusal to take any reward from the king of Sodom also attests to Abram's independence of any human support. God and God alone was his source of supply (14:22–23).

The first declaration of covenant (chapter 15). The main narrative, which ended at 13:18, picks up again here. The Lord had told Abram that He would make his seed as numerous as the dust (13:16), but now, years later, he had no children except for the adopted (thus "son of my house") Eliezer whom he had acquired in Damascus (15:2–3). The Lord assured him, however, that Eliezer would not be his heir—he would have a natural son. Hearing this word of hope, Abram "believed in the LORD" (literally, "leaned fully" on the Lord; 15:6).

This expression of confidence led to a covenant ritual in which the Lord, like a glowing and smoking censer, passed in a vision between divided carcasses (15:17). This "oath sealed in blood" was accompanied by a promise that Abram's descendants would (a) sojourn in a place of bondage for four hundred years, (b) be delivered with great riches, and (c) inherit all the land between the "river of Egypt" (present-day Wadi el-Arish) and the Euphrates River (15:13–16, 18–21).

Abram's own efforts to fulfill the covenant (chapter 16). Abram's faith, though sufficient for him to be pronounced righteous (15:6), was too weak for him to wait longer on the Lord for a son. Sarai was barren, thus precluding children by her, so she hit on the commonly accepted cultural strategy of having a child by proxy. Abram therefore undertook to sire a son, Ishmael, by Sarai's servant girl Hagar, a pregnancy that though it appeared to meet the need for a descendant proved to provoke Sarai, who sensed her inadequacy all the more. She began to make Hagar's life so miserable that Hagar fled to the desert.

> *Because of Abraham's confidence in God, God accounted his faith to him as righteousness, an example Paul cited of justification by grace through faith.*

There "the angel of the LORD" met her, provided for her needs, and counseled her to return to Sarai. She too would be blessed through her son Ishmael, for he would become founder of a vast multitude of descendants, the Arabs being prominent among them (see 25:12–18). Many Bible students identify the angel as a preincarnate embodiment of Jesus Christ, or he may have been an angelic being who was so closely identified with the Lord as to be addressed at times as God Himself (16:13; see also 21:17; 22:11–12; 32:24, 30).

The second declaration of covenant (chapter 17). About thirteen years after the first presentation of the Abrahamic Covenant (see 16:3, 16) and of God's promise to give Abram a son (15:4), the Lord appeared to him as El Shaddai ("God the All-Abundant One") and renewed the covenant pledge, this time in greater detail. Abram would father a multitude of nations under monarchic rule, and his descendants would inherit all the land of Canaan as a possession (17:6, 8). A sign of the Lord's commitment was the change of Abram's name to Abraham. No longer just the "exalted father" (*'abrām*), he would become "father of a multitude" (*'abrāhām*). Moreover, the Lord would seal and symbolize the covenant by the rite of circumcision, a mark that forever after would set the covenant people apart (17:10–14).

The promise of a son naturally involved Sarai as well, so her name too was changed. This time, however, there was no change in meaning (both *saray* and *sarâ,* mean "princess"). The change in the vowels was significant enough, however, for Sarah to know that she was about to enter a new phase of her life, one that would entail her becoming the mother of a son who, like Ishmael, would become the ancestor of many descendants (17:15–16). Hearing that his aged wife would bear a son, Abraham laughed (*yiṣḥāq*), so God told him the lad's name would be Isaac (*yiṣḥāq*). But Abraham's weak faith did not prevent his obedience, so he and all his family and servants were circumcised as evidence of that commitment to the Lord's covenant (17:22–27).

A heavenly visitation (18:1–15). The next encounter between the Lord and Abraham was to serve the same purpose as the previous one—to assure him of the birth of a son—but this time God came in human form as though to test him again at the point of faith. One day while the patriarch sat at his tent door, three "men" dropped by to visit. As was (and is) common in nomadic culture, Abraham urged them to break bread with him (18:1–8), thus "entertaining angels unaware" (Heb. 13:2).

The narrator made it clear that one of these guests was the Lord (Gen. 18:1), that is, the Angel of the Lord, who represented Him in a visible form (see, for example, 16:7–11; 21:17; 22:11, 15; Exod. 3:2; Judg. 6:11–22). He spoke to Abraham and Sarah, again promising the birth of the long-awaited son. So absurd was this to Sarah that, like Abraham earlier (Gen. 17:17), she laughed, only to be rebuked by the omnipotent One, who asked whether or not there was anything too difficult for Him (18:14). The final proof of His power and grace would be the birth of Isaac within the year.

B. Abraham the Intercessor (18:16–19:38)

An important element of the Abrahamic Covenant was the promise that all the peoples of the earth would be blessed through him (12:3; 18:18;

see also 22:18; 26:4; Gal. 3:8). The cities of the plain had experienced that blessing when Abraham delivered them from the eastern kings (Gen. 14:15–16), and now Abraham was about to intercede for these same cities when God revealed His intention to destroy them because of their unspeakable sins. Abraham and his descendants became channels of God's redemptive grace.

Abraham's intercession before God (18:16–33). After dinner (18:8) two of Abraham's guests set out for Sodom and Gomorrah for the purpose of warning Lot about the destruction of the cities of the plain (18:16, 22; 19:1). The third guest—the Lord Himself—remained to disclose to Abraham the judgment He was about to inflict. The reason He confided in Abraham was precisely because Abraham was God's instrument of intercessory blessing (18:17–18).

Hearing what the Lord was about to do, Abraham "bargained" with Him for the lives of the doomed citizens of Sodom, Gomorrah, and the other evil cities. After much negotiation the two agreed that judgment would be forestalled if only ten righteous persons might be found there.

The destruction of the cities of the plain (19:1–28). When the two angels reached Sodom, Lot met them, invited them in, and then tried to secure them against the homosexual mob that sought to seize and abuse them. Even the offer of his daughters failed to buy off the frenzied throng, so the angels, messengers of Almighty God, blinded and immobilized them (19:1–11). The angels then informed Lot as to the purpose of their visit: Sodom and everything in it was to be destroyed because of its irredeemable wickedness (19:13; compare 6:5; 11:6). Only Lot, his wife, and his two daughters would be spared and then only if they hurried and found refuge in the nearby city of Zoar (19:12–22).

At last convinced, Lot and his family ran for their lives, but his wife, curious about the awesome destruction behind her, turned to look and was immediately encrusted in a solution of salt raining from the skies. At the same moment that Lot's wife stood as a frozen pillar Abraham, miles to the west, stood also in dismay as he witnessed the sights and sounds of God's righteous fury (19:26–28).

The salvation of Lot and his daughters (19:29–38). Abraham's intercession had not been in vain, however, for Lot and his daughters arrived safely in Zoar and then went on to a cave to the east overlooking the Dead Sea (19:29–30). Once there it dawned on his daughters that they were now without marriage prospects, for all the young men they had known had been swept away in God's judgment. They therefore contrived a plan whereby they could bear children by their own father whom they rendered senseless by drunkenness. This resort to incest, though not to be justified, is not surprising in light of Lot's irresponsibility in rearing his children in such a morally bankrupt environment as Sodom (see 13:11–13).

The result of this turn of events was the birth of two sons, Moab and Ben-Ammi (19:37–38). Their descendants, the Moabites and the Ammonites, settled in the Transjordan, and beginning in Moses' day and throughout Old Testament history they became a source of constant irritation and spiritual disablement to the people of Israel, their distant cousins.

C. Sarah's Testings and Triumph (20:1–21:21)

Compounding Sarah's problem of barrenness, Abraham once again passed her off as his sister in order to preserve himself. But God used even this ruse to make Abraham and Sarah a blessing and, moreover, finally allowed Sarah to give birth to Isaac, a birth, however, that alienated Hagar and Ishmael from the Abraham family.

Abraham and the blessing of Abimelech (chapter 20). For reasons unstated Abraham moved south from Mamre to Gerar, home of a Philistine enclave ruled by Abimelech. Fearing for his life in that godless place (20:11), Abraham persuaded Abimelech that Sarah was his sister, not his wife, a lie he had used on Pharaoh years earlier (12:13). The Lord revealed the truth to Abimelech, however, before anything unfortunate happened to Sarah. Nevertheless He had already closed the wombs of the Philistine women because of Abimelech's evil (if misguided) intentions (20:18).

To demonstrate once more Abraham's role as an intermediary through whom God blessed others, the Lord urged Abimelech to solicit Abraham's prayers on his behalf that His potential wrath might be averted (20:6–7). This overture was accompanied by lavish gifts to Abraham, who then prayed for an end to the barrenness of the Philistines (20:17). This kind of ministry is linked in the narrative to Abraham's designation as a prophet (20:7). The gifts of Abimelech must not be construed as bribes or compensation to Abraham to induce him to pray. Clearly they were tokens of the generous spirit of a man who, once enlightened, desired to express regret for the way he had caused embarrassment to Sarah (20:16).

The birth and blessing of Isaac (21:1–21). The healing of the infertility of the Philistine women as an answer to prayer is matched now—at long last—by Sarah's conception and delivery of Isaac, the promised covenant son (21:1–3; see also 17:16; 18:10). With more than a bit of irony Abraham [(21:3, obeying God (17:19)] named him "Laughter" (*yiṣhāq*, "Isaac") for they had both once laughed at the very prospect of parenthood (17:7, 18:12). However, Sarah's laughter now was an expression not of incredulity but of joy (21:1–7).

After Isaac's circumcision and weaning, Abraham made a great festival to which Hagar and Ishmael were invited. When Sarah saw young Ishmael—now a lad of fourteen or fifteen years—making merry (another Hebrew pun on the word for Isaac), she demanded that Hagar and Ishmael be exiled from the community because she perceived Ishmael to be a threat to Isaac, the legitimate heir to the covenant (21:11).

God graciously intervened to preclude further family strife. He commanded Abraham to allow Hagar and Ishmael to depart for the Negev desert. There He met them and gave them food and water. More important, He promised them that Ishmael too would head a line of noble desert peoples, a promise that ultimately eventuated in the rise of the Arab tribes and their kinsmen (21:18; see also 16:10; 17:20; 25:12–18).

D. Abraham's Testings and Triumph (21:22–25:11)

Great faith is hammered out on the anvil of testing, something Abraham discovered throughout his remaining days. First, the Philistines of Gerar challenged him over water rights (21:22–34). Then the Lord commanded him to sacrifice his son Isaac (22:1–19). Next he lost his wife in death and struggled to find a suitable burial place (chapter 23). After that he was threatened by lack of progeny because his bachelor son Isaac had not married (chap. 24). Finally he died, full of years and rich in blessings (25:1–11).

Contention and covenant with the Philistines (21:22–34). Following the resolution of the conflict between Abraham and Abimelech of Gerar over Sarah (chap. 20), Abimelech seems to have violated an agreement between them by seizing some of Abraham's water wells. Abimelech denied any involvement, so Abraham, eager to patch things up and to show good will, made a covenant with him at Beersheba, the meaning of which is "well of the oath" (*be'ēr sāba'*) or "well of the seven," referring to the seven lambs Abraham offered as part of the covenant ritual.

The offering of Isaac (22:1–19). The testing implied in the previous episode is explicit here, for God "tested" Abraham's faith by asking him to do something that would effectively negate all the promises of covenant blessing—offer his only (literally, "solitary, unique") son Isaac as a burnt offering. All that Abraham and Sarah had dreamed and prayed for through all the years would, as it were, go up in smoke. More seriously, how could God's oath to make Isaac the channel of world redemption (17:15–21) be reconciled with His command now to Abraham to terminate that process?

With no recorded objection or resistance Abraham took his son to Moriah—where Solomon's temple would one day be located (2 Chron. 3:1)—and prepared to carry out the will of God. When Isaac asked him about the nature of the sacrificial victim Abraham replied in trustful resignation, "God himself will provide the lamb" (Gen. 22:8, NIV). Then, as Abraham raised the knife to slay his son, the Lord intervened and provided a substitute animal in Isaac's place. The purpose of the test then became clear: Because of Abraham's magnificent faith and obedience, the promise to make him the instrument of covenant blessing was repeated and reinforced (22:16–18). Any lingering doubts Abraham may have had about the constancy of God surely dissipated in the face of such a display of divine intention.

The death and burial of Sarah (22:20–23:20). After a brief résumé of more distant family ties (22:20–24), the narrative turns to the account of Sarah's death and Abraham's difficulty in securing a proper burial place. The point seems to be that though Abraham already possessed all of Canaan by promise (15:18–21), in actual fact he did not own enough ground to bury his beloved wife. The importance of his faith is thus underscored, for he still had to look to the future for a permanent city whose builder and maker is God (Heb. 11:10, 16).

After much bargaining with Ephron the Hittite, Abraham purchased a field with a cave near Kiriath-arba (or Hebron, Gen. 23:2). The place, otherwise known as Machpelah (23:17), became a cemetery not only for Sarah but also eventually for Abraham (25:9), Isaac (49:31), and Jacob (49:29–30; 50:13). Though they owned no land as such, these patriarchs, by faith, had a stake in the land, a magnetic point that would draw their descendants back to Canaan.

A search for a wife for Isaac (chapter 24). In a day when teenage marriages were common and customary, Isaac had reached the age of forty with no marriage prospects (25:20). Once more Abraham was put to the test, for if Isaac should fail to produce offspring, all the covenant promises would be to no avail. Abraham therefore sent his trusted servant Eliezer to Aram Naharaim (upper Mesopotamia), the place where he himself and his brothers had resided before moving to Canaan (see 11:31; 12:1). His assignment was simple—find a suitable wife for Isaac from within the extended family.

Arriving at the city of Nahor (site unknown), Eliezer met Rebekah and her family, and after some negotiation an arrangement ensued that all parties agreed was "made in heaven" (24:50–51). When Rebekah at last came to Isaac's dwelling place, the choice of Rebekah as his wife was soon confirmed as a wise one, for he fell in love with her and found her to be a source of great comfort in the loss of his mother (24:67).

The epitaph of Abraham (25:1–11). The story of Abraham closes with information about his lineage through a second wife, Keturah, the distribution of his estate to Isaac and his other sons, and his death and burial at Machpelah. Evidence of some healing of broken relationships between Isaac and Ishmael is apparent in their taking joint responsibility for their father's proper burial. But the line of promise would surely pass through Isaac; God blessed Isaac after his father's death. Though the patriarch died, the promise lived on.

III. THE ACCOUNT OF ISAAC (25:12–27:45)

The strong figures of Abraham and Jacob tend to overshadow Isaac, who seems to be only a link between them. Such an assessment, however, fails to recognize the central role Isaac had in transmitting the covenant promise, a role somewhat misjudged, perhaps, because it was carried out so faithfully and without fanfare. Whatever weakness of character he displayed was compensated by his very obvious desire to follow the will of God.

The descendants of Ishmael and Isaac (25:12–26). The names of Ishmael's twelve tribal descendants can be only partially linked with secular texts that provide further ethnic and geographic identification. On the whole, they describe Bedouin peoples of the central and northern Arabian peninsula (25:18).

Isaac's descendants were limited then to his twin sons Esau and Jacob, the point at hand being the circumstances of their birth (25:19–26). Their linkage with Abraham is established first, and then the miraculous nature of their conception. Like Sarah, Rebekah was barren, and only through divine intervention did she become pregnant. She at once recognized that her pregnancy was complicated, for she sensed that her unborn children were contending with one another even in her womb. When she asked about the meaning of the prenatal struggle, the Lord revealed to her that contrary to normal custom the elder of her twins would someday become subservient to the younger.

In due course the sons were born, the one named Jacob because he seized his brother's heel, thus delaying his birth (in Hebrew the name Jacob is *ya'ăqōb*, from *'āqēb*, "heel"), and the other named Esau, "the hairy one" (*'ēsāw*) (25:25). Esau was an outdoorsman, one who enjoyed hunting, whereas Jacob was more domestic, more inclined to house and home. Their differences in lifestyle led their parents to an unhealthy favoritism, Isaac preferring Esau and Rebekah catering to Jacob. Beyond this, however, was Rebekah's recollection that Jacob had been promised the preeminent position even before his birth.

The struggle over birthrights (25:27–34). Jacob, already a supplanter and conniver from his mother's womb, seized on his mother's favoritism to justify his robbing his elder brother of his birthright. A birthright usually allotted the elder son two-thirds of the father's estate, the other son(s) getting one-third (Deut. 21:17). Jacob's natural avarice found support also, he felt, in the promise that he would be master over Esau (Gen. 25:23). Jacob therefore caught his famished brother in a moment of weakness one day, and Esau, disregarding the seriousness and legality of the transaction, surrendered his claims to primacy for a bowl of red stew.

Isaac and Abimelech (26:1–33). As bearer of the covenant privileges, Isaac was no more exempt from testing than was Abraham. And as is often the case in families, weaknesses or proclivities of one generation are passed on to the next. An example of this is the story of Isaac's encounter with the Philistine king Abimelech, probably a son of the Abimelech known to Abraham (20:1–2). A famine had come, and Isaac, like his father before him, decided to go to Egypt for relief (see 12:10). The Lord intervened, however, and told him to reside among the Philistines at Gerar and there exercise his covenant role as blesser of the nations (26:3–4). While there, however, Rebekah caught Abimelech's eye, and he wished to add her to his harem, a desire encouraged by Isaac, who asserted that she was his sister, not his wife. The ruse was discovered before harm was done, and like his royal predecessor Abimelech not only desisted from his intentions but also commanded that Isaac and his wife were to be left alone (26:11; compare 20:14–16).

Isaac's failure to model God's righteousness with regard to Abimelech did not prevent God's blessings on him materially. He became so prosperous, in fact, that the Philistines envied him and set about to sabotage his efforts by filling his wells with dirt (26:15, 18–21). His patience in turning the other cheek and moving on helped offset his previous deceptions, and eventually he and his enemies achieved peaceful coexistence at Rehoboth, the "wide place" of God's fruitfulness.

The reason for this turn of events was the very evident blessing of God on Isaac that Abimelech was able to see. He therefore wanted to join in fellowship with the man of God, for he clearly saw in this affiliation a means whereby his own people would be blessed. This, of course, was the original purpose of the Abrahamic Covenant (26:4).

The struggle over blessings (26:34–27:45). The birthright consisted of the bequeathal of a material estate (see 25:29–34). The blessing, on the other hand, was spiritual in nature, the prayerful transmission of hopes and dreams and, in the case of the Abrahamic Covenant, of divine promises. Like the birthright, the blessing normally went to the elder son.

So Esau, though he had sold his birthright, was still heir to Isaac's blessing, something Rebekah wanted to preclude. The narrative hints at Esau's disqualification (26:34–35) and then goes on to disclose how Rebekah and Jacob concocted a plot that resulted in Isaac's mistakenly, but legally, transferring the blessing to Jacob rather than Esau. That blessing is clearly reminiscent of the one first given to Abraham and then channeled through Isaac (27:27b–29; see also 12:1–3; 22:17–18; 26:4). But just as God had reserved a blessing for Ishmael, who had been "cheated" out of what he thought was his (16:10; 21:17b–20), so He blessed Esau also with the promise that someday he would enjoy prosperity and independence (27:39–40). This hope did not assuage Esau's anger, however, so he plotted against the day when he could take vengeance against his cheating brother (27:41–45).

IV. THE ACCOUNT OF JACOB (27:46–37:1)

A. *The Blessing of Jacob in Aram (27:46–31:55)*

To save her son's life, Rebekah urged him to flee to her homeland under the pretext of finding a wife. After twenty years there he accumulated two wives, two concubines, at least twelve children, and vast holdings of livestock and other goods. All of this came about because of God's efficacious grace.

The journey to Haran (27:46–28:22). Impelled by concern for Jacob's deliverance from Esau and also his need to marry among his kinsmen, Rebekah and Isaac sent him off to Paddan Aram, Rebekah's homeland (28:1–8; compare 24:4, 10). The rather devious motivation behind this strategy should not obscure the fact that God was sovereignly at work behind the scenes. This is apparent in the divine visitation at Bethel in which the Lord reiterated His covenant promises to Jacob (28:13–15). So powerful was this encounter that Jacob marked the place by a pillar and named it Bethel, "the place of God."

Jacob's marriages (29:1–30). Encouraged by God's vindication, Jacob arrived at his destination, met and fell in love with Rachel, and worked out a marriage arrangement with her father, Laban. For seven years of labor, Laban said, Jacob could have the hand of Rachel, but once the time was over Laban "suddenly" remembered that elder daughters must marry first. Consequently Leah, rather than Rachel, became Jacob's bride. To reinstate good feelings Laban "threw in" Rachel as well but with the caveat that Jacob serve seven more years. His love for Rachel made it possible for Jacob to comply without further complaint.

Jacob's children (29:31–30:24). As a kind of compensation for her second-class status, the Lord gave Leah children while withholding them from Jacob's favorite, Rachel. In rapid succession she bore Reuben, Simeon, Levi, and Judah (29:31–35), until at last Rachel offered to Jacob her maidservant Bilhah by whom, in effect, she gave birth to Dan and Naphtali (30:1–8). Meanwhile, Leah, who found herself no longer able to conceive, employed her own slave girl Zilpah as a surrogate, having Gad and Asher in this manner (30:9–13). Once more God intervened on Leah's behalf and she herself gave birth to Issachar and Zebulun (30:14–21). Then at last Rachel bore Joseph. She gave him that name, which in Hebrew is *yôsēp*, "adding," because of her intense hope that God would give her even more offspring (30:23–24).

Jacob's labors and return home (30:25–31:55). Having served Laban for fourteen years in return for his daughters Leah and Rachel, Jacob requested that he be released from further responsibility and allowed to return home. Laban urged Jacob to remain, however, for he knew full well that his own prosperity derived from Jacob's having been with him (30:27). Pressed further, Jacob relented but only after having driven a hard bargain as far as wages and other provisions were concerned. Ever crafty, Laban agreed, but then he changed the terms of the agreement after it was in place (30:35–36).

If Laban was devious, Jacob was even more so, for he undertook measures to counteract Laban's chicanery. The result was increasing wealth for Jacob at Laban's expense (30:37–43). Clearly the situation was deteriorating, so Jacob, following divine prompting (31:3, 11–13), resolved to return to Canaan. Waiting until Laban was absent from home, Jacob fled with his family, servants, livestock, and movable goods. Meanwhile, Laban heard of Jacob's departure, set out after him, and, after both God's intervention and common sense prevailed, made a treaty with Jacob that neither would trouble the other again (31:44–54).

B. Jacob in Canaan (32:1–37:1)

Having functioned as a channel of blessing to Laban despite the differences between them, Jacob returned to Canaan in order to fulfill his covenant responsibilities there. God's continuing presence and blessing are apparent, but so are Jacob's character flaws and interpersonal insensitivities. These and other factors dictated the need for God to move His people out of Canaan and into Egypt, a place of moral and spiritual incubation.

The journey to Shechem (chapters 32–33). As Jacob crossed into the Jordan Valley he sensed the danger of a confrontation with his estranged brother, Esau. He therefore resorted to prayer and strategy to assure Esau of his good intentions and desire for reconciliation (32:1–21). Sending his family on ahead, Jacob remained east of the Jabbok River, where, in the middle of the night, he encountered a mysterious visitor—a manifestation of the Lord, as it turned out (32:28, 30)—and engaged him in a wrestling match. Because of Jacob's tenacity the heavenly opponent blessed him by changing his name to Israel (*yisrā'ēl*), for he had contended (*sārâ*) against God (*'ĕlōhîm*) and had prevailed (32:28). By a play on words, the meaning "contend with God" was transmuted into "prince of/with God."

The exhilaration of this experience soon turned to stark terror when Jacob heard of Esau's arrival to meet him. As it turned out, there was nothing to fear, for Esau greeted him warmly and even invited him to his own country, Seir (or Edom). Jacob respectfully declined but was able to resume his travels in peace (*sālēm*, perhaps "to Salem," that is, Shechem) until he at last reached Shechem.

> *God's people found comfort in returning to where God had something significant for them, Shechem, Bethel, and Gilgal. The Christian life also has its "holy ground," places marking conversion, baptism, and commitment of life. To revisit them can be a source of thanksgiving and renewal.*

He purchased property and decided to settle there, at least for a while, for Shechem was a place sanctified by Abraham as his first stop in the land of Canaan (12:6).

Trouble at Shechem and travel to Hebron (34:1–35:22a). Jacob and his family had barely settled down when the son of the city's ruler raped Jacob's daughter Dinah, a shameful act that prompted her brothers Simeon and Levi to take revenge (34:25–26). As serious as the whole episode was, it was only symptomatic of a deeper and more pernicious problem that was beginning to emerge. That was the problem of the contamination of God's elect people through intermarriage with or otherwise undertaking improper relationships with the pagan peoples of the land (34:30). Clearly, the only course of action at the moment was to leave the area of Shechem and return to the relatively safer environment of Hebron, where Isaac and his clan still awaited them.

Thus Jacob moved south toward Bethel, and as he entered that holy place where he had previously encountered the Lord in a glorious epiphany (see 28:10–22), the Lord appeared again and reaffirmed the terms and promises of the Abrahamic Covenant for which he had become responsible (35:9–15). Pressing on from there, the caravan reached Ephrath (perhaps Bethlehem of Judah, 35:16, 19) where Rachel died giving birth to Benjamin. This note of sorrow mixed with hope sharply contrasts with the observation that Reuben, Jacob's oldest son, had engaged in sexual relations with his father's own concubine (35:22). The corruption of Canaanite life was once more exhibited in graphic terms.

A genealogical footnote (35:22b–36:43). As a conclusion to the Jacob-Esau conflict and an opening to a new era, Moses included a list of Jacob's sons (35:22b–26), a brief note about Isaac's death (35:28–29a), and a hint at reconciliation between his sons (35:29b). This is followed by an extensive outline of Esau's descendants (36:1–19), a list of Horite rulers who had preceded Esau in Seir (36:20–30), a list of kings who followed these chieftains (36:31–39), and a summary of rulers of Edom who sprang from Esau (36:40–43).

V. THE ACCOUNT OF JOSEPH (37:2–50:26)

Signs of Israel's moral and spiritual peril had already come to the fore (34:1–17; 35:22), and one more would come to light (chap. 38) that would make it imperative for Israel to leave Canaan for an environment in which the budding nation could find productive soil. That place would be Egypt, so Joseph was sent there to pave the way for a more-than-four-hundred-year opportunity for growth in numbers and, more important, in spiritual maturity.

A. Joseph's Exile to Egypt (37:2–38:30)

Though often read as a tale of treachery, abuse, and profound sorrow, the story of Joseph is rather one of celebration of the sovereign if mysterious purposes of God. Sold into Egyptian slavery by his jealous brothers, Joseph eventually became their means of salvation and blessing.

What appears to be an interruption of the Joseph narrative is in fact its rationale. After a series of shortsighted blunders and moral lapses (38:1–11), Judah impregnated his own daughter-in-law, very likely a Canaanite woman, who had disguised herself as a prostitute (38:12–23). His sin was disclosed, but despite its gravity God allowed the twin sons born of the relationship to become heads of clans through one of which, Perez, eventually sprang King David and Jesus Christ Himself (Ruth 4:12; Matt 1:3, 16). The whole incident, however, illustrated powerfully the need for Israel to leave that corrupt and tempting culture.

B. Joseph's Fall and Rise (chapters 39–41)

Joseph at first rose through the ranks of Potiphar's servants, but because of false charges of sexual molestation by the Egyptian's wife, Joseph found himself in prison (39:1–20). The Lord blessed him there, however, and before long he became a trustee over the prison, one who also was known as an interpreter of dreams (39:21–40:8). Having successfully done so on two occasions, Joseph was invited by Pharaoh to interpret the king's troubling dreams (40:9–41:13). Joseph, admitting that only God could give such insight (41:16), revealed to Pharaoh what lay ahead. A famine would come, but by wise management its harmfulness to Egypt could be averted (41:14–36). The king was so impressed and convinced that he promoted Joseph to a high position, perhaps as minister of agriculture (41:37–57).

C. Joseph's Reunion with His Family (chapters 42–45)

Since God's purpose was for Jacob and his sons to find moral and spiritual refuge in Egypt, it was inevitable that He would create circumstances that moved them in that direction. The famine already referred to in Pharaoh's dream (41:14–36) provided the impetus, for it affected Canaan as well as Egypt. The first step Jacob took was to send his sons to Egypt to procure food supplies, a mission that required them to deal directly with their brother Joseph (42:1–17). Joseph, whom they did not recognize after more than a decade, promised relief but only if they left Simeon behind as a hostage until their youngest brother Benjamin should come on a future trip (42:18–25). To compound their apprehension, the money they had paid was slipped into their grain sacks without their knowledge, thus making them afraid ever to face Joseph again (42:26–38).

Face him they must, however, for the famine lingered on. After much persuasion, Jacob agreed to let Benjamin go with his brothers for more grain (43:1–15). This time, after protesting their innocence regarding the money and presenting their youngest brother to him, Joseph threw a lavish banquet for them (43:16–34). He then sent them on their way but again arranged for not only their money to be surreptitiously returned but his precious silver cup was tucked in as well. When he sent his men after them and they found the brothers in possession of all these things, he demanded that Benjamin be handed over to him as a slave (44:1–17).

The brothers' urgent pleas for Benjamin's release touched Joseph's heart so deeply that he could keep his secret no longer and revealed his true identity (44:18–45:15). Pharaoh, once apprised of the situation, then offered a generous invitation for Jacob and all his family to live in Egypt (45:16–28).

D. The Descent of Israel to Egypt (chapters 46–50)

Israel's settlement in the land of Goshen (46:1–47:26). To confirm to Jacob that the move to Egypt was part of a grand heavenly design, the Lord repeated to him the essence of the Abrahamic Covenant (46:1–4). Thus encouraged, Jacob and his caravans, seventy persons in all (46:27), arrived in Egypt, where Pharaoh allotted to them the region of Rameses

(Goshen; 47:11; see also 45:10; 46:28), a lush pastureland in the eastern delta of the Nile (46:5–47:12). In line with the promise of the covenant that Abraham's seed would be the means of blessing all nations, Joseph became the preserver and distributor of all the food supplies necessary for the Egyptians (47:13–26).

Jacob's blessing of his sons (47:27–49:28). Having reached advanced age and knowing death was near, Jacob first blessed the two sons of Joseph, Ephraim and Manasseh (48:13–22), and then his own sons and their descendants (49:1–28). Just as he, the younger son of Isaac, had received the patriarchal blessing (27:23), so Ephraim was blessed rather than his older brother (48:20). The point, of course, is that God acts in line with His own sovereign purposes even if these contravene human custom and tradition.

Of all the magnificent prophetic blessings of Jacob on his sons, the blessing on Judah is most theologically significant, for it identifies Judah as the tribe through which the future ruler would come (49:10–12). Later revelation puts beyond doubt that this regal person was first David (Ruth 4:12, 18–22), then his dynastic descendants (1 Chron. 3:1–24; Matt. 1:6–16), and finally and fully Jesus Christ (Acts 2:29–36).

Jacob's death and its aftermath (49:29–50:26). Having charged his sons to bury him in the patriarchal tombs at Machpelah (49:29; see also 47:30), Jacob died and was embalmed according to Egyptian practice (49:33–50:3). Joseph and his brothers then carried their father's body to Canaan for burial according to his wishes (50:4–14). Now with their father gone, Joseph's brothers feared that he might avenge himself against them for their past treatment of him (50:15–18). Joseph was quick to remind them, however, that all things had been done by the Lord, evil human intentions notwithstanding. What they meant for harm God had turned into good, both his and theirs (50:19–20).

Limited human experience and understanding make it difficult to see good in the sorrows and setbacks of life. These often come about, however, as God's means of achieving a higher good, for our blessing and not our hurt.

At length Joseph also died. Like his father, he asked to be buried in Canaan, but not immediately. That could await the day when Israel, in accord with God's gracious plan, would leave Egypt and enter the promised land of rest (50:22–26; see 15:12–16).

EXODUS
Deliverance to Covenant Privilege

AUTHOR

$\mathcal{T}$o the arguments advanced for Mosaic authorship of Genesis and the Pentateuch in general (see pp. 1–2) may now be added those that specifically address Exodus. The title of the book in Hebrew, "And These Are the Names," consists of the first two words of Exodus. The fact that the book begins with "And" suggests that Exodus continues the narrative that ends at Genesis 50:26. If one can make a case for the Mosaic authorship of Genesis, then one can surely do the same for Exodus, at least as far as this linkage is concerned.

Similarly, the literary bridging is also impressive. Exodus 1:1–7 is reminiscent of Genesis 46:8–27, which provides a list of Jacob's family members who migrated to Egypt. The Exodus list, while much shorter, picks up where the previous one left off and speaks of the prosperity and population growth in the centuries that had followed that migration (Exod. 1:7). This, of course, cannot prove that Moses was author of both books (or either), but it in no way flies in the face of ancient tradition to that effect.

The book's own testimony as well as that of the rest of the Bible is much more unambiguous and objective. In several places Moses is said to have spoken or written texts that help make up the contents of Exodus (15:1; 17:14; 24:4; 34:27). The Dead Sea Scrolls (CD 5:1–2; 7:6, 8–9; 1QS 5:15), other extrabiblical texts and traditions (for example, *Babylonian*

Talmud, Baba Bathra 14b–15a), and the New Testament (John 19:36; Acts 23:5; Rom. 9:17; 1 Cor. 10:7; 2 Cor. 8:15) all explicitly or implicitly endorse this view. The only way such unanimity of opinion can be overcome is by rejecting these testimonies as lacking in authority or by suggesting that they merely reflect a prevailing popular understanding of authorship that has no basis in actual fact. In short, nothing in Exodus or extraneous to it leads to anything but Mosaic composition.

UNITY

Source criticism (see pp. 2–3) divides Exodus among three major hypothetical constructs—J, E, and P. According to one analysis J (the so-called Yahwist) wrote much or most of chapters 2, 4–5, 8–10, 15, 34; E (the Elohist) contributed chapters 1, 3, 13, 17–18, 21–24, 32–33; and P (the Priestly source) was responsible for chapters 6, 12, 16, 20, 25–31, 35–40. Miscellaneous and/or editorial passages that join the others together are attributed to an anonymous redactor. Such analysis leaves no room for original Mosaic authorship of the whole, and it also presupposes originally independent, unrelated sources that gradually became patched together over five hundred years until they created the existing Book of Exodus.

Unfortunately for its adherents, this hypothesis cannot be validated by any data. It sprang out of a world-view that said religions developed gradually, and that divine revelation is not possible. Even though its philosophical underpinnings are nearly universally rejected, modern criticism dogmatically adheres to the hypothesis.

DATE

The question as to when Exodus was written obviously relates to the authorship and unity of the book. The view espoused here—that Moses wrote Exodus—allows some flexibility in the matter, at least the space of about thirty-eight years. The book could not have been written after 1406 B.C., when Moses died. On the other hand, it could have been completed as early as 1444 B.C., two years after the Exodus. There is no reason to think that Moses would not have written the book that early, since it certainly was important to him to record its contents in permanent (written) form as early as possible.

ADDRESSEES

The audience of Exodus—those who first heard or read the book—depends on its date. If it was composed right after the giving of the Sinai Covenant (around 1444 B.C.), the addressees would have been the generation of the Exodus deliverance itself. Besides incidental hints about Moses speaking to and even writing for the Sinai community (Exod. 17:14; 24:4; 34:27–28), the book speaks of no event after the covenant revelation. The only suggestion of a later time of composition is the observation in 16:35 that Israel ate manna for forty years, right up until they arrived at the border of Canaan.

On the other hand, since the setting of the book is limited to the Exodus and Sinai experiences, there would be reason to include later events. On balance it seems best to assume that Exodus, like Genesis, was addressed to the assembly of Israel in the plains of Moab. This also better accommodates such statements as the one about the manna.

PURPOSE

The purpose of the Book of Exodus is to celebrate God's gracious deliverance of His chosen people Israel from Egyptian slavery to the freedom of covenant relationship and fellowship with Him. It forms a bridge between the promises of the Abrahamic Covenant (concerning seed, land, and blessing) and fulfillment in a people constituted as a theocratic community through whom God's redemptive purposes would be achieved. Exodus contains the covenant text that gave Israel a legal and constitutional framework within which to carry out her divinely ordained responsibilities. It also mandated the mechanism by which the nation could have access to the Holy One and provided a means of renewing that access should it be disrupted by Israel's sin.

THEOLOGICAL EMPHASES

The overriding theological message of Exodus is that God had redeemed and made a covenant with a people who had sprung from the ancient promises given to the patriarchs. That covenant had not made them God's people—for they already were that (Exod. 19:4–6; Deut. 7:6–11)—but it had brought them into a relationship with the Lord whereby they could become the means by which He would bless all the nations of the earth (Gen. 12:3; 22:18; 28:14).

Secondary themes are (a) the electing and powerful grace of God, whose ways are past finding out but who nevertheless enters human history to perform His creation purposes; (b) God's faithfulness in keeping His promises to those to whom He commits Himself; and (c) the role of Israel as the peculiar people chosen to reflect the kingdom of God before the nations of the earth. Israel must also communicate to these nations the message of reconciliation to the One they had offended and alienated by their sinful rebellion. The human race has fallen woefully short of God's expectations, but He has provided a way through which it can become all He intended. That way was promised to the patriarchs, channeled through Israel, and incarnated in Jesus Christ. The Book of Exodus helps trace the history of that divine plan for redemption.

OUTLINE

I. Israel's Bondage and the Plagues (1:1–12:36)
  A. Historical Introduction (1:1–7)
  B. Historical Background (1:8–22)
  C. Preparation of Moses (chapters 2–4)
  D. Moses before Pharaoh (chapters 5–11)
  E. The Passover (12:1–36)
II. Israel's Exodus (12:37–18:27)
  A. Journey to the Red Sea (12:37–14:20)
  B. Journey to Mount Sinai (14:21–18:27)
III. Israel's Covenant and Fellowship (chapters 19–40)
  A. Preparation for Covenant (chapter 19)
  B. The Covenant Text (chapters 20–23)

C. The Covenant Ceremony (chapter 24)
D. The Preparations for the Covenant Dwelling Place
   (chapters 25–31)
E. Apostasy and Renewal (32:1–35:3)
F. Construction of the Tabernacle (35:4–40:38)

I. ISRAEL'S BONDAGE AND THE PLAGUES
(1:1–12:36)

The Genesis narrative leaves Israel in a state of well-being in Egypt, but Abraham had been told that his descendants would dwell in a foreign land where they would be oppressed for four hundred years (Gen. 15:13). Exodus 1 explains how the change from prosperity to persecution took place in the 280 years between Joseph's death and Moses' birth.

A. Historical Introduction (1:1–7)

This passage is a bridge to link the patriarchs to Moses and the ancient promises with the beginnings of fulfillment. Joseph had died near the end of the glorious Twelfth Dynasty of Egyptian history, a time of almost unparalleled power and wealth. In that era God gave His people Israel providential care and bountiful success, thus preparing them for something special.

B. Historical Background (1:8–22)

On the collapse of the Twelfth Dynasty, Egypt entered the chaotic era of the Semitic Hyksos rule, especially in the delta region of Israel's habitation, until new native Egyptian rebels rose up to overthrow the Hyksos and expel them from the land. This introduced the Eighteenth Dynasty of the so-called New Kingdom period, a regime which, while restoring Egypt's political, cultural, and imperialistic glory, turned against Israel, thus initiating the oppression from which she pleaded to be delivered.

The "new king" who did not know Joseph (that is, whose sympathies were no longer with the Hebrew people) was probably Ahmose, founder of the New Kingdom (around 1570 B.C.). Having just expelled the Hyksos, he put the Hebrews into slave labor because he viewed them as pro-Hyksos agents who could do harm to his government. Other pharaohs followed this policy and even intensified the persecution, going so far as to institute infanticide against all Hebrew male children. Despite this, some were saved by heroic midwives and still others, like Moses, by mothers who hid them.

C. Preparation of Moses (chapters 2–4)

God had sworn to Abraham that after four hundred years in a strange land He would deliver His people from bondage (Gen. 15:14–16). The time was now at hand and Moses was to become the agent of their deliverance. But he had much to learn before he was equipped for this seemingly impossible mission. Only after he had experienced a disciplinary wilderness in his own life would Moses be able to lead Israel in the wilderness journey that would end in the Promised Land. The chief thing he had to learn was who God is and what it meant to be fully obedient to Him.

The preservation of Moses (2:1–10). Moses was born about 1526 B.C., probably in the reign of Thutmose I. Because of the edict requiring all male infants to be slain, Moses' mother hid him away as long as she could and then entrusted him to the Lord by placing him in a reed basket in the Nile River (2:1–4). Pharaoh's daughter (possibly the famous princess Hatshepsut) found him there, and when she discovered that he was a Hebrew, she hired his own mother to be his nurse (2:5–12). The name she gave him (Hebrew, *mōšeh,* from *māšâ* "to draw forth") is similar to the common Egyptian name element Mose (or Mosis), as in the pharaoh's name Thutmose.

The exile of Moses (2:11–22). After forty years Moses, who enjoyed a position of royalty in Pharaoh's court (see Heb 11:24–27), slew an Egyptian foreman who had beaten a Hebrew slave. This act in which he identified with his own downtrodden people was misunderstood by some of them, who viewed him as an ambitious power-monger. Fearing detection, Moses fled for his life to Midian, east of the Sinai Peninsula. There he met Reuel (or Jethro; 3:1), a Midianite priest, whose daughter Zipporah he took as his wife. Plaintively, the narrator points out that the son of that union was named Gershom, "stranger there."

The call of Moses (2:23–3:22). After nearly forty more long years (see 7:7) the king of Egypt from whom Moses had fled (probably Thutmose III) died, thus making Moses' return to Egypt possible. Israel's plight had only worsened, but at long last the Lord heard them and called Moses to go back to lead them out, in line with His ancient pledge (2:23–25; Gen. 15:13–16). Moses meanwhile was in Sinai shepherding Jethro's flock when suddenly the Lord appeared in a flaming bush and identified Himself as the God of the patriarchs. He then spoke to Moses of His plan to make him the leader of his people, the one who would free them from bondage and take them to Canaan. Astounded by this theophany and command, Moses objected, but God reminded Him of His presence and power.

Moses still offered his feeble rejoinders, arguing next that he could not very well lead his people out on God's behalf if God had not even revealed the name by which He was acting. Then, in one of the most significant theological disclosures in the Old Testament, God identified Himself as "I AM WHO I AM" (*'ehyeh 'ăšer 'ehyeh*, Exod. 3:14). By that eternally present name and power He would deliver them. When expressed in the third person (*yihyeh*), the name is most commonly rendered "He is." An alternative form with the same meaning is Yahweh (sometimes rendered Jehovah), frequently translated "LORD."

When God added that He had not been known to the fathers by this name (6:2–3), the Lord intended Moses to understand not that they had never heard the name (see, for example, Gen. 12:1–4, 7–8; 13:4, 10, 13–14, 18; 15:1–18), but that they had never comprehended its full theological significance. It is the name of covenant redemption, and since that was precisely Israel's need in Egypt, that was the name by which Moses would introduce the Lord's salvation (Exod. 3:15–17). Moses' demand to Pharaoh to let Israel go would be met by stony resistance, but the "I Am" would be more than able to prevail and deliver them. He would work miracles of such amazement that not only would the king relent but also, ironically, the Egyptians would send the Israelites away loaded with wealth.

The return of Moses (chapter 4). Even in the strength of that commitment Moses continued to make excuses. The people will not believe You are with me, he said, so the Lord changed Moses' shepherd's rod into a snake and then back again to a rod. The rod or staff was symbolic of regal authority. The Lord showed Moses by this sign that He would bless his leadership. Next He made Moses' hand to become leprous and then whole. Like the rod, the hand was a metaphor for power. The wholeness of the hand attested to God's delegation of divine authority. If these signs failed to persuade the people, Moses would be able to turn the very waters of the river into blood. In this dramatic fashion the Egyptian river deities would be seen to be powerless, indeed, to be dead (4:1–9).

Finally Moses complained that he was ineloquent and thus unable to command respect as a spokesman. The Lord responded by reminding him that He is Creator of all things, even one's organs of speech. But in a most gracious act of deference the Lord agreed to let Aaron be his interlocutor. How He would do so provides unusual enlightenment as to the nature and function of a prophet. Aaron would be as a mouth to Moses, and Moses would be as God to Aaron (4:16; see also 7:1).

Persuaded at last, Moses made his way toward Egypt with his wife and sons. Along the way a most unusual encounter took place (4:18–26). The Lord had told Moses that he was to warn Pharaoh that his eldest son's life would be taken if he refused to let Israel, the Lord's firstborn "son," depart from the land. But Moses had not even identified his own firstborn son, Gershom, as a member of the covenant people by the rite of circumcision. Moses therefore had no credibility in this area of firstborn sons, so he stood in jeopardy before the Lord for this serious oversight (4:24). Only Zipporah's initiative in performing the act forestalled God's intention to slay Moses.

Back in Egypt the Lord had instructed Aaron to meet Moses. Through Aaron Moses spoke to the people, accompanied by all the signs that had been promised. It was then clear to all that God's day of deliverance would soon take place (4:27–31).

D. Moses before Pharaoh (chapters 5–11)

Moses had already been warned that his demand of Pharaoh to let Israel leave Egypt would be to no avail (3:19; 4:21). He was not surprised, then, when permission was withheld, despite a series of calamities that the Lord unleashed against Egypt and its recalcitrant ruler. However, Pharaoh's resistance led Moses again to question the call of God, especially since the Israelites themselves began to challenge Moses' leadership. At last Pharaoh would appear to relent, but no sooner would Israel begin its journey east than the king would set out to bring them back, a tactical blunder that would cost him and his kingdom dearly.

Request to worship the Lord (5:1–21). When Moses finally had an audience with Pharaoh (probably Amenhotep II), his plea that Israel might undertake a pilgrimage in the desert to worship the Lord was met with a resounding rebuff. To add insult to injury, the king concluded that his Israelite slaves had too much time on their hands and therefore should gather their own straw to make brick. Their inability to keep up the pace resulted in severe punishment.

When their foremen complained, Pharaoh only stiffened his resolve to exact the full quota of bricks. The Israelites therefore turned on Moses and Aaron, blaming them for the disastrous turn of events that had overwhelmed them.

Renewal of the promise (5:22–7:7). Just as the people murmured against Moses, so Moses murmured against the Lord (5:22–23). The Lord, unlike Moses, however, was able to offer hope. He, the God of the burning bush who had appeared as El Shaddai (the all-abundant One) to the patriarchs, had long ago promised that their descendants would inherit Canaan (6:1–5). The time had now come to implement the terms of the ancient covenant by redeeming Israel out of Egypt (6:5–6), by making a new national covenant (6:7), and by leading them into the Promised Land (6:8), all through the power of His name "I Am." In the strength of that name Moses should return once more to Pharaoh (6:10–13).

As though once more to assure Moses of his authority as leader of Israel, God reminded Moses of his ancestry. He descended from Levi through the clan of Kohath (6:16, 18). His father Amram married Jochebed and their sons were Aaron and Moses (6:20). Eventually Aaron became the chief priest and from him sprang the whole line of subsequent chief priests (6:23, 25). Moses thus was a Levite, with all the cultic and political privileges that accrued to that tribe. Beyond that, he stood in the very place of God before Pharaoh with Aaron as his prophet (7:1). On the basis of this pedigree and derivative authority Moses could now appear once more to Pharaoh and in the name of the Lord could demand that he set his Israelite kinsmen free (7:2–7).

Revelation through signs (7:8–11:10). At the first encounter of Moses and Aaron with Pharaoh (7:8–25), Aaron cast down his rod and it became a snake. When the Egyptian magicians replicated this sign, they were dismayed to see Aaron's rod-snake devour theirs (7:8–13). The rod here, as before (4:2–5), symbolized regal authority. The point was clear: The Lord and not Pharaoh was sovereign, and the Lord's servants Moses and Aaron represented that sovereignty.

Pharaoh was unmoved, however, so the Lord commanded Moses to take the rod and strike the waters of the Nile with it, an act suggesting dominion over not only creation but also over the gods of Egyptian mythology linked with the life-giving force of the river. Their "death" would become apparent by the transformation of the water into blood (7:14–19). When Moses and Aaron did as God said, the Nile in effect died, and the people had to dig for drinking water in order to survive (7:20–25).

This display of power against the very foundation of Egyptian ideology failed to soften Pharaoh's heart, so the Lord authorized another plague. This time frogs came out of the river and swarmed over the whole land, even into the kitchens and bedrooms of the people. Once more, the Nile and its deities that were supposed to provide nourishment to the land instead spewed out these ugly creatures that threatened to poison it (8:1–7). Though Pharaoh's magicians duplicated this wonder, he relented and agreed that if the frogs were removed (something his practitioners could not do), he would let the Hebrews undertake their religious pilgrimage. No sooner had Moses successfully interceded on Egypt's behalf, however, than Pharaoh once more stiffened his resistance against God's purposes (8:8–15).

As a result of the third plague the whole land became infested with gnats (8:16–19). When the Egyptian sorcerers attempted to imitate Moses and Aaron, they could not do so and had to concede that such a sign could come only from God, that is, the God of Israel (see also 7:5; 10:7). Pharaoh, however, became all the more resistant.

The next plague was a swarm of flies that clearly was a sign from God in that it did not affect Goshen, where the Hebrews lived (8:20–32). This separation of God's people from all others attested to their election by Him and His providential care for them. It also bore witness that Israel's God was Yahweh, Lord of all creation. The release of the flies proved to be more than Pharaoh could tolerate, so he gave permission for Israel to worship, but not outside Egypt's borders. When Moses protested, the king conceded to the extent of allowing the people to go to the desert but not the three days' journey Moses had requested. Once more the Lord delivered the land from plague, but once again Pharaoh reneged on his promise.

Pharaoh's stubbornness led to still another confrontation with Moses and his God (9:1–7), which resulted in the death of all the Egyptian cattle by disease (literally, "pestilence"). Israel's cattle were unaffected, however—evidence once more of God's special favor toward them.

The next judgment of the Lord on Egypt took the form of painful boils (literally, "inflammations") that affected human and animal life alike (9:8–11). Even the Egyptian magicians suffered and perhaps Pharaoh as well. But this time the king not only would not relent but could not, for the Lord had hardened his will (9:12). The lesson here is that when one ignores the prompting of the Lord time and time again (see 7:13, 22; 8:15, 19, 32; 9:7), the Lord will confirm that resistance and make belief impossible. Even this can be an expression of divine sovereignty (Rom. 9:14–18).

The threat of the seventh plague was much more ominous and direct (9:13–35). Moses said that the Lord would destroy the land with an unprecedented hail storm that would affect all of Egypt (except the Israelites), including Pharaoh himself. This would demonstrate the Lord's uniqueness among all the "gods" and would show by Pharaoh's humiliation that the Lord alone is Ruler over all. This time no offer of negotiation was given to Pharaoh. Instead, the heavens opened up and with thunder, lightning, and hail the Lord revealed His awesome power and judgment through all the land. Only Goshen, the land of the Hebrews, was spared (9:22–26).

Seeing his nation in ruins, Pharaoh offered at least the semblance of confession and repentance, though its lack of genuineness was quickly exposed once the ordeal was over (9:27, 34–35). Moses himself could see through the charade, but he continued his apologetic on God's behalf by declaring to Pharaoh that just as the plague itself witnessed to God's glory, so would its ending (9:29). The storm was no "freak of nature." It was an act of God from beginning to end, a display that testified to Israel's Creator as Lord over all things.

God said the plagues had been carried out to manifest His power among not only the Egyptians but also His own people Israel. In future years they would be able to recall these astounding displays of power and in light of them to confess that God is Lord (10:1–2). The next in the series was a judgment by locusts, a catastrophe so foreboding that it was feared that all Egypt would be destroyed (10:7). Pressed by his advisers, Pharaoh at first seemed conciliatory, and so he agreed to let Israel's men go worship the Lord in the desert. When Moses insisted that all Israel—human beings and even livestock—be permitted to leave, Pharaoh withdrew his offer entirely (10:8–11). The Lord then unleashed the locusts in such vast numbers that they covered the whole country, devouring every plant and leaving abject devastation in their wake. Again Pharaoh pleaded for relief with a superficial expression of contrition (10:16–17). But deep down he still rebelled, and when the locusts had been expelled he adamantly refused to let Israel go (10:20).

In a land of almost cloudless days year-round and of worship of the sun, darkness for seventy-two hours would certainly reveal the impotence of Egypt and her deities. This state of affairs now befell the land in the ninth plague, except for the territory of the Israelites, where the sun continued to shine (10:21–29). Pharaoh was so shaken by this assault on the very foundations of his belief system that he agreed to let all the people go to worship the Lord, but he said they must leave their livestock behind. This absurd proposal was, of course, rejected, so the king, infuriated by all that had led up to this, swore to kill Moses if he ever appeared before him again. In unmistakably ominous overtones Moses replied that Pharaoh indeed would never see his face again.

The Lord then told Moses that He would send one more judgment on Egypt, after which the Exodus would take place (11:1–10). Ten is a number of climax or completeness in the Bible, so a tenth plague would signal the finality of God's work of judgment and deliverance (compare Gen. 31:7, 41; Deut. 4:13; 10:4; 1 Sam. 1:8; Dan. 1:12–14, 20; 7:7, 20, 24). Ironically, though Pharaoh detested Moses and the Israelites, the common

their purses to them and

compared to this last one, to death. One cannot help included the slaughter of were turned, and not even s dire warning fell on deaf that he had learned noth-ght for the future (11:10).

dus

oils	9:8–12
ail	9:13–35
ocusts	10:1–20
arkness	10:21–29
eath of	
he firstborn	11:1–12:30

as not limited to Egyptians elief. This included the He-deemer would spare these sted visibly. When and only he Lord pass over and spare

ecause God's deliverance of orated, it was important to ations would commence on t of such moment that that irst of the religious calendar e was Nisan (Neh. 2:1). The the fall. Thus the Old Testa-f Trumpets) taking place on the first day of the seventh month

known as Rosh Hashanah.

The Passover ritual was to consist

lamb from the tenth to the fourteen

family and/or its neighbors would off

be eaten except for the blood, which

9:4; Lev. 17:10–16; Deut. 12:16), was

the houses of the Israelites who tr

12:6–10). The whole ceremony is ca

12:11) for in His destruction of Egy

over (*pāsaḥ*) the houses whose doorp

Blood as a symbol of atonement and

Inauguration of the Feast of Unlea

future, Passover was to be followed by

be eaten or even allowed in the hous

time it took for bread to rise would d

which was to be done in great haste.

the Israelites of the time when haste wa

lives from Egypt's pursuing army. To th

ened Bread, though it is usually so clo

has ceased to exist as a separate rite.

Implementation of the Passover (12

the instructions about Passover, the p

out. Again the prophet reminded the

them never to forget what they were do

teaching to all generations to come (12

visited Egypt with the tenth plague, th

of every unprotected home (12:29–30

Israelites fled with their unleavened br

tian friends and neighbors were divinely

Celebrating significant historical e

tions participate in the tragedies an

Thus Passover, Yom Kippur, C

a means of reliving the past and ex

Egyptians felt otherwise. God led them to open their purses to them and for Israel to enjoy their favor (Exod. 11:3).

All previous plagues pale into insignificance compared to this last one, for every family in Egypt lost its firstborn son to death. One cannot help but recall that Israel's oppression in Egypt had included the slaughter of its helpless male babies (1:16). Now the tables were turned, and not even the royal household was spared (11:5). Even this dire warning fell on deaf ears, however, for Pharaoh's heart was so stony that he had learned nothing from the past and therefore took little thought for the future (11:10).

The Ten Plagues in Exodus			
1. Nile turned to blood	7:14–25	6. Boils	9:8–12
2. Frogs	8:1–15	7. Hail	9:13–35
3. Gnats	8:16–19	8. Locusts	10:1–20
4. Flies	8:20–22	9. Darkness	10:21–29
5. Death of livestock	9:1–7	10. Death of the firstborn	11:1–12:30

E. The Passover (12:1–36)

The threat of the death of Egypt's firstborn was not limited to Egyptians alone but to all its residents who lived in unbelief. This included the Hebrews as well. So only faith in the Lord as Redeemer would spare these potential victims, a faith that must be manifested visibly. When and only when this display of faith was evident would the Lord pass over and spare the families that testified to it.

Inauguration of the Passover (12:1–14). Because God's deliverance of His people would henceforward be commemorated, it was important to note the dates of its occurrence. The preparations would commence on the tenth day of the month Abib (13:4), a fact of such moment that that month would from that time onward be the first of the religious calendar (12:2). In later terminology the month's name was Nisan (Neh. 2:1). The civil year would begin in the month Tishri in the fall. Thus the Old Testament speaks of New Year's Day (the Feast of Trumpets) taking place on the first day of the seventh month (Lev. 23:24; 27:1), an occasion now known as Rosh Hashanah.

The Passover ritual was to consist of the preparation of a yearling male lamb from the tenth to the fourteenth of the month, at which time each family and/or its neighbors would offer it up as a burnt offering. It was to be eaten except for the blood, which, besides being ritually taboo (Gen. 9:4; Lev. 17:10–16; Deut. 12:16), was to be used at the Passover to mark the houses of the Israelites who trusted God for deliverance (Exod. 12:6–10). The whole ceremony is called the Passover (Hebrew, *pesaḥ*; 12:11) for in His destruction of Egypt's firstborn the Lord would pass over (*pāsaḥ*) the houses whose doorposts were set apart by blood (12:13). Blood as a symbol of atonement and redemption is clearly in view here.

Inauguration of the Feast of Unleavened Bread (12:15–20). In Israel's future, Passover was to be followed by seven days in which no leaven could be eaten or even allowed in the house. The reason for this was that the time it took for bread to rise would delay Israel's departure from Egypt, which was to be done in great haste. Observing this feast would remind the Israelites of the time when haste was of the essence in preserving their lives from Egypt's pursuing army. To this day the festival is called Unleavened Bread, though it is usually so closely connected to Passover that it has ceased to exist as a separate rite.

Implementation of the Passover (12:21–36). After Moses had relayed the instructions about Passover, the people commenced to carry them out. Again the prophet reminded them of its meaning and commanded them never to forget what they were doing and to pass on its practice and teaching to all generations to come (12:21–28). That very night the Lord visited Egypt with the tenth plague, the destruction of the firstborn son of every unprotected home (12:29–30). Fearing for their very lives, the Israelites fled with their unleavened bread and all the goods their Egyptian friends and neighbors were divinely disposed to give them (12:31–36).

> *Celebrating significant historical events can help present generations participate in the tragedies and triumphs of their forebears. Thus Passover, Yom Kippur, Christmas, and Easter provide a means of reliving the past and experiencing its power.*

II. ISRAEL'S EXODUS (12:37–18:27)

Israel was already God's "son" (Exod. 4:22–23), so the need now was for Israel to be released from the illegitimate sovereignty of one king, Pharaoh, to the sovereignty of another, the Lord God. This required a miraculous intervention of divine power and a supernatural leading and provision along the way to the place where God was to encounter His people in covenant partnership. This section of Exodus creates a bridge from the Exodus to Sinai.

A. *Journey to the Red Sea (12:37–14:20)*

Israel's fears of Pharaoh were not unfounded, for no sooner had the people left Goshen (or Rameses, 12:37) than the mighty Egyptian army followed in hot pursuit (14:5–6). Meanwhile they reflected again on the meaning of what was transpiring. After 430 years (12:41; see Gen. 15:13; 46:5–7), they were leaving Egypt for the land God had promised to give them. He had spared them in the tenth plague, and so they were now free to depart. Thereafter the Israelites and those brought into covenant privilege with them would celebrate the Passover as a memorial to God's gracious initiative on their behalf.

A major point to the tenth plague was the fact that because Pharaoh would not allow Israel, God's "firstborn son," to leave Egypt, the firstborn sons of Egyptian families must forfeit their lives unless they were protected by sacrificial blood (Exod. 4:22–23; 11:5; 12:29). As a result of God's having preserved Israel's firstborn, they belonged to Him in a special way and must be set apart to Him for His use (13:1–2). This was a new element to be added to the annual celebration of the Passover-Unleavened Bread festival once Israel had settled in the Promised Land (13:3–10). Not only would the firstborn of the people be set apart, but also animals would be dedicated to the Lord. The firstborn of "clean" animals (that is, those ritually suitable) would be sacrificed, but animals such as asses could be redeemed, that is, replaced by a lamb. Human beings obviously could not be sacrificed so they too were to be redeemed by payment of a lamb. All of this would symbolize God's favor on Israel's firstborn at the time He judged Egypt for its sin (13:11–16).

The usual route to Canaan from Egypt was the so-called Via Maris, the "Way of the Sea," which followed the Mediterranean coastline closely. However, this required traveling through Philistine territory, a prospect that was likely to dishearten the Israelites and even cause them to return to Egypt (13:17–18). But these Philistines were not the ones encountered by Israel later in the times of the judges (Judg. 10:7; 13:1) and kings (1 Sam. 13:1–23). Instead they were the descendants of the Philistines with whom the patriarchs had had dealings (Gen. 20:1–18; 26:1–11). The major immigration of Philistines (also known as "Sea Peoples") took place around 1200–1150 B.C., 250 years after the Exodus.

The Lord thus led Israel straight east, toward the chain of lakes now joined together by the Suez Canal. Having arrived at Etham from Succoth (both places now unknown), they found themselves in a perilous condition, hemmed in on the left, right, and rear by the desert, and facing uncrossable waters just ahead. God had led them by fire and cloud but to what end? It seemed that only destruction lay ahead (Exod. 13:17–14:2).

God, however, had another reason for this strategy. The Egyptians once more would become filled with pride and self-sufficiency, and seeing Israel boxed in, they would view Israel's plight as a sign the Lord had abandoned His people. However, once the Lord gained the victory, He would gain great honor and all Egypt would see once more that He is God (14:3–9).

When Pharaoh's army arrived, the soldiers found the defenseless Israelites at Pi Hahiroth, whose location is presently unknown. Realizing their dire circumstances, the Israelites hurled bitter accusations against Moses for having led them there, to which he responded that all they needed to do was to be still and watch what God would do for them. He would fight for them, for it was His war, not theirs. This is the first example in the Old Testament of what some scholars call "holy war" or "Yahweh war." That is, this war was undertaken by the Lord in defense of His own reputation, promises, and self-interest (14:10–14; see also, for example, 15:3; Deut. 1:30; 3:22; 20:4). It is to be distinguished from "ordinary" war that Israel might undertake on her own (Num. 14:39–45).

One purpose of holy war was to bring glory to God in its successful prosecution. In Israel's hopeless situation here was an opportunity for the Lord to make clear that He is the God of creation and of history. He therefore commanded Moses to part the sea, an act that would exalt Him above Pharaoh and testify to Egypt that He alone is the Lord. The glowing cloud that would lead the way would symbolize God's presence and His role as divine Warrior on Israel's behalf.

B. Journey to Mount Sinai (14:21–18:27)

The Exodus (14:21–15:18). With great confidence in God, Moses extended his rod over the waters. They immediately parted and stood like walls on either side of Israel's highway through the sea (14:21–22). When the Egyptian troops attempted to pursue, their chariot wheels became mired in the mud (as some ancient versions read) or turned aside (Hebrew, *šûb*) so that they could not catch up. Recognizing that the Lord Himself was doing battle, the Egyptians attempted to wheel about and escape, but it was too late. Israel was safely on the other side when with a thunderous roar the walls of water collapsed and the entire enemy host was drowned. No wonder the Israelites responded with such awe and affirmation of both the Lord and His servant Moses (14:26–31).

The prose account of the Exodus is echoed by one of the most stirring exultations in the Lord to be found anywhere in the Bible (15:1–18). The overtones of holy war are unmistakable, making the point that the Exodus was divinely originated, supernaturally carried out, and miraculously consummated. Israel was involved, indeed, but only as a beneficiary—almost as a spectator—of the event. This, of course, is in line with the whole biblical doctrine of redemption. It is an act of grace conceived and effected by a loving God who, for reasons known only to Him, reaches down to the objects of His favor to deliver them from sin, slavery, and death.

The "song of the sea" begins with a description of the Lord as a "Man of war" who has brought about a triumphant work of deliverance (15:1–3). Specifically, He overthrew the Egyptians in the sea by a blast of His mighty breath. He divided the waters in this manner, and at His command they returned to their place, crushing Pharaoh's hosts before them (15:4–10). The lyrics next extol the Lord, the incomparable One, for this act of wrath was also an act of mercy. Egypt's death meant Israel's life. All the world heard of these saving acts and responded in terror before Israel's God (15:11–16). But the end was not yet, for the God who brought His people out of bondage would bring them into the land of liberty, the place He had prepared for both them and Himself. It was in Canaan that He would exercise His true and everlasting sovereignty (15:17–18).

The miracles of provision (15:19–17:7). After Miriam and the women of Israel responded to Moses' song of praise, Moses led the people first to Marah (literally, "bitterness"), where the bitter waters were sweetened, and then to Elim, an oasis with abundant natural springs (15:22–27). Between Elim and Sinai the people complained about an inadequate food supply, a complaint the Lord met by the miraculous provision of manna and quails. The breadlike manna (Hebrew, *mān hū'*, "What is it?") was distributed in such a way as to meet each day's need and no more. Those who took more than needed would see it rot away, and those who took too little would go hungry. Only on Sabbath eve could a double portion be collected, for no such activity must be done on that hallowed day. To commemorate this bountiful and supernatural provision Moses commanded that a potfull of manna should be kept by or in the ark of the covenant ever after (chapter 16).

Manna enough for a day at a time recalls the model prayer in which Jesus taught, "Give us this day our daily bread" (Matt. 6:11). The request is not so much that God would be generous as that we might be content with what each day provides and requires.

At the next place of encampment, Rephidim, the people again ran short of water. In desperation Moses turned to the Lord for counsel and was told to strike a certain rock with his rod and from it water would gush out. Though the place became one of blessing, its names thereafter memorialized Israel's criticisms and complaints. It would in the future be called Massah ("testing") and Meribah ("strife"), for those nouns best characterized Israel's faithless responses to God's good purposes (17:1–7).

The victory over enemies (17:8–16). Israel's first encounter with a hostile people also took place at Rephidim. An Amalekite raiding party swept down on Israel's weak and feeble stragglers (see Deut. 25:18), and for this cowardly attack the Amalekites suffered defeat at Israel's hands as God gave enablement. Joshua first came into prominence at this point as Moses' designated military officer (Exod. 17:9). The narrative also drops a hint as to his future role as theocratic administrator, for Moses was to declare to Joshua the punishment that Amalek must suffer in days to come (17:14). Moses was instructed here to keep a written record of Amalek's attack, a hint that he was already preparing materials for what eventually would be the Pentateuch.

The encounter with Jethro (chapter 18). At some stage of the itinerary Moses' father-in-law Jethro joined the Israelites, bringing with him Moses' estranged wife Zipporah and their sons (18:1–6; see 4:18–26). Jethro had already heard of the miraculous Exodus deliverance (18:1), but now Moses elaborated, stressing that what God had done had been done for Israel's sake (18:8). Hearing all this, Jethro, already a "priest of Midian" (18:1; see 2:16; 3:1), exclaimed over the incomparability of the Lord God of Israel (18:10–11). To cement this declaration he sacrificed a burnt offering, thus joining himself to Israel and Israel's God by covenant (18:12).

Before Jethro went his way, he observed how overtaxed Moses was in trying to administer the legal and social affairs of the whole community. The people continuously went to Moses to obtain justice from the Lord (18:15–16). Wisely, Jethro pointed out that if Moses continued at this pace, he would surely wear himself out. His advice was that Moses should continue to be the conduit through whom the people addressed the Lord and the communicator of God's will to the people, but that he should also appoint lower courts to hear cases that need not come directly to him. Only those beyond their capacity to judge need be referred to Moses himself (18:19–22).

III. ISRAEL'S COVENANT AND FELLOWSHIP (CHAPTERS 19–40)

An important reason for the Exodus was to bring Israel to the place— spiritually and geographically—of entering into covenant with God. As already noted, this was not a covenant that made Israel the people of the

Lord, for that had been done long before through God's covenant with Abraham. Rather, the covenant about to be implemented was one that would give Israel the opportunity to be God's servant people, the channel by which He would communicate and transmit His redemptive program to the whole world.

The remainder of the Book of Exodus consists of the offer and acceptance of the covenant (chapter 19), its text (chapters 20–23), the covenant ceremony (chapter 24), preparations for the Lord's dwelling place among His people (chapters 25–31), and the record of its construction (35:4–40:16). In the midst is the tragic story of Israel's apostasy, followed by a reminder of God's gracious forgiveness (32:1–35:3).

A. Preparation for Covenant (chapter 19)

Three months after the Exodus, Israel arrived at the mountain where the Lord had earlier said He would meet them (19:1–2; see 3:12). In a most theologically significant declaration He reminded them how He had defeated the Egyptians, delivered His own people, and brought them to Himself, that is, to the mountain of His revelation (19:4). Now, on condition of their obedience to His forthcoming covenant, He was prepared to make them His special possession, a precious gem, as it were, that He had selected from among all the nations (19:5). The role they were to play should they accede would be one of intercession between the Lord and the peoples of the earth. They would become a royal priesthood, a holy nation (19:6). Just as any priest bridged the gap between the transcendent God and His earthbound creatures, so Israel, already God's "son," would become a mediator between the ineffable One and all the nations that needed to be reconciled to Him.

When Moses communicated this astounding offer to them, the people immediately responded in the affirmative (19:7–8). The Lord then commanded Moses to prepare the people for His awesome encounter with them as the two parties—the Lord and Israel—came together to make their mutual pledges (19:9–15).

Such an encounter was by no means between equals. In fact, the holiness of God differs so greatly from the carnality of humanity that the

Israelites could not even look on His resplendent glory. In language wholly inadequate to describe the divine manifestation Moses spoke of it in terms of cosmic imagery—thunder, lightning, clouds, smoke, and earthquake. The usual theological term for this kind of visitation is *epiphany*, a display of the Lord's presence short of the revelation of His actual person.

The Israelites stood at the foot of the mountain trembling as they stared up at the terrifying scene above. The whole mountain seemed ablaze with God's presence, and it shook as He thundered forth His response to Israel's offer to make a covenant with them. Only Moses could stand between, and so he shuttled back and forth between Israel in the plains and the Lord God in the impenetrable heights of Sinai. The task of communicating between the two lay with him, for if the Lord spoke directly to the people they would die (19:16–25; see also Deut. 4:33; 5:4–5, 24–25).

B. The Covenant Text (chapters 20–23)

The Decalogue (20:1–17). The revelation God shared with Moses on the mountaintop was the "Book of the Covenant" (20:2–23:33), the first part of which is the Decalogue or Ten Commandments. The Decalogue is the constitution of the covenant community, as it were, and the remaining laws are amendments or clarifications of the commandments. In recent times scholars have drawn attention to the fact that the laws of the Decalogue are of one type or form (apodictic) whereas the others are of a different kind (casuistic). More important, it is clear in light of ancient Near Eastern (particularly Hittite) models that the Book of the Covenant (as well as Deuteronomy) is best described as a suzerain-vassal treaty text, one in which a great king (here, God Himself) makes a covenant with a lesser king. In such a form the will of the greater is imposed on the lesser, but the latter stands to gain great benefit if he accepts and obeys the terms of the covenant.

By form, the covenant documents contained a preamble and historical prologue as an introduction to the body of the stipulations proper. Here in Exodus the preamble and historical prologue are extremely brief, reported in 20:2. The first four commandments (20:3–11) regulate Israel's relationship to the Lord, and the last six (20:12–17) address the relationship between persons. In each section the most serious violation occurs first, and the least violation is at the end. Moreover, the first five commandments all refer to God directly or indirectly, whereas the last five do not. The "hinge" commandment is the fifth, the one enjoining honor toward one's parents. Though this is mainly on the "horizontal" plane, that is, one human being toward another, an appeal is made to "the LORD your God."

The first commandment (20:3) asserts that only God is to be worshiped, and the second (20:4–6) prohibits any attempt to make an image of Him or any other imagined deity. The third (20:7) forbids the misuse of the Lord's name by invoking it for no worthy purpose. The fourth commandment (20:8–11) concerns the setting aside of the seventh day as a day of rest and recollection of God's creative work. Since He rested after six days, so must His people.

After the command to honor one's parents (20:12), there are four that prohibit certain actions, again in an order of most significant to least significant: murder, adultery, theft, and false testimony (20:13–16). The tenth is remarkable in that it speaks not of an outward deed but of an inward disposition: "You shall not covet" (20:17). In a sense this is the most reprehensible of all though least detectable, for the desires and passions of the human heart often give rise to the violent and hurtful actions prohibited in the other commandments.

The people's reaction (20:18–21). The glory of God and all its cosmic manifestations that attended the scene of Moses' ascent of Sinai to receive the covenant text accompanied his descent as well. The two displays of divine presence form a bracket, as it were, around the text of the Decalogue itself (19:16–25; 20:18–21). The purpose clearly is to set off the Ten Commandments as the supreme expression of God's nature and purposes as they relate to Israel. From beginning to end they are God's words, not man's, and they must be viewed against the backdrop of His awesome majesty.

The Book of the Covenant (20:22–23:33). On the basis of this description in 24:7, the laws that follow the Decalogue are commonly viewed as a discrete composition designed to complement the Ten Commandments as a set of bylaws or amendments. The case for seeing it as such finds support in a prelude (20:22–26) and postlude (23:20–33) that share the common theme of the Lord's uniqueness and a strict prohibition against worshiping anyone but Him. To put it another way, the Book of the Covenant begins and ends with a focus on the first two commandments, thus establishing their importance as the foundation of the entire covenant relationship.

When Israel arrived in Canaan, it would be acceptable for places of worship to be established wherever the Lord made His presence known (20:24). These local shrines must not be confused with the central sanctuary described in Deuteronomy 12, to which the covenant community as a whole was to resort at least three times a year. Rather, they were places with altars of earth or fieldstone (as opposed to the hewed stone of Canaanite altars) set up for the convenience of worshipers in their own villages who could not easily travel to the central sanctuary. Many of these appear in the later historical record (see, for example, Judg. 6:25–27; 13:15–20; 1 Sam. 9:11–14; 16:1–5; 1 Kings 18:30–40).

The first section of the Book of the Covenant proper deals with the treatment of slaves, especially fellow Israelites who had come to that status because of debt (Exod. 21:1–11). They could not be forced to remain in that relationship for more than six years, so their debt was reduced *pro rata* every year until it was paid off at the end of the sixth. If they married and had children during that time, only the husband and father could go free. If they wished to remain with their creditor, they could do so and their choice would be legalized publicly by having their ear lobes pierced (21:1–6). If a man's daughter was delivered over to a creditor as an earnest toward repayment, however, she must be released also after six years unless she had become the wife of the creditor or his son. In that case other financial obligations entered in, depending on what other complications attended her status (21:7–11).

The second major section (21:12–36) pertains to various kinds of bodily harm inflicted by persons or even animals. Premeditated murder required the death penalty, but accidental homicide required only detention in the city pending a trial (21:12–14). Striking one's parents was a capital offense, as was kidnapping or even showing total disrespect of one's parents (21:15, 17). Injury short of death called for compensation, usually monetary (21:18–21). In an interesting specific case, if a man were to injure a pregnant woman so that she gave birth prematurely but with no serious aftereffects to her or the child, a mere fine paid to the husband was sufficient. However, if either the mother or child died, the attacker was to pay with his life. The principle here is *lex talionis*, punishment being commensurate with the crime (an "eye for [an] eye," 21:22–25).

Punishment for injury to slaves or injury caused by animals was generally less severe (21:26–32). In the former case, the slave must be set free, and in the latter case the animal's owner must die if the animal was known to be dangerous, or he could be merely fined if the ox, for example, had never before manifest such behavior. If a person caused an animal's death by leaving an open pit, he was required to recompense its owner (21:33–34). If one man's animal killed the animal of another, both animals were to be disposed of in a manner that would compensate the offended party (21:35–36).

The next collection of laws concerns theft and property rights (22:1–17). Compensation for the theft of animals that were later killed could be four or five times their actual value (22:17). Even if the thief kept the animal alive, he must pay its owner twice its value (22:4). If an owner apprehended and killed a thief breaking and entering in the nighttime, he was absolved of any culpability (22:2–3). Damage to a neighbor's property by careless release of animals on it or misuse of fire demanded financial restitution (22:5–6). If a person kept another person's property under his care and it became lost or stolen, the caretaker suffered penalty in proportion to his responsibility for its loss (22:7–9). This included the care of animals as well (22:10–13). On the other hand, if one borrowed something from another with no rental fee and then damaged or lost it, he must make compensation (22:14–15). Since a daughter was, in a sense, her father's "property," any man who violated (thus, stole) her must either marry her and pay a bride price to her father or, if the father would not let her marry the man, the perpetrator must make the payment (22:16–17). Property clearly did not compare in value to life and health, but it was still an important part of a family's well-being and so its misappropriation or loss demanded fair compensation.

The last major section of the Book of the Covenant is much more miscellaneous in content, but the dominant theme of the whole is religious in nature (22:18–23:19). It begins with the injunction to put fortunetellers to death (22:18) and ends with the strange prohibition against boiling a young goat in its mother's milk (23:19; see Deut. 14:21). The one has to do with pagan prophetic devices (see Deut. 18:9–14), and the other with an unnatural mingling of a source of life with its product. This provides the basis for the Jewish kosher tradition of not serving dairy and meat dishes at the same meal.

Included in the stipulations of this section are a prohibition against bestiality (Exod. 22:19), sacrifice to the Lord alone (22:20), fair treatment of the poor and helpless (22:21–27), proper respect for divine and human authority (22:28), the giving of one's best to the Lord (22:29–31), the pursuit of justice in everyday life (23:1–5) as well as in the courts (23:6–9), careful attention to the letter and spirit of the Sabbath (23:10–12), and, in summary, acknowledgment and worship of the Lord to the exclusion of all other "gods" (23:13).

The community or corporate nature of Israel lies at the heart of the need for her to assemble at the central sanctuary three times each year (23:14–17). The first gathering would be for the Passover–Unleavened Bread feast in the spring (23:14–15); the second was the Festival of Harvest, also known as the Festival of Weeks (34:22); and the third was the Festival of Ingathering or Tabernacles (Lev. 23:34, NIV). These times of assembly and worship would be in addition to whatever religious activity was carried on by individuals and families in local places. In any circumstance, proper protocol must be followed in making offerings to the Lord (Exod. 23:18–19).

The Book of the Covenant concludes with the Lord's promise to Israel to go with them all the way to Canaan and there to bless them (23:20–33). The "angel" (literally, "messenger") who would accompany them would be a representative of the Lord, so Godlike as to bear God's name and to have the authority to forgive sin (23:21). This is an example of a theophany, a manifestation of God in human form. Some see this Being as a preincarnate appearance of Jesus Christ. Whatever the case, He would lead Israel to triumph over the inhabitants of the Promised Land (23:23).

Once there the Israelites must refuse to yield to idolatry and must serve the Lord faithfully. This would ensure God's blessing on them in agriculture, health, posterity, and in military and political success. Violation of the covenant, however, would result in God's judgment (23:24–33).

C. The Covenant Ceremony (chapter 24)

An element in the process of covenant making was a ceremony, usually including a formal meal, that testified publicly to the binding nature of the agreements to which the contracting parties had sworn. This passage provides insight into this aspect of the Sinai Covenant.

It seems that Moses first ascended alone to the presence of the Lord (24:1–2), where he received the Decalogue and Book of the Covenant by God's gracious revelation. He then descended to the people with the "words" (commandments) and "laws" (that is, regulations; the Book of the Covenant) and presented them to the assembly, which swore to obey them (24:3). After writing down all these terms, Moses erected an altar (representing the Lord) and twelve pillars (representing Israel's twelve tribes). He then sprinkled the blood of a sacrifice on these objects, thereby symbolizing God's covenant union with His people (24:4–8). Moses, Aaron, Aaron's sons, and seventy elders then "met" the Lord in a display of His glory and shared with Him the covenant banquet (24:9–11).

The earthly or human side of the ceremony must be matched by the divine side, so Moses ascended once more to Sinai's summit, where he encountered the ineffably awesome presence of God (24:17). The Lord there gave him a duplicate set of the Commandments and Book of the Covenant (24:12), one that was identical to what Moses had already written (24:4). One copy was to be retained by the Lord, as it were, and the other by Israel, for it was traditional in the ancient world for both covenant parties to have a copy of their mutual agreement. After the whole arrangement had been consummated on the mountain, Moses returned to the people below (24:12–18).

D. The Preparation for the Covenant Dwelling Place (chapters 25–31)

The first set of instructions (chapters 25–27). Now that the Lord had made a covenant with Israel and, as part of it, had commanded Israel to appear before Him three times a year (23:14–17), a place for that encounter must be prepared, a place built according to strict specifications (25:1–8). The furnishings must include a wooden chest (the Ark of the Covenant) to contain the covenant tablets (25:16) and to serve as a throne or dais on which the Lord would "sit" invisibly as King (25:10–22). A table must also be fashioned to hold loaves of "showbread" (KJV, literally, "bread of [God's] presence") that would symbolize the Lord's provision for His people (25:23–30; see also Lev. 24:5–9). In addition, there must be a candelabrum with six branches, making seven lamps in all (Exod. 25:31–39). This represented the Lord's guidance. All was to be made according to a heavenly pattern revealed to Moses at Sinai (25:40).

Moses also received revelation about the curtains (26:1–6), roofing (26:7–14), and side boards (26:15–25) and bars (26:26–30) of the tent-like structure as well as the partition (the veil) that separated the two rooms (the Holy Place and Most Holy Place) from each other and the drapes that provided covering over the front door (26:31–37). Just in front of the tabernacle there was to be an altar of acacia wood covered with bronze, on which the priests would offer sacrifices (27:1–8). Around the entire complex a fence was to be built to enclose an area of 100 by 50 cubits (150 by 75 feet). This was to consist of posts and beautifully fashioned linen hangings (27:9–19). The interior of the building was to be illuminated by the candlelabrum which Aaron and his priestly descendants were to tend (27:20–21).

The clothing and consecration of the priests (chapters 28–29). The clothing of the priests was to be for glory and beauty, thus suggesting God's transcendence and His immanence (28:2). After providing a summary list of the various items (28:4–5), the Lord spoke of the specifications and significance of each.

The first garment is the ephod, an apronlike outer covering joined at the shoulders by straps on which were set two onyx stones containing the names of the tribes of Israel, six on each stone. Their placement would suggest the role of the priest in bearing the needs of the people before the Lord (28:6–14). A square plate was to be affixed to the front of the ephod and on it twelve more stones, each representing a tribe, were to be embedded. The purpose of this arrangement was to symbolize the compassion of the priest, who must constantly have his people's interests on his heart (28:29). Two other precious stones called Urim ("lights") and Thummim ("perfections") were to be suspended from the ephod, perhaps in a pouch or pocket of some kind (28:30; see also 1 Sam. 14:16–20). In some way these stones could be "read" by the priests as a form of divine revelation (Num. 27:21).

Under the ephod the high priest was to wear a blue robe decorated at the hem with bands of colorful pomegranates and bells (Exod. 28:31–35). His head covering was to be a turbanlike hat, on the front of which there was to be a gold plate bearing the inscription "Holiness to the LORD" (28:36). This set the priest apart as a kind of symbolical sin-substitute, one who bore the people's sins before a holy God (28:38). Other parts of the attire were an outer robe, sashes, and linen underwear designed to protect the modesty of the priests as they undertook their tasks (28:39–43).

The ritual of ordination required that the priests come attired in their finery to the altar, where they first would be anointed with oil as a sign of their separation to ministry (29:1–9). Then bulls and rams were to be offered up, the blood of the latter being applied to the right ear, right thumb, and right big toe of the priests. This probably symbolized their consecration to hear God's Word, do His will, and walk according to His precepts. Other parts of the sacrifices were burned or used as meat by the celebrants as a way of showing their fellowship with God as His special servants (29:10–37). As mediators between God and Israel, the priests would sacrifice the daily community offerings and otherwise represent the populace at the place of worship (29:38–46).

The second set of instructions (chapters 30–31). The remaining furnishings of the tabernacle now receive attention, namely, the incense altar, to be set just in front of the veil (30:1–10), and the bronze wash basin, to be placed between the great bronze altar and the entrance to the tabernacle (30:17–21). Interspersed are instructions concerning the "sanctuary tax" of a half-shekel to be paid annually by every adult male (30:11–16) and the formulas for making the spices and oils to be used in the tabernacle services (30:22–38). The incense altar typified prayer (see Rev. 8:4), and the basin typified the purification needed if one is to approach God in His holiness.

If the pattern of construction was heavenly, those who labored to build the tabernacle and its furnishings must have heavenly assistance. Two Judahites, Bezalel and Oholiab, were selected to head up the work; to prepare them for it the Spirit of God came on them (Exod. 31:1–11). The instructions for the preparation of God's sanctuary and the priests to officiate in its services conclude with another reminder to observe the Sabbath, the day when the tabernacle would be most in use (31:12–17).

E. Apostasy and Renewal (32:1–35:3)

While Moses was on Mount Sinai receiving the covenant revelation (31:18; see also 24:12–18), the people down below almost immediately began to break its stipulations, especially the first two commandments (32:1–6). They persuaded Aaron to lead them away from the Lord (commandment one) and to make a gold idol representing either the Lord or Egyptian deities (commandment two).

The Lord therefore told Moses that He would destroy Israel and make Moses the founder of a new nation, a second Abraham, as it were. Moses "reminded" the Lord of His promises to the patriarchs, however, and urged Him to consider the scandal if He were to break His word (32:7–14). When Moses saw the pagan revelries for himself, he began to understand the Lord's anger. Dashing the stone tablets in pieces, he chastised Aaron, destroyed the idol, and returned once more to plead for the Lord's forgiveness of His people. If they could not be restored, he wished that he too would be condemned forever (32:15–35).

> *Moses was so closely bound to his beloved people Israel that he refused to be delivered if the nation itself could not be forgiven. The greatest display of such a sentiment, however, is the love of Christ who willingly laid down His life for the world.*

The Lord heard His godly servant's intercession and commanded him to lead them on toward Canaan (33:1–6). The sign that God still endorsed Moses' leadership was His appearance in the cloud of glory at the "tent of meeting" (Hebrew, *ʾōhel mōʿēd*), a temporary structure to be distinguished from the tabernacle (*miškān*, "dwelling place"). Whenever the Lord spoke to Moses, He did so at that place (33:7–11). Because of the people's terrible apostasy, however, Moses needed extra assurance of God's continuing favor, and so he asked that He might show him a special measure of His glory. Reminding Moses of His holiness and of the inability of human beings to see Him in His unveiled glory, the Lord nonetheless passed near Moses in a display of His transcendent splendor (33:12–23).

Moses may have smashed the tablets of the Decalogue to bits, but God had remained true to His commitment to Israel. He told Moses to carve out two new tablets, and then He renewed His pledge to keep covenant with His chosen people (34:1–9). But Israel, too, had an obligation to the Lord. They must resolve to worship Him alone (34:10–17), to keep His festivals and sabbaths (34:18–24), and to desist from any ritual practices not appropriate for a holy people (34:25–26).

Moses complied with the Lord's directives and so magnificent was their encounter that when Moses next appeared to the people at the foot of the mountain his very face shone with God's reflected glory, so much so that he was forced to wear a veil in their presence (34:27–35; 2 Cor 3:7). He then urged them to construct the tabernacle, reminding them, however, of the need to abide by Sabbath law in the process (Exod. 35:1–3).

F. Construction of the Tabernacle (35:4–40:38)

The remainder of the Book of Exodus records, for the most part, the construction of the tabernacle and its furnishings as prescribed in chapters 25–27 and 30–31. Moses' appeal to the people for precious metals and stones met with a ready and generous response (35:4–9) as did his solicitation of workers to do the actual building (35:10–19). These were all men and women who willingly volunteered because their hearts "moved" them to do so. God's work can be done right only by godly and God-led servants (35:20–29). Over the whole project, of course, were Bezalel and Oholiab, men who had natural skills but whose gifts were augmented and perfected by the infilling of God's Spirit (35:30–36:1; compare 31:1–6).

In turn the workers made the curtains, coverings, boards, bars, and veil of the tabernacle (36:8–38). Next they built the ark of the covenant, the table of showbread, the candelabrum, the altar of incense, the great bronze altar of sacrifice, the wash basin, and the fence around the courtyard (37:1–38:20). Exodus 38:21–39:1 provides an inventory of all the materials used and their value.

The tailors also turned to their task, fabricating the ephod, breast-plate, robe, coats, headdress, and gold head plate (39:2–31) for the high priest and his sons. All was done according to divine specifications, for the Lord spoke not only through the oral and written word but also through the architecture and furnishings of His earthly dwelling place as well (39:32–43).

On the first day of the first month of the second year after the Exodus the tabernacle rose from the ground, completed at last (40:1–19). The Lord Himself then "moved into" His dwelling place, a move symbolized by the placement of the ark into the most holy place (40:21). That He felt very much at home is clear from the fact that He filled the tabernacle with His glory. When He was at "home," His glory was there. When He led His people onward through the desert, His glory left the tabernacle for the time and marched forward to the land of promise (40:34–38).

LEVITICUS
Handbook on Holiness

AUTHOR

*M*any critical scholars say the Book of Leviticus was written in postexilic Israel. This late date of around 450 B.C. obviously precludes authorship by Moses, who lived one thousand years earlier. As pointed out earlier, the bases on which this view rests—religious developmentalism and alleged evidence of literary redactionism under priestly influence—are without objective proof. In fact, scholars increasingly are coming around to the view that the worship system prescribed in Leviticus began in the Mosaic era.

On a positive note, Moses, though nowhere explicitly identified in Leviticus as its author, is its central figure, and to him God gave instructions throughout the book about Israel's mode and purpose of worship (1:1; 7:38; 8:4–6; 9:1, 5–7; 10:3–7; 11:1; 13:1; 16:1; 27:34). The location of the book in the middle of the Pentateuch, which, as a whole, claims Mosaic authorship, also witnesses powerfully to his having composed it. Also Jewish and Christian tradition attests to its Mosaic origin.

UNITY

Even critical scholars have little debate about the unity of the book in its present canonical form. Some, however, might argue that the various literary forms in the book suggest that independent compositions were stitched together to comprise the whole book, but this need have no bearing on common authorship and overall unity. For example, these forms include prescriptions for sacrifice and offering (chapters 1–8), narrative (chapters 8–10), definitions of ritual impurity (chapters 11–15), the ritual of the Day of Atonement (chapter 16), the so-called Holiness Code (chapters 17–25) and a blessing-and-curse section (chapter 26). These all fit together logically and thematically and contribute to a beautiful literary structure.

DATE

A good case can be made that Leviticus was Moses' first "publication." The other books of the Pentateuch seem to presuppose arrival at the plains of Moab, but Leviticus offers hints that its contents were all revealed at Sinai (Lev. 27:34) and before "the first day of the second month of the second year after the Israelites came out of Egypt" (Num. 1:1, NIV). The date of 1446 B.C. for the Exodus suggests that Leviticus was written around 1444 B.C.

ADDRESSEES

With the rest of the Pentateuch, Leviticus addresses all Israel (for example, Lev. 1:2; 4:2; 11:2) in general, but it also narrows its scope to particular persons or groups such as the priests and Levites (for example, 9:1–2; 13:1–2; 16:1–2; 17:1–2). In line with the proposed date of the book (around 1444 B.C.), the Israelites whom Moses addressed specifically would be the Exodus generation, the ones with whom the Lord had just made the covenant at Sinai.

PURPOSE

Exodus 19:4–6 describes Israel as "a holy nation," one set apart by the Lord to be His special people in accomplishing His special mission in the earth. Having accepted this role by affirming the Sinai Covenant, Israel became God's vassal, His minister to mediate His saving grace to all nations. To be a holy nation required Israel to have a means whereby that holiness could be maintained. Therefore there needed to be a set of guidelines stipulating every aspect of that relationship between the nation and her God. In this sense holiness as a position intersects with holiness as a condition. In the former, holiness means merely the establishment of a relationship whereby a person or even an object or institution is set apart for a particular function. It has no necessary ethical or moral corollary. In the latter sense holiness comes to embody purity and righteousness, for God's own personal holiness entails not only His remoteness and uniqueness but also His moral perfection. Persons that He sanctifies and declares holy must also therefore exhibit moral uprightness.

Fundamentally Leviticus describes the means by which Israel may approach God to offer appropriate homage and to cultivate and maintain the relationship brought about by the covenant. Since Israel (with all the human race) was inherently evil by virtue of the Fall, there must be a divinely originated apparatus or system to make possible the purification of the people and all they touch so that they might be qualified to approach and serve the Lord.

THEOLOGICAL EMPHASES

The theological meaning and abiding relevance of Leviticus lie in its timeless and irrevocable themes of the holiness of God, His covenant with Israel, and the resultant demands for holy living. The God who elected Israel to be His servant people is the same God who in Jesus Christ has redeemed a people in this day to serve a similar function. The sacrifices, rituals, ceremonies, and holy days have no legal status for the church, but the principles they embodied are those that must characterize the people of the Lord of every generation if they are to serve Him effectively as salt and light.

OUTLINE

I. Laws concerning Sacrifice (chapters 1–7)
   A. The Various Offerings (1:1–6:7)
   B. The Priests and the Offerings (6:8–7:38)

II. Establishment of the Priesthood (chapters 8–10)
   A. Consecration of the Priests (chapter 8)
   B. Proper Priestly Function (chapter 9)
   C. Improper Priestly Function (chapter 10)
III. Separation between the Clean and the Unclean (chapters 11–15)
   A. Clean and Unclean Animals (chapter 11)
   B. The Uncleanness of Childbirth (chapter 12)
   C. The Uncleanness of Skin Disease (chapters 13–14)
   D. The Uncleanness of Bodily Emissions (chapter 15)
IV. The Day of Atonement (chapter 16)
   A. The Form of the Ritual (16:1–28)
   B. The Importance of the Ritual (16:29–34)
 V. Laws concerning Holiness (chapters 17–25)
   A. Sacrifice and Blood (chapter 17)
   B. Sexual Relationships (chapter 18)
   C. Interpersonal Relationships (chapter 19)
   D. Capital Offenses (chapter 20)
   E. Worship and Holiness (chapters 21–22)
   F. Holy Days (chapter 23)
   G. Consecration and Desecration (chapter 24)
   H. Sabbatical and Jubilee Years (chapter 25)
VI. The Blessing and Curse (chapter 26)
   A. Blessing for Obedience (26:1–13)
   B. Curse for Disobedience (26:14–39)
   C. Hope through God's Grace (26:40–46)
VII. Offerings of Dedication (chapter 27)
   A. Regulations about What Could Be Given (27:1–25)
   B. Regulations about What Could Not Be Given (27:26–34)

I. LAWS CONCERNING SACRIFICE (CHAPTERS 1–7)

This first major unit of Leviticus concerns the nature, purpose, and ritual of sacrifice. As God's vassal people Israel was required to present to Him tokens of tribute and devotion, a protocol invariably linked to covenant making in the ancient world. This, furthermore, must be done with a willing spirit but also in line with clearly articulated and well-understood instructions. Since there was to be a variety of offerings with many different functions and meanings, an elaborate manual of procedure was necessary so as to ensure appropriate approach to the Lord God.

A. *The Various Offerings (1:1–6:7)*

The burnt offering (1:1–17). The term *burnt offering* derives from a Hebrew verb meaning "to go up, ascend." This suggests that the entire sacrifice ascended to the Lord by being totally consumed by the flames of the altar. The material of the offering could be an animal of the herd (1:3) or the flock (1:10) or even a bird (1:14). The purpose was to effect atonement for the offerer (1:4), a result symbolized by the laying of one's hands on the head of the victim, thus pointing to its substitutionary role. The animal was, in effect, taking on itself the sin of the person who had offered it to the Lord. The death of the substitute is described as a "soothing aroma" (1:9, 13, 17) before the Lord, a means of satisfying His sense of justice and achieving a harmonious relationship between Him and those men and women who had offended Him.

The grain offering (2:1–16). Offerings to the Lord must not be limited to animal sacrifices alone, for all the fruit of one's labor originated in His bountiful grace and must therefore be returned to Him in part and in kind. The name of the grain offering is the generic term *gift* or *present* (Hebrew, *minḥâ,*), a term most suitable in view of this particular kind of covenant. It seems to have followed the burnt offering in ritual sequence (see Num. 28:1–8), a fitting order in that its essence is not the overcoming of the sin barrier between God and man—the purpose of the burnt offering—but the recognition of a state of reconciliation. Thus it was not wholly consumed on the altar but was shared with the priests (Lev. 2:3). Moreover, the inclusion of salt, an ingredient commonly used to symbolize covenant fellowship (2:13; see Num. 18:19; 2 Chron. 13:5; Ezek. 43:24), also attests to the grain offering as one shared by the Lord and His people. This portrayed the Lord's satisfaction (Lev. 2:2, 9, 12) with those who served Him as agents of human redemption.

The peace offering (3:1–17). The fellowship aspect of the presentation of offerings is even more clear in the third example, the *peace offering.* This term (Hebrew, *šělāmîm,* from *šālôm,* "peace") can also (and perhaps better) be rendered as a "thank" or "fellowship" offering, for the root meaning of *šālôm* is wholeness or oneness. The idea here is not that the sacrifice is made to bring about reconciliation with God but to celebrate the unity already procured by such means as the burnt offering. It is like the grain offering (*minḥâ,*) in that it produced a soothing aroma before the Lord (3:5, 16), but it differs in that the offerings were animals and not the product of harvest. They could be from the herd of cattle, the flock of sheep, or even a goat (3:1, 6, 12), but in any case the sacrifice must represent a genuine self-denial on the part of the offerer. At the same time, the giver, as party to the covenant relationship, could participate in the meal afforded by the sacrifice. In a mystical sense the Lord, the priests, and the worshiper himself sat at a common table and partook of a common repast. The analogy between this ritual and the Lord's Supper is most apparent (Matt. 26:26–29). Neither suggests a means of salvation; instead both celebrate the oneness achieved through salvation.

The sin offering (4:1–5:13). While the burnt offering dealt with sin and its atonement in general (1:4), particular acts of sin, whether unintentional or not, were also addressed and in particular ways according to the persons and circumstances involved. The fellowship between the Lord and His people and among the people themselves could and would be interrupted by sin. This contingency thus called for remediation.

As with all the previous cases, the offering for sin required appropriate sacrifices. These could include a bull, lamb (here a female, 4:32), goat, dove, or even flour. The type of offering was determined by the status or role of the sinner. Should a priest sin, even inadvertently (literally, "through ignorance"; 4:3, 22, 27; 5:15), he must offer up a bull whose blood would be sprinkled in the holy place before the veil (4:1–12). Sin by the corporate community of Israel was dealt with in the same way, with the priests acting as mediators (4:13–21). The ruler's personal sin required the slaughter of a male goat and the application of its blood to the great bronze altar (4:22–26). The ordinary Israelite citizen who sinned must offer a female goat or lamb (4:27–35). All such sins of nonintentionality could be forgiven when dealt with in pure motive and by proper ritual procedure (4:26, 31, 35).

A subcategory of the sin offering had to do with sinful acts or omission of acts done without one's conscious knowledge of having done so (5:2–4). The kind of sacrifice was based on the financial ability of the guilty party. If the poor could not afford a goat or lamb, then they could present two doves (5:7–10) or even just a handful of flour (5:11–13).

The guilt offering (5:14–6:7). This term (Hebrew, 'āšām, "guilt") also conveys the idea of recompense or reparation. Should one sin in ignorance (4:2, 22, 27) in a matter concerning worship (5:14–16) or related areas (5:17–19) or openly transgress against a fellow member of the community (6:1–7), he must present appropriate compensation, namely, a ram without defect plus 20 percent of the ram's value in silver for sins against the Lord (6:16), and the same amount of penalty for having defrauded a fellow citizen (6:5). Both kinds of offense—unintended and deliberate—could be atoned for but must incur reparation. The point is that though forgiveness is a response of grace there are always damaging consequences of sin, especially as they impact other vulnerable human beings.

> *Illness, old age, and death are reminders of the reality of sin, but in heaven these cease to exist, as Christ's righteousness becomes effective in practice as well as in status.*

B. The Priests and the Offerings (6:8–7:38)

The sacrifices and offerings just described were to be mediated through the priests, so it was necessary for the priests to understand their role. Moses thus included a brief "handbook" for priests, one that generally follows the order of offerings presented in 1:1–6:7.

The priestly responsibility with regard to the burnt offering is directed here to the need to keep the altar fires burning day and night (6:8–13). He must also be careful to dispose of the ashes that would accumulate from the constant sacrificial offering of animals and grains. As for the grain offerings of the people themselves, nothing is added here with respect to priestly activity (6:14–18). What is new is instruction to the priests about the grain offerings they themselves must present to the Lord. They may keep none of it for their own use but must burn it all on the altar (6:19–23). Likewise the ministry of the priests with regard to the sin offerings finds little elaboration here except for the note to purify objects accidentally spattered by sacrificial blood (6:24–30).

The ritual for trespass (reparation) offerings does find greater detailed description here (7:1–10), particularly in listing the portions of animal sacrifices allotted to the priests. This is even more the case with the peace or fellowship offerings (7:11–21). Along with the offerer, the priests also came in for a share of the meat which they and the people in general must eat at appointed times and in an appropriate manner. The Lord, who "sat" with His people as Sovereign, received the best parts, namely, the fat and the blood (7:22–27). The priests also were favored with select portions, notably the breast and right thigh of the animals. These are described, in fact, as their "portions" (7:28–36).

Leviticus 7:37–38 summarizes the whole preceding section by listing the various kinds of offerings and by emphasizing that these came to Moses from the Lord by direct revelation. This latter point underscores the importance of proper ritual in approaching the sovereign Lord God under the terms of the Sinai Covenant mandate.

II. ESTABLISHMENT OF THE PRIESTHOOD (CHAPTERS 8–10)

Exodus 28–29 describes the procedures to be followed in selecting, anointing, and outfitting the priests of Israel so as to qualify them for ministry. Leviticus 8–10 records the implementation of these instructions and also recounts a series of sacrifices undertaken by Aaron and his sons as the first official act of their priesthood. Also these chapters specify the criteria of character and conduct by which the priests were to order their lives and ministry, criteria which, unfortunately, were violated by Aaron's own sons (10:1–7, 16–20).

A. Consecration of the Priests (chapter 8)

Employing a narrative style, Moses recorded the fact that all Israel assembled before the tabernacle to witness the ordination of Aaron and his sons to the priesthood (8:1–5). They first clothed themselves in the garments and trappings that set them off from all others and that spoke so beautifully of the role they were to play (8:6–9). Moses then anointed them (8:10–13), offering up on their behalf a sin offering (8:14–17), a burnt offering (8:18–21), and an offering of consecration to symbolize their total commitment to their high and holy office (8:22–30). Since this last offering was a fellowship offering (see 7:11–18), the priests partook of it throughout the seven days of purification (8:31–36).

B. Proper Priestly Function (chapter 9)

The ordination of Aaron and his sons officially qualified them to take the leadership of Israel's religious life, so they immediately set about their responsibilities. First, they prepared to offer sacrifices designed to effect and underscore the unity of the Lord with His people (9:1–7). He had appeared to them in a special way on this happy occasion, an appearance that called for response on their part. Aaron therefore presented a sin offering (9:8–11), a burnt offering (9:12–17), and a fellowship offering (9:18–21). The ceremony of animal sacrifice was capped off by a priestly blessing, an oral declaration that God was pleased with His people's worship and that He would reciprocate by showing His favor toward them (9:22–23a). The appearance of God's glory was further evidence of divine approval, but most impressive of all was the fire He sent down to consume the sacrifices (9:23b–24). There could be no room for doubt that the priestly office was ordained of the Lord and that Aaron and his sons were the chosen instruments to fill that office.

C. Improper Priestly Function (chapter 10)

Immediately following the narrative of the consecration of the priests are two incidents that illustrate not only the importance of their adhering to the guidelines regulating their office but also the severe consequences of not doing so. In the first instance two of Aaron's sons, Nadab and Abihu, burned incense ignited with "strange," that is, illicit, fire. Rather than taking coals from the great bronze altar before the tabernacle (see 16:12; Num. 17:11), they had obtained them from elsewhere, probably from profane or secular sources outside the tabernacle. Ironically, this unauthorized fire was met by the fire of God's glory and wrath, the same fire that had ignited the sacrifices following the ordination of the priests (Lev. 10:2; see also 9:24). Rather than attesting to the sanctification of Nadab and Abihu, the fire now consumed them. This was the penalty for failing to glorify God as His priestly representatives (10:3). Eleazar and Ithamar, Aaron's surviving sons, were not to mourn the death of their brothers, Moses said, for the harsh punishment they had received was fully justified in light of the privileges they enjoyed (10:6).

Moses then continued to instruct Eleazar and Ithamar as to the need for sobriety when they were engaged in tabernacle ministration, for to imbibe alcoholic beverages in such circumstances would blur the line of distinction between the ritually clean and unclean (10:10). That is, the priests of Israel, unlike those of the pagan world, must exemplify a lifestyle appropriate to the purity and holiness of the God whom they served.

The second illustration of priestly lapse was the oversight of Eleazar and Ithamar regarding the proper disposition of sacrificial meats to which they were entitled (10:12–20). The law allowed (in fact, commanded) the priests to share in the eating of grain and fellowship offerings as long as they did so in designated areas (10:12–15; see also 6:14–18; 7:28–34). It seems that after the tragic deaths of Nadab and Abihu, their brothers Eleazar and Ithamar had violated the regulation concerning the sin offering by failing to consume their allotted portion of it. Coming to their (and his own) defense, Aaron pleaded with Moses that the awesome events of that day had so unnerved him that he refrained from further activity lest he too should suffer calamity (10:19). Acting as God's agent, Moses accepted Aaron's explanation. The point had been clearly made, however, that God's business must be done in God's way.

III. SEPARATION BETWEEN THE CLEAN AND THE UNCLEAN (CHAPTERS 11–15)

Between the two episodes of priestly failure (Lev. 10:1–7 and 10:12–20), Moses had enjoined Aaron and his descendants to draw sharply the line of demarcation between the holy and the profane, the clean and the unclean (10:10). The underlying purpose was to instruct Israel as to its own unique nature and function, compared to all other nations of the earth. All of life, then, must be understood in terms of separation between what was acceptable to the Lord and what was not. The criteria by which He made these distinctions are not always self-evident. In fact, the whole point may be that persons and things are holy or profane simply by divine fiat. God's having declared them to be one or the other is enough to make them so.

A. Clean and Unclean Animals (chapter 11)

Land animals, primarily mammals, make up the first category (11:1–8). All clean animals of this group must be ruminants that have divided hooves. One of these characteristics by itself would not suffice to make an animal acceptable for table fare. In some instances their uncleanness may be related to their habits or to their likelihood of transmitting disease, but fundamentally their status as such was by arbitrary decree on God's part.

As for marine creatures (11:9–12), only those with both fins and scales could qualify. It is well known, of course, that shellfish improperly prepared and preserved can be hazardous to human health. Again, however, the distinctions drawn here have no apparent linkage to such concerns. The mere allocation of such creatures to one category or the other by an all-wise and sovereign God is sufficient.

Because of the sheer number of bird species and the lack of practical means of separating them into various categories, Moses provided a list of some twenty flying creatures whose flesh was considered unsuitable as food for humans (11:13–19). That is, to eat them was to violate God's own definition of moral and spiritual propriety. Once more, this was not so much because of inherent impurity as it was divine determination.

The remainder of the chapter deals with such matters as clean and unclean insects (11:20–23), uncleanness contracted by contact with carcasses

(11:24–38), uncleanness from touching the dead bodies of even clean animals (11:39–40), and a prohibition against eating any kind of crawling creatures (11:41–43). The reason for all these strictures was, as always, that because the Lord is holy His people must also be holy (11:44–47). Among other ways, that holiness was symbolized by what one touched or consumed, whether the rationale for such restriction was clearly understood or not.

> *Children often want reasons for parental prohibitions when those reasons are too complicated for pat answers. Often the response has to be simply, "Because I said so." Many of the standards of holiness demanded by an omniscient God for the Christian are beyond human understanding. We ought to be willing to conform to them if for no other reason than the fact that God has ordained them.*

B. The Uncleanness of Childbirth (chapter 12)

The act of giving birth in and of itself is never viewed as unclean in the Old Testament. It was the discharge of blood and other body fluids accompanying the birth process that brought about a state of ceremonial impurity. Just as her menstruation suggested an improper "use" of blood, so a woman's loss of blood in childbirth constituted a violation of blood's sanctity (15:19; 18:19). Following the birth of a son a woman was to remain unclean for seven days, and fourteen days after the birth of a daughter. At the end of the necessary time span the woman was to make burnt and sin offerings as an atonement for the blood flow, after which she could be declared clean.

C. The Uncleanness of Skin Disease (chapters 13–14)

Disease, like the emission of blood and other vital fluids, conjured up images of death and all its terror, for death often followed serious illnesses. Since death and dead things were considered ritually impure, so even disease, especially that as visible as skin impairment, rendered its victim unclean. This section thus concerns itself with the manifestation of various kinds of skin blemishes and eruptions that could affect not only one's body but also one's clothing and even houses that might become contaminated by it. This section also provides diagnostic analysis and prescribes remedies for its medical and spiritual cure.

The many symptoms and prescriptions listed in chapter 13 indicate a wide spectrum of afflictions. Their ritual cleansing after physical healing had occurred required the offering of sacrifices appropriate to each case (14:1–32). Similarly, clothing that had become polluted by such diseases were also to be treated by washing or, if that failed, by burning (13:47–59). Houses would manifest their contamination by mildew, a condition to be remedied either by repairing the affected part of the house or by tearing it down (14:33–53). The victim throughout the period of his illness and recovery was to live in social isolation. Whenever he ventured out among the public, he must announce his impurity by crying out "Unclean, unclean." His physical condition spoke all too eloquently of the separation caused by sin and death and of the need for a means of restoration to the community (see 13:45–46).

D. The Uncleanness of Bodily Emissions (chapter 15)

Corresponding to the uncleanness of childbirth (12:1–8) is a male's discharge of pus or other impurities caused by disease (15:1–12) or through the release of semen (15:16–18). These were to be redressed by proper rituals that included bathing and the offering of sin and burnt offerings (15:10–11, 13–15, 18). Female menstrual flow and other causes of blood fluxation also called for purification, not only of the woman herself but of objects or other persons brought into contact with the blood (15:19–24). Sin offerings and burnt offerings were applicable here as well, for though the loss of blood and other fluids was not inherently sinful, it symbolized the process of decay, disease, and death, all the fruits of human sin and fallenness.

IV. THE DAY OF ATONEMENT (CHAPTER 16)

The various occasions for and acts of atonement described thus far in Leviticus are mainly of a limited, even individual, nature. That is, they speak to the need for establishing harmony between a holy God and persons or groups that have sinned or otherwise become impure and therefore have become unable to approach Him. Moses now turned to the collective community of Israel as a whole and to its need as a corporate people of the Lord to deal with the matter of national alienation.

A. The Form of the Ritual (16:1–28)

The death of Aaron's two sons provided the impetus for instruction to Aaron about approaching the Holy One. He could do so even to the extent of entering the Most Holy Place but only once a year, on the day he would present there the blood shed for national atonement. Properly attired, he would enter the outer room of the tabernacle, the Holy Place, with a sin offering and a burnt offering. He would also set apart two goats and a ram for sacrifice. A bull had to be slain for Aaron's own atonement, and then one goat was to be selected as a sin offering and the other as a "scapegoat." The former would symbolize the propitiation for sin, that is, its being covered, and the other represented expiation, the removal of sin. Both of these were on behalf of the whole people.

The blood of the slain goat, like that of the bull, must be brought into the Most Holy Place and sprinkled on the ark of the covenant (16:14–15), representative of God's very throne. By this act not only the people but also the tabernacle and all its furnishings would become purified. The live goat must then be driven into the deserts bearing with him the aggregate sins of all Israel (16:22). Once he left the tabernacle Aaron must bathe himself, change his clothes, and then offer up sin and burnt offerings on the great bronze altar in the courtyard. The parts of the animals not consumed on the altar must be taken outside the camp and burned (16:27–28).

B. The Importance of the Ritual (16:29–34)

This sacred ritual was to take place on the tenth day of the seventh month each year, a day now known as Yom Kippur ("Day of Atonement"). It was to be a day of complete rest, when the whole nation could undertake intense introspection and, in light of its collective sin, seek and receive atoning grace so as to enter the new year in perfect fellowship with the Lord.

V. LAWS CONCERNING HOLINESS
(CHAPTERS 17–25)

A dominant motif of Leviticus, as noted at the outset, is that of holiness, the holiness both of the Lord, which is inherent to His nature and person, and of His people and even inanimate things that derive holiness from Him. This is so central to the book that its longest section (chapters 17–25) is commonly called "the Holiness Code." In this section Moses categorized a wide variety of regulations pertaining to the acquisition and maintenance of holiness under eight headings.

A. Sacrifice and Blood (chapter 17)

While Israel was in the desert sojourn, no slaughter of animals—for sacrifice or merely for human consumption—could be undertaken outside the camp, for the line of demarcation between ritual and domestic slaughter had not yet been drawn. That would await the sedentary life in Canaan when sheer distance from the central sanctuary would make slaying for meat alone a proper activity (Deut. 12:5–21). For now, however, all slaughter was sacred and must be conducted at the tabernacle (Lev. 17:1–9).

The blood of animal sacrifices therefore was holy and must not be eaten. Blood was a metaphor for life itself, a gift of God so precious as to have inherent sanctity (17:10–13). The life of an innocent animal could not impart its vicarious value by being ingested, then, but by being applied as blood on God's altar (17:14–16).

B. Sexual Relationships (chapter 18)

Having just come out of Egypt and on the verge of entering Canaan—places of the most obscene and disgusting sexual behavior—Israel must learn not to follow these pagan practices, many of which were done in the name of religion (18:3, 24–25, 27, 30). This is why this chapter is bracketed by the declaration "I am the LORD your God" (18:2, 30). To avoid these detestable acts and to heed, instead, the statutes of God's covenant with them would assure God's people of life (18:5). That is, sexual immorality leads to death, but adherence to holiness and purity results in both quality and quantity of life.

Though Israel was to be endogamous (marrying within the community), it was not, like the heathen, to be incestuous. Thus one could not have sexual relations with one's mother, sister, granddaughter, half sister, aunt, daughter-in-law, wife of a living brother, any woman and a close female relative at the same time, or the sister of one's wife (18:7–18). Other prohibitions had to do with adultery, homosexuality, and bestiality (18:20–23). It was for things like these that the occupants of Canaan would be expelled by the Lord, and if Israel followed their example they too would be excommunicated and/or driven from the land (18:24–29).

C. Interpersonal Relationships (chapter 19)

True holiness manifests itself in more than ritual and sexual behavior. Indeed, it pervades all of life both vertically (toward God) and horizontally (toward others). God's holiness and thus human holiness must provide the bases for all behavior. Not surprisingly, the Lord's statement about His holiness introduces this lengthy exhortation (19:1–4).

Holiness was to govern the way offerings were made (19:5–8), harvests were gathered (19:9–10), and people were treated as to their properties (19:11–14) and legal rights (19:15–16). In summary, one must love his neighbor as himself (19:18; see also Matt. 19:19). Illustrative of the separation of life that characterizes biblical holiness is the forbidding of crossbreeding animals, mingling seed and fabric, and cohabiting with a slave girl already engaged to a fiancé (Lev. 19:19–22). The last example has to do primarily with the violation of social taboos, the crossing of recognized class boundary lines. Because of class distinctions, such limitations have no immediate or practical relevance in the church, the body of Christ (see Gal. 3:23–29). The principle of separation from sin, however, does remain in force (2 Cor. 6:14–18).

Once in the land the Israelites could plant and eat the fruit of trees after a certain interval (Lev. 19:23–25), but they must at all cost avoid the pagan customs of eating blood, practicing the occult arts (19:26–28, 31), and submitting their daughters to cultic prostitution (19:29). On the other hand, they must observe the Sabbaths, respect the place of worship, honor the elderly, love strangers, and be fair and just in all interpersonal dealings (19:30–36). In short, they must manifest holiness by keeping all the covenant requirements (19:37).

D. Capital Offenses (chapter 20)

The chief offense against the Lord was idolatry, for it constituted rebellion and high treason against the Lord, the sovereign One who brought Israel into covenant relationship and into the expectation of loyalty attendant to such a relationship. One of the most extreme expressions of idolatry was the worship of Molech, the Ammonite god, to whom human sacrifices were offered (18:21; 1 Kings 11:5, 7, 33; 2 Kings 23:10, 13). There is little wonder that pursuit of such a deity would invoke the Lord's severest wrath (Lev. 20:1–5).

Akin to idolatry was the appeal to divination and incantation and the audacity to undercut the authority of one's parents who were the Lord's agents of sovereignty (20:6–9). Adultery, incest, homosexuality, and bestiality also come in for strong denunciation (20:10–16), as do other improper sexual relationships (20:17–21; see also 18:6–18). All these deviations were common among the nations whom the Lord would evict from Canaan (20:22–23). Because Israel had been called to be a separated (that is, holy) people, she must learn the principles of separation that govern all of life. The Lord is holy and so—as was stated repeatedly—Israel too must be holy (20:24–26; see also 19:2; 20:7).

E. Worship and Holiness (chapters 21–22)

If the laity were to be holy, how much more should the priests be holy, especially in their official capacity as leaders of the worshiping community. Unlike pagan officiants they must not come in contact with the dead (except for immediate family members; 21:1–4), they must not make incisions or other disfigurements on their bodies (21:5), and they must refrain from marrying prostitutes or divorcées (21:6–8). Should a priest's daughter disgrace him and his ministry by going into harlotry, she must pay with her life (21:9). The high priest must be held to an even higher standard (21:10–15). He must abstain from all contact with the dead and must never leave the sanctuary while in the process of ministry, even to mourn his dead (21:12). He could marry only a virgin and no one from outside the priestly line (21:14–15). The reason, as always, is that the high priest is holy, having been set apart by the Lord.

Priests must also be as perfect physically and outwardly as possible. They could have no birthmark or other blemish, nor could they be blind, lame, deformed, or emasculated (21:16–20). Should they become impaired while in office, they could remain in their ministry but could no longer enter the Holy Place or even offer sacrifices at the great bronze altar (21:21–23). The reason, of course, is not that physically deformed persons—even priests—hold less value in the eyes of the Lord. Rather, because the physical symbolized the spiritual, it was considered inappropriate for all but "perfect" specimens to represent the people before a perfect God. On the other hand, God is no respecter of persons (Acts 10:34), for He looks not on the outward appearance but on the heart (1 Sam. 16:7).

F. Holy Days (chapter 23)

As the great King, the Lord not only dwelt in a special place among His people (the tabernacle and later the temple) and there expected and received their tributes of sacrifice and offering, but He also set aside special times for the community as a whole to appear before Him to render account to Him and to celebrate their covenant relationship with Him. Exodus 23:14–17 introduces the matter by systematically listing the three annual festivals. Leviticus 23 amplifies that brief overview by describing the rituals to accompany the festivals and by adding others to them.

The first of the "set festivals" was the Sabbath, the seventh day of every week (23:1–3). Its purpose was to provide rest for God's people. The first of the pilgrimage festivals, however, was the Passover and Unleavened Bread, observances joined together to commemorate the Lord's deliverance of Israel from Egyptian bondage (Exod. 12:1–18). Here, however, only the agricultural aspects receive attention. The fifteenth and twenty-first days of the first month of the year were times of community convocation wherein no work was to be done. The fourteenth was the

Passover itself. All through the eight days, appropriate sacrifices of both produce and animals must be offered (Lev. 23:4–14).

The second national festival must take place fifty days after the first, that is, the day after seven sabbaths. Its name, therefore, was the Festival of Weeks or, in the Greek Bible, Pentecost (Greek, *pentēcostē*, "fiftieth"). Though many offerings must be presented, the principal agricultural significance was the marking of the wheat harvest (23:15–22). In Israel barley comes to fruition in the spring or Passover time (23:10), whereas wheat follows several weeks later (23:16). The first and best of each crop belonged to the Lord as a token of His blessing and as a sign of Israel's dependence and gratitude.

The third festival was to revolve around three major ideas: the new year, atonement, and another harvest celebration (23:23–44). The first of these, the Feast of Trumpets, came to be known in postbiblical times as Rosh Hashanah, "the first of the year." It was a day of rest requiring a burnt offering as part of its observance. The second, the Day of Atonement, was to follow ten days later. It too was a Sabbath day on which no work could be done. Furthermore, it must be a time of intense heart searching by the whole community, after which there must be a spirit of abject repentance for all sins committed in the previous year. The priestly ritual for this day has already been described (chapter 16). The third autumn festival was the Feast of Tabernacles, a celebration that lasted for seven days beginning with the fifteenth day of the month. This feast concluded on the eighth day with a community convocation featuring burnt offerings.

Here in Leviticus (and in Num. 28:16–31) the first two festival times—Passover and Weeks—are associated strictly with harvest times, with no attention to the historical circumstances that gave rise to them. This is not the case with their elaboration in Deuteronomy, where Passover is linked to the Exodus and Weeks is linked to the Egyptian sojourn (Deut. 16:1–12). The Feast of Tabernacles, on the other hand, is associated in Leviticus 23:39–44 with the desert wanderings, though this association is not stated in Deuteronomy (Deut. 16:13–15) or even Numbers (Num. 29:12–38). To help future generations to recall and relive the deprivations of their ancestors they were to erect crude huts in which they were to live for a week. Deuteronomy (but not Exodus, Leviticus, or Numbers) specifies that the crops to be presented to the Lord in the fall festival were to be from the threshing floor and winepress, that is, the grains and grapes (Deut. 16:13).

G. Consecration and Desecration (chapter 24)

A mark of separation or holiness was the means by which that status was brought to pass. Thus the menorah of the tabernacle must be fueled by olive oil especially prepared for that purpose (24:1–4). Likewise the bread of the table of covenant remembrance must be baked and set out properly. Symbolically it provided sustenance for the Lord, but it provided physical food for the priests (24:5–9). Moses described the bread as "a most holy part," that is, as a most sacred object by virtue of its having been set apart for holy purposes (24:9).

The Lord's very covenant itself with all its stipulations was to be viewed as holy (24:9–23). By way of illustration, a certain young man blasphemed God's holy name, thus violating the third commandment (Exod. 20:7; 22:28). The punishment for such a gross infringement on divine holiness was death at the hands of the entire assembly (Lev. 24:16). Infraction of all covenant law required penalty, in fact, for in an ultimate sense it was a trespass against the Holy One (24:22).

H. Sabbatical and Jubilee Years (chapter 25)

In Israel's sacred calendar certain years as well as days were to be set apart as holy times. For example, every seventh year must be a sabbatical year, that is, one set apart to the Lord and designed to allow the land to have rest from crop production (25:1–7). Beyond this, every cycle of seven sabbatical years would usher in a fiftieth year called the "Year of Jubilee." Like the forty-ninth year, it was a sabbatical in which the land must lie fallow. Moreover, those who held mortgages on properties or even persons must release them so as to reestablish social and economic equilibrium (25:8–17).

Israel need not have any fear of famine in the sabbatical years, for God would provide plenty of food to tide His people over (25:18–22). Also there was no need for mortgages to await the Year of Jubilee for their expiration, for the mortgagee could either pay them off from his own resources or he could receive release, thanks to a friend or relative who would serve as his redeemer by making payment for him (25:23–34). The theological implications of redemption at this level and for redemption at the level of spiritual need are clear. Christ's role as the Redeemer, who ransoms all who believe in Him, reflects this Mosaic regulation.

Turning to persons in a position to extend relief, Moses first prohibited loans at interest to a fellow Israelite (25:35–38). Even if the latter must become indentured, he must be treated as a brother and not a slave. He must be granted unconditional release in the Jubilee year (25:39–43). Aliens, however, could become not only vassals but actual property to be bought and sold (25:44–46). Such an allowance clearly must be understood as regulating an already existing ancient Near Eastern social reality and not an endorsement of slavery per se. Finally, if a non-Israelite brought an Israelite under conditions of economic servanthood, every effort must be made for him to be redeemed from that situation (25:47–54). In light of the fact that Israel was the servant of the Lord, it was most unseemly that she should remain in bondage to another lord (25:55).

VI. THE BLESSING AND CURSE (CHAPTER 26)

Covenant texts of the ancient Near Eastern world invariably contained blessing and curse sections that outlined what the subordinate party could expect as he or she conformed or failed to conform to the covenant stipulations. Leviticus, though not in itself such a text, is part of the covenant document introduced in the Book of the Covenant of Exodus 19–24. Furthermore, the term "covenant" (Hebrew, $b^e r\hat{\imath}t$) occurs frequently in this chapter (Lev. 26:9, 15, 25, 42, 44–45), a fact that makes the connection between covenant and the blessing and curse language here inescapable.

A. Blessing for Obedience (26:1–13)

After a brief introduction based on the first four commandments (26:1–2), the Lord set forth the conditions for covenant blessing: "walk according to my statutes and be careful to obey my commandments" (26:3). The statutes and commandments were the stipulations of the covenant, so the appeal in short was for Israel to keep covenant with the Lord. To do so would guarantee His favor.

The blessings in view are agricultural productivity, domestic tranquillity, victory over hostile nations, and the presence of the Lord among them (26:4–11). In the clearest terms of covenant relationship the Lord said, "I will . . . be your God, and you shall be My people" (26:12). All this is the result of His redemptive grace in bringing Israel out of Egyptian bondage and into His glorious freedom (26:13).

B. Curse for Disobedience (26:14–39)

If adherence to the covenant stipulations brings blessing, to spurn them is to invite judgment. Again technical terms ("commandments," "statutes," "ordinances") define the nature of the stipulations, but here the connection to the covenant is even more explicit. To violate the terms of the covenant is to break (Hebrew, *pārar*, "invalidate") the covenant itself as an organ of relationship (26:15). The curses that follow such disloyalty are almost a mirror image of the blessings but in reverse. They will include sickness and famine, defeat at enemy hands, lack of agricultural productivity, and attack by wild animals (26:16–22).

If these judgments fail to effect repentance and renewed obedience, the Lord would send more enemy invasion, more famine, and the annihilation of Israel's cities and illicit shrines (26:23–32). The greatest curse of all, perhaps, will be the scattering of the nation throughout the world and the consequent abandonment and desolation of the land (26:33). The land will remain that way as many years as the Sabbath years that Israel will have ignored and failed to observe (26:34–35). As for the remnant left behind, they will be so weak and demoralized as to be unable to resist any other judgment the Lord will allow to come on them (26:36–39).

C. Hope through God's Grace (26:40–46)

The apparent finality of Israel's rejection collides inevitably with God's covenant faithfulness, however, so even when it seems that all is lost He will interpose His word and work of grace to elicit national repentance and restoration. When the people of Israel are in distant lands, they will confess their sins of covenant disobedience, which resulted in their deplorable state (26:40–41). The point to be noted especially is that it is the Lord who initiates the confession. It is He who will lead His people to repentance (Rom. 2:4). Scarcely any passage in the Bible is more clear in asserting that conversion is in itself an act of divine grace.

Once the terms of renewal have been met, the Lord will reestablish the benefits of His covenant to Israel. He will "remember" His pledge to Israel, a promise resting on unconditional promises He had made long ago to the patriarchs (Lev. 26:42). For God to "remember" is not to suggest that He could possibly forget. It communicates the notion of reactivating a relationship that had, in a sense, been suspended because of Israel's stubborn rebellion. The remembering will issue in covenant renewal, a repair of the breach for the sake of the nation's ancestors with whom the Lord had made an irreversible commitment (26:43–45).

VII. OFFERINGS OF DEDICATION (CHAPTER 27)

In light of the blessings of God in general, and specifically those just mentioned as response to covenant obedience (26:1–13), Moses closed the Book of Leviticus by exhorting Israel to present to the Lord votive or dedicatory offerings. These were done not to gain favor with Him but as expressions of gratitude and commitment to Him for all the manifestations of His grace. But even voluntary offerings must follow a protocol and must not be done at the whim of the worshiper and in a self-chosen manner. This chapter provides the guidelines necessary to offer gifts to God in a way that pleased Him.

A. Regulations about What Could Be Given (27:1–25)

When one decided to present a votive offering of silver, he or she must do so according to gender and age criteria (27:1–8). For example, a man from twenty to sixty years old must give fifty shekels and a woman thirty. A man over sixty must present fifteen shekels and a woman ten. These sums represent requirements for persons of average means, but the votive offerings of the poor could be calculated according to their relative affluence. Since the average wage was about one shekel per month, offerings of silver would certainly have been rare.

A dedicatory animal once pledged to the Lord could not be retracted or exchanged for another. The offerer could, however, redeem it by paying its price plus 20 percent interest (27:9–13). The same rule applied to the setting apart of a house (27:14–15). Other regulations applied to the vowing of fields in general and in particular to their real or mortgage ownership in relation to the Year of Jubilee. Such properties would either go to the Lord (that is, the priests, 27:21) or to the original owner if the offerer had purchased it (27:22–24), or the owner could redeem it at its estimated worth plus 20 percent (27:19).

B. Regulations about What Could Not Be Given (27:26–34)

Firstborn ritually qualified animals such as oxen or sheep could not be vowed to the Lord, because they belonged to Him already (27:26; see also Exod. 13:2). All other animals could be, however (Lev. 27:27). Likewise, anything or anyone under God's ban could not be presented as a dedicatory offering, for these too were His by virtue of His having claimed them for His own use or purpose (27:28–29; see also Josh. 6:17–19). Finally, tithes of all goods and produce could not be vowed, for they belonged automatically to the Lord as Sovereign. The offerer could redeem them at their true value plus 20 percent if he chose to do so, but the payment plus interest would then be given over to the Lord.

Leviticus closes with the brief but important note that its contents came to Moses from the Lord at Mount Sinai (Lev. 27:34). This links the book inextricably to the whole covenant revelation at that place and to Moses as its mediator.

NUMBERS

𝒫ilgrimage to 𝒞ovenant 𝒫ossession

AUTHOR

𝐴rguments and evidences for Mosaic authorship of the Pentateuch as a whole obviously apply to all of its parts, including Numbers. This is particularly true given its location in the Pentateuch and its necessary function in providing a bridge between the covenant settings of Sinai (Exodus-Leviticus) and Moab (Deuteronomy), both of which are indisputably linked to Moses as their chief protagonist and spokesman (Exod. 19:7; 20:1; 24:4; Deut. 1:1; 31:24).

Moreover, Numbers itself bears explicit witness to its having come from the pen of Moses. For example, Numbers 33:2 states that "at the Lord's command Moses recorded [literally, 'wrote'] the stages in their journey." Though this most obviously applies to the following itinerary (33:3–49), that is only a recapitulation of the journeys that constitute most of the preceding content of Numbers, a fact that certainly does not weaken Mosaic authorship of the whole book. That impression finds confirmation in the very last verse of the book that summarizes its entirety: "These are the commands and regulations the LORD gave through Moses to the Israelites on the plains of Moab by the Jordan across from Jericho" (36:13). A stronger confirmation of Mosaic composition could hardly be expected.

UNITY

Though modern critics usually divide Numbers into sources such as J (the "Yahwist," Num. 11–12, 21–24, and parts of chapters 10, 13–14, 16, 20, 25–32) and P (the "Priestly," most of the rest of the book), the tradition of a unified Mosaic composition not only undercuts such alleged separate documents but does away with any need for them. Admittedly the book contains many distinctly different literary forms and styles as well as a variety of topical and theological themes. Such diversity, however, need not be explained on any other basis than that of a creatively gifted author who composed and/or collected texts of various genres and with wide-ranging interests and purposes.

As a whole, the book is narrative, an account of Israel's forty-year journey from Sinai to Moab. Moses was clearly the leader of the community in transit and also an eyewitness of all that transpired. His work as author might, then, be considered almost as a diary, a log, as it were, of his and Israel's experiences in interaction with the Lord and with other peoples. But the travelogue consists of many parts, some prose and some poetry. It embodies census lists (Num. 1:5–46; 3:14–39; 4:34–49; 26:5–51), instructions about travel procedures (2:2–31), regulations for the priests and Levites (3:40–4:33; 8:5–26; 18:1–32), protocol regarding sacrifice and ritual (5:1–7:89; 9:1–10:10; 15:1–41; 19:1–22; 28:1–30:16), and inheritance rights (30:1–12). Poetry is represented by whole or partial selections such as "The Book of the Wars of Lord" (21:14–15), the "Song of the Well" (21:17–18), the "Song of Heshbon" (21:27–30), and snatches from the oracles of Balaam (23:7–10, 18–24; 24:3–9, 15–24). Some of these may have already existed and then been incorporated into Moses' narrative. For the most part, however, it must have been he who first put them into writing and then synthesized them into the present product. Whatever unity or lack thereof may be apparent can be explained as well on the theory of an original author rather than on that of a much later redactor.

DATE

While allowance must be made for the possibility that parts of Numbers were collected and/or composed from the time of the Sinai sojourn (around 1444 B.C.), the book as a whole was not completed until Moses and Israel arrived in the plain of Moab just before the conquest of Canaan (Num 36:13). Given the date of the Exodus required by the Masoretic text (see pp. 40–41), the Book of Numbers must have achieved its final form by 1406 B.C.

ADDRESSEES

The initial readers of the Book of Numbers were the Israelites assembled in the plain of Moab just before the Conquest (36:13). Moses had, of course, spoken much of its contents to the people ever since they had been at Sinai (9:4; 11:24; 15:1–2, 17–18; 16:40; 29:40), but it must have become accessible to the whole community in its entirety only on the eve of the conquest of Canaan. Its recipients then were the younger generation that had survived God's purging judgment (14:26–35; see also Deut. 2:34–37). But the message of Numbers transcends its historical and cultural setting, and through it God continues to address His people. Its abiding relevance to the church is already clear to the New Testament writers, who cited it frequently for instruction and illustration (Luke 1:15; John 19:36; Acts 7:36, 39–40; 21:23–27; 1 Cor. 10:5, 8, 10; Heb. 3:11, 17).

PURPOSE

The overriding concern of the book is to detail Israel's journey from Sinai to the Promised Land, but not just in geographical terms. Of far greater importance is the spiritual pilgrimage and its success or failure depending on the obedience of the people to the covenant mandates revealed in the Sinai Covenant. As long as Israel walked in the divine footsteps, as it were, everything went well. When the people abandoned the pathway of God's purposes, however, the result was disaster. Journey, then, became a metaphor for national life. The way of the Lord through the desert—and Israel's response to it—provided instruction as to how her life in the land of Canaan must be pursued if she was to know the fullness of His blessing and the satisfaction of being His instrument of universal salvation.

Other purposes for the book include the organization of the loosely affiliated tribes into a more cohesive religious and political community that would be suitable for sedentary life in the land. At the same time it was clear that societal structures appropriate to the generations yet to come in the Promised Land were not always relevant to seminomadic conditions. Therefore a secondary purpose of Numbers was to provide guidelines for tribal life between its covenant purpose disclosed at Sinai and its fulfillment decades later in the conquest and occupation of Canaan. It would be left to Deuteronomy to address the religious and political concerns of that time and place.

THEOLOGICAL EMPHASES

The major theological theme of Numbers is reciprocal in nature: God has brought a people to Himself by covenant grace, but He expects of them a wholehearted devotion. Having accepted the terms of the Sinai Covenant, Israel had placed herself under obligation to obey them, a process that was to begin at once and not in some distant place and time (Exod. 19:8; 24:3). Proof of their loyalty began to be tested at the very beginning of their journey toward Canaan. Denied the food and other familiar benefits they had known in Egypt, the people complained against both the Lord and His servant Moses (for example, Num. 11:1–15; 12:1–8; 14:1–10; 16:1–14, 41–50). In this way they demonstrated their fickleness and faithlessness, but they also provided the occasion for God to display His gracious loyalty to His promises.

Nowhere is the latter more apparent than in the words of salvation uttered by the pagan prophet Balaam. Israel had already failed dismally in the desert and would continue to do so in the ages to come. Despite this, God would raise up from the remnant of the nation a Ruler who would at last bear and even become the message of reconciling grace. Of this one Balaam, overwhelmed by the Spirit of God, cried out in exultation: "A star will come out of Jacob; a scepter will rise out of Israel" (24:17, NIV). The message of the book is clear: Israel (and all of God's people) would fail to be faithful to His covenant expectations, but He would remain true. He cannot deny Himself.

OUTLINE

I. Preparation for Travel (1:1–10:10)
   A. Arrangement of the Tribes (chapters 1–2)
   B. Instructions to the Levites (chapters 3–4)
   C. Miscellaneous Ordinances (chapters 5–6)
   D. Instructions about the Tabernacle (chapters 7–8)
   E. The Passover (9:1–14)
   F. Preparation for the Journey (9:15–10:10)

II. The Journey to Kadesh Barnea (10:11–14:45)
   A. Departure from Sinai (10:11–36)
   B. Rebellion against Moses (11:1–12:15)
   C. Sending of the Spies (12:16–14:45)

III. The Journey to the Plains of Moab (15:1–22:1)
   A. Sacrifice and Service in the Promised Land (chapter 15)
   B. Rebellion and Vindication (chapters 16–17)
   C. Liturgical and Ritual Laws (chapters 18–19)
   D. Sojourn at Kadesh Barnea (20:1–21)
   E. Continuation of the Journey (22:22–22:1)

IV. The Encounter with Balaam (22:2–25:18)
   A. Balaam and His Journey (22:2–40)
   B. Balaam's Oracles (22:41–24:25)
   C. Israel's Apostasy (25:1–18)

V. Preparations for Conquest (chapters 26–36)
   A. Laws of Inheritance (26:1–27:11)
   B. Succession to Moses (27:12–23)
   C. Laws concerning Offerings (chapters 28–30)
   D. Punishment of Midian (chapter 31)
   E. Allocation to the Eastern Tribes (chapter 32)
   F. Summation of the Itinerary (33:1–49)
   G. Final Instruction about Conquest and Inheritance (33:50–36:13)

I. PREPARATION FOR TRAVEL (1:1–10:10)

The transition between Leviticus and Numbers marks a transition also in Israel's onward movement toward Canaan. The revelation of the covenant at Sinai was over, and the nation, now bound to the Lord by mutual commitments, was ready to press on to the fullness of the covenant promise, namely, a land in which Israel could undertake its role as God's redemptive agent.

Before the journey could resume, however, the vast throngs had to be organized by tribes, clans, and families both to expedite movement and to create an orderly worshiping community. Also the time of pilgrimage would be long, as it turned out, because of Israel's persistent disobedience. Life in the desert would require temporary social and religious measures that would be unnecessary later in the land but in the interim must be carefully spelled out. Numbers, then, is essentially a record of Israel's desert sojourn and a handbook prescribing her way of life until she finally entered the land of promise.

A. Arrangement of the Tribes (chapters 1–2)

More than a year had passed since the exodus from Egypt (1:1), most of the time being spent in the vicinity of Mount Sinai. Now the time had come to move on to Canaan, the land God had promised. The logistics of organizing and leading hundreds of thousands of people who had probably settled at Sinai in rather random fashion was enormous. The Lord therefore instructed Moses and Aaron to take a census of the people by tribe, clan, and family. The militaristic nature of the procedure is clear from the fact that only men twenty years old and above were to be included, that is, men suitable for war (1:3).

Discipline, structure, and order are inherent in the character of God and in all His works. The Creator who brought beautiful symmetry out of chaos in creation (Gen. 1:1–2) also said through Paul the apostle that everything should be done "decently and in order," especially in the church (1 Cor. 14:40, KJV). This principle underlies the organization of the tribes under Moses' leadership.

Tribal leaders, one over each tribe, must serve under Moses. The list of the tribes is based on their descent from Jacob through Leah (the first five tribes), Rachel (the next three), and the two maidservants, Zilpah and Bilhah (the next four). Levi is not listed because of that tribe's special place in the march and encampment (1:5–19). The order of the tribes in the actual statement of their totals is identical to the order in the list except that Gad follows Simeon rather than Asher (1:25; see 1:14). This is probably because of Gad's close association with Reuben in the later Transjordan settlement (32:1–5; Josh. 13:15–28). Reuben and Gad also appear together on the same side of the encampment around the tabernacle (Num. 2:10–16).

The grand total of adult males "able to go forth to war" was 603,550 (1:45–46, KJV). At a minimum one would have to suppose that the population of Israel as a whole exceeded 2.5 million. The practical implications of this are so profound that many suggestions have been made as to how to understand these figures. Liberal scholars simply dismiss them out of hand as having no historical basis, whereas many conservatives offer alternative understandings of the Hebrew term *'elep*, "thousand." They propose, for example, that *'allup*, "chieftain" or "clan," was intended, not *'elep*. This change involves only a revocalization of the Hebrew text, not a respelling of the consonants. (Verbal inspiration pertains only to the consonants of the original manuscripts.) By this view of vowel change the total would be 603 "clans" or other units plus some 550 other persons. If an *'allup* were only one hundred in number rather than one thousand, the total would be a more manageable 60,000 or so.

The reason for these proposals is the almost unimaginable scene of 2.5 million people leaving Egypt, wandering through the desert, assembling for two years at Sinai—all with flocks and herds dependent on them for food and water. The line of march alone, it is said, could stretch one hundred miles in length and be several miles in width. Therefore, it is argued, the numbers need to be brought down to a more manageable size.

However, there is no textual evidence for reading *'elep* as *'allup*, nor will the totals result in 603 clans. It seems best, then, to take the data at face value while recognizing the problems in doing so. After all, the whole point of the Exodus and wandering narratives is to magnify the God of Israel and to celebrate His unlimited grace and power (Exod. 7:5).

As already noted, the tribe of Levi does not appear in the census lists, because the Levites were ministers of religious affairs, not men of war. They were to attend to the tabernacle and its furnishings both in times of worship and in transition from place to place. Their role was so exclusively their own that anyone who attempted to infringe on it and approach the tabernacle must be slain (Num. 1:51). Even the location of this tribe in the camp shows the uniqueness of the Levitical office. Whereas the other tribes must pitch their tents in the periphery, the Levites could erect theirs all around the tabernacle. The tabernacle thus formed the focal point, the place where the Lord Himself dwelt, and the nation surrounded it at a distance. Between the Lord and His people were the Levites, forming both a barrier between the holy and the profane and a means of access to the Holy One by the profane people (1:53).

When the journey commenced, the tribes were to march and encamp in a stipulated order and manner. The tribes of Judah, Issachar, and Zebulun were to locate to the east of the tabernacle (2:1–9). Judah, under the leadership of Nahshon, was chief among that group. Nahshon appears later as an ancestor of King David (Ruth 4:20–21) and therefore of Jesus Christ (Matt. 1:4, 16). Because of Judah's prominence as the royal, messianic tribe, it was to lead the way whenever the tribes moved forward (Num. 2:9).

The second set of tribes—Reuben, Simeon, and Gad—camped on the south side. The tribe of Reuben, descendants of Jacob's eldest son, enjoyed primacy in this group and led the others in second place (2:16).

En route, these two tribal groups would precede, and right after them would come Levi with the tabernacle and all its equipment (2:17).

The third group consisted of the tribes of Ephraim, Manasseh, and Benjamin (2:18–24). Ephraim and Manasseh were sons of Joseph, who in turn was a son of Jacob's favorite wife, Rachel. Benjamin was Rachel's only other son, so that tribe's association with Ephraim and Manasseh is readily understandable. Ephraim—later a name for the whole Northern Kingdom itself (Isa. 7:2; Jer. 7:15; Hos. 4:17)—was the dominant tribe on the west side of the encampment.

The tribes of Dan, Asher, and Naphtali settled on the north side and made up the rear of this group. These three tribes shared in common a northern settlement allocation. Otherwise, the basis of their association is not entirely clear.

B. Instructions to the Levites (chapters 3–4)

A major element of God's gracious provision for His covenant people was the choice of men set apart to fill the office of priest. They would lead the people in worship and also provide mediation between them and the Lord (Exod. 28:1). Moses' own brother Aaron was the first of these priests, and only his descendants would thereafter be qualified to hold the office. Moses and Aaron were in the line of Levi (Exod. 6:16–20), so by virtue of this lineage all priests were to be Levites, that is, of the tribe of Levi.

On the other hand, not all Levites were priests, for not all were descendants of Aaron. However, they could serve the priests as assistants and thus enjoy access to the holy things of God that were denied to all other people. Aaron had four sons, two of whom died shortly after their anointing to the priestly ministry because of their boldness in offering "unauthorized fire" (Lev. 10:1–3). The other two, Eleazar and Ithamar, served with their father, and when Aaron died Eleazar succeeded him (Num. 20:25–28).

Thereafter it seems that only one high priest could serve at a time, though perhaps there was an exception for a short time in the time of David and Solomon when Abiathar and Zadok shared the office or at least overlapped (2 Sam. 20:25; 1 Kings 2:35; 1 Chron. 15:11). The Levites carried out the bidding of the priests, aiding them in sacrifice and worship and in all details having to do with the care of the tabernacle (Num. 3:5–10).

The Lord clarified His choice of the Levites as a people peculiarly related to Him (3:11–13). He had taken the lives of the firstborn of the Egyptians in the tenth plague, thus making them His own in the sense of their being "devoted" to him (Exod. 11:5; 13:15). He therefore could lay claim to the firstborn of Israel, but in life, not death (13:2; Num. 3:13). That is, Israel owed the Lord a great debt because of His redemptive grace, a debt to be paid in kind, as it were. But He showed even more grace by setting the Levites apart as substitutes for the firstborn of the other tribes. Rather than their being taken from their homes and pressed into sanctuary service, their places would be taken by the Levites.

The tribe of Levi consisted of three clans, Gershon, Kohath, and Merari. To each of these Moses assigned specific responsibilities (3:14–20). The Gershonites were to camp at the rear of the tabernacle, that is, to the west. They were to care for the tabernacle proper with all its coverings and drapes (3:21–26). The Kohathites (of whom Moses was one; Exod. 6:18, 20) were to the south. They were charged with the care and use of all the tabernacle furnishings (Num. 3:27–32). The Merarites, to the north, were concerned with the wood and metal parts of the tabernacle (3:33–37). The priests camped on the east side near the very entrance to the holy structure (3:38–39).

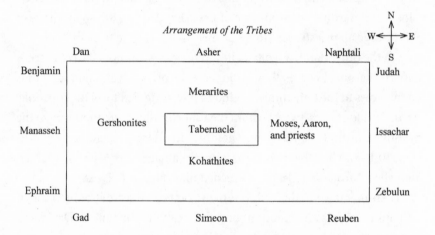

To determine whether the Levites were sufficiently numerous to match the number of firstborn sons of the other tribes, Moses undertook a count. He discovered there were 22,000 Levites and 22, 273 firstborn (3:39, 43). All those Levites were the Lord's (3:45), but so were the remaining 273 firstborn. The problem was resolved by allowing the extra 273 to be redeemed by monetary compensation at the rate of five shekels each (3:47). A silver shekel was about four-tenths of an ounce, so each redemption price was about two ounces. By today's standards at about $5.00 per ounce, the redemption could be made for $10.00. However, a better comparison is the amount to be paid to redeem a person from a vow to the Lord. This required five silver shekels for a boy from one month to five years old (Lev. 27:6). The best estimate is that a shekel was about one month's income, so the five-shekel redemption price was indeed precious.

Having delivered a grand total of 1,365 shekels over to the priests as redemption money (Num. 3:51), Moses ordered that a count be made of all the Levites from thirty to fifty years old by clans. The Kohathites totaled 2,750 (4:35), the Gershonites 2,630 (4:40), and the Merarites 3,200 (4:44). The full complement of 8,580 (4:48) would thereafter assume various responsibilities for tabernacle service according to their clan affiliation (4:1–3).

The priests, as Kohathites, led their kinsmen in the proper handling and transportation of the ark of the covenant, the table of showbread, the menorah, the incense altar, the altar of sacrifice, and other sacred furnishings of the tabernacle (4:4–14). These must all be wrapped in sealskin and blue cloth to prevent their being touched directly or even seen by those ritually disqualified from doing so. In fact, should a Kohathite other than a priest touch any of these articles (each one was a *qōdeš*, "holy thing," 4:15, NIV), he would surely die. Eleazar, son of Aaron, was designated as overseer of the entire process of dismantling and transporting the tabernacle (4:16).

To underscore again the holiness of the tabernacle and its service, the Lord directed Moses to implement safeguards whereby the Kohathites— who were most involved in the matters of the sanctuary and therefore most vulnerable—could be protected from inappropriate contact with what was off-limits to them (4:17–20). Specifically, they must never enter the tabernacle (*qōdeš* again, but here meaning the Holy Place) to look on its furnishings, lest they die. The idea was that the nearer one approached the presence of the Lord as represented by the ark, the more awesome was the effect of His glory. Only priests could enter the Holy Place, and only the high priest the Most Holy Place (Lev. 16:1–5).

The Gershonites, under Ithamar, Aaron's other son, were assigned the task of caring for and transporting the coverings, curtains, screens (or veils), cords, and all other similar materials pertaining to the tabernacle (Num. 4:21–28). Ithamar also directed the Merarites, who were responsible for the remaining parts of the tabernacle, that is, the wood and metal materials of which its sides were constructed (4:29–37). Thus the tribe of Levi, carefully numbered and divided by clan, assumed the great privilege of ministering the matters of the tabernacle in the transition from the Exodus to the settlement in Canaan (4:49).

C. Miscellaneous Ordinances (chapters 5–6)

Israel's life in the wilderness required certain regulations and stipulations appropriate to that situation. In addition to instructions about the tabernacle and its travels already addressed, Moses spoke here about the purity of the community (5:1–4), restitution for trespass (5:5–10), suspicion of marital infidelity and its evidence (5:11–31), standards pertaining to Nazirites (6:1–21), and the recitation of the priestly blessing (6:22–27).

In order for the community to exhibit moral and spiritual purity, it was required to deal with its symbolic outward manifestation, physical purity. Thus lepers, persons with abnormal flux (of pus, semen, blood, and the like; see Lev. 15), and those who came in contact with dead bodies (Num. 19:11) were to be quarantined outside the camp, for the Lord dwelt in the midst of the camp (5:3). This does not imply that diseased persons are inferior or are excluded from God's grace. These were temporary measures designed to highlight the principle of spiritual purity, which is invisible, by its analogy to the physical, which is visible (see 12:9–15).

No line was drawn in the theocratic community between sin against one's neighbor and sin against the Lord. If one person wronged another, then he or she must make full restitution plus 20 percent for any loss incurred by the offended party (5:7). If, however, neither the victim nor a next of kin survived to receive compensation, the restitution was to go to the priest, who of course represented the Lord Himself. In fact, the trespass is said to be against the Lord (5:6), and therefore its remedy must include proper sacrifices and offerings in addition to the restitution already demanded (5:8–10). Though the particular trespass is not stated, the similarity of this legislation to that of Leviticus 6:1–7 suggests that theft of property is in view, an interpretation strengthened by the insistence on restitution plus interest.

The next regulation has to do with an allegation by a husband that his wife has been adulterous. He has no witness, but a "spirit of jealousy" has come on him (Num. 5:14). That is, he has a "sneaking suspicion" that something is amiss in their relationship, though he has no solid proof. Again, this is a "religious" matter, so the man was to take his wife to the priest with a grain offering, the purpose of which was to expose the facts of the case. The Hebrew phrase reads literally, "a gift of remembrance bringing to mind iniquity." The idea is not so much that the offering would cause the woman to recall that she had sinned, but that the offering would expose that sin to public view.

What follows is commonly called "trial by ordeal," a form of judicial proceeding well known in the ancient Near East but found only here in the Old Testament. The procedure here consisted of the woman drinking a potion made up of "holy water" (that is, water set apart for the purpose), dust from the tabernacle floor, and the ink that dissolves from words written on a text of some kind. She must appear with disheveled hair (a sign of mourning), hold the grain offering in her hand, and then swear to her innocence. The priest would record the words of her oath and then dip the text into the vessel of water so that the ink would mingle with the dust in the water. The priest would offer the grain on the altar, and then the woman would drink the potion. If she were innocent, no harm would follow; if she were guilty, however, the water of bitterness—so-called because of its effects—would cause a swelling of the belly (perhaps her uterus) that would signify and result in infertility (5:28). In such a case the husband was exonerated (5:29–31). Nothing is said about his culpability should his suspicions turn out to be unfounded.

Though this may seem to resemble magic as practiced in pagan cultures, the association with God's tabernacle, the priests, sacrifice, and self-imprecation makes clear that this is a divinely sanctioned procedure, its "mechanical" nature notwithstanding. The Lord was at work (5:16, 18, 21, 25), using the well-known principle of psychosomatic relationship. The woman's body would reveal her innocence or guilt precisely because she was either innocent or guilty.

The next ordinance has to do with the Nazirite vow, a decision by a man or woman to be set apart for a time in order to give special attention to knowing and serving God (6:1–2). The concept, based on the term *nāzîr* ("to devote oneself"), involved essentially three kinds of self-denial: to refrain from alcoholic beverages or even their source, to allow one's hair to grow throughout the designated time, and to avoid contact with a dead body (6:3–8). If the vow was broken by contact with the dead, the individual had to undergo rituals of purification before resuming his or her status as a Nazirite (6:9–12). At the conclusion of the stated period of devotion, the Nazirite had to go through another ritual of sacrifice in order to be free of the restrictions sworn to at the beginning of the time of dedication (6:13–21).

Famous Nazirites in the Bible are Samson and Samuel (Judg. 13:2–7; 1 Sam. 1:9–11), both dedicated by their parents for a lifetime of separation, and Paul, whose dedication was for a limited time (Acts 18:18–21). Samson broke at least two of the stipulations of his vow (Judg. 14:5–9; 16:18–22), and there is no evidence that he ever undertook the rituals of reinstatement to his Nazirite position.

The final instruction of this section is directed to the priests who were to bestow a liturgy of blessing on the people of Israel (Num. 6:22–27). By performing this ministry the priests would "put the Lord's name" on them. That is, they would become identified with Him in such a way as to ensure His grace and goodness toward them.

D. Instructions about the Tabernacle (chapters 7–8)

The tabernacle had been built, but now there must be means of conveying it and also of maintaining its regular services, a fund for upkeep and continuation, as it were. The leaders of the tribes rose to the occasion and first presented carts and oxen to the Gershonites and Merarites to assist them in transporting their parts of the tabernacle and its furnishings. These were not provided to the Kohathites, however, for their cargo—the ark and other objects associated with the sanctuary—was too sacred to trust to any other means except poles carried on their shoulders (7:9; see also 4:15). Levites later under David presumed to move the ark on a wagon, much to their great sorrow (2 Sam 6:6–11).

Other gifts consisted of silver platters, silver bowls, gold spoons, and various sacrificial animals (Num. 7:12–17). Each of the tribal leaders in turn (in the same order as in 2:1–31) presented their gifts before the tabernacle on behalf of their people (7:12–83). As a result there was an abundant supply of materials dedicated to the service of the Lord (7:84–88).

Preparation of the Levites for this service was to follow precisely prescribed rituals, an order revealed by the Lord himself (7:89). The candelabrum had to be lighted correctly (8:1–4), the Levites purified and properly sanctified and ordained (8:5–10), and then presented as a tribe to the Lord as an offering (8:11–13). Only when they had undergone this initiation were the Levites qualified to lead in worship (8:14–19).

The Levites followed the Lord's requirements exactly and then commenced their ministry (8:20–22). The point is that it is God who calls to service and determines suitability for it and not persons who assume a ministry as though it were simply a matter of professional choice.

The maturity and physical well-being requisite to the Levitical office are clear from the stipulation that only men between twenty-five and fifty years old could serve in certain capacities (8:23–26). The minimum age of thirty mentioned earlier (4:3) may reflect a later period. That is, chapters 7 and 8 seem to be earlier chronologically than chapter 4. Perhaps at first age twenty-five seemed necessary in order to provide enough men, but later it became clear that by starting with age thirty enough men would be available. The upper age of fifty marked the point of retirement from active tabernacle service, but men older than that were to continue as watchmen guarding the premises (8:26).

E. The Passover (9:1–14)

At this point the account moves back a couple of weeks or so to the middle of the first month of the year (9:1; compare 1:1), the month of Passover (that is, Nisan or Abib; see Exod. 12:1–6; 13:4). The tabernacle having been erected, it became possible for such festivals to be observed in connection with it. Besides, the move out of Egypt was preceded by Passover, so it would be appropriate for the move from Sinai also to follow Passover.

After the service was concluded, Moses learned that certain persons had been prevented from participating because of their ritual disqualification for having touched a corpse (Num. 9:6; see also 19:11–22). This presented a dilemma for Moses who, not finding provision for such a contingency in the Law, appealed directly to the Lord (9:8). In a remarkable display of grace, the Lord said that under such circumstances Passover could be postponed (9:9–12). However, anyone who tried to take advantage of this loophole for no good reason would experience not grace but judgment. He would be "cut off from his people," that is, excommunicated from the nation and thus unable to enjoy its benefits.

F. Preparation for the Journey (9:15–10:10)

In another narrative retrojection Moses returned to the day the tabernacle had been completed and was infused with God's glory (9:15; see Exod. 40:1, 17, 34). That mark of His presence would thereafter signal both the movement of the camp forward and its resting place. When the fiery cloud rose up from the camp, the journey began, and when it settled down, the journey ended, whether it was for only a day or two or a year or more (Num. 9:22). Thus it was clear that the Lord led the way. He was headed for the Promised Land and Israel was to follow (9:23).

Movement of so many people called for military precision. Based on trumpet blasts of different number and intensity, various responses would occur. At times all the people would assemble, at other times only the leaders, and at still other times the tribes would march (10:3–6). Trumpets would also sound in battle, almost as a cue for the Lord to deliver His people (10:9). Also trumpets were to be blown to herald the beginning of a new month and the arrival of annual festival times (10:10).

II. THE JOURNEY TO KADESH BARNEA (10:11–14:45)

The journey from Sinai to the border of Canaan consisted of two major stages—many miles and a few weeks to Kadesh Barnea, and a few miles and many years from there to the plains of Moab. The difference is the crisis of unbelief and rebellion that took place at Kadesh Barnea, a spiritual malaise that sentenced Israel to aimless migration in hostile deserts. The crisis was already foreshadowed in the trek from Sinai to Kadesh Barnea, for in that short time the people repeatedly complained and resisted Moses' leadership.

A. Departure from Sinai (10:11–36)

More than a year after the Exodus and right after the delayed Passover (9:11–12), the cloud of God's glory rose up from the camp signaling that the time had come to leave Sinai and head north (10:11–13). The Judah contingent departed first (10:14–16). Then the tabernacle was dismantled, and the Gershonites and Merarites proceeded with their parts of it (10:17; see 4:21–33). Next came Reuben and its affiliated tribes (10:18–20) and the Kohathites carrying the sacred ark and other tabernacle furnishings (10:21). The Ephraimites and Danites brought up the rear (10:22–28).

At this point Moses related his encounter with his brother-in-law Hobab, who had either just joined Israel at Sinai or had been there with his father, Reuel (or Jethro; Exod. 2:18; 3:1), some months earlier (18:1–5). Since Hobab seems to have been familiar with the deserts of Sinai (Num. 10:31), Moses asked him to join the procession, promising that God would bless him for it (10:29, 32). It seems that Hobab refused (10:30), but, on the other hand, some of Hobab's kinsmen are mentioned later as having some connection with inhabitants of Canaan (Judg. 4:11).

With the migration underway, the priests with the ark moved to the front, for the ark symbolized the presence of the Lord, who of course was the real Leader of the people (Num. 10:33–34; see also 9:23). When the ark moved ahead Moses would cry out, "Rise up, O LORD! May your enemies be scattered!" (10:35, NIV). When it stopped, he proclaimed, "Return, O LORD, to the countless thousands of Israel!" (10:36, NIV). Clearly, then, Moses saw the ark as the very manifestation of the God of Israel.

B. Rebellion against Moses (11:1–12:15)

The trek to Canaan had hardly begun when the people began to complain in words and spirit so offensive to the Lord that He sent "fire" on them (11:1). There is no reason to take this other than literally, perhaps a conflagration triggered by lightning or a carelessly tended campfire. Exercising his mediatorial role, Moses prayed for God to stay His hand, and the Lord graciously relented. The incident gave rise to the name of the place, Taberah (from the Hebrew *bāʿar*, "to burn"), a site no longer identifiable.

Soon afterward complaint burst forth again, this time because of the unappetizing diet forced on the people. The griping began with disorganized clusters of people and spread to the community as a whole. They longed for the meats and vegetables of Egypt instead of the manna that formed the staple of their diet. They had grumbled about such matters even before they reached Sinai. In those days God had supplied them with miraculous provisions of quail and manna (Exod. 16:4–14), and now, the other side of His covenant grace and love, He did so again as a display of His dependability.

This fresh eruption of rebellion crushed Moses' spirit. Lashing out against the Lord, Moses accused Him of having placed the heavy load of His people on Moses' frail shoulders (Num. 11:10–12). He could not feed these people, he said, nor could he any longer withstand the pressures of leadership. If God really loved him, He would not permit such unfairness but instead would relieve his pain by taking his life (11:13–15; see also Exod. 32:32).

God's response was twofold: He would place His Spirit on seventy elders whom Moses was to select to share the burden of governance (Num. 11:16–17), and He would send quail in such abundance that the people would not only tire of it but would make themselves ill from stuffing themselves with it (11:18–20a). Thus they would suffer from having spurned God's gracious act of delivering them from Egypt (11:20b). Moses' skepticism about the provision of such a supply comes up hard against the rhetorical question, "Is the Lord's arm too short?" (11:23). Surely the God of the Exodus is also the God of supernatural preservation.

Moses complied with the Lord's instructions, and having gathered seventy elders to "the tent" (that is, the Holy Place of the tabernacle; see Exod. 27:21; 29:42), he witnessed the magnificent scene in which God placed on them the same Spirit that had come on Moses and empowered him (Num. 11:24–25). The sign of this divine investiture was an outburst of prophesying by the elders, a phenomenon not to be repeated by them (11:25b).

Though the Old Testament does not contain a fully developed theology of the Holy Spirit, it does reveal enough to show that the Spirit was a manifestation of God Himself and not merely a way of referring to some divine attribute (see, for example, Gen. 1:2; 6:3; Exod. 31:3; Num. 24:2; Judg. 3:10; 1 Sam. 10:6, 10; Isa. 11:2; 42:1; 61:1). Here the Holy Spirit attested to His presence by enabling untrained spokesmen to speak words otherwise impossible to them (see also 1 Sam. 10:5, 10–11, 13; 19:20–21, 24).

This gift was so uniquely that of Moses alone that when Eldad and

Medad, two men who had not joined the seventy, began to prophesy, Joshua protested to Moses that they had no right to do so. Joshua's loyalty to Moses and jealousy for his master's spiritual leadership is commendable, but his concern met with a most unexpected response. "I wish that all the Lord's people were prophets," Moses said, "and that the LORD would put his Spirit on them" (Num. 11:29). The work of ministry is too great for one person or for even a few. The whole body must be Spirit-filled and Spirit-led if God's purposes are to come to pass.

> One of the most difficult virtues of the Christian life is to "rejoice with those who rejoice" (Rom. 12:15). It is all too easy to feel that one has exclusive ownership of the grace and goodness of God, so when He blesses others there is often a reaction of jealousy or even hostility.

The second response to Moses' request—the need for food—followed in the form of a vast flock of quail that flew over the camp for miles on each side (11:31–35). They flew at such a low elevation that they could easily be plucked from the skies. Giving vent to their appetites, the people seized on this bounty with no sense of gratitude to God. But before they could even begin their gluttonous orgy, the Lord struck them down. Forever after, the site of this debacle became known as Kibroth-Hattaavah, "the graves of lust" (11:34).

The next stopping place was Hazeroth, perhaps modern 'Ayin Khodara (11:35; see also 33:17–18; Deut 1:1). There the next rebellious act took place; it was unexpected and serious because it arose from within Moses' own family. Joshua had already argued that only Moses was an authorized prophet (Num. 11:28). Miriam and Aaron now challenged that premise, and on the basis of the allegation that Moses had married improperly they asserted that they as well as he were qualified to be divine spokespersons (12:1–3).

The "Cushite woman" most likely was Zipporah, daughter of Jethro the Midianite (Exod. 2:21), who, of course, was a foreigner. By referring to "Cushan" and "Midian" together, Habakkuk 3:7 seems to favor the view that the Cushite woman was a Midianite. On the other hand, "Cushite" may refer to her having been from Cush in Africa (later known as Nubia), and so she may have been black. In either case Moses' siblings used this relationship as a pretext for undermining his unique authority.

God forbids doing harm to His prophets (Gen. 26:11; Ps. 105:15), so the Lord called Miriam and Aaron to account (Num. 12:4–5). Ordinary prophets (like Aaron and Miriam), He said, receive revelatory dreams and visions, but not so with Moses. To him God spoke openly (literally, "mouth to mouth"). His role was unique and should not be challenged (12:6–8; see also Deut. 34:10). To dramatize the seriousness of Miriam's insubordination and also to underscore Moses' mediatorial ministry, the Lord struck Miriam with a loathsome skin disease (probably not the same as modern leprosy), which forced her to be quarantined outside the camp (Num. 12:9–15). Only Moses' prayer brought about her restoration. The lesson is self-evident: God chooses whom He will to do His bidding, and that choice must never be criticized or undermined.

C. Sending of the Spies (12:16–14:45)

The next stage of the journey ended at Kadesh Barnea, in the Paran desert (12:16; see also 13:26). From this great oasis, the center of Israel's life for the next thirty-eight years (Deut. 2:14), Moses sent out a reconnaissance party of twelve men—one from each tribe—to explore Canaan in order to determine the feasibility of conquest and the nature of Canaan's resources (Num. 13:1–20). Included in the party were Caleb the Judahite and Hoshea (Joshua) the Ephraimite (13:6, 8). Moses had changed Joshua's name from a word meaning merely "salvation" to one meaning "the Lord saves." This is the Hebrew name of the Savior (Greek, Iēsous).

For forty days the spies searched out the land from the Zin desert in the south to Rehob in the north, somewhere near the source of the Jordan (see Judg. 18:28; 2 Sam. 10:6–8). En route they passed through Hebron, sacred because of its association with the patriarchs (Num. 12:22; Gen. 13:18; 23:2, 19; 35:27). The reference to its having been built seven years before Zoan (that is, Tanis, Egypt, in 1737 B.C.) suggests either that it took its name then or that the earlier named places were in the vicinity of Hebron.

An illustration of this follows. It seems that a certain man had, with "high hand," violated the Sabbath by gathering firewood on that day. Moses' verdict was unambiguous: He must be stoned to death by the community (15:32–36). The harshness of the penalty drove home the seriousness of the previous injunction against blasphemy. In order that they and their descendants might remember not only the fourth commandment but all of them, Moses instructed the people to wear tassels on their clothing. This would help direct their minds to who God is and what He had done for them (15:37–41).

B. Rebellion and Vindication (chapters 16–17)

Sometime during the stay at Kadesh Barnea a fellow Kohathite named Korah led a rebellion against Moses and Aaron, challenging their claim to unique priestly authority (16:1–3). Moses took up the challenge and instructed Korah and his Levitical cohorts as well as Dathan and Abiram, leaders of the Reubenites (16:12; see also 26:9), to assemble the next day for a contest to determine whom, in fact, God had chosen (16:4–11).

Since incense could be offered only by the priests, Moses told Korah as well as Aaron to appear at the tabernacle with their censers in hand to see how the Lord would respond (16:15–19). Fearful that the Lord would destroy the whole community (16:20–21), Moses and Aaron prayed that His judgment would fall on only the guilty—Korah, Dathan, Abiram, and their confederates (16:22–24). Moses then asserted that if God indeed had chosen him, the earth would open and swallow the rebels (16:25–30), a result that indeed followed immediately (16:31–34). Fire consumed others (16:35), and the censers they had used, even though illegitimately, had become "holy" (that is, used for sacred purpose) and therefore were converted into bronze sheets to cover the altar of burnt offering (16:36–39). From then on Israel would know that only priests could approach the Lord with incense (16:40; see also 2 Chron. 26:18).

One would think this would end the rebellion, but sadly this was not the case. The people accused Moses and Aaron of having slain the rebels, a charge so fallacious that the Lord once again threatened to annihilate the whole assembly (Num. 16:41–45). Ever the faithful mediator, Moses urged Aaron to make atonement for the people, and though a plague from the Lord had already begun, Aaron's priestly intercession brought it to an end (16:46–50). To cap off Aaron's claim to unique privilege as priest, the Lord commanded Moses to place twelve staffs—emblems of authority— before the Lord at the tabernacle (17:1–7). Each staff represented a tribe, with the one of Aaron standing for Levi. The next morning Aaron's staff had "sprouted" and "budded," producing almond blossoms and fruit (17:8–11). The staff was then placed near the ark of the covenant as a reminder of the sovereign grace of God who chooses whom He will to serve Him. This time the lesson seems to have struck home (17:12–13).

C. Liturgical and Ritual Laws (chapters 18–19)

To further affirm the role of the priesthood and to explain the relationship between the priests and Levites, the Lord spoke directly to Aaron about these matters (18:1–7). Only the priests could minister in the tabernacle proper; the Levites could assist but in a limited way. Only the priests could present and share in some of the sacrifices and offerings (18:8–20), whereas other offerings were designated for the Levites as tithes on which they could subsist (18:21–32).

Other rituals to be observed under priestly auspices had to do with purification by means of the blood and ashes of a red heifer (19:1–10). One who had become ritually impure because of touching a dead body, for example (19:11; see 5:2), could be cleansed by the application of water containing the ashes (19:12–13). Persons and even objects rendered impure by being in the presence of a corpse could also be rendered pure by this process (19:14–19). Those who refused to comply with such requirements for ritual cleansing must be excommunicated lest they contaminate the whole fellowship (19:20–22).

D. Sojourn at Kadesh Barnea (20:1–21)

After thirty-eight years at Kadesh Barnea, Israel prepared to resume the journey to Canaan but this time by following a route south of the Dead Sea and through Edom (20:14). Before this took place several incidents occurred in rapid succession. Miriam died and was buried at Kadesh (20:1); the people ran out of water and Moses, enraged by their incessant complaining, struck a rock from which God promised water if Moses only spoke the word (20:2–13); and Moses tried without success to get permission from the king of Edom to pass through his land on the so-called King's Highway (20:14–21).

Though understandable, Moses' loss of temper displeased the Lord and resulted in his being unable to enter the Promised Land (20:12; see 27:14; Deut. 3:26–27). Moses' disobedience as Israel's leader had damaged not only his own reputation in the eyes of the people but the Lord's reputation as well.

> Such punishment for what might seem to be a relatively minor offense underscores the principle that God expects more of those to whom He entrusts responsibility than He does from others. Jesus said, "From everyone who has been given much shall much be required" (Luke 12:48, NASB).

E. Continuation of the Journey (20:22–22:1)

Edom's defensible position in the mountains and canyons of the Transjordanian plateaus made it possible for that nation to deny Israel access to the north-south routes that passed through it. Moses decided therefore to skirt Edom on the south and travel northward along Edom's eastern border. On the way Aaron died at Mount Hor, south of the Dead Sea, and was buried there, and his son Eleazar succeeded him as high priest (20:22–29). Meanwhile, to ensure that Israel would not penetrate Canaan from the south, the king of Arad attacked them, but this time God gave His people victory (21:1–3).

This did not change the projected itinerary. Israel journeyed to the Red Sea (that is, the Gulf of Aqaba or Eilat, 21:4) and from there to Moab through the deserts east of Edom. Along the way the people complained again, so much so that the Lord sent poisonous snakes to bite them. The only remedy was to look in faith on a bronze snake raised above them on a pole (21:5–9; see John 3:14).

Once near the border of Moab at the Arnon River (Num. 21:13), Moses sought permission from Sihon, the Amorite king of the region, to pass through his territory toward the Jordan River (21:21–22). The request was denied; so what Israel could not do peaceably was accomplished militarily (21:23–31). The result was Israel's unintended conquest and occupation of the territory of the Amorites. Alarmed by Israel's success, Og, king of Bashan, attacked, but God delivered him and his nation into Israel's hands as well (21:33–22:1).

IV. THE ENCOUNTER WITH BALAAM (22:2–25:18)

Moab historically laid claim to all the Transjordan from the Zered River in the south to the Jabbok River in the north. In Moses' day, however, the Amorites had limited Moab to a zone south of the Arnon River (21:13). With Sihon's defeat, the Moabites once more were free to repossess their lands north of the Arnon River, but now in competition with Israel. Balak, king of Moab, determined to rid himself of Israel, something he knew he could not do militarily. He therefore engaged a pagan sorcerer to do it for him.

A. Balaam and His Journey (22:2–40)

King Balak, in alliance with Israel's enemies the Midianites, set out to hire a widely acclaimed prophet from Pethor far north on the Euphrates River to come and curse the threatening Israelites (22:2–6). Seeking counsel from Israel's God—who told him not to yield to Balak's blandishments— Balaam at first refused to go with Balak's emissaries (22:7–14). When offered more financial inducement, the pagan soothsayer changed his mind, and despite the Lord's warnings he decided to assist Balak in his schemings (22:15–34). Then in a remarkable display of sovereignty the Lord told Balaam to continue with his mission, but He let him know that he would be able to speak only what God permitted him (22:35–40).

B. Balaam's Oracles (22:41–24:25)

Two "specialties" in ancient pagan prophetism were divination and incantation. The former sought to understand the intentions and purposes of the gods, and the latter attempted either to support those intentions or, more often, to thwart them by ritual or other means. Balaam was known for expertise in both, but here his purpose was to subvert the intentions the Lord had for Israel by overturning God's blessings and making them curses. Over and over he tried to curse Israel, but in vain, for God spoke blessing when Balaam intended cursing (23:8, 12, 26; 24:13).

The blessings uttered against the will of the pagan prophet are among the most magnificent in the Bible. Israel would be a unique people, Balaam said (23:9), a people whose God would never leave them (23:21). Repeating the wording of the Abrahamic Covenant (Gen. 12:3), Balaam said that those who blessed Israel would be blessed, but those who cursed them would be cursed (Num. 24:9). Most remarkable of all was the messianic promise about the star from Jacob, a Ruler who would rise in powerful triumph (24:17; see also Gen. 49:10). Not even the most celebrated enchanter in the ancient Near Eastern world could change the saving purposes of Israel's God.

C. Israel's Apostasy (25:1–18)

What Balaam could not accomplish as an enchanter he managed to do behind the scenes, at least partially. Somehow he managed to seduce certain Israelites to worship the deity of the area, the Baal of Peor (25:1–3; see also 31:16; 2 Pet. 2:15; Jude 11). This god was particularly associated with the Midianites, apparently in connection with typically Canaanite fertility myth and ritual (Num. 25:6–8).

Phinehas, son of the priest Eleazar, was so incensed by this blatant idolatry that he led the judges of Israel in a slaughter of the guilty Israelites which, with a plague sent by God, took twenty-four thousand lives (25:4–5, 7–9). This guaranteed to Phinehas and his descendants a perpetual Aaronic priesthood (25:10–13).

V. PREPARATIONS FOR CONQUEST
(CHAPTERS 26–36)

After the disaster at Peor, Moses renumbered the people in anticipation of their imminent entry into Canaan. In the course of doing so, it was brought to his attention that families with no sons as heirs must have some provision for inheritance by daughters. This done, he addressed matters of sacrifice and festival, vows, vengeance on Midian, and the distribution of Transjordania among the two and a half eastern tribes. Then he outlined procedures for conquering and dividing Canaan, appointing cities of refuge, and the marriage of female heiresses. All that remained was his farewell address, in which he outlined the covenant renewal made necessary by life in the land of promise. That is the content of Deuteronomy.

A. Laws of Inheritance (26:1–27:11)

In order for the Promised Land to be fairly apportioned among the tribes, the Lord commanded Moses and Eleazar to number the people by tribe. Comparison of the tribe-by-tribe totals with the census nearly forty years earlier (Num. 1:1–46) yields some interesting facts. For the most part the totals are about the same, but Simeon's original 59,300 (1:23) was now 22,200, a drop explained by the role that Simeonites especially played at Baal Peor (25:14). Manasseh, on the other hand, grew by over 20,000 (1:35; 26:34), while Ephraim declined by 13,000 (1:33; 26:37). Asher also experienced significant growth, from 41,500 to 53,400 (1:41; 26:47). The grand total slipped by about 1,800, suggesting no overall growth in the forty years of rebellion.

The Levites, who would have no land inheritance, numbered 23,000 as compared to 22,273 at the beginning (26:62; 3:43). Moses then explained one reason for the apparent stabilization of the population—the totals were only of those qualified to enter the land, not those who had forfeited their rights by their disobedience (26:63–65; see 14:29–35).

The lack of Levitical inheritance gave rise to the matter of inheritance by daughters who had no surviving brothers (27:1–11). The solution was that women in that case had every right to their father's inheritance.

B. Succession to Moses (27:12–23)

Moses already knew that he would never enter Canaan (20:12), so he urged the Lord to select a successor to him. Certainly not to his surprise, the Lord revealed to Moses that his faithful attendant Joshua would be the man (27:18; see Exod. 17:9–14; 24:13; 33:11). The ceremony of succession would consist of a laying on of hands and the giving of a charge. The people would recognize the validity of Joshua's office as he inquired of the Lord through the priest and led them in all their national affairs.

C. Laws concerning Offerings (chapters 28–30)

Life in the land would require attention to sacrifices and offerings, festivals and holy days. These included the daily burnt offerings (28:1–8), the Sabbath (28:9–10), the new moon festivals (or Feast of Trumpets; 28:11–15; see 10:10), the Passover (28:16–25), the Firstfruits (or Feast of Weeks or Pentecost; 28:26–31; see Lev. 23:15–21), the New Year festival (later known as Rosh Hashanah; Num. 29:1–6; see Lev. 23:23–25), the Day of Atonement (Yom Kippur; Num. 29:7–11; see Lev. 23:26–32), and the Feast of Tabernacles (also called Succoth; Num. 29:12–38; see Lev. 23:33–35). In addition, they must observe proper regulation concerning vows, especially the women, who could not make them independent of their fathers or husbands (Num. 30:1–16).

D. Punishment of Midian (chapter 31)

Midian had been the principal ethnic or tribal group that, under Balaam's leadership, had seduced Israel into idolatry at Peor (25:1–18). Ironically, Moses was related to the Midianites through marriage, for Zipporah his wife was a daughter of a Midianite priest (Exod. 2:16–21). He must have found it painful therefore to engage Midian in holy war, but God's own justice must be paramount above all other relationships. Led by Phineas, twelve thousand men of Israel, one thousand from each tribe, marched forth, slaughtering all males they encountered, including Balaam (Num. 31:1–18). Contrary to the principles of holy war (see Deut. 20:16–18), they spared the women, an infraction severely condemned by Moses (Num. 31:9–16). So he ordered all except the unmarried women to be killed (31:17–18).

Such mass slaughter would cause ritual impurity, so Moses gave detailed instructions about purification for those who touched dead bodies. He also prescribed proper protocol for purifying the booty and distributing it to the victors (31:19–54).

E. Allocation to the Eastern Tribes (chapter 32)

Once the Israelites had conquered most of Transjordania, some of them—explicitly the tribes of Reuben, Gad, and half of Manasseh—asked permission to occupy it because of its rich pasturage (32:1–5). Moses at first rejected their appeal on the grounds that their refusal to join their brothers in the conquest of Canaan would be demoralizing (32:6–15). The tribal leaders responded by pledging that they would send their troops to Canaan to fight, and only after successful conquest would they rejoin their families in the east (32:16–19). Convinced of their sincerity, Moses relented after sanctioning the agreement before the priests and tribal leaders (32:20–32). He then allocated the eastern lands from south to north to Reuben, Gad, and Machir, a clan of Manasseh, respectively (32:33–42).

F. Summation of the Itinerary (33:1–49)

In a recapitulation of Israel's history since the Exodus, Moses recorded a narrative based on significant places and the important events associated with them. He began with the flight from Rameses (that is, Goshen) itself (33:3; see Exod. 12:37), a flight that flaunted the weakness of the Egyptians and their gods (Num. 33:1–4). From Rameses the route appeared to dead end at the Red Sea, but God led them through the sea until they reached Mount Sinai (33:5–15).

The next stage was from Sinai to Zin (or Kadesh Barnea), a journey that found them stopping at a number of sites not previously named and most of which cannot now be identified (33:16–36). After thirty-eight years they headed toward Canaan, burying Aaron along the way (33:38–39), until at last they reached the plains of Moab (33:40–49). The itinerary was written out by Moses himself (33:2), a hint that he was responsible for the record of all the events of the narrative.

G. Final Instruction about Conquest and Inheritance (33:50–36:13)

Though he could not go there, Moses obviously had a great interest in the land God had promised his ancestors. Directed by the Lord, Moses mapped out that land by regions, carefully delineating the borders. The southern extent would be marked by a line from the south end of the Dead Sea west to the "Wadi of Egypt" (modern Wadi el-Arish; 34:1–5). The western border would be the Mediterranean ("the Great Sea," 34:6). The northern frontier would extend from Mount Hor (not the burial place of Aaron but a peak somewhere north of Mount Carmel) to Hazar Enan (perhaps modern Qaryatein, seventy-five miles northeast of Damascus; 34:7–9). The eastern border would begin at Hazar Enan and run south on the east side of the Kinnereth (Galilee) Sea to the place where the Jordan River enters the Dead Sea (34:10–12).

Within this area the nine and a half western tribes would find their places. Eleazar and Joshua, representing the religious and political leadership respectively, were to work with leaders of each tribe in allocating the territories (34:16–29). Though the Levites would not receive territory as a tribe (see 18:23–24), they would be given forty-eight cities throughout the land, including six that would be places of refuge (35:1–8).

The purpose of refuge cities was to provide temporary sanctuary to anyone accused of homicide. If a person accidentally took the life of another person, he could run to one of these places and be protected from private vengeance until his case came to trial (35:9–15). If it were proven that the accused did not act with premeditation, members of the victim's clan or family could do him no harm. The perpetrator, however, would have to return to the city of refuge to which he had originally fled, and he would have to remain there until the high priest then in office would die. In a sense, the slayer was under house arrest as a punishment for taking human life even if with no evil intent. Should he leave early, however, the avenger on behalf of the victim could put the accused to death (35:22–28).

In a case of premeditated murder, no place of safety was available. In fact, the "blood avenger" could and must slay the criminal on behalf of not only the victim but also his family and the whole community (35:16–21). Clearly there must have been rules of evidence and other proper legal procedures in such cases, for otherwise vigilante justice would undermine the very basis of civil life (see Deut. 19:15–21).

The sanctity of human life is clear both from the fact of capital punishment as the only suitable punishment for murder (Gen. 9:5–6) and, on the other hand, from the prohibition against enacting the death penalty in cases where premeditation cannot be proved. To execute the innocent is as evil in God's sight as to exonerate the guilty.

Indication of this and also of the need to redress the act of homicide in particular follows (Num. 35:29–34). No vengeance could be undertaken without proper evidence. For example, the testimony of only one witness would be invalid. Also the punishment for murder must be death. No ransom (that is, compensatory payment) could substitute for the death of the assailant. The reason is that the blood of the victim would corrupt the very soil on which it fell, and the only way the pollution could be removed was by canceling it by the blood of the murderer. Besides being a Mosaic principle, this also was as ancient as the Noahic Covenant (Gen. 9:6).

Once more Moses had to address the matter of inheritance by daughters (Num. 36:1–13). He had already declared by the revelation of God that a man who died without sons could pass his estate on to daughters (27:1–11). Now the same case—that of Zelophehad's daughters—needed further refinement. The problem was the loss of territory to their tribe if they married men from without (36:3–4). In such a case the men's tribes would possess the estate. Moses' solution was clear and nonnegotiable: Zelophehad's daughters (and all women in that situation) could marry only within their tribes (36:6–8). Only this could guarantee the tribal territories assigned by divine decree.

In conclusion Moses summarized all he had written in Numbers as the "commands" and "regulations" of the Lord (36:13). The authority for them lay not in his having penned them but in God's having supernaturally revealed them.

DEUTERONOMY
Covenant Faith Reaffirmed

AUTHOR

*P*recritical Jewish and Christian tradition unanimously attributed the basic substance of Deuteronomy to Moses, though there have always been some who have argued for post-Mosaic additions such as the account of the great Lawgiver's own death (Deut. 34:5–12). The view that Moses wrote Deuteronomy is seen in the book's opening words, "These are the words which Moses spoke," a statement that attributes the immediately following passage and, by implication, the entire work to Moses. Throughout the Bible Moses is often referred to as this book's author (for example, Josh. 1:7–8; Judg. 1:20; 3:4; 1 Kings 2:3; 2 Kings 14:6; 2 Chron. 25:4; Ezra 3:2; Matt. 19:7; Mark 12:19; Luke 20:28; Acts 3:22; Rom. 10:19; 1 Cor. 9:9). There can be no doubt that the prophets, Jesus, and the apostles concurred with the witness of Deuteronomy as to its authorship.

UNITY

Traditionally Deuteronomy has been viewed as an address or collection of addresses delivered by Moses to a representative gathering of his Israelite compatriots, the whole of which was then put to pen and ink. Thus the book was viewed as more or less homiletical in style with a strong hortatory flavor.

A typical approach to the nature and structure of Deuteronomy is that of S. R. Driver, who wrote that "the book consists chiefly of three discourses, purporting to have been delivered by Moses in . . . Moab, setting forth the laws which the Israelites are to obey, and the spirit in which they are to obey them, when they are settled in the land of promise" (*A Critical and Exegetical Commentary on the Book of Deuteronomy* [Edinburgh: Clark, 1902], i). These discourses he identified as (a) the introductory discourse (1:6–4:40), (b) the exposition of the Law (5:1–26:19; chapters 27–28), and (c) the third discourse, which serves as a supplement (29:1–30:20). The remainder of the book consists of various introductions (1:1–5; 4:44–49), conclusions (31:1–8; 32:48–34:12), and other matters, many of which appear not to be integral to the overall structure. It is remarkable perhaps that Driver's analysis anticipates and largely conforms to the organizational pattern of Deuteronomy that more recent study of ancient Near Eastern suzerain-vassal treaty texts reveals.

Building on the publication and study of Late Bronze Age treaty documents found at Hattušaš (or Boghazkeüi, its modern name), the capital of the New Hittite Empire, George F. Mendenhall demonstrated that Deuteronomy (and Exodus 20–23, the so-called Book of the Covenant) contained all the essential elements of these Hittite treaty texts and in precisely the same order. He therefore concluded that the author(s) or redactor(s) of Deuteronomy must have patterned their work after the Hittite model. With this judgment a whole host of scholars have concurred, especially those of a conservative persuasion, though obviously others challenged the comparisons from the beginning and continue to do so to the present day. The current state of the debate will receive attention below.

The implications of these comparative studies are, of course, extremely profound. For example, if one can show that Deuteronomy is patterned after late Hittite exemplars, its date presumptively must be early (no later than 1300 B.C. or so) and its Mosaic authorship more assured. But for now it is important to see how the very literary structure and form of the book, in light of these clearly attestable similarities, yields insight into its function, purpose, and meaning.

Granting the remarkable parallels suggested thus far, it is still important to point out that Deuteronomy is more than a mere formal covenant text. For one thing, it is much longer than any extant documents of that kind. For another, it still presents itself as a farewell address by Moses, the covenant mediator, one filled with nonlegal passages such as itineraries, exhortations, hymns, and other poetic material. In other words, Deuteronomy is of mixed and varied genre. But all this does not vitiate the essential core of the composition as being covenant in style and purpose. It is covenant expressed in narrative and exhortation, the whole thing together comprising a farewell address.

DATE

Authorship by Moses presupposes certain chronological parameters. First, Deuteronomy itself claims to have originated in the "land of Moab" (Deut. 1:5) at the end of the wilderness journey and on the eve of the conquest of Canaan (4:44–49; 34:1–4). Second, this completion of the itinerary occurred precisely forty years after the Exodus, according to the biblical witness (2:7, 14; Josh. 5:6; see Num. 14:33–34). This reduces the matter of the date of Deuteronomy to a consideration of the date of the Exodus itself, a problem that can be addressed only briefly at this point.

First Kings 6:1 dates the founding of Solomon's temple to his fourth year, that year being, according to the best chronological reconstruction, 967–966 B.C. The fixed date with which this achievement is associated is the Exodus, which occurred 480 years earlier (1 Kings 6:1). The Exodus then can be assigned to the year 1447–1446 B.C. It follows that the wilderness era ended in 1407–1406 and that the Book of Deuteronomy must have taken shape at the same time. The communique of Jephthah the judge to the Ammonites bolsters this view of events, for according to it the Israelites of the Transjordan had been there for three hundred years, that is, from the time of the beginning of the Conquest until Jephthah's own day (Judg. 11:26). Since the judgeship of Jephthah can be determined with reasonably good precision as having fallen in the last decade of the twelfth century (around 1106–1100 B.C.), Jephthah's data clearly agree with those of 1 Kings. So the only biblical texts that directly attest to the dates of the Exodus and Conquest converge on 1447–1446 and 1407–1406 respectively, thus offering strong support for the date of 1400 or so for the composition of Deuteronomy. Even if one were to grant the dates of a "late" Exodus and Conquest (around 1275–1235 B.C.), Mosaic authorship is unaffected for the Mosaic chronology could itself, of course, be lowered accordingly. In fact, a thirteenth-century background would be all the more compatible with a comparison of Deuteronomy to Hittite suzerain-vassal treaty texts (a matter of supreme importance in understanding Deuteronomy's full implications), for these secular texts flourished in a period slightly later than 1400. Despite this, the traditional early date should be followed, for it is consistent with all other aspects of the problem.

ADDRESSEES AND PURPOSE

Deuteronomy (and most likely much of the rest of the Pentateuch as well) was written by Moses on the eve of the conquest of Canaan as a means of addressing a number of questions and concerns. First, it was important that the people understand who they were, where they originated, and what their God intended for them in the years to come. Genesis enabled them to trace their roots back to the patriarchs and to the patriarchal covenant that promised a people and a land. Exodus rehearsed the story of the growth of that people, their redemption from cruel and despotic bondage, and their covenant affiliation with the Lord, who called and equipped them to be a kingdom of priests and a holy nation (Exod. 19:4–6). The same book and Leviticus outlined the means by which the nation might have access to a holy God and how it must function as a holy people in fulfilling the covenant requirements. Numbers provides instruction for the people in movement from covenant to conquest. Finally, Deuteronomy reiterates the covenant, but it does so in a greatly expanded form and in terms appropriate to the new generation about to enter the Promised Land. The new generation, about to embark on conquest, stood in need of covenant reiteration and reaffirmation, a procedure in line with covenant relationships attested to throughout the ancient Near Eastern world. A covenant made between a great king and a vassal people must be renewed by his and their successors with the passing of the generations.

Second, Moses was about to die, so it was essential that he commit to writing the whole collection of tradition and truth that he understood to be the very revelation of God. This was especially urgent in the case of Deuteronomy, for that composition would serve as the corpus of law and practice for the covenant community from that day forward. For Moses to hand on to Joshua the mediatorship of the covenant necessitated the transmission of the covenant text itself. That this is precisely how both Moses and Joshua understood the matter is clear from Moses' injunctions to the Levitical priests concerning the reading of the Law (i.e., Deuteronomy) in years to come (Deut. 31:9–13) and his insistence that they carry it with the ark into the Promised Land (31:24–26). Joshua was confirmed in his mediatorial role by direct revelation and was told explicitly that he personally must be "careful to obey all the law my servant Moses gave you" (Josh. 1:7), an indisputable reference to Moses' writings and most likely to Deuteronomy especially. In other words, covenant leadership must presuppose and be accompanied by covenant transmission; hence there was need for a full and final statement of covenant requirements prior to Moses' death and Joshua's succession.

THEOLOGICAL EMPHASES

The theology of Deuteronomy cannot be separated from its form. As a covenant text it was the vehicle by which the sovereign God expressed His saving and redemptive purposes to His servant nation, His kingdom of priests whom He elected and delivered from bondage in response to the ancient patriarchal promises. This theme—that Israel is the mediator of God's gracious restorative purposes toward fallen humanity—is the great central theological statement of the book. It is that integrative principle that unifies the book and explains its place in the Scriptures.

While addressed specifically to ancient Israel, Deuteronomy also consists of timeless principles and theological truths that are very much appropriate to the modern church and world. The elements of covenant that make up the great bulk of the book are expressions of the very character of God. God prescribes and commands what He does because of who He is. This is particularly true of the Ten Commandments, which, though certainly time-bound in some respects such as the observance of the Sabbath as celebration of the Exodus, nevertheless articulate fundamental notions about the incomparability and uniqueness of God on the one hand and the expectation of universal human response to such a God on the other.

Basic to Deuteronomy is the fact that the God of Israel, who had redeemed them from bondage and chaos, chose to identify with them in an everlasting covenant bond. This very God, in and through His Son Jesus Christ, has graciously condescended to do likewise in a great saving act on behalf of all people. Deuteronomy may indeed no longer be directly applicable to today's church, but the principles on which it was based are as viable today as they were in the days of God's servant Moses.

OUTLINE

I. The Covenant Setting (1:1–5)
II. The Historical Review (1:6–4:40)
    A. The Lord's Past Dealings with Israel (1:6–3:29)
    B. The Exhortation of Moses (4:1–40)
III. The Preparation for the Covenant Text (4:41–49)
    A. The Cities of Refuge (4:41–43)
    B. The Setting and Introduction (4:44–49)
IV. The Principles of the Covenant (chapters 5–11)
    A. The Opening Exhortation (5:1–5)
    B. The Ten Commandments (5:6–21)
    C. The Sinai Revelation and Israel's Response (5:22–23)
    D. The Nature of the Principles (chapter 6)
    E. The Content of the Principles (chapters 7–11)
V. The Specific Stipulations of the Covenant (12:1–26:15)
    A. The Exclusiveness of the Lord and His Worship (12:1–16:17)
    B. Kingdom Officials (16:18–18:22)
    C. Civil Law (19:1–22:4)
    D. Laws of Purity (22:5–23:18)
    E. Laws of Interpersonal Relationships (23:19–25:19)
    F. Laws of Covenant Celebration and Confirmation (26:1–15)

   VI. Exhortation and Narrative Interlude (26:16–19)

  VII. The Curses and Blessings (27:1–29:1)

     A. The Gathering at Shechem (27:1–10)

     B. The Curses That Follow Disobedience of Specific
Stipulations (27:11–26)

     C. The Blessings That Follow Obedience (28:1–14)

     D. The Curses That Follow Disobedience of General
Stipulations (28:15–68)

 VIII. The Historical Review (chapters 29–30)

   IX. Deposit of the Text and Provision for Its Future
Implementation (31:1–29)

    X. The Song of Moses (31:30–32:43)

   XI. Narrative Interlude (32:44–52)

  XII. The Blessing of Moses (chapter 33)

 XIII. Narrative Epilogue (chapter 34)

I. THE COVENANT SETTING (1:1–5)

Moses introduced the great covenant text of Deuteronomy by establishing its geographical and chronological setting. Israel was in the Arabah, the lower Jordan River valley, but since the place names in 1:1 cannot be precisely identified, the exact location of the encampment cannot be determined. A location due east of Jericho is most likely. As for the date, Moses set it as the end of the fortieth year since the Exodus, August/September by the modern calendar. Sihon and Og had been defeated (1:4; see Num. 21:24–26, 33–35), so the way was clear for Moses to address the great assembly in preparation for the conquest of Canaan.

II. THE HISTORICAL REVIEW (1:6–4:40)

In their classic form Late Bronze Age covenant texts always contained a historical prologue, an account of the past relations of the parties entering into covenant relationship. Since Deuteronomy was patterned after such a form, it too contains a historical review. This review traces the account of the forty-year period since the Law was first given at

Sinai (1:6). Being only a survey, it does not provide the detail already covered in Exodus, Leviticus, and Numbers. Rather, it recites the major episodes and turning points in order to lay the foundation for what the Lord intended to reveal about His expectations for Israel in the Promised Land.

A. The Lord's Past Dealings with Israel (1:6–3:29)

Moses began his account of Israel's recent history by stating the Lord's command for them to leave Sinai (here Horeb and throughout Deuteronomy) and to head for the land of the promise, the place God had sworn to give to their patriarchal ancestors (1:6–9). They had become so numerous and contentious by then that Moses had found himself unable to lead them by himself, and so he had chosen subordinates to share the load of governance with him (1:9–18; see Exod. 18:13–26).

The next important stopping place had been Kadesh Barnea, from which Moses had sent out agents to inspect the land of Canaan in order to assess its defensibility (Deut. 1:19–25; see Num. 13:1–20). The majority of the twelve spies—all but Caleb and Joshua (Deut. 1:36, 38)—had demoralized the people by reporting that conquering Canaan would be an utter impossibility because the Canaanite cities were so well defended. Despite Moses' assurances that the battle was the Lord's, the people concluded that God hated (that is, rejected) them and thus had brought them into the desert to die (1:26–33).

The result of their rebellion was tragic indeed. That whole generation of adults would die in the desert, kept from entering Canaan and enjoying its blessings. Only Caleb, Joshua, and the young among them would participate in those privileges (1:34–40). Determined nevertheless to thwart the judgment of the Lord, the people headed north from Kadesh Barnea to penetrate Canaan on their own. This proved to be a fatal mistake, for the Amorites defeated them and forced them into inglorious retreat (1:41–46; see Num. 14:39–45).

After thirty-eight years (Deut. 2:14) they had resumed the journey again, this time heading south toward the Red Sea (that is, the Gulf of Aqaba or Eilat; Num. 21:4). The intention was to march north on the

King's Highway through Edom (the kingdom of Esau's descendants; Deut. 2:4), the most direct route to the plains of Moab. The Lord commanded them to avoid Edom, for He had given that area to the Edomites as their own inheritance (2:1–8; Num. 20:14–21). Edom refused to give Israel permission to pass through her territory.

The only route left was the desert highway leading from the Red Sea north to Moab, to the east of Edom. Again, Israel was instructed to respect the territory of Moab because of ancient kinship ties as well as God's sovereign allocation of the land to them (Deut. 2:8–15). The same disposition of inheritance was true of Ammon as well, so Israel had been told to refrain from infringing on their land holdings, which lay north and east of Moab (2:16–25).

The Amorites, however, were fair game. Moses had done them the courtesy of asking permission to traverse their territory north of the Arnon River (Num. 21:13), but Sihon their king had refused to grant it, a mistake that cost him his very kingdom (Deut. 2:26–37; see also Num. 21:21–32). Because the Amorites were among the peoples to be subjected to the curse of God (Deut. 7:1), He had led Israel's armies into unchallenged triumph (2:30, 33, 36).

All that had stood in the way then were the Bashanites who lived in central and northern Transjordania. Their king, Og, also stubbornly refused to capitulate, and so he met the same fate as Sihon, the loss of all his lands (3:1–11). The people of Bashan were, furthermore, Amorites and thus subject to the ban (Hebrew, *ḥērem*, 3:6; see 2:33). All the Transjordan area was now open to Israel, from the Arnon River in the south to Mount Hermon in the north (3:8).

Reuben, Gad, and half the tribe of Manasseh had then sought and obtained permission to settle in Transjordania on the condition that they first help their fellow tribes conquer the Canaanites on the other side of the river (3:18–20; see Num. 32:1–32). This done, the land was divided, with Reuben and Gad taking the southern areas and Manasseh the north (Deut. 3:12–17). Moses then encouraged the other tribes not to fear, for just as the Lord had defeated the Amorites so He would do to the Canaanites (3:21–22). The prospects of that glorious land to the west so moved Moses that he asked once more to be allowed to go there with his people. His impatience in the matter of the smiting of the rock made this impossible, however, so Moses had to be content with viewing the land from afar (3:23–29; see 1:37; Num. 20:10–13).

B. The Exhortation of Moses (4:1–40)

God's faithfulness to Israel in the past gave Moses a basis on which he could assure Israel of God's ongoing commitment to them and at the same time appeal to them to respond to Him in obedience. The Lord had given them a covenant law at Sinai, and He was about to reveal another, this one a greatly enlarged version appropriate to life in Canaan. To keep its terms would bring life (4:1), but to violate them would invite the same kind of divine displeasure they had experienced at Baal Peor (4:2–4; see Num. 25:1–9). Moreover, observance of the covenant terms (that is, decrees, laws, regulations) would cause other nations to marvel at Israel's wisdom and thus to stand in awe of Israel's God (Deut. 4:6–8).

To press the matter home, Moses recounted the scene at Mount Horeb (another name for Mount Sinai) where God had revealed Himself in theophanic glory by an awesome display of fire and darkness (4:9–11). The occasion was the revelation of the covenant, specifically the Ten Commandments, which the Lord commanded Moses to teach the people (4:12–14). This raised the question as to the nature of God. The people had seen no form (4:12, 15), so therefore they must refrain from representing Him by an image or idol (4:16–18). Even the stars and planets could not capture His essence and so must not become objects of worship (4:19). God's claims to exclusive worship by His people followed from His redemptive activity on their behalf. He had delivered them from the fiery crucible of Egypt, but if they became apostate rebels He would devour them in fiery wrath (4:20, 23–24).

This would be true of future generations as well. If Israel should later embrace idolatry, God would scatter them far and wide (4:25–28). However, His irrevocable covenant pledges to them would cause them to repent, and in response to that repentance the Lord would bring them back again to the land (4:29–31; see also Lev. 26:40–45; Deut. 30:1–10).

He would do this because only He is God and because Israel was His chosen people. In all the history of the world, Israel alone had witnessed the kind of self-revelation and redemption that the Lord had displayed (4:32–34). This was done precisely to assert His uniqueness (4:35; see also Exod. 8:10; Isa. 40:18, 25; 46:5, 9) and His elective grace (Deut. 4:36–38). Surely this was sufficient reason for Israel to be loyally obedient to all the terms of the covenant about to be disclosed (4:39–40).

III. THE PREPARATION FOR THE COVENANT TEXT (4:41–49)

A. The Cities of Refuge (4:41–43)

In Numbers 35 Moses had made provision for places of sanctuary for persons accused of homicide (Num. 35:9–34; see also Deut. 19:1–13). Three of these cities of refuge were to be in Canaan and the other three— Bezer, Ramoth, and Golan—in the Transjordan.

B. The Setting and Introduction (4:44–49)

By way of secondary introduction to the covenant (see 1:1–5), Moses spoke of it as a "law" consisting of "stipulations, decrees, and laws." That is, "law" is a way of describing the covenant text as a whole, and the other terms, which occur repeatedly throughout the book, refer to the stipulations of the covenant. Moses' repetition of the setting of his address (4:46–49) is typical of Semitic prose, which clarifies and emphasizes ideas by repeating them.

IV. THE PRINCIPLES OF THE COVENANT (CHAPTERS 5—11)

The Deuteronomic covenant has two main divisions—the general stipulations and the specific stipulations. The former are principles, whereas the latter reflect case law, that is, they deal with particular instances and situations. The principles flow out of and are elucidations of the first two commandments, and the specific stipulations amplify the intent and application of the remaining eight.

A. The Opening Exhortation (5:1–5)

This new section begins in typically Mosaic fashion with brief allusions to the past. Israel is enjoined to give heed to the forthcoming terms of the renewed covenant just as they had to the Law revealed originally at Horeb. Moses had been the Lord's mediator then and would be the same now to the new generation at Moab.

B. The Ten Commandments (5:6–21)

The form and contents of the Decalogue in Exodus 20:1–17, have already received attention, so the present discussion deals only with differences between the two versions. Only two are significant at all, the lesser being in the tenth commandment. The Exodus rendition lists the neighbor's house first and then the wife and makes no reference to his field (Exod. 20:17). Deuteronomy lists the wife first and then the neighbor's house and field (Deut. 5:21).

A greater difference exists with reference to the fourth commandment—observance of the Sabbath day—but only in the "motive clause," that is, the statement as to why it should be kept. Exodus 20:11 draws attention to God's rest on the seventh day of creation as the rationale for Sabbath rest, whereas Deuteronomy 5:15 links the Sabbath to the Exodus liberation. Israel had been enslaved in Egypt and then set free from oppressive labor. So it was appropriate that the Israelites should celebrate that fact by granting relief to their slaves, animals, and even themselves by resting on the Sabbath.

C. The Sinai Revelation and Israel's Response (5:22–33)

At this point Moses harked back to the scene of the first revelation of the commandments at Horeb. Accompanied by fearful displays of His glory (5:22, 24; see 4:33, 36), God had written the commandments on duplicate stone tablets which He handed over to Moses. Moses here reminded the people of the terror they had experienced (5:24–26) and how they had implored him to serve as a mediator between themselves and such an awesome God (5:27). Through him the Lord had expressed the wish that the reverence with which the people regarded Him at that moment might be true always. Then He could bless them with long life and well-being (5:28–33).

Special events in God's redemptive program are marked and remembered on special days. The Sabbath celebrated two such events in Old Testament times—Creation and the Exodus. The former called to mind Israel's (and the world's) inception, and the latter spoke of her release from Egyptian bondage. Incorporating but eclipsing both is the glorious resurrection of Jesus Christ, which accomplished a new creation and full redemption. No wonder the apostles set aside a new day—Sunday—as the day of commemoration. Jesus' resurrection is not significant because it took place on a Sunday. To the contrary, Sunday is special because the Lord arose from the dead on the first day of the week.

D. The Nature of the Principles (chapter 6)

The basic principles of the covenant are expressed in the Ten Commandments, the essence of which is the Shema (which means "Hear"): "Hear, O Israel: The LORD our God, the LORD is one. Love the LORD your God with all your heart and with all your soul and with all your strength" (6:4–5). This, with all the rest of the covenant Law, was to be embraced and obeyed by the nation when they settled in the land of promise (6:1–3).

So important was the Shema (see Matt. 22:37; Mark 12:29–30; Luke 10:27) that Moses commanded all parents to teach it and the rest of the book to their children and even to adorn themselves and their very dwellings with portions of God's commands as reminders to be forever obedient to them (Deut. 6:6–9). The tendency in Canaan would be to take all of God's provisions there for granted and thus to forget that He is the Source of all blessing (6:10–12). As for the gods in whom the Canaanites put their trust, these must be repudiated not only because of their powerlessness but also because worship of them would be a breach of the first two commandments (6:13–15).

From a positive point of view, Israel must worship the Lord by keeping His covenant mandates, for in doing this they would find favor with God (6:16–19). In time to come they could explain to their descendants that these stipulations reflected the relationship Israel enjoyed with the Lord as a consequence of His having redeemed them from Egypt and having brought them into the land promised to the patriarchs (6:20–23). Obedience to them would constitute a state of righteousness, that is, a position of unfettered fellowship with God. Only this would guarantee His continuing blessing on the nation in days to come (6:24–25).

E. The Content of the Principles (chapters 7–11)

Dispossession of nonvassals (chapter 7). The only way to ensure that Israel would be able to occupy the land fully and to remove the temptation to idolatry was for her to utterly destroy the inhabitants (7:1–2a). *Ḥāram* (Hebrew for "to destroy") means to give something over to the Lord, often by destroying it. In 7:26 the verb is rendered "set apart for destruction" (see also Num. 21:2–3; Deut. 2:34; 3:6). Failing this, they were not to make any covenants with them, including the covenant of marriage (7:2b–3). Such relationships would inevitably lead to moral and spiritual compromise, even to the extent of idolatry (7:4). Thus all pagan paraphernalia such as altars, pillars, and *asherim* (symbols of the pagan goddess Asherah) must be eradicated (7:5; see also Exod. 23:24; 34:13).

The reason for such drastic action was Israel's uniqueness as the people of the Lord (Deut. 7:6–11). They had been elected by Him to serve a certain purpose (7:6; see Exod. 19:4–6). This sovereign choice was based on no other principle than sheer grace, for Israel had nothing by which to commend herself. Grace brought the people out of Egypt, grace established them in covenant with Him, and grace would provide lavish blessings in return for their obedience.

These blessings would include fertility of man and beast, productivity of field and vineyard, and deliverance from the ailments common to the wicked nations around them (Deut. 7:12–16). If they should wonder how these nations could be overcome, they must recall that God had delivered mighty Egypt into their hands; what He had done in history He could and would do in the future (7:17–24). The battle was His, not theirs. He would lead the charge and guarantee the victory. In other words, this was "holy war," designed to exalt the Lord in the midst of the people in their own land (Exod. 23:20–22, 27; Deut. 20:10–18). When He had won the battle, His people must annihilate the kings of those nations as well as all the objects associated with their despicable religions (7:25–26).

The Lord as the source of blessing (chapter 8). According to Canaanite mythology, all the blessings of nature derived from nature deities whose powers could be unleashed through proper sacrifice and ritual, often of the most perverted kind. In contradiction to this, Israel must understand that the Lord, and only He, was responsible for all good things. He would lead them into the land and there would care for them in every area of life (8:7–10). At the same time they must know that material things alone are not satisfying. They must also learn that "man does not live on bread alone but on every word that comes from the mouth of the Lord" (8:3, NIV; see Matt. 4:4; Luke 4:4).

If Israel forgot this in times of prosperity and took credit for it as a product of their own intelligence and hard work, they could expect the same fate as the pagan nations that failed to recognize that God is the ultimate Cause of everything worthwhile (Deut. 8:20). He had brought them out of Egypt, sustained them in the deserts, and would soon take them into Canaan (8:14–18). The gods of the nations could take no credit, and for Israel to attribute to them what only the Lord could do was the height of arrogant blasphemy.

Blessing as a product of grace (9:1–10:11). Moses now resumed the subject of holy war to impress on Israel once more that any success they would enjoy in conquering Canaan must be attributed to the Lord (9:1). It would not be as a reward for their righteousness either, for grace is not based on human effort or even human perfection. Rather, God would expel the heathen of the land for His own sake—He had sworn to the patriarchs that He would do so (9:4–5; see Gen. 15:18–21; 26:3–4). Moreover, Israel hardly merited any of God's favors in light of recent history. From the time God had brought them into covenant at Sinai they had rebelled, even to the extent of making a golden calf (Deut. 9:6–12). And even after they had left the holy mountain, they continued their pernicious ways (9:22–24).

As a result God threatened to disown His people and to make Moses the founder of another chosen race (9:13–14). Had Moses not interceded in fervent prayer, God's judgment surely would have fallen (9:18–20). But with his prayer Moses also reasoned with the Lord, arguing that His promises to the patriarchs to keep His covenant with them gave the Lord no option but to save their descendants now, no matter what evil they had done (9:25–27). Besides, what would the godless nations say about Israel's God if it appeared that He was unable to take them into the land of Canaan (9:28–29)?

The Lord had responded in a magnificent act of grace. He had instructed Moses to prepare two more stone tablets on which He would inscribe the very words of the Decalogue that had perished when Moses dashed the first tablets to the ground. Moses must also build an ark, a richly decorated wooden chest, in which to place the tablets (10:1, 3, 5; see Exod. 25:10). When the Israelites resumed their journey to Canaan, the Lord set apart the tribe of Levi to carry and attend to the ark, a privilege that would more than compensate for the Levites' lack of a territorial inheritance in the land (Deut. 10:6–11). The Lord Himself would be their inheritance. That is, the opportunity to serve Him would be the richest of rewards (10:9; see also Num. 18:20; Deut. 18:2).

Love of the Lord and love of others (10:12–22). The only proper response to God's faithfulness in the past, Moses said, was for Israel to submit willingly and gladly to the terms of the covenant the Lord was making with them (10:12–13; see 6:4–5). He had chosen them out of all the nations, and as Sovereign over them He had a right to expect them to express undivided loyalty to Him and proper regard for their fellowman. Jesus later spelled out the two greatest commandments in similar terms: " 'Love the Lord your God with all your heart and with all your soul and with all your strength and with all your mind'; and, 'Love your neighbor as yourself' " (Luke 10:27, NIV).

Obedience and disobedience and their rewards (chapter 11). Again appealing to the past performance of the Lord on Israel's behalf (Num.

11:1–7), Moses urged them to comply wholeheartedly with the covenant, for only such obedience would guarantee their blessing in the beautiful, productive land to which they were going (11:8–12). The land would have abundant and timely rains as well as bountiful crops if the people remembered that the Lord is the Source of all good things (11:13–17).

As he had done before (6:7–15), Moses enjoined the people to remember forever these teachings and also to instruct their children in them in every way possible (11:18–21). Compliance would result in conquest and occupation of the land, but disobedience clearly would not (11:22–25). In more formal, legal terms Moses offered the people two options: blessing and curse. The one follows obedience, the other disobedience, particularly the rejection of the Lord in favor of other gods (11:26–28). The ceremony of affirmation by which Israel could swear her fidelity would take place at the mountains of Gerizim and Ebal in Canaan, a place sanctified by God's ancient revelation of covenant to Abraham (11:29–32; see Gen. 12:6–7; Deut. 27:11–14; Josh. 8:30–35).

V. THE SPECIFIC STIPULATIONS OF THE COVENANT (12:1–26:15)

What seem to be collections of miscellaneous case laws and regulations in this section are, on closer investigation, systematic expositions of the Shema and the Ten Commandments. Moses thus turned from the establishment of foundation covenant principles to applications of these principles in everyday life. Viewed from this perspective, a number of the laws transcend Old Testament Israel and take on relevance for today. Covenant stipulations are reflections of the nature and character of God Himself and therefore in their essence are never obsolete (though, of course, the Mosaic Law, as a way of life, was abrogated at the Cross; Rom. 10:4; Gal. 3:24–25).

A. The Exclusiveness of the Lord and His Worship (12:1–16:17)

Since only the Lord is God (5:6–10), only He should be worshiped and only in places designated for that purpose. The pagans worshiped their gods at many shrines and altars, but these would have to be demolished to give way to the worship of the Lord at a single central sanctuary, the place where He would "cause His name to dwell" (literal translation, 12:5). This expression suggests that God is too transcendent to be localized on earth (see 1 Kings 8:27), so His unique presence in the tabernacle would be represented by its being the place associated with His name. He would there hold court, as it were, as the great Sovereign and would receive the sacrifices and other acts of worship of His people (Deut. 12:8–12). All other places would be taboo as centers of national religious assembly (12:13–14).

> Jesus taught the woman at the well that the time would come when neither Mount Gerizim, the Samaritan holy place, nor Jerusalem, the site of the temple, would be exclusive places of worship (John 4:21). In saying this, however, He did not repudiate the Old Testament idea that God invests certain places with His peculiar presence. This notion, in fact, is what underlies the importance of New Testament corporate worship in specially designated places and times (1 Cor. 11:18, 20; Heb. 10:25).

The sanctity of blood (12:15–28). Offerings made to the Lord must be slaughtered in designated sacred places (including the central sanctuary), but slaughter for food could be done anywhere, provided the blood was properly disposed of (12:15–25). It could not be eaten but must be drained from the animal and poured out on the ground (12:16, 23, 25; see Gen. 9:4). The reason is that the blood is a metaphor for life itself, and as such it is too sacred to be consumed as ordinary nourishment (Lev. 17:10–13).

Along with sacrificial animals, all other kinds of offerings must be taken to the places chosen by the Lord for His worship (Deut. 12:26–28). These places would provide a venue not only for encounter with the Holy One but also for fellowship with His people, especially Levites and socially and economically disadvantaged citizens who could share in the produce brought to those places.

The abomination of pagan gods (12:29–32). In stark contrast to the purity of the worship of the Lord was the devotion of the nations to their imaginary gods. And yet the very sensuality of these deities would powerfully affect God's own people. So by all means they must resist these allurements and remain true to the Lord alone.

The evil of false prophets (chapter 13). False gods imply also false prophets, for every religious system has its spokesmen. Moses did not limit these to the Canaanites, however, but noted that false prophets would arise even within Israel. The question was how to recognize them and what to do about them.

First, they could perform extraordinary signs, that is, read portents that would actually come to pass. However, that alone could not qualify them as authentic, for they could use those powers to induce God's people to abandon Him in favor of other gods (13:1–2). But such gifts come ultimately from God Himself, who would allow these counterfeit prophets to employ them as a means of testing the loyalty of His people. They must not succumb to these siren calls but instead must put to death any prophet who proclaimed a message designed to lead Israel astray (13:3–5).

This radical remedy must be applied even if the false spokesman was a member of one's own family (13:6–10). Only such drastic action could stop further efforts at undermining total obedience to the Lord (13:11). False prophetism at distant places in the land must also be judged (13:12–18). In fact, any town in which this was tolerated must come under the Lord's ban, that is, total annihilation (13:15). No town would ever again be built on its ruins. Only this stern measure could turn aside God's wrath and permit His mercy and grace to come to the forefront again (13:16–18).

The distinction between clean and unclean animals (14:1–21). A fundamental theological idea in the Old Testament is that God is absolutely holy and He requires corresponding holiness from those who confess Him as Lord. This idea is expressed here (14:1–2) and finds practical outworking in distinctions drawn by the Lord between clean and unclean animals, that is, those fit for human consumption and those not suitable for humans to eat. The rationale for the separation into these categories may have some connection to physical health (prohibition of shellfish, for example; 14:9–10), but on the whole an animal was clean or unclean because God declared it so. Similarly He also chooses people or nations as objects of His elective grace (Exod. 19:4–6; Deut. 7:6–8; Acts 10:15).

The list here (Deut. 14:3–20) is virtually identical to the one in Leviticus 11:1–23. In addition Deuteronomy 14:21 includes the prohibition against eating the meat of animals that have died a natural death and the rather enigmatic injunction not to boil a young goat in its mother's milk (see Exod. 23:19; 34:26).

Tribute to the Sovereign (14:22–16:17). An understanding of Deuteronomy as a suzerain-vassal treaty text (see under "Unity") provides insight into the relationship between the Lord, who reigns from a central place (14:23; see also 12:5), and His vassal Israel, who must regularly offer Him sacrifices and offerings. Annual tithes of the crops must be submitted to both the Lord and the Levites who serve Him (14:22–27). In fact, the entire tithe of every third year would go to the Levites and all others who lacked independent means of support (14:28–29).

A sign of appreciation for the Lord's redemption and release of His people from Egypt (15:15) would be their willingness to release from debt fellow Israelites who had been forced into economic servitude. Every seventh year was to be a year of release in which all debts must be canceled. On the other hand, if a poor person needed relief, one must willingly provide it with no thought of either putting him in servitude or extracting repayment from him (15:7–11).

Should an Israelite enter into what might be called "debt service," that is, a relationship in which a debtor worked off his loan to his creditor, he must be released from that status after six years and with financial resources sufficient to give him a new start (15:12–15). If he chose to remain in that arrangement, however, he could do so and would indicate his assent to it by having a hole bored through his ear lobe. This would signify that he had relinquished all rights to independence (15:12–18; see also Exod. 2:2–6; Lev. 25:39–43).

Also reminiscent of the Exodus deliverance was the claim the Lord had on the firstborn males of all Israel's flocks and herds (Deut. 15:19–23). He exercised this claim because He had spared Israel's firstborn of man and beast when He destroyed those of Egypt (Exod. 13:2, 11–16). Those ritually suitable for sacrifice must be slain and offered as fellowship offerings (Deut. 15:20–22; see Lev. 7:11–18).

Another major element in the sovereign-vassal relationship was the requirement that all Israelite males appear three times a year at the central sanctuary to celebrate certain annual festivals (Deut. 16:1–17; see Exod. 23:14–17; Lev. 23:4–36; Num. 28:16–29:38). The Passover and Unleavened Bread festivals must take place in the spring, Weeks (or Pentecost) in the summer, and Tabernacles in the fall (16:1–17). These were to be times of national acknowledgment of God's mighty acts in history on their behalf and also of His beneficent care in providing for His people by blessing the labor of their hands.

B. Kingdom Officals (16:18–18:22)

Judges and officials (16:18–17:13). The principle of authority implicit in the fifth commandment ("Honor your father and mother") is broadened in this section to include all who are in positions of authority. But they must recognize their limitations and exercise their offices in strict conformity to fairness and righteousness (16:18–20).

Among the matters the judges must address are those concerning idolatry (16:21–22), improper sacrifice (17:1), and apostasy, the pursuit of other gods (17:2–3). Such cases must be carefully investigated, and if sufficient witnesses bore testimony to one's guilt, the offender must be executed under the direction of the officials in charge (17:4–7). If the case were too complicated for the local court, the case could be appealed to the priests at the central sanctuary, who served as a kind of supreme court (17:8–10). Their verdict, which was final, must be carried out scrupulously. Failure to do so would bring heavy penalty on those charged to execute it (17:11–13).

Kings (17:14–17). The time would come when Israel would demand a king like those of other nations, and when that happened royal protocol must already be in place. The king must be an Israelite chosen by God, and one who had no ambition to accumulate horses, wives, or too much money. Solomon, of course, was one who abused all of these qualifications (1 Kings 10:23–11:3). Kingship as such was not contrary to God's purposes, however. He had promised Abraham and Sarah that they would sire kings (Gen. 17:6, 16), and Jacob prophesied that a ruler would come from Judah (49:10; see also Num. 24:17). Samuel's later protest about

Israel's demand for a king had to do not with kingship per se but with a premature insistence on it (1 Sam. 8:4–9; 13:14).

The legitimacy of kingship is clear from the guidelines outlined here (Deut. 17:18–20). The future king must retain and regularly read a copy of Deuteronomy, obey the covenant requirements, and exhibit unswerving fidelity to its great teachings. This is not a concession to a demand for a king but the regulation of an institution that was integral to God's administration of His earthly kingdom.

Priests and Levites (18:1–8). Sacred affairs in the kingdom fell within the domain of the priests and Levites. They had no tribal allotments (18:1–2), but they would enjoy the inestimable privilege of serving God and being sustained by offerings from God's people. There must be no discrimination between Levites of the central sanctuary and Levites who came there from outlying villages. They must all serve and share alike (18:6–8).

Prophets (18:9–22). The messages of the prophets often included warnings and exhortations addressed to both the population at large and other national leaders. However, prophetism was by no means unique to Israel; in fact, as already seen (13:1–18), it was a major feature of Canaanite culture and of the entire ancient Near Eastern world. Moses here listed the wide variety of forms pagan prophetism took (18:9–14), most of which were either divinatory or incantational in nature. The former performed rituals designed to discover the intentions of the gods, whereas the latter attempted to alter those intentions for good or ill if possible (compare Num. 22:2–6).

In any case such godless practices were abhorrent to the Lord and must be avoided at all cost by His people (Deut. 18:13). In their place He would raise up an order of prophets like Moses, spokesmen for God called and empowered by Him (18:15–19). The Lord would speak to and through them, and anyone who failed to obey their words could expect His severe displeasure. Later revelation made clear that the prophets in view included individuals like Samuel (1 Sam. 3:1–21) and Elijah (1 Kings 17:1–7; Mal. 4:4–6) and especially Jesus Christ, the Prophet par excellence (Acts 3:18–26; 7:37).

As for prophets in general, the acid test of their authenticity would be the fulfillment of their predictions (Deut. 18:20–22). Those who failed in this respect must thereby be branded as false, speaking words out of their own imaginations. There was no reason to fear them.

C. Civil Law (19:1–22:4)

All organized societies require structures within which individual and community behavior can take place. This would be no less true of Israel in its domesticated life in Canaan. The first set of regulations here relates to the sixth commandment, "You shall not murder" (5:17). If someone is murdered, the accused must have a means of preserving himself from family vengeance until his case could gain a fair hearing. This matter had already received extensive treatment (19:1–13; Num. 35:9–34).

Proper legal procedure in cases such as homicide or even the misplacement of boundary markers (Deut. 19:14) included multiple and unimpeachable witnesses (19:15–20; see also 17:6–7; Num. 35:30) and a punishment commensurate with the crime. In legal terms this is known as *lex talionis*, or "eye for [an] eye" (Deut. 19:21; see also Exod. 21:23–25; Lev. 24:19–20).

The Old Testament recognizes the lamentable reality of warfare, including its occasional necessity. Sometimes the only way for Israel to overcome its (and the Lord's) enemies was to engage them in battle in His name. This was certainly God's means for conquering Canaan and expelling its illegitimate occupants from the land.

The covenant stipulation here has to do with homicide but of a kind sanctioned by the Lord as both defensive and divinely ordained offensive military operations. The chapter discusses not only the carrying out of war against distant foes but also "holy war" (see Deut. 7:1–5) against the irredeemable inhabitants of Canaan. In either case, when the war was justified God would be in it, leading His people to battle (20:1–4).

In "ordinary" war, recruits could be excused for a number of reasons (20:5–9). When the army was finally drawn up, it must first offer terms of surrender to a city before attacking it (20:10–11). If the enemy would not capitulate, the city could be captured and all its men put to death (20:12–15). But in holy war everyone and everything must be totally destroyed

(20:16–18). In both kinds of conflict, anything useful like fruit trees should be spared. Besides, such a living thing has committed no evil (20:19–20).

Occasionally a homicide victim would be found in an open field with no clue as to who his assailant was. In such a case the people of the village nearest the corpse must assume culpability to the extent of acting corporately to remove guilt from them (21:1–9). The priests near the scene were to undertake a ritual consisting of the breaking of the neck of a heifer and the washing of hands by the village elders whereby they would disavow any connection of their community with the crime.

This sense of corporate identity, though lacking in the modern western world, is also an important concept in the New Testament church (Eph. 3:6; 4:1—7, 16; Col. 1:18; 3:15).

Still in the context of war and death, Moses spoke of the treatment of female prisoners (Deut. 21:10–14). When taken from distant lands (20:14), they were allowed to become wives to Israelite men but only after having time to go through proper rituals of lament and purification. This led to the possibility of multiple marriage and the allotment of inheritance rights (21:15–17). If a man had two wives, one loved more than the other, he must give the regular double portion of his estate to his eldest son, even if the son was born to the less-loved wife. His feelings toward his wives must have nothing to do with the higher priority of primogeniture.

Moses also addressed the problem of disrespectful and insubordinate children (21:18–21). If parental discipline failed, such children could be brought to the village elders and publicly executed. If the bodies of criminals like these were hanged as a public display, they must not remain in that state overnight for the curse of God visited on the guilty individual would then be applied to the whole community (21:22–23).

This provision gives extra meaning to the crucifixion of Jesus whose body, according to the Law, had to be removed from the cross before sundown (John 19:31).

The final statute has to do with returning lost animals to their owners or helping fallen animals to their feet (Deut. 22:1–4). One may not ignore such situations under the pretense of not seeing them, for that is a form of theft or at least a lack of brotherly love.

D. *Laws of Purity (22:5–23:18)*

Israel's call to be a holy people, set apart from all others, prompted a host of statutes illustrative and supportive of that principle. Thus men and women must not dress in each other's clothing (22:5), mother birds were not to be taken as food (22:6–7), rooftops must have guardrails to prevent someone falling off (22:8), fields must not be sown with mixed seed (22:9) or plowed with a mixed yoke (22:10), and one must not wear garments of mixed fabric (22:11). To remind themselves of these prohibitions, the people must wear tassels on their hems (22:12).

Illicit sexual relations were particularly indicative of a lack of a proper attitude toward the Lord and His holiness. Young women must be virgins at marriage, and if they were shown not to be they must be publicly executed (22:13–21). Both male and female adulterers were also subject to the death penalty (22:22). An engaged woman who had sexual relations in a village with someone other than her fiancé must die along with her partner (22:23–24). However, if the act took place in the countryside, it would be considered rape and only the man must die, for the presumption is that she would have cried out but no one could hear (22:25–27). Sexual intercourse with an unbetrothed virgin required the man to take her as his wife and to pay her father fifty shekels of silver (about four years' wages; 22:28–29). The monetary assessment was compensation for her loss of service to her father.

Purity of body and behavior symbolized purity of heart and motive. So there were sanctions against incest (22:30), emasculation (23:1), illegitimacy of birth (23:2), access to the covenant community and its privileges by Ammonites and Moabites (23:3–7), offspring of Lot's incest with his daughters (Gen. 19:30–38), unlimited access by the Edomites (Deut. 23:7–8), and bodily emissions of soldiers in camp (23:9–14). Grace is seen in the law that prohibited giving an escaped slave back to his master, but condemnation rested on male and female prostitutes and on the income derived from their profession which they had the audacity to offer to the Lord as a votive gift (23:15–18).

E. Laws of Interpersonal Relationships (23:19–25:19)

Application of the Ten Commandments to life continues in this section in a variety of ways. There is prohibition of loans with interest to fellow Israelites (23:19–20), the requirement that vows made to the Lord be paid (23:21–23), and permission to pluck grapes and grains from a neighbor's fields, provided one did so with no harvest implement in hand (23:24–25). Most important are regulations pertaining to divorce (24:1–4). Though divorce is contrary to the creation purposes of God (Gen. 2:24; Matt. 19:3–12), it was practiced by Israel, but such practice was to be strictly regulated. Here the issue is divorce because of "something indecent" (Deut. 24:1; see also 22:13–21) in the woman and the prohibition of her remarriage to her original husband once she had been divorced and taken a second husband.

Statutes here also cover exemption from military service for newly-weds, the need to return pledges on loans that were necessary to livelihood, the death penalty for kidnapping, proper ritual in cases of leprosy, timely payment of wages, individual responsibility for sin, fair and merciful application of justice, and provision for the poor by leaving gleanings in the vineyards, orchards, and fields (24:15–22).

Various laws, customs, and penalties were to apply to Israel's life in the Promised Land. But in their enactment there must be mercy and grace. For example, in punishment by flogging the culprit could receive a maximum of forty blows (25:1–3). Even animals must be recipients of kindness (25:4). When a man died without an heir, his brother was expected to father a son by his widow (the so-called levirate law; see Gen. 38:8; Ruth 4:1–6; Mark 12:18–27) in order to preserve the dead brother's name into the future (Deut. 25:5–10). The brother who refused to do this would be publicly disgraced (25:9–10). A woman who attempted to emasculate a man must lose her hand (25:11–12), weights and measurements must be accurate (25:13–16), and Amalek, Israel's prototypical enemy, must someday be punished for having attacked Israel in the desert (25:17–19; see Exod. 17:8–16).

F. Laws of Covenant Celebration and Confirmation (26:1–15)

When Israel was securely settled in Canaan, the people must, as part of the Festival of Weeks (26:2; see 16:9–12), perform the ritual of presenting a firstfruits offering and confessing the great acts of God's salvation and sustenance from the dawn of their existence (26:1–11). Then as part of their responsibility to the Levites, they must turn over to them the tithe of their produce at the end of every third year (26:12–15). Having sworn before God that they had held nothing back, they could rest in the assurance of His continued blessing.

VI. EXHORTATION AND NARRATIVE INTERLUDE (26:16–19)

Moses concluded the lengthy exposition of general and specific stipulations of the covenant by reiterating his injunction to obey them and by reminding the people that they are God's special people.

VII. THE CURSES AND BLESSINGS (27:1–29:1)

Covenants have no value if there is no inducement to abide by their conditions. Negatively, these inducements would be in the form of punishment for violation; positively, they would consist of reward. In covenant terms these are the curses and blessings respectively. Deuteronomy, as a covenant text, provides lengthy clauses outlining the curses and the blessings.

A. The Gathering at Shechem (27:1–10)

The setting for the ceremony of curses and blessings was to be at the ancient and sacred place where the Lord first appeared to Abraham, namely, Shechem (Gen. 12:6–7; see also 35:4; Deut. 11:26–30; 27:12–13; Josh. 8:30–35; 24:1–3). After they had occupied the land, the people must erect a monument there on whose plastered surface they must inscribe the covenant text, and then they were to declare their affiliation with and loyalty to the Lord God.

B. The Curses That Follow Disobedience of Specific Stipulations (27:11–26)

In preparation for the recital of curses and blessings, the people would be divided into two groups, with six tribes standing on Mount Gerizim and six on Mount Ebal. The ark and its Levitical attendants were to remain in the valley between them (Josh. 8:33). The Levites would then read off the curses (twelve in all) to which the people would assent by crying "Amen." The violations of covenant listed here are representative, not exhaustive.

C. The Blessings That Follow Obedience (28:1–14)

Adherence to the covenant terms would bring God's promotion, prosperity, and victory over enemies. Israel would become the head of nations and not the tail.

D. The Curses That Follow Disobedience of General Stipulations (28:15–68)

In this section Moses did not list particular instances of covenant disobedience. Instead he listed the judgments that could be expected when the covenant as a whole was ignored (28:15). The various curses (28:16–19) included agricultural disaster (28:20–24), invasion by enemy forces and deportation (28:25–26) that will create all kinds of international chaos (28:27–35), diminishment of reputation among the nations (28:36–46), famine leading even to cannibalism (28:47–57), and eventually a kind of reverse exodus in which Israel would be delivered to the nations and not from them (28:58–68).

VIII. THE HISTORICAL REVIEW (CHAPTERS 29–30)

After a brief narrative interlude (29:1), Moses, in typical fashion, reviewed the past (29:2–9), enjoined present obedience (29:10–13), and pointed to the future with all its possible (indeed, likely) prospects for disobedience and consequent judgment (29:14–21). That judgment would be so awesome that it would cause the nations to be astonished at its severity. The reason for it, they would learn, was Israel's unfaithfulness to the Lord and His covenant expectations (29:22–29).

But the God of wrath is also the God of grace, who would manifest that attribute by leading His people to repentance (30:1–2), restoring them to their land after having scattered them (30:3–6), cursing their enemies with the curses they had experienced (30:7), and pouring out on Israel the blessings they had previously enjoyed (30:8–10).

The power necessary to obedience was readily available to Israel; in fact it was in their minds and hearts (30:11–14; see Rom. 10:6–8). They could and must choose what they would do (Deut. 30:15). They could obey and receive blessing (30:16) or they could disobey and experience wrath (30:17–19a). Moses' appeal, of course, was for his people to choose the better thing (30:19b–20).

IX. DEPOSIT OF THE TEXT AND PROVISION FOR ITS FUTURE IMPLEMENTATION (31:1–29)

When two parties entered into a treaty arrangement in the ancient Near East, copies of the treaty were filed for future reference. Having come to the end of his life, Moses was concerned that this be done with Deuteronomy, the covenant document. He urged Joshua and Israel to be courageous in view of the imminent conquest (31:1–8) and also to place a copy of the Law in the ark of the covenant so that it could be easily accessible for public reading every seven years (31:9–13). This was in order to remind Israel to keep its terms and thus avoid spiritual decline.

The Lord knew that this would not avail, and in fact He shared His sentiments with Moses, instructing him to compose a song which, when sung by Israel in the future, would serve as an indictment of their wicked behavior (31:14–21). Moses did so and taught the people to sing it then and there (31:22). Offering Joshua a word of personal encouragement, Moses oversaw the deposit of the text into the ark in a solemn ceremony in which he invoked divine wrath against future generations that would depart from its teachings (31:23–29).

X. THE SONG OF MOSES (31:30–32:43)

The text of the song Moses had been commanded to compose (31:19) opens with an appeal to the heavens and earth to bear witness to the people's pledge to remain true to the Lord (32:1). It then celebrates the person and the power of the Lord (32:2–4), who, despite Israel's wickedness (32:5), had led them from Egyptian bondage to the blessings of the present moment (32:6–14). Speaking both historically and prophetically, Moses recited Israel's idolatry and spoke of a time when God would defeat and scatter them among the nations (32:15–26a).

This judgment would have been permanent were it not for God's faithfulness to His own promises (32:26b–27). Israel would continue in rebellion and would be threatened with obliteration (32:28–35), but God at last would reveal Himself as a powerful Deliverer, who would heal His own people and destroy their enemies (32:36–43). Sin would abound, it is true, but grace would much more abound (Rom. 5:20).

XI. NARRATIVE INTERLUDE (32:44–52)

After Moses taught the song, he again told the people to take it to heart for it would be to them a matter of life and death. The Lord then told Moses to ascend Mount Nebo and prepare to die there. Because of his sin at Meribah he would not cross the Jordan River into Canaan, but at least he could view it from a distance (Num. 27:12–14).

XII. THE BLESSING OF MOSES (CHAPTER 33)

Just as Jacob had blessed his sons on his deathbed (Gen. 49:1–27), so now Moses blessed their tribal descendants as his final public act. Following a brief note of praise in which he extolled the Lord and His covenant sovereignty (Deut. 33:2–5), Moses addressed each tribe in turn (33:6–25). He concluded with a general blessing for all Israel, one whose very possibility lay in the nature of God as Creator and Lord and in His saving work in bringing Israel to Himself (33:26–29).

XIII. NARRATIVE EPILOGUE (CHAPTER 34)

As God had commanded (32:49), Moses climbed to the top of Mount Nebo where he could view the entire land of promise from Dan in the north to the Negev and Dead Sea in the south (34:1–3). This was the territory sworn to the patriarchs as an everlasting possession (34:4; see Gen. 12:7; 26:3; 28:13). For a final time God told Moses he could see the land but could not enter it (Deut. 34:4).

Moses' epitaph follows (34:5–12). Ancient Jewish tradition suggests that Joshua penned these words as an addendum to Deuteronomy, a view that has much to commend it. Though Moses was 120 years old, his strength and vitality were unabated. His death, then, could be considered premature, something necessitated by the need for Israel to undertake the conquest at once. Joshua succeeded his master, but of him as well as others who followed it was said, "No prophet has risen in Israel like Moses, whom the LORD knew face to face" (34:10). This assessment remained true until One came who was *the* Prophet without compare, Jesus Christ the Lord (see 18:15–18).

JOSHUA
Conquest: The Ideal versus the Real

AUTHOR

*A*ncient Jewish tradition attributes the Book of Joshua as well as the last eight verses of Deuteronomy to Joshua himself (Babylonian Talmud, *Baba Bathra* 14b). While this is possible, nothing in the book explicitly asserts this to be the case, and in fact there are a few references to events long after Joshua's time that would presuppose a later writing and/or later additions (for example, Josh. 4:9, 14; 7:26; 8:28–29; 9:27; 10:27; 14:14). The clearest evidence has to do with Joshua's death (24:29) and the statement that Israel was faithful to the Lord through all the years of Joshua's life and throughout the days of the elders of Israel who outlived him (24:31). Since some of these elders could have been mere children at the time of the Conquest (Num. 14:29; 32:11), the oldest of them would likely have lived eighty or ninety years beyond the Conquest, that is, as late as 1320 B.C. Final touches on the book could certainly be that late. On the other hand, the account states that the Jebusites lived in Jerusalem and could not be expelled by Israel (Josh. 15:63). David eventually did so (2 Sam. 5:6–10), and thus the Book of Joshua in its present form must precede David's conquest of Jerusalem in 1000 B.C. Perhaps the best position on the matter is to presume that much of the book comes from Joshua's own memoirs and personal records but that an unknown compiler or compilers composed the book in its extant form.

159

UNITY

Scholars who view Joshua as part of the "Hexateuch" (that is, the Pentateuch plus Joshua) suppose that it, like the Pentateuch, shows evidence of originally independent sources (J E D P, see p. 2) having been edited into the canonical book. S. R. Driver, for example, suggests that Joshua 1–12 is a continuation of the J E source, and that the topographical descriptions in chapters 13–24 are P material. The whole book, however, was assembled and elaborated, he says, by an editor who wanted to emphasize how careful Joshua was to fulfill Moses' covenant mandates.

Increasing skepticism about the validity of the documentary hypothesis leaves this analysis with little to commend it. Still others say the book records actual events that were greatly amplified and embellished in the exilic or postexilic period. However, not a shred of objective evidence supports this view as well. An unbiased reading of the book gives the impression of a unity of composition and an early date, the few editorial insertions referred to above being the exceptions.

DATE

Inasmuch as the question of authorship cannot be resolved, the exact date of the writing of the Book of Joshua cannot be determined. But clearly it is later than Joshua's own lifetime and earlier than David's time. On the whole, a date of around 1300 B.C. seems reasonable.

ADDRESSEES AND PURPOSE

Nothing in the book indicates a specific setting or audience for its message. It certainly was intended for the benefit of the Israelites who conquered Canaan and/or those who lived after the Conquest. The purpose was to provide a historical narrative of God's faithfulness to His covenant promises in taking the people into the land of Canaan and enabling them to stake out their claim there. As long as they were obedient, things went well, but when they took matters into their own hands, they suffered God's severe displeasure. The book thus provides a paradigm, a template as it were, of the blessings attendant to covenant loyalty and the curses that follow anything less. A secondary purpose was to account for tribal allocations, the identity and location of Levitical cities, and the like. If questions would arise later about such matters, the answers could be found in this ancient record.

THEOLOGICAL EMPHASES

The underlying theological theme of Joshua is that the Lord is a covenant-keeping God who, having made promises to the ancestors of Israel, will see them to perfect fulfillment (Josh. 1:2–6; see Gen. 15:18–21). The inheritance of the land is particularly in view, for the nation's destiny as a priestly mediator would be impossible without the geographical dimension (Exod. 19:4–6; 23:20–33; Deut. 8:1–10). Broader than the promise is the whole concept of covenant, the instrument by which God had brought Israel into a saving and serving relationship with Himself. Land inheritance is just a part of the blessings of the covenant (Gen. 15:1–11; 17:1–14; 26:2–4).

The Book of Deuteronomy is essentially a covenant text, and in that treatise the Lord had commanded Joshua through Moses to reaffirm the covenant on Israel's behalf once they had entered the Promised Land (Deut. 27:1–8). This is one of the first things Joshua did after the central campaign was over and he had access to Shechem, the place designated for covenant renewal (Josh. 8:30–35). Then at the end of his life and following the conquest, Joshua gathered Israel there once more for covenant celebration (24:1–28). Covenant renewal marked the initiation and completion of the conquest of the Promised Land.

Also the Book of Joshua centers on the sovereignty of God as the overarching truth that explains all the rest. God was the One who would grant Israel victory over her enemies (1:7–9), who led them through the raging Jordan (3:7–17), and who enabled them to see the fulfillment of all His promises with their own eyes (21:45; 23:14; 24:13). This proved that though they were up against humanly impossible odds (Deut. 7:1; 9:1–3), God was with His people as their Deliverer. The message is clear: He is God also of all the nations of the earth, and whether they recognize this or not they must and will succumb to His sovereignty (see Josh. 2:9-14; 9:9–10, 24).

OUTLINE

I. The Crossing of the Jordan (chapters 1–5)
   A. The Command to Joshua (1:1–9)
   B. The Command to the People (1:10–15)
   C. The Response of the People (1:16–18)
   D. The Sending of the Spies (chapter 2)
   E. The Miracle of the Crossing (chapters 3–4)
   F. Covenant Renewal (chapter 5)
II. The Central Campaign (chapters 6–9)
   A. The Defeat of Jericho (chapter 6)
   B. The Defeat at Ai (chapters 7–8)
   C. The Alliance with Gibeon (chapter 9)
III. The Southern Campaign (chapter 10)
IV. The Northern Campaign (chapter 11)
V. Subsequent Attempts at Settlement (chapters 12–22)
   A. A Summary of the Conquests (chapter 12)
   B. Eastern and Western Allotments (chapters 13–19)
   C. The Cities of Refuge (chapter 20)
   D. The Levitical Cities (chapter 21)
   E. The Departure of the Eastern Tribes (chapter 22)
VI. Joshua's Farewell Address (chapters 23–24)
   A. Exhortations and Warnings (chapter 23)
   B. The Assembly at Shechem (24:1–28)
   C. Joshua's Death and the Conclusion of the Book (24:29–33)

I. THE CROSSING OF THE JORDAN (CHAPTERS 1–5)

Before the conquest of Canaan could begin, the river that blocked access to it from the east also had to be conquered. It was in the spring, at flood stage, that the effort would be made, as though to suggest that the God who could overcome natural barriers could also defeat human opposition. The crossing of the Jordan, then, was not just another stage in the advance of Israel toward the land of promise. It was, rather, an opportunity for the Lord to demonstrate His sovereign grace and power in conquest just as He had done at the Exodus.

A. *The Command to Joshua (1:1–9)*

Almost without interruption the narrative of Joshua picks up from the end of Deuteronomy. Moses had died (Deut. 34:5–8) and the mantle of leadership had fallen on Joshua (Josh. 1:9; see also Num. 27:18–20, 23; Deut. 31:7–8, 14, 23). It was his task now to take the nation across the river, something that would be easily done, for the Lord would be with him as He had been with Moses (Josh. 1:5). The crossing would result in the inheritance of the land that God had promised to the patriarchs as a part of His covenant program (1:6; Gen. 15:18–21).

However, there were conditions to be met if all these things were to come to pass as the Lord intended. Joshua himself must learn to trust God with all his heart, and he must realize that success in the work of the Lord comes only in obedience to His word. When this is the case, there is every reason to expect success (Josh. 1:6–9).

B. *The Command to the People (1:10–15)*

The moment of truth had come. Within three days the masses would form up and begin the journey west across the river. Meanwhile the Reubenites, Gadites, and East Manassehites must remember that their soldiers, though eventually permitted to live in the Transjordan, must help their brother tribes in the conquest of Canaan (see also Num. 32:20–27; Deut. 3:18–20). The rest of the people could, of course, settle into the territories already allocated to them (Num. 32:33–42).

C. *The Response of the People (1:16–18)*

Joshua's smooth transition to leadership is affirmed by the people's pledge to follow him just as they had followed Moses. In fact, anyone who refused to recognize Joshua's role and rebelled against him must die (1:18)! There was but one small caveat—it must be apparent that the Lord was with Joshua as he had been with Moses (1:17). This is not an unreasonable stipulation, for no man or woman has a right to demand a following in the spiritual realm if there is no evidence of the presence of God in that person's life.

D. The Sending of the Spies (chapter 2)

Joshua had once been sent on a mission to spy out the land of Canaan (Num. 13:8), and now he sent two others to assess its strength, particularly in and about Jericho. This city lay beside the major route into central Canaan, and as long as it stood its defenders would be a threat to Israel. Their immediate destination—the house of a harlot—seems strange at first, but two reasons may explain their selection. First, the house was part of the construction of the wall itself and therefore was more accessible and could more easily be a point of escape. Second, strange men at a harlot's place of business would hardly raise suspicion.

Their ruse was discovered, however, and so Rahab had to hide the men on her roof lest they be apprehended (Josh. 2:2–7). When it was safe, she informed them that the whole land was terrified of them and their God because of their miraculous deliverance from Egypt and their recent victories over the Amorites of Transjordania. Surely only the true God could do such things, she concluded (2:8–11). She then exacted from the spies a promise that Israel would spare her and her relatives in return for her having given them a hiding place (2:8–14).

She then lowered them over the wall with a rope, and the spies told her to mark her section of the wall with the same red rope so that she could be saved from destruction. Only if her whole family gathered there could they be saved, but if a word of their plans should be disclosed they would all perish (2:15–21). After a three-day wait in the mountains until the way was clear, the spies returned to Joshua with the same message he and Caleb had once delivered to Moses: God would give them glorious success (2:22–24; see also Num. 13:30).

> *The message that the God of Israel is also the God of grace who wishes all people to be saved finds exquisite demonstration in the story of the Canaanite Rahab. Despised, a foreigner, a prostitute, a liar, a traitor—all these terms describe her. But by her faith in the only true God she was spared death in the Conquest and even became grafted into the ancestral lineage of Jesus the Messiah Himself (Matt. 1:5).*

E. The Miracle of the Crossing (chapters 3–4)

The crossing of the Jordan, like the passing through the Red Sea, would be an act of God in which He displayed His conquering power as divine Warrior (Exod. 14:13–14, 25, 30–31; 15:3). The symbol of His presence was the ark of the covenant, which served metaphorically as His throne (25:10–22; Deut. 20:1–4; 1 Sam. 4:1–11). He would lead the way in the person of the priests and Levites bearing the ark (Josh. 3:1–6).

The supernatural character of the crossing would be apparent by the otherwise unexplainable damming up of the river at the moment the priests' feet touched the water (3:13). Some scholars account for the stoppage by a landslide farther up the Jordan River where it passes through a narrow chasm. However, this hardly reduces the element of miracle, for the timing in this case was divinely ordained. The point is that once the ark neared the raging torrent, the river would become docile, testifying thereby to the sovereignty of the God of Israel over all creation (3:7, 10).

To underscore that the work was all of God, He had commanded Israel to undertake the crossing at the worst possible time. It was harvesttime, that is, springtime just following the latter rains (3:15). The Jordan, usually a narrow muddy creek, overflowed its banks at that season, sometimes sweeping away everything that failed to reach higher ground. Against such odds the priests, in a mighty act of faith, marched into the maelstrom, which immediately receded, leaving a dry river bottom. There the priests stood until the whole throng of Israel had passed over (3:14–17).

Meanwhile twelve men had been chosen to take twelve stones from the riverbed, one for each tribe (4:2). These were to be set up as a memorial cairn on the west bank of the Jordan to testify to yet unborn generations of the grace and power of God who had brought them into the land (4:4–7). The place selected for the erection of the memorial was Gilgal ("rolling"; 5:9), somewhere between the Jordan and Jericho (perhaps near present-day Khirbet el-Metjir).

The Lord had led the way through the river, but He in the person of the priests remained there until every last Israelite had passed over (4:11). One cannot help admire the faith of the priests, who must have stood for many hours in the place that should have been under many feet of water and perhaps would be again at any moment. To mark that place of God's special intervention Joshua said that a heap of stones should also be erected there—right in the midst of the river—as a perpetual memorial. The narrator wrote that the stones "are there to this day" (4:9), meaning, of course, until the time that he himself saw them there years later. The whole process brought glory to God, and it also affirmed Joshua's leadership, who from then on was regarded as almost a second Moses (4:14).

At last the priests were allowed to ascend the west bank of the Jordan, and as soon as they did the river returned to full flood stage (4:18). At the first formal assembly of Israel in the land of promise the people gathered around the memorial stones at Gilgal where Joshua pointed out their significance. From then on those stones would testify to the fact that the God of the Exodus was the God of the Conquest of the river and of the nations that occupied the land of promise. The stones would also remind people everywhere that Israel's God is indeed sovereign over all (4:19–24).

F. Covenant Renewal (chapter 5)

Once word of the crossing had spread, the people of Canaan lost all heart to resist the Israelites (5:1; compare 2:10–11). But before the pagan nations had real cause for alarm, the men of Israel had to certify their covenant loyalty to the Lord through the rite of circumcision (5:2). Until Israel was covenantally compliant, they had no right to expect God's blessing. Somehow the ceremony had been ignored all the years in the desert (5:7), and for this reproach to be lifted it must be done then.

Passover was another sign of God's covenant favor. The season was on them to celebrate this festival that marked their redemption from Egyptian bondage, so they did so. With great relief the people saw the disappearance of the manna and its replacement by the crops of the land (5:10–12). The Lord in a sense brought His work of salvation full circle. He had appeared to Moses in a burning bush to announce that work, and now He appeared to Joshua as Commander of heaven's angelic host to proclaim its completion (5:13–14). Like Moses, Joshua was aware that he stood on holy ground (5:15).

II. THE CENTRAL CAMPAIGN (CHAPTERS 6–9)

Joshua's military strategy has long been admired as a model of intelligence and efficiency. Simply put, it was one of divide and conquer. Canaan consisted of two major power blocs, the Amorites to the south and Canaanites to the north. If Joshua could drive a wedge between them, he could prevent their forming an alliance against him and thus could dispose of them each in turn. But this wedge could be effected only by first penetrating into Canaan's central highlands, a task that required bringing Jericho and other strongholds under Israelite control.

A. The Defeat of Jericho (chapter 6)

In perhaps the strangest plan of attack ever devised, the Lord revealed to Joshua that because the battle was His, only His methods could bring success. Moreover, Jericho, perhaps as an example to all other Canaanite cities, would fall under the Lord's judgment, His *ḥērem*, which would require total annihilation of human and animal life as well as destruction of all material things except those devoted to the Lord for His use (6:17–19, 24). (See comments on the related verb *ḥāram* on pages 140–41).

The nature of the campaign as a holy war (7:1–5; 20:1–20) explains the role of the priests and the ark. The priests must lead the armies around the city once a day for six days and seven times on the seventh. Then they would blow trumpets, the people would shout, and the walls would collapse (6:1–7). By faith they pursued this bizarre attack, and at the end the promised results took place. The walls fell down, the city was looted, and all but Rahab and her family fell victim to the sword (6:17, 22–25; see 2:13–14).

So symbolic was Jericho of the irremedial presence of apostasy and moral degeneracy among the Canaanites that a curse was put on anyone who ever tried to rebuild the city (6:26). It would cost the lives of the very children of those who thought they could circumvent this divine decree (see 1 Kings 16:29–34). Though all the inhabitants of Canaan were subject to the penalties of *ḥērem* to some degree, only Jericho, Ai, and Hazar were burned to the ground (Josh. 8:28; 11:11–13). The other cities were left standing to provide Israel with ready-made housing (Deut. 6:10–11).

B. The Defeat of Ai (chapters 7–8)

Joshua had no sooner uttered the curse about Jericho and its properties than a man named Achan took some of the plunder that belonged to the Lord (6:19) and kept it for himself (7:1). This set in motion a series of disasters that affected not only him but also the whole community.

The next phase of Israel's strategy revolved around a military encampment named Ai ("ruin"), the modern location of which is still unknown. It lay east of Bethel, with a deep valley lying between them (8:9). Joshua thought (perhaps somewhat overconfidently) that this comparatively small place could be taken by two or three thousand men, a reasonable estimate except for one mitigating circumstance—there was sin in Israel's camp (7:11). The result was that Joshua's force was routed and several lives were lost (7:1–5). Shaken by this unexpected reversal, Joshua fell on his face before God in shame and penitence (7:6–9). The Lord then told him to arise and to set in motion a process that would reveal who in Israel had broken the terms of the ḥērem, thereby invoking divine judgment (7:10–15).

Probably by means of the Urim and Thummim (see Num. 27:21), Joshua narrowed the investigation down to the tribe of Judah, the clan of Zeraḥ, the extended family of Zabdi, and the single individual Achan (Josh. 7:16–18). Knowing that self-defense was impossible, Achan confessed to his theft and produced those items that should have been handed over to the Lord in the first place (7:19–23). But the unpardonable had been done and Achan and his immediate family—who must have been involved in or at least aware of Achan's wrongdoing—were themselves placed under ḥērem and destroyed (7:24–26).

With this matter behind them, the Lord now authorized Joshua and his troops to attack Ai once more. Like Jericho it was to be razed and all its citizens and properties delivered over to divine wrath (8:1–2). Employing sound tactics of ambush and inducement, Joshua achieved a stunning victory. Drawing Ai's troops from their protective walls, he set on them, leaving not a single survivor. Meanwhile, other Israelites entered the unguarded city, slew its remaining inhabitants, and burned it to the ground (8:3–23). So thorough was its devastation that it became known from that time onward merely as "the ruin" (Hebrew, ʿay).

With the removal of Ai, Israel had free access to the central hill country. Joshua therefore celebrated God's faithfulness in giving the nation victory by convening them in assembly at Shechem, some twenty miles north of Ai. This suggests that the entire central Canaan region was either subdued by or had formed an alliance with Joshua and his armies.

The purpose of the assembly was to engage in covenant affirmation, something Moses had instructed them to do once they had arrived in the land (Deut. 27:2–8). Joshua built an altar that doubled as a stela and on it wrote a Mosaic text, probably Deuteronomy. Half the people stood at the foot of Mount Gerizim and half in front of Mount Ebal, the two mountains overlooking Shechem. There the whole nation swore covenant fidelity to the Lord (Josh. 8:30–35).

C. The Alliance with Gibeon (chapter 9)

Having learned of Israel's success, the city-states of Canaan began to form coalitions to protect themselves (9:1–2). The people of the nearby town of Gibeon took a different tack, however. They sent a delegation to Joshua, men disguised in such a way as to appear to be from a distant land and thus exempt from ḥērem (Deut. 20:10–18). Without seeking divine counsel Joshua foolishly made a pact with them (Josh. 9:3–15), learning too late that they were in fact Hivites and should have been put to death (9:16).

The only thing that could be done, given the binding nature of the treaty, was to subject the Gibeonites and their neighbors to Israel's overlordship. They therefore became servile vassals of Israel, woodcutters and water carriers (9:16–21). This position they held for ages to come, presumably down to the days of Saul, David, and the united monarchy (2 Sam. 21:1–14). Once more Israel paid the bitter price for not seeking the mind and will of God at every step of the way (Josh. 9:22–27).

III. THE SOUTHERN CAMPAIGN (CHAPTER 10)

Jerusalem, a Jebusite city, was only ten miles south of Ai, so its citizens became terrified when they heard of Ai's total destruction. The king of the city-state, Adoni-Zedek, decided that only a strong alliance of Amorite rulers could possibly save them all from a similar fate. So he persuaded his fellow kings from Hebron, Jarmuth, Lachish, and Eglon to join him in provoking Israel so that Israel would be encouraged to retaliate. The plan was to invade and punish Gibeon for having made peace with Israel, a tactic that would force Israel to come to the aid of its little ally (10:1–5).

Apprised by the Gibeonites of their peril, Joshua made an overnight march from Gilgal, Israel's temporary capital, arriving in time to engage the Amorites in fierce battle. But Israel was not alone, for again the battle was the Lord's. While the Amorites fled before Joshua down the descent of Beth Horon, the Lord sent huge hailstones that slew more than Israel did with the sword. Moreover, He extended the length of the day to nearly double its usual time, thus giving Israel ample daylight to finish the job. So marvelous was this divine intervention that it was set to verse and recorded not only here but in a noncanonical work known as the Book of Jashar (10:6–15; see also 2 Sam. 1:18).

The Amorite kings managed to escape to Makkedah, some twenty miles or so southwest of Gibeon. They hid themselves in a cave there, but not for long. Joshua learned of their whereabouts, sealed up the cave, and proceeded to decimate the Amorite populations in the vicinity (Josh. 10:16–21). Joshua then dragged the five kings from the cave, slew them in a public execution, and impaled their bodies on five posts until sundown (see Deut. 21:22–23). Having in this gruesome manner demonstrated the awfulness of God's judgment on those determined to resist him, Joshua converted the hiding place into a mausoleum, covering the cave's opening with large stones that, the narrator pointed out, were there to this very day (Josh. 10:22–27).

Summarizing the southern campaign, the record lists the various cities that fell to Israel (10:28–39). They include Makkedah itself, Libnah, Lachish, Gezer, Eglon, Hebron, and Debir. The full extent of the territory is described in 10:40–43. It embraced roughly everything from Kadesh Barnea in the northern Negev to Gibeon in the north and from the hill country west to Gaza on the Mediterranean.

IV. THE NORTHERN CAMPAIGN (CHAPTER 11)

The third phase of Joshua's strategy was an attack on a Canaanite coalition that had formed north of the Jezreel Valley under the leadership of Jabin, king of Hazor (11:1–5). As before, the battle was the Lord's, so there was no need for Israel to be afraid (11:6). When the armies met, the Canaanites fell before the hosts of the Lord until no Canaanite was left (11:7–9). Joshua then took Hazor, the largest city in the northern part of Canaan, burned it to the ground and slaughtered its populace at the same time. But in line with policy stated long before by Moses (Deut. 6:10–11), Joshua spared the remaining cities in order to provide places for his own people to live (Josh. 11:10–15).

The entire conquest to that point is summarized in 11:16–23. Virtually everything in the central hill country of the land had fallen. The Lord had put within the hearts of the enemy kings a fierce resistance to His will, and on the basis of that recalcitrance—known by Him to be irreversible—He had enabled Joshua to prevail. Only in the lower coastal plain, later Philistia, did pockets of independence remain.

V. SUBSEQUENT ATTEMPTS AT SETTLEMENT (CHAPTERS 12–22)

Whereas the former chapters speak of conquest, these chapters speak of settlement, and therein lies a certain difficulty. The optimistic appraisal of the Conquest, a period of perhaps as short as seven years (14:7–10), seems undercut by Israel's failure to occupy and dominate the land in the ensuing half-century or so. This part of the book is an eloquent witness to the difference between what Israel could have been under God and what she in fact became in the course of seeking her own independent pathway.

A. A Summary of the Conquests (chapter 12)

Beginning with the Transjordanian conquests under Moses, the narrator continued with a list of the kings of the west, thirty-one in all, whose territories were to be divided among the tribes of Israel.

B. Eastern and Western Allotments (chapters 13–19)

The narrative here opened with the impression of some years having passed since the completion of the initial conquest. The rest of the section speaks of what remained to be taken and how the tribes were to determine and appropriate their allocations.

The land unpossessed (13:1–14). Reuben, Gad, and half of Manasseh had already been assigned their Transjordanian inheritances (see 1:12–18), but the western tribes had not. In fact, they could not until they removed the last occupants of the land, those who lived primarily in Philistia (11:2–3) and in the far north (11:4–7). At least allocation could be made in the hope that complete domination of the land would someday become a reality.

The territories of Reuben, Gad, and East Manasseh (13:15–33). The area of Reuben was from the Arnon River in the south to Heshbon in the north and from the Dead Sea and the Jordan River eastward. Gad's region was north of Reuben to the vicinity of the Sea of Chinnereth (Galilee) near the Jordan. And East Manasseh embraced everything east and north of Gad to the Golan region and perhaps even beyond. Thus the eastern tribes (minus Levi) found a home in the old Amorite kingdoms (see 12:1–5).

The allotment to Caleb (chapter 14). After summarizing the eastern land distribution and pointing out once more Levi's lack of territory, the narrator focused on the story of one man, Caleb, and how his faithfulness to the Lord made it possible for him to gain an estate for himself. He reminded Joshua that Moses had promised such a boon forty-five years earlier, and now, though he was eighty-five years old, he was prepared to repel whatever people stood in the way of that promise. Joshua gladly complied and assigned Caleb the city of Hebron.

One of the remarkable things about the Bible is its attention not only to nations and peoples but also to individuals. This underscores the fact that He who "loved the world" provided the means of redemption whereby "whoever believes" may be saved. In a generation of apostates Caleb remained true to the Lord, and for his faithfulness he was singled out as a recipient of God's gracious blessings.

The territory of Judah (chapter 15). This large region lay north of a line from the south end of the Dead Sea to the "river of Egypt" (that is, the Wadi el-Arish) and north to a line just south of Jerusalem. Its western border was the Mediterranean Sea, and its eastern border was the Dead Sea and lower Jordan Valley. Caleb's inheritance lay within this territory (15:13–19).

The territories of Ephraim and West Manasseh (chapters 16–17). Ephraim was north of Judah as far as Shiloh and between the Mediterranean and the Jordan. The large district of the western half of Manasseh extended north of Ephraim to the Galilee region just south of Carmel and the Sea of Chinnereth (Galilee).

The location of the tabernacle (18:1). After the conquest the leaders of Israel moved the tabernacle (and thus the religious center of the nation) from Gilgal to Shiloh, a much more central location. It was approximately on the border between the two important tribes of Ephraim and Manasseh.

The territory of Benjamin (18:2–28). Rachel was the mother of both Joseph and Benjamin, and Joseph was the father of Ephraim. The tribe of Benjamin was located just south of Ephraim and north of Judah. It included Jerusalem within its holdings.

The territory of Simeon (19:1–9). In effect Simeon had no independent allocation. It was absorbed by Judah eventually and lost its tribal identity. Perhaps this was attributable to Simeon's drastic population reduction following that tribe's special culpability in the apostasy of Baal Peor (Num. 25:14; also compare Num. 1:23 with 26:14).

The territories of Zebulun and Issachar (19:10–23). Zebulun was north of the Plain of Jezreel and just west of the Sea of Chinnereth. The region occupied by the tribe of Issachar was between Zebulun on the north and West Manasseh on the south. Its eastern border was the Jordan River.

The territories of Asher, Naphtali, and Dan (19:24–48). The small tribe of Asher lay along the Mediterranean coast north of Mount Carmel. It was bounded on the east by the tribes of Zebulun and Naphtali. Upper Galilee provided the setting for the people of Naphtali. Their lands lay north of Zebulun and east of Asher as far as the upper Jordan and beyond. Originally assigned a region west of Benjamin and Ephraim, the Danites soon left there and moved north of the Sea of Chinnereth to a place called Laish (or Leshem, 19:47; see Judg. 18:29). They took the area by force and eventually established an independent religious system there (Judg. 18:1–31).

The allotment to Joshua (19:49–51). Joshua was an Ephraimite (Num. 13:8), and so he received his promised inheritance in Ephraim. The site selected was Timnath Serah (perhaps Khirbet Tibneh, around fifteen miles southwest of Shechem), otherwise known as Timnath Heres (Josh. 24:30; Judg. 2:9). With this final and climactic allotment the process of distributing the Promised Land to its tribal and individual tenants was complete. It had been done by divine direction, and thus there is implicitly a sense of responsibility on their part to occupy well and faithfully.

C. The Cities of Refuge (chapter 20)

At an earlier time Moses had set forth provisions for persons accused of homicide to find sanctuary pending a formal trial. Such sanctuary was to be available in a number of towns scattered throughout the land (Num. 35:6–34; Deut. 4:41–43; 19:1–3). With the Conquest over, these places were now designated by name—Kedesh of Naphtali, Shechem, and Hebron in Canaan proper; and Bezer, Ramoth, and Golan in Transjordania.

D. The Levitical Cities (chapter 21)

Because the tribe of Levi had been set apart to the ministry of the tabernacle and other sacred responsibilities (Num. 3:11–51), it would have no territorial allotment as such (35:1–8). Instead, the Levites and their families would reside in forty-eight cities scattered throughout the land (Josh. 21:41), six of which were the cities of refuge referred to above (21:11, 21, 27, 32, 36, 38).

E. The Departure of the Eastern Tribes (chapter 22)

Following the conquest of the Transjordan some years earlier, the tribes of Reuben, Gad, and East Manasseh had requested of Moses that they be allowed to settle there rather than in Canaan. Moses had granted the request with the proviso that their fighting men should assist their fellow tribes in conquering Canaan, after which they could return to their families (Num. 32:1–32; Josh. 1:12–18). The Conquest was now effectively over; so Joshua excused these men from further involvement, and with his blessing he sent them back to their homes. His parting words admonished them to covenant obedience, because the fact they lived east of the river did not mean they had no further obligations to the Lord and His chosen people (22:1–6).

The warning was justified because when the men reached the Jordan, they built an altar which, to the Israelites of Canaan, appeared to be evidence of a religious center in competition with the central sanctuary at Shiloh (22:10–12). A delegation, in fact, went to the place of the altar and accused its builders of that very thing (22:13–20). The Law stated clearly that the Lord would place His name in one place only (Deut. 12:1–7), and the action of the eastern tribes was in direct violation of that stipulation.

In response, the eastern leaders explained that what they had erected was not an altar in competition with the authorized one at Shiloh but merely a memorial. They said that later generations would view it not as a sign of the division of the tribes but of their unity despite their separation by the Jordan River (Josh. 22:21–29). Phinehas and the others were persuaded by this explanation, and instead of disciplining the eastern tribes, the leaders commended them for their commitment to the things of God. Thereafter the altar was called Ed ("witness") because it testified to the ongoing allegiance of the Transjordan tribes to the whole nation.

VI. JOSHUA'S FAREWELL ADDRESS (CHAPTERS 23–24)

Like Moses before him, Joshua at last came to see that his life was nearly over and that he needed to provide a legacy to his people in the form of (a) a reminder of their need for covenant commitment (23:1–16), (b) a review of God's past blessings on them (24:1–13), and (c) a renewal of the covenant relationship (24:14–28). The book then ends with a brief postlude tending to "unfinished business" (24:29–33).

A. Exhortations and Warnings (chapter 23)

Sometime after the Conquest was over (23:1) Joshua convened an assembly of Israel in order to deliver, in effect, a farewell address (see also Moses' farewell address in Deut. 29:2; 31:1–2). He reminded them of God's goodness in overcoming their enemies and assured them that He would continue to do so until the task was completed once and for all (Josh. 23:2–5). This, however, would be largely conditioned on their faithfulness to the Lord and on strict obedience to the terms of the covenant He had made with them and their ancestors (23:6–13).

If they should fail in this respect, they could expect the reverse of all these good things. Instead of being established in the land, they would be torn up and "transplanted." Their violation of the covenant—especially the first two commands of the Decalogue—would invite swift and sure judgment, resulting in their total decimation (23:14–16; see Deut. 28:20–24).

B. The Assembly at Shechem (24:1–28)

The review of sacred history (24:1–13). At the conclusion of the first phase of the Conquest, Joshua had gathered the people at Shechem to renew their covenant with the Lord (8:30–35). Now at the end of his life he returned there for a similar occasion, a time of national recommitment to their covenant calling and purpose. The account here is much more expansive, particularly because it contains a lengthy historical prologue narrating God's gracious relationship with His chosen people from Terah's time to their own (24:2–13; see also Deut. 1:6–4:40). The highlights of the sacred history were the election of the fathers (Josh. 24:3), the deliverance from Egypt (24:5–7), the desert sojourn (24:8), the conquest of Transjordania (24:9–10), and the present situation in which they lived in towns and houses they had not built (24:11–13).

The call for decision (24:14–25). Such providential care should elicit only one response: obedience. But the decision had to be theirs. They could follow the God who had brought them to that hour or they could go after the gods of the land. As for Joshua and his family, they would serve the Lord (24:14–15). With obvious superficiality the throng confessed that it was God who had indeed redeemed them and therefore there was no question as to where they stood (24:16–18). Joshua knew, however, that there were already the inroads of idolatry among them, and almost sarcastically he challenged them to prove the seriousness of their confession by repudiating these incipient signs of paganism, something they swore to do. Joshua therefore sealed the national commitment in a formal covenant ceremony (24:19–25).

Membership in the covenant community of Israel was in itself no guarantee of God's favor. Each individual in Israel must trust in the Lord and obey Him. So Joshua led his family to declare their commitment to truth and obedience no matter what others might do. No less is expected of those who name the name of Christ. Each is accountable, and from each the Lord expects obedience and responsible stewardship (Luke 19:11–27).

The stone of witness (24:26–28). To make this event one forever enshrined in Israel's national consciousness, Joshua added "these words" (that is, the very words of their affirmations) to "the Book of the Law of God." This likely refers to an addendum to the Pentateuch, a work which gave rise to the Book of Joshua itself. In addition he erected a stone monument there as witness for all time to the vows they had made to the Lord.

C. Joshua's Death and the Conclusion of the Book (24:29–33)

Sometime after his farewell address, Joshua died at the age of 110 and was buried at Timnath Serah, his private estate (see 19:50). As long as he and his contemporary elders lived, Israel remained true to the Lord (24:31). The implication, however, is that things changed after that, a point explicitly made in Judges 2:10. The reference to Joshua's death leads to the narrator's observation about the disposal of two other famous persons, Joseph and Eleazar. Joseph had asked that his remains be taken from Egypt to be buried in Jacob's properties at Shechem, a request now honored (Josh. 24:32; see Gen. 50:24–25; Exod. 13:19). As for Eleazar, the high priest and son of Aaron, his own son Phinehas saw to it that he was interred in a property set aside for him in the territory of Ephraim (Josh. 24:33).

JUDGES

Anarchy versus Divine Sovereignty

AUTHOR

*A*ccording to the Babylonian Talmud (*Baba Bathra* 14b), Samuel wrote Judges as well as 1 and 2 Samuel. Inasmuch as everything in the book chronologically precedes Samuel's death, this is a reasonable suggestion. The book itself offers no clue as to its authorship, however, nor is there internal witness to it elsewhere in the Bible. It seems best to leave it as an anonymous composition, one likely stitched together from a number of originally independent texts. Such an admission does not deny the book's divine inspiration or its character as inerrant revelation.

UNITY

Evidence of the composite nature of the book lies in a careful look at its contents. Judges 1:1–3:6 somewhat overlaps with and forms a transition from the Book of Joshua. This section also introduces the spiritual decline of the nation, which gave rise to the need for God's judgment followed by His deliverance through judges. The narratives about the judges comprise a distinct unit (3:7–16:31) consisting of accounts about these men and one woman. The last five chapters (along with the Book of Ruth) focus on events associated with Bethlehem, perhaps suggesting that they were composed as late as the time of David's anointing to be king of Israel. The two stories

179

also feature Levites under less than flattering circumstances, the first Levite becoming priest of an apostate cult (Judg. 17–18) and the other the hapless husband of a murder victim (Judg. 19–21).

Earlier criticism traced the alleged sources J (the Yahwist) and E (the Elohist) throughout Judges, attributing a few odd parts to P (Priestly) and the final editing of the whole to a late redactor. More recently Judges, with Joshua, has been more severely disconnected from the Pentateuch and viewed as a part of the massive theological history known as the "Deuteronomic History" (Josh.–2 Kings). Among other things, this would presuppose a time as late as the postexilic period for the final shape of the book. It furthermore suggests that Judges reflects not actual historical events but a theologized version of the premonarchy period designed to justify the need for and development of the Davidic regency. There is no objective evidence supporting such reconstructions, however. It is preferable, instead, to understand the Book of Judges as a reliable historical account of a period that was chaotic and wicked, and which also provided a theological interpretation of life lived apart from the sovereignty of God. The two stories at the end are not mere appendages; they serve to illustrate graphically how perverse the days of the judges really were.

DATE

If, as some of the ancient Hebrew canonical traditions assert, Judges and Ruth comprise one book, the earliest possible date for its final form would have to be sometime after David's selection to be king of Israel. The reason for this is the reference to David as the great-grandson of Ruth (Ruth 4:17, 22). David was born in 1041 B.C. and was likely fifteen or so years of age when Samuel anointed him as Saul's successor (1 Sam. 16:1–13). That suggests a date for the completion of Ruth (and therefore of Judges) shortly after 1025 B.C. It is likely, however, that incidental details were added to the text as late as the fall of Samaria in 722 B.C. (see also Judg. 18:30).

Even if Ruth is detached from Judges, the latter must have been written no earlier than around 1084. This is based on the fact that Samson exercised his judgeship from about 1104 to 1084 B.C., and the account carries forward to the end of that period (15:20; 16:31). The repeated observation that in those days "there was no king in Israel" (17:6; 18:1; 19:1; 21:25) seems to presuppose that there was a king at the time the statement was made. Saul began his rule in 1051 B.C., so Judges must have attained its final shape sometime after that.

ADDRESSEES

The preceding case for a date in the period of the monarchy plus the lamentable political and spiritual plight of the nation throughout the era of the judges because of a lack of central authority provide a likely occasion for the production of the book. The "audience" would have been the whole nation of Israel, who were in transition from at least a quasi-theocracy to a human monarchy.

PURPOSE

The purpose, given the scenario just proposed, is to show Israel how tragic life can be when God's people refuse to acknowledge His sovereignty and instead everyone does "what [is] right in his own eyes" (21:25). True, the Lord had made provision for human kingship as early as patriarchal times (Gen. 17:6, 16; 35:11; Deut. 17:14–20), but in the interim it was His intention to rule over them directly in a theocratic framework (1 Sam. 8:7; 10:19). The judges were merely administrators of this regency with no pretensions to royal authority of their own (Judg. 8:22–23). The Book of Judges recounts how serious was Israel's misunderstanding of God's design and how devastating were the consequences. It thus sets the stage for the arrival of a truly God-ordained king, a man after God's own heart (1 Sam. 13:14; Acts 13:22), who would found a dynasty of rulers through whom the Lord could exercise His dominion over all creation (2 Sam. 7:8–17).

THEOLOGICAL EMPHASES

A leading theological theme in Judges is the consequences of sin in the life of a nation (or an individual) when it refuses to abide by the clear-cut will of God. Such behavior results in spiritual, moral, and political chaos and, unless checked, in eventual destruction. A contrasting theme, however, is the redemptive grace of God, which, while not condoning such sin, is able to undo its baleful effects when nations and people repent and turn to God for forgiveness and restoration. This is seen best, perhaps, in the so-called cyclical pattern of Judges 2:11–19. The Israelites would follow after other gods (2:11–13), the Lord would bring punishment (2:14–15), they would cry out to Him (2:18), He would raise up judges to deliver them from oppression (2:16), they would disregard the judges and go back to their idolatry (2:17, 19), and thus the cycle would repeat itself. Sadly, the more dominant voice is that of judgment, for on the whole the book reveals a people insistent on spurning the overtures of divine intervention.

OUTLINE

I. A Review of the Conquest (chapter 1)
   A. The Conquest by Judah and Simeon (1:1–20)
   B. The Failure of the Other Tribes (1:21–36)
II. The Theme of the Period (2:1–3:6)
   A. The Theophany at Bochim (2:1–5)
   B. Joshua's Death and Its Aftermath (2:6–10)
   C. The Cycle of Sin and Deliverance (2:11–23)
   D. The Nations Left in the Land (3:1–6)
III. The Narratives of the Judges (3:7–16:31)
   A. Othniel (3:7–11)
   B. Ehud (3:12–30)
   C. Shamgar (3:31)
   D. Deborah (chapters 4–5)
   E. Gideon (chapters 6–9)
   F. Tola and Jair (10:1–5)
   G. Jephthah (10:6–12:7)
   H. Ibzan, Elon, and Abdon (12:8–15)
   I. Samson (chapters 13–16)

IV. The Introduction to Israelite Idolatry (chapters 17–18)
   A. Micah's Images (chapter 17)
   B. Dan's Idolatry (chapter 18)
V. The Internal State of the Tribal Alliance (chapters 19–21)
   A. The Crime against the Levite (chapter 19)
   B. Civil War against the Tribe of Benjamin (chapter 20)
   C. Revival of the Tribe of Benjamin (chapter 21)

I. A REVIEW OF THE CONQUEST (CHAPTER 1)

The close connection between the Book of Joshua and Judges is apparent from the fact that Judges picks up where Joshua left off, but it does so by overlapping Joshua to some extent. (This is also true of the ending of 2 Chronicles and the first part of Ezra.) The overlapping is not in identical terms, however, nor is it complete. In fact, it focuses on the phase of the Conquest that followed Joshua's death and, moreover, makes clear that the Conquest even then was not successful.

A. The Conquest by Judah and Simeon (1:1–20)

In light of the likelihood that Judges was composed as late as David's reign over Judah at Hebron, it is not surprising that so much attention is paid to Judah's successful conquest of its allotted area. After Joshua died (1:1), the first assault was made against the city of Bezek (perhaps Bezqa, northeast of Gezer), whose king, Adoni-Bezek, was captured (1:2–7). Then Jerusalem fell—clearly only temporarily since David had to capture it later (2 Sam. 5:6–10)—as did Hebron (Judg. 1:8–10). Caleb, a Judean (Num. 13:6), had already been granted a territory in Judah (Josh. 14:13–15; 15:13–19), the occupation of which is recounted here (Judg. 1:11–15). Finally, other places came under Judah's control, all except those in the valleys that were occupied by the Canaanites. These could not be dislodged, because the Canaanites had the use of ironclad chariots (1:16–20).

B. *The Failure of the Other Tribes (1:21–36)*

On the whole, the other tribes were not so successful in occupying their allotted territories. Benjamin could not drive out the Jebusites in Jerusalem (1:21), Ephraim's conquest was limited only to Bethel in the record (1:22–26; see also 1:29), and Manasseh had to leave much of its allotment to the Canaanites (1:27–28), as did Zebulun, Asher, and Naphtali (1:30–33). Dan could not evict the Amorites from the coastal lowlands and had to remain content with a small settlement in the hills (1:34–36).

II. THE THEME OF THE PERIOD (2:1–3:6)

Joshua and his contemporaries were not long off the scene when Israel began to defect from the covenant and go into idolatry. This they did for centuries despite God's punishment and gracious restoration. This seemingly endless cycle of fall and favor is encapsulated here. Its description serves almost as a table of contents for the whole book.

A. *The Theophany at Bochim (2:1–5)*

Here the author went back to an experience of Israel otherwise unmentioned but clearly in the time of Joshua (2:3, 5; see Josh. 23:13). The Angel of the Lord—a common manifestation of the Lord in the book (Judg. 6:11–24; 13:2–21)—had come to warn the people to keep covenant with Him lest they be unable to come into their inheritance. They wept so loudly at the prospect that the place became known as "Weeping" (Hebrew, *bôkîm*).

B. *Joshua's Death and Its Aftermath (2:6–10)*

The overlap of the Book of Judges with the Book of Joshua is clear again in its repetition of the notice of Joshua's death (see Josh. 24:28–31). The point here, however, is to show how the death of the great leader and his contemporary leaders was soon followed by a generation of people who no longer knew or desired to serve the Lord.

C. The Cycle of Sin and Deliverance (2:11–23)

The initial defection that followed Joshua's death inaugurated a pattern of life that continued throughout the period of the judges, more than 250 years (around 1330–1080 B.C.). This pattern, in fact, is one of the major theological issues of the book. The people would go into idolatry, they would suffer at the hands of foreign invaders, they would cry out to the Lord, He would raise up judges to save them, they would enjoy rest, and then they would lapse once more into apostasy.

D. The Nations Left in the Land (3:1–6)

The incomplete nature of the Conquest is asserted once again (see 1:1; 2:3), but this time God allowed Canaanites and others to remain in certain areas in order to discipline His people and to use them as a form of testing to determine the extent of their loyalty to Him. Unfortunately it did not take long for their covenant infidelities to show themselves, for they betrayed them in one of the clearest means possible—intermarriage with the pagan people (3:6; see Exod. 34:15–16; Deut. 7:3–4; Josh. 23:12).

III. THE NARRATIVES OF THE JUDGES (3:7–16:31)

The main characters of the Book of Judges are the persons described by that title. The word *judges* refers not so much to those who presided over trials at court but rather to men and women raised up by the Spirit of God to establish and maintain domestic law and order, adherence to covenant principles, and deliverance from foreign oppression. They were chosen arbitrarily by the Lord with no particular notice given of their qualifications or even their character. Their office furthermore was non-hereditary. A judge's children did not automatically succeed him or her in office. The point clearly being made is that the Lord alone is King and that He can and does choose the most surprising channels through whom to administer His dominion.

A. Othniel (3:7–11)

The first of the judges was a nephew of Caleb and also his son-in-law (3:9; see 1:13), a fact that places his judgeship late in the fourteenth century B.C. Israel's apostasy after Joshua's death resulted in an eight-year oppression by an Aramean kingdom from which Othniel brought deliverance.

B. Ehud (3:12–30)

The next oppression came from the Moabites, just east of the Jordan River. Their king, Eglon, kept Israel in cruel bondage, at least in Jericho and vicinity, for eighteen years (probably around 1300–1280 B.C.). Because Jericho was in Benjamin, Ehud, a judge from that tribe, went to Moab to pretend to offer tribute to the king. Gaining private access to Eglon, Ehud assassinated him and managed to escape to Ephraim. There he gathered a body of troops, which he led against the advancing Moabites with triumphant success. Eighty years of peace followed, at least in that part of the land.

C. Shamgar (3:31)

All that is known of this judge is that he killed six hundred Philistines with an oxgoad. This took place probably around 1200 B.C. or a little earlier, since Philistines were not in Canaan in large numbers before then.

D. Deborah (chapters 4–5)

Sometime after Ehud's death (probably in the latter half of the thirteenth century), Israel again turned from the Lord and this time suffered judgment at the hands of northern Canaanites centered in Hazor. For twenty long years their leader, Jabin, made life miserable for Israel until at last God called Deborah to save her people. This surprising use of a woman underscores the principle in the book that the status of the individual is not of paramount importance. The kingdom was the Lord's, and He would deliver as He chose to do.

Deborah called on Barak, a northern officer, to accompany her to Mount Tabor where the Canaanites had assembled. There God gave Israel great victory (4:12–16). The Canaanite commander Sisera fled for his life, but instead of saving his life he met death in the tent of an Israelite sympathizer (4:17–22). After that, the Canaanite oppression quickly withered away (4:23–24).

The story of Deborah's exploits appears also in poetic form (chapter 5). After celebrating the Lord's conquests in the past (5:1–5), the poem speaks of the terrible days of the immediate period (5:6–11), a situation that called for pan-tribal cooperation under Deborah's leadership (5:12–18). It celebrates God's victories through her (5:19–23) and singles out the heroism of Jael, the Kenite woman who put mighty Sisera to death (5:24–31).

E. Gideon (chapters 6–9)

Sometime around 1200 B.C. Israel's wickedness prompted God's judgment in the form of a Midianite conquest that devastated much of central Israel. The Midianites—and their Amalekite allies (6:3)—were desert tribes from the region south and east of the Dead Sea. After seven years God called Gideon from Ophrah (perhaps modern Afula in the Jezreel Valley). He appeared to him as the Angel of the Lord, and Gideon offered a sacrifice to Him there as the representative of the Lord (6:11–24).

If Gideon was to be the leader of God's people, however, he had to destroy the pagan objects with which even his own family had been involved. This done, the enemy came against him, forcing Gideon to call for help from neighboring tribes, especially in the north. Then, to seek a sign from God that He was with him, Gideon asked for and was granted the miracles of the wet and dry fleece (6:25–40).

Gideon then gathered his thirty-two thousand troops at Jezreel, but the Lord told him to pare the numbers back lest the Israelites take credit for what God was going to do. Twenty-two thousand availed themselves of the opportunity to leave (7:1–3), but ten thousand were still too many. When at last only three hundred remained Gideon was ready for battle (7:4–8). That evening a Midianite dreamed of disaster to be brought through Gideon and Gideon's God. Encouraged by this, Gideon attacked with his small troop, but all they had to do was stand aside and watch the Lord gain the victory (7:9–23).

After pursuing the remnants of the enemy across the Jordan, Gideon returned in triumph, having slain the hosts of Midian and Amalek and their kings (7:24–8:21). He then faced a most unexpected request—that he allow himself to become king over all Israel. Gideon realized the inappropriateness of this overture, for he was spiritually and theologically sensitive enough to know that only the Lord was King (8:22–23). However, he conceded to the extent of fabricating an ephod of gold, an object whose original function was to serve as part of the high priest's attire (Exod. 28:6–35) but which in this instance became an object of worship in itself (Judg. 7:24–27). The form and function of the ephod here is not clear, but it probably was woven of golden threads that made it stiff enough to stand in place like an image or idol (see 17:5; 18:14–20).

The people's demand for a king did not cease with Gideon's death. Abimelech, one of his sons by a concubine, sensed this desire and capitalized on it by offering himself as king (8:29–9:6). The whole setting of this move reflects the theme of the book—everyone doing what was right in his own eyes. Gideon was no sooner off the scene than Israel turned to Baal worship, especially at the ancient and sacred site of Shechem (8:33; 9:1).

From Shechem, his hometown, Abimelech launched his political campaign. He appealed to the people for their favor and then slew his own half-brothers in order to eliminate rival candidates. Gideon's youngest son, Jotham, survived, however, and by means of a fable, spoke to the Shechemites about Abimelech's twisted character and devious intentions (9:7–21). He was unsuccessful for the moment, for Abimelech claimed to be king over Shechem and reigned for three years.

Meanwhile, the Shechemites became estranged from Abimelech and welcomed among them a man named Gaal who offered his own services as king (9:22–29). Zebul, the mayor of Shechem, was loyal to Abimelech, however, and informed him of the conspiracy (9:30–33). Abimelech had been absent from Shechem because of the threats against him (9:25), but now he realized he must return and reclaim his kingship before it was too late. He laid siege to Shechem, but Gaal soon emerged, confident that he could put Abimelech to rout. He underestimated his foe, however, and was himself put to flight (9:34–40).

Zebul then prevented Gaal and his followers from returning to

Shechem. This gave Abimelech opportunity to attack them as well as people yet remaining in the city. He destroyed them and the lower city, flattening it and sowing it with salt so nothing would ever grow there again. He then attacked the heavily fortified citadel, set it on fire, and watched as one thousand people died there (9:41–49).

Other rebels lived at Thebez (modern Tubas, about ten miles northeast of Shechem), so Abimelech took that town as well. However, in his attempt to storm the citadel a woman dropped a heavy millstone on his head, mortally wounding him. Rather than suffer the disgrace of having been slain by a woman, Abimelech asked one of his attendants to put him out of his misery (9:54).

F. Tola and Jair (10:1–5)

Tola, a minor judge of the tribe of Issachar, made his headquarters in Ephraim. Through him God delivered His people from unnamed antagonists. No enemy is mentioned in connection with Jair, who judged the eastern tribes of Gilead for twenty-two years. His power and affluence are seen in his large family and vast real-estate holdings.

G. Jephthah (10:6–12:7)

Near the end of the twelfth century (around 1125 B.C.) Israel again lapsed into unrestrained idolatry. They began to worship not only the gods of Canaan but also those of surrounding nations. In His wrath the Lord brought in two instruments of judgment simultaneously, the Philistines from the west and the Ammonites from the east. For eighteen years the latter oppressed Israel severely until the people repented and called on the Lord (10:6–9). They admitted they had followed this pattern of disobedience throughout their history, but once more they asked for God's intervention in such plaintive tones that He was moved (10:10–16).

Believing the Lord was with them, the people assembled at Mizpah in Gilead (see also 11:29), right in the staging area of the Ammonites. There they began to seek a leader who could deliver them (10:17–18). Before long it was clear that Jephthah, a son of a prostitute and a social outcast, was their man, for despite these faults he was renowned for his heroism (11:1–8). He agreed to lead them, but only if his leadership would continue to be recognized after the emergency was over (11:9–11).

Jephthah first tried negotiating with the Ammonites. He reminded them that Israel had lived peaceably among them for three hundred years, so why should they now raise claims of territorial occupation (11:12–28)? The Ammonites paid no attention to this logic, however, so Jephthah was forced to march against them to their lands south of Gilead. Before he left he made the rash and tragic mistake of promising to offer the Lord a sacrifice of whatever met him if and when he returned victoriously to his home (11:29–33). Sadly, his own daughter came out to greet him after the battle was won, and the narrative says that Jephthah "did to her according to the vow which he had made" (11:39). Whether or not this resulted in human sacrifice, the painful lesson is that one must never in haste promise the Lord what cannot be paid with moral and spiritual integrity.

The Ephraimites meanwhile were displeased that Jephthah had not invited them to share in the battle and thus its spoils. The matter came to a violent head, and Jephthah resorted to an extreme course of action. He decided to slay all the Ephraimites on the east side of the Jordan, but the only way he could tell if they were native Ephraimites or not was for them to pronounce the Hebrew word *šibbōlet* ("ear of grain"). West Israelites pronounced it *sibbōlet* (with an initial "s" rather than "sh"), thus betraying their true identity (12:1–6).

H. Ibzan, Elon, and Abdon (12:8–15)

Another minor judge over a limited territory, Ibzan of Bethlehem was distinguished primarily for having thirty sons and thirty daughters. A lesser figure, Elon, a Zebulunite from the north, was buried there. Apparently his administration was rather localized. Abdon, another man with prolific descent, hailed from Ephraim and was buried there, in the town of Pirathon (probably modern Fer'ata, about five miles southwest of Shechem).

I. Samson (chapters 13–16)

Because of the tales of his superhuman exploits, Samson is best known of all Israel's judges. He is also the last judge recorded in the Book of Judges. The historical setting of his birth was a forty-year oppression of Israel by the Philistines that commenced around 1120 B.C. (10:7). The need for deliverance coincided with the childlessness of a Danite couple who, in answer to their urgent prayer, received the joyful news from the Angel of the Lord that they would soon have a son. He would be a Nazirite, which meant he must be separated from all others and devoted entirely to the Lord (13:1–7; see Num. 6:1–21).

Once this had been communicated to him (Judg. 13:14), Manoah, the husband, made a sacrifice on a large nearby rock, but before he could build a fire the Lord sent a flame from heaven to ignite it, thus validating the Angel as the messenger of God Himself (13:15–23). In due time the son was born and named Samson ("little sun"). As he grew, the Spirit of God came upon him, indicating that the Lord had planned something special for him (13:24–25).

Samson, however, turned out to be a man of badly flawed character. Despite his Nazirite status and the visitations of the Spirit, he fell victim to pride and lust, particularly as it pertained to women. When he reached the age of twenty—the age he became judge and began to deliver Israel (16:31)—he had his first romance. Having met a Philistine girl from Timnah (modern-day Tell Batash, eighteen miles west of Jerusalem), he fell in love with her and eventually married her. In the process of all the wedding arrangements, he broke his Nazirite vow by touching a dead body (14:9). Later, when Delilah, another Philistine, pressed him to reveal the secret of his strength, he broke his vow again by allowing her to cut his hair (16:19).

Despite these failings and many others, God displayed His grace toward Samson by using him as an instrument for delivering Israel from Philistine threat. He slew thirty Philistines at Ashkelon after his wife's betrayal (14:19–20), set fire to their wheat fields because his wife married a Philistine (15:1–6), killed many others when they took revenge (15:7–8), and then killed one thousand at one time with a donkey's jawbone as a weapon (15:9–20). Betrayed by another Philistine lover, Delilah by name, Samson was taken prisoner to Gaza where, cruelly blinded, he was forced to grind grain like an ox (16:1–22). So persuaded were they that their god Dagon had given them this illustrious captive, the Philistines brought Samson into their temple to mock him (16:23–27). This time, knowing that his strength lay only in the Lord, Samson pulled the pillars of the temple down, destroying more Philistines in his death than in all his life (16:28–31). Even in death he was a victor.

> Samson's life illustrates the great theological truth that the work of the Lord depends, in the final analysis, not on human means but on divine enablement. God used a flawed instrument to bring glory to Himself. How much better it would have been for Samson to have surrendered himself to God in character as well as accomplishment——but how comforting to know that God triumphs despite us if not through us.

IV. THE INTRODUCTION TO ISRAELITE IDOLATRY
(CHAPTERS 17–18)

The last section of the Book of Judges consists of two narratives (chapters 17–18 and 19–21), sometimes called indexes to the book. They, along with the Book of Ruth, make up a trilogy of stories whose setting is in the period of the judges of Israel (around 1330–1080 B.C.) and that have in common an interest in Bethlehem, the birthplace of David (and, of course, Jesus Christ). The story of Ruth, however, stands in sharp moral and spiritual contrast to the two in Judges whose dominant theme is the anarchy brought about because of Israel's rejection of the Lord as King (Judg. 17:6; 18:1; 19:1; 21:25).

A. Micah's Images (chapter 17)

One of the principal characters of this story is Jonathan, grandson of Moses (18:30), a fact that sets it somewhere early in the time of the judges, probably around 1300 B.C. The main actor is Micah, a syncretist who established an idolatrous cult in Ephraim. Lacking a proper priest, he engaged the services of a wandering Levite from Bethlehem, whom he hired to officiate at his shrine under the mistaken impression that this would guarantee the Lord's good favor.

B. Dan's Idolatry (chapter 18)

Meanwhile the people of Dan found it impossible to occupy the land that had been assigned them (Josh. 19:40–48), so they sent a scouting party to the north to find an alternative site. On the way they encountered Micah's priest, who predicted success in their enterprise (Judg. 18:1–6). Encouraged, they made their way to Laish, a remote region north of the Sea of Galilee. When they returned home, they assured their fellow tribesmen that the area was theirs for the taking (18:7–10).

A military contingent then headed toward Laish, stopping at the house of Micah along the way. They robbed him of all his gold and silver idols and persuaded his priest that he would be better off with them. Realizing the prestige he would have as priest of a whole tribe and not just a household, he went along with the Danites, Micah's feeble protests notwithstanding (18:11–26). When the small army reached Laish, they slaughtered the peaceful population and rebuilt the ruined city, naming it Dan. For centuries thereafter Dan was associated with an aberrant form of Yahweh worship, especially following the selection of the site by King Jeroboam as one of two places of bull worship (1 Kings 12:25–29).

Astoundingly the narrator revealed the name of this hireling priest at the end of his account—it was none other than Jonathan, Moses' grandson (Judg. 18:30)! Within two generations at least one tribe of Israel had lapsed from covenant faithfulness to the Lord to the beginnings at least of outright paganism (18:27–31).

V. THE INTERNAL STATE OF THE TRIBAL ALLIANCE (CHAPTERS 19–21)

The previous narrative dealt with spiritual apostasy; this one recounts the sorry saga of moral pollution. Abandonment of the Lord and of His covenant principles inevitably leads to both of these results. The internecine struggle that resulted from the moral indifference of the tribe of Benjamin almost spelled doom for the entire nation. Only the grace of God preserved it from that fate.

A. The Crime against the Levite (chapter 19)

Ironically the lead character in this episode is a Levite with Bethlehem connections, as was the case in the previous story. This Levite was from Ephraim, however, with his wife being a Bethlehemite. She became estranged from him and returned to her family. The Levite pursued her to Bethlehem, hoping that she would return to him (19:1–9).

At last she agreed, and after some delay the two set out for home. They came by Jerusalem, which at that time was independent of Israel, and finding no access there they decided to spend the night in Gibeah, the chief city of Benjamin (19:10–15). They knew no one there, and as they prepared to sleep in the streets, a stranger offered them shelter from the dangers of exposure (19:16–21).

That night a gang of sodomites beat on the door, demanding that the Levite come out so they could brutalize him. The host offered them his own daughter, but they refused. Then in a despicable act of cowardice and selfishness, the Levite thrust his own wife out the door. All night she suffered the attack of the savage mob, and when the Levite arose early in the morning he found her dead at the threshold (19:22–26). What follows next is almost beyond comprehension. Filled with outrage and yet helplessness, the Levite carried his wife's body home where he dissected it and sent its parts through the length and breadth of the land (19:27–30). The purpose of this grisly display was to evoke what indeed transpired— the pricking of the national conscience to an awareness as to just how low the moral barometer had sunk.

B. Civil War against the Tribe of Benjamin (chapter 20)

The rape and murder of the Levite's concubine galvanized the whole nation of Israel. By the thousands they gathered at Mizpah (modern-day

Tell en-Nasbeh, about eight miles north of Jerusalem) to determine what measures to take. The consensus was that since the crime occurred in Gibeah that city must be punished (20:1–11). To isolate the actual perpetrators, the Benjamite leaders were asked to disclose their identities so that they alone would bear the penalty, thus absolving the whole nation of blame. The Benjamites refused to betray their fellow tribesmen, however, and instead prepared for war against the other tribes (20:12–16).

After seeking counsel from the Lord, the decision was made for Judah to launch the attack first. The result was disastrous. Judah suffered a devastating defeat, and a second effort by other Israelite troops fared no better (20:17–25). With great lamentation and supplication before the Lord at Bethel—the location of the ark and the tabernacle—the Israelites asked one more time about the wisdom of a third attack. This time the Lord promised them success (20:26–28). It was only after Israel recognized that the battle was not theirs but the Lord's that they were able to prevail.

This time Israel set ambushes around Gibeah, and when the Benjamites emerged from the city to meet them, the Israelites surrounded them and the Lord Himself gave them victory (20:29–35). Meanwhile the city itself was set on fire, and when the Benjamites in the surrounding areas saw the smoke, they broke rank and divided into small contingents that could easily be overcome. Before long the tribe was decimated, and vengeance was complete (20:36–48).

C. Revival of the Tribe of Benjamin (chapter 21)

Too late it dawned on Israel that in their zeal to avenge the Levite and root out moral corruption they had virtually lost an entire tribe. Only a few hundred Benjamite men survived, and all the women had perished. Moreover, the Israelites had made a solemn oath not to give their daughters as wives to Benjamin (21:1–7).

The remedy was to look for women from among Israelite towns that had not participated in the war. Among these was Jabesh Gilead, across the Jordan and just south of the Sea of Galilee. There they found four hundred single women, whom they brought back after destroying their city (21:8–15). However, two hundred more were still needed (see 20:47).

Someone recalled that there was an annual festival at nearby Shiloh where young women participated in ritual dancing (21:16–19). Since it would have been taboo to marry Canaanites and other foreigners, these must have been Israelites who, like those of Jabesh Gilead, had not shared in the battle. The fathers of the girls would not be at fault since their daughters were taken from them by force.

The remaining Benjamites therefore went to Shiloh, captured as many wives as they needed, and thus guaranteed the continuing existence of their tribe (21:20–24). A descendant of this policy was King Saul, a Benjamite whose Jabesh Gilead roots are clearly implied (1 Sam. 11:1–11; 31:7–13). But nothing could justify this solution to a problem that was only symptomatic of the whole era, one reflected again in the very last and summarizing verse of the book: "In those days Israel had no king; everyone did as he saw fit" (Judg. 21:25).

RUTH
God's Surprising Grace

AUTHOR

The attachment of the Book of Ruth to the Book of Judges in the twenty-two-book arrangement of the Hebrew Bible implies common authorship or compilation of the two books, a view supported by the Babylonian Talmud as well (*Baba Bathra* 14b). There is no reason to reject the Jewish tradition that Samuel was responsible for the whole, though admittedly there is no explicit internal evidence to support it.

UNITY

The tightly knit structure of this short story presupposes its original unity. Nothing can be taken from it without doing harm to its overall message, nor need anything be added. The book's later use in the liturgy for the Feast of Weeks (or Pentecost)—and hence its location in the Kethubim ("Writings") or third major part of the canon—also has no bearing on either its authorship or unity.

The only section whose originality to the book is questionable is the concluding genealogy (4:18–22). However, the reference to David's ancestry in 4:11–12, 17 clearly paves the way for the genealogy, which is necessary if the blessing of the elders is to have its intended fulfillment.

DATE

The latest datable event in the book is the birth of David, which occurred in 1041 B.C. (2 Sam. 5:4; see also 1 Kings 6:1). David's significance was not in his birth, however, but in his selection by the Lord to be king, a selection ratified by his anointing by Samuel about 1025 B.C. A date of 1020 or so for the book's final form is quite reasonable and even compatible with authorship by Samuel (see 1 Sam. 25:1).

ADDRESSEES

Saul's disobedience and rejection by the Lord (1 Sam. 13:1–13; 15:17–23) gave rise to the need for God's own choice as ruler, the "man after [God's] own heart" (13:14). Samuel (or whoever was the author) would have used the Book of Ruth as a way of informing the nation as to the legitimacy of this choice.

PURPOSE

As suggested, the basic purpose of the Book of Ruth is to clarify the fact that David was fully qualified to be king not only because God had chosen him but also because of his pedigree that connected him directly back to Judah, the tribe through which the promised Ruler would come (Ruth 4:18; see also Gen. 49:10; Matt. 1:3–6). A secondary purpose is to extol the virtues of the principal characters of the story, who, though they lived in the corrupt days of the judges, stood in sharp contradiction to their culture.

THEOLOGICAL EMPHASES

The key theological idea of Ruth is that the sovereign God who deigns to rule through human institutions—specifically through the Davidic dynasty over Israel—is universal in His ultimate intentions. Nothing could be more ironic than the fact that the great-grandmother of King David was a pagan, indeed, a detested Moabite (Deut. 23:3–6; see also Gen. 19:30–38). Such grace paved the way for David's great Son, Jesus Christ, to become not just King but also Savior of all those who would embrace Him as such (Matt. 1:6–16; John 3:16).

OUTLINE

I. The Moabite Sojourn (chapter 1)
II. Ruth's Encounter with Boaz (chapter 2)
III. Ruth's Proposal to Boaz (chapter 3)
IV. Ruth's Marriage to Boaz (4:1–17)
V. The Genealogy of David (4:18–22)

I. THE MOABITE SOJOURN (CHAPTER 1)

The connection between the books of Ruth and Judges is apparent at the outset for the setting of the story is "when the judges ruled" (1:1). Since Ruth was a great-grandmother of David, the Ruth narrative may have taken place around 1200 B.C. A famine had struck Judah, so Elimelech, his wife Naomi, and their two young sons set out for Moab, where food was in plentiful supply. The sons married Moabite girls, but both the boys and their father died, leaving three widows (1:1–5).

Naomi, learning that the famine was over, decided to return to Bethlehem. One daughter-in-law opted to remain in Moab, but the other, Ruth, not only resolved to accompany Naomi but to embrace her God, the Lord of Israel (1:6–18). Once back, Naomi was warmly embraced by her community, but bereft of both family and possessions Naomi perceived her situation to be bleak indeed. She was no longer *nāŏmî* ("pleasant") but *mārā'* ("bitter") (1:20).

II. RUTH'S ENCOUNTER WITH BOAZ (CHAPTER 2)

Because of their poverty-stricken situation Ruth gained permission from Naomi to avail herself of the Mosaic provision that allowed the poor to gather scatterings of the harvest as they chose (2:2; see Lev. 19:9–10). As it "happened," she came to the fields of Boaz, a prominent citizen who, when he saw Ruth, inquired as to her identity (Ruth 2:3–7). Boaz was so impressed with her care for her mother-in-law that he urged her to remain on his property where she would be shown special favors (2:8–16).

Boaz clearly was aware of his responsibility as a near relative to Naomi (2:1), and perhaps he had also been struck with the charm and vulnerability of the young widow Ruth. In any event Naomi certainly saw the providence of God in directing Ruth to Boaz, and so she began to strategize a plan whereby both her and Ruth's adverse situations could be remedied (2:17–22).

III. RUTH'S PROPOSAL TO BOAZ (CHAPTER 3)

Naomi's plan was far more complicated than Ruth could have realized. First, Naomi had been reduced to such financial straits that she had been forced to mortgage all her late husband's properties in order to survive (4:3; see Lev. 25:23–28). Only a wealthy relative could or would be able to redeem it back for her. Second, Naomi's sons had died with no sons of their own to carry on their name. Again, only a near kinsman could marry a surviving widow and raise up a son in the name of the deceased (Ruth 4:5; see Deut. 25:5–10). In this case Boaz was able and morally obligated both to repurchase the property and to marry Ruth—or so it seemed.

With this in mind Naomi told Ruth to visit Boaz in the night as he slept near his threshing site. There she must make her wishes known by "uncovering his feet," that is, by symbolically indicating her interest in marriage. Such a bold move appears to modern Western custom to be out of line, but this was not the case at all in ancient Israel. Ruth therefore did as she was told (Ruth 3:1–7). When Boaz awakened in the night, Ruth, in effect, proposed marriage under the terms already stated. He agreed, but then he made the startling disclosure that he was not the nearest relative (3:8–12). Another citizen had first refusal, but Boaz said he would follow up the matter with him to see what his reaction would be (3:13). Ruth then returned to Naomi, carrying a large load of grain Boaz had given her as a sign of his good faith (3:14–18).

IV. RUTH'S MARRIAGE TO BOAZ (4:1–17)

True to his word, Boaz confronted the near relative and in a public legal venue informed him of Naomi's plight and of his opportunity to deliver her from it (4:1–4). The relative agreed to redeem the property, but when Boaz added that the whole transaction included marriage to Ruth as well, the deal was off. The reason, the man said, was that children born to Ruth and him would jeopardize the inheritance rights of his existing family (4:5–6).

In line with ancient custom, the near kinsman took off his sandal—that part of his attire that trod on the ground—thus relinquishing any claim to or responsibility for Naomi's estate. Boaz therefore was free to take Ruth as his wife and to discharge all the duties incumbent on him (4:7–10). The witnesses took note and then pronounced the blessing that Boaz and Ruth might, like their famous Judean ancestors, be blessed with worthy and abundant offspring (4:11–12). In due course a son, Obed, was born, the harbinger of even greater blessings to come (4:13–17).

V. THE GENEALOGY OF DAVID (4:18–22)

The birth of Obed to Ruth was under less than ideal circumstances for a number of reasons. She was a Moabite, a widow, and poverty stricken. But these kinds of liabilities harked back to the time of Judah, founder of the tribe of which Boaz was a member. Judah had produced a son by his own daughter-in-law Tamar, who had seduced him by pretending to be a prostitute (Gen. 38:12–23). That son was named Perez (Ruth 4:12), and through him the line of Boaz originated. But the intrigue does not end there, for Boaz is said to be a descendant also of Salmon, whom the New Testament identifies as the husband of Rahab the harlot (Matt. 1:5)! How mysterious and gracious are the ways of the Lord who, by means of this infamous linkage of generations, brought forth not only David (Ruth 4:22) but also Jesus Christ the Lord (Matt. 1:16).

Little did Ruth know that she would become not only a great-grandmother of King David but also an ancestor of God in the flesh, the very One whom she embraced as her God at a moment of personal decision. Choices we make at the prompting of God's Holy Spirit have ramifications for good beyond our wildest dreams.

1 SAMUEL
The Movement toward Monarchy

AUTHOR

The Babylonian Talmud (*Baba Bathra* 14b–15a) attributes the authorship of 1 and 2 Samuel (originally considered one work) to Samuel the prophet: "Samuel wrote the book which bears his name and the Book of Judges and Ruth." The fact that his death is recorded in 1 Samuel 25:1 led to further reflection on the matter, however, and the observation that "it was completed by Gad the seer and Nathan the prophet." While this falls short of proof, it is not inherently impossible. Gad lived at least as late as the time of David's purchase of the temple property at Jerusalem, a transaction that took place not long before David's death. In any case, Gad would have known of this since David inquired of him as to the propriety of building an altar there (2 Sam. 24:18). As for Nathan, he played a major role in the transition between David and Solomon which took place after the times recorded in Samuel (1 Kings 1:8–45). Besides, both Gad and Nathan—in addition to Samuel—are recognized as having composed accounts of the life and times of David (1 Chron. 29:29–30). There is no reason to question that their writings together make up the books of Samuel.

UNITY

The view of authorship just proposed does not negate the likelihood that Samuel is a collection of writings edited into their canonical form by an unknown composer or perhaps by Nathan himself. On the other hand, the view that Samuel is a constituent part of the massive work known as the "Deuteronomistic History," a work that achieved final form only in the postexilic period, has less to commend it. While not necessarily inimical to a high view of Scripture, it simply lacks any objective internal support, to say nothing of any compatibility with ancient tradition. Nothing in its present form presupposes any need for the account to have been edited as it left the pen of a tenth-century B.C. author.

The major narratives of 1 Samuel are (1) the birth, dedication, and call of Samuel (chapters 1–3); (2) the ark stories (chapters 4–7); (3) the Saul narratives (chapters 8–15); and (4) the "history of the rise of David" (1 Sam. 16–2 Sam. 5). According to the book's own witness, Samuel could have written chapters 1–24, including, on the basis of oral information, the story of his own birth and early childhood (chapters 1–2).

DATE

Granting the reliability of both biblical and talmudic tradition regarding Nathan's role in recounting the history embodied in Samuel, a date of about 960 for its essentially completed rendition is not wide of the mark. Solomon succeeded David as king in 971 B.C., and Nathan had a hand in recording some of the events of Solomon's reign (2 Chron. 9:29). It would seem that he must have lived for at least a few years of Solomon's tenure in order for it to have been considered important enough to mention.

ADDRESSEES

The intended hearers and/or readers of the book would potentially be the entire nation of Israel in Solomon's time and every generation since. There clearly is no lesser group in view, though the book, like most of the rest of the Old Testament historical books, makes no comment on the matter.

PURPOSE

This is somewhat easier to determine because of the selective nature of the narratives as well as the incidental comments by their protagonists and the observations offered by the unknown authors. Overall, 1 Samuel is an apology for the validity of human monarchy as a God-ordained institution, but particularly the monarchy of David and his dynastic successors. Following the dismal failure of the theocratic community of the era of the judges, it was important to make clear that God would continue to reign. He would do so through people whom He himself would elect. The "experiment" with Saul was a last opportunity for Israel to see that even monarchy was no better than anarchy if the right person was not on the throne. The choice of David and the evident signs of God's blessing on him gave the nation great hope that the long-awaited promise of a Judean ruler (Gen. 49:10) was about to come to pass.

THEOLOGICAL EMPHASES

In line with the statement of purpose above, a careful reading of 1 Samuel reveals at least three principal theological strands that inform and unify the book. First, the ancient promise of God that kings would issue from the patriarchs (Gen. 17:6, 16; 35:11), specifically a line of rulers from Judah (49:10), comes to the forefront as something about to be fulfilled. The way had been paved for this by the instructions in Deuteronomy as to how the kings were to conduct themselves (Deut. 17:14–20). Abortive attempts to establish human kingship in the times of the judges also show that this was a common and well-understood anticipation (Judg. 8:22–23; 9:1–2).

Second, the book reveals the error of attempting to run ahead of the promises of God and to bring to pass with human effort what only God can and should do. The demand for a king arose from the desperation of the people who could no longer tolerate the moral and spiritual collapse of the years of the judges and who saw no hope in the sons of Samuel who would succeed him (1 Sam. 8:1–9). Despite Samuel's strong protestations that the desire for such a king was wrong because it was premature (8:10–18), the people insisted anyway (8:19–20). The Lord therefore authorized Samuel to choose Saul, though he was not the long-awaited shepherd God had in mind (8:21–22; see also 13:14). The result of this demand by the people was politically and spiritually devastating.

Third, the book teaches the principle that the all-wise and all-powerful God is sovereign, and when nations or individuals submit to His dominion there is great blessing. The story of David's rise from humble obscurity to the threshold of kingship is eloquent witness to this truth. The elective grace of God in choosing him was reciprocated by David's faith and faithfulness, a combination of the divine and human that not only guaranteed a happy outcome three thousand years ago but that also undergirds any hope of God's blessing for the believer of the present day.

OUTLINE

I. The Preparations for the Monarchy (chapters 1–9)
  A. Samuel's Birth and Childhood (chapter 1)
  B. Hannah's Song (2:1–10)
  C. The Situation at Shiloh (2:11–36)
  D. Samuel's Call (chapter 3)
  E. The Story of the Ark (chapters 4–7)
  F. Selection of a King (chapters 8–9)
II. The Period of Saul (chapters 10–31)
  A. Saul's Ascendancy (chapters 10–14)
  B. Saul's Rejection (chapter 15)
  C. Saul and David (chapters 16–26)
  D. Saul's Death (chapters 27–31)

I. THE PREPARATIONS FOR THE MONARCHY (CHAPTERS 1–9)

As the last of the judges (1 Sam. 7:15), Samuel paved the way for the transition between the theocratic ideal of the period of the judges and the monarchy. When it was apparent that Samuel's sons whom he had appointed to replace him were not fit candidates, the people demanded a king, a demand to which Samuel reluctantly acceded once the Lord made it clear that he was to do so (8:1–9; 9:16).

A. Samuel's Birth and Childhood (chapter 1)

The circumstances of Samuel's birth are similar to those of Samson with whom Samuel was contemporary (Judg. 13:1–7). His father, Elkanah, had two wives, one of whom, Hannah, was barren. She would go regularly to Shiloh, the location of the temple, from her hometown a few miles west. There she would pray that God would give her a son (1 Sam. 1:1–8). When Eli the priest noticed the intensity of her prayer and thought that she was drunk, Hannah explained that she desperately wanted a son and that if God gave her one she would dedicate him to the Lord as a Nazirite (1:9–18; see Num. 6:1–21; Judg. 13:5).

Assured by the priest that God had heard her, she returned to her home and in due time gave birth to Samuel. When he was weaned after a few years, his mother took Samuel to Shiloh, where, true to her vow, she dedicated him to the Lord as a Nazirite. Samuel was placed under Eli's tutelage in preparation for the priesthood. Though he was from Ephraim, Samuel, being a descendant of Levi, was qualified to serve (1 Chron. 6:33–34, 38).

B. Hannah's Song (2:1–10)

In a great expression of praise—one imitated later by Mary in the Magnificat (Luke 1:46–55)—Hannah celebrated the goodness and grace of God in giving her a son. She, the lowly one, had become exalted (1 Sam. 2:1) in the same way God always exalts the humble and brings down the proud (2:7–8). Climactically she anticipated the coming of a king, one to be known as *māšîaḥ* ("Messiah"). This finds fulfillment in David (2 Sam. 7:8) and then most magnificently in Jesus Christ, the son (descendant) of David (1 Sam. 2:10; see Matt. 21:9).

C. The Situation at Shiloh (2:11–36)

Shiloh was selected as the site of the tabernacle as early as the days of Joshua (Josh. 18:1), but before long it accommodated elements of paganism that continued down to Samuel's time two hundred years later (Judg. 21:19–21). Eli the priest was godly enough, but his undisciplined sons took advantage of their position by stealing the best of the sacrifices (1 Sam. 2:12–17) and by engaging in so-called sacred prostitution right in the vicinity of the tabernacle (2:22–26).

Meanwhile Samuel continued to mature in his training for the priesthood (2:18–21). This was in view of the fact that the Lord, having confronted Eli with his disobedience and the wickedness of his sons, was about to terminate his priesthood and replace it with one that was more faithful to Him (2:27–36). The first sign of this would be the violent death of his sons (2:34). Eventually the line of Eli, descendants of Ithamar, became secondary to the line that produced Zadok, a descendant of Eleazar (1 Chron 24:1–6; see also 1 Kings 2:26–27).

D. Samuel's Call (chapter 3)

Samuel was born about 1120 B.C., ending a period of many generations in which revelation from the Lord was a rarity (3:1). God at last broke the silence and spoke to Samuel, who until that time had never encountered the Lord in this manner (3:7). Thinking at first that the voice he heard was Eli's, Samuel at last knew that the Lord was calling. The message was astounding. God would judge the family of Eli until it no longer existed (3:10–14). The next morning Samuel relayed to Eli the devastating message, one Eli knew was from God and therefore irrevocable (3:15–18). Beginning with that word from God, Samuel came to be known as a prophet as well as a priest. Everything he spoke came to pass, thus authenticating his new role (3:19–21).

E. The Story of the Ark (chapters 4–7)

These chapters are designed to reveal how Eli's family came to a tragic end but, more importantly, to underscore the political and military circumstances that gave rise to Israel's demand for a king. The Philistines, having been in the region for about a century, now entertained ideas about dominating the whole land. They marched against Israel in the lowlands just west of Shiloh and defeated Israel's army. Israel attributed the setback to the absence of the ark—the symbol of God's presence among them—and so the ark was brought from Shiloh to the battlefield (4:1–4).

This superstitious use of God's holy ark was totally ineffective. The Philistines defeated Israel again, captured the ark, and slew Eli's evil sons (4:5–11). When Eli heard the news he dropped dead. A daughter-in-law of Eli, learning of the death of her husband, gave birth to a child prematurely, a boy whom she named Ichabod, which means "no glory" (4:12–22). With the ark in enemy hands the glory had indeed departed, for God's abode among His people was represented by that symbol.

With unbridled glee and pride the Philistines took the ark, which they considered an image of Israel's God, and placed it at the feet of Dagon, the grain-and-fish deity who headed their pantheon. The next day the idol lay prostrate before the ark. It was re-erected only to fall again, this time with broken limbs (5:1–5). This contest persuaded the Philistines of Ashdod that Dagon was no match for the Lord, so they sent the ark to a sister city, Gath, whose citizens were soon struck with a plague. The same thing happened to the people of Ekron when the ark was forwarded there (5:6–12).

After seven weeks the Philistines sought some way to return the ark to Israel. They at last decided to place it on a driverless oxcart along with some golden pacification offerings. If the animals took the ark straight back to Israel, then the ark's damage to them was clearly an act of Israel's God. If, however, they meandered around, then their series of disasters was just a fluke (6:1–9).

The behavior of the animals confirmed the Philistines' worst fears— the ark was indeed powerful and something to be feared. They were immensely relieved to see the cart disappear over the horizon toward Beth Shemesh. There the Levites celebrated with a great sacrifice, offering up the animals that had pulled the wagon and accepting the gold objects as evidence of the defeat of their Philistine enemies (6:10–18). The joy was short-lived, however, for a great number of the people died because of their irreverent act of peering into the ark (6:19–20). The penalty paid by God's own people for their sacrilege was much greater than that of the pagan Philistines, for God's expectations of those to whom He has revealed Himself are always much greater.

Like the Philistines, the people of Beth Shemesh had no desire to hold on to the ark, so they sent it on to Kiriath Jearim, a few miles west of Jerusalem (6:21–7:1). There it remained at the house of Abinadab for about a century. The twenty years referred to (7:2) speaks only of the time between the return of the ark and the beginning of Samuel's leadership.

The first thing Samuel did was to persuade the people to quit their idolatry (7:3–4), and then he convened a great assembly at Mizpah (7:5;

see Judg. 20:1). The ceremony, which was for national repentance, was briefly interrupted by a Philistine attack, but God Himself intervened and sent the enemy away in panic (1 Sam. 7:5–11). Samuel erected a monument there to commemorate God's victory and gave it the name Ebenezer, "stone of [God's] help" (7:12). The outcome was so decisive that the Philistine threat was greatly reduced (7:13–14). As for Samuel, he served the Lord for the rest of his days, particularly in the Benjamite hill country, residing in Ramah, his birthplace (7:15–17; see 1:1, 19; 2:11).

F. Selection of a King (chapters 8–9)

For reasons not stated, Samuel's sons, much like Eli's, fell short of their father's standards of behavior and therefore were felt by Israel to be disqualified from leadership (8:1–5). The Israelites therefore requested that Samuel appoint them a king like those who ruled other nations. Samuel protested, but when he consulted the Lord, He told the prophet to grant their request, for it was He, the Lord, whom they were repudiating and not Samuel (8:6–9).

This premature demand for a human king would be costly, however, for the ruler they would get in their impatience would exploit them, God said, for his own selfish ends (8:10–18). Despite this warning the people insisted, so the Lord set in motion the process by which the king would be identified (8:19–22).

The narrator now turned to a Benjamite named Kish, who had a most imposing and promising young son named Saul (9:1–2). In order to bring this candidate for king to Samuel's attention, the Lord caused some donkeys belonging to Kish to go astray. Kish then sent Saul and a servant to search for the animals, but to no avail. When they were about to give up, the servant recalled that a seer lived nearby, a prophet who might be able and willing to deal with such a mundane matter (9:3–10). They therefore headed for the prophet's home of Ramah, only to learn that he had gone to a nearby shrine to officiate at a festival (9:11–14).

The seer, of course, was Samuel. While the Lord was leading Saul, He was also leading Samuel, instructing him that His choice for king was on his way. When they met, Samuel revealed the whereabouts of the donkeys but also told Saul to meet him the next day to learn about the great things God had in store for him, a prospect that to Saul seemed incredible (9:15–21). The rest of that day Samuel entertained Saul with a lavish banquet, and the next morning he prepared him to hear the word of the Lord (9:22–27).

II. THE PERIOD OF SAUL (CHAPTERS 10–31)

Samuel's warnings about the king on whom the people insisted were not long in being fulfilled in Saul. He began well, but within a short time he displayed the willfulness and spiritual insensitivity that opened him up first to the prophet's rebuke and then to the Lord's overt rejection of him and his dynasty. Along with Saul's decline was the election of David to kingship, a choice which, when made public, turned David into a detested rival in Saul's eyes, one to be hunted down and destroyed if at all possible. At the end, God, as always, would have His way and would seat on His earthly throne the man after His own heart.

A. Saul's Ascendancy (chapters 10–14)

As God's theocratic administrator (7:6; 8:4–7), Samuel had the responsibility to carry out God's will on behalf of the community. He therefore anointed Saul to be king (10:1) as the Lord had earlier told him to do (9:16). Since he knew Saul would seek confirming signs of this wholly unexpected turn of events, Samuel told him that the lost donkeys would be found (10:2), that he would meet men who would provide him with bread (10:3–4), that he would encounter a band of prophets near Gibeah and would join them in their prophesying (10:5–7), and that he should go to Gilgal to await Samuel who would offer up sacrifices there (10:8).

The first three of these occurred the next day, accompanied by a radical change in Saul's own life and disposition (10:9–16). The Lord "gave him another heart" (10:9, KJV), a phrase that should not be understood in terms of Christian conversion but as indicative of a giftedness to reign as prince over his people. The need for this change was apparent in the public assembly that Samuel convened in order to present Saul to the nation (10:17–24). Having narrowed the choices down to Saul alone, Saul was not to be found; for in his modesty he had hidden himself (10:22). Despite this disclaimer of royal privilege, the people as a whole hailed him as their king (10:24). Samuel then sealed the arrangement with appropriate ceremony (10:25–26). Ominously, however, the narrator noted that not all were pleased with the choice that had been made (10:27).

As though to silence his critics, Saul launched an attack against the Ammonites who had laid siege to Jabesh Gilead (11:1–12), the town from which Saul's own maternal ancestors had likely sprung (Judg. 21:14). So desperate was the plight of the city that the people even considered agreeing to the loss of their right eyes as a term of peace (1 Sam. 11:2). However, they turned to Saul instead, a resort permitted by the Ammonites who viewed Saul with great disdain at best (11:3–5).

Though chosen prematurely, Saul was still used by God to deliver His people. The Holy Spirit came on him, and with a hastily gathered militia he marched to Jabesh Gilead and defeated the Ammonites (11:6–11). Saul's Israelite critics began to melt away, for it was clear that God was with him (11:12–13). Once more an assembly was gathered, this time at Gilgal, the place of Israel's first encampment in the Promised Land (11:14–15). The purpose was to reaffirm Saul's kingship and to link it with the initial efforts of Israelite conquest under Joshua (Josh. 5:2–9).

Some years passed by (1 Sam. 13:1), and Samuel, now advanced in age, gathered the people of Israel together for a farewell address, much as Moses had done nearly four centuries before (12:1; see Deut. 1:1). He first established his personal credibility among them over a lifetime of ministry (1 Sam. 12:2–5), and then he reminded them of their sacred history from the time of the Exodus to the present moment (12:6–13). Over and over God had proved Himself faithful even though Israel's record was one of sin and rebellion. In light of that review of God's loyalty to His covenant pledges, Samuel challenged the throng to reciprocate, to walk with God in the future (12:14–15). As a sign that God would continue to be with them, He sent thunder and rain in response to Samuel's prayer, something unheard of in the time of wheat harvest (12:16–18).

The result of this marvelous display was a confession by the people of their sin in asking for a king and their plea to Samuel that he would pray for them (12:19). Samuel took this request as a privilege and also a solemn duty. He said, in fact, that to fail to pray would be to sin against God (12:20–23). This would not alleviate Israel of its obligation to serve the Lord, however (12:24–25).

Soon after that, Samuel's worst fears about Saul's kingship began to be realized. Saul had engaged the Philistines in fierce battle at Micmash, and when it seemed that he would be overcome, he and his troops retreated east to Gilgal (13:1–7). This was the place Samuel had mentioned to Saul as the site of sacrifices that the prophet would make on Saul's and Israel's behalf (10:8). The only stipulation was that Saul must wait for one week until Samuel arrived. Threatened by the Philistines, Saul offered the sacrifices himself, but as soon as he had done so Samuel arrived (13:8–10). Saul tried in vain to excuse his inappropriate assuming of the work of a priest. Because Saul had rejected the Lord, Samuel said, the Lord would reject Saul. The dynasty that could have been his would die with him for he would be replaced by the man of God's elective choice (13:11–15). That man, of course, was David.

> *A proper understanding of the phrase "a man after [God's] own heart" (13:14) yields the glorious truth that salvation and selection for service depend not on what He sees in us but on His own free will. That we are chosen is testimony to His grace, not to our goodness.*

Stinging from this rebuke, Saul nonetheless moved back up to the hill country to encounter the Philistines once again (13:16–18). Crippled by the knowledge that he had lost the favor of the Lord, Saul was further handicapped militarily. The Philistines had a corner on the iron market and thus held tactical military advantage over the Israelites, who were still in the Bronze Age, as it were (13:19–23).

Saul, with commendable courage, persisted in the defense of Israel's hill country against superior Philistine forces. His son Jonathan, with only a single soldier with him, decided to undertake a daring maneuver whereby he would penetrate enemy lines and await a sign from the Lord as to how to carry out the battle (14:1–15). If the enemy told them to remain in place, they would not advance, but if they taunted them to come forward they would, knowing by this that God was with them. Thus armed with divine strength, the two of them slew about twenty Philistines.

Meanwhile, Saul's forces were defecting, and to his dismay he learned that Jonathan was among the missing (14:16–17). Saul therefore appealed to the Urim and Thummim (implied by the presence of the ark and the gesture of withdrawing the hand; 14:18–19; see also 14:40–42). Encouraged by what these sacred lots communicated, Saul attacked and achieved success (14:18–23).

Saul had apparently sworn the army to a vow that they would fast until God intervened on their behalf (14:24–30). Jonathan had not known of the vow, however, and had eaten some wild honey. When Saul found this out later, he attributed Israel's comparative lack of military predominance to Jonathan's disregard of the vow, a charge Jonathan would rightly reject as baseless. Saul's suspicions that someone had broken the vow found little relief by the further disclosure that some of his men, having seized Philistine livestock, had slaughtered and eaten it in violation of Mosaic regulations (14:31–35; see Lev. 17:10–13). This prompted Saul to perform certain sacrificial rituals before taking up the pursuit of the Philistines again (1 Sam. 14:36–42). This included seeking counsel from the Lord by means of the Urim and Thummim as to the advisability of continuing the conflict (14:36–37) and also to determine the identity of the culprit who had broken the vow. To Saul's dismay, the lot revealed that the culprit was his own son Jonathan (14:38–42).

When confronted by his father, Jonathan readily confessed what he had done and furthermore was prepared to pay with his life for violating the vow. The people opposed this, however, and they delivered Jonathan from his father's cruel wrath (14:43–46).

The narrator concluded this part of the Saul saga by summarizing the king's military exploits in a positive manner and by listing his sons, daughters, and other near relatives (14:47–51). The section ends with the note that Saul never ceased battle with the Philistines, a fact that caused him constantly to seek out choice young warriors. Thus the way was paved for the introduction of David, a man whose ascent would mean Saul's demise (14:52).

B. Saul's Rejection (chapter 15)

Saul's dynasty had already been foreclosed because of his preemptive sacrifice at Gilgal (13:13). Now his personal reign would come to an end. Centuries earlier, the Lord had commanded Moses to record the Amalekite massacre of Israel's stragglers in the Sinai desert (Exod. 17:8–16). The time had now come for divine justice to be levied, a task God had reserved for Saul (1 Sam. 15:1–3). With a vast army Saul marched into the central Negev region, where the Amalekites made their home. He was to destroy them completely (see Deut. 20:16–18), but his obedience was not complete. For reasons not stated, he spared Agag the king and the best of the Amalekite livestock (1 Sam. 15:4–9).

Such disobedience angered the Lord, as it did Samuel when he heard about it. The prophet summoned the king, who, in a hypocritical show of deference and piety, bowed to Samuel and spoke a greeting in which he claimed to have fully carried out the will of God (15:10–13). The very sound of the animals betrayed him, however, and Saul's assertion that they had been spared as sacrifices to the Lord only stiffened Samuel's words about God's intended judgment. The Lord, he said, had elevated Saul to a position of great authority and responsibility (15:14–17). Sent now on a simple mission where the lines of obedience and disobedience were clearly drawn, Saul had failed. Though he tried to blame others, the fault was his. No amount of superficial religiosity could take the place of heartfelt obedience to God. Saul must, then, lose his throne (15:21–23).

Saul's repentance was no more sincere than his claims to obedience (15:24–31). His absolute rejection of the Lord was at last met by the Lord's rejection of him. This had nothing to do with eternal salvation, of course, but only with his position and role as king. That was forever finished, and his kingly office would be transferred to another, "[one] better than you" (15:28).

What Saul failed to do, Samuel accomplished. He slew Agag, and then he and Saul separated, Samuel to his home at Ramah and Saul to Gibeah. Never again did Samuel visit Saul, though he mourned for him the rest of his days. As for the Lord, He regretted the outcome of His having chosen Saul to be king in the first place (15:32–35).

C. Saul and David (chapters 16–26)

The long narrative of the relationship between Saul and David contains two major phases: on friendly terms (chapters 16–17) and on unfriendly terms (chapters 18–26).

On friendly terms (chapters 16–17). By the time he met David, Saul had reigned for about twenty-five of his forty years. David came to Saul's attention after the Lord had sent Samuel to Bethlehem to select the young son of Jesse to be the long-awaited ruler whom God had chosen (16:1; see also 13:14; 15:28). Jesse proudly paraded his sons before the prophet by descending age until only David—who was out tending the sheep—was left. Jesse had to learn that human criteria for greatness are not always the Lord's. Man looks on the externals, but God sees the heart (16:7). When the unlikely lad at last was brought, Samuel knew at once that he was God's chosen vessel. His anointing was confirmed by the powerful presence of God's Spirit on his life from then on (16:13).

Meanwhile that same Spirit left Saul, to be replaced by demons that haunted and incapacitated him (16:14–23). Only sweet music brought him peace, and by the providence of God that music came from the gifted fingers of the shepherd boy David, who must have composed and played on the harp many melodies of worship and praise on the Judean hillsides. Several of the biblical psalms find their settings in those times and places.

Saul's rejection did not mean the immediate end of his reign and responsibilities. War continued, especially with the Philistines. The most famous battle was that of the Valley of Elah, where Israelite and Philistine armies engaged in a standoff that they agreed should be settled by the combat of individual heroes from each side. Goliath, a nine-foot giant, represented Philistia, but no volunteer could be found in Israel until David happened on the scene bearing supplies for his army brothers. David's connection with Bethlehem (17:12, 15) again suggests either that his stay with Saul at Gibeah had been sporadic or, more likely, that it had come to an end for a while. This would explain why Saul seems to have failed to recognize David later on (17:56).

In any event David convinced Saul to let him represent Israel's forces. With only a sling and great confidence in God David put Goliath to death

(17:24–49). He decapitated the Philistine with the giant's own sword, which he then took, with the head, to the vicinity of Jerusalem (17:50–54; see 21:1, 8–9). Saul, having become reacquainted with David, determined then to make him part of his permanent retinue (17:55–58).

This choice would bring intense sorrow to both. Saul brought David to Gibeah, where he formed strong bonds of friendship with Saul's heir apparent, his son Jonathan.

On unfriendly terms (chapters 18–26). David soon became celebrated as a war hero, the object of adulation by the women of Israel, who sang of his exploits in terms much more enthusiastic than their praises of Saul (18:1–7). This so enraged Saul that he tried to kill David more than once. God was with David, however, and increasingly he became the favorite of Israel (18:8–16).

Saul had promised to give his daughter as wife to any man who could slay Goliath (17:25), so the time now came to deliver. First promising the elder daughter Merab, Saul reneged and offered Michal instead, but only on the condition that David could give evidence of having slain one hundred Philistines. This bizarre request was made in the hope that David might perish in the effort (18:17–25). But to Saul's surprise David was delighted by these terms, and in short order he doubled that tally and thus was free to take Michal as his wife (18:26–29). This course of action elevated David's esteem all the more in the eyes of his countrymen (18:30).

Saul then openly disclosed his intentions to do away with David, who found an ally and confidant in the king's son Jonathan (19:1–7). The pressure and danger became so intense, however, that David had to leave Gibeah and his family altogether and find refuge from Saul (19:8–17). Knowing that he would be safe with Samuel, David made his way to the aged prophet's home at Ramah. Saul found him there, but despite his best efforts to do so he could not capture him; for the Spirit of God overwhelmed him and his men, thus immobilizing them in a state of uncontrolled delirium (19:18–24).

David knew that he would be safe at Ramah only temporarily, so he met with Jonathan in order to plot further strategy (20:1–3). The next day was the beginning of a new month, and Saul would expect David to attend the festival marking the occasion (Num. 28:11–15). If his absence were excused, that would be a sign of Saul's favor; if, however, Saul was angry that David was missing, that would be a bad omen. In the latter case David told Jonathan to tell him the truth so that he could escape (1 Sam. 20:4–11).

Since it would be hazardous for Jonathan to be seen with David again, the two devised a plan by which Jonathan could communicate Saul's reaction to David. Jonathan would pretend to do archery practice, and if David's life was in danger Jonathan would tell the boy who fetched his arrows to look farther out. Otherwise he would instruct him to come nearer (20:12–23). Swearing to their covenant bonds once more, the two separated. Jonathan returned to the palace and informed Saul of David's plans to miss the festival. With great rage Saul turned on his son, reminding him that unless David died the throne would never be handed on to him. Saul then punctuated his wrath by trying to kill Jonathan with his spear (20:24–34).

Jonathan arrived at the unmistakable conclusion that the rift between Saul and David was permanent and irreparable. He therefore went to the prearranged meeting place and shot arrows out into the field. He then told the boy with him to go farther out to retrieve the arrows and then to return home with them. Once more embracing and pledging their mutual loyalty, Jonathan and David sadly parted, painfully aware that things would never be the same again (20:35–42).

Cut off from friend and family, David had to fend for himself (21:1). He had come to know Ahimelech, the high priest of the sanctuary at Nob, for he had taken Goliath's head and sword there sometime earlier (17:54). So he went first then to Nob—probably on the hill now known as Mount Scopus—for he needed food for himself and his men and also he needed a weapon. The latter was ready at hand, the sword of Goliath (21:8–9). As for food, all Ahimelech had was day-old showbread, but that could be eaten only if the men were ritually pure. David assured the priest that they were, so they ate of it despite its sacred character (21:5–6).

One of Saul's mercenaries, an Edomite named Doeg, happened to be there. He later disclosed to Saul what David had done at Nob and how Ahimelech had assisted him and his party of outlaws. David, sensing his imminent peril, left the country and found sanctuary among the Philistines of Gath. This was rather like leaping from the frying pan into the fire, for David had slain multitudes of Philistines in the past. Ironically he came now to Gath, the home of Goliath, whose sword he now carried for self-protection. Only by feigning madness did David escape with his life, for Achish, the ruler of Gath, shared the superstition that it was bad luck to kill a madman (21:10–15).

Achish had no need of more madmen, he said, so he sent David back to Judah, where he found refuge in caves at Adullam (perhaps modern-day Tell esh-Sheikh, between Jerusalem and Lachish). By then, word was out that David had taken up the lifestyle of a bandit, foraging as best he could from place to place. Before long others joined him, until he had a small army of four hundred men (22:1–2).

Knowing that his loved ones were in danger of guilt by association, David took them to Moab, the home of his great-grandmother, Ruth (22:3–4; see Ruth 1:1). Gad the prophet then told David to leave Adullam and find a hiding place in the forest of Hereth (1 Sam. 22:3–5). Saul's rage was continuing to build, and when he learned from Doeg that Ahimelech the priest had come to David's aid, he ordered that the priest and all his subordinates be put to death, despite the fact that they affirmed their innocence. Nob itself was destroyed along with all its inhabitants (22:6–19). Abiathar, a son of Ahimelech, escaped, however, and told David of the massacre. David then swore to make Abiathar his own priest, a role that eventually broadened to that of high priest in David's monarchy (22:20–23; 1 Kings 2:26–27).

Word of the purging of the priesthood seems to have severely altered David's strategy for some reason, for when he heard of Philistine attacks against his Judean countrymen at Keilah (probably modern-day Khirbet Qila, west of Hebron) he decided to go on the offensive, a decision sanctioned by his appeal to the Urim and Thummim in the hand of Abiathar (1 Sam. 23:1–6). This brought Saul into the conflict, for he heard that David was in Keilah, and he determined to apprehend him there (23:7–8). Again appealing to the ephod, that is, the Urim and Thummim, David received guidance from the Lord that the Keilahites would prove to be treacherous and that he and his men should flee before Saul arrived (23:9–14).

For one last time Jonathan made contact with David and assured him that in the end he would survive and, in fact, would become king of Israel. He himself would take a subservient position (23:15–18). Little did

Jonathan know that he would not live long enough for this part of his expectation to become a reality (see 31:2; 2 Sam. 1:17).

Again David was betrayed by fellow Judahites, this time at Ziph, five miles southeast of Hebron. Before Saul could make it to Ziph, David moved once more, this time to the Maon desert south of Hebron (modern-day Khirbet el-Ma'in). Saul pursued him there as well, but before he could find him he was called away to deal with a Philistine invasion (1 Sam. 23:19–27). David used this respite to find more secure quarters for his little army. He finally set out for the Dead Sea and found exactly what he needed at En Gedi with its many cliff-side caves (23:28–29).

Security even at En Gedi was not long-lasting. Somehow Saul learned that David was there, and Saul soon found the very caves in which David and his men were hiding. This time David had an opportunity to destroy his nemesis once and for all when he encountered Saul in an unguarded moment. David's opportunity was outweighed by his theology, however, for he recognized that Saul's kingship, though possible only by divine concession, was nevertheless sacred. David knew that if Saul were to die at all it would be at God's hands, not David's (24:1–7).

Saul must be made to understand this act of grace, however, so David disclosed his whereabouts to the king. Holding aloft the skirt of Saul's robe that he had cut off in the cave, he dramatically made clear that it could just as well have been Saul's head he was holding (24:8–15). The truth hit home like a sledgehammer. Crushed by his own guilt and by the enormity of David's forbearance, Saul at last was forced to confess that David, indeed, would be king someday. All he asked was that in that day David would smile kindly on Saul's offspring (24:16–22).

After a brief note about Samuel's death (25:1), the narration continues with the account of David's exile in the Judean deserts. Leaving En Gedi, David returned to the region of Maon, a place he had frequented before (23:25). For the time being Saul left him alone, but life was hard enough in that harsh wilderness. Food and drink were in short supply, so David was forced to turn to the largesse of his fellow tribesmen to sustain himself and his entourage. This was not asking too much, for David had provided protection (25:16) and had never extorted supplies from them (25:7).

A rich livestock owner, Nabal by name, had especially benefited, so David asked him for help, a request that was brusquely denied (25:2–11). Enraged by this lack of gratitude and hospitality, David urged his men to attack Nabal, a plan that was thwarted only by Nabal's beautiful wife, Abigail, who persuaded David that her husband acted as he did only because, as his name indicated, he was a fool (Hebrew, *nābāl,* "fool," 25:25). What's more, she provided what he had refused—bread, wine, sheep, grain, raisins, and figs (25:18). Thus she became the means of Nabal's escape from death.

When David and Abigail met, she fell prostrate before him with earnest intercession on behalf of her foolish husband (25:23–31). David responded with deep gratitude, both for the provisions and for Abigail's wisdom in preventing what surely would have been the massacre of Nabal's household. When Abigail returned home and told her husband of his narrow escape, the very thought of it brought a heart attack and death shortly thereafter (25:32–38). Deeply impressed by both her beauty and her wisdom, David took Abigail as his wife (25:39–42), an arrangement complicated by the fact that he already had one wife and would later add another (25:43–44). Polygamy, even by David, has no biblical sanction. It merely reflects the unfortunate accommodation by believers at times to the mores of a fallen, pagan culture.

Following this episode the Ziphites, who had already displayed the most hateful treachery toward their kinsman David (see 23:19–23), tipped off Saul that David was in their vicinity (26:1–5). In what would prove to be his last effort to apprehend his rival, Saul moved against David deep into the Negev desert. He set up his camp, but David soon discovered where it was and, with a nephew, Abishai, made a bold penetration of the Israelite defensive perimeter. To prove Saul's vulnerability, David approached the sleeping king despite the presence of Abner and other bodyguards. Though Abishai would have slain Saul then and there, David only took his spear and water bottle for, as always, he recognized that Saul was the anointed of the Lord with whom God Himself would deal (26:6–12).

Once at a safe distance, David called out to Saul and Abner, taunting them with the reality that Saul's head could have been removed as easily as was his spear (26:13–16). In a final affirmation of his innocence, David asked why Saul had been so relentless in pursuit of him since the Lord clearly was not in the matter (26:17–20). Then, perhaps for the first time,

Saul was forced to confess in true contrition and repentance that God had His hand on David and that inevitably he would prevail and rule over Israel (26:21–25). Sadly, he came to understand all too late that the sovereign purposes of God may be resisted but can never be overcome.

> *Personal ambition and private vengeance seem endemic to human nature, even among believers. David taught by example that God alone has the right to promote and demote. The biblical truth is that vengeance belongs to the Lord (Deut. 32:35; Rom. 12:19), and it is His prerogative to do what He will with those who call Him Lord (9:19–21).*

D. Saul's Death (chapters 27–31)

David at Ziklag (chapter 27). David was not so optimistic about Saul's pledges, however, and so he went a second time to the Philistine city of Gath, hoping to find refuge (27:1–4). The previous time he had convinced Achish, the Philistine ruler, that he was a madman (21:10–15), but this time David appealed to the rupture between himself and Saul as a basis for forming a league with Achish against their common foe, Israel. Clearly persuaded, Achish treated David as a vassal ruler, giving him the town of Ziklag as a fiefdom (27:5–7). To prove his loyalty, David undertook raids against Judah's perennial enemies in the south, pretending to Achish that he had attacked and decimated his own fellow Judeans (27:8–12). The goods he seized he presumably bestowed on these very countrymen (see 30:26–31), thus buying their favors against the time when he would claim his kingship over them (27:8–12).

Saul at Endor (chapter 28). David's pact with Achish brought with it unforeseen consequences, however, for the Philistines set up a plan for a military showdown with Israel, thus placing David on the horns of a dilemma. By treaty he must be loyal to the Philistines. By ethnic, tribal, and theological heritage, on the other hand, he must be loyal to Israel (28:1–2).

Meanwhile, Saul, having gone to the place of attack in the Jezreel Valley, found himself without guidance as to his course of action, for Samuel the prophet was dead and Saul had banned all means of pagan divination (28:3–7). One survivor of his purge, however, was a witch from the nearby town of Endor. Disguised as best a seven-foot-tall man could be, Saul went to Endor and asked the woman to conjure up the spirit of Samuel from Sheol, a request that violated the Law of Moses (Deut. 18:9–12) as well as his own edict. Assured that no harm would come to her, the woman employed her occultic powers, and to her great amazement she saw a spirit rise before her (1 Sam. 28:8–14). The amazement was because the apparition came not because of her power but by the power of God.

Whether the figure that arose was actually Samuel or just a vision of Samuel is incidental to the narrative. The point is that God spoke to Saul in this manner, reminding him of his disobedience and of the Lord's choice of David to be king. Even more distressing was the message that Saul and his sons would soon join Samuel in death (28:15–19). Devastated by the news, Saul could hardly stand to his feet. After a hearty meal, however, he regained his strength and set his face toward destiny (28:20–25).

David's return to Ziklag (chapters 29–30). The two mortal enemies squared off against each other in the Valley of Jezreel, with David in the uncomfortable position of having to fight against his own people. His quandary was soon relieved, however, for the Philistine rulers prevailed over their compatriot Achish of Gath, persuading him that David could hardly be counted on in the heat of battle. Surely, they said, David's natural instincts would force him to side with his own people (29:1–5). Reluctantly Achish agreed and sent David—much to David's relief—back to his home in Ziklag (29:6–11).

But when David returned, he saw to his horror that his city had been raided by Amalekites, who had burned it to the ground and had taken property and persons with them, including David's wives (30:1–6). He therefore sought divine direction by means of the priestly ephod (the Urim and Thummim; 23:9), and the Lord permitted him to pursue the Amalekites to their campsites. When they arrived at the Wadi Besor (just south of Gaza), they divided into units of four hundred and two hundred men, the latter to remain behind to guard the supplies (30:7–10).

David was stymied at this point, unable to determine the whereabouts of the enemy. A wandering Egyptian provided intelligence, however, leading them to the Amalekite bivouac (30:11–15). Without hesitation David attacked. Only a few Amalekites escaped and all the people and possessions of Ziklag were recovered intact (30:16–20). On his return to Besor, David shared with the two hundred troops there the booty he had acquired from the Amalekites. Over the protests of the four hundred who had actually done the fighting, David established the policy that prevailed thereafter that those who do their duties behind the lines must share equally with those in the front lines (30:21–25).

When he returned to Ziklag, David made the politically astute move of distributing Amalekite spoil among all the settlements of Judah. Listed last is Hebron, for it was at Hebron that he would establish his first capital as king over all Israel (30:26–31; 2 Sam. 2:1–4).

The battle of Gilboa (chapter 31). Back at the battle scene in Israel, the Philistines quickly gained the upper hand, pursuing Saul and his sons to Mount Gilboa. The latter were slain, and Saul, knowing that he could not long hold out, asked his own attendant to kill him. This he would not do, so Saul fell on his sword, ending his life by suicide (31:1–6). This cut out the heart of Israelite resistance, thereby enabling the Philistines to control the entire Jezreel region. They decapitated Saul's remains, impaling his body on the wall of Beth Shan and taking his armor (and perhaps his head) as a trophy of victory back to their pagan temples (31:7–10). Out of gratitude to Saul, who in his first public act as king had delivered them from Ammonite siege, the people of Jabesh Gilead, just across the Jordan River, removed Saul's body from the wall and gave it a proper burial in their own city (31:11–13; see 11:1–13).

2 SAMUEL
The Davidic Promise and Prospects

AUTHOR

*M*any of the issues of introduction that concern 1 Samuel pertain to 2 Samuel as well and therefore need not be repeated here. Thus the unity of the whole Book of Samuel as attested to by both ancient tradition and internal evidence presupposes common authorship and/or composition, probably, as suggested earlier, by Nathan or Gad or both (1 Chron. 29:29–30). Nothing in 2 Samuel suggests that it was written later than 960 B.C. or so, the early years of Solomon's reign.

Such views of authorship and composition do not preclude the likelihood of sources having been collected and, under the direction of the Holy Spirit, included in the book. First Samuel 16 through 2 Samuel 5 is a narrative describing the rise of David to kingship. Shorter segments are the ark narrative (2 Sam. 6), the covenant promise of a Davidic dynasty (2 Sam. 7), a summary of David's military engagements (8:1–14), and a list of his public officials (8:15–18). The next large block is the so-called Succession Narrative (2 Sam. 9–20 and 1 Kings 1–2). The intervening material consists of narratives about the Gibeonites (2 Sam. 21:1–14) and Philistines (21:15–22), a Davidic psalm of praise (chapter 22), David's "last words" (23:1–7), a list of heroes (23:8–39), and the story of David's census and its resultant punishment (chapter 24).

PURPOSE

Second Samuel records the fact that David became the legitimate king of Israel because of being chosen by the Lord. The book intends, then, to show how all this came to pass. But, as many scholars have shown, its purpose is also to display the faithfulness of the Lord in ensuring the continuation of David's dynasty despite his many sins and the sins of individuals associated with him. The story of 2 Samuel properly ends not with its last chapter but with 1 Kings 2, where Solomon is said to be firmly established on David's throne as the first member of his dynastic succession.

A more important purpose than these is to introduce the Davidic Covenant, that instrument by which the Lord disclosed His sovereign choice of a human ruler through whom He would exercise dominion over all His creation both historically and in the end times. The theological import of this purpose will be addressed presently.

THEOLOGICAL EMPHASES

The overriding theological theme of 2 Samuel is the Davidic Covenant, the instrument of promise and commitment whereby the Lord would bring to pass in human government His pledges to the patriarchs about a nation (Gen. 17:6), a dynasty of rulers (17:6, 16), and a land (17:8; see also 15:18–21). These would find expression not only in David and his time, however, but in the future with David's royal Descendant (Jesus Christ) whose reign would never end (2 Sam. 7:12–13). The book describes how that fulfillment took place, a process not unmarked by sin and setbacks but one that nevertheless resulted in the enthronement of Solomon, the first of those many whose line would eventually reach climactic perfection in Jesus Christ (Matt 1:6–16).

OUTLINE

    I. David at Hebron (chapters 1–4)
        A. Lament for Saul and Jonathan (chapter 1)
        B. Battle between David and Abner (chapter 2)

    C. Conflict between Joab and Abner (chapter 3)

    D. Death of Ish-Bosheth (chapter 4)

II. David's Prosperity (chapters 5–10)

    A. The Capital at Jerusalem (chapter 5)

    B. The Return of the Ark (chapter 6)

    C. The Davidic Covenant (chapter 7)

    D. David's Campaigns and Officials (chapter 8)

    E. David's Kindness to Saul's Family (chapter 9)

    F. Abuse against David's Ambassadors (chapter 10)

III. David's Sin and Internal Problems (chapters 11–21)

    A. David's Adultery (chapter 11)

    B. Nathan's Rebuke and David's Punishment (chapter 12)

    C. The Sin and Murder of Amnon (chapter 13)

    D. The Estrangement of Absalom (chapter 14)

    E. Absalom's Revolution (chapters 15–18)

    F. David's Return to Power (chapter 19–20)

    G. The Slaughter and Burial of Saul's Sons (21:1–14)

    H. Miscellaneous Philistine Encounters (21:15–22)

IV. David's Final Years (chapters 22–24)

    A. David's Song (chapter 22)

    B. David's Farewell Address (23:1–7)

    C. David's Heroes (23:8–39)

    D. David's Census and Its Punishment (chapter 24)

I. DAVID AT HEBRON (CHAPTERS 1–4)

The death of Saul removed the only obstacle to David's installation as king of Israel except for Saul's only surviving son, Ish-Bosheth, and his mentor Abner, who continued to hold at least nominal power. The tribe of Judah was solidly in support of David, however, because he was a son of that tribe and he had also done much to gain its favor (1 Sam. 30:26–31). Once the leaders of Judah were aware of Saul's demise, they proceeded to acclaim David as their ruler and to localize his kingship at Hebron, the chief city of the region.

A. Lament for Saul and Jonathan (chapter 1)

David, having just returned to Ziklag from his campaign against the Amalekites (1 Sam. 30:1), received the tragic news of the death of Saul and his sons from, ironically, an Amalekite messenger who, in fact, claimed to have killed Saul with his own hands (2 Sam. 1:1–10). To the amazement of the deceitful braggart, David was not at all grateful for his having killed Saul. In fact, David viewed Saul until the very end as the anointed of the Lord against whom no human hand should be raised (1:14; 1 Sam. 24:6; 26:9). The penalty for such a heinous breach of divine purpose was instant death, this time, not for what the Amalekite actually did but for what he claimed to have done (2 Sam. 1:11–16).

David, who had often played and sung soothing music in times of Saul's madness (1 Sam. 16:14–23), now composed a lament to express his and Israel's sorrow at the death of Saul and his sons (2 Sam. 1:17–27). Its title was "The Bow," a composition the narrator said was also part of an anthology known as the Book of Jashar (1:18; see also Josh. 10:13). In it David, with pure and sincere brokenheartedness, acknowledged that Saul, "the glory of Israel," had died, but he cautioned the people against publicizing the fact lest the Philistines rejoice in it (2 Sam. 1:19–20). He then uttered an imprecation against Gilboa, the place of the tragedy (1:21–22), as though it bore some culpability. Then he urged the Israelites to weep for Saul and Jonathan because of all the good they had done (1:23–25). And in a most personal word, he reflected on the deep love and friendship he and Jonathan had enjoyed (1:26–27).

B. Battle between David and Abner (chapter 2)

Abner was a cousin of Saul (1 Sam. 14:50) and therefore uncle to Ish-Bosheth, Saul's only surviving son and heir apparent to the throne of Israel. Acting out of personal self-interest, Abner arranged for Ish-Bosheth's coronation, knowing full well that his weak nephew would be only a puppet through whom he himself could rule (2 Sam. 2:8–9).

Meanwhile David was installed as king over Judah at Hebron (2:1–4a) and offered his services obliquely to all of Israel (2:4b–7). For seven years (around 1011–1004 B.C.) the kingdom remained divided in this manner, until at last both sides decided to settle the issue of national kingship by a contest of champions (2:12–17). David's contingent prevailed, and Abner and his forces retreated in disarray.

Three of David's nephews—Joab, Abishai, and Asahel (1 Chron. 2:13–17)—were not content, however, and chased after the fleeing Abner. Asahel caught up with the older man but underestimated Abner's prowess and died at the point of his spear (2 Sam. 2:18–23). Joab and Abishai kept up the chase but recognized that they were no match for Abner and his allies. They had to reconcile themselves to a stalemate, at least for the time (2:24–29). With sorrow Joab buried his brother Asahel, all the time plotting his revenge (2:30–32).

C. Conflict between Joab and Abner (chapter 3)

This chapter begins with the ominous note that David's "house" (that is, Judah) became stronger and stronger, and Saul's "house" (that is, Israel) weaker and weaker (3:1). Evidence of David's success is seen in his political alliances and in the increasing size of his family (3:2–5). Israel's weakness is apparent in the struggle between Ish-Bosheth and Abner, who made clear his designs on the kingship (3:6–7). Charged with this allegation, Abner determined to cast his lot with David and thus deliver Israel over to him (3:8–11).

Abner, true to his threat, notified David of his desire for rapprochement, an arrangement David accepted on condition that Abner restore his wife Michal to him (3:12–16; see 1 Sam. 18:28). Once this was done, Abner used his good offices in Israel to persuade the nation to make a covenant with David and to submit to his lordship (2 Sam. 3:17–21). Joab, Abner's mortal enemy, had been gone from Hebron all this time, and when he found out that David had made league with Abner, he was furious (3:22–26). Feigning noble intentions, Joab sent for Abner to return, and when the two met, Joab murdered him in revenge for the death of his brother Asahel (3:27–30).

One suspects that Joab had other motives as well, including his fear that Abner might preempt his own role as commander of David's troops. This fear was only compounded by David's reaction to this bloody turn of events. As he had mourned for Saul and Jonathan, so now he mourned for Abner, a reaction that surely left Joab stunned. The people as a whole were pleased with David, not only in that matter but in the whole tenor and tone of his leadership (3:31–39).

D. Death of Ish-Bosheth (chapter 4)

Though Abner was clearly a threat to the incompetent Ish-Bosheth, Abner's death left Saul's successor fearful for the future. That fear was well-founded, for two assassins set on him while he was napping, slew him, and took his head as a grisly trophy to King David (4:1–3, 5–8). It seems these murderers had learned nothing from David's treatment of the Amalekite who had claimed to be responsible for Saul's death (1:13–16). Citing that instance (4:10), David ordered that these too should pay with their lives (4:9–12). To David, a son of Saul was to be honored almost as one anointed by the Lord.

II. DAVID'S PROSPERITY (CHAPTERS 5–10)

David's reign may conveniently be divided into two parts: before his great sin with Bathsheba and afterward. This section reviews those glory days when David experienced blessing after blessing, victory after victory, and divine visitation after divine visitation. The high point of it all was God's revelation of the Davidic Covenant, in which He informed David of all His saving intentions by means of the dynastic succession, climaxing in the perfect Ruler. David neither earned the right to receive such revelation and privilege nor could his sin later on cancel it out, for the initiative was the Lord's and His word must stand firm.

A. The Capital at Jerusalem (chapter 5)

With virtually the last vestige of the house of Saul out of the picture, the need to fill the power vacuum in the north was acute. David was firmly in place at Hebron, he was hailed as a hero in the days of Saul's monarchy, and there was general recognition that God willed that he be the king over the whole nation. Israel's leaders therefore went to Hebron to crown him king (5:1–3). He had reigned there for seven and a half years and would reign over all Israel for an additional thirty-three years (5:4–5).

Hebron, a Judahite city, would never work as a national capital, however, for such a choice would smack of regional favoritism. For the same reason a northern site would be unsuitable. The logical solution was to find a neutral place between Judah and Israel, and that could be only one city—Jerusalem. There was only one problem. For centuries Jerusalem had remained in Jebusite hands (Judg. 1:8, 21) and its defensibility seemed to make it an unobtainable prize. Undeterred, David took the city, changed its name to "the City of David," and commenced major construction activity in and around it (2 Sam. 5:6–10).

Further evidence of David's increasing power and prosperity were his alliance with King Hiram of Tyre, whose contractors erected a royal palace for David, and the enlargement of his harem and proliferation of offspring (5:11–16). This did not go unchallenged, however, especially by the Philistines. Stung by his defection from them and alarmed by his growing power base, they attacked David in successive campaigns, but all to no avail. God clearly was showing His favor (5:17–25).

B. The Return of the Ark (chapter 6)

Among the structures David built was a tabernacle in which to house the ark of the covenant (6:17). That symbol of God's presence had remained at Kiriath Jearim (called Baalah of Judah in 6:2, KJV), for nearly one hundred years (1 Sam. 7:1–2), eighty years since Samuel's conclave at Mizpah (7:5). Oblivious of proper protocol in handling the ark (see Num. 4:5–6, 15, 17–20), David and his procession laid it on a cart for the ten-mile trip up to Jerusalem (2 Sam. 6:1–5). Along the way the oxen stumbled, and to keep the ark from falling off, a well-intentioned but ritually disqualified man named Uzzah seized it to prevent such a calamity (6:6). Good motives notwithstanding, judgment was swift and sure. Uzzah died on the spot and David, chagrined and terrified, left the ark where it was for three more months (6:7–11).

The reason for God's severe displeasure is not difficult to find. God's work (and even worship) must be done in God's way, in line with His instructions. The ark was too holy for even His priests and Levites to touch it. It must be carried by them on staffs inserted through rings in its corners. When David returned to move the ark once more, he did so with utmost care. Donning priestly garments in line with his role as a Melchizedekian priest (see Gen. 14:18–20; Ps. 110:4; Heb. 5:5–10), David entered Jerusalem with joy and triumph, depositing the ark in the sacred tent he had erected there (2 Sam. 6:12–15).

His wife Michal observed what was to her his shameless celebrating and dancing, and she chided him for it. Not to be overlooked is the note that she was the daughter of Saul (6:20). The implication seems clear: She was jealous for her father's fame and could not stand to see her husband take it on himself for whatever purpose. David had to remind her that God had chosen him even over her father in line with His eternal plan. Sadly, their dispute over the matter resulted in a rupture between them that never was healed (6:16–23).

C. The Davidic Covenant (chapter 7)

The highlight of David's life was God's revelation to him of His covenant purposes. Through no merit of his own he was the object of divine grace, the one after God's own heart (1 Sam. 13:14; Acts 13:22). The time had now come for the reality of what had up to this point been only promised (Gen. 49:10; Num. 24:17; 1 Sam. 16:1, 13). The impetus for the covenant revelation was, ironically, David's desire to build a substantial temple for the Lord, not just the temporary tabernacle he had already installed (2 Sam. 7:1–2). Through the prophet Nathan, however, the Lord made clear that rather than David making a house for Him, *He* would make one for David, that is, a royal dynasty (7:11). David's name would become famous (7:9), and Israel, the nation over which he ruled, would forever be established in the land (7:10).

Even more astounding than all this, the Davidic dynasty would endure without end (7:16). Solomon, David's immediate successor, would build a temple for the Lord (7:14–16). If he or any of his descendants sinned they would be punished, but God would forever keep His promise regarding the dynasty (7:12–17). All this was more than David could comprehend. How could one who had come from such lowly circumstances be so favored? How could the blessings promised to him have such far-flung implications? The answers lay only in the promises and gracious elective purposes of God (7:18–21).

> *Sometimes life's greatest blessings flow out of its profoundest disappointments. David wanted nothing more in life than to build a temple for the Lord, but God said no! This crushing denial was then followed by a stunning word of promise—God would build him a house! Our willingness to do what little we can for Him will be repaid many times over by the outpouring of His lavish and surprising acts of grace both now and in the ages to come.*

The incomparable God of Israel had redeemed that nation from Egypt to make them His servant people forever (7:22–24). On the basis of that sacred history—and God's faithfulness to the nation—David could be confident that the covenant made now with him would also come to fruition. What had begun with sheer amazement at the eternal plan of God, (7:18) ended with David's declaration of confidence in God's intention to fulfill His promises (7:29).

D. David's Campaigns and Officials (chapter 8)

The narrative is interrupted here to provide a catalog of David's military exploits and a list of his military and civilian officials. The point is not to glorify war but to show that God gives victory over the enemies of those who love and serve Him. He is the One who "gave David victory everywhere he went" (8:6, 14). These victories over the Philistines, Moabites, Arameans, and others (8:1–8) resulted in the payment of monetary tribute to David (8:2, 6, 10) and also their incorporation into what might be called an "Israelite empire." For the first time Israel's territory extended beyond its allotted borders.

David's reign was marked by justice and righteousness (8:15). To ensure that, David put in place a number of trusted public officials who served as military officers, chroniclers, priests, and scribes (8:16–18). The reference to David's own sons as priests (8:18) has to do not with the Aaronic priesthood served by Zadok and Ahimelech but that of Melchizedek, with which David had already become identified (6:12–15).

E. David's Kindness to Saul's Family (chapter 9)

The solidifying of David's rule enabled him to give attention to matters important to him but till then not possible to resolve. Not least was his concern for the offspring of Saul, a concern he had told Jonathan he would keep uppermost in his mind (1 Sam. 20:12–16). After a thorough search David learned of Jonathan's son Mephibosheth, a young man crippled in his feet from having fallen from his nurse's arms when he was but a five-year-old child (2 Sam. 4:4). Mephibosheth was some distance away, in Lo Debar, east of the Jordan (17:27), but David sent for him and promised him lifetime security because of the vows David had made to Jonathan years earlier (9:1–8). Saul's own servant Ziba and his family would from then on be responsible for tending to Mephibosheth's every need (9:9–13).

F. Abuse against David's Ambassadors (chapter 10)

Among David's allies at first was Nahash, king of Ammon. When David heard that his friend had died, he sent a delegation to Rabbah, the Ammonite capital, to convey his condolences. Hanun, successor to his father's throne, listened to the false testimony of his counselors who said the Israelites were on a spy mission, and so Hanun treated them most shamefully by cutting off half their beards and shortening their cloaks (10:1–4). Embarrassed by their immodesty, David's men refused to return home until their beards were fully grown (10:5).

Hanun knew full well that such a breach of international relationships would not go unrequited, so he quickly formed alliances with the Arameans of various city-states (10:6–8). Meanwhile Joab had led Israel's army to the field of battle, encouraging his brother Abishai and other commanders to trust God and act like men (10:9–12). With little effort, it seems, they repelled the Aramean-Ammonite coalition and returned victorious to Jerusalem (10:13–14). Not easily dissuaded, the Arameans formed an even larger force, with some troops even coming from beyond the Euphrates River. But again Israel prevailed, this time with David himself in command (10:15–18). Having learned their lesson, the Arameans became tributary to David (see 8:6) and resolved never again to go to Ammon's aid (10:19).

III. DAVID'S SIN AND INTERNAL PROBLEMS (CHAPTER 11–21)

If the first half of the story of David in 2 Samuel rises to a crescendo with the accounts of his domestic and foreign successes, the second half makes a dizzying plunge from that lofty height and becomes a litany of personal and national failure broken only here and there by glimpses of renewal and reversal. But despite human failing there was heavenly forgiveness. The sorry story of sin and its inevitable aftermath finds more than a match in the restorative grace of God, whose ultimate objectives will always come to the fore.

A. David's Adultery (chapter 11)

With the onset of the dry season David sent his troops to Rabbah (now Amman, Jordan), capital of the Ammonite kingdom, to finish the campaign he had begun earlier (10:14). This time David stayed home, a decision innocent perhaps in itself but one that would prove to be his undoing. On a certain day he saw his beautiful neighbor Bathsheba bathing, and against his better judgment he seduced her, leaving her pregnant (11:1–5). To cover up his mistake, he called her husband, Uriah, back from the battlefield, almost begging him to go home to enjoy his wife (11:6–13). When this failed, David sent Uriah back to battle with a note ordering Joab to place Uriah in a vulnerable spot where he would likely be attacked (11:14–21). The strategy worked and David soon learned that he was not only an adulterer, but also a murderer. The narrative ends with the disarming understatement that "the thing David had done was evil in the sight of the LORD" (11:27).

B. Nathan's Rebuke and David's Punishment (chapter 12)

The prophet Nathan, whom God had sent to bear the good news about the Davidic Covenant (7:1–17), appears now as the messenger of God's displeasure. After relating the parable about the poor man's lamb (12:1–6), Nathan identified David as the rich man who had stolen that lamb; that is, he had stolen Bathsheba from her husband and, beyond that, had orchestrated his death (12:7–9). For these terrible sins, David's family would be visited with similar judgment (12:10–12).

With profoundest remorse David confessed and heard the undeserved words of forgiveness (12:13; see Pss. 32; 51). But forgiveness did not annul consequences. His and Bathsheba's illegitimate son died despite David's earnest intercession, an outcome he accepted with amazing equanimity (2 Sam. 12:14–23). As though to demonstrate that grace is greater than sin, the Lord allowed Bathsheba to become pregnant again. This time she gave birth to a son named Solomon, a name based on šālôm, "peace." He received another name as well, Jedidiah, "loved by the Lord," a sign that God was not through with David and his dynasty (12:24–25).

In due time Joab captured Rabbah of Ammon but rather than take credit for its fall himself, he invited David to come and complete the conquest (12:26–31). This he did, and most successfully. The pity is that David had not gone to war the first time around, thus avoiding the temptations of the flesh that spelled his moral downfall.

C. The Sin and Murder of Amnon (chapter 13)

The next repercussion of David's sin arose from within his dysfunctional family, an appropriate description in view of the problems attendant to polygamy and its resultant offspring. David's eldest son, Absalom, had a full sister, Tamar, who innocently incited her half-brother Amnon with lust (13:1–6). Pretending to be ill and in need of her care, Amnon prevailed on David to allow her to tend to him, a flaw in judgment that resulted in her shameful rape (13:7–19).

Absalom could not allow his sister's honor to be violated so unjustly. Biding his time, he arranged a sheep-shearing festival two years later, to which he invited the unsuspecting Amnon. Absalom's servants plied Amnon with wine, and when he was sufficiently drunk, they put him to death (13:20–29). When

David heard the news, he was devastated, mainly because of the erroneous report that all his sons had died (13:30–33). But Amnon's demise alone caused him great sorrow, so much so that Absalom knew that he must go into exile in order to evade David's anticipated revenge (13:34–38). Little did Absalom appreciate David's capacity for forgiveness. Once he had grieved for his dead son, Amnon, David yearned for the return of the son who had slain his brother (13:39).

D. The Estrangement of Absalom (chapter 14)

Noting David's changed attitude toward Absalom, Joab put in motion a plan to effect a reunion between the two. He engaged the services of a wise woman from Tekoa (the home also of the prophet Amos, just south of Bethlehem; Amos 1:1) who appeared before the king in mourning apparel. When David asked the cause of her grief, she related the sad story that one of her sons had killed another and now the family avengers were seeking the murderer's life (2 Sam. 14:1–7).

Touched deeply by this poor woman's plight, David assured her that her surviving son would live under royal protection (14:8–11). She then revealed to David that it was he to whom she referred and that it was he who must forgive and forget the wrongdoings of his estranged son (14:12–17). The king surmised correctly that Joab was the instigator of this plot (14:18–20), a stratagem that he now endorsed by sending Joab to bring Absalom back home (14:21–24). When Absalom came back, however, he kept his distance from his father for two full years, mainly because David showed no signs of initiating further contact. Meanwhile the narrator commented on Absalom's physical attractiveness and enlargement of family, hints of troubling times to come (14:25–27). As for Joab, he failed to do his part in achieving father-son reconciliation until Absalom burned his barley fields, thereby getting his attention (14:28–33).

E. Absalom's Revolution (chapters 15–18)

The sloppy and insensitive way the whole matter was handled only increased Absalom's antagonism toward his father. By display of personal interest in the well-being of citizens who felt deprived of justice, Absalom slowly but surely gained popular support (15:1–6). At the opportune moment he went to Hebron, where he met with collaborators who publicly proclaimed him king in place of his father (15:7–12). By the time David heard of the insurrection, it was too late. He had either been unaware of Absalom's machinations or had underestimated their importance. In any event he felt temporary exile from the country was his only recourse (15:13–18).

David's most loyal troops went with him, as did the priests Zadok and Abiathar bearing the ark of the covenant (15:19–29). In a sense the presence of the ark represented the presence of God. David felt this to be presumptuous, however, for if God was with him in truth, he would return to Jerusalem anyway in God's good time. He did not need the ark to provide that assurance. Zadok and Abiathar therefore returned the ark to the tabernacle on Mount Zion (15:29).

To add insult to injury, David learned that his longtime counselor, Ahithophel, had joined forces with Absalom. He therefore sent a loyal friend, Hushai, back to Jerusalem to undermine Ahithophel's counsel and also to gain information for David about Absalom's plans and policies (15:30–37). As he crossed the Mount of Olives, David met Ziba, Mephibosheth's servant, who told him—falsely as it turned out (19:24–30)—that Mephibosheth also had gone over to Absalom (16:1–4). His disappointment at this news was exacerbated by his encounter with Shimei, a relative of Saul, who threw stones and heaped verbal abuse at David as the king's party made its painful trek to the east. Even this, David saw in a positive light, for he said that perhaps God would turn the cursing into blessing (16:5–14).

Back in Jerusalem Absalom confronted Hushai, who soon persuaded him that he had defected from David and would now serve Absalom. For the interim, however, Absalom followed the advice of Ahithophel, who suggested that he make David's concubines his own, thus asserting publicly that he was now the legitimate ruler of all Israel (16:20–23). Ahithophel also advised Absalom to launch an immediate attack against David before the latter had a chance to build up his forces (17:1–3). Before Absalom could act on this counsel, however, Hushai offered a counterproposal, namely, that Absalom should bide his time until he could enlist a larger army and overwhelm David by sheer force of numbers (17:4–14).

Viewing this as a better plan, Absalom postponed pursuit of David for the moment. David's spies in Jerusalem soon got word to the king about the delay, enabling David to leave his temporary hiding place for more secure quarters in Mahanaim, east of the Jordan (17:15–26). When Ahithophel realized his counsel had been spurned, he took his own life out of sheer frustration (17:21–23). David found warm hospitality in Mahanaim (17:27–29), but he continued to be in danger for Absalom and his army had also arrived in Transjordania (17:24, 26).

In preparation for the inevitable conflict, David divided his small regiment into three parts. The commanders of these companies were given strict instruction not to do Absalom any harm (18:1–5). Unfortunately Absalom, riding through a dense thicket, became entangled in low-lying oak boughs from which he could not quickly escape. Joab was directed to the scene and without a second thought he ran three javelins through Absalom's heart (18:6–15).

After some indecision as to how or even whether David should be notified, runners were dispatched with the news that David's son and royal rival was dead (18:16–32). The reason for Joab's ambivalence was his past experiences of similar circumstances. David seemed to have a way of rejoicing at the calamities of his friends and mourning the death of his enemies—or so Joab, at least, interpreted it (19:6; see 1:17; 3:31–34). He was not surprised, then, when David once more lamented the death of one who had sought to harm him (18:33).

F. David's Return to Power (chapters 19–20)

This time Joab had had enough of David's apparent disregard for those who best tried to serve him, and he lashed out at the king with words of recrimination and advice. The only way David could regain the confidence of the people, Joab said, was for him to pay more attention to them and their needs (19:1–8). Strong talk about rejecting David's return had already begun to emerge, especially in the north (19:9–10). David therefore undertook a campaign of reconciliation, beginning in his own country, Judah. He went so far as to promise Amasa, whom Absalom had made commander of his army, that he would now lead David's army in place of Joab (19:11–15).

David's efforts to regain a following in the north were even more demanding of diplomatic skill. On his return to the west, he encountered a delegation of Benjamites, members of Saul's own household (19:16–20). Among them was Shimei, the same man who had stoned and reviled David earlier (see 16:5–8). Amazingly, David received and forgave him, an act that clearly had at least some political overtones. Abishai, always quick to use the sword on David's behalf, would have done so again against Shimei had David not intervened (19:21–23).

Mephibosheth appeared next, and when David asked him why he had remained in Jerusalem and on Absalom's side, the poor cripple pleaded for mercy. He had been unable to travel but, more important, his servant, Ziba, had lied about his disloyalty (see 16:3–4). Ziba had hoped to seize all of Mephibosheth's estate by this means, but now that his treachery was exposed he was forced to return half of what he had taken (19:24–30). David allowed Ziba to keep half of the estate only because he was a Benjamite and David was trying to win that tribe especially back to his rule.

A large company of Gileadites had accompanied David as far as the Jordan River so as to give him a proper farewell. One of them, Barzillai, had provided hospitality to the king in his dark days of exile, so David invited him to Jerusalem where he could live out his days in peace and prosperity. Barzillai asked to be excused from such a generous offer for he was old and wanted to be buried with his fathers in his own land (19:31–39).

David had anticipated grave difficulty in reclaiming his throne, so he hardly expected the overwhelmingly favorable reception he experienced when he arrived at Gilgal. But there was a downside even to this, for both Israel and Judah tried to lay claim to having the greater loyalty to David, with Judah pressing the matter more effectively (19:40–43). This so offended certain Benjamites, that is, partisans of Saul, that they made a declaration of independence from David and Judah (20:1–2).

David therefore went to Jerusalem, formally reclaimed his kingship (20:3), and ordered Amasa to march north to put down the rebellion. Along the way Amasa encountered Joab who, jealous for his old job as commander (19:13), stabbed Amasa to death (20:4–10a). Joab then took up the chase of the rebels until he arrived at a place called Abel Beth Maacah, just west of Dan (20:10b–14). Sheba, the leader of the Benjamite faction, had taken refuge in a fortress there. A wise woman, fearing that Joab was about to destroy the whole place for the sake of one man, agreed to toss Sheba's head over the battlements if Joab would desist. True to her word, the deed was done, and Joab returned triumphantly to Jerusalem (20:15–22).

G. The Slaughter and Burial of Saul's Sons (21:1–14)

At some point in the past Saul had massacred the Gibeonites, a Canaanite people within his own Benjamite borders (21:1). This was particularly heinous and unforgivable because Joshua had made a covenant with these people centuries earlier, although under devious circumstances (Josh. 9:3–27). Man may forget but God does not, so the Lord at last brought judgment to Israel for Saul's sin. When David asked the Gibeonite survivors what vengeance would satisfy them, they said that nothing but the execution of seven of Saul's sons (male descendants) would do (2 Sam. 21:2–6).

> David, though flawed in many ways, is a model of gracious forgiveness of those who had wronged him. This was particularly true of his relationship with Saul and his offspring. With no one holding him to account or even expecting or understanding such magnanimity, David, motivated only by his own tender spirit, modeled what Paul would later teach about overcoming evil with good (Rom. 12:20–21).

Mephibosheth was spared because of David's special protection, but seven others were impaled near a rocky ledge. The mother of two of them remained nearby to protect their unburied corpses (21:7–10). This grisly scene reminded David that the remains of Saul and Jonathan had never been retrieved from Jabesh Gilead and given proper burial in their home town Gibeah. He therefore brought back their bones to the family sepulcher so they could be buried with their ancestors (21:11–14). Though the text is silent on the matter, it is likely that the watchful mother now was free to bury her own sons. In a strange kind of way Saul's whole family had become reunited.

H. Miscellaneous Philistine Encounters (21:15–22)

The beginning of David's reign was marked by Philistine antagonism (see 5:17–25), and the historian closed his account with a summary of the Philistine wars and the heroes of Israel whom God used to bring victory.

IV. DAVID'S FINAL YEARS (CHAPTERS 22–24)

Except for chapter 24, this section consists of two poetic compositions by David (chapter 22 and 23:1–7) and a list of his mighty men (23:8–39). Thus it matches in some ways the opening of the book with its poetic lament over Saul and Jonathan (1:19–27) and the exploits of David's heroes (2:1–5:10). Moreover, the theme of chapter 24—the acquisition of a temple site—corresponds to the ark narrative (chapter 6) and David's desire to build a temple in the first place (7:1–2).

A. David's Song (chapter 22)

This magnificent composition (repeated as Psalm 18) is a hymn extolling the person of the Lord and celebrating His exploits. He attended to his servant David, shaking the very earth and heavens as evidence of His power. He also delivered David from his many enemies. All His ways are just, David proclaimed, and His excellence is seen in the strength He affords the weak, the protection He brings to bear in times of trouble, the victory He achieves over those who threaten His own beloved ones, the provision He made for David's rule, and the salvation He provided and would continue to provide for David and his descendants.

B. David's Farewell Address (23:1–7)

Like Jacob (Gen. 49:1–27) and Moses (Deut. 33:1–29) before him, David spoke and/or penned a valedictory to his people. In his address he recognized his own role as the anointed king (2 Sam. 23:1), one to and through whom God had communicated revelation (23:2–3). Yet he expressed astonishment that God had made a covenant with him, a word so sure that evil men who tried to subvert it would meet with certain and awesome judgment (23:4–7).

C. David's Heroes (23:8–39)

This lengthy list consists of two parts, five men whose exploits are described anecdotally (23:8–23), and thirty-two others whose names are merely mentioned (23:24–39), a total of thirty-seven (23:39). However, the thirty chief men referred to in verse 13 and the five in verses 8–23 total thirty-five. Possibly the word "thirty" was a technical term for David's select men of *approximately* thirty—here thirty-two. Or the word "thirty" means exactly thirty, with some soldiers replacing others as they were killed in battle (such as Uriah; 23:39).

Among all these were David's own nephews Abishai (23:18) and Asahel (23:24), but conspicuous by his absence was another nephew, Joab. The obvious reason for this omission was Joab's fall from favor because of his stubborn resistance to David (19:5–7, 13). Benaiah (23:20), distinguished by his bravery in slaying both men and lions, later became Solomon's chief military officer (1 Kings 2:35).

D. David's Census and Its Punishment (chapter 24)

For reasons undisclosed, Israel invoked the wrath of God, who then permitted David to undertake a census that would result in great loss of life (24:1). The chronicler, however, attributed the incitement to Satan, not the Lord (1 Chron. 21:1). The most satisfying resolution of this apparent dilemma is the assumption that the temptation to take the census came from Satan, but was allowed by the Lord (a similar "causal chain" is recorded in Job 1:6–12; 2:6).

Taking census of David's military might was considered sinful probably because that would cause David to trust his own human resources rather than the Lord. Joab seems to have understood this (2 Sam. 24:3), but David nonetheless commissioned Joab to go throughout the land and bring back the totals of those qualified to bear arms (24:2–9). Only after he had done so did David come to see the sin involved in the act. It was too late, however, and all David could do was accept one of three punishment options—famine, enemy invasion, or disease. Knowing God to be fair and just, and man to be quite otherwise, David chose to leave the matter with the Lord (24:10–14).

The wrath of the Lord was thus unleashed in a great plague that killed seventy thousand people (24:15). Then, just as God was about to strike Jerusalem itself, He relented in a display of undeserved mercy. That restraint enabled David to see all the more clearly that he had sinned and that he, not the people, should be held accountable (24:16–17). The angelic sword had been held back at a ledgy outcropping of Jerusalem owned by a Jebusite named Araunah (24:16). David therefore decided to build an altar there on which to offer sacrifices that would move the Lord to bring judgment to an end. When Araunah learned that David wanted to erect an altar on his property, he offered it to David as a gift (24:18–23). David refused, however, recognizing full well that gifts given to God that cost the giver nothing can never be considered sacrifices. With all this God was well pleased and graciously brought to an end the plague David had brought on his nation (24:24–25).

1 KINGS
The Slippery Slope to National Ruin

AUTHOR

*I*n all ancient Jewish canons 1 and 2 Kings are, correctly, considered to be one book, the present division no doubt being a concession to the practical need to avoid having such a lengthy composition on one scroll. The smooth flow of the narrative between the two books further confirms their original unity. The process by which the extant work came together is addressed next under "Unity."

The most reliable early Jewish witness to the authorship of Kings is the Babylonian Talmud (*Baba Bathra* 15a), which states that "Jeremiah wrote the book which bears his name, the Book of Kings, and Lamentations." This testimony asserts the unity of 1 and 2 Kings ("the Book of Kings") and links Kings to Jeremiah. Scholars have long noted the similarities of style and content between Kings and the Book of Jeremiah. While this alone cannot prove Jeremiac authorship of Kings, there is nothing in Kings that would seriously preclude his having done so with the possible exception of the reference to the release of King Jehoiachin from Babylonian house arrest in 560 B.C. (2 Kings 25:27–30). This late date and the location of the incident might suggest that those verses were added after Jeremiah's time, because he would by then have been nearly one hundred years old and, if living, would have been in Egypt, far from Babylon.

Apart from this Jewish tradition, however, there is no explicit state-ment of authorship either in 1 and 2 Kings or in other extrabiblical writings.

UNITY

Joshua, Judges, and Samuel all seem to have originated as separate com-positions. The same can be said of 1 and 2 Kings in general, the main exceptions, perhaps, being 1 Kings 1–2, commonly linked to 2 Samuel 9–20 as part of the so-called Succession Narrative, and the note about King Jehoiachin referred to above.

Whoever wrote Kings, it is clear that he drew on already existing records and traditions which he, directed by the Holy Spirit, arranged into the present shape of the book. The major blocks are the history of Solomon (1 Kings 1:1–11), the divided monarchy to the reign of Ahab (chapters 12–16), the narratives of Elijah (chapters 17–22 and 2 Kings 1:1–2:14) and Elisha (2 Kings 2:15–9:37), the reign of the Ahab dynasty (chapters 1–8), the reign of the Jehu dynasty (9:1–15:12), the decline and fall of Israel (15:13–17:41), the reign of Hezekiah (chapters 18–20), the evil reigns of Manasseh and Amon (chapter 21), the reign of Josiah (22:1–23:30), the decline and fall of Judah (23:31–25:26), and the epilogue concerning King Jehoiachin (25:27–30). The narratives of Elijah and Elisha coincide with or overlap those of kings Ahab through Joash, so there is clearly no way that some or even most of these larger blocks can be viewed as origi-nally separate compositions.

The author did suggest, however, that he was aware of and no doubt utilized other writings in preparing his own account of history. He knew of noncanonical proverbs and songs composed by Solomon (1 Kings 4:32) and such compositions as the book of the annals of Solomon (11:41), the book of the annals of the kings of Israel (for example, 14:19; 15:31; 16:5, 14, 20, 27; 22:39), and the book of the annals of the kings of Judah (for example, 14:29; 15:7, 23; 22:45). He must surely have depended on a num-ber of other, unnamed, sources in researching and compiling the book that lies at hand.

DATE

The latest event in 1 and 2 Kings for which there is indisputable evidence is the release of King Jehoiachin of Judah from Babylonian imprisonment (2 Kings 25:27–30). This occurred in the thirty-seventh year of the exile of Jehoiachin, that is, about 560 B.C. Nebuchadnezzar reigned until 562 and was succeeded by Amel-Marduk (562–560), known in the Old Testament as Evil-Merodach. A number of other times the phrase "until this day" or similar statements appear, thus suggesting some dating frame of reference (see 1 Kings 9:13, 21; 12:19; 2 Kings 2:22; 8:22; 10:27; 16:6). Unfortunately the settings of these phrases are so vague as to make it impossible to date them.

ADDRESSEES

The intended readers of 1 and 2 Kings were the whole community of Israel and Judah, including those who were living at the time the books were written and future generations. As the Word of God, these books have applicability to the church as well.

PURPOSE

One overriding purpose stands out, namely, to document the history of a people that, despite God's elective and providential grace, failed to live up to its covenantal privileges and responsibilities. And that history is not of a political or social nature as most historical texts are. Rather it is "theological history," that is, a record of persons and events in interaction with the Lord. In other words, it is history written from the heavenly viewpoint, one that is more concerned with meaning than with merely "brute fact."

THEOLOGICAL EMPHASES

Among a plethora of possibilities, two major theological themes stand out in 1 Kings. First, the point is made that disobedience to God's covenant commands leads to national and personal disintegration. This truth finds its fruition in 2 Kings, but it is articulated in 1 Kings as well (11:4, 9–12; 13:33–34; 14:7–10, 22–28; 16:29–33). The converse was also true—those who were obediently loyal to the Lord enjoyed His good favor (for example, 15:9–15; 22:42–43). Unfortunately these were few and far between.

A second principal theological motif in 1 Kings is the concept of the sovereignty of God, which, despite human failings, continues to carry forward His eternal purposes. Along with this is the unconditional nature of the covenant that God had made with the patriarchs and with David, a notion which, while not commonly affirmed explicitly in the book, runs through it undeniably as a coordinating thread. For example, the Lord chided Solomon for having transgressed the covenant but added quickly that the kingdom would continue, if only in a smaller form, because of David's sake (11:13, 32, 36; 15:4–5). The vindications of Elijah the prophet also attested to the incomparability of Israel's God and to His ultimate triumph (17:24; 18:24, 39; 20:13).

OUTLINE

I. The Period of Solomon (chapters 1–11)
  A. The Struggle for Succession (chapter 1)
  B. David's Death and Solomon's Solidification (chapter 2)
  C. Solomon's Power and Wisdom (chapters 3–4)
  D. Solomon's Building Activities (chapters 5–8)
  E. The Covenant with Solomon (9:1–9)
  F. Solomon's Glory (9:10–10:29)
  G. Solomon's Sin and Death (chapter 11)
II. The Period of Jeroboam's Dynasty (12:1–15:32)
  A. Rehoboam's Threat (12:1–15)
  B. Israel's Rebellion (12:16–24)
  C. Jeroboam's Idolatry (12:25–13:34)
  D. Jeroboam's Rejection by the Lord (14:1–20)
  E. The Reign of Rehoboam (14:21–31)
  F. The Reign of Abijam (15:1–8)

    G. The Reign of Asa (15:9–24)

    H. The Reign of Nadab (15:25–32)

  III. The Period of Baasha's Dynasty (15:33–16:14)

    A. The Reign of Baasha (15:33–16:7)

    B. The Reign of Elah (16:8–14)

  IV. The Period of Anarchy (16:15–22)

   V. The Period of Omri's Dynasty (16:23–22:53)

    A. The Reign of Omri (16:23–28)

    B. The Beginning of Ahab's Reign (16:29–34)

    C. Elijah the Prophet (chapters 17–19)

    D. The Siege of Samaria (chapter 20)

    E. Naboth's Vineyard (chapter 21)

    F. Ahab's Death (chapter 22)

I. THE PERIOD OF SOLOMON (CHAPTERS 1–11)

In size, power, and material prosperity, no other period of Israel's history could match the golden years of Solomon's forty-year reign. He was only twenty years old when he succeeded his father as king. Acutely aware of his limitations, he sought wisdom from God, who gave him not only that but much more—fame, wealth, and international respect. Sadly the spiritual tone of his early years gradually eroded away, and at the end, Solomon, influenced by his many pagan wives as well as by his own worldly ambition, sank to the level of an oriental despot. The glory of his youth faded into the shame of his old age.

A. *The Struggle for Succession (chapter 1)*

David's latter years found the king in a state of physical and mental deterioration that, in effect, left him incapable of making firm decisions. Capitalizing on this, his son Adonijah, fourth in line to succeed him by ordinary policy, determined to seize the throne. Two of his elder brothers, Amnon and Absalom, had died (2 Sam. 13:29; 18:14), so the way seemed clear to him. He therefore convened an assembly of leaders to install him as king before another could step in (1 Kings 1:1–10).

David had previously established Solomon as his royal heir, however (1 Chron. 22:9–13), so Nathan, ever faithful to David, told the queen mother, Bathsheba, about Adonijah's plot. She went to the king, joined later by Nathan, and reminded him of his expressed intentions (1 Kings 1:11–27). Recalling then what he had previously determined—and swayed as well by the appeal of Bathsheba, mother of Solomon—David instructed Zadok the priest and others to arrange for a preemptive coronation of Solomon (1:28–37). This was done before Adonijah and his followers could interfere. Once Adonijah was convinced that his father had enthroned Solomon with his blessing, he knew that further steps toward his own kingship would be futile (1:38–48). He therefore fled for sanctuary to the tabernacle, fearing rightly that his life was now in jeopardy (1:49–53).

> *David's sins of adultery and murder, while forgiven, resulted in unforeseen consequences, especially in his family life. Even on his deathbed his succession was in jeopardy as his children jockeyed for power. The lesson is clear: God forgives and even forgets our sins when we repent (Heb. 8:12), but their aftereffects may never be eradicated this side of heaven.*

B. David's Death and Solomon's Solidification (chapter 2)

The last recorded act of David was his injunction to his beloved son to keep the whole Law of Moses, that is, all the terms of the covenant made with the ancestors and also with David himself (2:1–4). In addition he offered practical advice as to how to deal with Joab, his traitorous general (2:5–6); Barzillai, who had befriended him while he was on exile from Absalom (2 Sam. 17:27–29); and Shimei, the Benjamite who had cursed him when he was in flight from Jerusalem on that occasion (1 Kings 2:7–9; see also 2 Sam. 16:5–8).

After a long reign of forty years, David died and Solomon commenced his sole and undisputed regency (1 Kings 2:10–12). Meanwhile Adonijah had not given up, and under pretense of acceding to Solomon's kingship he came to Bathsheba with what seems like a strange but harmless request: He wanted David's companion Abishag as his wife (2:13–18). This overture was not as innocent as it seems, however. To take a former king's wife or concubine as one's own was to lay claim to his office, and Abishag was in a similar position (see 2 Sam. 16:20–23; 20:3). Solomon understood this fully, so when his mother spoke to him of the matter he saw that Adonijah was still seeking the throne for himself. He therefore ordered his henchman Benaiah to kill Adonijah and thereby avert further threat from that quarter (1 Kings 2:19–25).

Solomon then turned to the turncoat priest, Abiathar (1 Sam. 22:20; 23:6; 1 Kings 1:7) and stripped him of his office. Next he directed his attention to Joab, who saved his own life only by fleeing to the tabernacle and finding refuge there. Solomon paid no heed to the tradition of sanctuary at the holy place, however, and told Benaiah to put him to death there if he refused to leave. Benaiah then became chief officer of Israel's army, and Zadok took Abiathar's place as high priest.

Only Shimei remained to be dealt with. His fate was to remain forever in Jerusalem, failing which he would surely die. He kept these terms for some years, but in foolish pursuit of some escaped slaves he left the city, a mistake for which he paid with his life. No wonder, after all this, the narrator could write, "The kingdom was now firmly established in Solomon's hands" (2:46).

C. Solomon's Power and Wisdom (chapters 3–4)

The story of Solomon's rise to power and glory is prefaced by a reference to his marriage to an Egyptian princess, an entanglement which, like others, would bring about his eventual decline and the demise of the united monarchy (3:1–3; see also 11:1–13). Most likely before that marriage took place, young Solomon had gone to the original Mosaic tabernacle at Gibeon to offer sacrifices to the Lord (3:4; see 1 Chron. 16:39; 21:29). The fact that David had also built a tabernacle in Jerusalem in which to house the ark shows that until Solomon constructed his temple there were two authorized places of worship in Israel (2 Sam. 6:17).

As Solomon worshiped the Lord, He appeared to him and told him he could have whatever he requested. Recognizing his immaturity—the Hebrew *na'ar* in 1 Kings 3:7 means not a child but an immature person—

Solomon asked for wisdom to lead the people (3:4–9). Because he sought first God's kingdom, God also added "all these things" (Matt. 6:33) to him as well. Moreover, his loyal commitment to the Davidic and Mosaic covenants would assure the continuation of God's blessings on him all his days (1 Kings 3:10–15).

The nature of biblical wisdom is clear from the story of the two prostitutes who came to Solomon for counsel (3:16–28). It seems that each had a baby but one smothered hers by rolling over on it. She therefore took her friend's infant, claiming it as her own. Solomon suggested cutting the living child in two, knowing full well that the maternal instinct to let the child live would outweigh any other consideration. He rightly concluded that the woman who was willing to give up her baby was the true mother. This just decision reflected the presence of God in Solomon's role as judge.

Solomon's wisdom was also expressed in the matter of statecraft. He appointed various religious and secular officials, drew up a plan whereby each of the twelve districts (roughly equal to tribal territories) would provide food and other supplies to the central government, and established political and military control over all the territory from the Euphrates to the border of Egypt (4:1–21). From the areas under his extended sovereignty he demanded taxes and tribute, so much so that with his income from within Israel as well he became wealthy beyond measure. More important, he brought peace to the land through all the years of his administration. All of this testified to his God-given skills (4:22–28).

Solomon's wisdom was apparent in his understanding of creation and the lessons to be learned from closely observing it. More than all the fabled wise men of the east and Egypt (4:29–31), he drew forth principles of life and behavior from plants and animals of every kind (4:33; see also Prov. 6:6–11; 30:24–28), teaching what he learned by composing thousands of proverbs and songs (1 Kings 4:32). No wonder he came to enjoy an international reputation for wisdom, one that led others to seek him from near and far (4:34).

D. Solomon's Building Activities (chapters 5–8)

Solomon's international fame led to contacts with leaders throughout the eastern Mediterranean world. Among them was King Hiram of Tyre (around

980–947 B.C.), a Phoenician nation just north of Israel. The Phoenicians were celebrated as mariners but also as master architects and builders. Solomon therefore negotiated with Hiram to send timber from Lebanon as well as skilled workmen so that he could commence building a temple for the Lord, something David had been forbidden to do (5:1–6).

A deal was struck and Hiram proceeded to provide Solomon with all the cedar and fir he needed in return for vast quantities of Israelite wheat and olive oil to be delivered year after year (5:7–12). Ordinary labor came from within Israel itself and operated within a system whereby ten thousand men a month were deployed to the forests of Lebanon and twenty thousand worked on the project in Jerusalem. At the end of the month, the men in Lebanon returned and were replaced by ten thousand more from Israel. By rotation they served one month away and two months at home. In addition there were seventy thousand carriers and eighty thousand stoneworkers, all under the supervision of thirty-three hundred foremen (5:13–18).

Solomon—like David his father—had an intense burden to erect a temple worthy of his great God and to do so as quickly as possible. Once he had established himself politically, he commenced the project, laying the foundations in his fourth year (966 B.C.), exactly 480 years after the Exodus of his ancestors from Egypt. All its parts were prefabricated, the whole being a work of exquisite beauty and craftsmanship (6:1–10, 14–36). Though not a large building by modern standards, Solomon's temple was roughly twice the size of the Mosaic tabernacle and was obviously designed for the ages.

For seven years the project went forward, and by 960 B.C. it was completed (6:37–38). Meanwhile the Lord had promised Solomon that if he were faithful to the Sinaitic and Davidic covenant stipulations, He would ensure the stability of Solomon's regime and would forever dwell among His people Israel (6:11–13). Sadly enough, the building stood for only 380 years. The Babylonians razed it to the ground in 586 B.C., and with its destruction the Lord Himself departed from Jerusalem, awaiting the day when the messianic temple will take its place (2 Kings 25:9; Ezek. 11:23).

Second in order was Solomon's own palace, a project that took thirteen years to complete (1 Kings 7:1–8a). Along with it he provided a residence for Pharaoh's daughter (7:8b), whom he had married (3:1). Like the temple these buildings were of the finest materials and handiwork (7:9–12). A prime example of a craftsman with artistic skill was Hiram of Tyre, a half-Israelite worker in bronze (not to be confused with Hiram, the king of Tyre). All the bronze features of the temple—the freestanding pillars, the sea and its stands, the wash basins, and miscellaneous vessels—were forged and shaped by his gifted hands (7:13–47).

The most precious furnishings were made of gold—the incense altar, the table for the memorial bread, the menorahs, and various pots and pans. When all these things were finished, they were taken into the temple to become part of the apparatus of worship (7:48–51).

When all was ready, the ark of the covenant itself was brought from David's tabernacle on Mount Zion (2 Sam. 6:17), and with great reverence and solemnity it was installed in the Most Holy Place of the temple (1 Kings 8:1–3). In addition Solomon took the ancient tabernacle of Moses and its furnishings from its location at Gibeon and stored them somewhere in the temple complex (8:4; see 3:4; 2 Chron. 1:3–4). When all this had been done, the cloud of God's glory filled the temple, symbolizing the fact that He had taken up residence among His people in that earthly place (1 Kings 8:5–11; see Exod. 40:34–35).

Solomon responded by acknowledging the presence of the Lord and by addressing the assembly gathered for the dedication of the temple. He reminded them that the Lord had done without a permanent dwelling place since the Exodus and had refused to allow David to build him one despite his earnest desire to do so. That privilege must await his son Solomon, a privilege having now come to fruition (1 Kings 8:12–21).

The king next stood before the temple, and in the longest prayer in the Bible Solomon raised his voice in praise and petition to the Lord on behalf of himself and the nation (8:22–53). He first extolled Him as the God of the covenant and implored Him to continue His favor on the house of David forever. He then acknowledged that though the magnificent temple could not begin to house the Lord, there was something about it that marked the point of contact between Him and His chosen people. When they prayed they should do so by facing the temple, exactly as Daniel did four hundred years later (Dan. 6:10). The temple would be a place of justice, one to which the people could look in times of defeat because of their sins against God. This would be true in times of drought and agricultural blight as well (1 Kings 8:31–40).

Even foreigners who came to believe in the Lord could look to the temple in faith and find there that the God of Israel was their God also (8:41–43). If Israelites went to war and even ended up captives in distant lands because of their disobedience, they could still turn toward God's house in their prayers and find forgiveness and deliverance (8:44–52). The reason, Solomon said, was that Israel was the elect vessel of the Lord whom He had gloriously redeemed from Egypt (8:53).

Rising from his knees, Solomon blessed the throng, reminding them of God's faithfulness in the past and assuring them of His dependability in the years to come. He wished for them that the Lord would always turn their hearts to Him so that in their obedience they could display the sovereignty, incomparability, and exclusiveness of the Lord before the nations that they might believe in Him as well (8:54–61).

The prayer and blessing were followed by a massive sacrifice of fellowship (or peace) offerings. Thousands of animals were offered up to the Lord by tens of thousands of worshipers from all over the land and beyond. For a solid week the dedicatory services continued, until at last on the eighth day Solomon sent the people away to their towns and villages (8:62–66).

E. The Covenant with Solomon (9:1–9)

Following David's expression of desire to build a temple for the Lord, the Lord had made a covenant with him in which he established David's dynastic succession forever (2 Sam. 7:11–16). Now that Solomon had finished the temple in fulfillment of God's promise, he too was challenged to be obedient and was promised an everlasting descendancy. Disobedience, on the other hand, would result in destruction of the temple and dispersal of the people of Israel to foreign lands. The covenant with David and his dynasty was unconditional and eternal, but its benefits came only to those of each generation who were loyal to its terms.

F. Solomon's Glory (9:10–10:29)

Solomon's massive building programs were completed after twenty years, halfway through his reign (9:10). They were not without their difficulties, however, as the historian pointed out. Most serious was the misunderstanding between Solomon and King Hiram of Tyre as to the terms of their agreement. As payment for Hiram's raw materials, Solomon had ceded to him twenty Galilean villages, which, when Hiram saw them, he spurned as worthless (thus naming the area Cabul, "as good as nothing"; 9:10–14).

The work of building in Jerusalem and elsewhere fell to recruited laborers, mainly from among Canaanites, Amorites, and other indigenous peoples in the land. They constructed fortresses and supply centers throughout the land, most notably at Hazor, Megiddo, and Gezer (9:15–21). Israelite manpower was generally reserved for the military (9:22). Among other miscellanea the narrator spoke of Solomon's labor overseers (9:23), the move of Pharaoh's daughter into her new facilities (9:24; see 7:8), and Solomon's care to keep the annual festivals (9:25). Also the narrator drew attention to Solomon's fleet of ships and his and Hiram's sailors at Ezion Geber on the Red Sea (that is, the Gulf of Aqaba or Eilat). From there Solomon conducted trade in all kinds of goods, especially gold (9:26–28).

Solomon's accomplishments gave rise to international fame. His reputation spread as far away as Sheba on the south Arabian peninsula, more than twelve hundred miles from Jerusalem. The ruler of that land, an unnamed queen, was impressed with rumors of Solomon's wisdom, so she traveled that great distance to interview him. She took with her vast quantities of exotic and valuable goods, but these paled in comparison to what Solomon already had. "The half was not told me," she said as she marveled at Solomon's wisdom and glory. More importantly, she recognized that Israel's blessings were due to a gracious and beneficent God (10:7–10).

When the queen departed, Solomon loaded her caravans with fabulous treasures (10:13), goods he had imported from far and near (10:11–12, 14–22). His annual income of gold—not including what was imported— amounted to 666 talents or about twenty-five tons! It was no exaggeration to claim that Solomon was the richest and wisest of all the kings of the then known world. No wonder people sought him out to see and hear how God had blessed him (10:23–25).

Among Solomon's many business pursuits was his interest in horse trading (10:26–29). He had an enormous chariotry corps and became rich by serving as a middleman in the purchase and sale of horses and chariots, especially between Egypt and the lands of Cilicia and Aramea.

G. Solomon's Sin and Death (chapter 11)

The story of Solomon's rise to power had begun with an apparently irrelevant note that he had married a daughter of Pharaoh, probably Siamun of dynasty 21 (3:1; see also 7:8; 9:24). Far from irrelevant, however, that bit of information anticipated the sin that would eventually bring both Solomon and his kingdom to ruin, namely, his foreign entanglements and the idolatry and religious syncretism that ensued. Granted, these marriages and concubinages were largely for political purposes, but the effect was the same—"his wives turned his heart away" (11:3).

To accommodate his wives and the religious traditions they represented, Solomon established pagan shrines throughout the land (11:1–8), a compromise that evoked a severe reprimand from the Lord (11:9–13). The covenant with David's dynasty would stand, but all the tribes except Judah—David's own tribe—would be torn away from the kingdom to form a separate entity.

> One of the most puzzling aspects of the life of Solomon was the fact that he, the wisest of all men, could be so foolish, particularly in the last years of his reign. What must be understood is that the very basis, in fact, the essence of biblical wisdom is to fear God (Prov. 1:7). It was precisely when Solomon neglected this principle that he began the slippery slope to folly (1 Kings 11:9).

Thus began the disintegration of Solomon's empire even while he was still alive. First to break away was Edom under the leadership of Hadad, an Edomite prince who had fled to Egypt in David's time but returned now to deliver his people from Israel's domination (11:14–22). To the north the Aramean city-state of Damascus became independent of Solomon, as a result of the instigation of Rezon (also known as Hezion; 11:23–25; 15:18). Most painful and damaging of all was the secession of the ten northern tribes (all but Benjamin; 12:21) through the influence of Jeroboam, one of Solomon's most trusted officials. Jeroboam of Ephraim was in charge of Solomon's conscripted labor in his district, and he proved to have sterling leadership qualities. Moreover, the prophet Ahijah revealed to him clearly that the Lord would appoint him ruler over the northern kingdom, that is, over everything but the dynasty of David, which would forever remain independent because of God's irrevocable covenant. Furthermore, if Jeroboam would be faithful to that same covenant, he and his descendants could expect a long and prosperous tenure.

When Solomon heard of Ahijah's message, he tried to apprehend and kill Jeroboam. He was too late, however, for Jeroboam escaped and found refuge with Pharaoh Shishak of Egypt. Shortly thereafter Solomon died, having reigned for forty years, and he left his truncated kingdom in the hands of his son Rehoboam.

II. THE PERIOD OF JEROBOAM'S DYNASTY
(12:1–15:32)

The orientation of Israel's history as recorded in 1 and 2 Kings is toward the Northern Kingdom and not Judah. The reverse is true in the account in 1 and 2 Chronicles. The following discussion therefore will be in terms of the successive dynasties of Israel, with the affairs of Judah and its kings described in reference to these northern rulers. The first of these dynasties was founded by Jeroboam and extended through only two generations, his own and that of his son, and for only twenty-two years (931–909 B.C.).

A. Rehoboam's Threat (12:1–15)

Rehoboam, son of Solomon's Ammonite wife Naamah, began to occupy Israel's throne in 931 B.C. and reigned for seventeen years (14:21). Since Jeroboam had already been informed that he would be king in Israel,

Rehoboam went to the old northern covenant site of Shechem (Gen. 12:6; Josh. 24:1; Judg. 9:1, 3) to preempt Jeroboam's regency (1 Kings 12:1–5). Jeroboam showed up, and on behalf of the people there he urged Rehoboam to relax the severe fiscal policies of his father Solomon.

Rehoboam's senior counselors advised him to heed the people, but his peers encouraged him to exacerbate the situation in order to show who really was in control. Foolishly the young king took the latter tack and threatened to increase the burdens of an already overburdened populace. But this rash decision had divine overtones, for its repercussions would result in the purpose that the Lord had in mind all along, namely, the division of the kingdom and the rule of Jeroboam (12:6–15).

B. Israel's Rebellion (12:16–24)

Rehoboam's surly response to the assembly prompted an immediate declaration of independence by Israel under Jeroboam's leadership. He himself was proclaimed king at Shechem—which became the first capital of the Northern Kingdom—and Rehoboam was forced to retreat in ignominious humiliation. Back in Jerusalem, however, he raised a large army and determined to march north to reclaim his lost territories. The prophet Shemaiah interdicted this course of action, reminding Rehoboam that all these terrible series of events were part of an irreversible plan of God Himself and were therefore irremedial.

C. Jeroboam's Idolatry (12:25–13:34)

After solidifying his position at Shechem, Jeroboam shored up his control of the Transjordan and then addressed the possibility that his people might have second thoughts about their break from Judah and give up their plans for an independent state (12:25–33). The key motivation for this, he knew, would be religious, not political. The temple was in Jerusalem, so the people who wished to participate in the regular and mandatory festivals would have to go to Judah in order to do so. Gradually, he feared, their hearts would be turned toward reunification. To preclude this, Jeroboam set apart two places of worship in Israel, one at Dan in the north and the other at Bethel in the south. There he installed golden calves and, like Aaron and his cohorts centuries earlier (Exod. 32:4), declared these to be the gods of the Exodus deliverance (1 Kings 12:28). Most likely the calves were intended to be iconic representations of the Lord.

Beyond this, Jeroboam appointed non-Levitical priests and changed the liturgical calendar so that the Feast of Tabernacles, for example, would be observed in the eighth month rather than the seventh (12:31–33). Such blatant perversion of the worship of the Lord could not go unchecked. The Lord therefore sent an anonymous prophet from Judah to Bethel to confront Jeroboam, who, in fact, was in the act of offering incense when the prophet arrived (13:1). Though kings could function as priests in certain circumstances (2 Sam. 6:12–15), it was strictly forbidden for them to offer incense for this was limited to the Aaronic priests alone (Num. 16:39–40; 2 Chron. 26:16–18).

Confronting the king, the prophet predicted that the time would come when a Davidic king, Josiah by name, would demolish these pagan shrines and slay the priests associated with them (1 Kings 12:2–3; see 2 Kings 23:15–16). Infuriated, Jeroboam reached out to seize the prophet, only to find his own arm paralyzed and helpless. As a sign of future destruction, the altar of incense collapsed and the ashes were scattered. Jeroboam therefore pleaded for healing of his paralysis and, when this was done, he invited the prophet home for a reward. The prophet sensed that this was an inappropriate accommodation to the wicked king, and therefore he turned his back and headed home (1 Kings 13:4–10).

Meanwhile a prophet from Bethel, having heard of all that had transpired, caught up with the young prophet from Judah and induced him to break bread with him at his home, claiming that the Lord had instructed him to do so. Naively forgetting that God never countermands His own decrees without informing the original recipient, the prophet sat down with the old man, who then revealed to him a true revelation: Because he had not gone straight home as originally commanded, he would meet a tragic and untimely death by the mouth of a lion (13:11–25).

After this came to pass, the old Bethelite prophet—smitten perhaps by his own duplicity—buried the corpse in his own tomb. He then requested his sons to bury him there as well, for he had come to recognize that the young prophet's predictions about God's judgment on Bethel would surely come to pass. Perhaps he felt that association with a true prophet of the Lord, even if only in death, would help erase his disobedience in life and ministry. Whatever he might have learned was lost on Jeroboam. He, in fact, became a paradigm against which all future wicked kings of Israel were compared (13:26–34).

> *God never contradicts Himself and therefore never reveals anything contrary to the Bible, His written Word. Any message that purports to be from the Lord but that finds no biblical sanction is a false message, one to be ignored.*

D. Jeroboam's Rejection by the Lord (14:1–20)

Signs of the Lord's displeasure with Jeroboam were not slow in coming. His son Abijah fell deathly ill, so Jeroboam sent his wife, heavily disguised, to Ahijah, the prophet who had first revealed to Jeroboam that he would be king (14:1–3; see 11:29–31). Though blind, Ahijah "saw through" Jeroboam's treachery and told his wife that the message she must carry to the king was not at all pleasant. Despite God's grace in bestowing kingship on him, Jeroboam had become the polar opposite of David. He had gone into idolatry, and for this and other violations of God's trust he and his family would come to a sudden and gruesome end. The Lord would then raise up another line of kings, one that would, however, be no better. In the end, Israel was destined to deportation because of its hopeless addiction to the sinful pattern begun by Jeroboam.

Jeroboam's wife no sooner reached the capital (now Tirzah, modern–day Tell el-Far'ah) than her child died, a loss shared by the entire nation. Sometime later Jeroboam also died, leaving affairs of state to another son, Nadab, whose reign would be of only fleeting duration.

E. The Reign of Rehoboam (14:21–31)

Rehoboam, the third ruler of the Davidic dynasty, occupied the throne in Jerusalem for seventeen years (931–913 B.C.). Having learned all too well from his father Solomon's example in his later years, Rehoboam ardently embraced the trappings of idolatry for which the Lord had punished his ancestors long before him. By his fifth year, the Lord allowed King Shishak (Sheshonq in Egyptian texts) of Egypt to besiege and plunder Jerusalem itself en route to other military objectives farther north. Besides all this, Rehoboam was in constant conflict with Jeroboam, his adversary in Israel, until at last he died at the age of fifty-eight.

F. The Reign of Abijam (15:1–8)

Rehoboam's son Abijam (one of twenty-eight sons; 2 Chron. 11:21) succeeded him with a brief reign of three years (914–911 B.C.). Like Rehoboam—but unlike David, the model of royal godliness—Abijam was evil. Yet, for David's sake the dynasty was not destroyed, no matter the behavior of any of its representatives, including Abijam. This underscores the indissolubility of God's covenant promises. Abijam knew nothing but war with Jeroboam until his abbreviated reign gave way to death.

G. The Reign of Asa (15:9–24)

The downward spiral of Judean kings at last was reversed by Asa, son of Abijam, who enjoyed forty-one years of rule (911–870 B.C.). He instituted programs of reform, going so far as to remove his own grandmother from her office as "Great Lady" (Hebrew, gebîrâ, 15:13) because of her idolatrous influence. (She was not his mother as 15:2, 10 together make clear). Asa's major secular concern was his incessant war with Israel, especially with King Baasha (15:16–22). When Baasha threatened Judah by building border fortifications, Asa bribed Ben Hadad of Damascus into attacking Israel's northern areas. This forced Baasha to leave off his hostilities toward Judah for a time, so Asa was able to take the building materials of Baasha's fortresses and use them to construct his own. In his old age Asa suffered from a foot disease, possibly gout, and appointed his son Jehoshaphat as his coregent for a brief time (873–870 B.C.; 15:23–24).

H. The Reign of Nadab (15:25–32)

Jeroboam's son and only successor reigned for only two years (910–909 B.C.), a time of continuing apostasy. The instrument of his punishment was Baasha, a king prophesied earlier without name (14:14). Baasha killed Nadab in battle and then went on to annihilate the entire Jeroboam family.

III. THE PERIOD OF BAASHA'S DYNASTY (15:33–16:14)

A. The Reign of Baasha (15:33–16:7)

The founder of the second dynasty of the Northern Kingdom, Baasha reigned for twenty-four years (909–886 B.C.) all within the time period of Asa's rule in Judah. He, like Jeroboam, was evil and heard a word from a prophet condemning him and his dynasty to destruction (see 14:6–11). He apparently died of natural causes in Tirzah, his capital, something of a rarity in those turbulent times.

B. The Reign of Elah (16:8–14)

Elah, like Nadab, ended the dynasty of his father within two years of succeeding him (886–885 B.C.). He met his fate at the hand of an assassin, Zimri, who followed this up by exterminating all of Baasha's family. Ironically this is precisely what Baasha had done after slaying Jeroboam's son Nadab.

IV. THE PERIOD OF ANARCHY (16:15–22)

Zimri held forth for only a week at Tirzah when Omri, commander of Israel's armies, learned of Elah's murder and came to Tirzah to avenge it. When Zimri saw that all was lost, he set the palace afire and died in its flames. This opened the way for an intense struggle for power. Half the population favored Omri, and the other half favored Tibni, whose demise is described rather simply by the words "so Tibni died" (16:22).

V. THE PERIOD OF OMRI'S DYNASTY (16:23–22:53)

The third true dynasty of Israel was founded by Omri and continued for five generations after him (885–841), only two of which—those of Omri himself and his son Ahab—receive attention in 1 Kings. More important than either king, however, was the mysterious and powerful prophet of God, Elijah the Tishbite. Narratives of his accomplishments dominate the remainder of the book.

A. The Reign of Omri (16:23–28)

Assyrian inscriptions celebrate this ruler who earns only six verses in the biblical text. This short sketch does take note, however, of Omri's moving of the capital from Tirzah to Samaria in his sixth year (around 880 B.C.), its site from then until the Assyrian conquest in 722 B.C.

B. The Beginning of Ahab's Reign (16:29–34)

Wicked Omri was followed by even more wicked Ahab (874–853 B.C.). As though he needed help in his apostasy from the Lord, he married the Sidonian princess Jezebel, who further encouraged him in his pursuit of Baal worship. He built a Baal temple in Samaria itself and set up other pagan worship centers throughout the land.

C. Elijah the Prophet (chapters 17–19)

The flow of the narrative of political history is interrupted by the appearance of Elijah, one of the most striking figures in all the Bible. He appeared suddenly on the scene, announcing to Ahab that God was about to send a drought because of Israel's sin (17:1–7). Running out of food and water himself at the brook Kerith, Elijah went to Sidon (the home, ironically, of Jezebel), where God sustained him through the care of a poor widow who herself, with her son, was about to perish. Were it not for a miracle of God who kept her grain and oil from running out, all three would have died (17:8–16).

Further evidence of God's favor on Elijah was his power in resuscitating the widow's son, who had died of some illness. This miracle elicited from her the testimony that Elijah was a man of God whose words came from the Lord (17:17–24). This foreigner's confession was in stark contrast to the unbelief among Elijah's own Israelite countrymen. Even three years of drought failed to convince most of them to repent. Finally Elijah sought out an official in Ahab's palace, Obadiah by name, and told him to inform the king that he would meet with him with a word from the Lord. Predictably Ahab blamed the prophet for all his woes, but Elijah confronted him with the truth—it was Ahab's idolatry that lay at the heart of all of Israel's troubles (18:1–19).

To make an empirically demonstrable case, Elijah challenged Ahab to gather his prophets at the high place at Carmel and there to have them call on their gods to ignite a sacrifice while he implored the Lord to do the same. When all was ready, the Baal prophets did all in their power to induce their god to send lightning to consume the sacrifice, but to no avail (18:20–29). But when Elijah offered a simple prayer, the Lord responded with a mighty conflagration that burned up not only the sacrifice but also the altar itself and the water poured on and around it to create an even more impossible test (18:30–38). The result was clear to all—only the Lord is truly God (18:39).

With this issue settled, Elijah had the false prophets put to death (18:40) and then warned Ahab that the drought was about to end, for rain clouds were gathering on the western horizon (18:41–46). But those were not the only ominous clouds, for Jezebel determined to kill this troublemaker Elijah for having publicly embarrassed her and her religious establishment. Elijah therefore fled far to the south, arriving eventually at Horeb, the sacred mountain of Moses. There the Lord encountered him in whispers of revelation and heard the prophet complain that only he was faithful of all the people of God (19:1–14).

Offering him comfort and assurance, the Lord commissioned Elijah to return to Israel and to anoint Jehu as the next king of Israel, Hazael as king of Damascus, and Elisha as his prophetic successor. He did only the last of these immediately on his return (19:15–21).

D. The Siege of Samaria (chapter 20)

Meanwhile the Arameans attacked and besieged Samaria, demanding that Ahab pay a heavy ransom to spare his city. Ahab refused, however, and, bolstered by the encouragement of an unnamed prophet, he launched his own attack, forcing the Arameans to retreat. A year later they returned and once more fell before Israel's armies. This time King Ben Hadad was besieged, holing himself up in the Israelite city of Aphek. His counselors advised him to appeal to Ahab on the basis of their brotherhood and the promise of attractive treaty arrangements. Ahab, foolishly, complied. A prophet, by means of a parable, rebuked Ahab and told him he would pay for his folly with his life.

E. Naboth's Vineyard (chapter 21)

Ahab's weakness and shortsightedness are clear also from the story of Naboth and his vineyard. Ahab coveted this lush property of his neighbor, but Naboth was unwilling to part with it. Jezebel therefore fabricated charges of blasphemy against him, charges that stuck and resulted in Naboth's stoning. This gave Ahab undisputed rights to the property. Elijah encountered the wicked king once more and informed him that this was the last straw. He and his pagan queen would die a miserable death. Because of his repentance, however, his dynasty would end not with him but with a later descendant.

F. Ahab's Death (chapter 22)

First Kings ends with the narrative that describes Ahab's final days (22:1–40) and the transition of rule that followed (22:41–53). For three years there had been peace between Israel and Aram, but Ahab was unhappy that certain Transjordanian parts of his kingdom were still under Aramean control. He enlisted the support of King Jehoshaphat of Judah, and the two decided to liberate those occupied territories (22:1–4). First, however, Jehoshaphat had to be sure that the Lord was in it and would give victory. Ahab's own prophets offered such assurance, but Jehoshaphat knew they were charlatans and insisted that a true prophet be sought (22:5–12).

There was such a man, Micaiah son of Imlah, but he was in prison because of the unpopularity of his message. When he appeared before the kings, at first he sarcastically assured them of victory (22:15), but then he addressed them with the truth—Ahab's prophets were liars and the outcome would be disastrous (22:13–23). For telling the truth Micaiah was remanded once more to the dungeon. Ahab and Jehoshaphat then sallied forth to battle, but before sunset of the first day of conflict Ahab was dead, pierced by a "random" arrow of an Aramean soldier. His remains were returned to Samaria, where he was buried (22:24–40).

Jehoshaphat, Ahab's ally, succeeded his father Asa and reigned for twenty-five years (873–848 B.C.). He enjoyed a generally favorable rating, but the negative note is made that he was on peaceful terms with wicked Ahab (22:41–44). He otherwise engaged in the removal of idolatry from Judah and the development of a trading industry (22:45–50). His younger contemporary was Ahaziah son of Ahab (853–852 B.C.), who like his father forsook the Lord and encouraged the worship of other gods (22:51–53).

2 KINGS
Destruction and Deportation

$\mathcal{F}$irst and Second Kings form a unitary composition, and therefore most matters of introduction relative to 2 Kings have already been addressed in the section on 1 Kings. However, two matters peculiar to 2 Kings—author and date—must be addressed here.

AUTHOR

The ancient Talmudic tradition that Jeremiah wrote 1 and 2 Kings, though without either internal or other explicit external support, remains a viable option for the book as a whole. An exception may be the last four verses of 2 Kings, a passage that recounts the release of King Jehoiachin from Babylonian internment and the benefits extended him for the rest of his life (25:27–30). The date of his release was 560 B.C., when he was only fifty-five years old. Had he lived to the age of seventy-five—not unrealistic for the time—the account at the end of 2 Kings could have been penned as late as 540 B.C. This would surely preclude Jeremiah's authorship since by then the prophet would have been well over one hundred years old (Jer. 1:1–3).

If an anonymous author added the information about Jehoiachin to the existing composition of 2 Kings, it is possible—even likely—that his hand may be seen elsewhere in the book, though why and where is impossible to recover. It seems best to view the book as essentially the work of one man (Jeremiah?) but with the likelihood of additions here and there by other inspired contributors.

DATE

On the supposition that King Jehoiachin lived for a few years after his release from house arrest, one may date 2 Kings as late as 550 B.C. or so. Lack of reference to Cyrus and his decree permitting the Jews to return to their homeland from Babylonian exile appears to rule out any possibility that any part of the book is later than 540. If Jeremiah was author of most of the book, as Jewish tradition attests, 1 and 2 Kings must have been completed shortly after 586 B.C., the date of the fall and destruction of Jerusalem, for Jeremiah's known public ministry came to an end shortly after that event (2 Kings 25:8, 22–26; Jer. 41:1, 43:6–7).

OUTLINE

I. The Continuation of Omri's Dynasty (1:1–8:15)
   A. The Reign of Ahaziah (chapter 1)
   B. Elijah's Departure (2:1–11)
   C. Elisha the Prophet (2:12–8:15)
   D. The Reign of Jehoram of Judah (8:16–24)
   E. The Reign of Ahaziah of Judah (8:25–29)
   F. The Anointing of Jehu of Israel (9:1–13)
   G. The Deaths of Joram and Ahaziah (9:14–28)
II. The Divided Monarchy from Jehu to the Captivity of Israel (9:29–17:6)
   A. The Reign of Jehu (9:29–10:36)
   B. The Reign of Queen Athaliah (chapter 11)
   C. The Reign of Joash (chapter 12)
   D. The Reign of Jehoahaz (13:1–9)
   E. The Reign of Jehoash (13:10–14:16)
   F. The Reign of Jeroboam II (14:17–29)
   G. The Reign of Uzziah of Judah (15:1–7)

    H. The Reign of Zechariah of Israel (15:8–12)

    I. The Reign of Shallum (15:13–15)

    J. The Reign of Menahem (15:16–22)

    K. The Reign of Pekahiah (15:23–26)

    L. The Reign of Pekah (15:27–31)

    M. The Reign of Jotham of Judah (15:32–38)

    N. The Reign of Ahaz of Judah (chapter 16)

    O. The Reign of Hoshea (17:1–6)

III. The Kingdom of Judah to the Captivity by Babylonia (17:7–25:7)

    A. Theological Explanation for the Fall of Israel (17:7–41)

    B. The Reign of Hezekiah (chapters 18–20)

    C. The Reign of Manasseh (21:1–18)

    D. The Reign of Amon (21:19–26)

    E. The Reign of Josiah (22:1–23:30)

    F. The Reigns of Josiah's sons (23:31–25:7)

IV. The Babylonian Captivity (25:8–30)

    A. The Pillaging of Jerusalem (25:8–17)

    B. The Deportation of the People (25:18–21)

    C. The Establishment of a Local Government (25:22–26)

    D. The Release of Jehoiachin from House Arrest (25:27–30)

I. THE CONTINUATION OF OMRI'S DYNASTY
(1:1–8:15)

A. The Reign of Ahaziah (chapter 1)

The account of the accession of Ahaziah, son of Ahab, to the throne of Israel appears in 1 Kings 22:51–53. In his brief two-year reign (853–852 B.C.) he did evil, particularly in worshiping Baal. But Baal of Samaria was not at the center of his religious devotion. One day the king suffered what proved to be a fatal accident, and rather than call on the Lord he sent a delegation to Ekron to plead his case before the Philistine deity of that place, a god with the pretentious name of Baal-Zebub, meaning "exalted lord." Along the way they encountered Elijah, who told them in no uncertain terms that their evil king would not recover.

Disconcerted by this word, the king's men returned to Samaria, and when they described to Ahaziah the strange man with the foreboding message, he knew at once it was his nemesis Elijah. He therefore sent a second entourage that, attempting to challenge the prophet, was consumed by heavenly fire. A third contingent met the same fate (1:11–12), so the leader of the third party, chastened and educated by the tragic end of his predecessors, bowed before Elijah in deep humility. This time the Lord told Elijah that it was safe for him to come from his hilltop refuge and to go to Samaria with the message Ahaziah had already heard from his own messengers: He would never rise from his sickbed. The judgment soon came to pass and Ahaziah passed his rule on to his own brother Joram.

B. Elijah's Departure (2:1–11)

The Lord decided that Elijah, like Enoch before him (Gen. 5:24), should not die but should be translated to heaven. The visible vehicle of his removal would be a whirlwind (2 Kings 2:1) that manifest itself to onlookers as a fiery chariot (2:11). When Elisha learned that his master was about to leave this world, he insisted on following him from Gilgal to Bethel to Jericho, all places associated with Elijah and his prophetic movement, otherwise called "the sons of the prophets."

Arriving at the Jordan River, Elijah parted its waters as Joshua had done more than five hundred years before. He then told his protégé to ask one blessing of him before he was taken up. Without hesitation Elisha prayed that he might have Elijah's spirit in double portion, a blessing Elijah said would surely be granted.

When given the opportunity to fill in a blank check, as it were, Elisha chose not silver and gold but something incomparably better—a double portion of Elijah's prophetic spirit. Like Solomon before him he sought "first the kingdom of God, and His righteousness" (Matt. 6:33, KJV), and the Lord therefore gave him additional unexpected blessings.

C. Elisha the Prophet (2:12–8:15)

As Elijah ascended, he bequeathed Elisha his prophetic mantle, and like his master, Elisha struck the water with it, with the same results. The water parted so he could cross once more to the west bank (2:12–14). Both he and the sons of the prophets understood this miracle to be God's affirmation of Elisha as the true successor of Elijah (2:15–18), a contingency that had been promised long before in Elijah's experience at Mount Horeb (1 Kings 19:16, 19–21). Elisha's leadership was soon put to the test, both internally and from without. He first made the bitter waters of Jericho potable (2 Kings 2:19–22), and then, mocked and ridiculed by some blasphemous youth of Bethel, he invoked divine judgment in the form of two ferocious bears who mauled them (2:23–25).

The prophet soon found himself caught up in the larger arena of national and international affairs. Ahaziah having died, his brother Joram succeeded him on the Omride throne (3:1–3). Sometime in Joram's twelve-year tenure, Moab, a vassal state to Israel, rebelled under its energetic and ambitious ruler, Mesha, a rebellion attested to also in the famous "Moabite" (or "Mesha") inscription. Joram solicited the aid of Jehoshaphat of Judah as well as that of the king of Edom, and the three headed toward Moab. They soon ran out of water, and in desperation they sent for Elisha who, they hoped, could come to their rescue (3:4–12).

For Jehoshaphat's sake Elisha reluctantly agreed to help. Dig trenches throughout the countryside, he said, and God would fill them with water. They did so, and the Lord, true to the word of the prophet, provided water in abundance (3:13–20). Meanwhile the Moabites saw the redness of the morning sky reflecting in the channels of water, and assuming it to be the blood of their enemies, they cast caution aside and moved forward to seize the spoils of war (3:21–23). Too late they came to see their error and fell beneath the savage Israelite attack. Even Mesha's desperate act of offering his own son as a sacrifice proved to be of no avail (3:24–27).

Apart from this incident (and one or two others such as the healing of Naaman; chapter 5), Elisha's ministry was on behalf of "little people," especially those of his own prophetic circle. God used him to provide a miraculous supply of oil for a prophet's widow (4:1–7), a male child for a barren couple who had provided generous hospitality to him on numerous occasions (4:8–16), and the raising up of that same child who died of sunstroke sometime later (4:17–31). Through prayer and physical contact he proclaimed the God of Israel to be the Giver and Sustainer of life (4:32–37).

Back among his prophetic disciples, Elisha delivered the community from a noxious broth concocted unwittingly by one of their number (4:38–41), and, like Jesus, he was able to multiply twenty small loaves of bread until it was sufficient for a hundred people with much left over (4:42–44). Clearly his prayer for a double portion of Elijah's spirit was answered and then some. What is important to note is that the miracles were done not just for their own sake or even for the benefit of those blessed by them. Rather, they were evidences of the power of God in an age of increasing moral and spiritual decay and decline. God was raising up a whole new institution—that of the canonical prophets—and it fell to Elijah and Elisha to bear testimony to the divine origin and sanction of that institution.

One of the most delightful narratives of the ministry of Elisha is the story of the healing of Naaman, an Aramean soldier. It demonstrates that God loves the nations of the world as much as He does His special servant-people Israel. The point of the story is that Gentiles find salvation in the God of Israel as the nation is faithful to bear witness to Him in line with the principles and promises of the Abrahamic Covenant (Gen. 12:1–3; 22:18; 26:4).

Naaman was commander of the army of the king of Aram, probably Ben-Hadad II, but all this honor, power, and prestige was to no avail to him because he had contracted leprosy and thus was condemned to ostracism and loss of a leadership role. It "happened," however, that he had an Israelite servant girl in his household who told him that he could find deliverance through Elisha, a prophet of Israel's God. The king of Aram therefore sent a letter to the king of Israel (probably Joram) urging him to use his good offices to see to it that Naaman found a cure. The Israelite ruler misconstrued the intent of the appeal, however, concluding that to ask for such an impossibility was a provocative act leading to war between them (2 Kings 5:1–7).

When Elisha heard of his king's dilemma, he told Naaman's servants to send for Naaman and then instructed him to immerse himself seven times in the Jordan River. Angry at this suggestion of healing by "long distance"—and especially at the indignity of bathing in Jordan's muddy waters—Naaman at first refused but then relented at the urging of his servants. His faith, meager as it was, resulted in his complete healing (5:8–14).

More importantly, Naaman experienced spiritual cleansing. He confessed that there was no God but the God of Israel, and in gratitude to Him he offered Elisha payment for his services. The prophet refused, so Naaman made another request: that he be allowed to take some of the sacred soil of Israel back to his own land to serve, perhaps, as a base on which he could erect an altar for making sacrifice to the Lord. Moreover, he pleaded in advance for God's forgiveness for his forced future participation in the worship of Rimmon, an Aramean god, since his king would expect him to do so as part of his official responsibilities (5:15–19).

Meanwhile Elisha's assistant, Gehazi, had seen the treasures Naaman had offered Elisha. Overcome with greed, he caught up with Naaman and fabricated a story about some unexpected guests whom Elisha needed to entertain at great personal cost. Touched by this need, Naaman responded lavishly. Elisha must have suspected something underhanded about Gehazi's deportment, however, for he confronted him about his recent whereabouts. Exposed as a hireling unfit for prophetic ministry, Gehazi contracted the leprosy from which Naaman had been cured and thus was forever disqualified from service to Elisha and the Lord (5:20–27).

At this point Elisha's private and more public ministries are juxtaposed once again. He performed the miracle of retrieving an iron axhead from the murky waters into which it had fallen (6:1–7) and then played a role in the ongoing conflict between Aram and Israel. It seems that no matter what strategy the Arameans devised, Israelite intelligence was aware of it and interdicted it. At last it was disclosed that Elisha the prophet was responsible for leaks of information (6:8–13).

When Ben-Hadad, the Aramean king, heard that Elisha was in Dothan, he sent a large force there to put the prophet out of commission. But Elisha saw in a vision that God was with him and that the hosts of heaven far outnumbered those of Aram. He prayed that God would strike blind those who sought his life, a request God honored (6:14–19). Elisha then offered to guide the blinded Arameans back to their homeland, but instead he led them to Samaria. The Lord opened their eyes there but forbade any further harm to them. With profound thanksgiving and much the wiser, the Arameans went home, never again to raid Israel with small contingents (6:20–23).

Sometime later, however, Ben-Hadad launched a major invasion of Israel and laid Samaria the capital under a long and devastating siege. Food became so expensive and scarce that the population finally resorted to cannibalism, a situation over which Israel's king himself was powerless (6:24–31). King Joram refused to accept responsibility for his people's plight, vowing instead to punish Elisha who, of course, had been instrumental in freeing the Aramean army when it had last been in Samaria. Elisha put the finger of blame on the king and predicted that the siege would soon end, and the inflationary prices would drop precipitously (6:32–7:2).

This came about through a rumor to the effect that Hittite troops were marching against the Arameans. This so terrified them that they fled to their own land, abandoning all their possessions and supplies in their wake. Some lepers outside the city walls discovered the empty Aramean tents and the piles of food that had been left untouched. Convicted by their selfishness, they shared the good news with their fellow citizens in Samaria and thus the city was saved (7:3–20). In this manner it became clear that deliverance comes not from human effort but ultimately from the grace and help of a loving God.

Once more the narrator joined stories of the private and public ministries of Elisha. In a flashback he related how Elisha had advised the woman of Shunem to leave her home for seven years because of an impending famine and how, after she returned, she had found her property appropriated by somebody else. Using his influence with the king, Elisha saw to it that justice was done and that the woman regained all that was hers (8:1–6).

The prophet's larger ministry this time involved his visit to Damascus where, as Elijah had been commissioned to do (1 Kings 19:15), he announced that Hazael would succeed Ben-Hadad as king. It seems that Ben-Hadad was ill, and Elisha came with the enigmatic message that though he would recover from his illness he would die nevertheless. Hazael, the king's confidant, took this to mean that he was free to take matters into his own hands, which he did by smothering his king to death. God's purposes were thus accomplished but surely the means employed could not have met with His approval. But the larger lesson is that God is the Lord not just of Israel but of the whole world. The nations will be blessed by Him but they are also accountable to Him (2 Kings 8:7–15).

D. The Reign of Jehoram of Judah (8:16–24)

The historian next related the accession of Jehoram son of Jehoshaphat to the kingship of Judah. Sadly, his eight-year rule (848–841 B.C.) was marked by disobedience, a situation explained but not justified by his marriage to a daughter of wicked King Ahab of Israel. His spiritual weakness was matched by a political and military decline that permitted Edom to become independent of Judean rule. On his death, Jehoram's throne became occupied by his son Ahaziah, named obviously for his evil uncle, King Ahaziah of Israel (1 Kings 22:51).

E. The Reign of Ahaziah of Judah (8:25–29)

Ahaziah reigned for only one year (841 B.C.), a brief but eventful tenure that reflected the apostasy associated with the Northern Kingdom. His mother was Athaliah, daughter of Ahab and Jezebel, so he was nephew to Joram, his contemporary in power in Israel. Joram capitalized on that relationship to induce Ahaziah to go to war with him against Hazael of Aram, a decision that would soon result in the death of both kings at the same time. Joram was wounded and went to Jezreel to recover. There his nephew joined him to encourage him in his recuperation.

F. The Anointing of Jehu of Israel (9:1–13)

At Horeb Elijah had been commissioned by the Lord to do three things: anoint Elisha as his prophetic successor, anoint Hazael to be king of Aram, and anoint Jehu to be king of Israel (1 Kings 19:15). Only the third of these remained to be done, and it fell to Elisha to bring it about. Jehu was an Israelite commander who was engaged in battle against Aram at Ramoth Gilead. Elisha sent a young prophet to that distant place in Transjordan to notify Jehu of his appointment by the Lord to be Israel's next king. He anointed him privately and then presented him publicly to his troops, who immediately acclaimed him king.

G. The Deaths of Joram and Ahaziah (9:14–28)

Without further ado Jehu headed west to Jezreel to do what had to be done to secure his reign—eliminate Joram and all the rest of the Ahab dynasty (9:14–16). When Joram learned of Jehu's coming, he and Ahaziah rode out to meet him to inquire as to the purpose of his visit. Without mincing his words, Jehu told the king that God had sent him to punish Joram's wickedness. Joram then tried to flee but Jehu slew him personally and laid his bloody corpse in the vineyard Ahab had stolen from Naboth at the cost of Naboth's very life (9:17–26; 1 Kings 21:1–26).

Ahaziah fared no better, for his family connection to Joram implicated him as well. Tracking him down, Jehu killed Ahaziah and then went on to Jezreel, where he located the evil queen mother Jezebel. Elijah had prophesied a gruesome end to this fountainhead of Israelite idolatry (21:33), and the Lord used Jehu to bring it about (2 Kings 9:30–37).

II. THE DIVIDED MONARCHY FROM JEHU TO THE CAPTIVITY OF ISRAEL (9:29–17:6)

The usual formula to introduce a king is lacking in the case of Jehu because of the unique and violent nature of his rise to power. There was a public acclamation of his kingship but it was at a distance, not in the capital (9:13). And his actual tenure could not begin until he had removed King Joram of Israel from the throne, an action that hardly provided suitable occasion for a ceremony of investiture, particularly since it had to be followed up immediately by further purging.

Jehu's accession nevertheless marked a transition from the era of the Omride dynasty to a new one founded by Jehu and extending for four generations through the reign of Zechariah (841–753 B.C.; see 15:8–12). But in the final analysis the Jehu family was hardly an improvement, and that dynasty paved the way for the virtual anarchy that characterized the last thirty years of Israel's history until that nation fell to the Assyrians in 722 B.C.

A. The Reign of Jehu (9:29–10:36)

One may somewhat arbitrarily commence the reign of Jehu with his slaying of both Joram of Israel and Ahaziah of Judah at the same time, in 841 B.C. Jehu held the reins of leadership for twenty-eight years (841–814 B.C.), a time of reformation in some respects but of continuing apostasy in other respects. The elements of reformation included Jehu's removal of Jezebel (9:30–37), his extermination of the remainder of Ahab's family in both Israel and Judah (10:1–17), and his eradication of Baal worship, at least as a formal institution (10:18–28).

On the other hand, Jehu not only tolerated the idolatry associated with Jeroboam's golden calves at Dan and Bethel but participated in it (10:29–31). The Lord therefore punished him and his kingdom by allowing Hazael of Aram to chip away at Israelite territory, especially in the Transjordan (10:32–33). This was only the beginning of a trend that would at last result in Israel's being deported to Assyria.

B. The Reign of Queen Athaliah (chapter 11)

The death of young King Ahaziah of Judah at the hands of Jehu (9:27–28) left him with no heir except a year-old infant son named Joash (11:2). Seizing the opportunity, Ahaziah's mother Athaliah declared herself ruler, a position she secured by slaughtering all other claimants to the throne. This, of course, meant the members of her own family.

For six years (841–835 B.C.) this wicked daughter of Ahab and Jezebel held office, a tenure that had no legitimacy at all since she was not a descendant of David. Meanwhile, Jehoiada the priest and other godly leaders had secluded young Joash, waiting for an opportune time to present him as Judah's true monarch. When the boy was seven years old, the trap was sprung. When all was ready Jehoiada assembled a throng around the temple and led the people in a loud announcement of the investiture of Joash as king (11:4–12).

Hearing the tumult, Athaliah arrived at the temple, saw her young grandson already installed as ruler, and then met the bloody fate she had inflicted at the beginning of her own grab for power (11:13–16). Jehoiada then presided over a covenant-renewal ceremony binding the king and the people to the Lord and also the king to the people. This was followed by a destruction of the Baal temple and its priests and the appointment of righteous servants of the temple of the Lord (11:17–21).

C. The Reign of Joash (chapter 12)

The Davidic dynasty continued under the boy-king Joash, who reigned for forty years (835–796 B.C.). His record was favorable for the most part, most notably because of his leadership in repairing and renewing the temple, which had fallen into ruin (12:1–8). The response by the people for funds was overwhelming, and the level of mutual trust was inspiring. No detailed records of income and expense were necessary, for those who handled the monies were fully trustworthy (12:9–16).

Unfortunately much of the revenue had to be expended for a most unworthy cause—the buying off of Hazael who had laid siege to Jerusalem and was threatening to capture it and lay it waste (12:17–18). Perhaps because of this sign of weakness on the part of Joash, some of his own men rose up against him and assassinated him. This paved the way for his son Amaziah to succeed him, though clearly Amaziah was not involved in the coup that brought him to power (12:19–21; see 14:5).

D. The Reign of Jehoahaz (13:1–9)

The second ruler of the Jehu dynasty occupied that role for seventeen years (814–798 B.C.), paralleling the latter years of Joash of Judah. Jehoahaz, like his father, embraced the heresy of the golden calves and so experienced God's judgment by foreign oppression, especially from Hazael and Ben-Hadad, the kings of Aram. The Lord heard his cry for relief, however, and raised up a deliverer—probably King Adad-Nirari III of Assyria—who pressured the Arameans to leave Israel alone. The respite did little good spiritually, for Israel under Jehoahaz persisted in its idolatrous ways.

E. The Reign of Jehoash (13:10–14:16)

Jehoahaz was followed by his son Jehoash (also spelled Joash; 13:9) who reigned for sixteen years (798–783 B.C.). Consistent with the pattern of the house of Jehu, Jehoash was evil despite the good influence of the prophet Elisha, who had lived on into the early eighth century. On his deathbed the prophet challenged the king to trust God for victory over the Arameans, but Jehoash failed to avail himself of all that God could and would have done for him (13:14–19). After Elisha died, Israel suffered invasion from Hazael and Ben-Hadad in turn. Three times Jehoash was able to repel his enemies as Elisha had promised, but in the final analysis he failed to gain the victory that could have been his.

Aram was not alone in harassing Israel, for Judah, under its new king Amaziah (796–767 B.C.), also became a source of consternation. Amaziah's assessment is generally favorable, though he was somewhat derelict in failing to remove all vestiges of idolatry from his kingdom (14:1–7). He was militarily ambitious, as seen in his defeat of Edom and his challenge to Jehoash of Israel to confront him in battle. Disregarding the warning of the latter (14:8–10), Amaziah met him at Beth Shemesh where, to his dismay, Johoash more than met his match. Jehoash took the Judean king captive and then, having breached the walls of Jerusalem, sacked the treasures of the temple and royal palace. The victorious Israelite army then returned to Samaria, and Jehoash must have died shortly thereafter (14:11–16).

F. The Reign of Jeroboam II (14:17–29)

King Amaziah of Judah outlived Jehoash of Israel by fifteen years (14:17), falling at last to a party of conspiratorial assassins. For all this time Israel was ruled by Jeroboam II, the next in the line after Jehu, who retained his throne for forty-one years (793–753 B.C.). His reign not only embraced the latter years of Amaziah but went well into that of Azariah (Uzziah) of Judah as well.

Predictably perhaps, Jeroboam carried on the tradition of religious syncretism initiated by his namesake Jeroboam I. On the other hand, he proved to be a powerful deliverer of Israel from enemy encroachments, going so far as to regain territories that had been lost to them. This, the narrator stated, was in line with the prophetic word of Jonah, a citizen of the Northern Kingdom. God proved His faithfulness to even disobedient Israel, for He could not go against His own word.

G. The Reign of Uzziah of Judah (15:1–7)

Uzziah (also called Azariah; 15:1, 13, 30), whose reign is described much more fully in 2 Chronicles 26:1–23, sat on David's throne for fifty-two years (790–739 B.C.). His record, like that of his father, is basically positive, though he did tolerate such pagan elements as the high places (2 Kings 15:4). The historian here did not disclose the reason for Uzziah's suffering at the hands of the Lord, but the chronicler stated that the king had taken on himself the Aaronic priestly privilege of offering incense in the temple (2 Chron. 26:21–23). For this he contracted leprosy and was forced to yield his kingship to his son Jotham and live a private life for the rest of his days (2 Kings 15:5–7).

H. The Reign of Zachariah of Israel (15:8–12)

The last of the Jehu dynasty reigned for only six months (753 B.C.), a brief span terminated by Zechariah's assassination by a commoner, Shallum. Like all his forebears he was evil, and because of his and their sins the Jehu dynasty did not endure. Indeed, its demise had been predicted in its first generation, when Jehu had been informed that his house would survive for only four generations (10:30).

I. The Reign of Shallum (15:13–15)

Shallum, the murderer of Zechariah, lasted for only one month (752 B.C.) and was in turn put to death by Menahem, a revolutionary from the rival political center of Tirzah (15:33).

J. The Reign of Menahem (15:16–22)

Menahem, known for his brutality, situated himself in Samaria, where he reigned for nine years (752–742 B.C.). Though not a descendant of Jeroboam or Jehu, he retained their propensity for idolatry, behavior that prompted the Lord to send judgment in the person of King Tiglath-Pileser (here called Pul, 15:19; see also 15:29; 1 Chron. 5:26) of Assyria. This inaugurated a succession of Assyrian campaigns that led to Israel's collapse and deportation thirty years later. On this occasion Samaria was spared only because Menahem paid a heavy tribute to the Assyrian king, thus inducing him to lift his siege.

K. The Reign of Pekahiah (15:23–26)

The Menahem dynasty ended with his son Pekahiah, who ruled for only two years (742–740 B.C.). His personal, political, and spiritual wickedness brought swift and sure retribution from Pekah, one of his trusted officers.

L. The Reign of Pekah (15:27–31)

Apparently a Gileadite, Pekah had already created a power base at the beginning of the reign of Menahem, so much so that he was considered by the historian to be at least a provincial ruler for about twelve years (752–740 B.C.) and, after Pekahiah's death, king of all Israel for eight more years (740–732 B.C.). His accession did nothing to elevate the nation's moral temperature, however, for he sinned as much as any of his predecessors.

As a result, the Lord unleased Tiglath-Pileser once more, this time allowing the Assyrians to capture many towns and cities of the Upper Galilee region. As for Pekah, the proverb "he who lives by the sword will die by the sword" came true, and Hoshea, Israel's last king, slew him and took his place.

M. The Reign of Jotham of Judah (15:32–38)

Jotham's reign of sixteen years (750–735 B.C.) partly overlapped that of his father Uzziah, who was set aside because of his leprosy (15:5). He was viewed with favor generally but, like Uzziah, was overly tolerant of the people's resort to high places (15:35). Toward his latter years Aram and Israel formed a coalition against his kingdom Judah, one that was finally broken up by the inroads of Assyria.

N. The Reign of Ahaz of Judah (chapter 16)

Ahaz coreigned with his father, Jotham, from 735 to 731 and then commenced his sole reign of sixteen years, continuing until 715. His wickedness is compared to that of Israelite kings, for he went so far as to practice infant sacrifice (16:3). His turning to Assyria for aid against the threat of the Aramean-Israelite alliance did little to enhance his reputation, for in appealing to Tiglath-Pileser he emptied the temple and palace treasuries, in return for which the Assyrians captured Damascus. But the cost to Ahaz was not just monetary. He visited Tiglath-Pileser at Damascus, and seeing there a great pagan altar he was so impressed by it that he commanded one just like it to be erected in Jerusalem. He then offered sacrifice on it rather than on the bronze altar authorized by the Lord. In addition, he made other alterations in and around the temple, thus desecrating it even more. Judah was clearly in need of massive reformation, a turning to the Lord that Ahaz's godly son Hezekiah would lead.

O. The Reign of Hoshea (17:1–6)

The last of Israel's kings reigned for only nine years (732–722 B.C.). Though the record states that his behavior was comparatively better than that of his predecessors, it was a matter of too little too late. Having apparently come to power with Assyrian permission, Hoshea withheld tribute and thus incurred the wrath of Shalmaneser V, Tiglath's successor. Hoshea also had sought the help of Pharaoh So (also known as Osorkon) of Egypt against Assyria. This final straw provoked an Assyrian siege of Samaria, which fell after three years. Israel then suffered massive destruction and deportation from which it has never recovered to this very day.

III. THE KINGDOM OF JUDAH TO THE CAPTIVITY BY BABYLONIA (17:7–25:7)

Judah survived the collapse of her sister kingdom by fewer than 140 years. Though there were bright spots from time to time—notably the reigns of Hezekiah and Josiah—on the whole the house of David was represented by evil rulers who presided over an evil people. The rest of 2 Kings chronicles this sorry state of affairs.

A. Theological Explanation for the Fall of Israel (17:7–41)

Second Kings recounts and evaluates the history of Israel and Judah in terms of the adherence of those kingdoms to the covenant principles of Deuteronomy, and this is especially clear in 2 Kings 17:7–41.

The historian noted that the Assyrian deportation of Israel occurred for a number of specified reasons. Throughout their three-hundred-year history the Israelites had worshiped other gods (17:7–12). They ignored the warnings of the prophets and had rejected the terms of the covenant that God had made with them (17:13–18). Judah was no better, but up to that time only the Northern Kingdom had fallen (17:19–23).

> *The history of any nation—not just Israel—must ultimately be judged according to its faithfulness to the Lord. "Righteousness exalts a nation, but sin is a disgrace to any people" (Prov. 14:34). The author of 1 and 2 Kings, in unmistakable terms, explained Israel's demise as a direct consequence of her sin. The same is true, of course, of the life of any individual who persists in rebellion and unrepentance before God.*

Bringing the discussion around to his own time, the narrator described the Assyrian policy of replacing deported peoples with others who were brought in from distant places (17:24–26). While effective in discouraging rebellion, such a policy tended to cause peoples to lose their own cultural and religious identity. The Assyrian kings therefore authorized priests to return to Samaria to teach the things of the Lord but to do so alongside the pagan teachers who ministered to the foreign immigrants. This produced an intolerable syncretism (17:27–33), which resulted in Israel's abandoning the Lord and the covenant principles to which He had called them (17:34–41).

B. The Reign of Hezekiah (chapters 18–20)

The history of Judah as an independent entity began most auspiciously under Hezekiah, whose sole regency began a few years after Israel's collapse (715–686 B.C.) He got rid of pagan practices and led his kingdom to the exclusive worship of the Lord (18:1–8). While serving as coregent with his father Ahaz, Hezekiah had witnessed the demise of the Northern Kingdom (18:9–12), but in his own fourteenth year he himself came under Assyrian siege. Hezekiah first attempted to buy off the Assyrian King Sennacherib with an enormous sum of money, but Sennacherib was content with nothing less than Jerusalem's total capitulation, so he refused to lift the siege (18:13–18). With jeers and taunts, the Assyrian envoys pointed out to Hezekiah how fruitless it was to trust in Egypt or even the Lord his God (18:19–25).

Turning to the ordinary citizens, the Assyrian spokesmen pointed out how impotent was their King Hezekiah and their God. No other gods of any other nations had withstood the mighty Assyrian armies. Why, then, did they imagine their God could do any better (18:26–35)? Unable to respond, the people turned to Hezekiah to see what plan he might offer for their deliverance (18:36–37).

With deep concern and contrition Hezekiah sought the counsel of the prophet Isaiah, who assured the king that God would intervene on Judah's behalf (19:1–7). Meanwhile Sennacherib had gone to Libnah to confront the Egyptian army, which he understood to be on its way to Palestine. He had not forgotten his intention to capture Jerusalem, however, and he sent a letter to Hezekiah to warn him that he would soon be back (19:8–13). All Hezekiah could do was open the letter before the Lord and pray earnestly for divine intervention (19:14–19).

The Lord answered, but He did so through the words of Isaiah. Mighty Assyria would experience the terrible wrath of the Lord. He who had used Assyria as His own instrument of judgment would now turn against them because of their shameless arrogance (19:20–28). They would benefit from their siege for the moment, but Judah would be saved and enjoy prosperity in the end for Jerusalem was the city of David, a place precious in the eyes of the Lord (19:29–34). That very night the Lord's avenging angel annihilated the Assyrian army, leaving only Sennacherib and a few others to return ignominiously to Nineveh (19:35–37).

Just before that event Hezekiah had become deathly ill, but God heard his fervent plea for life and promised that He would deliver Jerusalem from the Assyrians and that He would grant Hezekiah fifteen more years (20:1–7). He then confirmed His word by the miracle of the lengthening of the day, a sign of the lengthening of his life (20:8–11). His recovery gained international attention, for Hezekiah soon received a delegation representing Merodach-Baladan, ruler of an Assyrian vassal state known as Babylonia or Chaldea. They came ostensibly to congratulate Hezekiah on his recovery, but clearly their real motive was to enlist Judah as an ally against their common Assyrian foe.

Flattered by such attention, Hezekiah showed the entourage all the treasures of his kingdom (20:12–15), a display of pompous pride that Isaiah said would cost him all he owned. The descendants of these very Babylonians would someday return and loot Judah's treasuries of all those things in which Hezekiah now boasted (20:16–21).

C. The Reign of Manasseh (21:1–18)

The good days under Hezekiah find striking contrast in the abysmal conditions rampant through most of Manasseh's fifty-five-year reign (695–642 B.C.). He restored the pagan shrines demolished by his father, placing some even in the sacred precincts of the temple (21:1–9). He went so far as to practice human sacrifice, just as his grandfather Ahaz had done (21:6; see 16:3). Besides these transgressions, Manasseh "filled Jerusalem with blood," that is, tolerated and promoted murder and mayhem of all kinds (21:16–18). No wonder the Lord said that Judah would suffer Israel's fate, for Judah's sin was every bit as great (21:10–15). The chronicler indicated that Manasseh repented at last (2 Chron. 33:12–13), but the word of national judgment was never repealed.

D. The Reign of Amon (21:19–26)

Amon's brief term (642–640 B.C.) was a mirror image of his father's. Lest it extend over such a long time, however, conspirators took Amon's life. They themselves were slain by a party that installed Amon's young son Josiah. Very likely this latter group was a pro-Amon faction that hoped Josiah would carry on his father's wicked policies. This was not to be, however, for Josiah became the godliest of the Old Testament kings who descended from David.

E. The Reign of Josiah (22:1–23:30)

Josiah, who commenced his reign at the tender age of eight, ruled for thirty-one years (640–609 B.C.). No occupant of the Davidic throne matched him for godliness of life and commitment to covenant principles (22:2; 23:25). In his young manhood he initiated a temple restoration project, one that resulted in the discovery of a long-lost copy of the Pentateuch or at least of Deuteronomy (22:3–13). Not knowing what to do in response to its message of condemnation for sin, Josiah appealed to the prophetess Huldah, who informed him that though the nation would suffer divine wrath, Josiah himself would not live to see it happen (22:14–20).

When Josiah read the scroll, he determined to lead his people in a great spiritual reformation (23:1–3). As a whole community they swore to obey God's covenant, a pledge that was followed by a wholesale destruction of pagan paraphernalia in and about Jerusalem (23:4–14) and even as far afield as Bethel, the site of Jeroboam's golden calf (23:15–20; see 1 Kings 13:1–3). The climax was the celebration of the Passover in a manner and on a scale unprecedented since the days of the judges more than five hundred years earlier (2 Kings 23:21–23). Notwithstanding Josiah's strict adherence to all the conditions of the covenant, the nation had defected from it so badly that God's judgment on Judah was irrevocable (23:24–27). An early sign of its approach was the devastating defeat of Judah's army by the Egyptians at Megiddo, a conflict in which Josiah himself lost his life (23:28–30). But even this was a blessing, for Josiah did not live to see his beloved land delivered over to the Babylonians.

F. The Reigns of Josiah's Sons (23:31–25:7)

Between the date of Josiah's death (609 B.C.) and the fall of Jerusalem (586 B.C.), four descendants of Josiah reigned in rapid succession, three sons and a grandson. The first son, Jehoahaz (23:31–35), held on for only three months. Pharaoh Necho of Egypt then took him prisoner to Egypt and set his brother Jehoiakim on Judah's throne. This suggests, of course, a rising Egyptian presence, thanks to Assyria's demise as a major world power.

Jehoiakim (609–597 B.C.), an older brother of Jehoahaz, was at first an Egyptian vassal but then, with the domination of Judah by Nebuchadnezzar and the Babylonians, Jehoiakim found himself answerable to the Babylonians. After a short time Jehoiakim rebelled, but before Nebuchadnezzar could address the situation Jehoiakim died, having sullied his reputation by all kinds of evil conduct. Already it was clear that Judah's tragic end was near at hand.

Jehoiakim's eighteen-year-old son Jehoiachin succeeded him and reigned for only three months (597 B.C.). Having prevailed over crises elsewhere, Nebuchadnezzar now was able to turn to the west again, so he came with a vengeance against Jerusalem. He captured the city, looted its treasuries, and carried off a number of prisoners including Jeroiachin (24:8–16) and Ezekiel (Ezek. 1:2; 40:1). Jehoiachin remained alive in Babylon for many years thereafter (2 Kings 25:27), but the kingship in Judah was handed over to his uncle Zedekiah (24:17).

Zedekiah, the last of David's descendants to occupy his dynastic seat in Old Testament times, hung on for eleven years (597–586 B.C.). No less evil than many of his forebears, he shared with some of them the foolhardiness of rebelling against the Babylonians (24:18–20). Nebuchadnezzar therefore came one more time to punish the little vassal state of Judah but this time with utter finality. Zedekiah tried to escape but was captured, blinded, and taken off to Babylon (25:1–7).

IV. THE BABYLONIAN CAPTIVITY (25:8–30)

The sad story of Judah's failure to conform to the Lord's covenant expectations and responsibilities concludes with the violent destruction of

Jerusalem and its temple and the deportation of a large and important segment of the population to far-off Babylon. Only the reinstatement of King Jehoiachin to personal freedom after many years provided hope that someday God's whole people would be free again.

A. The Pillaging of Jerusalem (25:8–17)

Leaving nothing to chance, this time Nebuchadnezzar ordered his troops to demolish the city of Jerusalem with all its public buildings, especially Solomon's temple and the royal palace. They then systematically looted all its treasures and carried off all the upper classes of the population. Only the peasants were left to work the soil and otherwise keep things intact for the benefit of the Babylonians, who viewed Judah as a vassal state.

B. The Deportation of the People (25:18–21)

Though most of the captives were taken to Babylon and kept alive, others, especially those who were political and religious leaders, ended up in Riblah to the north, where they were executed in the presence of Nebuchadnezzar himself.

C. The Establishment of a Local Government (25:22–26)

The Babylonian policy was not to eradicate all life off the land of Judah but only to so interrupt its existing political, social, and religious structures as to make it amenable to Babylonian sovereignty. Thus with the removal of Judean kingship, a new system of government was installed, consisting of appointees who would be subservient and directly answerable to the Babylonian central government. Gedaliah was the first of these so-called governors, but the strength of the underlying currents of resistance to Babylonian control is apparent in Gedaliah's assassination by fellow Jews, who themselves escaped to Egypt to forestall Babylonian retribution. The Book of Jeremiah provides more information on these events (Jer. 40:1–41:18).

D. The Release of Jehoiachin from House Arrest (25:27–30)

Only Jehoiachin, of all the house of David, survived the Babylonian conquest of Jerusalem. After a hiatus of more than twenty-five years in the record, the historian concluded his account by alluding to Jehoiachin's release from internment in the reign of Evil-Merodach (called Amel-Marduk in Babylonian texts), immediate successor to Nebuchadnezzar (562–560 B.C.). His rise to a position of favor in the eyes of his captors gave to Jehoiachin and to the Jews in general a cause for hope that the line of David would again be restored over a returned and rebuilt nation.

Sometimes in the blackest midnight of hopelessness and despair, a pinpoint of light begins to shine and offer renewed prospects for the future. God had promised David that his messianic dynasty would know no end (2 Sam. 7:16). Jehoiachin's release from Babylonian imprisonment was the ray of light that helped affirm the reliability of that ancient covenant promise.

1 CHRONICLES
Israel's History from a Global Perspective

AUTHOR

𝒯he lack of compelling evidence on the authorship of 1 and 2 Chronicles has led modern scholars to speak of the author(s) or compiler(s) of the books of Chronicles as "the chronicler." While this may lack precision, it reflects all that can be known on the matter to this point. Moreover, the term "author" itself may be somewhat inaccurate, given the apparent literary diversity of the material. Rather, one might better speak of a compiler of texts who selected them and frequently left them unchanged.

At the same time, the suggestion that the chronicler was more or less an editor should not denigrate his original contribution, for the skill with which he fashioned the end product out of such a breadth of diverse sources leads one to respect him as a highly creative artist. Close comparison of the chronicler's work to Samuel-Kings, his primary source, demonstrates clearly his capacity to adapt and refashion texts in the interest of his own peculiar approach to writing the history of his people.

The primary ancient source of information relative to the authorship of 1 and 2 Chronicles is the Babylonian Talmud, which states that "Ezra wrote the book that bears his name [that is, Ezra-Nehemiah] and the genealogies of the Book of Chronicles up to his own time. . . . Who then finished it [the Book of Chronicles]? Nehemiah the son of Hachaliah" (*Baba Bathra* 15a). This tradition thus identifies the chronicler as two persons—Ezra and Nehemiah, and in that sequence. In addition, it pre-supposes a common composition of Ezra–Nehemiah and Chronicles, a point of view that is discussed in the introduction to Ezra-Nehemiah.

UNITY

Regardless of authorship, the scholarly consensus is that Chronicles is one book, the division into 1 and 2 Chronicles having come about for practical reasons such as the unwieldiness of a single scroll of such length. In addition the major themes and emphases of 1 Chronicles continue in 2 Chronicles, and the overall literary structure yields patterns that suggest a single, unitary composition. This is in line with the Jewish tradition and ancient canon lists which invariably speak only of Chronicles and not of constituent parts. Division into two sections is attested to only in the Septuagint (the Greek translation of the Old Testament) and later versions.

DATE

This complicated question relates directly to that of authorship which, as has been pointed out, is itself most problematic. If Ezra was responsible for the bulk of the book, then his part at least could not be much later than 445 B.C., the date of his participation in the covenant renewal cer-emony led by Nehemiah (Neh. 8:1–12). Nehemiah seems to be a better candidate as far as some of the later genealogies are concerned, but even he recounted no historical events later than his return to Jerusalem from Susa in 432 B.C. (13:6). It is unlikely that he would have failed to continue the historical record if he were responsible for genealogies which appear, in fact, to have included names much later than his own time.

The Chronicles narratives end with the decree of Cyrus in 538 B.C. (2 Chron. 36:22–23), thus suggesting that most of the book was com-pleted by then. There are, however, incidental clues here and there that point to a date of 400 B.C. or even later for the production of the book in its final form. For example, Zerubbabel's genealogy contains names six generations after his own time (1 Chron. 3:19–24), thus as late as 400 B.C. The best view is that Chronicles as a whole was in place by 500 B.C., but that additions as late as the early fourth century continued to be added, especially genealogies, under the inspiration of the Holy Spirit.

ADDRESSEES

Chronological considerations alone make clear that the intended recipients of Chronicles were the postexilic Jewish community. In addition the message of hope centered in the restoration of the Davidic dynasty with all its political and religious significance is particularly appropriate to a people recently returned to the homeland and yet not fully established. On the other hand, lack of reference to the actual return of the exiles and to the problems they encountered in rebuilding their secular and sacred communities suggests that the initial readers of the book were the earliest phase of returnees, those who as yet were not fully aware of all that would be involved in their reconstitution as God's covenant people.

PURPOSE

If Chronicles was addressed to the earliest of the returned Jews, it must have been composed to meet the most profound needs of that community. Surely the uppermost question was whether the Lord could and would restore the house of David to its former glory and grandeur. Were the ancient promises to the ancestors now null and void in light of Israel's sin, or might it yet be possible that they were still in effect? The constant attention in Chronicles to the Davidic Covenant and its eternal nature was intended without doubt to build confidence that what God had begun He would complete, in spite of the sins of His people.

THEOLOGICAL EMPHASES

The most important theological ideas in Chronicles are (a) the centrality of the Davidic dynasty, founded on the unconditional covenant God made with him; (b) the role of David and his royal successors in establishing the temple and its services; and (c) the very evident purpose of selecting Israel under David's rule as the vehicle by which God would extend His saving grace to the whole world. These emphases pervade both 1 and 2 Chronicles extensively.

OUTLINE

I. The Genealogies (chapters 1–9)
   A. The Patriarchal Genealogies (chapter 1)
   B. The Genealogy of Judah (2:1-4:23)
   C. The Genealogy of Simeon (4:24–43)
   D. The Genealogy of Reuben (5:1–10)
   E. The Genealogy of Gad (5:11–17)
   F. The Hagrite Campaign (5:18–22)
   G. The Genealogy of Transjordan Manasseh (5:23–26)
   H. The Genalogy of Levi (chapter 6)
   I. The Genealogy of Issachar (7:1–5)
   J. The Genealogy of Benjamin (7:6–12)
   K. The Genealogy of Naphtali (7:13)
   L. The Genealogy of Western Manasseh (7:14–19)
   M. The Genealogy of Ephraim (7:20–29)
   N. The Genealogy of Asher (7:30–40)
   O. The Genealogy of Benjamin (chapter 8)
   P. The Settlers of Jerusalem (9:1–34)
   Q. The Genealogy of Saul (9:35–44)
II. The Rise of David (10:1–22:1)
   A. The Death of Saul (chapter 10)
   B. The Succession of David (chapters 11–12)
   C. The Movement of the Ark (chapter 13)
   D. The Establishment of David's Rule (chapter 14)
   E. The Arrival of the Ark and Its Installation (chapters 15–16)
   F. David's Concern for a Temple (chapter 17)
   G. David's International Relations (chapters 18–20)
   H. David's Census and Its Aftermath (21:1–22:1)
III. The Preparation for Succession (22:2–29:30)
   A. David's Preparation for the Temple (22:2–19)

B. David's Preparation of Religious and Political
   Personnel (chapters 23–27)
C. David's Great Assembly (28:1–29:22a)
D. The Succession of Solomon (29:22b–30)

I. THE GENEALOGIES (CHAPTERS 1–9)

What may seem at first glance to be material of little or no historical or theological value, namely, the genealogies of Chronicles, turns out, quite to the contrary, to be of major significance. The first word in this long section is "Adam," and the section closes with the genealogy of Saul and an introduction to his ill-advised reign as the king of Israel permitted but not endorsed by the Lord. The purpose is clear—to link God's creation purposes with David, whose divinely appointed role is recounted at the end of the first long narrative in the book, the one describing Saul's miserable failure (10:14). The fact that David's tribe, Judah, appears first among the tribes in the chronicler's list (2:1–4:23) also underscores the importance of David in the redemptive scheme.

A. *The Patriarchal Genealogies (chapter 1)*

The full genealogies of this chapter are virtually identical in wording to those of Genesis. Clearly, the chronicler made use of Genesis in compiling his lists, though he did omit some of the Genesis data where they seem not to have served his special purpose. Most notable are the truncated genealogies of verses 1–4, which summarize Genesis 4:25–5:32, and of verses 24–27, which summarize Genesis 11:10–26. The purpose is to make the connection as quickly as possible between Adam and Shem on the one hand and between Shem and Abraham on the other. First Chronicles 1:34 likewise gets to the heart of the matter by linking Abraham to Israel (not called Jacob here), thus paving the way for the introduction of David's (and the Messiah's) tribe, Judah, the subject of chapters 2–4.

B. The Genealogy of Judah (2:1–4:23)

After listing the sons of Israel in their correct birth sequence (2:1–2), the author turned immediately to the fourth son, Judah, for it was through Judah's line that God's plan of redemption would be transmitted and find fulfillment. This found its earliest clear expression in the blessing of Jacob, who prophesied that the messianic ruler would descend through that tribe (Gen. 49:10–12). This was despite Judah's less than sterling character and behavior, especially in regard to his marriage and his treatment of his daughter-in-law and children (Gen. 38).

By his daughter-in-law Tamar Judah had two sons, Perez and Zerah (1 Chron. 2:4), the former of whom became the transmitter of the tribal blessing (Ruth 4:18–22). The Perez line was distinguished by such notables as Boaz, the husband of Ruth (Ruth 4:13, 21; Matt. 1:5); Jesse, father of David (1 Chron. 2:12); and, of course, David himself (2:15). David became the recipient of a covenant that made it clear that his descendants would have the privilege of bearing the news of redemptive grace to the whole world (17:7–14). The New Testament provides specific identification of the last of those descendants—Jesus Christ Himself (Matt. 1:16).

Other famous descendants also are mentioned in the Judah genealogy, such as Achan (1 Chron. 2:7; see also Josh. 7:1), Bezalel (1 Chron. 2:20; see also Exod. 31:2), and Caleb (1 Chron. 2:42; see also Judg. 1:12–15). Of these, little is said, however, for the attention, as always in Chronicles, is on David and his descendants. Even here it is focused on particular descendants, those who culminate in the messianic promise. Thus David's sons born while he was ruler at Hebron are listed—including Amnon, Absalom, and Adonijah (1 Chron. 3:1–2)—as are those born later in Jerusalem (3:5–8). The most prominent of those born in Jerusalem was Solomon (3:5), so the record ignores the rest of the sons and begins to focus on him alone.

Solomon must have had a great number of children, considering the size of his harem (1 Kings 11:3), but only one is named here in his genealogy, namely, Rehoboam (1 Chron. 3:10). The reason is that the chronicler was interested not in recording a full family tree but in narrowing his scope to the royal line that would eventually issue in David's greatest Son, that is, the Messiah. The Old Testament record does not carry the matter that far, of course, for it traces the Davidic and Solomonic descent only to the end of the Old Testament historical period. The New Testament then provides the linkage between the last significant figure of the Chronicles list, namely, Zerubbabel, and Jesus Christ the Savior (Matt. 1:13–16; see also Luke 3:23–27).

The latter part of the Solomon genealogy (1 Chron. 3:20–24) provides a clue as to the earliest possible date for the composition of Chronicles since it contains the names of six generations of Zerubbabel's descendants. Zerubbabel was governor of Judah near the end of the sixth century (520 B.C. and later; see Hag. 1:1). He was certainly of middle age by then, because he was already among the leaders of the Jews when they returned to Jerusalem from Babylon in 538 B.C. (Ezra 2:2). On this assumption, and the further assumption that a generation was roughly twenty-five years in length, Zerubbabel's son Hananiah was born around 540 B.C. and his last named descendant, Anani, around 415. Chronicles thus must be later than 415 according to this line of evidence.

The Judah genealogy closes with other descendants more peripheral to the redemptive line (1 Chron. 4:1–23). Most of these names are associated with places in and about the territory assigned to Judah but otherwise are unknown except for a few like Othniel (4:13) and Caleb (4:15).

C. The Genealogy of Simeon (4:24–43)

Simeon appears next in the list because his tribe eventually was assimilated into Judah, losing its independent identity (Josh. 19:1–9). The chronicler suggested that the reason for this was Simeon's small population, a fact attributed to a low birth rate (1 Chron. 4:27). By David's time, Simeon no longer was a separate entity at all (4:31). However, some Simeonites apparently retained their tribal identity, for they moved aggressively to other places such as the territory of the Meunites and Amalekites, where they still remained as a recognizable people as late as the chronicler's own time (4:41, 43).

D. The Genealogy of Reuben (5:1–10)

As the eldest son of Jacob, Reuben should have been his father's heir, at least in terms of birthright if not of messianic blessing. The birthright, however, fell to Joseph (and through him to his sons Ephraim and Manasseh) because of Reuben's sexual intimacy with his father's concubine Bilhah (5:1; see Gen. 35:22; 49:4). As for the blessing, it was bestowed on Judah by divine elective grace (49:8–10). The Reubenites lived in Transjordania as late as the Assyrian exile of 722 B.C. at least, for the historian noted that Tilgath-Pileser took many of them captive at that time (1 Chron. 5:6).

E. The Genealogy of Gad (5:11–17)

The Gadites lived just north of the Reubenites in the Transjordan area known as Bashan. Besides this information the chronicler pointed out the interesting fact that a census of Gadites was undertaken in the days of the kings Jotham of Judah and Jeroboam II of Israel (5:17). Since these reigns did not overlap, it seems there must have been two such calculations sometime between 790 and 730 B.C. Perhaps they were done because of the need to determine military strength in light of the increasing threat by the Assyrians, who later captured Israel and much of Transjordania by 722 B.C.

F. The Hagrite Campaign (15:18–22)

Attention to the Transjordan prompted the chronicler to recall a resounding victory by the eastern tribes over an enemy known as the Hagrites, desert peoples who lived east of Gilead (5:10). This triumph, attributed to divine intervention (or "holy war"; 5:20, 22), took place in the time of King Saul (5:10), though it is nowhere else attested. This is an example of the chronicler's use of a source unknown to or at least not utilized by the author of 1 and 2 Samuel.

G. The Genealogy of Transjordan Manasseh (5:23–26)

At the time of the conquest of the Transjordan, half the tribe of Manasseh sought and received permission from Moses to settle in that area along with the tribes of Reuben and Gad (Num. 32:1–42). Gradually they fell away from the Lord and became idolatrous, a covenant defection that issued in their conquest and deportation by the Assyrian king Pul, also known as Tiglath-Pileser. Pul's dates (745–727) suggest that Manasseh's fall to Assyria occurred several years before that of the western tribes in 722 B.C.

H. The Genealogy of Levi (chapter 6)

The underlying purpose of this table, it seems, is to legitimate and clarify the role of the priests and Levites in the service of the temple (6:31). The tribe of Levi consisted of three clans, the members of which were entrusted with separate and discrete functions. Priests must descend from Aaron, a Kohathite, and the chronicler here listed all the chief priests from Aaron to Jehozadak, the priest in office in the days of the Babylonian destruction of the temple (6:3–15). In all there were twenty-two, including Aaron and Jehozadak, who occupied the ministry for a period of 860 years, or about thirty-nine years each on the average.

Other Kohathites plus the Merarites and Gershomites (6:16–30) exercised nonpriestly functions such as vocal and instrumental music (6:31–48). But all sacrifice at the central sanctuary had to be made exclusively by the priests (6:49–53).

The chronicler also addressed the matter of settlement patterns. The priests were assigned thirteen towns, all in Judah and Benjamin (6:54–60). The Levites received thirty-five cities within the territories of Manasseh, Issachar, Asher, Naphtali, East Manasseh, Reuben, Gad, and Zebulun (6:61–65) and apparently thirty-one more within Ephraim, Manasseh, East Manasseh, Issachar, Asher, Naphtali, Zebulun, Reuben, and Gad (6:66–81). Verses 66–81 list the cities of the Levites that are only totaled and unnamed in verses 61–65. The "missing" four cities (thirty-one rather than thirty-five) came from Dan, as the parallel list in Joshua 21:23–24 makes clear. Why the chronicler did not refer to Dan is not clear. In any case, the total of forty-eight priestly/Levitical cities is in line with the ancient Mosaic allocation of that many places (Num. 35:6–7; see also Josh. 21:41–42).

I. The Genealogy of Issachar (7:1–5)

The population figures here, probably referring to military strength, compare the eras of David (22,600; 2 Sam. 24:1–9) and the chronicler himself (36,000). The grand total of 87,000 must include contingents not further identified.

J. The Genealogy of Benjamin (7:6–12)

The Benjamites, divided into the clans of Bela (7:6–7), Becher (7:8–9), and Jediael (7:10–12), consisted of 22,034; 20,200; and 17,200 warriors, respectively, for a grand total of 59,434.

K. The genealogy of Naphtali (7:13)

This brief note simply lists five clans or subgroups.

L. The Genealogy of Western Manasseh (7:14–19)

The principal items of information here are (a) the recognized connection between West and East Mannaseh through the reference to the Transjordanian persons and/or areas of Gilead and Maacah (7:14–15), and (b) the mention of Zelophehad, a son of Manasseh, who had no male heirs and whose daughters' inheritance required a special legal dispensation (7:15; see Num. 36:1–12). Why the chronicler included these matters is not apparent. In the latter case it might be that in his time there was still some question of territorial claims in instances where there were no male heirs to an estate.

M. The Genealogy of Ephraim (7:20–29)

After a brief narrative about some land holdings of the Ephraimites that were seized by "men of Gath" (perhaps early Philistines), resulting in Ephraimite loss of life, the focus is on the genealogy of the famous Ephraimite Joshua son of Nun. Then follows a description of the large territory of that tribe and its principal cities.

N. The Genealogy of Asher (7:30–40)

Apart from the note that this Mediterrean coastal tribe mustered 26,000 men (7:40), this passage merely lists the four sons or clans of Asher and their sister together with their principal descendants.

O. The Genealogy of Benjamin (chapter 8)

The tribal genealogies end with Benjamin just as they begin with Judah, for Judah gave rise to the legitimate king long promised as a means of achieving God's redemptive design and from Benjamin came Saul, the outcome of human choice and strategy. The two, then, bracket all the rest as though to suggest that the whole nation was trapped in that tension between divine purpose and human ambition.

After an extensive list of families and their interconnections and various brief anecdotal notations (8:1–28), the chronicler directed attention to the cities of Gibeon and Jerusalem and the families associated with these places. Chief among them is the family of Ner, the grandfather of Saul (8:33; Ner is not mentioned in verse 30 but is included in the list in 9:35–44). The genealogy of Saul then continues for about eleven generations after him or a minimum of 275 years. The records cease after this, perhaps in the mid-eighth century B.C.

P. The Settlers of Jerusalem (9:1–34)

Having looked at the genealogical records of the tribes of Israel in general, and from a more distant historical perspective (9:1), the chronicler then moved closer to his own time and provided information about the postexilic settlers of Jerusalem and vicinity. These he categorized as Israel, the priests, the Levites, and the Nethinim (9:2).

By *Israel* is meant the non-Levite Israelites. These derived mainly from Judah, Benjamin, Ephraim, and Manasseh (9:3–9). The religious personnel were priests (9:10–13), Levites (9:14–16), porters (9:17–27), singers (9:33–34), and various other temple servants (9:28–32). The porters had first been under the direction of the chief priest Phinehas (9:20) and were later organized and assigned duties by Samuel and David (9:22).

Q. The Genealogy of Saul (9:35–44)

The family of Saul had been mentioned as an element within the overall genealogy of Benjamin (chapter 8). Now, as a way of introducing his reign as Israel's first king, the historian repeated the names of the principal ancestors and descendants of Saul, this time including a few names not given in the previous list (9:35–37; compare 8:29–31). The literary strategy was to locate Saul "in time and space" in preparation for the narrative that would describe his tragic end.

II. THE RISE OF DAVID (10:1–22:1)

Though the chronicler did not repeat the long account in 1 Samuel of the complicated relationship between Saul and David that resulted in their irreconcilable parting of the ways, he did clearly, though succinctly, point to its underlying theological basis—Saul, Israel's choice as king, must give way to David, chosen by the Lord from the beginning (10:13–14; 11:2). He then recorded his own version of David's illustrious reign, emphasizing, in line with his own peculiar historiography, David's concern with matters of worship.

A. The Death of Saul (chapter 10)

The historian added very little to the account of Saul's death related already by the author of 1 Samuel (1 Sam. 31:1–13). He did, however, make the observation that Saul's demise was punishment for his disobedience of covenant principles, and paved the way for David's succession (1 Chron. 10:13–14).

B. The Succession of David (chapters 11–12)

The story of David's succession is much more detailed and expansive here than in 2 Samuel. "All Israel" came to Hebron to recognize his kingship, and "all the elders of Israel" anointed him to that office (1 Chron. 11:1–3; see also 12:38–40). Skipping over the seven years at Hebron (2 Sam. 5:4–5), the narrator indicated that David captured Jerusalem with ease and made it Israel's capital with no sectional opposition (1 Chron. 11:4–8). David, in fact, became greater and greater because the Lord was with him (11:9).

Evidence of his greatness is seen in the stories of the heroic exploits of the men he gathered about him. They slew the Philistines, provided David with drinking water at great personal risk, and engaged both wild beasts and human giants in hand-to-hand combat (11:10–25). The names of more than thirty of these valiant warriors appear in a hall of fame of David's mighty men (11:26–47).

Not all of David's comrades in arms were sons of his own tribe of Judah. In fact, some of Saul's own Benjamite kinsmen joined David (12:1–7), as did others from the northern tribes of Gad (12:8–15), Manasseh (12:19–22), Simeon, Levi, Ephraim, Issachar, Zebulun, Naphtali, Dan, Asher, and the tribes of Transjordania (12:23–37). In other words, the impression is that the whole nation rallied behind their new king. The leaders, surprisingly enough, came from Benjamin as well as Judah. Because of Saul's affiliation with the tribe of Benjamin, David required that they especially swear to him their loyalty (12:16–18).

C. The Movement of the Ark (chapter 13)

To the chronicler, David's greatest achievement was the establishment of Israel's apparatus of worship, so he turned first to David's initial attempt to bring the ark of the covenant into Jerusalem. It had been housed at Kiriath Jearim through all the years of Saul (13:3), but now that David had built a tabernacle for it (see 15:1) it seemed appropriate that the ark find its place there (13:1–8). Unfortunately it was mishandled, and David had to postpone its further movement (13:9–14; see 2 Sam. 6:6–11).

D. The Establishment of David's Rule (chapter 14)

Before David's efforts to retrieve the ark, he had engaged King Hiram of Tyre to build a royal palace for him (14:1). This accompanied David's other affirmations of God's blessings such as a large harem (14:3), many children (14:4–7), and victories over his foreign enemies, especially the Philistines (14:8–16). He perceived correctly that the Lord had called and endorsed him as king (14:2), something that all the other nations came to recognize as well (14:17).

E. The Arrival of the Ark and Its Installation (chapters 15–16)

Before David expressed any desire to build a temple for the Lord, he erected a tabernacle in Jerusalem as a place of worship (15:1). Having learned that the holy ark must be transported according to proper protocol (Num. 4:15; 1 Chron. 13:9–10), David authorized the priests and Levites to enshrine it in the place he had prepared for it (15:3–5). The procession to the tabernacle included singers and instrumentalists who lifted their musical praises to the Lord (15:16–24). All along the way the Levites offered up sacrifices, as did David himself, the priest-king authorized to do so by virtue of his association with the order of Melchizedek (15:25–28; see 2 Sam. 6:12–15; Ps. 110:4). Even his wife Michal's jealous sulking in memory of her father, Saul, could not put a damper on the joyous festivities (1 Chron. 15:29).

The installation of the ark was a glorious event. David offered sacrifices at the tabernacle and the musicians continued to voice their expressions of worship and adoration of the Lord God of Israel (16:1–6). Among the musical selections were psalms composed either by David or someone else (perhaps Asaph; 16:7). These were all collected here by the chronicler as one hymn, or conversely this long piece was subsequently divided up into shorter compositions and/or appropriated by later psalmists. Verses 8–22 are the same as Psalm 105:1–15; verses 16–33 are the same as Psalm 96:1–13; verse 34 is essentially the same as Psalm 106:1; and verses 35–36 are close in wording to Psalm 106:47–48.

With the ark in place David appointed various personnel to minister at the tabernacle in Jerusalem (1 Chron. 16:37–38). Though an explicit statement is lacking, it seems reasonable to suppose that Abiathar was the chief priest there, since there were two such officers at that time (see 15:11; 1 Sam. 22:20; 2 Sam. 15:24; 1 Kings 4:4) and Zadok served at the old Mosaic tabernacle at Gibeon (1 Chron. 16:39; see 2 Chron 1:1–16; 5:2–5). This irregular practice of having two chief priests seems to have remained until Solomon built his temple and did away with the two separate tabernacles (1 Kings 2:27, 35).

F. David's Concern for a Temple (chapter 17)

A tabernacle symbolizes mobility and impermanence, both of which characterized Israel in the desert and, to a lesser extent, all through the years of the Conquest and the judges. David's acquisition of Jerusalem and construction of his own palace put in stark contrast the comparative flimsiness of the tabernacle he had erected on Mount Zion, so he expressed his wish to make a temple suitable for the Lord (17:1–3). The Lord had other plans, however. Temple-building was a peacetime pursuit and, in fact, a sign of completed conquest. David must therefore not build a temple; rather, God would build *him* a house, that is, a dynasty, that would be stable and everlasting. This Davidic Covenant would provide the way for a son of David whose throne would be eternal (17:11–15).

> David's desire to build a temple for the Lord, though not granted, reflects his heart for God. Often those who have been most blessed in the things of the world are least inclined to recognize the generous hand of the Lord and to reciprocate by honoring Him with their substance and other tokens of devotion. God took note of David's sacrificial offer and surprised him with the announcement that He would build him an everlasting house, a dynasty that would know no end.

Overwhelmed by this revelation, David could only marvel at the grace of God (17:16–19). In a profound but clear confession he acknowledged the sovereign pleasure of the Lord who, for reasons known only to Himself, chose Israel as his people out of all the nations of the earth (17:20–22). And now He had spoken of the future in which He would establish David's lineage forever (17:23–25). For all these evidences of God's favor and faithfulness, David could only affirm that He indeed is Lord, the Source of every blessing (17:26–27).

G. David's International Relations (chapters 18–20)

The Lord had responded to David's request to build a temple by implying that such a thing could be done only when Israel's enemies were subdued

(17:8, 10; see also 22:7–10). The account in chapters 18–20 lists the various military engagements David undertook as a man of war until the day when peace would prevail under the leadership of his son. He subdued the Philistines, Moabites, and Arameans (18:1–8), all because the Lord Himself gave Israel victory (18:6). Others voluntarily submitted, such as the kingdom of Hamath, and became tributary to Israel (18:9–11). Whether in Edom (18:12–13) or anywhere else, God blessed David, making it possible for him to create a nation of order and stability (18:14–17).

A particularly persistent foe was Ammon, the nation in Transjordania just east of Israel. Through a misunderstanding, it seems, the king of Ammon had humiliated a delegation David had sent to him to offer condolences on the death of his father (19:1–5; see also 2 Sam. 10:1–19). Fearing reprisal, Hanun, the Ammonite ruler, had hired mercenaries from nearby nations to assist him against an anticipated Israelite invasion (1 Chron. 19:6–9).

The attack indeed came to pass. Joab, commander of Israel's armies, led his division against the Arameans and deployed his brother Abishai's division against the Ammonites. The Arameans retreated at once to their own lands, so the Ammonites followed suit, finding refuge in their capital city of Rabbath Ammon (19:10–15). Meanwhile the Arameans augmented their forces and made a second foray into the Transjordan. David himself led Israel once more to victory, so decisively that Aram never again came to Ammon's aid against Israel (19:16–19).

Ammon, now on its own, was an inviting target, so David sent his troops to besiege the capital city. The king stayed home in Jerusalem this time, opening himself up to the temptations and resultant sins spelled out in detail in 2 Samuel 11–12 but not included by the chronicler. To tell the sordid tale again was unnecessary, and it would add little or nothing to the chronicler's principal interest, namely, the glory of the Davidic dynasty and establishment of its religious structures.

In any case Israel conquered and sacked Rabbah along with other Ammonite towns (1 Chron. 20:1–3). The same success attended conflicts with the Philistines despite their formidable size and strength (20:4–8).

H. David's Census and Its Aftermath (21:1–22:1)

David's great success on the battlefield seems to have given him the impression that victory comes through human strength and not the power of God. To test him in that area the Lord permitted Satan to induce David to take a census of his military forces, perhaps in anticipation of still more and greater international conflicts (21:5; see 2 Sam. 24:1). Though reluctant to do so, Joab carried out David's wishes and returned with a report that Israel could muster 1.1 million men and Judah 470,000 (1 Chron. 21:2–6).

This attitude of self-reliance displeased the Lord, who then offered David three punishment options. David wisely decided to let the Lord be the Agent of discipline, so God chose a pestilence rather than famine or war. But this was hardly just a slap on the wrist, for seventy thousand Israelites fell to the plague. Jerusalem itself was in danger of succumbing, but the grace of God intervened and the city was spared. David then understood that it was his confidence in the flesh that had brought disaster to his people, and he prayed earnestly that the plague might be lifted (21:7–17).

The Lord graciously relented and then instructed David to erect an altar at the threshing place of Ornan (spelled Araunah in 2 Sam. 24:16) the Jebusite. David refused to accept the property as a gift, so after paying for it he built the altar, offered burnt offerings, and thus fulfilled his role as a priestly mediator (1 Chron. 21:18–27). The author appended here the interesting note that one reason David sacrificed where he did is that the great altar of sacrifice made by Moses was at Gibeon, but David was afraid to go there because of God's avenging angel (21:28–30). It seems that the angel's threatening presence may have been one way to make it clear to David that Ornan's threshing floor was to be the site of Solomon's temple (22:1; see 2 Chron. 3:1).

III. THE PREPARATION FOR SUCCESSION (22:2–29:30)

David's inability to build the temple did not diminish his interest in the project. He set about gathering materials for it and establishing the temple personnel who would attend to its ministries. He then communicated to Solomon the plans and specifications that he had received by divine revelation. David thus paved the way for his son and successor to preside over both the political and spiritual spheres of Israel's national life.

A. David's Preparation for the Temple (22:2–19)

Once David understood the God-ordained location of the temple, he undertook the work of providing for and preparing the stones, timbers, metals, and other materials necessary for its construction (22:2–5). He then reminded Solomon that he, as a man of peace (the name "Solomon" is a derivative of šālôm, "peace"), must carry forward the project as a direct mandate from the Lord. If he remained faithful and obedient to the Lord, David said, Solomon would experience heaven's richest blessings (22:6–13). And there was no time to waste. The materials and men were at hand, so Solomon should not delay in pursuing the grand and glorious task God had given him (22:14–16). David turned also to Israel's leaders and charged them to cooperate with Solomon in providing a residence for the Lord that was worthy of Him (22:17–19).

B. David's Preparation of Religious and Political Personnel (chapters 23–27)

A temple and its services as massive in scope as the one just announced would require an enormous staff of multitalented and godly persons. First was Solomon himself, whom David appointed as his vice-regent (23:1; see also 28:5; 29:22). Then David numbered the Levites, divided them into four groups or courses, and assigned them the tasks of overseeing the temple in general, serving as officers and judges, working as porters, and leading in worship through instrumental music (23:2–6).

The chronicler included lists of Levites by clan and family (23:7–23). He then observed that their ministries would begin a new phase, for there would no longer be a need to assemble, disassemble, and transport the tabernacle. With the temple would come the Lord's ongoing presence among His people. From now on the Levites would assist the priests in the maintenance of the temple and with all the acts of worship that would take place there (23:24–32).

As for the priests, they too would serve in courses according to their lineage from Aaron. Only two sons of Aaron had survived—Eleazar and Ithamar (Exod. 6:23; Lev. 10:2)—and of these Eleazar had the larger number of descendants. Zadok was head of the line of Eleazar in David's time, and Ahimelech led the line of Ithamar. They and David appointed sixteen priests of Eleazar's clan and eight of Ithamar's to serve the temple on a rotating basis (1 Chron. 24:1–6). Their names appear in 24:7–18 as leaders of their courses, though surely other priests and/or Levites served under them. Perhaps some of the latter appear in the following list (24:20–31) for it is said that "These also cast lots just as their relatives the sons of Aaron" (24:31). Those lots may have determined the order in which they would serve in the temple.

Because music was so central to temple worship, David took care to appoint descendants of Asaph, Heman, and Jeduthun to lead the choirs and orchestras. Both men and women participated (24:5–6) according to a rotating schedule similar to that which regulated the ministries of the priests and Levites (25:1–8). There were 288 musicians in all, divided into twenty-four groups of twelve each. The Hemanites made up half of these groups, whereas Asaph and Jeduthun contributed only six groups each (25:9–31). All of these apparently belonged to the Levitical clan of Kohath (see 6:33, 38).

The responsibility for guarding and opening and closing the temple gates fell to the line of Korah, son of Izhar, son of Levi (26:1; see Exod. 6:21). The subclans of Korah plus Hosah, a subclan of Merari (1 Chron. 26:10), contributed over ninety men (26:2–11), who performed their assignments by lot as did the other Levites. Each group, moreover, was stationed at specified sides of the temple (26:12–19).

Other Levites oversaw the treasury of the temple, much of the receipts of which came from the spoils of war and other sources not connected to regular tithes and offerings (26:20–28). Still others were involved in the administration of more "secular" affairs such as peace officers and judges (26:29). There were several thousand of these throughout the kingdom. Their task is stated in rather general terms; they were to oversee every matter pertaining to God and the king (26:30–32).

The administration of the affairs of a rapidly growing kingdom and all its bureaucracy demanded the enlistment of thousands of major and minor public servants. David devised a system whereby each of the twelve administrative districts was responsible for one month to do whatever needed to be done during that time. The twenty-four thousand who made up each contingent were likely soldiers who perhaps functioned as a kind of national guard. However, there is nothing in the text that explicity indicates this (27:1–15). At the same time, tribal identity and structure were still in place and tribal government continued to be necessary. David therefore named or sanctioned the appointment of rulers of the various tribes (27:16–22). He desisted from a full census of the people, however, both because of God's promise that He would multiply Israel like the stars of the sky (27:23) and the divine judgment that had fallen when David had earlier asked Joab to do that very thing, that is, to determine Israel's military strength (27:24; see 21:1–7).

Royal officials included treasurers over various collections of revenue and managers of agricultural industries (27:25–31). David reserved positions of privilege and responsibility for family and friends such as his uncle, Jonathan, who was a scribe; Ahithophel, his counselor; Hushai, David's friend and confidant; and his own nephew, Joab, who served as commander of Israel's army (27:32–34).

C. David's Great Assembly (28:1–29:22a)

After all the practical matters of royal succession had been addressed, David convened a great assembly of Israel's officials and leading citizens to spell out to them what lay ahead and what he expected of them. He first shared with them what he had already disclosed to his son Solomon, namely, his desire to build a great temple to the Lord in Jerusalem (28:1–2; see also 17:1–2; 21:6–16). That hope had been dashed, however, for David was a warrior, and only when war was over and peace had come would temple building be appropriate (28:3; see 22:8–9). Nevertheless David, his tribe, and his dynastic descendants had been divinely chosen (28:4–5), an act of grace that now would result in the construction of God's house among them. Solomon would have the privilege of bringing it to pass, and if he and the nation remained faithful to the covenant they too would endure forever (28:6–8).

Turning to Solomon, David challenged him to be perfect before God, and if he failed in that, he should turn to the Lord in repentance. God had chosen him for the very special task of building the temple, a task that surely required a right relationship to the Lord (28:9–10). But this was to be no ordinary building concocted by human architects. David therefore turned over to Solomon a pattern that he had received by the Spirit of God (28:11–12, 19); one, it seems, that was based on a heavenly model. The whole building and everything in it must conform to this design, for in part and in whole the temple would be a metaphor of powerful significance (28:13–18). This is evident from the fact that the temple plans, like Scripture, were inspired and "authored" by Almighty God (28:19).

> *A problem in many churches today is the failure to recognize that corporate worship is an experience to be governed to a certain degree by order and propriety. David did not concoct the design of the temple by his own imagination, nor could Solomon build it as he pleased. The very architecture of the place was intended to teach Israel important lessons about the glory, grandeur, and awesomeness of their God. Christian worship that does less should be called into serious question.*

Concluding his remarks to Solomon, David encouraged him with the word that God would never abandon him. Besides this most wonderful assurance David could tell his young son that everything humanly possible had also been done to see that everything was in place for his kingship (28:20–21).

Once more David spoke to the people about the temple and its uniqueness as the house of God (29:1). He also made an appeal to them to make financial contributions toward its construction just as he had done. This they did willingly, causing David's heart to well up in joy and gratitude (29:2–9). Only God could have brought such a turn of events, as David well knew. He therefore raised his voice in praise, blessing the Lord for who He is and what He had done (29:10–13). Even the gifts he and the people had made were tokens of God's grace. They could give Him only what He had first given them (29:14–16).

Yet, David realized, God holds people accountable. He understands their motives and private ambitions. This is why Solomon needed a heart to love and obey God as he contemplated the awesome challenge of leading the nation in the future as well as undertaking the immediate task of building the temple (29:17–19).

Facing the crowds for a final time, David urged them to join him in blessing and worshiping the Lord, and with unanimity of mind and spirit they did so (29:20). In what is clearly a covenant-renewal ceremony, they sacrificed thousands of burnt offerings and then, expressive of their partnership with the Lord of the universe, joined David in eating and drinking around the festive table (29:21–22a).

D. The Succession of Solomon (29:22b–30)

David had previously installed his son as his vice-regent (23:1), but now, knowing he was about to die, David turned over to Solomon the full responsibility of government. By his side he appointed Zadok to be chief priest, thus limiting that office once more to only one claimant (29:22). The chronicler omitted any reference to the struggle for succession, for all these machinations and conspiracies were well documented elsewhere (1 Kings 1–2). They would detract from the idea that God was behind all that happened in the transfer of authority, so that human interference was not worth mentioning.

On Solomon's formal accession, the intense loyalty of the people toward David was immediately directed toward Solomon. And no wonder, for God had put His unmistakable approval on the young man, endorsing him as He had never done before with tokens of royal magnificence (1 Chron. 29:23–25).

The chronicler concluded this part of the account with an epitaph summarizing David's life and labors (29:26–30). David had reigned for forty years in all, and at the end of his life he could reflect on God's goodness in giving him many years, abundant riches, and great honor. These blessings and more were all well attested, the historian pointed out, and one need only research the records of Samuel, Nathan, and Gad to read them for oneself.

2 CHRONICLES
The House of David: An Uncertain Future

*A*ncient tradition as well as modern literary assessment of the two books of Chronicles indicate they were originally one book. So matters of introduction discussed in 1 Chronicles need not be repeated here.

OUTLINE

I. The Reign of Solomon (chapters 1–9)
   A. The Assembly at Gibeon and Solomon's Might (chapter 1)
   B. The Building of the Temple (2:1–5:1)
   C. The Dedication of the Temple (5:2–7:10)
   D. The Conditions of Covenant Blessing (7:11–22)
   E. Solomon's Accomplishments (chapters 8–9)
II. The Dynasty of David: Rehoboam to Uzziah (chapters 10–25)
   A. The Reign of Rehoboam (chapters 10–12)
   B. The Reign of Abijah (13:1–14:1)
   C. The Reign of Asa (14:2–16:14)
   D. The Reign of Jehoshaphat (chapters 17–20)
   E. The Reign of Jehoram (chapter 21)
   F. The Reign of Ahaziah (22:1–9)
   G. The Interregnum of Queen Athaliah (22:10–23:21)
   H. The Reign of Joash (chapter 24)
   I. The Reign of Amaziah (chapter 25)

III. The Dynasty of David: Uzziah to the Restoration Community
    (chapters 26–36)
    A. The Reign of Uzziah (chapter 26)
    B. The Reign of Jotham (chapter 27)
    C. The Reign of Ahaz (chapter 28)
    D. The Reign of Hezekiah (chapters 29–32)
    E. The Reign of Manasseh (33:1–20)
    F. The Reign of Amon (33:21–25)
    G. The Reign of Josiah (chapters 34–35)
    H. The Reigns of Jehoahaz, Jehoiakim, and Jehoiachin
       (36:1–10)
    I. The Reign of Zedekiah and the Fall of Jerusalem (36:11–21)
    J. The Decree of Cyrus (36:22–23)

I. THE REIGN OF SOLOMON (CHAPTERS 1–9)

Apart from a few incidents recorded by the chronicler but not included in 1 Kings (or vice versa) and some minor rearrangement of the narratives, the reign of Solomon as documented by the chronicler differs little in substance from its parallel account in 1 Kings. The more subtle undertones, however, are perceptible and are much in line with the author's intention of glorifying the Davidic dynasty as the vehicle by which God will accomplish His plans. That is, the chronicler seemed more the theologian whose concern was not so much to provide personal and political information as it was to demonstrate that history is part of a grand design, a plan devised and sovereignly administered by the Lord God of Israel. For that reason also the story depicts Solomon as somewhat less morally and spiritually blemished than 1 Kings. For example, nothing is said in Chronicles about Solomon's idolatry and pagan marriages, though perhaps there is a hint of the impropriety of the latter in the reference to Solomon's Egyptian wife (2 Chron. 8:11).

A. The Assembly at Gibeon and Solomon's Might (chapter 1)

After David's death Solomon, only twenty years old, made the transition from vice-regent with his father to full, independent kingship. Fully aware of his limitations and need for divine guidance, he made a pilgrimage to Gibeon, the site of the Mosaic tabernacle, some seven miles northwest of Jerusalem. The ark of the covenant was then in the tabernacle that David had made on Mount Zion (1:4; see 1 Chron. 15:1–15), but Solomon's desire was to offer up burnt offerings at the great bronze altar of Moses. To do that he had to go to Gibeon (2 Chron. 1:5–6).

God responded to the young king's piety by revealing Himself and offering to give Solomon the desire of his heart (1:7). Without hesitation Solomon asserted his need for wisdom (1:9–10). This unselfish petition so moved the heart of the Lord that He promised Solomon not only wisdom but also wealth and honor as well. No king before him (that is, Saul, David, and the earlier Canaanite rulers) nor after him could compare to the glory Solomon would enjoy (1:11–13).

Very quickly these things fell into place. Solomon established fortifications, amassed great personal and national wealth, and gained a monopoly on the horse-trading market (1:14–17). He imported Egyptian horses and chariots at low prices and resold them to the Hittites and Arameans at a handsome profit.

B. The Building of the Temple (2:1–5:1)

These military and commercial enterprises meant little to Solomon, however, compared to his desire to build a temple worthy of the Lord. He therefore entered into negotiations with Huram (spelled Hiram in 1 Kings 5:1), king of Tyre, to send him a skilled contractor as well as timber from Lebanon in order to make the project possible. Only the best would do, for, as Solomon said, "Our God is greater than all other gods" (2 Chron. 2:5, NIV). In return for Huram's help, Solomon would supply him and his workers vast quantities of food and drink (2:1–10).

Huram was delighted to be able to honor the Lord (2:11–12), so he appointed a half-Israelite (named Hiram also; 1 Kings 7:13) to oversee the project, and he pledged to provide all the timber necessary. It would be floated down the Mediterranean coast to Joppa and then transported overland to Jerusalem (2 Chron. 2:13–16). Solomon then divided his own work force into three groups. Seventy thousand porters, eighty thousand stonemasons, and thirty-six hundred foremen were recruited from among the alien classes (2:17–18).

When all the men and materials were in place, the work began. For the first time the threshing floor of Ornan (also called Araunah; 2 Sam. 24:16), the place chosen by David for the temple location (see 1 Chron. 21:28–22:1), is identified also as Mount Moriah, the site of Abraham's offering of Isaac to the Lord (2 Chron. 3:1; Gen. 22:2). The foundations of the temple were laid in Solomon's fourth year, the 480th year after the Exodus according to the account in 1 Kings 6:1. This was 966 B.C. according to the best chronological reconstruction.

The outer chamber of the temple (the Holy Place) as well as the inner chamber (the Most Holy Place) was decorated with lavish objects and lamination of gold and expensive wood (2 Chron. 3:3–9). In the latter room the artisans crafted beautiful cherubim overlaid with gold. Their outstretched wings reached from wall to wall thus overshadowing or covering (Hebrew, kᵉrûb, "cherub," "guarding one") the ark of the covenant (3:10–14; see 5:8). Two pillars, apparently freestanding, stood in front of the temple. One bore the name Jachin ("He will establish") and the other the name Boaz ("in it [or Him] is strength"). These were apparently memorial stelae designed to call attention to the Lord's presence (3:15–17).

Other temple objects were the great bronze altar, which rested on a foundation elevating it high above the ground; a large vessel called a "sea," supported on the backs of manufactured oxen; ten wash basins adjacent to the sea and altar; ten lampstands and ten tables for the outer chamber; and all kinds of pots and pans and other utensils and decorative items, all of which were placed in and about the temple according to their various functions (chapter 4).

When everything was finished, Solomon furnished the temple and filled its treasuries with the riches David had accumulated (5:1). It was time then, after seven years of careful construction (1 Kings 6:37–38), for Solomon to dedicate this glorious building to the Lord.

C. The Dedication of the Temple (5:2–7:10)

The most solemn act of all was the transfer of the ark from its place in David's tabernacle on Mount Zion to its new home in the temple. This was done in the seventh month, the time of covenant renewal associated with the fall festivals (5:3; see Deut. 31:9–13). As David had done when the ark first entered Jerusalem (2 Sam. 6:12–19; 1 Chron. 15:25–28), so Solomon and his entourage sacrificed and celebrated before the Lord in glorious procession (2 Chron. 5:2–6). Climactically the ark was installed in the Most Holy Place beneath the wings of the cherubim (5:7–10). Then when the priests withdrew and the Levitical choirs lifted up their voices in praise, the cloud of God's glory filled the temple, signifying that He was pleased and had come to dwell among His people in this symbolic way (5:11–14; compare Exod. 40:34–35).

> *As magnificent and enthralling as "natural" revelation might be (Ps. 19:1–6), without the interpretive word of Scripture it can never lead to the meaning of human existence, to the conviction of sin, or to the gospel message of forgiveness and life (19:7–14). God's magnificent display of glory at the temple needed the exposition in language that Solomon went on to provide.*

Solomon, in response to this manifestation of theophanic presence, addressed the assembled throngs with a word of theological interpretation (2 Chron. 6:1–11). He reminded them that up till now the Lord had refused to authorize a temple because His people had been wanderers (6:1–5). Now, however, peace prevailed and Jerusalem had become the place of permanent location for both the palace and the temple. At last it was fitting for the Lord to settle with His people in a more established manner (6:6–11).

The king then offered up to God a magnificent prayer (6:14–42). Falling on his knees on a platform built for the occasion, Solomon displayed his humility as a model for the people (6:12–13). He first acknowledged the Lord as the only God, the Covenant-Maker and Covenant-Keeper who had fulfilled His promise to David about dynastic succession (6:14–17). He then marveled that such a God—one utterly transcendent to His creation—could and would take up His residence, as it were, in such a frail, man-made structure (6:18–21).

That God had done so could not be denied. Sinners therefore could appeal to Him there for forgiveness, whether individuals or the entire nation (6:22–25). If famine, pestilence, enemy invasion, plague, sickness, or anything else came on them, they could know that God was in His temple and that from that place He would bestow forgiveness, grace, and deliverance (6:26–31). This would come, of course, only as a result of deep and genuine repentance. The God who knows people's hearts (6:30) could not compromise His holiness and justice to forgive on any other terms. Solomon dared to pray that this same loving response might bless even non-Israelites, foreigners who would also look to that place in faith (6:32–33).

Anticipating the likelihood of war and even deportation, Solomon prayed that God would give victory as the people of the Lord prayed toward the temple (6:34–35). But if they ended up in captivity because of their sin and then turned again to the Lord in repentance, Solomon prayed that God would hear even from distant places and that He would forgive and restore his wayward community (6:36–39). This calls to mind godly Daniel who, in far-off Babylon, never failed to pray daily with his face toward the Holy City (Dan. 6:10).

In a final petition, Solomon pleaded that the Lord would hear his prayer that very day (2 Chron. 6:40). Then in a most remarkable request, he urged the Lord to move into the temple along with the ark—the sign of His presence—and in that place to remember forever the sacred promises He had made to David and His descendants (6:40–42).

The Lord's response was immediate and terrifying. Fire from heaven consumed the sacrifices, and God's glory as a cloud permeated every part of the temple. So much was this the case that the priests would not enter the building and the people, awestruck, could only fall on their faces in praise and worship. Solomon added more sacrifices to these as an act of great dedication. All the time the musicians joined in with great vocal and orchestral celebration. All the people could do was stand in rapt wonder and amazement at all they saw and heard (7:1–7).

For seven days the festivities continued, climaxed by a massive convocation on the eighth. At last it all came to an end and the people returned to their homes, having come from as far away as Hamath in the north and the river of Egypt (Wadi el-Arish) in the south (7:8–10).

D. The Conditions of Covenant Blessing (7:11–22)

Sometime after the temple had been completed, the Lord revealed Himself to Solomon with the assurance that He had heard and would answer Solomon's prayer about the people in days to come. However, His blessings on them, God said, would be contingent on their seeking His face in humility and contrition. These conditions met, He would hear from His temple, the special point of contact between Himself and the chosen people whom He had elected and brought into covenant fellowship with Him. Should they fail to meet His terms, however, they could expect to be uprooted from the land of the temple and become a proverb, incarnating what it means to be a disobedient servant of the most high God.

E. Solomon's Accomplishments (chapters 8–9)

Midway through Solomon's reign (around 951 B.C.; 8:1), he took a greater interest in international affairs. He occupied cities that Huram had given him and brought others outside his borders under his control (8:2–4). He also fortified places within his kingdom and built still others from scratch, all to assert and maintain his strong leadership (8:5–6). He subjected non-Israelites to forced labor, but his own citizens were exempt, serving rather as overseers (8:7–10). One foreigner whom he obviously favored—his own wife, a daughter of Pharaoh—he allowed to reside in Jerusalem but only after facilities could be provided in a part of the city not considered holy (8:11).

Solomon meanwhile did not neglect public worship. He was careful to observe the sacrifices, festivals, and other matters of Levitical worship and to see to it that priestly personnel were available and attentive to their tasks (8:12–16).

Solomon's wider horizons are reflected by his interest in international maritime trade (8:17–18) and in the interesting account of a visitor, the queen of Sheba, from the distant land of south Arabia. Having heard of his legendary wisdom, she made the long journey of twelve hundred miles to visit Solomon to see if what she had heard was indeed true. It did not take long for her to realize that the reality far exceeded the grandiose rumors (9:1–8). Solomon was wiser and richer than anyone else she had ever known.

This evidence of God's blessings prompted the woman to make him even richer. She lavished him with many treasures, but Solomon was no less generous and sent her back home with more than she had brought in the first place (9:9–12). This anecdote prompted the chronicler to continue speaking of Solomon's prosperity. By trade and taxation his kingdom was awash in gold, ivory, and other tokens of exorbitant wealth (9:13–20). His ships imported exotic products from all over the known world. There can be little exaggeration to the claim that he was the richest king in the world (9:21–22).

His wisdom was still the great attraction, and rulers came from far and wide to learn the truths that God had put in his heart (9:23). Some came involuntarily, for Solomon had carved out an empire of vassal states from which he exacted heavy tribute (9:24). Such heavy-handed rule necessitated a strong army and stout fortifications (9:25), but the cost of such things seemed to Solomon to be worth it, considering the luxurious lifestyle it afforded (9:21–28).

In concluding his story of Solomon, the chronicler noted that more records appeared in the histories by Nathan and Ahijah as well as the recorded oracles of the prophet Iddo. After a long and prosperous reign of forty years Solomon died and was succeeded by his son Rehoboam (9:29–31).

II. THE DYNASTY OF DAVID: REHOBOAM TO UZZIAH (CHAPTERS 10–25)

Though somewhat more positive than the author of Kings, the chronicler nevertheless drew attention to the evil undercurrents of the history of the divided monarchy, undercurrents that all too often erupted to plain view. And this was not limited to Israel. Unlike his rather selective rendering of the lives and reigns of David and Solomon, the narrator held up the lives of their successors to close inspection and was not slow to point out their foibles as well as their strong points. It is as though he was preparing the reader—even as early as the time of the division of the kingdom—for the eventual disaster of Judah's dismantling and deportation.

A. *The Reign of Rehoboam (chapters 10–12)*

Since the city of Shechem was the power base of the northern tribes (Judg. 9:6), Rehoboam made a concession to them by traveling there to gain their support for his kingship. Jeroboam meanwhile returned to Shechem from Egypt, where he had been forced to flee because of Solomon's disfavor. It seems the people were willing to accede to the dynastic principle of succession, but they first wanted to wring some concessions from Rehoboam, especially in terms of what they perceived to be excessive taxation (2 Chron. 10:1–5). Otherwise they would turn their support to Jeroboam.

Repudiating the counsel of his father's advisers, Rehoboam consulted his peers, who told him he should not give an inch and in fact should increase the pressure on the people (10:6–11). Foolishly Rehoboam agreed and thus forfeited the Northern Kingdom (10:12–14, 16). But the historian was quick to point out that the young king's stupidity was itself playing into the will of God, who had already decreed that the kingdom should split (10:15; 1 Kings 11:29–39). Rehoboam's last-ditch efforts at reconciliation failed, and the kingdom was irremediably torn asunder (2 Chron. 10:19).

What Rehoboam could not do by diplomacy he now hoped to accomplish by military means. Raising a huge army, he was ready to attack, but the prophet Shemaiah informed him that the enterprise was hopeless for God Himself would oppose him (11:1–4). Rehoboam therefore poured his energies into an elaborate defense system (11:5–12). Meanwhile the true priests and Levites had fled from the north to Judah because of Jeroboam's wholesale introduction of idolatry (1 Kings 12:28–33). They became a great asset to Rehoboam, at least in the early years of his reign when he walked in obedience to the Lord (2 Chron. 11:13–17).

The first hints of trouble in Rehoboam's leadership appear in his predilection toward polygamy, exacerbated by its incestuous overtones (11:18–22). The historian mitigated this somewhat by commenting on Rehoboam's wise use of his many sons as local administrators and his foresight in providing for them (11:23), but he then stated most frankly that the king "forsook the law of the LORD" (12:1). This led to divine judgment at the hands of the Egyptian king, Shishak, who, in Rehoboam's fifth year (926 B.C.), invaded and would have completely subdued Judah had the king and people not repented. Judah did, however, become tributary to Egypt (12:2–8).

Rehoboam surrendered to Egypt many items from the temple and royal places, including the precious gold shields of Solomon to be replaced by cheap bronze replicas (12:9–11). Though Rehoboam repented and regained much of his power and glory (12:12–13), the overall indictment was still negative: "He did not set his heart to seek the LORD" (12:14). Documentation for all this and other matters may be found, the narrator wrote, in the records of Shemaiah and Iddo (12:15–16).

B. The Reign of Abijah (13:1–14:1)

Abijah, son of Rehoboam's favorite wife, Maacah, had been groomed by his father to succeed him (11:21–22). Abijah's reign, though eventful, was brief, lasting only three years (914–911 B.C.). His major project was his attempt to bring Israel back under Davidic control by force. He first tried to negotiate with King Jeroboam of Israel by reminding him that Israel belonged to the Davidic dynasty by divine fiat and that its rebellion in the first place was contrary to the will of God (13:1–8). Moreover, Jeroboam had no moral leverage because of the apostate nature of his religious leadership (13:9). With more than a little hypocritical self-righteousness, Abijah then contrasted the state of his own kingdom to that of the north. Judah (and he) had been faithful to the Lord in every way, he asserted, so for Israel to do battle against Judah was the same as fighting against God Himself (13:10–12).

Not persuaded, Jeroboam launched an attack, but the Lord fought for Judah and delivered them from defeat. This was not so much because of Abijah's personal piety, for that is never asserted, but because of the Lord's commitment to David and his ongoing dynasty. The chronicler noted that the battle was the Lord's, and the ultimate victory was His (13:13–18). Judah recovered some territory from the north, including Bethel, and Jeroboam never again became powerful enough to take it back (13:19–20). Abijah, however, did not live long enough to enjoy the fruits of God's grace. After only three years he died, yielding his throne to his son Asa (13:21–14:1).

C. The Reign of Asa (14:2–16:14)

The implicit evil of Abijah's reign is clear from the fact that his son and successor was highly commended for eradicating all the inroads of paganism that had been allowed or even promoted by Abijah and perhaps Rehoboam as well. Asa followed this up by encouraging his subjects to return to covenant fidelity. This brought peace to the kingdom, at least for a time, allowing Asa to shore up his defenses and to prepare for whatever threats might come from the outside (14:2–8).

Such threats were not long in materializing. First came Zerah of Ethiopia, the ruler of Egypt. A million strong, his army advanced to Mareshah on Judah's southern border. Hopelessly outnumbered, Asa cried out to the Lord, and in His character as divine Warrior the Lord achieved a great victory, forcing Zerah and the remnants of his troops to retreat to the safety of their own land (14:9–15).

The spiritual battle was not yet over, however, so the prophet Azariah challenged Asa to continue the struggle in this area of national life. God would be with Judah, he said, but only to the extent that the king and the people were loyal and obedient to Him (15:1–2). History should teach them of God's faithfulness, even in the days of the judges when virtual anarchy prevailed. Surely He would be with Judah now (15:3–7). Inspired by these words, Asa renewed his efforts at reformation. He uprooted idolatrous shrines and replaced them with the altar of the Lord at the temple, the only legitimate place of national worship. The effect was contagious, for when the people saw how God was blessing the efforts of their king, they rallied to his cause from all over Judah and beyond, even from as far away as Manasseh (15:8–9). Asa decided to formalize the movement by gathering a vast assembly at Jerusalem, a convocation capped off by a ceremony of covenant renewal (15:10–15).

Central to the Mosaic Covenant was insistence on the worship of the Lord alone and its corollary—the rejection of idolatry in all its forms (Deut. 5:7–10). As a logical outgrowth of Asa's reformation, therefore, he removed the trappings of paganism from the land and deposed those who led in its promulgation, including even his own grandmother (1 Kings 15:2), Maacah (2 Chron. 15:16). He did leave the high places untouched, but despite this the chronicler viewed him favorably on the whole (15:17–19).

Late in his reign (around 875 B.C.) Asa, under intense threat from Baasha, king of Israel, robbed the temple and national treasuries of their gold in order to hire Ben-Hadad of Aram to come to his assistance (16:1–3). This required Ben-Hadad to break his treaty with Baasha, which he was quite willing to do under the circumstances. Aram then attacked northern Galilee, thus diverting Baasha from his planned attack against Judah. Asa took advantage of this reprieve to secure his border with Israel by building defensive positions at Geba and Mizpah (16:4–6).

Such dependence on a foreign power—especially Aram—displeased the Lord, for Asa should have turned to Him, the God who had historically proved to be powerful and faithful on behalf of His people. For this callous disregard of the real source of blessing, Asa would be plagued with incessant warfare from that time on (16:7–10). This was not all. For the last three years of his reign he suffered from a foot disease, perhaps gout, during which time his son Jehoshaphat co-reigned with him. Even in this condition Asa looked to human physicians and not to the Creator, who alone has power to heal. His elaborate funeral service nonetheless attested to the favor he enjoyed in the eyes of his subjects (16:14).

C. The Reign of Jehoshaphat (chapters 17–20)

Asa's son Jehoshaphat followed up on his father's strategy of building defensive posts throughout the land, particularly along the northern border with Israel (17:1–2). Moreover he emulated the heart for God that Asa had shown in his earlier years, and for this the Lord granted Jehoshaphat a secure hold on the throne (17:3–6). One of Jehoshaphat's concerns was that the Law be taught throughout his kingdom, so he sent itinerant teachers to do that very thing (17:7–9).

The very evident signs of God's blessing on Jehoshaphat led surrounding nations to have a healthy respect for him. They lost their appetite for aggression against Judah and even sent gifts with the obvious intent of cultivating good relations (17:10–11). Taking nothing for granted, however, Jehoshaphat built even more fortifications and raised a vast army in anticipation of whatever change of heart might occur on the international scene (17:10–19).

The first sign of a weakness of character or at least a mistake in policy was Jehoshaphat's alliance with Ahab of Israel, who had just recently come to the throne of that nation. After some years that pledge of mutual support was put to the test when Ahab prevailed on Jehoshaphat to join him in recovering certain Transjordanian territories that Israel had lost to the Arameans (18:1–3). Unwilling to do so without a sure word from God, Jehoshaphat rejected the counsel of Ahab's own hireling prophets and insisted that a true prophet, Micaiah, be allowed to speak (18:4–11). Micaiah, brought to the two kings from prison, spoke a word of terrifying judgment—the king of Israel would not return from battle well and whole (18:12–27).

Ahab and Jehoshaphat, rashly ignoring God's word through the prophet, advanced on Ramoth Gilead, where Ahab was mortally wounded. He was barely able to make it back to his northern capital Samaria, where he died just as the prophet had said he would (18:28–34; see 1 Kings 22:27–38). Jehoshaphat managed to survive and return to Jerusalem, but there he was confronted by the prophet Jehu, who took him to task for his ungodly alliance with wicked Ahab (2 Chron. 19:1–3).

Severely chastened by this experience, Jehoshaphat commenced an energetic program of reformation and revival. He encouraged spiritual renewal and then set in place a network of judges whom he instructed to adjudicate cases with fairness and integrity as unto the Lord (19:4–7). For more difficult cases requiring appeal, Jehoshaphat appointed a supreme court in Jerusalem. Again the standard by which they must exercise justice was to be the covenant Law, and their motive must be the fear of the Lord (19:9–10).

Sometime later Moab and Ammon collaborated to invade Judah (20:1–4). Jehoshaphat quickly determined that his only hope was in the Lord. He therefore voiced a public prayer in which he rehearsed the attributes of God and the major events of divine deliverance throughout Israel's sacred history (20:5–9). Based on his faithfulness in the past, Jehoshaphat now appealed to the Lord to deal with the present emergency and to give his people success (20:10–13). In response the Spirit of God came on the Levite Jahaziel who, as a spokesman for God, reminded the assembly that the battle was not theirs but the Lord's (20:14–15). They would not have to lift so much as a finger but need only stand back and watch what God would do (20:16–19).

The next day Jehoshaphat prepared the people for "holy war," for he believed the message that the battle was the Lord's. Such war always involved priests and Levites (Deut. 20:2), so Jehoshaphat appointed sacred singers as part of the mobilization (2 Chron. 20:20–21). Meanwhile, the Lord had brought the people of Seir (that is, Edomites) into the mix, with the result that Moab and Ammon first attacked them and then each other. So all Judah needed to do was gather the spoils of war (20:22–25). Such an astounding victory prompted praise and joy among the Lord's own people but tremendous fear among their enemies (20:26–29).

The epitaph of Jehoshaphat is generally favorable. He lived in peace and walked in the path of his godly father, Asa, except for his failure to remove the high places (20:30–33). He never fully learned the bitter lesson of the unequal yoke, however, for he made an alliance with Ahab's son Ahaziah just as he had with Ahab. This time it was not for war but for international trade. The motives and results were exactly the same— Jehoshaphat's ships were destroyed before they could ever set sail (20:35–37).

E. The Reign of Jehoram (chapter 21)

Jehoshaphat tapped his eldest son to succeed him as king. But because he also had given his other sons gifts of lands and goods, his heir, Jehoram, feared that his own position might not be altogether secure; so he slew all his brothers to preclude their possible personal ambitions (21:1–4).

Such ruthless behavior set the tone for Jehoram's stormy reign of eight years (848–841 B.C.). He married Ahab's daughter Athaliah and, with her, introduced to Judah much of the paganism of the northern kingdom (21:5–6). Only because God was committed to His promises to David did Judah escape His awesome wrath (21:7). There were losses, however, including the revolt of Edom against Judah, which resulted in Edom's independence (21:8–10). Moreover, Jehoram heard in a letter from Elijah that he and his evil cohorts would not escape God's judgment entirely (21:11–14). The king himself would, in fact, suffer an excruciating disease of the bowels that would result in his death (21:15). Strangely the author of 2 Kings did not mention this turn of events.

Before he died Jehoram suffered the loss of his personal wealth and all the members of his family to bands of Philistines and Arabs. Only his son Jehoahaz (also known as Ahaziah; 22:1) survived so that the line of David would not be completely obliterated. Death must have been a welcome relief to this evil man after two years of unrelenting suffering. It was a relief to his people as well, who did not even accord him the usual honors of a royal burial (21:18–20).

F. The Reign of Ahaziah (22:1–9)

The instability of the kingdom in the aftermath of Jehoram's death is clear from the fact that his son was appointed king by the people and did not just automatically succeed him (22:1). This tenuousness of the Davidic line underscores the remarkable faithfulness of the Lord to His promise that the line would never end (1 Chron. 17:12; Ps. 89:35–37). But Ahaziah too was a weak link. His one-year reign was marked by the evil of his mother, Athaliah, and all his ungodly counselors (2 Chron. 22:2–4).

Ahaziah's tragic end coincided with that of his uncle, King Joram of Israel, whom he had joined in an ill-fated campaign against the Arameans (22:5–6). Both died on the same day at the hands of Jehu whom God had raised up to purge evil from both kingdoms. But Ahaziah's death only paved the way for his vicious and wicked mother to usurp the throne of David (22:7–9).

G. The Interregnum of Queen Athaliah (22:10–23:21)

Having gained political leadership in Judah by virtue of her marriage to King Jehoram, Athaliah, daughter of the nefarious Ahab and Jezebel of Israel, seized on her son Ahaziah's death to proclaim herself queen of Judah. To facilitate this she killed all possible candidates for the throne except one, her infant grandson Joash, whom Jehoiada, the chief priest, managed to hide (22:10–12).

THE OLD TESTAMENT EXPLORER

Six years later Jehoiada brought young Joash to the temple plaza and there publicly proposed his kingship, all without Athaliah's knowledge (23:1–3). He then outlined a strategy by which the evil woman could be put out of the way. The people would be placed in such locations as to make escape impossible, and then Athaliah would be lured into the trap (23:4–7). Joash then came forward, and with loud fanfare the populace proclaimed him king (23:8–11). Hearing the commotion, Athaliah rushed to the temple, where, too late, she saw her only grandson bedecked in the robes and insignia of kingship. As she started to escape, she was arrested and put to death at once (23:12–15).

Jehoiada then led the people in a covenant-renewal celebration in which the people pledged their loyalty to both the Lord and the king. The priest then destroyed the Baal objects and reestablished the worship of the Lord according to the Law. Joash's sitting on David's throne was a visible sign that the promise of an everlasting dynasty was still intact (23:16–21).

H. The Reign of Joash (chapter 24)

At first under the tutelage of Jehoiada and then on his own, Joash undertook a series of reforms to restore Judah back to the glorious years of Jehoshaphat. First on the agenda was the repair of the temple which had fallen into grievous ruin. Money would be needed, so the king launched a fund-raising campaign (24:4–7). He had a chest constructed and placed outside the temple into which donations could be made. To his surprise it was filled over and over again because of the people's enthusiasm for the project (24:8–11). With the money left over after the reconstruction phase, the king and Jehoiada authorized the purchase of all the implements necessary for temple worship (24:12–14).

After Jehoiada's death, Joash had to face the problem of the encroachment of idolatry into the royal family itself, a problem that even the prophets of the Lord could not resolve (24:15–19). One of them, Zechariah, stood in the power of the Lord to condemn their violation of the covenant, an act of holy boldness that cost him his life. Sadly, Joash himself had succumbed to the pressures of the mob and thus was an accomplice in the death of the son of his own mentor, Jehoiada (24:20–22).

Someone long ago remarked, "The blood of the martyrs is the seed of the church." Jesus Himself observed that the enemies of truth have always opposed its spokesmen in violent ways, extending "from the blood of the righteous Abel to the blood of Zechariah" (Matt. 23:35). The Zechariah in view is this prophet of the days of Joash, a true martyr for the faith. Our Lord thus saw the whole Bible as a book of martyrdom, from its beginning in Genesis to its end (in the Hebrew canon) in 2 Chronicles.

Judgment fell and quickly. First, the Aramean army came and despoiled Jerusalem, killing the sinful princes of Judah in the process. Then Joash's own servants turned on him, assassinated him, and refused him royal burial (24:23–26). Further details of his reign, the historian wrote, may be found in "the annotations on the book of the kings" (24:27).

I. The Reign of Amaziah (chapter 25)

One of Amaziah's first official acts was to execute those who had killed his father, though, in line with the Mosaic Law, he spared their children (25:1–4; Deut. 24:16). He then organized a great military force including one hundred thousand mercenaries from Israel (2 Chron. 25:5–7). A prophet chided him for engaging "foreign" troops because God, the prophet said, is well able to help His own without outside assistance (25:8). But since Amaziah had already paid the Israelites, how could he get a refund? Again the prophet spoke: "The Lord can give you much more than that" (25:9).

Having sent the Israelites away, Amaziah led a successful campaign against Edom, Judah's perennial enemy. Meanwhile the mercenaries, frustrated at being released from duty, pillaged Judean towns on their way back to Israel (25:11–13). On his return Amaziah challenged Jehoash (spelled Joash here) of Israel to do battle over the pillaging incident, a challenge Jehoash readily accepted (25:17–19). The result was a humiliating defeat for Judah. Amaziah was captured, Jerusalem breached, and the temple and royal treasuries looted (25:20–24).

The reason for this devastating setback was Amaziah's folly in bringing back to Judah the gods of his defeated foes, the Edomites (25:14).

How foolish to trust in gods that could not even deliver their own people (25:15–16). But the stubborn king would not listen, so the chronicler noted that Amaziah's defeat by Israel was an act of divine planning and purpose (25:20). Amaziah lived on after the death of his Israelite counterpart but seems to have learned little or nothing from his experiences. Like others before him, he died at the hands of assassins. At least he had the honor of being buried with his royal ancestors (25:25–28).

III. THE DYNASTY OF DAVID: UZZIAH TO THE RESTORATION COMMUNITY (CHAPTERS 26–36)

With the exception of Hezekiah and Josiah, most of the kings of Judah from 800 to 586 B.C. were disappointing as scions of the messianic line of David. Gradually it became apparent that the kingdom was headed for disaster in the form of massive deportation. Second Chronicles records this era of fearful expectation and documents the destruction of Jerusalem and the temple. It ends, however, on a note of hope—the return of the Jews from exile, thanks to the merciful decree of King Cyrus of Persia. Clearly God was not yet through with His chosen people. The house of David would continue on as the Lord had promised until it achieved its redemptive purpose.

A. The Reign of Uzziah (chapter 26)

Amaziah must have lived in fear of an untimely death, for he appointed his son Uzziah as his co-regent, a position he held for twenty-three years. At the same time it is clear that this appointment was an act of the people as well (26:1), thus suggesting that they too were concerned for Amaziah's longevity. By 767 B.C. Uzziah reigned alone. He had been well tutored by godly Zechariah (see 24:20–22) in his early years and set about to honor the Lord. The historian observed that as long as Uzziah sought the Lord, the Lord made him prosper (26:5).

Like Jehoshaphat a century earlier, Uzziah built strong fortifications throughout the land and was successful in waging war against surrounding peoples such as the Philistines, Arabs, Meunites, and Ammonites

(26:6–15). He had a special interest also in agriculture and made the hills and valleys verdant with produce (26:10). Sadly, near the end of his life he transgressed the Law by offering incense in the temple, a ministry limited to the Levitical priests alone (26:16–18; Num. 16:39–40). For this act of proud defiance he became leprous and was forced to live in seclusion until his death (2 Chron. 26:19–20). Uzziah's son Jotham took over the reins of government for about a decade, and then when Uzziah died, Jotham reigned in his own right (26:22–23).

B. The Reign of Jotham (chapter 27)

Jotham continued the godly lifestyle of his father and exceeded it in some ways, for he learned from Uzziah's mistakes and did not repeat them. He also carried out Uzziah's domestic and foreign policies, enjoying particular success against Ammon, which he brought under Judah's hegemony. All this, the chronicler pointed out, was because Jotham lived in accord with the will of God; "he walked steadfastly before the LORD" (27:6). After sixteen years of rule he died at the young age of forty-one and passed the crown on to his son Ahaz.

C. The Reign of Ahaz (chapter 28)

Ahaz was the antithesis of Jotham in every way. His spiritual models were the evil kings of Israel, whom he mimicked by establishing idolatrous worship centers throughout the land of Judah (28:1–4). Not surprisingly, God visited judgment on him and his kingdom by delivering him over to Rezin, king of Aram, and Pekah, king of Israel (28:5–7; see also Isa. 7:1). Pekah, however, overplayed his hand, and because he went too far in his rage against Judah, the Lord threatened him with disaster unless he released his Judean prisoners of war. Pekah's officers took the threat seriously and convinced him to set their southern brothers free (2 Chron. 28:8–15).

Ahaz, spared for the time being, requested Assyrian aid in anticipation of still more trouble from Aram and Israel. Moreover, other enemies such as the Edomites and Philistines had also begun to exert pressure, going so far as to achieve independence from Judean control (28:16–18;

see 25:14; 26:7). These setbacks came because of Ahaz's rebellion against the Lord. Appeal to Assyria brought little results, for after Ahaz paid the Assyrian king a handsome fee for his help, that help did not materialize (28:19–21). It is true that Tiglath-Pileser captured Damascus, thus allaying the Aramean threat (2 Kings 16:9), but this turned out to have serious spiritual consequences for Ahaz.

Second Kings 16:10–16 records a visit by Ahaz to Damascus, where he saw Aramean altars and other religious objects that deeply impressed him. The chronicler omitted reference to this visit, but he did point out Ahaz's apostate worship of Aramean deities and the corresponding abandonment of the worship of the Lord. Such wicked behavior precluded his burial with his fathers in the sepulchers of the kings (2 Chron. 28:22–27).

D. The Reign of Hezekiah (chapters 29–32)

After a long co-regency with his evil father Ahaz, Hezekiah commenced his rule as full regent in 715 B.C., seven years after the fall of Israel to the Assyrians. He immediately set about to reverse the damage done to the political and religious life of the nation under Ahaz, charging the priests and Levites to refurbish the temple and to prepare the people for covenant renewal. This they did in Hezekiah's very first month (29:11–19). Once the temple was cleansed and refitted, the king led in a great service of sacrifice of sin offerings for the nation and the temple (29:20–24). Everything was done according to the pattern established by David for temple worship (see 8:14–15). The musicians, the priests, and the people all joined in with joyous celebration, singing the praises of the Lord according to the ancient texts of David and Asaph (29:25–30).

The sin offerings were followed by thank offerings appropriate to the condition of unbroken fellowship that now existed between the Lord and His people. So vast were the offerings that poured in, the priests were overwhelmed and unable to manage it all and had to call on the Levites for assistance. God had indeed done a wonderful work of spiritual renewal, and for this the king and people alike rejoiced in thanksgiving (29:31–36).

Hezekiah, though ruling after the collapse of Israel to the north, remained sensitive to the spiritual needs of those who survived and still lived there. He therefore sent an invitation throughout the Northern Kingdom for all who wished to join their Judean brothers in a great Passover celebration to be held in the second month, the first month being impossible because of all that had to be done in preparation. The northerners were included in order to encourage them to return to the Lord and, unlike their forebears, to serve Him with all their hearts (30:1–9).

The response to this urgent and generous appeal was crushing. Hezekiah's messengers were ridiculed by all but a few, but these few, along with the Judeans themselves, entered into the Passover festivities with great anticipation (30:10–13). The arrangements, though postponed, were still made in such haste that many of the priests were not ritually qualified to minister nor were the people, especially from the north, qualified to participate, according to the strict requirements of the Law (30:14–18a). Hezekiah, recognizing that true religion is in spirit and attitude, prayed that God would overlook the letter in this case and allow all who had gathered to participate (30:18b–19). The Lord looked with favor on this request, and the Passover went forward with great joy and thanksgiving (30:20–21).

At the end of the feasts of the Passover and Unleavened Bread there was no desire to interrupt what God was doing for His people, so they continued for another week. The historian noted that there not had not been such an occasion in Jerusalem since the days of Solomon (30:23–27).

This precedent-setting Passover paved the way for other forms of reformation and revival. The high places in more remote areas were demolished, the priests and Levites were reorganized, their means of support put back in place (31:1–10), and a system for the collection and storage of temple offerings was devised (31:11–19). Most important, the chronicler drew attention to the fact that Hezekiah led in all these things, not out of a sense of kingly responsibility but as a heartfelt act of worship and obedience toward the Lord (30:20–21).

Fourteen years into his reign (701 B.C.; see 2 Kings 18:13), Hezekiah came face to face with his biggest external challenge—the invasion of the army of mighty Assyria under Sennacherib. Hezekiah quickly mobilized. He shut off water supplies from the approaching Assyrians, strengthened his fortifications, and raised a strong and well-equipped militia (2 Chron.

32:1–8). An Assyrian delegation then appeared on the scene and tried first to demoralize the Jews by recounting how powerless the gods of other nations had been before Sennacherib. How could they now have any confidence in Hezekiah and their god, the Lord (32:9–15)?

Day after day this barrage of propaganda continued, first by oral speech and then by letters (32:16–19). Hezekiah, together with Isaiah the prophet, did all that could be done, given the odds against them—they prayed to the God of heaven. An angel came and in a single stroke devastated the Assyrian host, forcing Sennacherib to retreat in painful shame. Before long, Sennacherib fell to assassins, but Hezekiah lived on, the object of international favor and respect (32:20–23).

Toward the end of his days, Hezekiah became ill and even though the Lord healed him, he failed to respond with proper gratitude, at least for a while (32:24–26). On the whole, however, the verdict on his life and leadership was favorable. He greatly strengthened the kingdom, and in the process he and his people enjoyed remarkable prosperity (32:27–30). Only in the matter of the boastful display of his riches to the Babylonian ambassadors did he stain his reputation (32:31; see also 2 Kings 20:12–15; Isa. 39:1–8). For further information about Hezekiah's reign, the historian cited such records as those of Isaiah, which seem to have been included in a work known as "the book of the kings of Judah and Israel" (2 Chron. 32:32–33).

E. The Reign of Manasseh (33:1–20)

It is often said that one's faith is always within one generation of dying out. This observation finds validation over and over in the Old Testament record. No sooner had Hezekiah died than his son Manasseh began to subvert all the good things his father had done. Most particularly Manasseh reintroduced idolatry to Judah, going so far as to practice human sacrifice and to place images within the holy temple of the Lord (33:1–9). Prophetic warnings fell on deaf ears, so the Lord allowed the Assyrians under Esarhaddon (681–669 B.C.) or Ashurbanipal (668–627 B.C.) to enter Jerusalem and take Manasseh as a prisoner back to Babylon, then an Assyrian provincial capital (33:10–11). The account in 2 Kings says nothing of this, but the chronicler described the king's "conversion," as it were

(2 Chron. 33:12–13). As always the chronicler sought to put the best possible face on the Davidic dynasty.

On his return from exile to Jerusalem, Manasseh undertook massive construction projects and, more importantly, he removed the pagan worship renters, replacing them with the true worship of the Lord at the temple (33:14–17). The historian closed his account of Manasseh's reign by referring to other documents such as "the annals of the kings of Israel," and "the records of the seers [prophets]" (33:18–20).

F. The Reign of Amon (33:21–25)

Manasseh's son Amon learned nothing from the tragic example of his father, it seems, for he repeated all his sins without emulating his repentance. After a reign of only two years (642–640 B.C.) Amon fell to assassins, who in turn were slain by "the people of the land," that is, the middle classes. They then set Josiah, son of Amon, on the Davidic throne.

G. The Reign of Josiah (chapters 34–35)

At last the long drought of spiritual decline came to an end again in the person of Josiah. Only eight years old when he inherited the regency, Josiah had a long reign of thirty-one years (640–609 B.C.), a time of fresh spiritual awakening but one too late to stem the tide of divine judgment. While only sixteen years old, Josiah had a great personal experience with God (34:3), and four years later he translated that to the whole nation in a massive reform effort that resulted in the eradication of heathen worship practices (34:1–7).

After six more years Josiah addressed the need for cleansing and refurbishing the temple that had fallen into such abysmal disrepair in the seventy years or more since Hezekiah's time. He first gathered workmen qualified to do all that was necessary and then accessed sums of money adequate to pay them and to purchase materials (34:8–13). One day when the temple treasury was being explored, the chief priest, Hilkiah, found a scroll which he identified as a copy of "the Book of the Law." Shaphan the scribe took the scroll at once to Josiah who, when he read it, recognized it as the very Word of God. So great was its impact on him that he tore his clothes in contrition and lamented that for all these past years the nation had failed to observe its covenant requirements (34:14–21).

The exact identity of the scroll remains a matter of scholarly debate, but as the narrative unfolds one must conclude that it contained at least Deuteronomy. When the prophetess Huldah became aware of the text, she spoke of the curses in the book, clearly a reference to Deuteronomy 28, where curses for covenant violation are listed. She then predicted imminent judgment on Judah because of the nation's long history of disobedience, but young godly Josiah would be exempted because of his heart for God. His eyes would not have to look on the demise of his own people (34:22–28).

Josiah then led the nation in a great ceremony of covenant renewal based on the newly discovered scroll (34:29–33). Then, like Hezekiah before him, he authorized the observance of the Passover, a festival that seems not to have been kept for many years. Once the priests and Levites were ready, the king and other leaders provided massive quantities of animals for sacrifice (35:1–9). Then the officiants carried out the service according to all the stipulations of the Law (35:10–15). The chronicler noted that this was the greatest sacrifice in Israel's history since Samuel, outstripping, it seems, even that of Hezekiah (35:16–19; see 30:26).

Meanwhile Assyria had been brought to its knees by the rapidly rising Neo-Babylonian Empire and other factors. In a last-ditch effort at survival, the Assyrian army had taken refuge in a fortification at Carchemish on the upper Euphrates River. The Babylonians attacked them there and inflicted a devastating defeat. Egypt, fearing Babylonia more than Assyria, had attempted to rush north to assist Assyria, but Josiah, a Babylonian ally, intercepted and detained Pharaoh Neco and his army at Megiddo. Unfortunately Josiah lost his life in this ill-conceived adventure, thus leaving Judah bereft of any further spiritual leadership (35:20–27).

H. The Reigns of Jehoahaz, Jehoiakim, and Jehoiachin (36:1–10)

Because of the almost total social and political breakdown that followed the untimely death of Josiah, "the people of the land" took charge and placed Jehoahaz, a younger son of Josiah, on Judah's throne. Egypt, however, now exercised authority over Judah, and Pharaoh Neco of Egypt deposed Jehoahaz and replaced him with his older brother, Eliakim, changing his name to Jehoiakim (36:1–4).

Jehoiakim held the reins for eleven years (609–598 B.C.) but as a vassal now of Babylonia after Babylonia's defeat of Egypt in 605 (see 2 Kings 24:7). Nebuchadnezzar of Babylonia punished Jehoiakim for his disloyalty to him but did allow Jehoiakim to remain in power until his (apparently) natural death (2 Chron. 36:5–8; see also 2 Kings 24:1–6).

Young Jehoiachin succeeded his father, Jehoiakim, but for only three months. Then he was taken captive to Babylon, where he remained under mild detention until his release thirty-eight years later by Nebuchadnezzar's successor Evil-Merodach (2 Chron. 36:9–10; see also 2 Kings 25:27–30).

I. The Reign of Zedekiah and the Fall of Jerusalem (36:11–21)

The last of Judah's kings, Zedekiah, was another son of Josiah, perhaps the worst of the lot. He rebelled against the Lord (36:12, 14–16) and Nebuchadnezzar (36:13), and for the latter indiscretion he paid not only with his own life but also will that of a great many of his fellow citizens. With fury the Babylonians came, decimating the population, robbing and destroying the temple and city, and carrying off those who remained alive (36:17–20).

J. The Decree of Cyrus (36:22–23)

The deportees remained in exile until shortly after the end of the Babylonian Empire in 539 B.C., seventy years in all. The Lord raised up a deliverer, a pagan named Cyrus, whom He used to return His people to their land (36:22–23; see also Isa. 44:28–45:4). Second Chronicles ends, then, not in despair but in great hope for the messianic figure Cyrus (the "His anointed," as he is called in Isa. 45:1) pointed forward to the ultimate Messiah, who in His redemptive work would bring the nation to life and service once again.

The mysterious ways of the Lord are nowhere more plainly seen than in His having raised up a pagan king to provide for the postexilic redemption of His chosen people. In startling language, Isaiah referred to Cyrus as God's "anointed" one (Isa. 45:1). How remarkable that God should display His universal sovereignty by calling a Persian king to be the type of the Savior of all who will believe, even Jesus Christ.

EZRA–NEHEMIAH

Building a New Community of Faith

According to ancient Hebrew tradition these two books were originally one composition. Only with the development of the Septuagint and
other versions and translations did they come to be viewed as separate
works. The following discussion offers arguments as to why the Hebrew
tradition is correct and why it is preferable to consider the two books
together.

AUTHOR

Ezra–Nehemiah contains numerous occurrences of first-person pronouns
("I," "me," "my," and so forth), especially in Nehemiah, but this falls short
of establishing the authorship of either book or of the combination of
the two, since all it shows is that there were at least some sources composed in the first person. As noted in the introduction to Chronicles, the
Jewish Mishnah attributes Ezra–Nehemiah to Ezra and all of Chronicles,
except for some of the genealogies, to Nehemiah. However, no case can
be made for common authorship of Chronicles and Ezra–Nehemiah, and
if either Ezra or Nehemiah were the author of the two books, the latter
would better qualify since he lived and ministered later than Ezra. On the
other hand, strong evidence of some additions to the book after
Nehemiah's time suggests that his work as well as Ezra's was incorporated
into a larger work by an anonymous compiler. Hints of such stitching

together of original Ezra and Nehemiah material may be seen in Ezra 1:1, 5–8; 3:1–13; 4:1–6, 7–11a, 17a; 5:6–7a; 7:11; Nehemiah 7:73b–8:18; and 9:1–10:39. Again this in no way challenges the doctrine of the divine inspiration of Scripture, for a compiler could have been guided by the Holy Spirit, just as were the authors whose names we know.

UNITY

Despite the evidence of multiple sources Ezra–Nehemiah demonstrates a remarkable unity of construction, patterns, concerns, and themes. This could, of course, be explained by either common authorship or by a final process that attempted to bring about this very result. Space does not permit a detailed analysis of the parts of the books and their creative integration into the finished product. Recent rhetorical studies have revealed an overall architecture that provides compelling evidence of unity. The following chiastic structure is typical:

A. Zerubbabel's return and list of returnees (Ezra 1–2)

    B. Building of the temple and opposition (Ezra 3–6)

        C. Return of Ezra (Ezra 7–8)

            D. Center: Purification of people (Ezra 9–10)

        C.' Return of Nehemiah (Neh. 1–2)

    B.' Building of the walls and opposition (Neh. 3:1–7:3)

A.' Zerubbabel's return and list of returnees; final reforms (Neh. 7:4–13:31)

DATE

The latest recorded event in Ezra–Nehemiah is Nehemiah's return to Jerusalem in 432 B.C. following a brief absence in Susa (Neh. 13:6). While it is impossible to assign a precise date to the final work, the book cannot have been written much later than 425 B.C.

ADDRESSEES

In general terms Ezra–Nehemiah was intended for the whole postexilic Jewish community, but in particular it was addressed to those in and immediately around Jerusalem. As part of the Word of God, of course, it transcends those narrow geographical and historical constrictions and speaks its message to all the people of the Lord in all ages. Its message, in some respects at least, is as relevant to any modern reader as it was to the fifth-century Jewish community that first heard and read it.

PURPOSE

Though the city of Jerusalem and its temple had largely been rebuilt by the end of the sixth century B.C., constant harassment by surrounding enemies had impeded the work and in fact had resulted in actual further destruction from time to time (Neh. 1:3). More serious were the inroads of social and religious elements from both foreign and domestic sources that threatened to undermine the moral and spiritual foundations of the struggling postexilic Jewish community. Ezra—Nehemiah recounts these concerns, and by detailing the lives and labors of the men whose names it bears it provides direction to that community as to how to avoid the covenant violations that had issued in the terrible judgment of the Lord on their fathers in the first place.

THEOLOGICAL EMPHASES

The overriding theological issue in fifth-century Judea was the viability of the community that God had restored from Babylonian exile. At stake was the very possibility of the continuation and fulfillment of the promises made to David that his royal descendants and the nation over which they were to rule would never end. Though there was superficial resemblance of a national and religious entity, fissures were beginning to appear that signaled the likelihood of total and complete disintegration unless radical steps of reformation could soon be put in place.

Ezra and Nehemiah exerted their efforts toward both exposing these tendencies and severely rebuking those especially responsible for them, and calling for deep, genuine, and universal repentance. They were fundamentally reformers, and their message was one of reformation. Not to be lost is their recognition of the Lord as the sovereign One, the God not only of Israel but also of all the nations. His purposes can be achieved with or without human cooperation, but His special plan for Israel inspired Ezra and Nehemiah to encourage their fellow Jews to line up with these purposes for their own good and for God's glory.

OUTLINE

I. Return from Exile (Ezra 1–2)
   A. Proclamation of Permission (chapter 1)
   B. List of Returnees (chapter 2)

II. Rebuilding of Worship and Community (chapters 3–6)
   A. Preparation for Rebuilding (chapter 3)
   B. Opposition to Rebuilding (chapter 4)
   C. Continuation of Rebuilding (chapter 5)
   D. Completion of Rebuilding (chapter 6)

III. Return of Ezra (chapters 7–8)
   A. Arrangements for His Return (chapter 7)
   B. Entourage with His Return (chapter 8)

IV. Ministry of Ezra (chapters 9–10)
   A. Sin of the People (9:1–4)
   B. Ezra's Prayer for the People (9:5–15)
   C. Ezra's Leadership in Reformation (chapter 10)

V. Nehemiah's Dilemma (Neh. 1:1–11)
   A. Report of Jerusalem's Condition (1:1–3)
   B. Nehemiah's Prayer (1:4–11)

VI. Nehemiah's Plan (chapter 2)
   A. His Request of the King (2:1–8)
   B. His Return to Jerusalem and Plan to Rebuild (2:9–20)

VII. Nehemiah's Building (chapters 3–4)
   A. His Organization (chapter 3)
   B. His Opposition (chapter 4)

VIII. Nehemiah's Domestic Reforms (chapter 5)

IX. Nehemiah's Determination (chapters 6–7)

X. List of Returnees (7:5–73a)

XI. Covenant Renewal (7:73b–10:39)
   A. Its Preparations (7:73b–9:4)

B. Its Proclamation (9:5–10:27)
C. Its Stipulations (10:28–39)
XII. Rededication of Jerusalem (11:1–13:3)
A. Lists of People and Priests (11:1–12:26)
B. Ceremony of Celebration (12:27–13:3)
XIII. Return to Former Sins and Second Reformation (13:4–31)

I. RETURN FROM EXILE (EZRA 1–2)

The narrative in Ezra is a continuation of that in 1 and 2 Chronicles, as the repetition of the so-called decree of Cyrus makes clear (Ezra 1:1–4; 2 Chron. 36:22–23). Whereas the chronicler had left the matter of the return of the Jews from Babylon unresolved, Ezra described that return and included a list of the clans and families involved.

A. Proclamation of Permission (chapter 1)

Though Cyrus, king of Persia, had assumed full regency over his empire by 550 B.C., his first year as ruler of Babylon was 539. It was then that he was led by Israel's God to issue a famous decree permitting all captive peoples in Babylonia, including the Jews, to return to their homelands. But this was not merely an empty gesture, for Cyrus provided the where-withal for the Jews not only to go back to Jerusalem but also to undertake the reconstruction of their ruined temple (1:1–4).

Duly authorized, those of the Jews impressed by God's Spirit to do so picked up their belongings and the costly furnishings of the old temple of Solomon and set out for the land most of them had never seen (1:5–7). Their leader was Sheshbazzar, "the prince of Judah" (1:8), probably the same man as Shenazzar, a son of Jehoiachin (1 Chron. 3:18) and therefore uncle of Zerubbabel, the postexilic governor of the Jews. With meticulous detail, the recorder of these events listed the various precious temple objects by number as though doing an inventory to compare to what had been stolen from Jerusalem fifty years before (Ezra 1:9–11).

B. List of Returnees (chapter 2)

The list that follows must have been an official record long antedating both Ezra and Nehemiah, for the latter, citing it almost exactly, said he came across it by researching the matter (Neh. 7:5). The eleven leaders of the returnees include such well-known persons as Zerubbabel, grandson of King Jehoiachin, and Jeshua, chief priest of the restored community. The Nehemiah of the list is not the famous governor, for that Nehemiah went to Jerusalem nearly a century later, in 445 B.C. Nor is Mordecai the kinsman of Queen Esther. He would have had to be just a child in 539 since he was a high Persian official no later than 475 B.C. or so. Besides, there is no hint that Esther's Mordecai had ever lived in Babylon, to say nothing of Jerusalem (Ezra 2:1–2).

The list of returnees is subdivided into "the men of the people of Israel" (2:3–35); the priests (2:36–39); the Levites (2:40–42); the Nethinim, a kind of temple servant class (1 Chron. 9:2; Ezra 2:58; 8:20); "the children of Solomon's servants" (2:55–58, KJV); and a miscellaneous group from various parts of the Jewish dispersion who could not document their ancestral affiliations (2:59–63).

Altogether there were 42,360 who made up this first major return. All of them began to settle down, probably in the villages of their ancestors as much as possible (2:68–70).

II. REBUILDING OF WORSHIP AND COMMUNITY (CHAPTERS 3–6)

The willingness to rebuild soon found expression in actual performance. With might and main the leaders and people alike took to the task and made a remarkable beginning. Before long, however, opposition set in and continued to plague the process from its beginning down to Ezra's own time, eighty years later. Over and over God encouraged His people through prophets and by other means, and time and again they appealed to the Persian central government for its intervention and protection. Gradually the physical structures began to take shape, but the moral and spiritual life of the community left much to be desired.

A. Preparation for Rebuilding (chapter 3)

In the seventh month of the first year of the return (about 537 B.C.)—the month of New Year's Day, the Day of Atonement, and the Festival of Tabernacles—Jeshua the priest and Zerubbabel the governor erected an altar to the Lord as the first step in rebuilding the whole community (3:1–3). They then officiated at the Festival of Tabernacles, a celebration which, among other things, provided occasion for covenant renewal (3:4–6a; see Deut. 31:9–13). There could hardly have been a more appropriate time to do so.

Seven months later (536 B.C.), the men and materials having been gathered, the construction of the temple foundation commenced (Ezra 3:8–10). For fifty long years God's house had lain in ruins. No wonder the people erupted into praise and thanksgiving when they beheld this new beginning with their own eyes (3:11). Some of the older among them, however, did not rejoice at all for they could not help comparing the modest dimensions of this building with the magnificent size and scope of the temple of Solomon (3:12–13; see also Hag. 2:3).

B. Opposition to Rebuilding (chapter 4)

Any good work for God can expect opposition from Satan and his cohorts. Not surprisingly, then, the Jews' enemies drew near when they learned of the building project. At first they offered to join in, claiming as Samaritans that they too worshiped the Lord and in an appropriate way (Ezra 4:1–2; see 2 Kings 17:32–33). Zerubbabel and Jeshua declined the offer, no doubt sensing it as a ploy by which to gain some kind of legitimacy and advantage (Ezra 4:3). The adversaries responded to this rebuff by trying to undermine the morale of the builders and otherwise frustrate its progress. This, the historian noted, they did all through the reigns of the Persian kings Cyrus (538–530), Darius (522–486), and Ahasuerus (also known as Xerxes, 486–465). This brings the records down to the time of Ezra himself, who, of course, was an eyewitness to this opposition (4:4–6).

Ezra therefore most likely wrote of the persecution of the Jews in the reign of Artaxerxes (464–424), for it was under the protection of this king that he and his entourage made their own return to Jerusalem (7:1).

Having failed to deter the Jews by other means, their foes composed letters to Artaxerxes in which they pointed out that the Jews had finished the walls of Jerusalem and other projects with the intention of gaining independence from Persia (4:7–12). This would cut off from the king a valuable source of revenue and could even mean the loss of all his territories west of the Euphrates (4:13–16). This produced its desired effect, for the king, searching the archives, learned that the Jews had indeed proved to be a headache in the past. He therefore decreed that all work cease (4:17–23). The reference to the cessation of work in 4:24 applies to the note in 4:5 concerning Darius. That is, the narrative of verses 5 and 24 is interrupted by a catalog of oppressions that came to Ezra's mind as he considered the earliest years of opposition.

C. Continuation of Rebuilding (chapter 5)

Continuing his résumé of the history of rebuilding and the opposition to it, the narrator focused on the period of King Darius to which he had just referred (4:24). At that time (520 B.C.), he said, two prophets of the Lord— Haggai and Zechariah—had encouraged Zerubbabel and Jeshua to move forward on the temple project (5:1–2). This they did, but opposition surfaced immediately from Tattenai, governor of the whole province, and his fellow officials (5:3–5). They decided to draft a letter to Darius, inquiring as to whether the construction work had imperial authorization. They first informed Darius as to the state of affairs and then told him how they had challenged the Jewish leaders about the legality of what they were doing (5:6–10). The Jews, Tattenai said, claimed they were building for their God and that they had permission to do so from King Cyrus himself (5:11–16). In conclusion Tattenai advised Darius to search the royal archives to see if there were any truth to these claims by the Jews (5:17).

D. Completion of Rebuilding (chapter 6)

Thus apprised, Darius ordered that the search be made for the documents in question and at length they were uncovered in a palace of Cyrus in

Media (6:1–2). Sure enough, the Jews were right. Cyrus had indeed approved the rebuilding of Jerusalem and the temple and had even provided material assistance (6:3–5). On the basis of this precedent established by his illustrious predecessor less than twenty years earlier, Darius had no option but to inform Tattenai that the projects must be allowed to continue, and with his full blessing and support. Anyone who stood in the way could expect to be severely punished (6:6–12).

With this obstacle behind them the Jews pressed on until the temple was finished in Darius's sixth year (516 B.C.). This was exactly seventy years after the destruction of the temple of Solomon. With great joy and praise to God, they celebrated His goodness to them (6:16–17). After organizing the priests and Levites by courses and assignments, the leaders observed the Passover on a massive scale (6:18–22). This type of festival-keeping was typical of such momentous events in the spiritual history of Israel (see 2 Chron. 30:1–27; 35:1–19).

III. RETURN OF EZRA (CHAPTERS 7–8)

This section describes events contemporary with Ezra himself, especially his return to Jerusalem from Persia with a large contingent of fellow Jews. There is every likelihood that Ezra is the author of this section and also of the rest of the book that bears his name.

A. Arrangements for His Return (chapter 7)

About fifty-eight years after the temple was completed, Ezra, a priest and scribe of the Jewish exilic community of Babylon, decided to emigrate to Judea, the land of his fathers. As a direct descendant of Aaron (Ezra 7:1–5), his priestly credentials were impeccable. Furthermore he obviously enjoyed favor and status among his exilic compatriots as well as with King Artaxerxes and other Persian leaders. When the king knew of Ezra's desire to lead his people back to Jerusalem, he readily granted his permission, and so in the king's seventh year (458 B.C.) Ezra and his party set out (7:6–9). His motives in going back are crystal clear: to seek the Law of the Lord, obey it himself, and then to teach it to his countrymen (7:10).

A sign of Artaxerxes' great fondness for Ezra is the letter of conveyance he composed on Ezra's behalf (7:12–26). After giving formal acknowledgment of Israel's God (7:12), the king issued a decree authorizing the return of the Jews (7:13) and their right to transport silver and gold with which they could purchase animals for sacrifice and other things necessary to the proper worship of the Lord at the temple (7:14–19). If this were not enough for their needs, they could draw more assets from the royal treasuries in the Persian province in which Judea was located (7:20–22). Above all, Artaxerxes insisted, was the need to do whatever was necessary to please and enjoy the favor of Israel's God (7:23).

Beyond all this, the king went on to command that all personnel associated with the ministry of the temple be exempted from taxes and tribute. Moreover, Ezra could appoint his own Jewish officials, instructing them in God's laws. Anyone who disputed this decree would answer to the king himself and would suffer dire consequences (7:24–26).

For such generosity Ezra lifted his heart and voice in praise to God. The heart of the king was truly in the hand of the Lord, who turned it whichever way He wished (Prov. 21:1). With such encouragement, Ezra gathered his band together and they set out on the long journey home (Ezra 7:27–28).

B. Entourage with His Return (chapter 8)

Ezra listed the names of the leaders of the various clans and families who accompanied him to the first assembly point (8:1–14). To his dismay, he noticed no Levites among them, and therefore he sent messengers to a place called Casiphia where he knew Levites could be found (8:15–17). These were obviously necessary for the proper function of the temple and worship there. Once these had been found and had joined his entourage, Ezra led the whole procession in intense prayer and fasting, beseeching the Lord that He would grant safety and success for the journey ahead (8:18–23).

Next Ezra distributed the sacred temple vessels among twelve priests for their safekeeping until they arrived in Jerusalem. These men were set apart to the Lord to do this, for holy tasks can be assigned only to holy people (8:24–30). With everything now ready, the several thousand pilgrims directed their faces to the land of promise. They arrived there without mishap and Ezra immediately took charge as chief priest. He delivered the sacred objects to the temple, offered up an enormous sacrifice, and then informed the Persian king's provincial officials of his decree and its provisions (8:31–36).

IV. MINISTRY OF EZRA (CHAPTERS 9–10)

Ezra wasted no time in addressing spiritual issues that had arisen early in the life of the postexilic community and that had continued off and on from that time to the present. Chief among these in Ezra's view was the problem of intermarriage of the Jews with their pagan neighbors, a problem that preoccupied him to the exclusion of all others, at least as far as the account in the Book of Ezra is concerned.

A. *Sins of the People (9:1–4)*

One of the principal covenant stipulations was that God's people must not intermarry with unbelievers lest they be drawn away to their heathen religious and moral practices (Exod. 34:15–16; Deut. 7:3–4). Ezra soon learned that this is precisely what the Jews had done when they returned from captivity (Ezra 9:1–2). Unable to contain his sorrow and anger, Ezra sat stunned for a while and then convened an assembly in order to issue his judgment on the matter (9:3–4).

B. *Ezra's Prayer for the People (9:5–15)*

That evening Ezra lifted up his hands to God in a prayer of confession and deep contrition in which he did not exonerate himself but, as spokesman for the whole nation, freely acknowledged the sins of the people. It was because of their history of disobedience that their fathers had gone into captivity in the first place (9:5–7). Now the Lord had brought them back, going so far as to give them favor in the eyes of the Persian kings. They had been able to rebuild their city and temple (9:9b), but despite all these displays of divine grace they had transgressed the Law of the Lord, particularly in the area of forbidden marriage (9:10–12). How then could they expect to escape God's judgment for doing the same things their fathers had done? In fact, they had no reason at all to claim exemption from His wrath (9:13–15).

C. Ezra's Leadership in Reformation (chapter 10)

Ezra's public (and presumably loud) prayer attracted attention, and before long the plaza in front of the temple was filled with people weeping over their sins (10:1). They readily confessed their wrongdoing in marrying pagan wives and pledged to do something about it, namely, to divorce and disown these wives and the children born to them (10:2–4). Convinced that this was the right course of action, Ezra arranged for a great conclave of all the people to take place so that he could outline a plan to bring it about (10:5–8).

Within three days the whole population gathered at the temple in a driving rain to hear the verdict. Ezra got straight to the point: He declared that the illicit marriages were sinful, that they must confess this sin to the Lord, and that they must dissolve these marriages at once and completely (10:9–11). The people agreed to all this but because of the inclement weather and the sheer logistics of implementing the divorce decree throughout the whole land, they requested that they have some more time in which to carry it out (10:12–15).

Ten days later the process was set in place, and within two months it had been accomplished (10:16–17). Ezra completed his account by listing a number of the men who had been involved in these drastic actions, including priests, Levites, singers, and the laity (10:18–44). The whole manner of Ezra's disposition of the problem is, of course, a matter of disagreement and debate, especially in light of Malachi's observation that God hates divorce (Mal. 2:16). Moreover, the Bible nowhere else sanctions divorce from non-Christian partners simply because they are unbelievers. Perhaps Ezra's action can be best understood as an extreme remedy for an extreme situation. If these huge numbers of unbiblical marriages had been tolerated, it could well have spelled the end of the postexilic community as the people through whom God would eventually bring redemption to the world.

V. NEHEMIAH'S DILEMMA (NEH. 1:1–11)

While Ezra was struggling with the issue of mixed marriages in Jerusalem, his younger colleague Nehemiah was enjoying the luxuries of the lavish court of King Artaxerxes in Susa. His heart, however, was in Jerusalem, and within thirteen years of Ezra's departure Nehemiah set out to join him.

A. Report of Jerusalem's Condition (1:1–3)

One day while on the job as Artaxerxes' butler, Nehemiah learned from his brother and others who had just come from Jerusalem that the Jews there were suffering persecution and that the city walls and other structures lay in ruins. This could not have been the result of the Babylonian destruction of 140 years earlier, for Nehemiah was surely aware of that. It must, rather, refer to damage done just recently, though nothing is said of it in the Book of Ezra.

B. Nehemiah's Prayer (1:4–11)

The job as taster of all the king's food and drink was a most important one, a task not to be entrusted to just anybody. Nehemiah knew, therefore, that only the Lord could persuade Artaxerxes to release him for a time, so he offered up a desperate prayer of appeal. God's people were suffering, he said, and despite their sin God had made a covenant to them. The king must now grant his permission for Nehemiah to minister to his needy people, and God must make the king to be so inclined.

VI. NEHEMIAH'S PLAN (CHAPTER 2)

A. His Request of the King (2:1–8)

One day as Nehemiah was serving Artaxerxes, the king observed that he was morose and so he inquired as to Nehemiah's state of mind (2:1–2).

Breathing up a prayer, Nehemiah disclosed all that was troubling him, and to his amazement he found the king most amenable to his request for a leave of absence (2:3–6). Moreover, the king provided letters officially endorsing Nehemiah and his mission and ordering his officials in the provincial government to grant whatever Nehemiah might need (2:7–8).

B. His Return to Jerusalem and Plan to Rebuild (2:9–20)

On his arrival in the province in which Judea was located Nehemiah presented himself to the governor. The latter's obvious favor toward him infuriated the Jews' enemies such as Sanballat and Tobiah, who began then to plot how to get around the king's decree of protection (2:9–10). Meanwhile Nehemiah rode his horse around the perimeter of Jerusalem by night in order to assess the damage and determine what it would take to re-erect the fallen walls. He then made his report to the city officials and urged them to get on with the project, the ridicule of their adversaries notwithstanding.

VII. NEHEMIAH'S BUILDING (CHAPTERS 3–4)

A project of the urgency and magnitude that lay ahead required the utmost careful planning. It also called for leadership, the kind that a seasoned administrator like Nehemiah could provide. But it also elicited a bitter reaction from the Jews' enemies, who were, in the final analysis, the adversaries of the Lord Himself. For the work to succeed, the builders would therefore have to be vigilant.

A. His Organization (chapter 3)

Nehemiah's strategy was to assign different village and family groups to various sections of the wall, divided roughly into segments between the seven gates of the city. No class, occupation, age, or gender was exempted, for the work was God's work, and the benefits would be enjoyed by all without discrimination.

B. His Opposition (chapter 4)

The ridicule with which Sanballat and his coconspirators had greeted the announcement of the construction project (2:19) intensified now that the work was actually underway. The project would get nowhere, they said, and Tobiah taunted that if even a small fox were to try to scale the wall it would come crashing down (4:1–3). This bravado was more wishful thinking than anything else, however, for it was clear that the Jews were serious and that they would let nothing stand in their way. On the other hand, taking nothing for granted, Nehemiah prayed that God would give him success (4:4–5).

After the wall reached half its projected height, Sanballat and the others realized that mockery alone would get them nowhere, so they contemplated the use of military force (4:7–8). It was too little too late, however, for the walls were now high enough to afford protection, and Nehemiah put in place extra security to guard the workers. More important, he appealed to the Lord for help and encouraged the others to do so as well (4:9–14). The Jews' detractors became dispirited and backed away, but Nehemiah continued to exercise due caution. He divided his crews into builders and defenders, and some held a sword with one hand and a trowel in the other, so intent were they on finishing the job (4:15–20). Even such necessities as bathing occasionally went by the board in the interest of accomplishing the task (4:21–23).

VIII. NEHEMIAH'S DOMESTIC REFORMS (CHAPTER 5)

The rebuilding of the walls at last had to give way to the rebuilding of the social and spiritual life of the community. Some had become financially impoverished to the extent that they had to mortgage their properties and even indenture their children in order to pay their debts (5:1–5). This filled Nehemiah with rage, for while it was permitted for Jews to exact interest from foreigners, to do so from a fellow Jew was intolerable (5:6–7; Exod. 22:25). Moreover, the Jews had ransomed one another from gentile ownership; how then could they put their very own kinsmen in a similar position (Neh. 5:8)? Besides all this, for one Jew to mistreat another in this way besmirched their reputation and, worse still, that of their God in the eyes of the surrounding peoples (5:9).

The remedy for this ill was complete restoration of all mortgaged properties and a vow never again to apply the world's standards to the economic life of the covenant community. This they all swore to do, thus ending this particular issue (5:10–13). Almost parenthetically Nehemiah recounted how he never laid claim to the benefits he could have enjoyed for twelve years as governor, unlike those who had preceded him in the office (5:14–15). In fact, he had turned the governor's mansion almost into a boardinghouse where he entertained his own and foreign officials at his own cost (5:16–18). The reason he mentioned this is to show that his scolding of others for their mercenary spirit was not at all hypocritical for he had practiced what he preached. No wonder he dared to pray that God would remember him for good (5:19).

IX. NEHEMIAH'S DETERMINATION (CHAPTERS 6–7)

At this point the narration returns to the events surrounding the completion of the city walls (4:21–23). Apparently never weary of their efforts to subvert the reestablishing of the Jewish state, Sanballat and his friends changed their tack and invited Nehemiah to enter into negotiations with them at a neutral place. Nehemiah saw through their scheme, however, and despite their repeated efforts to change his mind, he refused to meet with them (6:1–4). They then began to circulate a letter in which it was alleged that Nehemiah had a hidden agenda, one designed to make him a king independent of the Persian rulers. This, of course, was nonsense, as Nehemiah quickly reminded them (6:5–9).

Next, it seems that one of Nehemiah's own confidants had been influenced by Sanballat to induce Nehemiah to seek refuge in the temple in anticipation of an attack on his life (6:10). Nehemiah did not fall for this either, for he knew God was not in it. Moreover, if he tried to protect himself in this way, he would lose credibility as a leader (6:11–14).

Such discernment and boldness on Nehemiah's part contributed greatly to the success of his leadership. The wall was finished in such a brief time that the opposition had to acknowledge that the work was of God (6:15–16). Nevertheless they would not let up; instead they spread all kinds of false rumors about Nehemiah as a man and a leader and continued to send him threatening letters to harass and intimidate him (6:17–19).

Undeterred, Nehemiah pushed forward, directing his attention to matters of community organization. He appointed his own brother Hanani as co-mayor of Jerusalem with Hananiah, and he warned them to be constantly vigilant in matters of security. Part of the problem of the city's vulnerability was its sparse population, a problem he later addressed (7:1–4; 11:1).

X. LIST OF RETURNEES (7:5–73A)

With the social and civil situation more stabilized, Nehemiah decided to take a census of the population, probably to determine settlement locations and hereditary claims. This required research into the genealogical connections of the people, so appeal was made to old documents that listed the original returnees from Babylon. This is the same list Ezra had consulted earlier (Ezra 2:1–70). The minor differences there and here in Nehemiah are matters of slight copyist variations. The total number of free laity in both passages is 42,360, and in addition there were 7,337 servants and 245 singers (Neh. 7:66–67). The cities in which they settled were presumably the ones in which their preexilic ancestors had lived. Nehemiah's census may have been for the purpose of validating or contesting claims of property rights and similar matters.

XI. COVENANT RENEWAL (7:73B–10:39)

In the seventh month (Tishri), the month of the great fall festivals of the New Year, the Day of Atonement, and Tabernacles, the people's thoughts turned to the need for covenant renewal. This was precisely the time mandated by Moses, who said this was to take place on a regular basis at least every seven years (Deut. 31:9–13). Heeding their request, Ezra and Nehemiah led the assembly in the celebration of the Festival of Tabernacles followed by the presentation and acceptance of a covenant text appropriate to their time and place as a postexilic community.

A. Its Preparations (7:73b–9:4)

The remarkable thing about the spiritual renewal in Nehemiah's day is that it was initiated by the people themselves and not by the governor, priest, or some other leader. "As one man" they gathered in the plaza near the Water Gate, and they asked Ezra to read to them "the book of the law of Moses," that is, at least Deuteronomy (Deut. 31:24–26), if not the entire Pentateuch (Neh. 7:73b–8:1). The occasion was New Year's Day (now called Rosh Hashanah), the perfect time for beginning again (8:2).

Standing high on a wooden platform, Ezra read the Word of God to the people all morning long. With him stood a number of assistants who, in turn, clarified the reading and meaning of the text for these Aramaic-speaking Jews who, ironically, no longer spoke Hebrew in ordinary discourse (8:3–8). Their deep reverence for the Scriptures is reflected in their standing to their feet as Ezra commenced the reading (8:5). He would read a verse or two and then the interpreters rendered a translation with appropriate comments designed to provide a running commentary (8:7–8). Many scholars trace the origin of the Aramaic Targums (Old Testament paraphrases) to this oral rendition.

> *The reaction of Ezra's audience to his reading of God's Word is worthy of emulation, at least in spirit if not in physical terms. It was as if God Himself were speaking, which indeed is true once one recognizes that the Bible is in a real sense God's voice.*

God's word brought deep conviction as well as nostalgic memories, and the people began to weep. Ezra and Nehemiah told them to stop, however, for it was a day of joy and not sorrow. They could best express their overpowering emotions by looking to one another's needs, an appropriate response at the time of the fall harvest (8:9–12).

The next day's reading brought them to the passage outlining the purpose and procedures of the Feast of Tabernacles, perhaps Deuteronomy 16:13–17. This included the erection of huts made from brush and branches, so the people scoured the countryside for these materials and made these fragile structures as the Law of Moses required (Lev. 23:39–44). For seven days they kept this festival, with Ezra reading the Law throughout. The whole was capped off by a great assembly on the eighth day, which was also mandated by the Law (Neh. 8:13–18).

Immediately following the Festival of Tabernacles—and no doubt as its aftermath—the people became acutely aware of their failings as a covenant nation. For three hours the sacred text was read and for three more the audience responded in corporate confession (9:1–4). Surely the Lord was doing a great work among them to prepare them for renewal.

B. Its Proclamation (9:5–10:27)

The privilege of leading the nation in covenant renewal fell to the Levites who are listed in 9:5. After exhorting the crowd to stand and praise the Lord, they addressed Him in prayer, recognizing His incomparability and glory. The prayer itself follows, at least in a general way, the pattern of covenant texts found elsewhere in the Old Testament and in the ancient Near East as well (see the introduction to Deuteronomy). On the other hand, it lacks a body of stipulations and the blessings and curses sections, for these already existed in the Mosaic formulations and did not need to be repeated here. What is left basically is a history of Israel's relationship with the Lord since the making of the original covenants at Sinai and the plains of Moab.

In a preamble the Lord is confessed as the one and only God (Neh. 9:6a). The historical prologue then traces his role as Creator and as the One who made a covenant with Abraham (9:6b–8). The proclamation then recounts the Egyptian oppression followed by the Exodus and God's leading them to Mount Sinai, where He revealed His covenant plan for Israel (9:9–14). From there He had taken them through a route to Canaan that would have been impossible except for His miraculous supply (9:15).

Israel's response to all this grace had been one of obstinate rebellion. They rejected the leadership of Moses and turned to idols in defiance of

God's loving care for them (9:16–18). Despite this, the Lord in His mercy continued to lead them onward, supplying manna from heaven and giving them victory over their enemies (9:19–22). At last He had taken them into the Promised Land itself where they had dispossessed the peoples who lived there and occupied their dwellings and lands as their own (9:23–25). Even there Israel turned away from God until there was no remedy but judgment from outside enemies. God raised up judges to deliver them, but to no avail for they continued in their evil ways all through their history, until at last He had given them over to exile (9:26–30).

The postexilic community itself could testify to the fact that God had left a remnant through whom He would continue to carry out His plan of human redemption (9:31). The Levites therefore pleaded that He would look with favor on them because of their sufferings, and that despite His justice He might display grace (9:32–35). They lived among pagan peoples and under the imperialistic yoke of a foreign power, but their hope now was freedom from all this as a result of their present vows to the Lord (9:36–38).

After this lengthy prayer devoted primarily to the dismal history of Israel's past failures contrasted with the unlimited patience and grace of God, the secular and religious leaders whose names appear in 10:1–27 affixed their signatures to the covenant text, the provisions of which follow in 10:28–39.

C. Its Stipulations (10:28–39)

In line with usual covenant language one might describe this section as stipulation. However, it is in fact a statement of commitment to stipulations already incumbent on the nation by virtue of the Mosaic Covenant texts of which they had just been freshly reminded by the public reading of the Law of Moses. In what appears to be a univocal response, all segments of the community pledged themselves to keep all the terms of the Law that God had revealed to Moses long before (10:28–29). Addressing an issue that Ezra had already dealt with, they promised never again to intermarry with the heathen (10:30; Ezra 9:1–10:44). Besides this, they vowed to honor the Sabbath, to pay the required temple taxes, to offer the firstfruits of their labor, and to care for the needs of the Levites (Neh. 10:31–39).

XII. REDEDICATION OF JERUSALEM (11:1–13:3)

For reasons not entirely clear, the city of Jerusalem, though rebuilt and refortified, was underpopulated. Nehemiah therefore took measures to redress this lack, after which he dedicated the city walls and reorganized the temple personnel so that the worship of the Lord could take place in an appropriate manner.

A. Lists of People and Priests (11:1–12:26)

A shortage of residents in Jerusalem seems apparent in the need to guarantee that at least 10 percent of the total population would live there, and Nehemiah had already explicitly mentioned the problem (7:4–5). A list now follows of those who willingly moved into the city (11:2), as well as those who did so more under compulsion (11:3–24). Also appended is a list of the villages in which both citizens and religious personnel took up residence (11:25–36). Reference to the latter prompted the editor of the account to present a roster of priests and Levites who had come back with Zerubbabel and Jeshua at the very first return in 538 B.C. (Ezra 2:1–2). Though many of these names appear elsewhere (2:36–42; Neh. 7:39–45), the list as it stands occurs only here.

B. Ceremony of Celebration (12:27–13:3)

Another reason for the listing of past and present Levites now becomes clear. The wall of Jerusalem was now completely rebuilt, and Nehemiah was eager to dedicate it and the city to the Lord who had made its successful reconstruction possible. This required the services of the Levites and priests for this was not a secular matter but one of an intensely spiritual nature. Nehemiah therefore summoned religious personnel from near and far so the dedication could be done according to proper protocol (12:27–30).

When everyone had assembled, Nehemiah directed the political and religious leaders to ascend the wall and then to divide into two groups and proceed to march around the city in opposite directions (12:31–43). All along the way both processions gave thanks to God in vocal and instrumental music (12:27, 41–42). The people below were caught up in the excitement and glory of it all, and they too burst out in expressions of praise (12:43). Riding the crest of the wave, as it were, that very day Nehemiah appointed temple ministers in line with the ancient prescriptions of David and Solomon (12:44–46; see 1 Chron. 25:1; 26:1). He also saw to it that the material needs of these servants of the Lord would be met by the community that depended on them (Neh. 12:47). On a more negative note, the Mosaic Law forbidding access by some to the sacred assembly was also put into force, thus precluding the mixed multitude (that is, non-Israelites; see 9:2) from temple worship (13:1–3).

XIII. RETURN TO FORMER SINS AND SECOND REFORMATION (13:4–31)

At some point near the end of the twelve-year period of Nehemiah's governorship, he had gone back to Persia for undisclosed reasons. In his absence things had begun to deteriorate badly in Judea, a fact that may have prompted him to seek a second leave of absence from King Artaxerxes in 432 B.C. (13:6; see 5:14). Perhaps the most terrible wrong was the appropriation of a temple apartment by the Jews' notorious enemy, Tobiah (2:10; 6:1, 17–18), whom the chief priest, Eliashib, had befriended (13:4–7). In addition, Tobiah had married a daughter of Shecaniah, a leading citizen (6:18), thus gaining a further foothold into Jewish life. This carried no weight with Nehemiah, however, and his first act when he returned to Jerusalem was to evict Tobiah and his belongings from the temple and then purify the place from the ritual contamination that had resulted from this profaning of a sacred place (13:8–9).

Another problem was that the Levites had not been receiving the support from the people required by the Law of Moses (10:37–39), with the result that they had been forced to resort to secular employment in order to provide for their families (13:10). Nehemiah severely reprimanded the derelict community leaders. Then he appointed supervisors over the storehouses to ensure the proper distribution of tithes and offerings that were already beginning to pour in to meet the Levites' needs (13:11–14).

A third problem was gross violation of the Sabbath, especially by merchants who brought their wares into the city on the Sabbath day in order to ply their trade (13:15–16). Nehemiah's response was swift and sure. First, he chided the city officials for permitting such a thing, reminding them that disregard of the Sabbath in the past had resulted in God's judgment (13:17–18; Jer. 17:21–23). His second step was more forcible. He ordered the city gates to be locked by sundown on the eve of the Sabbath and not reopened until Sabbath was over (Neh. 13:19). Testing the limits, some of the traders lingered about the gates all day long on the Sabbath, waiting for business hours to begin. Viewing this as a breach of the spirit of the Law, Nehemiah said that anyone caught doing so in the future would be harmed physically (13:20–22).

Fourth, the persistent problem of mixed marriages had once again become a matter of concern during Nehemiah's absence and certainly even during his earlier governorship. The extreme measures of Ezra—a forced and wholesale edict of divorce—apparently had no lasting results or had not been universally applied. The "mixed marriages" of God's elect people so angered Nehemiah that he physically punished some of the guilty ones and made all the others swear that they would not do such a thing in the future (13:23–27). Interestingly Nehemiah did not compel divorce, perhaps because he had no scriptural grounds for doing so.

A celebrated case of intermarriage was that of a grandson of Eliashib the priest, who had wed a daughter of Sanballat, leader of the anti-Jewish movement from the very beginning (see 2:10, 19). Nehemiah exiled the young man from the community because he had desecrated the priestly office (13:28–29). Nehemiah concluded his memoirs by summarizing his efforts to bring about reform, and he prayed that God would bless him for his faithfulness (13:30–31).

ESTHER
Help from a Hidden Source

AUTHOR

 he Jewish historian Josephus (around A.D. 37–100) was the earliest authority to address the question of the authorship of the Book of Esther. He proposed Mordecai, a hero of the book, as its author. However, this seems unlikely, given the lavish praise heaped on Mordecai throughout the narrative (Esth. 6:11; 8:2; 8:15; 9:4; 10:3). The Mishnah, which records many Jewish traditions, merely notes that the "Men of the Great Assembly" were responsible. At the present no better answer is forthcoming.

UNITY

A common opinion among critical scholars is that the Book of Esther is the result of the joining of chapters 9–10 to an earlier narrative (chapters 1–8). In turn, the larger piece originally consisted of as many as three anecdotes— those of Mordecai, Esther, and perhaps Vashti. There is no way to prove this hypothesis, however, and so one should assume a fundamentally unified composition by the same author or at least the same final editor.

DATE

The latest date implicit in the book itself is about 470 B.C. (Esth. 3:7), and there is no reason to argue for its much later composition. The Hebrew of the book is in line with that of other sixth- or fifth-century works such as Ezra–Nehemiah; the use of Persian words is certainly to be expected in a work whose setting is in Persia; and the Festival of Purim, though not popularly celebrated until Hasmonean times (in the second century B.C.), is best dated in the Persian period. There is no occasion in later Jewish history that is as suitable.

ADDRESSEES

The readership of the book would initially have been the universal Jewish community of the dispersion. Then with the increasing significance of the Festival of Purim, it became the text of the celebration of that joyous annual event, still celebrated by Jews today.

PURPOSE

The purpose of the Book of Esther is to show that God can use ordinary people to accomplish His saving purposes. Beyond this is the idea that God is sovereign. Even though His name never occurs in the book, there can be no doubt that He has dominion over all nations and history itself.

THEOLOGICAL EMPHASES

Underlying everything in the Book of Esther is the fact that the God of Israel, who has made a covenant with the nation and has pledged to see it through to fruition, can and will do so no matter what opposition evil nations may raise against it. His lordship is not limited to a single people, place, and time, but is universal and omnipotent in its scope.

OUTLINE

I. Esther's Elevation to Power (chapters 1–2)
   A. The Demand of Xerxes (1:1–12)
   B. The Decrees of Xerxes (1:13–2:4)

    C. The Choice of Esther to Be Queen (2:5–18)

    D. The Discovery of a Plot against Xerxes (2:19–23)

 II. Esther's Role as Deliverer (chapters 3–7)

    A. The Decree against the Jews (chapter 3)

    B. The Vulnerability of the Jews (chapters 4–5)

    C. The Deliverance of the Jews (chapters 6–7)

III. Esther's Establishment of Purim (chapters 8–10)

    A. The Decree Favoring the Jews (chapter 8)

    B. The Implementation of Deliverance (9:1–16)

    C. The Celebration of Deliverance (9:17–32)

    D. The Advancement of the Jews (chapter 10)

I. ESTHER'S ELEVATION TO POWER (CHAPTERS 1–2)

The setting of the Book of Esther is Susa, the capital of the mighty Persian Empire, in the glorious days of one of its most illustrious rulers, Ahasuerus (also known as Xerxes), who ruled from 486 to 465 B.C. He was the immediate predecessor of Artaxerxes, who showed such favor to both Ezra and Nehemiah. Through a series of providential circumstances, Vashti, Xerxes' wife, was deposed and the beautiful Jewish maiden, Esther, took her place as the king's favorite wife.

A. The Demand of Xerxes (1:1–12)

Early in his reign, Xerxes celebrated some recent successes by hosting a lavish banquet for all of his courtiers in the magnificent splendor of the royal palace (1:1–8). When he had become thoroughly intoxicated by the endless supply of wine, some of his underlings challenged the king to summon Vashti, his queen, so all could admire her famed beauty. Flattered by this thought, Xerxes ordered his wife to come, but she was too noble to put on such a display and refused her husband's command (1:9–12).

B. The Decrees of Xerxes (1:13–2:4)

Completely at a loss, Xerxes turned to his counselors for advice. They first pointed out that Vashti's insubordination to her husband would set the example for all Persian wives everywhere to disobey their husbands (1:13–18). The only remedy was to depose her and to find a more compliant queen. The advisers said that when wives throughout the empire learned of this, they would immediately forget any ideas of women's liberation (1:19–20). This made sense to Xerxes, so he issued a decree that every man should be the head of his own home (1:21–22). He then began a search to find a replacement for Vashti, one more amenable to his lordship (2:1–4).

C. The Choice of Esther to Be Queen (2:5–18)

The narrator shifted the scene now to a Benjamite Jew named Mordecai, a leader of the Jewish populace in Susa. He had a beautiful cousin named Esther (Hadassah in Hebrew) whom he adopted as his own daughter after the death of her parents (2:5–7). When search was made for a suitable candidate for queen, Esther came to the attention of the king's messengers and was brought, along with many others, into his harem. Before long she became a favorite and was provided with the best of attention and accommodations. However, she did not disclose her Jewish identity, for Mordecai had counseled her against doing so (2:8–11).

The Persian custom was for the women of the king's harem to satisfy him on a rotating basis. In her own turn Esther was summoned and so impressed was Xerxes that he made Esther his queen in place of Vashti (2:12–18).

D. The Discovery of a Plot against Xerxes (2:19–23)

Sometime later Mordecai, who seems to have enjoyed special favor with those high up in Persian government and society, was sitting near the gate of the palace when he overheard an assassination plot against the king. He immediately communicated this information to his young cousin, who passed it on to Xerxes in time for him to apprehend the conspirators and put them to death. Esther had still not revealed her ethnic identity, for that must be kept hidden until it could be used to best advantage.

II. ESTHER'S ROLE AS DELIVERER (CHAPTERS 3–7)

The increasing favor with which Jews were being held in Persia produced a violent anti-Semitic backlash that threatened to annihilate the whole Jewish population. Unwittingly Xerxes signed a decree authorizing the slaughter of the Jews, only to find out, almost too late, that Esther, his beloved wife, was a Jew. Meanwhile Xerxes had learned of his indebtedness to Mordecai for his uncovering a plot against the king's life. He thus was constrained to promote Mordecai to even higher status, thereby frustrating anti-Semitic tendencies in this way as well.

A. The Decree against the Jews (chapter 3)

Haman, the arch-villain of the story, now made his appearance. He was second only to the king, but though all other officials did him obeisance, Mordecai the Jew refused him this honor (3:1–2). As time went by, Haman became filled with rage, and at last he hit on a solution—extermination of Mordecai and all the Jewish community (3:3–6). The pretext to the king was that the Jews were disloyal malcontents whose laws and customs were antithetical to Persia's and likely to poison the entire Persian way of life. Xerxes gullibly accepted this analysis of things and anthorized Haman to draw up a plan to solve the problem (3:7–11). Haman then dispatched couriers throughout the empire to order local officials to attack all Jews and put them to death on the thirteenth day of the month Adar (3:12–15).

B. The Vulnerability of the Jews (chapters 4–5)

Hearing of this devastating news, Mordecai and all the Jews of the empire began to weep, fast, and pray for divine intervention (4:1–3). Esther was no exception, for though no one knew she was Jewish, she felt keenly for her Jewish kinsmen. She therefore sent a messenger to Mordecai to learn the details of the decree; he in turn replied with an earnest request that she use her influence with her husband, the king (4:4–8). Her response was that it was dangerous for anyone—even her—to appear before the king uninvited, but Mordecai retorted that deliverance would come anyway, whether or not she was willing to get involved. Convicted by Mordecai's persistence and great faith, Esther agreed to do what she could. All she asked was that Mordecai and all the Jews fast for her for three days, and then she would enter the king's presence regardless of the consequences (4:9–17). Though God is nowhere explicity mentioned, He is implicit in the words "another place," from which the Jews could expect salvation (4:14).

> Though God chooses to use people, He is by no means dependent on them. Many believers act as though they are indispensable to the Lord's purposes, and if they refuse to do His bidding God's work will grind to a halt. Mordecai's challenge to Esther must be heard and heeded. Our sovereign God will accomplish all His objectives with or without us. He calls us not out of His need for us but for our need to find fulfillment in serving Him.

At the end of three days Esther laid her life on the line and entered the throne room unbidden. Far from being upset, however, Xerxes was delighted to see his beautiful wife and offered to grant her whatever request she might have, no matter how outlandish (5:1–3). All she wanted, she said, was to host a banquet at which Haman would receive special honor (5:4). The king readily acceded to this request, and when the occasion was underway he asked her again what boon he could grant her. As though she needed more time to think about it, Esther urged the king and Haman to come to the banquet hall the next day for a continuation of the festivities (5:5–8).

Haman's ego had become so inflated that he could hardly contain himself. As he set out for home, however, he encountered his hated nemesis Mordecai, who refused even to rise in his presence. Even when Haman related his good fortune to his wife, his excitement was mitigated by his every thought of Mordecai. His wife, Zeresh, recommended that he and his friends build a gallows on which to hang the hated Jew, and he was pleased with this suggestion (5:9–14).

C. The Deliverance of the Jews (chapters 6–7)

The night Haman was sleeping so well, the king tossed and turned on his pillow, unable to find rest. He called for the official chronicles to be read to him, a pastime that surely would bring on drowsiness. The reader at length came to a notice about how Mordecai had alerted the king concerning an assassination attempt (see 2:21–22). Xerxes interrupted to ask what had been done to reward such loyalty, and he was told that nothing had been done. Just then Haman came in, and Xerxes asked him how he could best honor a worthy servant. Self-centered as ever, Haman thought he was the intended recipient and advised the king to pull out all the stops for such a person (6:1–9). The king's response was crushing: Do all you have recommended for Mordecai the Jew. Speechless, Haman carried out the king's command and when he returned home that evening he heard his wife and his advisers predict his own demise (6:10–14).

Unable now to get out of the situation, Haman returned to the banquet. Once more Xerxes offered to grant Esther's every wish, and this time she begged for the deliverance of her Jewish people from the king's ill-advised decree (7:1–4). When the king asked who was behind this sinister plot to begin with, Esther pointed to Haman, their dinner companion. Enraged, Xerxes went to the garden to cool off, but when he returned he found Haman begging for his life on Esther's couch. He concluded at once that Haman was making amorous advances toward his wife and ordered that Haman be hanged on his own gallows without further delay (7:5–10).

III. ESTHER'S ESTABLISHMENT OF PURIM (CHAPTERS 8–10)

In a magnificent display of God's grace, the Jews were not only saved from a Persian holocaust but were also able to turn the tables on their enemies. The implements by which this was to be done—lots cast by the Jews—gave rise to the name of the celebration marking this deliverance, namely, Purim (Hebrew for "lots").

A. The Decree Favoring the Jews (chapter 8)

Again with disregard for her own life Esther entered the presence of Xerxes, pleading with him to reverse his previous decree to slaughter the Jews. Moved by her tears and logic, the king told Esther and Mordecai to prepare the text of another decree and to authorize it by the king's own seal (8:1–8). Once more the word went forth throughout the empire, but this time the decree gave the Jews permission to arm themselves and do whatever was necessary to survive (8:9–14). Encouraged beyond measure, they began to rejoice and celebrate despite the rapidly approaching day of reckoning, Adar 13 (8:15–17; see 3:13).

B. The Implementation of Deliverance (9:1–16)

When Adar 13 finally arrived, the enemies of the Jews became paralyzed with fear and fell easily before the Jewish onslaught (9:1–10). Thousands were slain, but even then Xerxes offered still more blessings to Esther if only she would make a request. All that remained, she said, was final vengeance on the household of Haman, that is, retribution against his ten sons. This was done, and so at last the Jews could live in peace (9:11–16). Esther, the instrument of her invisible but omnipotent God, had been the means of establishing justice in the earth. The story serves in a sense as a prototype of the future when all the injustices and inequities of this world will at last be resolved by the sovereign rule of the holy God.

C. The Celebration of Deliverance (9:17–32)

Adar 14, the day after the deliverance, became thereafter a special day in the Jewish calendar, a day of rejoicing and exchanging of gifts (9:17–19). The festival was authorized by Mordecai himself as a memorial of God's protection of the Jews against wicked Haman and his henchmen (9:20–25). From then on it was to be called Purim because of the casting of lots, which was designed to harm the Jews but which became in their hands a symbol of heavenly protection (9:26–32).

D. *The Advancement of the Jews (chapter 10)*

Xerxes completed his generous work of deliverance by recording for all posterity his promotion of Mordecai and protection of the Jewish people, a record to be found, the historian wrote, "in the book of the annals of the kings of Media and Persia" (10:2).

JOB
Resting in the Mystery of God

AUTHOR

Though the Babylonian Talmud claims that the Book of Job, like the Pentateuch, was from the pen of Moses (*Baba Bathra* 14b), there is no evidence in the book itself to this effect. In fact, the book offers no clue as to its authorship. The setting itself is from an ancient period, probably as early as that of the biblical patriarchs, but by itself this can tell us little about who wrote the book or when it was written.

UNITY

There are three major parts to the book—an introduction or prologue (chapters 1–2), the dialogues (3:1–42:6), and an epilogue (42:7–17). Some scholars limit the dialogues to chapters 3–31 and view chapters 32–37 (Elihu's monologue) and 38:1–42:6 (the speeches of the Lord) as originally separate pieces that were eventually incorporated into the whole. Critics have pointed to the fact that the prologue and epilogue are prose and the rest poetic and concluded that this proved that these parts also existed at one time independent of each other. More recent studies of comparative ancient Near Eastern literature have shown that the mere alternation of prose and poetry does not rule out literary unity. As it stands, the Book of Job is a wonderfully conceived composition, whose parts comprise a literary masterpiece.

DATE

As already stated, since the author of the Book of Job is not known, the date of the writing of the book is also unknown. The setting is clearly ancient, but this cannot prove anything about the date of the book. Scholars propose anything from the time of Moses (1400 B.C.) to the postexilic period (250 B.C. or even later), with many conservatives opting for the time of Solomon or a little later. This has in its favor the fact that wisdom and wisdom literature are closely connected to Solomon and his times. Some Bible students suggest that Elihu or even Job himself was the author.

ADDRESSEES

By its very nature, wisdom literature (and thus Job) is trans-Israelite or universal in its scope. It touches on themes and issues common to all humanity, and therefore it addresses persons of every place and time. Obviously Job was intended in the first instance to be a message to the covenant community of Israel, perhaps to provide a word of hope to those who may have wondered where God was in the midst of the calamities of personal or even national life. Its relevance far outstrips such local concerns, however, and is applicable to all who struggle with such matters.

PURPOSE

As suggested, the purpose of Job is to grapple with the question of the nature of God and His ways among mortals. How can a God who elsewhere in Scripture is described as the very essence of love and grace initiate or even allow suffering in the lives of His saints? How can His attributes be reconciled with His actions, especially when those actions appear to run counter to all He claims to be? Along with this central purpose are concerns to show the limitation of human knowledge, the inadequacy of man-made theologies, and the sufficiency of absolute trust in God no matter the circumstances.

THEOLOGICAL EMPHASES

Two primary theological ideas stand out in the Book of Job. First, there is a difference between popular, "empirical" theology on the one hand and true biblical revelation on the other; and second, when these two appear to be at odds and incapable of resolution, one must learn to trust and submit to the sovereignty of God who, in His omniscience, knows and does what is best. This is sometimes called "theodicy," that is, the justification of God and His activity in human affairs despite human inability to comprehend it. Human experience and divine intentionality may be conceived of as converging lines that never intersect in this life but that meet in a heavenly apex that resolves all mysteries of life, suffering, and death.

OUTLINE

I. The Prologue (chapters 1–2)
II. The Dialogue with the Three Friends (chapters 3–31)
   A. The First Cycle of Speeches (chapters 3–14)
   B. The Second Cycle of Speeches (chapters 15–21)
   C. The Third Cycle of Speeches (chapters 22–31)
III. The Four Speeches of Elihu (chapters 32–37)
   A. Elihu's First Speech (chapters 32–33)
   B. Elihu's Second Speech (chapter 34)
   C. Elihu's Third Speech (chapter 35)
   D. Elihu's Fourth Speech (chapters 36–37)
IV. The Two Divine Speeches (38:1–42:6)
   A. God's First Speech (38:1–40:5)
   B. God's Second Speech (40:6–42:6)
V. The Epilogue (42:7–17)
   A. Reconciliation of Job (42:7–9)
   B. Restoration of Job (42:10–17)

I. THE PROLOGUE (CHAPTERS 1–2)

The prose narrative here introduces the setting of the following dialogue section and permits the reader to have privileged information as to the causes of Job's theological dilemma. It locates him in time and space, thus securing his identity as an actual historical figure, but it also draws back the curtains of heaven, as it were, to reveal the ultimate struggle of the universe—that between an absolutely sovereign God and Satan who, though powerful, acts only according to God's own grand design.

The human protagonist of the story, Job, lived in Uz, a land in the upper Arabian desert (Jer. 25:20; Lam. 4:21). Like Noah (Gen. 6:9) he was an upright man, one whom God had blessed with a large family and vast holdings of livestock and other assets (Job 1:1–3). But his greatest possession was his piety, a godliness that caused him constantly to be vigilant regarding the spiritual well-being of his children (1:4–5).

Unknown to Job, Satan appeared one day before the Lord as was his habit and when questioned as to his recent whereabouts he explained that he had been "going back and forth" in the earth (1:7), that is, had been exercising his dominion over the fallen creation. The Lord did not challenge this assertion of satanic rulership for, indeed, the Lord had ceded to the evil one a temporary lordship over the earth (John 12:31; 2 Cor. 4:4; Eph. 2:2; 6:12). However, the Lord was quick to point out that Satan's dominion is not complete and unexceptional, for Job was one person over whom he had no control (Job 1:6–8). Satan's repartee was that Job had vested interest in serving the Lord, for God had protected and blessed him in a special way. If that protection were taken away, Job too would deny God's rule over him (1:9–12).

> While one should never minimize the power of the devil, it is important at the same time to recognize that his power can be exercised only to the extent that God permits it. This means that pain, illness, death, and even evil are somehow embraced within His sovereign plan. As difficult as this might be theologically, the alternative is to posit a dualism, a belief in a God of good and a god of evil, the two locked in irresolvable conflict. This, of course, is an idea completely foreign to God's Word.

The Lord granted Satan access to all of Job's properties, goods, and even children, and in a series of cataclysmic disasters they were all taken from him (1:13–19). This, however, did not move Job from his determination to serve God (1:20–22). Again Satan challenged the Lord, this time urging him to allow Job to suffer grievous illness of the body (2:1–6). Once more the Lord stepped aside, and Job was struck with painful boils over all his body (2:7–8). Despite his wife's advice that he curse God and die, however, he continued to rest in the underlying providence of God: He who gives good also permits harm (2:9–10).

Meanwhile, three friends of Job had heard of his stricken condition, and they came from neighboring lands to lament with him and offer their consolation and advice. When they saw him with their own eyes, they were so dumbstruck that they could only sit silently for seven days (2:11–13).

II. THE DIALOGUE WITH THE THREE FRIENDS (CHAPTERS 3–31)

By far the longest section of Job is the series of dialogues he carried on with his three visitors. These were delivered in turn, friend by friend, and Job responded after each one. The common theme of all the interchanges is the theological conclusion of the friends that Job's suffering was the result of sin on his part, and his retort was that he was innocent and therefore was suffering for no good reason.

A. The First Cycle of Speeches (chapter 3–14)

Job's lament (chapter 3). Job commenced the conversation by publicly cursing the day of his birth, a reaction to suffering that Jeremiah would later embrace (Jer. 20:14–18). Job intensified his disgust for that day by hoping that on every anniversary of his birth the sun might be hidden so that thick darkness could cover the earth (Job 3:1–10). Even better, he said, would have been death in his mother's womb. To have been stillborn would have precluded him from all the sorrows of life and opened up the rest that only the dead can know (3:11–19). Since those options were obviously impossible, Job finally longed for death. Why is it, he asked, that those who wish for death more than anything else are unable to enjoy its sweet release (3:20–26)?

Eliphaz's reply (chapters 4–5). Job's first respondent, Eliphaz, was from Teman (perhaps Tema) in the Arabian desert (see 2:11; 6:19). He first rebuked Job for his lack of composure in difficulty, especially since Job himself had comforted others in similar circumstances (4:1–4). But he then drove straight to the heart of the issue: No one ever suffered or died prematurely without sin having brought it on. Job therefore must have sinned (4:5–11). To buttress his logical deduction, Eliphaz related a vision in which a spirit appeared and instructed him about the finiteness of mere humanity. Since a human being is mortal and limited, what right does he have to assert his innocence in the face of such overwhelming empirical evidence to the contrary? Sinners suffer because they sin; to say otherwise is to ascribe injustice to the Lord (4:12–21).

Continuing his charge against Job, Eliphaz became decidedly more personal. He had seen people who started out well but whose worlds later came crashing down because of their sin. They suffered calamities similar to those of Job—the loss of their own children and the ruin of their crops. And this could not be attributed to "bad luck" or external causes. Judgment is inherent in the playing out of sinfulness (5:1–7).

The only solution for Job, Eliphaz said, was for him to turn to the Lord, who is the Creator, the omniscient One, and the Savior of all who will commit themselves to Him (5:8–16). What God did in Job's case, Eliphaz implied, was to bring suffering into his life as a wake-up call, an alarm to help him come to grips with the reality of his sin. If Job would make things right with God, he would find relief from his fears and would once more enjoy the blessing of many children and abundant riches (5:17–27).

Job's rejoinder (chapters 6–7). In his response to Eliphaz, Job admitted that he may have been a little rash in his initial complaint, but he still underscored the heaviness of his suffering (6:1–3). It was as though his body were full of poison, draining his life away (6:4). Were his agony not real, he would not be lamenting his condition, any more than an animal calls for food when it has plenty (6:5). Pat answers to his profound troubles will not do. They are as dissatisfying as unflavored eggs (6:6–7).

What Job really wanted was not to complain but to have the hope of an early death, thus preventing the possibility that he would deny God (6:8–10). How can he wait, however, and why should he (6:11)? Could it be that God had in fact already left him to his own devices (6:12–13)? Turning to address his friends, Job asked whether a person has the right to expect comfort from a friend even if he is in the wrong (6:14). Indeed he does, but his friends have proved to be as useless as dry riverbeds (6:15–18) or as disappointing as oases with no wells (6:19–20). They are altogether disloyal for no good cause (6:21–23). On the other hand, if they could point out sin in his life, he would certainly admit it (6:24). They should not judge him on the basis of intemperate remarks he may have made because of his intense pain (6:25–27). If he had done wrong in some way, he would be the first to know about it. His lack of conviction of sin led him to the conclusion that his suffering must be explained in some other way (6:28–30).

Job now pursued another tack. Life, he said, is like a term of service whose end is something to be desired (7:1–2). In his case, it is so burdensome that it seems to lack any meaning or purpose (7:3–4). Yet he was acutely aware that life is fragile, slipping away from him toward a certain and gloomy end (7:5–8). He would move into another realm, one from which he would never return, or so he was convinced at this stage of his thinking (7:9–10).

Perhaps this very hopelessness caused Job now to lash out at God (7:11). Why did God "pick on" him? Job was a mere speck in God's universe, so why should he be the object of so much attention (7:12–15)? God surely has many other more important matters to deal with than humankind (7:16–19). Even if Job had sinned, can that so throw off the moral equilibrium of the universe that God has to single him out? Why not just forgive him outright if he is such a problem (7:20–21)?

Bildad's reply (chapter 8). The second of Job's friends brought up the principle of moral cause and effect. Job's professions of innocence were empty (8:1–2) for God is equitable in His dealings with people (8:3). The judgment of Job's own children attested to this (8:4). Godly repentance, however, would avail to turn things around and restore all that Job had lost (8:5–7).

The proof of the principle may be seen in history. All human experience is common (8:8), and all human perspective limited (8:9). One must therefore draw on the accumulated wisdom of the past (8:10). Other proof derives from nature. As water provides nourishment to the reed, so faithfulness to God guarantees life. The lack thereof brings serious consequences (8:11–15). Likewise, as roots are essential to the whole plant, so is righteousness the foundation of human life and experience (8:16–20). Job's repentance would bring joy to him (8:21) but profound embarrassment to his enemies (8:22; see 42:7–9).

Job's rejoinder (chapters 9–10). Job's first address to Bildad was a magnificent confession of the sovereignty of God. He is absolute in both His arguments (9:1–3, 14) and His power (9:4–13). He cannot be questioned in His actions on earth (9:4–6) and in the heavens (9:7–9). If the great creatures submit to him, how can a lowly mortal challenge His motives and His doings (9:10–14)? Yet Job's recognition of God's sovereignty is more fatalistic than grounded in the nature of God as a just and righteous One. He is arbitrary, offering no basis for appeal (9:15), and His dealings with Job seem to be capricious (9:16–18), without consideration for Job's righteousness (9:19–21). It even seems that God allows evil to prevail (9:22–24).

God's apparent distance from Job made it impossible for him to put on a good front (9:25–28) or to purify himself sufficiently to bring the Lord nearer to him (9:29–31). In short, there was no communication because of the natural chasm between God and man (9:32–33) and because of Job's great fear of God (9:34–35).

Notwithstanding this massive gap, Job was determined to defend himself. He argued that a just God cannot punish the righteous (10:3), and since he is righteous (10:4–7) God cannot fairly punish him (10:2). Moreover, as a creation of God whom God has blessed and nurtured from before his birth (10:8–12), Job believed he deserved some special consideration. If he had sinned, he deserved all he was getting (10:13–17), but if he had not, then why did he suffer? Far better that he had not been born or, at least, that he be allowed to die in peace (10:18–22; see 3:11–13).

Zophar's reply (chapter 11). Zophar launched into a personal attack on Job himself, in effect calling him a hypocrite for protesting his innocence in the face of contrary evidence (11:1–6). What Job lacked, among other things, was a healthy respect for the wisdom of God, the omniscient One who knows all about human wickedness despite efforts to conceal it (11:7–12). All Job could do in light of that reality was to come clean (11:13–14). This would take care of his fear, misery, confusion, despair, and alienation from God (11:15–19). To refuse to repent would invite abject hopelessness (11:20).

Job's rejoinder (chapters 12–14). Zophar's counsel was met with ridicule. Why, Job asked, do his friends think they have more insight than he does (12:1–3)? He wishes they could understand that disaster often comes on those least prepared and least deserving of it (12:4–6). Once more he reflected on the sovereign ways of God as manifest in nature (12:7–9) and in man's very existence (12:10). In light of this lofty concept, the arguments of his friends seem shallow indeed (12:11–12). The only way Job could explain his condition is that God's omniscience and omnipotence with respect to nature (12:13–15), individuals (12:16–21), the mysteries of the unseen (12:22), and the affairs of whole nations (12:23–25) somehow has something to do with even Him.

Again, compared to these theological profundities the counsel of his friends is nothing more than common knowledge (13:1–2). It falls far short of the wisdom of God, and for that reason Job wished he could speak directly to God (13:3). Their speeches were deceptive, without value (13:4–5), and they should no longer profess to be speaking for God (13:6–9). In fact, they should be in mortal terror on account of their glib solutions for such complicated problems (13:10–12).

It is far better, Job said, for him to put himself in God's hands despite his ignorance of God's purposes for him. He could not save himself, after all (13:13–14), so no matter what God did to him—even to the point of taking his life—he would trust Him (13:15–16). By thus submitting himself, Job was not conceding that his friends' indictment of him was justified. Indeed, he maintained that his defense before them was unassailable (13:17–19).

Job then turned to the Lord with two requests and five questions. He begged for God to take away His hand of wrath and to deliver him from fear (13:20–21). He demanded to know precisely what he had done and, in the absence of such knowledge, how God could be fair in punishing him (13:22–25). To Job it seemed that God had put him in the impossible situation of holding him accountable for misdeeds that He refused to disclose to him (13:26–28).

From his own experience Job concluded that man by nature and from his birth is hopelessly fragile and impaired. His existence is temporal (14:1–2), his days are foreordained (14:3–5), and his life is without any apparent significance (14:6). Even a tree has hope; when it is cut down its root system survives, and the tree begins to grow again (14:7–9). A person's end, to the contrary, is final—there is no coming back (14:10–12). Job was unable to live with this moral conundrum, however. His burning desire and hope was that his suffering and death would give way to divine vindication (14:13), an appointment with God that presupposes life after death. If this were possible (and he seemed unsure), Job would gladly wait for it to come (14:14–15). His present condition seems, however, to rule out any such pleasant prospect (14:16–17). He can only resign himself to his fate. As the natural world erodes away, so does a person's hope (14:18–19). His ultimate disintegration is inevitable, leaving him no hope in this world nor any for a world to come (14:20–22).

B. The Second Cycle of Speeches (chapters 15–21)

Eliphaz's reply (chapter 15). The heated exchange between Job and his friends intensified in this second round. Eliphaz again led the way by suggesting that Job's words were self-condemnatory. He was his own best cross-examiner and critic (15:1–6). Job's fundamental problem, he added, was one of self-righteousness. He thought his knowledge was superior to others by virtue of age (15:7, 10) and a perceived special access to God (15:8–9). At the same time, he rejected God's gentle conviction (15:11–13) and failed to understand the fact of universal sin (15:14–16).

Job may try to dodge the issue, but he couldn't ignore the principle that wickedness brings disaster (15:17–20). The wicked (like Job) experience fear, deprivation, and uncertainty, all because of their hostility toward God (15:21–26). As Job should well know, material prosperity is no hedge against trouble (15:27–30), nor can false hope preclude the reality of inevitable judgment for sin (15:31–35).

Job's rejoinder (chapter 16–17). To all the previous allegations Job simply responded, in essence, "I've heard it all before. You are all worthless comforters" (16:2). Their language is trite, he said, and if he were in their place (and they in his), he would show them what constructive advice was all about (16:3–5)! All he could do now, though, was endure his pointless suffering, for whether he spoke or remained silent it was all the same (16:6). God had stripped him of everything (16:7–8) and exposed him to merciless torment. This came from his enemies (including the "friends"?) and even directly from the Lord Himself, who had, in a sense, used him for target practice (16:9–14). Most dispiriting of all, Job had gone through at least the outward show of repentance but to no avail (16:15–17).

Such a thought elicited from Job a heart-rending appeal to earth and heaven to vindicate him. He prayed that his case would not be forgotten, (16:18) and that God, his witness in heaven, would someday make right everything that was now so terribly wrong (16:19–21). Since there is no hope of that in the present time, it must await some other place and time (16:22–17:2). Raising his cry directly to the Lord, Job prayed for divine vindication. Only God is just and fair; human counselors at their best are deluded and perverse (17:3–5).

For the time being, however, there was not much cause for optimism. God had chosen to make Job an example (17:6–7), perhaps so those inclined to godliness might learn some valuable lessons (17:8–9). His friends, obviously, have learned nothing from his experience (17:10). All that remains is for him to go unjustified to the grave. If that is all there is, then what is the basis for any hope at all (17:11–16)?

Bildad's reply (chapter 18). In his second encounter with Job, Bildad sarcastically rebuked his friend for the futility of his speech (18:1–2), his arrogant self-righteousness (18:3), and his intemperate anger (18:4). He then launched into a lengthy discourse on the fate of the wicked, a review of what clearly was the theology of the day from the human perspective. First, he said, the wicked are unenlightened (18:5–6). They fall easily into the snares of their own folly (18:7–8), as well as those that come on them unexpectedly from all sides and over which they have no control (18:9–11).

The sinner, moreover, will die. Weakened by disaster and devastated by disease, he will inevitably succumb to the "king of terrors," death itself (18:12–14). In that mysterious realm of the dead he will be forgotten. His lands will become desolate (18:15), and his posterity at last will be cut off forever (18:16–19). The only good thing he will leave will be the warning that those who follow him in evil may expect a similar fate (18:20–21).

Job's rejoinder (chapter 19). To Bildad Job replied that he had grown quite weary of the empty platitudes of his friends. Ten times (that is, over and over) they had repeated their theological clichés (19:1–3), but all they had done was reveal their own lack of true perception (19:4). Furthermore, their insensitivity toward him had only compounded the burden that God had laid upon him (19:5–6). Saddest of all, God had counted him as an enemy, or so it seemed. He had been unresponsive to Job's pleas for help (19:7), frustrated him as he had looked for answers (19:8), reduced him to poverty and hopelessness (19:9–10), and laid siege to him, giving him no avenue of escape (19:11–12).

This harsh—indeed, irreverent—language continued in Job's lament that not only God but all human acquaintances had abandoned him. Those closest to him had forgotten him already (19:13–15). His servants no longer obeyed him, and his wife regarded him as a stranger (19:16–17). All who knew him had forsaken him (19:18–19) and had even turned against him (19:20–22). Is it not bad enough that God had done so? Job asked. Did those most dear to him have to treat him in such a shameful manner?

When it seemed that Job had spent himself with despair and self-pity, his spirits rallied and a ray of hope once more penetrated his gloom. He wished first that there could be a present but permanent record testifying to his innocence before God (19:23–24). That record then could be validated by his Redeemer, that is, by the Lord Himself, who someday will take his place of judgment on the earth (19:25). "To redeem" in this context is to vindicate, to attest to one's righteousness. For that to happen, Job himself must be present and therefore alive after death. In one of the grandest resurrection texts of the Old Testament, Job affirmed that he would survive death and not just in some disembodied form. From within his body he would see God and with literal, physical eyes (19:26–27). Though this is no thorough presentation of the doctrine of bodily resurrection as in 1 Corinthians 15, Job's confidence in God's integrity as a Vindicator can rest only in the necessity of resurrection.

Job's confidence in vindication after death presupposes bodily resurrection, a truth made possible in reality by the raising of the Lord Jesus Christ from the dead. Resurrection, then, is necessary not only to ensure unending life but also to certify the fact that God is just. If there is no resolution of moral inequities in this life, there must be one in the life to come. Otherwise, God is not fair—an unthinkable conclusion.

The other side of vindication is the punishment of those who falsely judged. Vindication for Job has, as its necessary corollary, judgment on his friends who so hardheartedly and erroneously condemned him (Job 19:28–29).

Zophar's reply (chapter 20). Undeterred by such radiant hope on Job's part—and perhaps even infuriated by it—Zophar underscored once more the true but misapplied doctrine of the mortality of the wicked. To him it is so obviously true as to require little or no thought (20:1–3). The apparent success of the sinner is but a mirage. His time on earth is short, and whatever victories he seems to claim will inevitably be reversed (20:4–7). Eventually he himself will disappear, and his possessions will be gone (20:8–10). Any hope of escape just because one is in the full bloom of youth is merely wishful thinking. Old age will surely come, and he will make his bed in the dust of the earth (20:11).

Zophar then added that things do not always go as well with the wicked as some might think. Sin tastes good in the mouth but creates terrible cramps and nausea in the stomach (20:12–14). Riches when first sampled seem delightful, but they too have no lasting benefit and will be vomited up again (20:15–17). What one acquires unjustly will all have to be surrendered again, and thus it affords no lasting pleasure (20:18–19).

In the end the wicked have no prospect but judgment. Because of their greed they will lose everything; because of their underhanded way of becoming rich they will become poor; and because of their selfishness they will suffer at the hands of others (20:20–22). And their punishment will come quickly and unexpectedly. It will strike in the midst of their bounty and with devastating results and utter finality (20:23–26). God Himself will be the judge, and all creation will bear witness against evil persons (20:27–29).

Job's rejoinder (chapter 21). Job had no difficulty in recognizing himself as the anonymous "wicked man" of Zophar's speech. He therefore pleaded for an opportunity to be heard one more time. It was only fair, after all (21:1–3), and the wretchedness of his condition certainly entitled him to speak (21:4–6).

The essence of this address is Job's perplexity concerning the wicked. First, they seem to live prosperously without God, something irreconcilable with Job's theology and with popular theology in general. Their families are large, their heritage long outlives them, and they seem never to know fear in the family circle (21:7–9). They prosper financially (21:10), they enjoy a rich and happy social life (21:11–13), and, astoundingly, not only are they secular but also they openly defy and reject God (21:14–16). Despite this, it seems that they rarely suffer in this life (21:17–18), nor do they seem to have any concern about judgment now or in the future. The attitude of the sinner seems to be, "Why should I worry about what happens after I die?" (21:19–21). So as far as Job can tell, death comes to all alike, whether they are righteous or evil (21:22–26).

This is Job's greatest theological difficulty at this point. The wicked never receive just retribution. If they lose everything, it is only an appearance of loss (21:27–28). As for ultimate and final judgment, who knows for sure whether they will face it (21:29–30)? From Job's perspective evil people escape punishment, and at death they rest in pleasant peace (21:31–34).

C. The Third Cycle of Speeches (chapters 22–31)

Eliphaz's reply (chapter 22). Eliphaz concluded his part of the dialogue by finally zeroing in on the real meaning of Job's suffering. First, he said, Job's self-righteousness has no value to God (22:1–3). In fact, his suffering was precisely related to the fact that his profession of godliness is without substance. Since when would God punish someone for doing good (22:4)? To the contrary, Job's predicament is demonstrable evidence of his having violated God's moral standards. He clearly must have done such things as taking advantage of the poor, withholding food and drink from the hungry, and neglecting widows and orphans (22:5–9), all of which show callous disregard for God's covenant law (Exod. 22:21, 26; Deut. 24:17). What further proof is necessary that sin brings suffering than to look at the example of Job (Job 22:10–11)?

Another problem with Job, Eliphaz continued, is that he had a limited understanding of God. He failed to see that though God is transcendent He is very much aware of all that transpires on the earth below (22:12–14). Job could hardly hope to hide from God or to keep secrets from Him. Moreover, Job repeated the mistakes of others in the past who failed to note and appreciate the goodness of God (22:15–18a). Instead, he was in danger of being hopelessly cut off from God's righteous ones, that is, as Eliphaz sees it, from him and his friends (22:18b–20).

As though to show his concern for Job and to offer him some hope after all, Eliphaz urged him to repent and make things right with God. He should return to the Lord (22:21–23), surrender his pride (22:24–25), and recognize that God will hear and answer his prayers (22:26–29). If he did this, he could become God's channel of blessing to others. Eliphaz clearly had in mind his own ministry to Job as a helpful counselor (22:30).

Job's rejoinder (chapters 23–24). Eliphaz's reminder that God is in heaven (22:12) may have triggered Job's lament about God's inaccessibility. First, he wanted to make it clear that his suffering was even worse than it appears or than he could describe (23:1–2). This made it all the more urgent that he be able to confront God in a legal setting and arrive at a fair resolution of his case. Job believed that if only he could meet God face to face, he could persuade Him of his innocence (23:3–7). Of course, that is not possible, Job concluded, and so he must remain with his frustration (23:8–9).

Job's inner turmoil was only exacerbated by his realization that though God knows he is innocent, He seemingly remains inflexibly apathetic (23:10–12). He seems to act not in response to Job's righteousness and appeals for exoneration but according to some principle of predestination (23:13–14). This being the case, what grounds of hope can there be (23:15–17)? God's seeming indifference extends to His failure to reward the righteous (24:1) and punish the wicked. Sinners dispossess the poor (24:2–4), deny them their basic rights (24:5–8), and deprive them of the necessities of life (24:9–12). They murder in secret, commit adultery under cover of night, and break in and steal in the hours of darkness (24:13–17).

According to the theology of the friends, the wicked will someday be judged and the righteous vindicated and blessed (24:18–23). But Job is unconvinced of this, for there is nothing in his observation of others or in his own experience that leads him to believe that the end of the righteous is any better than that of sinners (24:24–25).

Bildad's reply (25:1–6). Bildad's brief parting shot is a summation in which he celebrated the loftiness of God (25:1–3) and acknowledged the lowliness of humanity (25:4–6). God is the all-powerful, omnipresent Sovereign of the universe, whereas humans are sinners of such impurity that God in His holiness cannot look on them.

Job's rejoinder (chapters 26–31). This lengthy, uninterrupted discourse is Job's final sustained self-defense and search for vindication. Zophar, the third friend, kept silent afterward, concluding perhaps that Job had already anticipated any response he might make or that Job was a hopeless case, unable to learn from further counsel.

Job began by ridiculing the "comfort" of his friends, saying, in effect, that it had offered no help at all (26:1–4). He then launched into a magnificent and theologically sound exposition of the character of God. He is the omniscient One (26:5–6), who has created all things and keeps them under His control (26:7–10). All creation recognizes His dominion, even hostile and wicked forces, described here as monsters such as Rahab and the "fleeing serpent" (26:11–14; see also 9:13; Ps. 89:10; Isa. 27:1; 30:7; 51:9).

Fully aware of all these qualities of God, Job continued to protest his innocence (Job 27:1–6). Not even God could convince him otherwise. His friends, therefore, had been wrong in their assessment of him, and for this reason they and not he should have received divine condemnation (27:7–12). The plight of these and all evil people is tragic, indeed. They lose their children prematurely to death, and they themselves die with no mourners, not even their widows (27:13–15). They also forfeit their worldly goods. Whatever they accumulate in this life will be divided up by others (27:16–19). Everyday existence is filled with terror for them, along with overwhelming fear because of both human and divine antagonism (27:20–23).

The centerpiece of Job's soliloquy is an exquisite poem on wisdom (chapter 28), one seemingly so interruptive of his general flow of discourse as to cause many scholars to view it as an independent composition later inserted into the Book of Job at this place. While that is possible, it is unnecessary, for as Job reflected on the mysteries of God, of human life, and of his own painful experience, it would be natural for him to find meaning, if any at all, in God's wisdom. If he, Job, could not fathom these profundities, then surely God can and perhaps would graciously make him privy to at least some of them.

In discussing the source of wisdom, Job employed the analogy and imagery of mining. Gold, silver, and precious stones lie beneath the earth's surface all the time, but they can be extracted only by arduous and even dangerous labor. They are hidden and therefore are of no practical value until they are found and brought to light (28:1–11). The same is true of wisdom. It too lies hidden but even more so than mere stones and metals (28:12–14). It is far more valuable than these (28:15–19) precisely because it is so inaccessible and difficult to recover (28:20–22).

True wisdom, in fact, cannot be mined from the earth but must come from God, who alone knows where it is to be found (28:23). The workings of nature with its balance, its seasonal alterations, its magnificent displays of power and beauty—all this points to the Author of wisdom, for only God can bring such things to pass. It is only when one fears God, that is, reveres, confesses, and worships Him, that he can know anything of genuine wisdom. One cannot separate godliness from the kind of wisdom that makes sense of human life (28:23–28; see Ps. 111:10; Prov. 1:7; 9:10).

Having concluded his spontaneous reverie on wisdom, Job reflected back on the days before all these evil things had befallen him. He indulged in a bit of nostalgic longing for those times when all was well with him. His family was then intact (Job 29:1–5), he had enjoyed respect and even worshipful attention from his fellow citizens (29:6–11), he had been in a position to minister to those in need (29:12–17), and he had every right to think that he would live out his days in peace, enjoying his position of influence in the community (29:18–25).

All that had come crashing to the ground, however. Now those who had showered adulation on him—who themselves were the very dregs of society—mocked and ridiculed him (30:1–8). With venomous hostility they composed songs and proverbs that made him the butt of every kind of joke (30:9). They ostracized him, treated him as an outcast, and in every way made life miserable for him (30:10–15). Worst of all, it was the Lord who allowed this to happen (30:11).

Job could see no way out of his present condition. Day and night brought unrelenting misery (30:16–17). He was physically deformed, filthy in his appearance (30:18–19), and bound for a cruel death (30:20–23). In the past he had rendered aid to those in need (30:24–25), but when trouble came his way no one had risen in support (30:26–28). Instead he had become so repulsive to both himself and others that his lot was cast with those who lived in desert places like animals (30:29–31).

In one final plaintive defense of his integrity, Job recounted his life of moral integrity (31:1–4). He had been scrupulously honest in all his business dealings (31:5–8), had never committed the heinous sin of adultery (31:9–12), had treated his servants humanely and with respect (31:13–15), had met the needs of the poor and needy (31:16–23), had resisted the allurements of materialism (31:24–25), had not fallen into idolatry (31:26–28), had not engaged in personal vengeance (31:29–30), was careful to entertain strangers (31:31–32), did not conceal his sins (31:33–34), and did not abuse his stewardship of fields and properties (31:35–40). His only regret was that God seemed not to have noticed all this, no matter how obvious it should have been (31:35–37).

III. THE FOUR SPEECHES OF ELIHU
(CHAPTERS 32–37)

When it was apparent that Job's three friends and Job himself had worn themselves out with fruitless dialogue, a young listener, up till now hidden from the reader's view, enters the discussion with a lengthy discourse from his own peculiar vantage point. His name is Elihu ben Barachel, and he is identified further as a Buzite of the family of Ram. According to Genesis 22:21, Buz was a brother of Uz (see Job 1:1) and thus Job and Elihu traced their lineages back to a common source. Elihu challenged both Job and the three but in the final analysis had nothing substantially new to contribute to the problem of Job's suffering.

A. Elihu's First Speech (chapters 32–33)

Job's three friends at last give up, concluding that Job was hopelessly self-righteous and beyond instruction. This view was also held by young Elihu, who apparently had overheard the entire conversation (32:1–2). But Elihu also had no patience with the three, for they could only condemn Job without offering him sensible explanations (32:3–5).

With at least a claim to reluctance because of his youth, Elihu said he had waited until now to interject his opinion (32:6–7). He soon made the point, however, that wisdom is not limited to the aged but in fact derives from the Lord (32:8–10). Moreover, he had heard nothing from the friends to suggest that they had anything helpful or even true to say to Job (32:11–14). Meanwhile his thoughts had so welled up within him that he could remain silent no longer. He must speak or he would burst (32:15–20)! At the same time he said he would not take sides or resort to flattery for that simply was not his style (32:21–22).

Addressing Job, Elihu set forth his credentials. He would speak truth, he said, as God's Spirit enabled him to do so. He could do nothing else or claim anything more for he, like Job, was an ordinary man. Job therefore should not be intimidated by him (33:1–7). On the other hand, he had overheard everything Job had said, and to prove it, he proceeded to quote Job. What stands out are Job's professions of innocence (33:8–11), statements that Elihu rejected in light of what he knew about the justice of God (33:12).

Job's problem, Elihu said, was that he had not been content with his lot in life. He had tried to make God accountable to him when, in fact, God is under no obligation to share His plans and purposes with a mere human being (33:13). He does reveal Himself in dreams and visions on occasion, doing so in order to deliver a person from his own self-destructive tendencies (33:14–18). Beyond this, He instructs through suffering and tribulation (33:19–22). Job should have realized that in his own experience the Lord had been attempting to teach him important lessons.

Job's dullness notwithstanding, God still desired to break through in a merciful act of salvation. He would provide a way out whereby Job could be completely restored to the Lord as well as to the happy days of his earlier life. He could then sing of the great benefits of grace that come from heartfelt repentance (33:23–28). All these happy prospects flow from the very nature of God whose intentions always are to redeem. Elihu said he would be glad to share what God had laid on his heart if Job was willing to listen (33:29–33).

B. Elihu's Second Speech (chapter 34)

Hearing nothing from Job, Elihu commenced his second address with a scathing criticism of Job's hypocrisy and cynicism. He said he could discern the flavor of Job's speech and could expose it as a feeble attempt at self-justification (34:1–6; see 13:18). In reality, however, Job was no better than the sinner who loves to say that it never pays to serve the Lord (34:7–9). Like the friends, however, Elihu must conclude on theological grounds that since God is holy and just, the reason for Job's suffering lies with Job himself (34:10–12). God is sovereign over all His creation (34:13–15), and so He cannot be coerced or persuaded by earthly rulers to do what is unjust (34:16–19). Such beings, powerful as they are, will die, but God lives on, dealing with human beings only as they deserve (34:20).

Elihu then pointed out that God's fairness is a function of His omniscience. He can be just because He understands all that goes on in the secret places of one's life (34:21–23). When He acts in judgment, He does so with perfect knowledge of circumstances (34:24–28). Likewise, when He is seemingly unresponsive to a person's pleas, who can rightfully question Him (34:29–30)? This being the case, Job should choose the path of repentance, for that leads to forgiveness and restoration. If he refused, Job would find the consequences distasteful (34:31–33). Anyone with any spiritual intuition could understand Job's real problem: He had hardened himself against God, and the only remedy for him was more of the kind of suffering he had already experienced (34:34–37).

C. Elihu's Third Speech (chapter 35)

Once more alluding to a previous statement by Job, Elihu challenged the idea that the righteous are no better off than the wicked (35:1–3; see 21:15). Such an arrogant conclusion is tantamount to claiming that one is more righteous than God Himself (35:2). What Job needed to know is that God is not influenced toward a course of action by either one's goodness or his evil (35:4–6). This may influence human behavior, but it makes no impact on God whatsoever (35:7–8). At the same time, though the righteous and the wicked seem to be no different, in some ways they are different in the view of the Lord, who therefore responds to each on the basis of grace if not of necessity.

What Job needed to do, Elihu suggested, is to stop complaining and turn to God, who alone has the answer to his plight (35:9–11). But Job's cry must be genuine, from the heart, and not merely more self-justification (35:12–14). So far he had refrained from real repentance because the Lord had not yet poured out on him the full strength of His wrath. This had encouraged Job to continue in his present, self-deceiving course of action (35:15–16).

D. Elihu's Fourth Speech (chapters 36–37)

Lest Job fear that repentance might be in vain, Elihu took pains to elaborate on God's mercy. With more than a tinge of spiritual pride, he professed to speak for God on the matter (36:1–4). He reminded Job of God's power to punish the wicked, to reward the righteous, and even to establish kings in their rule (36:5–7). God can make sense of the predicaments in which people find themselves, and when they see that it is because of their wrongdoing He can lead them to repentance (36:8–10). If they respond positively to His corrections, they will enjoy lifelong blessing, but if not they face inevitable judgment (36:11–12). The trouble with sinners, however, is that they never seem to learn. They pay no attention when the Lord extends mercy and, like Job, they must suffer the consequences of their stubbornness (36:13–16).

According to Elihu, Job desperately needed to repent, for God's judgment was already apparent in his life (36:17). Therefore he must not spurn

God's overtures of grace. He must seek the light and not the darkness, the desired effects of his suffering and not the pursuit of iniquity (36:18–21). No one has the right to challenge what God does or to accuse Him of injustice (36:22–23). Job should therefore praise God and not complain against Him, for all His works are perfect, including His work of chastisement. His power and glory may be seen in the water cycle (36:24–29) as well as in the light of heaven and the mystery of the depths (36:30). The creation itself provides humankind with instruction about God's bountiful provisions and perfections. Everything He has made is an instrument in His hand designed to alert people to His presence (36:31–33).

Elihu's reflection on the power and beauty of the Lord as revealed in creation led him to a magnificent expression of praise in which he extolled God's sovereign majesty. The very lightning and thunder herald His awesomeness (37:1–5), the snow and rain testify to His lordship over the elements (37:6), and his display of power silences every person and frightens every beast (37:7–8). The cyclical patterns of the weather are not just natural phenomena; they are expressions of the dependability of God, who brings everything to pass in its season (37:9–12). He uses them also as means of blessing or as implements of judgment (37:13).

In light of this, Elihu asked, how can a mere mortal question the ways of God? Does Job understand the mysteries of the cosmos? Can he bring about the climatic changes that he observes all about him (37:14–18)? The very thought is preposterous. No one knows how to speak to God about such matters, to say nothing about trying to understand Him (37:19–20). At the change of the seasons when the sky is free of clouds and dust, its brightness can hardly be endured. How much greater is the God who has created these things and who displays His sovereign majesty through them (37:21–24).

IV. THE TWO DIVINE SPEECHES (38:1–42:6)

When Job and his friends with all their accumulated and collective wisdom had no more to say, God at last had the final word. Job and his "comforters" had repeatedly spoken of the popular but misguided theology of their day, a theology based on deduction, intuition, observation, and sometimes mere feeling. Though some correct conclusions and in fact marvelous declarations about God and His ways surfaced from time to time, the premises on which the spokesmen based their fundamental theological arguments were totally flawed. God must speak, then, in order to allow revelation to correct and clarify the theological musings of men who without such revelation are left to speculation.

A. God's First Speech (38:1–40:5)

With no forewarning the Lord appeared to Job by the theophany of a whirlwind, the same phenomenon associated with the taking of Elijah up into heaven (38:1; 2 Kings 2:1, 11). He then engaged Job as though he were on trial in a courtroom, asking challenging questions and demanding appropriate responses (Job 38:2–3). It turns out that the questions were rhetorical, for Job had no suitable response and furthermore was too terrified to answer them.

The dominant theme of the Lord's address is that of divine sovereignty, the idea that because He is God all that He does is just and right even when it can't be comprehended by human beings. This begins historically with creation itself. Turning to Job specifically, the Lord asked where Job was on that momentous occasion (38:4–7). Since Job himself did not then exist, he obviously had no comment, no word of wisdom. Similarly, he had nothing to say about the limitation of the seas (38:8–11; see Gen. 1:6–10), the ordering of time and seasons (Job 38:12–15; see Gen. 1:14–19), and the details of the structure of the cosmos with its perceived layers of compartments (Job 38:16–38).

What did Job know of the nether world, that mysterious realm of the dead deep beneath the sea and earth (38:16–18)? And even though Job lived on the earth, what did he really understand about such elemental things as light and darkness, snow and hail, rain and ice (38:19–30)? These things he no doubt took for granted, but in reality they could be traced only to the omnipotent God who created and regulated them for humankind's benefit. Even more awesome, perhaps, were the splendors of the heavens. Could Job account for the starry constellations (38:31–33)? Could he summon the refreshing rains and command the fearsome lightning (38:34–35)? Could he count the clouds and force them to release their life-giving showers (38:36–38)? The answer to these questions is quite obvious.

God's dominion extends also over the animal world. He alone can provide food for the ravenous beasts (38:39–41), and only He knows the length of their gestation, the time and place of their birth, and the mystery of their maturation and eventual independence (39:1–4). He controls all these characteristics and habits. He tends to the wild ass of the desert (39:5–8) and manages the unbroken ox, which no man can domesticate and put into service (39:9–12). He cares for the stupid ostrich that has too little sense to care for itself and its young (39:13–18). He has made it this way in order to display His providential care. Can Job take credit for the proud and powerful horse that charges fearlessly into battle (39:19–25)? Such a magnificent animal testifies to a Creator who has conceived of and who cares for creatures like this, animals beyond human origin and able to survive without human supervision. Birds of prey—wild and untamed—also submit to the hand of God alone. Only He has provided them with incredible gifts necessary to their survival, and only He could imagine the benefits it yields to His creation (39:26–30).

Pausing for the moment, the Lord gave Job opportunity for rebuttal or at least some kind of response (40:1–2). In view of God's wonderful declamation of His creative power and sovereignty, all Job could say is that he had nothing to say. He had spoken once, he said, and now found himself unable and unwilling to add anything further (40:3–5).

B. God's Second Speech (40:6–42:6)

This being the case, the Lord continued His interrogation. First, He challenged the insolence of Job. Who did he think he was that he could question the ways of God? Did he imagine himself to be wiser and more powerful than God (40:6–9)? If Job thought of himself this way, then let him present himself in his royal dignity and bring the proud to account. Let him exercise his powers of authority and judgment against evil men until they have been brought low (40:10–13). If he could do this, the Lord would have to concede that Job indeed was someone to be reckoned with, one well able to deliver himself from all his troubles (40:14).

Without even waiting for Job to offer a possible but meaningless rejoinder, God then spoke of two exemplary creatures—one on the land and the other in the water—that serve to provide analogies by which God's sovereignty can be understood and appreciated. The first is called "behemoth," a term which, by its plurality, suggests an animal in the abstract but clearly a powerful and fearsome beast. Many scholars identify behemoth as the hippopotamus, an attractive suggestion given the description that follows (see Ps. 8:8; 50:10; 78:22; Joel 1:20; 2:22; Hab. 2:17). Behemoth has powerful muscles and legs like iron (Job 40:15–18). He lies serenely in the watery thickets, unperturbed even by the river in floodtime (40:19–23). He fears no man, scoffing at those who would attempt to capture him (40:24).

The creature of the waters—leviathan—may be the crocodile, an animal so fearsome and strong that he came to represent or epitomize the enemies of the gods of Canaanite mythology. Even the biblical writers adopted this imagery, applying it to the devil and thus viewing him as a snake or dragon (Gen. 3:1; Pss. 74:12–14; 104:25–26; Isa. 27:1; Rev. 12:9; 20:2). The Lord who created such a beast asked Job whether he was prepared to go after the leviathan and draw it from its lair (Job 41:1–2). Could Job persuade the leviathan to obey him like a household pet (41:3–5)? Can commercial fishermen catch him for profit (41:6–7)? Try it once, said the Lord, and you will never try it again (44:8–9)!

If one fears only an animal—no matter how terrifying it might be—should he not fear God all the more, since He is the one who has created leviathan and who directs its every move (41:10–11)? To underscore the comparison, the Lord continued His description of the animal. It is powerful, unable to be skinned, armed with massive teeth, and covered with impenetrable armor (41:12–17). The spume of its mouth is like smoke and its eyes glow like burning coals (41:18–21). Its every move elicits terror (41:22–25), and if one is bold or foolish enough to attack it, it is all in vain, for the leviathan fends off blows like drops of rain (41:26–30). It stirs up the waters, and in its wake it leaves a foam like floating frost (41:31–32). No wonder the whole world quakes in its presence, for none is equal to it (41:33–34).

At last Job found words but no longer words of complaint or self-pity.

Brought to his senses by this recounting of God's unfathomable, inexpressible sovereignty, all Job could do is confess that he had spoken amiss and out of turn. He had tried to come to terms in logical, empirical ways with mysteries whose resolution must lie deep within the heart and purposes of an infinite God. When he was questioning before, he should have been praising. What he thought he knew about God by popular theological rumor, he now had come to know by experience of revelation. The answer now was obvious—repentance and full trust in his God (42:1–6).

> *Sometimes the best answers to life's most baffling and troubling questions lie not in what God says but in who He is. When believers recognize that truth, they begin to see that God does not just know the answers but, in fact, is the answer. To know Him is to know all one needs to know. The rest may come later but is unnecessary for now (1 Cor. 2:9; 1 John 2:2–3).*

V. THE EPILOGUE (42:7–17)

A. Reconciliation of Job (42:7–9)

Once Job had finally come to terms with God as well as with his suffering, God vindicated his newfound faith by affirming Job in the company of his friends. Having pleaded for an arbiter before (9:33; 16:19), Job himself now became one, an intercessor between his self-righteous friends and a holy God with whom he interceded on their behalf.

B. Restoration of Job (42:10–17)

On the basis of Job's mediatorial ministry, the Lord blessed him with double what he had before (42:10). His relatives drew around him with their belated expressions of consolation (42:11), he regained his vast holdings of livestock (42:12), and God gave him another generation of children (42:13–15). His daughters were especially precious to him, beautiful young women to whom he allotted equal shares of his estate with their brothers. The capstone of God's favor was Job's longevity. The years of his suffering, painful as they were, must have faded from his memory in the 140 years God granted him to live (42:16–17).

PSALMS
Human Response to Divine Presence

AUTHOR

Of all the books of the Old Testament, the Book of Psalms can best be defined as an anthology, that is, a collection of compositions. In this case the works of many poets are included, so one should speak of a multi-authored production. In addition, evidence exists that editors took up the individual psalms and collected and arranged them into their present order in the book (Ps. 72:20). Many of the psalms are of anonymous authorship and of the others David is most prominent with at least seventy-two credited to him. Other contributors were "the sons of Korah" (Pss. 42, 44-49, 84-85, 87-88), Asaph (50, 73–83), Solomon (72, 127), and even Moses (90).

UNITY

Many scholars have attempted to discern some kind of structural pattern for the Psalms collection but with little success. Clearly the division of the whole into five "books" suggests some attempt at systematizing by authorship and certain key theological terms and ideas, but even here there is no absolute consistency. For example, Book I (Pss. 1–41), which is largely Davidic, uses the name Yahweh predominantly, whereas Book II (Pss. 42–72), prefers Elohim. Even where the psalms are essentially identical

(Pss. 14 and 53; 40:13–17 and Ps. 70), Book II uses Elohim where Book I has Yahweh. Only in smaller units, for example, the so-called pilgrimage psalms (Pss. 120–134), is there semblance of a purposeful collection.

DATE

In a general way it seems that the collection of psalms reflects a chronological process. That is, the indisputably earliest examples tend to occur in the first parts of the Psalter and the latest in the latter parts. For example, the bulk of the Davidic psalms are in Books I and II, and Psalm 137, an exilic poem, is in Book V (Pss. 107–150). The absence of ascription of authorship does, of course, complicate the issue, as does the appearance of such an ancient text as Moses' Psalm 90 as the opening piece in Book IV (Pss. 90–106). Apart from these aberrations, which arose probably from thematic and/or theological considerations, the book may be said to cover the period from 970 to 550 B.C.

ADDRESSEES

The initial readership is difficult if not impossible to determine in a specific sense for most of the psalms because of anonymous authorship, lack of a chronological setting, and the inability to know the situations out of which they arose. Some may have been intended originally as expressions of private worship, whereas others were likely commissioned by kings, priests, and other leaders for use in public worship at the temple. Regardless of the initial readers and hearers, there can be no doubt that the Psalter eventually became the hymnal of Judaism and of the early church. Indeed, it continues to serve that purpose for all who love to worship the Lord. Individual laments, petitions, praises, thanksgivings, and hymns became the common property of all Israel, and to this day they articulate those same responses to God and His ways and works among His people.

PURPOSE

Theology is concerned not only with God's nature, character, and self-revelation but also with human response to divine initiative. That is, it is in the nature of a two-way conversation. This does not diminish the revelatory significance of the whole, for while Psalms and the wisdom literature are indeed the product of human reflection and response, they never canonize theological notions that are contrary to the whole body of revealed truth, the Scriptures. The questions, challenges, and even conclusions that are reached may occasionally exhibit a less-than-orthodox point of view, but it is always clear that these reactions are not intended to reflect God's own perspective. The Lord let the poet or sage speak his mind, but then He either guided him to a correct assessment of reality or interrupted his musings with a word of truth. The result is conformity to the uncorrupted truth of God's person and purposes. The purpose of Psalms, then, was to provide a vehicle by means of which individuals as well as the community of Israel could respond in multifaceted ways to their experiences in life as they lived it in the presence of their God.

THEOLOGICAL EMPHASES

The overwhelmingly predominant theological thrust of the Book of Psalms is its God-centeredness. Whether describing the attributes of God or praising Him for them and His mighty acts, the psalms focus on the God of Israel and the Lord of all the earth. Even the songs of lament that reflect the despair and hopelessness of the human condition are aware of the existence of God and confess the complainant's dependence on Him. In fact, those psalms always end on a note of confidence that God will hear and deliver those who trust in Him. No depository of divine revelation is more replete with testimony to theology proper than Psalms. It is here that one must look if he or she is even to begin to penetrate the mystery of God's nature and to fathom His purposes for creation and history.

A second theme centers on humankind, especially Israel as a covenant people and individuals in that community. At times the psalmists cried out on their own behalf, at other times on behalf of the community, perhaps as its official or at least self-appointed spokesmen. The whole range of emotional, psychological, spiritual, and even physical experience is described in Psalms. Human beings at their worst and at their best appear as authors and/or subjects of these works, almost always in struggle with one another or with the Lord. They laid bare their inner selves, and whether in praise or lament they made themselves vulnerable to the prying eyes of the reader. It is this very fact that gives the psalms their abiding relevance. Every believer of every age can see himself in the ineffable joy as well as the impenetrable gloom of the poets as they recount the reality of their experiences.

Third, the Book of Psalms speaks of the resolution of the tension between God in His transcendent holiness and humankind in its apparently irremedial alienation from Him. There is hope, after all, a hope grounded in the covenant that God made with Israel and that has atoning, redemptive benefits not only for Israel but for every person who has faith in Him. Sin, which marks human existence at every level—individual and corporate—can be forgiven and one can have life abundant now and forever. Though one must not force New Testament revelation onto Old Testament texts, it is clear from Psalms that God has provided a messianic Deliverer whose atoning work will at last accomplish the reconciliation with Him for which the psalmists consistently yearned (Pss. 2 and 110).

CHARACTERISTICS

As a collection of poetry, the Book of Psalms must be interpreted according to the principles appropriate to Hebrew poetic literature. This includes figures of speech, chiasms and other formal structural patterns, and above all, poetic parallelism in which lines appear in close literary and semantic relationship to each other. Among these are synonymous, antithetical, emblematic, climactic, and synthetic parallelisms. These will be pointed out in the analysis of the various individual psalms.

Beyond this is the recognition that the psalms were composed according to certain literary genres or forms, the study of which is popularly called "form criticism." This approach seeks to determine the literary character of a composition and the situation in life (*Sitz im Leben*) in which it originated. That is, is the psalm a hymn, a praise, a thanksgiving, a lament, or the like, and who composed it and for what reason?

Regarding the *Sitz im Leben*, the settings of the psalms can rarely be determined with any confidence, especially if they have no title. Even psalms with titles usually lack precise information about the life situations of their authors—in fact, some scholars question whether the titles were part of the original composition. Some psalms do, of course, lend themselves to a rather accurate assessment of their background, Psalm 51 being a case in point.

Form criticism is more helpful in its analysis of the psalms in terms of genre, style, and unique literary peculiarities. Though there is nothing approaching unanimity in the matter, the following major types or categories of psalms are these: hymns, communal laments, individual laments, royal psalms, and individual songs of thanksgiving. Less common are songs of pilgrimage, communal songs of thanksgiving, wisdom psalms, and liturgical psalms. Most of these will be pointed out in the analysis of the psalms to follow. Without overstating the case, one should recognize the fact that form not only is indicative of function in general, but in the case of the Bible is essential to meaning, especially in the Book of Psalms.

OUTLINE

The heterogeneous nature of the psalms and the lack of a convincingly discernible pattern in their arrangement precludes any attempt to construct a satisfying detailed outline of the entire book. It seems best, therefore, merely to follow the ancient tradition of the Psalter itself and to list the "books" into which it is divided:

Book I	Psalms 1–41
Book II	Psalms 42–72
Book III	Psalms 73–89
Book IV	Psalms 90–106
Book V	Psalms 107–150

BOOK I: PSALMS 1–41

PSALM 1

A. The Comfort of the Godly (1:1–3)

B. The Condemnation of the Ungodly (1:4–5)

C. The Contrast between the Godly and the Ungodly (1:6)

This is a wisdom psalm considered by many scholars as an introduction to the whole Psalter. Its purpose is to support the idea espoused elsewhere in the wisdom literature that knowledge of and obedience to the Lord is the secret to success in life (Prov. 1:7; 9:10; 15:33; Ps. 111:10). It emphasizes the need to saturate oneself in the word of God (1:2), an idea greatly elaborated in the 176 verses of Psalm 119.

PSALM 2

    A. Rebellion of the Nations (2:1–3)
    B. Retribution on the Nations (2:4–6)
    C. Rule over the Nations (2:7–9)
    D. Refuge of the Nations (2:10–12)

Though it lacks a title and any hint of authorship here, apostolic tradition attributed the psalm to David (Acts 4:25). This is reasonable in view of the contents, which speak of David as God's son (2:7) and as the anointed one who ruled under divine authority (2:2). The term "anointed one" translates the Hebrew *māšîaḥ*, "messiah," and so the psalm also clearly anticipates One who goes beyond David in both His nature and His function. The early church correctly understood the psalm to be messianic (Matt. 26:63; John 1:50), but this does not preclude reference to David as well (2 Sam. 7:11–16; 1 Chron. 17:13). The great message of the psalm is that the sovereign God and His anointed earthly rulers will prevail over all evil antagonists and will at last bring them into submission to His lordship. Only those who make peace with Him can expect to be spared.

PSALM 3

    A. David's Lament of Distress (3:1–2)
    B. David's Lift of Deliverance (3:3–4)
    C. David's Lying in Peace (3:5–6)
    D. David's Lesson in Faith (3:7–8)

This psalm, the first attributed to David by title, is designated as an individual lament. The title also suggests that the occasion for the poem was David's flight into Transjordanian exile from his son Absalom (2 Sam.

15–17). One can hardly imagine the anguish of spirit that David must have experienced when not only his son but also the whole nation seemed to have turned against him. Even more troubling would be the thought that God, the Covenant-Maker, had allowed the rebellion to take place despite the promise that David would never lack a descendant to sit on his throne (7:12–16). The psalm, however, reveals David's confidence that God would put down his enemies and give him ultimate victory (Ps. 3:8).

PSALM 4

    A. Call for God (4:1)
    B. Confidence in God (4:2–3)
    C. Communion with God (4:4)
    D. Countenance of God (4:5–7)
    E. Contentment in God (4:8)

This individual lament by David also seems to relate to Absalom's rebellion (4:6; compare 3:2). This psalm is the first to take note in the title of such matters as purpose (for the "[choir] director") and instrumentation ("on stringed instruments"), both of which were of importance to David as leader of Israel's temple worship (1 Chron. 25:1–8). The initial note of despair quickly turns to one of hope as David saw already that deliverance is on the way. Those who scoff at the idea of God's presence (Ps. 4:6) seem to have never experienced His salvation in their own lives (4:1b, 3). David, however, already was joyful, knowing that the darkness of his night of travail would give way to the daylight of divine safety.

PSALM 5

    A. Introduction (5:1–3)
    B. The Holiness of God (5:4–6)
    C. The Hatred toward God (5:7–10)
    D. The Help of God (5:11–12)

Still another lament by David, this psalm, also dedicated to the choir director, was to be played on wind instruments, according to the title. Inasmuch as Psalms 3 and 4 seem to have some setting in the Absalom rebellion, one may surmise that Psalm 5 too finds its roots in that circumstance. If so, it seems that the revolt had not yet become public. After invoking God's attention, David pointed out that the Lord, the Holy One, has no patience with evildoers. They rebelled against God but he, David, had remained steadfastly loyal (5:7). No matter what happens, the Lord would care for him and for all who trust Him (5:11–12).

PSALM 6

    A. The Chastisement of the Lord (6:1–3)
    B. The Concealment of the Lord (6:4–7)
    C. The Compassion of the Lord (6:8–10)

The lament psalms continue with this prayer for mercy, one set to the *sheminith* ("eight"), that is, perhaps, to a higher octave. Some scholars call this a penitential psalm, along with six others of the same type (Pss. 32, 38, 51, 102, 130, 143). What occasioned David's composition cannot be determined. But he had experienced God's disfavor for some sin, and before he died he wanted the Lord to extend His forgiving grace (6:4). Confident that the Lord had heard him, he was able to silence the taunts of his enemies (6:10).

PSALM 7

    A. David's Trust (7:1–2)
    B. David's Testimony (7:3–5)
    C. David's Travail (7:6–8)
    D. David's Trial (7:9–10)
    E. David's Tribute (7:11–13)
    F. David's Triumph (7:14–17)

This strongly emotional lament (thus Hebrew *shiggaion* in the title) very likely issued from David's persecution under Saul during the decade he lived in the Judean desert (1 Sam. 24–26). The reference to "Cush, a Benjamite" favors this view. David recounted his pursuers (Ps. 7:1) and said he deserved to be overtaken by them if he had truly sinned against the Lord (7:3). He, in fact, had not, however, and therefore he prayed for divine vindication and deliverance (7:9). God is righteous, David said, and He will punish those who refuse to repent (7:12). They will receive the same kind of judgment that they had hoped to inflict on the innocent (7:16).

PSALM 8

    A. The Praise of God (8:1–2)
    B. The Priority of God (8:3–5)
    C. The Purpose of God (8:6–9)

This magnificent hymn was a favorite of the New Testament writers, especially the author of Hebrews, who used it in support of the incomparability of Jesus (Heb. 2:6–8; see also 1 Cor. 15:27). It also serves as a commentary on Genesis 1:26–28, explaining the importance and role of humanity in God's creation of all things. True to its hymnic nature, the psalm is filled with praise of God—His name and attributes; His awesome power and glory, especially revealed in His creation of the human race; and His grand design in creation.

> *The universe testifies to the power and glory of God but somewhat as a foil against which to measure the centrality of humankind in the divine design. But beyond this is the perfect One of whom men and women at their best are only a dim foreshadow—Jesus Christ the Savior and Lord.*

PSALM 9

    A. Exaltation of God (9:1–4)
    B. Extermination by God (9:5–6)
    C. Exoneration through God (9:7–10)
    D. Extolment of God (9:11–12)
    E. Exhibition of God (9:13–16)
    F. Expectation from God (9:17–20)

This work by David defies easy categorizing. Its basic note is thanksgiving for some triumph, perhaps David's defeat of the Arameans and Ammonites at Rabbah (2 Sam. 12:31). Stylistically it is noteworthy as one of nine psalms composed alphabetically. Together with Psalm 10 its verses begin with successive letters of the Hebrew alphabet, except for five letters that are omitted. This may suggest that at one time Psalms 9 and 10 were one unified composition. The Septuagint, the Greek translation of the Old Testament, renders it as such. The defeat of David's enemies had caused him to acknowledge that the Lord is truly King (9:7). And what He has done in history, He will do again in the coming day of judgment (9:16–20). The righteous, however, will enjoy His mercy and grace and will praise Him for it (9:12–14).

PSALM 10

 A. The Absence of God (10:1–2)
 B. The Attack on God (10:3–4)
 C. The Attitude toward God (10:5–11)
 D. The Address to God (10:12–15)
 E. The Answer from God (10:16–18)

This psalm continues Psalm 9 formally and stylistically and, one presumes, in subject matter as well. Here, however, the wicked who were condemned to judgment in 9:17 scoff at the message of wrath and act as though God does not exist or at least has no interest in human affairs (10:11). David, clearly the author because of the ascription of Psalm 9, pleaded with the Lord not to remain silent in the face of such arrogance but rather to exercise His sovereign rule (10:16; compare 9:7). At the end David was convinced that God indeed will vindicate His poor and oppressed people by removing forever those evil ones who dare to oppose His lordship (10:17–18).

PSALM 11

 A. Counsel to David (11:1–3)
 B. Confidence of David (11:4–6)
 C. Conclusion by David (11:7)

This may be a so-called psalm of confidence in which the original cause for lament has been overcome and its expression is therefore not included by the poet. The setting is not known, though such an occasion as the beginning of Absalom's revolt is possible. It seems that David had been advised by counselors to escape from Jerusalem, but his reliance on the Lord was so strong as to make this option unthinkable. Indeed, he was confident that the Lord would remove the threat by overcoming those who would do him harm.

PSALM 12

    A. Condition of the Times (12:1–2)

    B. Condemnation of Boasters (12:3–4)

    C. Consolation from the Lord (12:5–6)

    D. Confidence in the Lord (12:7–8)

Some scholars label this psalm a community lament, for though it is attributed to David he seems to be a spokesman for the whole community. Things were going poorly for there was an absence of godly men. Rather, Israel's leaders saw themselves as self-sufficient, and from that vantage point they became oppressive of the poor and weak. David was confident, however, that the Lord would do what is right, for His words of commitment are worth their weight in silver (12:6).

PSALM 13

    A. The Perplexity of David (13:1–2)

    B. The Petition of David (13:3–4)

    C. The Praise of David (13:5–6)

An individual lament psalm, this work by David is appropriate for anyone who has cause to lament for any reason. David complained that God seems to have forgotten him, so he implored Him to make His presence known. Gaining such assurance, he praised God for His ongoing faithfulness (Hebrew, *ḥesed*, 13:5), a conviction that enabled him to act as though the desired deliverance had already taken place (13:6).

PSALM 14

    A. The Testimony of Fools (14:1)
    B. The Test of Fools (14:2–4)
    C. The Terror of Fools (14:5)
    D. The Triumph over Fools (14:6–7)

The term "fool" in the Old Testament is regularly a synonym for "sinner," for it is the fool who has no place for God in his life. This psalm of exhortation seeks to encourage the Lord's people to seek Him and thus to be delivered from the onus of the epithet "fool." A fool, David said, turns aside from God, becomes morally corrupt, and mistreats the righteous. When exposed, they become terrified (14:5). David's request was that they themselves might be put to shame in the full light of the Lord's triumph (14:6).

PSALM 15

    A. Demand for Purity (15:1–2)
    B. Definition of Purity (15:3–5)

This psalm was possibly a liturgical psalm, sung in connection with Israel's worship as a community. It insists that only those who are right with God have the right to worship Him with the community, for the way to righteousness is adherence to the stipulations of the Covenant (15:3–5). The Law—even here—is not said to be the way to purity, but faithfully obeying it is indicative of one's purity before a holy God.

PSALM 16

    A. The Refuge of the Saints (16:1–3)
    B. The Rejection of the Sinners (16:4)
    C. The Riches of the Steadfast (16:5–8)
    D. The Redemption of the Saints (16:9–11)

This *miktam* (perhaps from the Hebrew *kātab*, "to write") of David is a psalm of confidence penned at some period of his life when he was unusually hard-pressed. Its climax (16:10–11) contains one of the few clear references to resurrection in the Old Testament, a point underscored by its use by the apostles to prove the resurrection of Jesus (Acts 2:24–32;

13:35–37). David acknowledged his security in the Lord as well as the folly and futility of paganism. The righteous, he wrote, enjoy the blessings of God in this life, and beyond all that they can have confidence in a life to come, one filled with felicity and joy.

The resurrection of Jesus Christ lies at the very heart of the Christian message. Without it, "we are to be pitied more than all men" (1 Cor. 15:19). David understood this a millennium before it happened, for he saw clearly that the righteousness and justice of God could not be realized in human experience without the possibility of life after death.

PSALM 17

    A. David's Plea (17:1–2)
    B. David's Profession (17:3–5)
    C. David's Petition (17:6–7)
    D. David's Position (17:8–9)
    E. David's Peril (17:10–12)
    F. David's Portion (17:13–15)

One of five psalms described technically as a prayer (Hebrew, *t'pillâ* see also Pss. 86, 90, 102, 142), this lament of David is filled with strong pathos. Its language of struggle suggests, like Psalm 16, that the author was undergoing some kind of severe trial, but, like that psalm, it ends on a note of certainty that God will hear and deliver. David defended his integrity and pleaded for vindication (17:7). He was surrounded by enemies who had put him in mortal peril. Only God could remedy the situation and, indeed, David was confident that He would do so even if it were not till after death (17:15).

PSALM 18

    A. The Extolling of the Lord (18:1–3)
    B. The Exploits of the Lord (18:4–19)

    C. The Equity of the Lord (18:20–30)

    D. The Excellence of the Lord (18:31–50)

Most critics identify this as a "royal psalm," but one with heavy overtones of an individual song of thanksgiving. It appears in almost identical form in 2 Samuel 22. There—as here—it serves as a praise to the Lord for having delivered David from his enemies, including Saul (2 Sam. 22:1). The title refers to David as "the servant of the Lord," a messianic term supported also by David's description as "His anointed" (*māšîaḥ*, "messiah") in Psalm 18:50.

    After praising God in general (18:1–3), David recited His mighty deeds that call for such praise. The Lord had attended to David personally (18:4–6), thereby manifesting His power on earth (18:7–8) and in the heavens (18:9–15). These references to earthquakes, eclipses, and storms show that the God of nature who could display such power is the One who cared for him personally. God could therefore immobilize David's enemies (18:16–19) and establish the righteous who sought refuge in Him (18:20–30). He provides strength to the weak (18:31–34), protection to the vulnerable (18:35–40), support to David in his claims to kingship (18:41–45), and salvation for him and all his dynastic descendants (18:46–50).

PSALM 19

    A. The Works of God (19:1–6)

    B. The Word of God (19:7–14)

One of the most beautiful and favorite of all the psalms, this hymn by David praises God for the excellence, extent, and profound effect of all His creative works. This "general revelation" by which His power and glory may be seen is complemented by the "special revelation" of God's Word, which enables people to understand Him as One who gives wisdom (19:7–9) and who provides a means by which sin can be forgiven and reconciliation achieved (19:10–14).

PSALM 20

    A. Encouragement of the King (20:1–5)

    B. Expectation concerning the King (20:6–8)

    C. Exhortation on behalf of the King (20:9)

A royal psalm, this piece, written by David or perhaps on his behalf, finds strong affinities with Psalm 21, with which it may have originally been joined. It is a community petition to the Lord to preserve King David, who may have been preparing for battle against some foreign nation (20:5). The people believed that God would do so, for the king, as God's "anointed" (20:6), can call on heavenly resources unknown to other rulers. So much so is this the case that the poet merged the idea of Davidic kingship with that of the Lord, whom he called King in the greatest sense of that term (20:9).

PSALM 21

    A. Proclamation of Answered Prayer (21:1–2)
    B. Product of Answered Prayer (21:3–6)
    C. Providence through Answered Prayer (21:7–8)
    D. Protection through Answered Prayer (21:9–12)
    E. Praise for Answered Prayer (21:13)

This royal psalm—possibly a continuation of the previous one—celebrates some great victory God had brought to David and for which David praised Him. The singer announced that God had answered prayer on the king's behalf (21:1–2), an answer seen in the assertion of his royalty (21:3), the extension of his life (21:4), and the exaltation he enjoyed among others (21:5–6). This followed the king's confident trust in God (21:7–8), who had destroyed every hand raised against the king and who would continue to do so in the future (21:9–12). Just as it begins, so the psalm ends on a note of praise of God, the exalted and powerful One (21:13).

PSALM 22

    A. David's Cry (22:1–11)
    B. David's Condition (22:12–21)
    C. David's Consolation (22:22–31)

Clearly a song of individual lament, this psalm plumbs the depths of human despair. With its counterpart, Psalm 69, it reflects David's profound depression, perhaps during the time of Saul's persecution of him (1 Sam. 23:25–29). It is set musically to a melody called "Deer of the Dawn," no doubt a tune of somber and mournful quality. The experiences of David anticipated those of Jesus, who quoted parts of it as He was suspended on the cross (on Ps. 22:8 see Matt. 27:39; on Ps. 22:9 see Matt. 27:43; on Ps. 22:18 see John 19:24; on Ps. 22:23 see Heb. 2:12). Thus this is a messianic psalm in which David's suffering is typical of Christ's suffering.

Sensing his isolation from even God, David asked how God could forsake him (Ps. 22:1). He had not abandoned the fathers of old, but now David saw himself in a condition far worse than theirs. All human companions had shunned him; in fact, they mocked and ridiculed him (22:7). All he had left was the Lord (22:11). Like a hunted prey David was attacked by his fierce enemies, who already counted him as good as dead as they made plans to divide his goods among them (22:18). Only God could avail. After God had heard and delivered him—or, more likely, in anticipation of deliverance—David celebrated God's goodnesses to him. The Lord's deliverance of him, he believed, would testify to the nations of His power and glory and therefore they too would turn to Him for salvation (22:27).

PSALM 23

    A. The Lord's Provision (23:1–3)

    B. The Lord's Protection (23:4–5)

    C. The Lord's Promise (23:6)

This psalm—perhaps the best known of the entire Psalter—is an individual psalm of confidence. In it David recalled his days as a shepherd in Bethlehem's fields and how he tenderly cared for the defenseless and naive animals under his authority. If he, a human shepherd, could exercise such vigilance over mere animals, how much more must God guard those persons created in His very image. He provides for every need, and no matter the danger He guarantees protection for the present and throughout life and beyond.

PSALM 24

    A. Ascent to the Temple (24:1–6)

    B. Access to the Temple (24:7–10)

Comparison of this psalm to Psalm 15 leads to the conclusion that this too is a liturgical song, one composed perhaps for such an occasion as David's triumphant march with the ark into the Zion tabernacle (2 Sam. 6). Franz Delitzsch suggests that part one consists of an introit by a choir (Ps. 24:1–2), followed by a single voice raising a question (24:3), to which another provided response (24:4). The choir then concluded with a note of promise (24:5–6). The second part follows the same pattern except for the choral interruption between the two solo voices: chorus (24:7), solo (24:8a), chorus (24:8b–9), solo (24:10a), chorus (24:10b, c). The whole ends with a marvelous declaration of the kingship of the Lord.

PSALM 25

    A. Introduction (25:1–3)
    B. Request for God's Favor (25:4–7)
    C. Rehearsal of God's Goodness (25:8–10)
    D. Reliance on God's Forgiveness (25:11–22)

This nearly complete acrostic poem (one Hebrew letter is missing) is clearly an individual lament. After an opening appeal to the Lord for victory over his enemy, David pleaded first for divine guidance based on God's past faithfulness, especially in the forgiveness of his sins (25:6–7). He then recited the attributes and qualities of the Lord, including His grace (25:11), His covenant loyalty (25:14), and His power to save (25:15, 20). As king, David's concern was not just for himself but for Israel, the people of the Lord. They too must be delivered from their troubles (25:22).

PSALM 26

    A. Integrity of the Psalmist (26:1–3)
    B. Isolation of the Psalmist (26:4–5)
    C. Innocence of the Psalmist (26:6–8)
    D. Importunity of the Psalmist (26:9–11)
    E. Epilogue (26:12)

Another psalm of individual lament, this prayer of David may have originated in an experience such as his expulsion from the land in the Absalom revolt, though there is no way to be certain. As is often the case in lament psalms, the complainant asserted his own innocence and/or uprightness (26:1; see also 7:8; 17:3; 25:21), but he also was aware that his relationship with the Lord could not be taken for granted. He stood constantly in need of grace and forgiveness (26:6–7), so that he might be able to worship the Lord in His holy place (26:8). His prayer, then, is that he might not be like the sinners, who were bound to destruction, but that he would be a person of integrity before God (26:9–11).

PSALM 27

    A. Confidence of Faith (27:1–3)
    B. Comfort in Faith (27:4–5)
    C. Consequences of Faith (27:6)
    D. Desire for the Lord (27:7–8)
    E. Dependability of the Lord (27:9–10)
    F. Deliverance by the Lord (27:11–12)
    G. Delight in the Lord (27:13–14)

Though this psalm includes both an expression of confidence (27:1–6) and an individual lament (27:7–14), David no doubt composed it as a single piece. After proclaiming his confidence in the Lord, he delighted in anticipating a lifetime of fellowship with Him (27:4–5), a hope that inspired him to praise God (27:6). On a more negative note, perhaps, David pleaded for the Lord not to reject him but to receive him, even though all others—including his parents—should refuse to do so (27:10). He was especially concerned that the Lord deliver him from those hostile toward him. He was so confident that all of this would come to pass that he concluded by exhorting others also to trust God (27:13–14).

PSALM 28

    A. Supplication to the Lord (28:1–5)
    B. Satisfaction in the Lord (28:6–9)

The title provides no information as to the setting of this psalm of individual lament, but the reference to hypocritical plotting (28:3) and to the threat to his kingship ("His anointed," 28:8) could well fit the occasion of Absalom's revolution. David feared that if the Lord would not hear him, he would be as good as dead (28:1). He then wished that God would judge his adversaries (28:4). As he reached a degree of certainty that God had heard him, David rejoiced in the Lord and in his anticipated salvation (28:7). All would be well as God restored him and manifested also His own kingship (28:9).

PSALM 29

    A. Source of the Thunder (29:1–2)
    B. Strength of the Thunder (29:3–9)
    C. Serenity after the Thunder (29:10–11)

A classic hymn, this poem is thought by a number of scholars to have Canaanite origins, with the name of Yahweh taking the place of Baal. Though there are themes and motifs in common, the theological differences are so profound as to rule out any possibility of dependence. More likely the psalm is a polemic against paganism, one that attributes to the Lord the power and glory that the heathen ascribed to their own deities.

Seven times the voice of the Lord thundered forth. He manifested his sovereignty over the seas, the mountains, the deserts, and the forests (29:3, 5, 8–9). In fact, He is Ruler over all things, enthroned in splendor and bestowing strength and peace to His people (29:11).

PSALM 30

    A. Rejoicing in the Lord (30:1–3)
    B. Reward of the Lord (30:4–5)
    C. Rejection of the Lord (30:6–7)
    D. Request to the Lord (30:8–10)
    E. Response of the Lord (30:11–12)

This is an individual song of thanksgiving (see also Pss. 9–10) composed to celebrate a healing of David from what he perceived to be a terminal illness (30:2–3). The psalm's superscription, on the other hand, relates it to the dedication of a house of worship. Perhaps David's illness was more spiritual than physical and the occasion was his aborted attempt to take the ark of the covenant to his Zion tabernacle, a failure that brought him to the depths of despair (2 Sam. 6:1–11). When it was done properly later, he surely would have dedicated the ark and its new resting place. The term for "dedication" (*ḥănŭkkâ*) was later applied to Hanukkah, the postexilic Jewish festival marking the dedication of the Hasmonean temple.

In any case, David rejoiced in his healing after what seemed to be an interminable time of suffering but was, in fact, but a brief moment (Ps. 30:5). He thought God had forsaken him, (30:7) and in his despondency he had cried out for deliverance (30:10). God had heard and had responded, an act of mercy that elicited great praise from David and a pledge to thank Him forever (30:12).

PSALM 31

    A. A Prayer for Deliverance (31:1–8)

    B. A Picture of Despair (31:9–13)

    C. A Protest against Destroyers (31:14–18)

    D. A Plea for Dedication (31:19–24)

The extended persecution and isolation described in this psalm of individual lament suggests a setting such as David's ten-year alienation from Saul, though, of course, that must remain only a matter of speculation. The poet prayed earnestly that God would preserve him, but in the end he was willing to commend his spirit to the Lord, words Jesus also spoke on the cross (31:5; Luke 23:46). The language of David's suffering, though perhaps somewhat hyperbolic, is nonetheless soul-stirring in its imagery (Ps. 31:10, 12). No wonder he cried out for vindication. Anticipating that God at last would do this very thing, David exhorted the people of the Lord to have confidence in Him and to love Him because of His goodness and grace (31:23–24).

PSALM 32

    A. The Blessing of Forgiveness (32:1–2)

    B. The Basis of Forgiveness (32:3–5)

C. The Benefits of Forgiveness (32:6–10)

D. The Benediction of Forgiveness (32:11)

According to the title this is a *maskil*, that is, a song skillfully (from *śākal*, "to be insightful") composed. By genre, however, it is most likely an individual song of thanksgiving. David had committed some terrible sin—perhaps a reference to his adultery with Bathsheba and the murder of her husband Uriah—and had suffered terrible emotional and spiritual anguish as a result (32:3–4). But he had confessed and had sought the Lord's forgiveness (32:5) and thus began to enjoy God's blessings in a new way (32:7, 10). He coveted these blessings for others in a similar situation, urging the forgiven to be joyful and to express that joy with all their being (32:11).

PSALM 33

A. Call to the Righteous (33:1–3)

B. Care of the Righteous (33:4–5)

C. Creation on Behalf of the Righteous (33:6–9)

D. Counsel for the Righteous (33:10–11)

E. Concern for the Righteous (33:12–19)

F. Confession of the Righteous (33:20–22)

This stirring hymn makes appeal to the saints of God to praise Him for it is the right and natural thing to do (33:1). He is worthy of praise because of His providential care of His own, commencing with creation and continuing on in the lives of every generation. Those who know Him as God and Savior are the special subjects of His favor and can rest in His strength and security (33:18–19). The appeal by which the anonymous poet introduced the psalm is matched by a conclusion in which the righteous ones whom he had addressed respond in confession and continued trust in their Lord (33:20–22).

PSALM 34

A. David's Praise of the Lord (34:1–3)

B. David's Prayer to the Lord (34:4–6)

    C. David's Prosperity in the Lord (34:7–10)

    D. David's Proclamation of the Lord (34:11–14)

    E. David's Preservation in the Lord (34:15–22)

An individual song of thanksgiving, this psalm, according to the title, originated in the days when David was "on the run" from Saul. A slight problem is apparent in the title in that David actually feigned madness before the Philistine ruler Achish, not Abimelech (1 Sam. 21:10–15). On the other hand, Abimelech may be a title for any Philistine ruler. That seems to be the case in the dealings of the patriarchs with the Philistines (Gen. 20:1–18; 21:22–34; 26:1–17). In all, eight psalms are assigned to this decade of David's life, the chronological sequence perhaps being 7, 59, 56, 34, 52, 57, 142, and 54. Of further interest is the fact that this is an alphabetic acrostic with all but one letter of the Hebrew alphabet beginning each verse in sequence.

David began by urging others to join him in praising the Lord, and then he recounted how God had heard his prayers and delivered him (Ps. 34:6). Those who depend on the Lord, said the poet, will lack nothing (34:10). Those who expect His blessings must, of course, depart from evil. When they do so, they, like him, will see how faithful the Lord is. The evil will surely meet judgment, but the saints of the Lord will never be held guilty in His eyes (34:22).

PSALM 35

    A. Imprecation on the Wicked (35:1–10)

    B. Iniquities of the Wicked (35:11–18)

    C. Innocence before the Wicked (35:19–28)

Though this is an individual lament, it seems to form a pair with the preceding psalm. For example, only these two psalms refer to the "angel of the LORD" (34:7; 35:5–6). On the other hand, the lack of a title makes it difficult to place the psalm in the same historical context as Psalm 34, at least with any certainty. An important feature of this psalm (along with Psalms 7, 69, and 109 especially) is its imprecatory language, that is, it is bold in its demand that God deal with the wicked with utmost severity. This is not contrary to the Christian gospel, for the New Testament also is clear in its denunciation of sin and in its proclamation of a day in which God's wrath will be poured out on those who refuse His grace (John 3:36; 1 Thess. 2:16; Rev. 6:16–17; 14:19). The psalmist's imprecation is not in defense of his own person but on behalf of God's honor. David thus referred to salvation by the Lord as he contended with his enemies (Ps. 35:9–10). They had mistreated him in such a way that surely God could not help but take vengeance (35:17). God must therefore act according to His own righteousness (35:24) and be magnified in the vindication of His suffering saints (35:27).

PSALM 36

    A. Description of the Wicked (36:1–4)
    B. Distinction from the Wicked (36:5–10)
    C. Destruction of the Wicked (36:11–12)

Though usually categorized as a psalm of individual lament, this Davidic piece also contains elements of wisdom (36:1–4) as well as a hymn (36:5–10). Here the poet spoke of the folly of the wicked who think their evil will never be discovered. Rather, they go on planning iniquity day and night. What they should recognize is that the Lord is the source of all blessing (36:7–8). He indeed is the very fountain of life (36:9; Jer. 2:13). Disregard of this basic truth will eventually lead to the destruction of the foolish.

PSALM 37

    A. Security of the Righteous (37:1–11)
    B. Support of the Righteous (37:12–20)
    C. Sustenance of the Righteous (37:21–26)
    D. Salvation of the Righteous (37:27–40)

This is clearly a wisdom psalm, one composed as an alphabetic acrostic. (Pss. 9–10, 25, and 34 are also acrostic psalms.) As opposed to the fool in the previous psalm, the wise, that is, the righteous one, of this psalm enjoys the favor of the Lord in a variety of ways. He need not fear the evil one, for the sovereign Lord is in control and would provide protection. In fact, the wicked will perish and thus no longer be a threat (37:10).

Meanwhile the weapons of the unrighteous will be turned to their own devastation (37:15). They will have no success over God's own people, for the little that they do have in the providence of the Lord far outmatches all the might of the godless (37:16). No matter how desperate their plight may seem, the people of the Lord have resources at their disposal that can more than address just their basic needs. Sometime they will become heirs of the land itself (37:22). They are marked as men and women of wisdom (37:30) and obedience to the Law (37:31). Contrary to the wicked, who will soon pass away (37:35–36), the righteous will be preserved because they have taken refuge in the Lord (37:40).

PSALM 38

    A. The Suffering of the Psalmist (38:1–8)

    B. The Supplication of the Psalmist (38:9–15)

    C. The Salvation of the Psalmist (38:16–22)

This psalm of individual lament may find its source, like several others (see Pss. 6, 32, 51), in the life-changing sins of adultery and murder that made such a profound impact on King David. The title includes the petition "for a memorial," that is, to invoke the Lord to note the psalmist's sincere confession (see also Ps. 70). He has suffered the painful wounds of his own conscience, conviction of sin so enervating as to affect even his physical health (38:7). His friends have all forsaken him, so that all he can do is turn to the Lord. Only in Him does he have any hope of comfort and healing (38:15). Unless the Lord intervened on his behalf, David feared he would be overcome by those who hate him (38:19). His plea was that he might soon enjoy God's favor and salvation (38:22).

PSALM 39

    A. The Frailty of Mankind (39:1–5)

    B. The Finiteness of Mankind (39:6–11)

    C. The Futility of Mankind (39:12–13)

This psalm of individual lament seems to form a pair with Psalm 38 (see 39:2 and 38:13), but its setting is not as clear. David dedicated it to Jeduthun (also in the titles of Pss. 62 and 77), one of his choir directors (1 Chron. 16:41; 25:1). David confessed his profound limitations as a mere man (Ps. 39:4), and extrapolated from his own experience that the human race as a whole is empty and hollow in its natural condition (39:11). Only in God is there hope for this life and beyond (38:13).

PSALM 40

    A. Works of the Lord (40:1–5)
    B. Worship of the Lord (40:6–8)
    C. Witness to the Lord (40:9–10)
    D. Waiting on the Lord (40:11–17)

Basically a psalm of individual thanksgiving, this poem includes touches of other elements as well. Verses 1–10 clearly express thanksgiving, but verses 11–17 are similar to a lamentation. David was especially grateful for God's redemptive grace that had delivered him from some actual or anticipated disaster and had set him on a firm foundation (40:2). This elicited from him what he said was the highest form of sacrifice to the Lord, namely, obedience to the will of God (40:8). The author of Hebrews quoted this text to speak of the atonement secured by the perfect obedience of Jesus Christ (Heb. 10:5–10).

David then declared that the salvation granted to him must issue in his bearing witness of it to others. The song concludes, however, with a plea that the salvation will be ongoing. David's own sin and the dangers he faced threatened to undo him. But past deliverance gave him confidence that whatever arose would be dealt with by God's intervention (Ps. 40:17).

PSALM 41

    A. Reward of the Righteous (41:1–3)
    B. Reproach of the Righteous (41:4–9)
    C. Renewal of the Righteous (41:10–12)
    D. Epilogue (41:13)

Another psalm of individual thanksgiving, this composition concludes Book I. Its connection to Psalm 1 may be seen in the use of the word "blessed" at the beginning of each of the two psalms. The setting is perhaps the rebellion of Absalom, and Ahithophel is possibly the unfaithful "friend" mentioned in verse 9 (2 Sam. 16:23). Later Jesus used these same words to speak of His "friend" Judas, who betrayed Him (Matt. 26:50; John 13:18). David was not lamenting here, however; he was rejoicing in God's salvation.

The Lord cares for the weak (Ps. 41:1) despite the reproaches and threats of their enemies. All that remained was for the Lord to exercise retribution on those who purposed to do David harm (41:10). The epilogue (41:13) rounds off not only the psalm but also the whole section (Pss. 1–41).

BOOK II: PSALMS 42–72

PSALM 42

A. Thirsting for God (42:1–5)
B. Trusting in God (42:6–11)

A song of individual lament, this first psalm in Book II uses the word Elohim ("God"). The whole section, in fact, is marked by this feature. In Psalms 42–72 the name "Elohim" occurs 164 times, compared with 30 uses of Yahweh ("LORD"). This psalm also seems to have been written by or under the auspices of the "sons of Korah" along with several others in Book II (Pss. 44–49). Korah, a great-grandson of Levi, rebelled against Aaron's leadership (Num. 16:1–2), but his own descendants distinguished themselves as leaders in Israel's worship (1 Chron. 6:32–38).

The psalmist's "thirst" for God must be seen not only in the comparison he made ("as the deer pants after streams of water") but also against the background of the deserts with which he was apparently most familiar. To him, fresh water was not just a refreshing luxury—it was tantamount to life itself! How much more so is a life-giving relationship with Jesus Christ.

The unknown author spoke of his intense longing for God and his desire to worship Him with others in the temple (Ps. 42:4). It seems that for some reason he had been denied access to this holy privilege, hence his bitter lament. Unless the language of verse 6 is to be taken figuratively, one must conclude that the poet was a long distance from Jerusalem. While he experienced a great longing for the temple and its services, he was aware of God's presence and he knew that God was not geographically limited (42:11).

PSALM 43

    A. The Prayer of the Psalmist (43:1)

    B. The Problem of the Psalmist (43:2)

    C. The Proposal of the Psalmist (43:3)

    D. The Promise of the Psalmist (43:4)

    E. The Praise of the Psalmist (43:5)

Though the psalm bears no title, it is likely to be attributed to the sons of Korah because it is in the list of such psalms. Moreover, it may have been part of Psalm 42 at one time (compare 43:5 with 42:5, 11). Like Psalm 42, it is a song of individual lament. Here, however, the psalmist complained not because he was absent from the temple but because his enemies were oppressing him (43:2). The answer, nevertheless, was the same—to worship the Lord in His sacred temple (43:3).

PSALM 44

    A. Past Deliverance (44:1–3)

    B. Present Determination (44:4–8)

    C. Present Dishonor (44:9–16)

    D. Present Despair (44:17–26)

The setting of this communal lament is unclear, but its message is relevant to God's people of every generation. The poet recounted the Exodus and Conquest from his nation's ancient history and then acknowledged that the God who made those marvelous accomplishments possible was also His God (44:4). His people were in distress—perhaps already in

Assyrian or Babylonian exile (44:11, 14)—and had become the object of international ridicule (44:13). With more than a little blindness to his nation's faults, the psalmist argued that this had happened undeservedly. Almost like Job he asked God to point out to him where and how the people had failed (44:17–21; see Job 23). Indeed, the psalmist said, it was for God's sake that they were suffering (Ps. 44:22). His appeal, then, was that God would rise up on their behalf and deliver them from all their distress (44:26).

PSALM 45

    A. Description of the King (45:1–8)

    B. Desire of the King (45:9–11)

    C. Dignity of the King (45:12–17)

As a royal psalm this lovely poem was almost certainly composed on the occasion of a royal wedding. Quite possibly it was the marriage of young King Jehoram of Judah to Athaliah, daughter of Ahab and his Tyrian wife, Jezebel (45:12; 2 Kings 8:16–18; 2 Chron. 21:1–6), though, of course, that cannot be proved.

The poet described the groom in glowing terms appropriate to a descendant of David and human prototype of Jesus Himself (Ps. 45:2–5). He even called him "elohim," that is, "mighty one," the one who represents God on the earth (45:6). His bride was beautiful, but despite her regal standing she honored the king (45:11). Together with all their attendants the royal couple entered the palace, where in due time they would establish their own line of Davidic descendants (45:16). The glory of his Davidic association was so magnificent that the psalmist said the newly married king would never be forgotten. God Himself would cause the people to praise him as a messianic figure forever (45:17).

PSALM 46

    A. The Presence of God (46:1–3)

    B. The Protection of God (46:4–7)

    C. The Promise of God (46:8–11)

A so-called Song of Zion—one thematically linked to Psalms 47 and 48—this praise for a significant victory may have arisen out of a circumstance such as Jehoshaphat's triumph over the Moabites and their allies (2 Chron. 20:1), a "holy war" campaign accompanied by the singing of hymns (20:21–22). The psalm begins with the confession that God is a refuge (Ps. 46:1), a point that summarizes the next two main sections as well (46:7, 11). So long as God is with His people, they need have no fear (46:2). Zion itself is secure from all the threats of the nations because of God's role as a defensive fortification (46:7). And this is no temporary measure either, for He will usher in a day when all the nations will acknowledge His lordship (46:10).

PSALM 47

    A. The Authority of God (47:1–4)

    B. The Absoluteness of God (47:5–8)

    C. The Adoration of God (47:9)

A royal psalm, this one goes beyond the human realm and speaks of the Lord's enthronement as King over all the earth (see also Pss. 93, 96–99). That sovereignty, however, is in reference to Israel, who, with the Lord, will exercise dominion (47:3). There is no limit to His rule—it is absolute and universal (47:8). In time to come, the nations will recognize this fact and, with Abraham and his descendants, will form one mighty people of God (47:9).

PSALM 48

    A. The Description of Zion (48:1–2)

    B. The Defense of Zion (48:3–8)

    C. The Destiny of Zion (48:9–14)

Another song of Zion, this tribute to the city of David celebrates it as the special earthly residence of the Lord. In almost mythic language—mythic because it responds resoundingly to pagan ideas about holy places—it describes Jerusalem as a place of beauty and prominence. Those who attempted to gain illegitimate access to it or otherwise do it harm were disappointed, for God was its protection (48:3). From it He will radiate His glory in ages to come, and as the capital of His kingdom it will be the center of His sovereign rule (48:14).

PSALM 49

A. Introduction (49:1–5)
B. Importance of Riches (49:6–12)
C. Insecurity in Riches (49:13–15)
D. Impermanence of Riches (49:16–20)

This wisdom psalm deals with a perennial problem—the proper estimation of wealth. After an introduction in which the sage called for a hearing, he declared how worthless material things are in comparison to the truly important things of life such as redemption from death or even the ongoing of this present life (49:12). Evil men who make riches their security will face inevitable death, while those who trust in the Lord will rule over them. The righteous ought not to envy the wealthy, therefore, because when they pass from this earth they cannot take their material things with them (49:17).

PSALM 50

A. The Coming of Judgment (50:1–6)
B. The Conditions of Judgment (50:7–15)
C. The Condemnation through Judgment (50:16–21)
D. The Consideration of Judgment (50:22–23)

Asaph is the attributed author of this psalm along with a number of others (Pss. 73–83), all of which use the divine name Elohim. Its approach is highly prophetic in tone and its themes center on ritual and worship. Some scholars therefore describe it as a prophetic liturgy. Asaph was a Levite whom David appointed to have oversight of the musical aspect of temple worship (1 Chron. 6:31–40; 15:17–19; 16:5, 7, 37).

The poet wrote of God's establishing a judicial setting to which He will summon His people to accuse them before witnesses (Ps. 50:4). He would not condemn them for failing to provide sacrifices to Him for they had gone through the motions of doing so, and in any case He is not dependent on them for His survival (50:12). What He had wanted but had not received was the thanksgiving of His people and their sense of dependence on Him (50:14–15). He would also charge them with covenant violation (50:16). They had systematically broken His commandments, thinking that His silence on the matter was a sign of His approval or His indifference (50:21). Only by redressing these things could they hope to receive God's forgiveness and deliverance (50:22–23).

PSALM 51

    A. Recognition of Sin (51:1–2)

    B. Recital of Sin (51:3–5)

    C. Repentance of Sin (51:6–9)

    D. Restoration from Sin (51:10–12)

    E. Restitution for Sin (51:13–17)

    F. Epilogue (51:18–19)

This famous confession by David, a psalm of individual lamentation, was composed in the aftermath of his sins of adultery and murder (2 Sam. 11). It is the first of the psalms of David in which he employed the divine name Elohim, a choice that perhaps reflects his sense of distance from God as Yahweh, that is, the covenant God. The psalm is a model of how one ought to address sin in his life. David first acknowledged that he was a sinner, and then he noted that though he did wrong against other people his sins were ultimately against God (51:7). He then pleaded for forgiveness from God (51:9–10) and restoration to fellowship with him (51:11). The genuineness of his repentance is seen in his pledge to praise God and to bear witness to others of God's saving grace (51:13, 15).

> *Once we understand that no sin is against a fellow human being alone and that all sin is transgression against God, we will no longer treat it so lightly. To violate one created as the image of God is to grieve Him to whom we are all accountable, even the Creator.*

PSALM 52

    A. Denunciation of the Wicked (52:1–3)

    B. Destruction of the Wicked (52:4–5)

    C. Delight over the Wicked (52:6–9)

This psalm of exhortation is the first of four Davidic psalms (Pss. 52–55) that are called *maskil*, that is, "skillfully composed." Its setting, as indicated by the title, is when David was running from Saul. The particular subject in view is Doeg, an Edomite henchman of Saul who betrayed the priests of Nob for having provided assistance to David and his men (1 Sam. 22:6–10). No doubt Doeg is the one who is referred to in Psalm 52:1, 7. David condemned him as a lying braggart, whose destruction by the Lord was just a matter of time (52:5). His judgment would display the futility of a sinful life and would cause the righteous to rejoice in the Lord, who is faithful to do what is right in dealing with human behavior (52:8).

PSALM: 53

    A. Description of the Fool (53:1)

    B. Depravity of the Fool (53:2–4)

    C. Dispersal of the Fool (53:5–6)

Another psalm of exhortation, this one describes the condition of those who attempt to live without God. Its wording is similar to Psalm 14, of which this may be a later variation. David stated that the height of folly is to deny that God exists or that He is present in human affairs (53:1). Those who try to live as though God does not exist are hopelessly corrupt (53:3) and can look forward only to God's severe indictment and judgment (53:5).

PSALM 54

    A. Cry of the Psalmist (54:1–3)

    B. Confession of the Psalmist (54:4)

    C. Confidence of the Psalmist (54:5–7)

This psalm of individual lament was written when David was pursued by Saul, specifically David's betrayal by the Ziphites, some of his fellow

Judahite tribesmen (1 Sam. 23:19–23; 26:1–5). In his distress David cried out to God (Ps. 54:1), confident that he would be heard and delivered (54:4). David was so sure of this that he pledged that he would offer sacrifices of thanksgiving (54:6).

PSALM 55

A. The Complaint of David (55:1–8)
B. The Confusion of David (55:9–14)
C. The Condemnation by David (55:15–21)
D. The Comfort of David (55:22–23)

Some scholars suggest that David was in a foreign city when he penned this psalm of individual lament. He complained that he was in a place from which he could not easily extricate himself (55:6–8). He was ill at ease there, and moreover, he lamented having been betrayed. One thinks of the disloyalty of his counselor Ahithophel, whose duplicity contributed to David's having been forced into exile in Transjordania (2 Sam. 15:12; 16:15–23; 17:14). He perhaps was the "friend" referred to in Psalm 55:13. In a strong imprecation David urged God to deal with these traitors as they deserved (55:15). Their hypocritical professions of friendship were treacherous (55:20–21), but God would have the last word, vindicating the righteous and condemning the wicked (55:22–23).

PSALM 56

A. Threat to the Psalmist (56:1–2)
B. Trust of the Psalmist (56:3–4)
C. Trials of the Psalmist (56:5–6)
D. Triumph of the Psalmist (56:7–9)
E. Thanksgiving by the Psalmist (56:10–13)

The setting of this psalm of individual lament by David is, according to its title, his having taken up temporary residence among the Philistines at Gath (1 Sam. 21:10–15). The enemies in the psalm were not the Philistines, however, but Saul and his cohorts, who were constantly attempting to take David's life. Ironically, David said his trust was in God when, in fact, he had sought protection with Achish, the Philistine ruler (Ps. 56:3–4). Saul had dogged his steps (56:6), but God was well aware of that and now, David knew, He would begin to deliver him (56:9). The lament thus turns to praise. Even though David's rescue from Saul was not yet an accomplished fact, he felt it was as good as done because of God's utter reliability (56:11).

PSALM 57

    A. Peril of the Psalmist (57:1–5)

    B. Protection for the Psalmist (57:6)

    C. Praise by the Psalmist (57:7–11)

In this psalm of individual lament, which the title associates with David's refuge in a cave (possibly Adullam, 1 Sam. 22:1–2; or En Gedi, 24:1–7, NIV), the psalmist uttered an urgent cry for protection from the "lions" who sought to devour him (Ps. 57:4). He delighted to see, however, that his enemies had fallen into their own trap (57:6), and for this reason he burst out in exultant praise of God (57:9).

PSALM 58

    A. The Character of the Wicked (58:1–5)

    B. The Condemnation of the Wicked (58:6–8)

    C. The Consummation of the Wicked (58:9–11)

Usually considered a community lament, this psalm clearly is similar to the previous one (compare 57:4 and 58:6). In it David described sinners as being wicked from their very birth (58:3) and as the source of moral and spiritual venom (58:4). He prayed that God would destroy them (58:6), so that the righteous may rejoice in the justice of the Lord toward those who know and love Him (58:11).

PSALM 59

    A. Plot of the Enemy (59:1–7)

    B. Punishment of the Enemy (59:8–15)

    C. Praise for Victory over the Enemy (58:16–17)

This psalm of individual lament seems to have arisen from the earliest days of David's flight from Saul. In fact, the title implies that David was still in Gibeah, protected by his wife from assassins bent on killing him (1 Sam. 19:11–17). He was, of course, aware of their evil designs (Ps. 59:1), and he invoked God's wrathful intervention on his behalf (59:11). This would make clear to Israel and everyone that God is sovereign and has everything under control (59:13). Already assured of God's deliverance, David thanked and praised Him (59:16–17).

PSALM 60

    A. The Smiting of the Lord (60:1–4)

    B. The Sovereignty of the Lord (60:5–10)

    C. The Sufficiency of the Lord (60:11–12)

The title of this communal lament links it to military campaigns not recorded in the Old Testament, though they may be included in the lists of David's wars with surrounding nations (2 Sam. 8:13–14; 1 Chron. 18:3–4, 12–13). The poet first complained about God's chastisement of the nation (Ps. 60:1), but then he confessed and exulted in the sovereignty of God, who is Lord of all the nations. In conclusion he expressed hope that though Israel had suffered defeat in the past, God would enable her to prevail over all her foes (60:12).

PSALM 61

    A. Preservation of the Psalmist (61:1–4)

    B. Praise of the Psalmist (61:5–8)

Another psalm of individual lament by David, this composition may also be described as a royal supplication. The reference to the prolonging of the king's life (61:6) may suggest that David penned these words after his return from Absalom's rebellion. However, this cannot be stated with certainty. In any event, David spoke of his need for divine favor and protection (61:2) and concluded on a note of confidence that God would do for him all that he needed (61:5).

PSALM 62

    A. God as a Rock (62:1–4)

    B. God as a Refuge (62:5–8)

    C. God as a Rewarder (62:9–12)

In this psalm of confidence—which logically and thematically follows Psalm 61 (compare 61:4, 8 with 62:8b; 61:4 with 62:7)—David employed the metaphor of a rock to suggest God's permanence and reliability (62:2). Having demonstrated this in his own experience, he exhorted everyone to learn to trust in the Lord and stand on Him as a foundation (62:8). This would not be in vain, for the time will come when God will reward those who give him priority in their lives (62:12).

PSALM 63

    A. The Psalmist's Thirst (63:1–3)

    B. The Psalmist's Trust (63:4–8)

    C. The Psalmist's Triumph (63:9–11)

In this psalm of individual lament David seems to have been recalling the days of his exile when he was forced out of the land by Absalom. In any case the time was sometime after he had become king of Israel (63:11; see 2 Sam. 15:23, 28; 17:16, 29). The thirst he described may have been physical, but in a deeper sense it reflected his longing for the Lord and the tabernacle (Ps. 63:1–2). He believed the time would come when he would return home and once more enjoy the benefits of God's more immediate presence. Then he would also prevail over those who sought to do him harm (63:11).

PSALM 64

    A. The Brazenness of the Enemy (64:1–4)

    B. The Boasting of the Enemy (64:5–6)

    C. The Brokenness of the Enemy (64:7–10)

Still another psalm of individual lament, this treatise by David registers his amazement at the boldness of his enemies who dared to attack the righteous ones of the Lord. They also boasted that they would never be found out and brought to account (64:5). Those who shoot at God's people (64:4) will, however, someday become the target of His judgment (64:7), a turnabout that will cause people everywhere to acknowledge God's power and His own people particularly to be glad for His deliverance (64:10).

PSALM 65

    A. The Grace of God (65:1–4)

    B. The Glory of God (65:5–8)

    C. The Goodness of God (65:9–13)

This is a communal thanksgiving hymn celebrating Elohim as the God of the natural world. He hears prayer, forgives sin, and bestows blessing on the basis of His sovereign power and grace. His very creation attests to that sovereignty (65:7–8) but not just in ways that terrify those who observe His works. Indeed, the bountiful harvests that sustain the human race are evidences of God's generosity and goodness (65:11).

PSALM 66

    A. The Praise of the Lord (66:1–4)

    B. The Power of the Lord (66:5–7)

    C. The Providence of the Lord (66:8–12)

    D. The Payment to the Lord (66:13–15)

    E. The Proclamation of the Lord (66:16–20)

Another communal thanksgiving psalm, this one extols God's power in general (66:1–4), and then specifically by recounting the Exodus as a supreme example of His power (66:6). The anonymous poet celebrated God's sustaining grace through difficult times and then, on the community's behalf, promised to offer up sacrifices of appreciation (66:13). The poem ends with a personal testimony of God's goodness to the author and a solemn reminder that God hears only those who have dealt with their sin (66:18).

PSALM 67

    A. The Salvation of God (67:1–2)

   B. The Sovereignty of God (67:3–4)

   C. The Satisfaction of God (67:5–7)

This communal thanksgiving hymn seems to be a song of celebration for the ingathering of the harvest (67:6). The poet appealed to the Lord to bless His people so that all the world would praise Him (67:2). In this way He could also display His kingship over the whole earth (67:4). The psalmist's desire was that everyone would come to recognize that life's blessings are from God and that therefore He should be glorified (67:7).

PSALM 68

   A. The Majesty of God (68:1–6)

   B. The Memory about God (68:7–14)

   C. The Mountain of God (68:15–18)

   D. The Mercies of God (68:19–27)

   E. The Mightiness of God (68:28–35)

The setting of this communal hymn of thanksgiving is unclear, though perhaps it describes the movement of the ark of the covenant into battle against the Ammonites (2 Sam. 10:6–8; 11:11). In any case the tone is decidedly militaristic with God in the role of the divine Warrior waging holy war. David portrayed Him as the triumphant One whose very presence causes His enemies to faint and fade away (Ps. 68:2). David then rehearsed God's leadership of Israel through the Sinai deserts, to the holy mountain, and beyond, even to the conquest of Canaan (68:12, 14). In light of all this, Bashan in Transjordania would be no obstacle at all to God's triumph. Since Ammon and its capital were in the area here epitomized as Bashan, there may be some support to the suggestion that David's Ammonite campaigns are in view.

Returning again to the Exodus and wilderness experience of Israel (68:22–23, 25; see Exod. 15:20), David expressed his confidence in what God would do on Israel's behalf. As the powerful One, His victories would be so impressive that the rulers of the earth would be forced to concede that He is Lord and thus would praise and worship Him (Ps. 68:30–31).

PSALM 69

A. The Psalmist's Distress (69:1–12)
B. The Psalmist's Desire (69:13–21)
C. The Psalmist's Denunciation (69:22–28)
D. The Psalmist's Deliverance (69:29–36)

This is a psalm of lament with heavy overtones of imprecation. One might also describe it as typically prophetic because of the many New Testament citations of it (compare Ps. 69:4 with John 15:25; Ps. 69:9a with John 2:17; Ps. 69:9b with Rom. 15:3; Ps. 69:21 with Matt. 27:34; and Ps. 69:25a with Acts 1:20). The likely setting is sometime in the decade when Saul was pursuing David in the desert. David complained that he was nearly overwhelmed by his threatening circumstances, troubles that had come because of his steadfast loyalty to the Lord (Ps. 69:7, 9). He was an object of ridicule by those whom he encountered publicly (69:12). He sensed that he was close to death (69:15) and that only divine intervention would save him (69:18). Human beings had offered no help, and in fact they only made his situation worse (69:21).

> Many people struggle with the idea of divine retribution against unrepentant sinners. But Jesus' appeal to forgive one's enemies must be balanced by His role of Avenger, the One who will judge those who remain in obstinate rebellion against Him (Rev. 19:11–16).

In response to all this, David uttered imprecations against those who had made his life so miserable (Ps. 69:22–28). This is not petty human vindictiveness, for in the context of David's suffering as a representative of the Lord (69:7, 9) David was eager to defend God's honor and reputation. He therefore denounced those who sinned so openly and grievously against God. In conclusion David was confident that the Lord would deliver him, and so he praised God for this and encouraged others to do so as well (69:34).

PSALM 70

    A. Rejection of the Wicked (70:1–3)

    B. Rejoicing of the Righteous (70:4–5)

This psalm of individual lament by David is similar to Psalm 40:14 except that the earlier psalm employs the name Yahweh. Here David prayed that the evil actions of his enemies would be brought to naught and conversely that those who love the Lord would glorify him for His beneficence (70:4).

PSALM 71

    A. Reflection on the Past (71:1–6)

    B. Request for the Present (71:7–12)

    C. Resolution for the Future (71:13–18)

    D. Restoration at the End (71:19–24)

An anonymous psalm of individual lament, this poem seems to have been composed later than Psalms 31 and 35, as its similarity to those psalms makes clear (compare 71:1–3 with 31:1–3; 71:13 with 35:4; and 71:15 with 35:28). Psalm 71 is the testimony of an old man who pondered God's goodness to him over the years but who also had ongoing needs in his golden years (71:9). Still threatened by those who would do him harm (71:13), he prayed that God would continue to preserve him (71:18), and promised to proclaim His name to all who would hear (71:16). Beyond this life there is still hope, he said, for God will vindicate the sufferings of this world with renewed life in the world to come (71:20).

PSALM 72

    A. Character of the King's Reign (72:1–4)

    B. Completeness of the King's Reign (72:5–8)

    C. Conquests in the King's Reign (72:9–11)

    D. Compassion of the King's Reign (72:12–15)

    E. Continuation of the King's Reign (72:16–17)

    F. Epilogue (72:18–19)

This is a royal psalm attributed to Solomon and composed, no doubt, on the occasion of some anniversary. Like the wisdom writings of Solomon, it is proverb-like, especially in its use of figures from the natural world (72:5-6, 16). Its wisdom character forms a fitting conclusion to Book II, which opens with a psalm exhibiting similar motifs (42:1, 6–7).

Psalm 72 is bold in its declaration of the king as the custodian of divine character and privilege (72:1; see also 2 Sam. 7:13–14). Through him the Lord will reign forever (Ps. 72:5) and universally (72:8). He will have dominion over Israel and the whole earth (72:11). Just as the Queen of Sheba had given gifts to Solomon (72:10; 1 Kings 10:1), so all earthly rulers will one day acknowledge the lordship of Israel's God. His reign will be compassionate (Ps. 72:12–15), and it will endure eternally as a regime in which the earth will enjoy unprecedented blessing and all nations will utter unparalleled praise (72:16–17). The psalm and Book II end with a doxology extolling the Lord's person and works.

BOOK III: PSALMS 73–89

PSALM 73

    A. The Envy of the Man of God (73:1–14)

    B. The Enlightenment of the Man of God (73:15–20)

    C. The Enjoyment of the Man of God (73:21–28)

Psalms 73–83 are all attributed to Asaph (as is Ps. 50), and they all refer to God as Elohim. Psalm 73 is a wisdom psalm whose sentiments are similar to those of Psalm 1. The psalmist admitted that in the midst of life's difficulties and dangers he had perceived that evil people seem exempt from such things (73:5). They arrogantly refuse to consider God (73:11), and they seem to be blessed in spite of such arrogance (73:12).

Having come to his senses, Asaph described his change of heart as almost a conversion. He began to understand that the prosperity of sinners is only a mirage and that they are headed for certain disaster (73:18). In reality the righteous are the ones who are blessed with divine insight and guidance (73:23–24). It is they who have hope in both heaven and earth (73:25). The righteous must therefore celebrate this hope and share it with others who need it (73:28).

PSALM 74

    A. Desperation of the Psalmist (74:1–3)
    B. Description of the Psalmist (74:4–8)
    C. Despair of the Psalmist (74:9–11)
    D. Demonstration by the Psalmist (74:12–17)
    E. Desire of the Psalmist (74:18–23)

This lament was composed by Asaph on behalf of the community. Because of its connections to the Book of Lamentations (compare Ps. 74:7 with Lam. 2:2; Ps. 74:4 with Lam. 2:7; and Ps. 74:9 with Lam. 2:9), many scholars view the destruction of the temple by the Babylonians as the likely setting for this psalm. However, this view is problematic since the psalm is ascribed to Asaph. Besides, it is quite possible that the author of Lamentations picked up terms and topics from Psalm 74. On the other hand, reference to Asaph may mean only that the psalm is in a collection instigated by Asaph and not necessarily that it was composed in all its parts by him.

The poet lamented God's abandonment of Israel, which seemed obvious in light of the temple itself (74:3, 7). In his despair he registered a profound pessimism (74:9), and yet, reflecting on the mighty acts of God in the past—particularly the Exodus—he awakened to the possibility of divine intervention and renewal (74:12, 15). On the basis of God's covenant promises (74:20), he pleaded that God would take vengeance on those who brought Israel so low (74:22).

PSALM 75

    A. The Warning of God (75:1–5)
    B. The Works of God (75:6–8)
    C. The Worship of God (75:9–10)

Sometimes described as a prophetic exhortation, this poem warns against proud self-dependence (75:4). God, the Judge of all the earth, will not countenance this spirit, and in fact He will force the wicked to drink the cup of their own making, a bitter wrath that comes from Him in response to sin (75:8). The thought of such perfect justice caused the psalmist to exult in the Lord, the Judge who rewards the righteous and condemns the wicked (75:10).

PSALM 76

    A. The Praise of God (76:1–3)

    B. The Punishment by God (76:4–6)

    C. The Pronouncement of God (76:7–9)

    D. The Predominance of God (76:10–12)

Like Psalms 46 and 48 this psalm too is a song of Zion. Perhaps this hymn was written in celebration of the defeat of Sennacherib in Hezekiah's time (2 Kings 19:35–36), though ascription to Asaph again makes this somewhat problematic (see comments on Ps. 74). In typical fashion the hymn begins with praise to God for His powerful intervention (76:3), specifically His overthrow of a threatening army (76:6). God Himself had announced His intentions beforehand (76:8). Amazingly, far from diminishing His glorious reputation, the hostile forces ended up praising God (76:10).

PSALM 77

    A. The Psalmist's Complaint (77:1–3)

    B. The Psalmist's Concern (77:4–9)

    C. The Psalmist's Conviction (77:10–15)

    D. The Psalmist's Comfort (77:16–20)

This psalm of communal lament may be a composite of the lament proper (77:1–15, 20) and a later insertion of four verses (77:16–19) of three lines each. The psalmist expressed his past and present fears and wondered if God indeed was willing and able to address those concerns (77:9). His uncertainty soon gave way to confidence, a conviction that what God had done in the past He was well able to do again (77:11, 14). In particular he recalled the Exodus, the grand event in Israel's history (77:15). At that time the whole earth trembled as the sea parted, and God's people experienced His miraculous deliverance (77:16–20).

PSALM 78

    A. The Covenant of the Lord (78:1–11)

    B. The Compassions of the Lord (78:12–29)

    C. The Condemnation of the Lord (78:30–37)

    D. The Cataclysms of the Lord (78:38–51)

    E. The Concern of the Lord (78:52–59)

    F. The Choice of the Lord (78:60–72)

This magnificent psalm contains all the significant moments of Israel's history with appropriate theological commentary. Asaph began with an appeal to his audience to reflect on the past, particularly on the occasion of the giving of the Sinai Covenant (78:5). Sadly, the tribes did not go long before breaking its stipulations (78:10). This happened despite God's power and grace in delivering them from Egypt through the Exodus and providing for them in the wilderness (78:13, 15–16). The more He did for them, the more they rebelled (78:19). The miraculous supply of water, manna, and quails filled their stomachs but did little to fill them with gratitude (78:22).

At length the patience of the Lord was spent, and He poured out His wrath on those sinners (78:31). Though they supposedly repented, it was only a hypocritical turning back to God (78:35–36). It seems they had completely forgotten the slavery of Egypt and the plagues with which the Lord had demoralized Pharaoh until at last Israel was permitted to leave (78:42). All the while the Lord had tolerated Israel's lack of faith and disobedience for He knew full well how frail and mortal its people were (78:38–39).

The rebellion did not cease with the conquest of Canaan, for though the Lord had dispossessed the people of the land, the tribes of Israel persisted in their wickedness, this time going so far as to embrace pagan idolatry (78:58). After many generations of this waywardness, God permitted the Shiloh sanctuary to be removed and the ark delivered over to the Philistines (78:60–61; 1 Sam. 4:11, 17). But Israel's godlessness continued unabated until only Judah was left (Ps. 78:68) with David and his descendants as God's agents of earthly rule (78:70). At long last stability and righteousness prevailed, with this situation clearly in place at the time of the composition of the psalm (78:72).

PSALM 79

    A. Ruin by the Nations (79:1–4)

    B. Revenge on the Nations (79:5–8)

    C. Rejoicing over the Nations (79:9–13)

This communal lament shows clear connections to Psalm 74. Its setting is unmistakably the destruction of the temple in 586 B.C. by the Babylonians. Its being attributed to Asaph must therefore be taken in the sense of its being part of an Asaph collection. Jerusalem lay in ruins (79:1), a situation that the poet felt should surely elicit divine retribution on Babylon (79:5). And in light of the special relationship between Israel and the Lord (79:10), God owed it to His own reputation, if nothing else, to vindicate His people by forgiving and restoring them (79:9, 13).

PSALM 80

A. Approach to God (80:1–3)
B. Anger of God (80:4–7)
C. Appeal to God (80:8–19)

The last verse of the preceding psalm and the first of this one share so much in common that it is safe to say that their juxtaposition is deliberate. Both also are communal laments. The psalmist here appealed to God as Israel's shepherd whose powerful arm is needed in moments of crisis (80:3). God had allowed enemies to come as an expression of His anger against His people (80:4) but now, said the poet, He must respond to their repentance. Besides, He had brought Israel out of Egypt and had planted her like a vine in the Promised Land (80:8). How could He now abandon her in her ruinous state? He must come and empower the king (the man of his right hand, 80:17) to lead the nation once more to victory (80:19). Meanwhile the poet promised that the people would not repeat their waywardness but would call on Him as their God (80:18).

PSALM 81

A. Call for Celebration (81:1–5)
B. Cause for Celebration (81:6–10)
C. Condition for Celebration (81:11–16)

This song of exhortation (see also Pss. 14, 50, 52, 53, 75) gives evidence of belonging to Psalms 77 and 78 as a unit. It celebrates a new moon festival, probably on the first day of Tishri, the seventh month, also known as Rosh Hashanah or New Year's Day (81:3; see Lev. 23:24). The psalmist appealed to the people to observe the festival because of God's faithfulness in the past in delivering Israel from Egypt (Ps. 81:6) and providing for her in the wilderness (81:7). Israel had rebelled against the Lord, however, and even in the psalmist's day she had continued to do so (81:13). If the people would repent, the Lord would forgive and enable them to prevail over their enemies (81:14).

PSALM 82

   A. Command from God (82:1–4)
   B. Condemnation by God (82:5–7)
   C. Call to God (82:8)

This communal lament takes the form of a legal setting in which the Lord called to account the leaders of Israel with whom He was greatly displeased. These were judges and other public officials (82:2) who had betrayed their important positions through bribery and other inducements. Having commanded them to amend their ways (82:3–4), God questioned whether they would do so because of their blind insensitivity (82:5). The Lord had gone so far as to call them "gods" (that is, "mighty ones"; 82:1, 6), an idea Jesus cited when accused of claiming deity for Himself (John 10:34). If mere men of the Old Testament could be called gods, why was it wrong for the very Son of God to consider Himself as such?

PSALM 83

   A. The Counsel of the Enemy (83:1–4)
   B. The Covenant of the Enemy (83:5–8)
   C. The Condemnation of the Enemy (83:9–12)
   D. The Confusion of the Enemy (83:13–16)
   E. The Confounding of the Enemy (83:17–18)

The last of Asaph's psalms, this one is also a communal lament. Internal evidence suggests that it arose from Jehoshaphat's conflict with Edom and its allies (83:6–8; see 2 Chron. 20:1–30), though, of course, this cannot be proved. Israel's (Judah's) enemies had conspired to destroy her

PSALMS: HUMAN RESPONSE TO DIVINE PRESENCE

(Ps. 83:4), even entering into a formal alliance to do so. Appealing to history, the poet cried out to the Lord to deal with these foes just as He did in the days of Deborah (83:9–10; see Judg. 4–5) and Gideon (Ps. 83:11–12; see Judg. 7–8). As He had defeated and decimated the Canaanites and Midianites centuries earlier, Asaph wanted God to overwhelm those in his own day who were bent on harming the Lord's chosen ones (Ps. 83:13–16). By this means they would come to know that God alone is Lord over the whole earth (83:18).

PSALM 84

    A. Desire for God's House (84:1–4)
    B. Directions to God's House (84:5–8)
    C. Dedication to God's House (84:9–12)

> *Some Christians seem to lack any concern about regular and consistent corporate worship. This "hit-or-miss" attitude runs up against the solid wall of truth conveyed by Psalm 84. True faith finds expression not only in private meditation but also in public convocation as part of the body of Jesus Christ.*

This song of Zion, a song of pilgrimage, is associated with the sons of Korah (see also Pss. 42 and 43) whose duties included being gatekeepers of the temple (1 Chron. 26:1, 12–19). The psalm expresses special concern for David as the anointed one of the Lord (Ps. 84:9). The author also revealed his intense longing for God's house, his desire, perhaps, to be there even when off duty as a porter (84:10). The author of Hebrews captured this idea when he urged Christians to be faithful in assembling for worship (Heb. 10:25). The psalmist added that the impulse for worship ought to be so strong as to overcome any obstacle that might stand in the way of the pilgrim on his way to the temple (Ps. 84:7). God was there, and to worship Him there was the height of all joy and blessing (84:10).

PSALM 85

    A. Restoration from the Lord (85:1–3)
    B. Request of the Lord (85:4–7)
    C. Redemption through the Lord (85:8–10)
    D. Righteousness with the Lord (85:11–13)

A communal lament, this appeal to the Lord seems to have arisen out of the bleak circumstances of the Babylonian exile. The author was confident that God had forgiven Israel's sins (85:2), but now he implored the Lord to restore His people (85:6). Only He could bring full reconciliation to the people and return to the land the glory that had long since departed (85:9; see Ezek. 11:22–25). Once that had taken place, the psalmist was confident that his people would once more enjoy the benefits for which they were created and called (Ps. 85:11–13).

PSALM 86

    A. Request of the Lord (86:1–5)
    B. Recognition of the Lord (86:6–13)
    C. Relationship to the Lord (86:14–17)

This individual lament attributed to David reflects some trial in his life that threatened to undo him, though he described it so generally as to make it impossible to isolate any particular event. This fact makes this psalm and many others pertinent to believers of any generation. David believed that God could and would deliver him because he understood God's nature (86:5). He alone is God (86:8), and therefore only He is worthy of praise (86:12). Because David was God's servant, he had special claim on God's mercy and grace which, when bestowed on him, would put to shame those who sought to do him evil (86:17).

PSALM 87

    A. Glory of Zion (87:1–4)
    B. Grace to Zion (87:5–7)

This brief song of Zion by the sons of Korah was apparently written after some occasion when Jerusalem was delivered by divine intervention. It speaks of the centrality of the holy city and of the privilege of those fortunate enough to have been born there (87:5). In the future that will continue to be an evidence of grace, so that when the final records are kept it will be especially noted who was native to Zion and who was not (87:5–6).

PSALM 88

    A. Despair of the Psalmist (88:1–7)

    B. Desolation of the Psalmist (88:8–12)

    C. Distress of the Psalmist (88:13–18)

Attributed to Heman the Ezrahite, perhaps the same as the wise man compared to Solomon (1 Kings 4:31), this individual lament depicts its author as one who is as good as dead (Ps. 88:4), lying already it seems in the depths of the earth (88:6). Like Job, he seemed all alone, cut off from family and friend (88:8; see Job 19:13, 19). If he died, his desolation would be all the worse, for in death even God is absent—or so the psalmist feared (Ps. 88:11). Again like Job, he lamented God's refusal to reveal Himself (88:14; see Job 13:24), concluding in most pessimistic terms that his case was hopeless (Ps. 88:16).

PSALM 89

    A. The Covenant of the Lord (89:1–4)

    B. The Conquests of the Lord (89:5–18)

    C. The Constancy of the Lord (89:19–37)

    D. The Chastisement of the Lord (89:38–45)

    E. The Concealment of the Lord (89:46–51)

    F. Postlude (89:52)

This royal psalm by Ethan the Ezrahite (see 1 Kings 4:31) focuses on David as the servant of the Lord whose messianic descendants—culminating in One who will reign forever—represent the rule of the Lord on the earth. In an affirmation of the promises initially made to David himself, the psalmist declared that God's covenant with David is unconditional and everlasting (Ps. 89:3–4; see also 2 Sam. 7:16; Isa. 9:7). Its guarantee lies in God's faithfulness to Israel in the past, in His triumph over Egypt and the

Red Sea (Ps. 89:10), and in His dominion over all His creation (89:11–12). His choice of David (89:20) assured the psalmist that God would never forsake King David (89:24). Indeed, God will exalt him to the highest position, one so eminent that David would be able in a unique way to call God "Father" (89:26). But such blessings would not be exhausted in David, for his royal descendants would also inherit the covenant promises (89:29). Even if they sinned, the Lord would punish, of course, but He would never go back on His word to David (89:35).

Then, in a sudden change of mood, the author lamented a tragedy that had occurred, one so severe as to call into question the faithfulness of the Lord to His covenant pledge (89:39). Possibly the tragedy was the invasion and pillaging of Jerusalem by Shishak of Egypt in the days of Rehoboam, David's grandson (1 Kings 14:25–28), though this is only a guess. In any case the king had been humiliated and his glory tarnished (Ps. 89:44–45). God seemed to have hidden Himself, and so naturally there was a theological conundrum: How could the Lord's unconditional promise of an eternal Davidic dynasty be reconciled to the reality of its imminent danger of collapse? Unable to offer a satisfactory response, the psalmist could only appeal to God, who is altogether reliable (89:52).

BOOK IV: PSALMS 90–106

The next major section of the book of Psalms opens with a psalm attributed to Moses, and it closes with a psalm in which Moses is the dominant figure (Ps. 106). The two thus envelope the collection, the major elements of which are hymnic praises to God, particularly addressing His kingship (Pss. 93, 96–99).

PSALM 90

    A. Eternality of God (90:1–4)

    B. Examination by God (90:5–8)

    C. Entreaty of God (90:9–12)

    D. Expectation through God (90:13–17)

In this communal lament Moses extolled the attributes of God (90:2, 14,

16, 17), but he also rehearsed his own sins and those of his people which brought on them God's severe displeasure. The eternal God, he said, exists in strict contradiction to the mortality of humankind (90:2; see also 90:5–6). Yet He is aware of and concerned about their sins (90:8). Moses therefore pleaded that the chasm between the infinite God and a sinful humanity might be bridged by God's gentle instruction (90:12) and forgiveness (90:13). Once done, this would bring untold satisfaction to God's children and would redound to His great glory (90:16).

PSALM 91

    A. Speaker One (91:1)
    B. Speaker Two (91:2)
    C. Speaker One (91:3–8)
    D. Speaker Two (91:9a)
    E. Speaker One (91:9b–13)
    F. Speaker Three: the Lord (91:14–16)

This wisdom psalm may be seen as two speakers interacting antiphonally with a third speaker, the Lord, providing a fitting resolution. The interchange opens with an assurance of security for those who abide in the Lord (91:1), followed by a response in which the speaker agreed to put his trust in Him (91:2). The first speaker then added many more promises concerning God's care, especially in the face of danger from hostile forces (91:3–8). The second speaker concurred by addressing the Lord once more as his refuge (91:9a; see 91:2). The first speaker continued to add assurances, this time suggesting that God's angels are instruments of protection to the righteous (91:11–12). Then the Lord Himself capped the discussion with His own personal affirmation of what the first speaker had said (91:14–16).

PSALM 92

    A. Propriety of Worship (92:1–3)
    B. Praise for God's Works (92:4–6)
    C. Punishment of the Wicked (92:7–9)

    D. Prosperity of the Righteous (92:10–12)

    E. Perpetuity of the Righteous (92:13–15)

This individual song of thanksgiving was written, according to the title, to accompany the Sabbath celebration. The psalmist noted that worship is a good thing (92:1), if only for the magnificent works that God has done (92:4). The overthrow of the Lord's enemies is also an occasion for praise (92:9). Most of all, His goodness toward the righteous ought to elicit heartfelt thanksgiving from them (92:12, 15).

PSALM 93

    A. The Majesty of the Lord (93:1–2)

    B. The Mightiness of the Lord (93:3–5)

This psalm celebrates the Lord's kingship, one of several that do the same (Pss. 47, 96–99). He deserves acclaim for the splendor of His person (93:1) and His everlasting existence (93:2). He also reigns because of His transcendent power, an attribute to which all nature bears witness (93:5).

PSALM 94

    A. Request to the Lord (94:1–7)

    B. Retribution of the Lord (94:8–15)

    C. Refuge in the Lord (94:16–23)

In this communal lament the anonymous psalmist pleaded to God as a Judge and Avenger to bring the wicked to account (94:3). Addressing such sinners, he reminded them of God's omniscience (94:9), fairness (94:10), and desire to correct them (94:12) so that they might repent and begin to enjoy God's blessing (94:15). Turning to his own concerns, the poet acknowledged God's protective grace toward him (94:17). Evil ones had risen up against him, but God had been a fortress in which he had found security (94:22).

PSALM 95

    A. Praise of the Lord (95:1–2)

    B. Power of the Lord (95:3–7b)

    C. Punishment of the Lord (95:7c–11)

A psalm of exhortation, this one invites the reader to praise God (95:1–2) because of His dominion over all people and things, especially His chosen ones (95:3, 7b). Those who fail to acknowledge His lordship will, like their ancestors in the wilderness, perish and be unable to enter the rest God has prepared for the obedient (95:11; see Num. 14:23, 28–30; Heb. 3:7–11, 15).

PSALM 96

    A. The Song of Yahweh (96:1–3)
    B. The Strength of Yahweh (96:4–6)
    C. The Service of Yahweh (96:7–9)
    D. The Sovereignty of Yahweh (96:10–13)

This is another of the psalms that celebrates the Lord's kingship. The author urged God's people to sing a new song to Him, one that proclaims His glory to all the earth (96:3). It is right to do so because He alone is God (96:5). A proper response ought to consist of sacrificial offerings and abject humiliation before Him (96:8–9). Along with God's reigning is His ultimate judgment. At last the skewed sense of right and wrong in this world will be corrected, and true and righteous government will prevail (96:13).

PSALM 97

    A. Description of Yahweh (97:1–3)
    B. Deeds of Yahweh (97:4–5)
    C. Demonstration of Yahweh (97:6)
    D. Deference to Yahweh (97:7–9)
    E. Deliverance by Yahweh (97:10–12)

This song of Yahweh's kingship, defined further by some scholars as an enthronement psalm, describes Him as the holy, transcendent One (97:3), who manifested Himself that way in the past, particularly at Sinai (97:4–5). The whole universe continues to attest to these things (97:6), so it is only appropriate that everyone in it bow down before His majesty (97:7). He will preserve the righteous—those who already recognize Him as Lord—from all evil and harm (97:10).

PSALM 98

    A. The Salvation of the Lord (98:1–3)

    B. The Song of the Lord (98:4–6)

    C. The Sovereignty of the Lord (98:7–9)

In this psalm of the Lord's kingship, the poet first drew attention to God's deliverance of His people based on His covenant with them, which expressed His love and faithfulness (98:3). Such grace elicited praise in vocal and instrumental music (98:6). In fact, all nature bursts out in song in anticipation of His glorious coming to usher in universal righteousness (98:7, 9).

PSALM 99

    A. He Who Is to Come (99:1–3)

    B. He Who Is (99:4–6)

    C. He Who Was (99:7–9)

The last of the five psalms of the Lord's kingship, this one is divided into thirds by the thrice-repeated statement that God is holy (99:3, 5, 9; see also Isa. 6:3). Each part views Yahweh's sovereignty from a different chronological aspect. He will assert universal dominion in time to come as He already does, though then especially in and through Israel (Ps. 99:4). All this is predicated on history, on God's revelation of His power and glory at Sinai, and in subsequent experiences of His people (99:6).

PSALM 100

    A. The Greatness of the Lord (100:1–3)

    B. The Goodness of the Lord (100:4–5)

A favorite hymn of Israel and the church, this psalm may have originated when thank offerings were presented at the temple. It urges God's people to worship Him because He is their God and they are His people. Beyond that, He has poured out His goodness on them, and they should at least reciprocate by presenting thank offerings to Him (100:4).

PSALM 101

    A. David's Praise (101:1)

    B. David's Promise (101:2)

    C. David's Purity (101:3–4)

    D. David's Protection (101:5–6)

    E. David's Purging (101:7–8)

This is usually described as a royal psalm, one with a heavy autobiographical flavor. David first offered praise to God, then committed himself to live an upright life before Him (101:2). David said he would avoid anything that might cause him to stumble, including people whose own lifestyles are incompatible with God's standards (101:5). Rather, he would count among his associates those who also are upright (101:6). The impure, in fact, could not serve David as king and would be removed from Jerusalem, "the city of the LORD" (101:8).

PSALM 102

    A. The Psalmist's Plight (102:1–11)

    B. The Psalmist's Prospect (102:12–22)

    C. The Psalmist's Promise (102:23–28)

This is clearly a psalm of individual lament, as the title suggests, one in which the anonymous sufferer gropes for words adequate to describe his miserable condition. Like Job, his speech is filled with simile, metaphor, and hyperbole, for ordinary language could not plumb the depths of his despair (compare 102:3, with Job 30:30; Ps. 102:4 with Job 33:20; Ps. 102:5 with Job 19:20; and Ps. 102:10 with Job 27:21). The situation that called forth such grief was probably the Babylonian exile, for Zion was in ruins and was in desperate need of rebuilding (Ps. 102:13–14). Only God could do this, and so the psalmist hoped for a day when God would hear the prayers of His saints and would release them from their physical and spiritual bondage (102:17, 20). Then they could resume their worship and praise of the Lord in Jerusalem (102:21–22). The author of the poem believed that this would happen, for the Creator of all things—He who lives forever (102:27)—will be faithful to carry to fruition all He has begun.

PSALM 103

    A. The Favors of the Lord (103:1–5)

    B. The Fairness of the Lord (103:6–10)

    C. The Forgiveness of the Lord (103:11–14)

    D. The Faithfulness of the Lord (103:15–18)

    E. The Finality of the Lord (103:19–22)

This great Davidic hymn blesses God for who He is and for all the blessings He has bestowed on David. Having been forgiven and redeemed, David felt like a new man (103:5). Throughout Israel's history God was just in all His ways, and because of His mercy He had not poured out the wrath they deserved (103:10). He, the Creator, understands human mortality (103:14). He recognizes the temporal nature of human existence but offsets it with His covenant loyalty to those who keep its terms (103:15–18). David proclaimed the heavenly and eternal nature of Yahweh's sovereignty (103:19), a state of affairs that should elicit praise from all creatures everywhere (103:22).

PSALM 104

    A. The Preeminence of God (104:1–4)

    B. The Power of God (104:5–9)

    C. The Provision of God (104:10–15)

    D. The Protection of God (104:16–18)

    E. The Planning of God (104:19–23)

    F. The Providence of God (104:24–30)

    G. The Praise of God (104:31–35)

This hymn celebrates God as Creator and serves in a general sense as a theological commentary on Genesis 1:1–2:3. The unknown author affirmed that God is utterly transcendent, visible only in the glory of light and clouds. He established the earth in the watery depths and then caused the waters to part so that dry land could appear (Ps. 104:6–7). He then provided springs and rainfall to water the earth, thus allowing for plant life necessary for the survival of animals and humans (104:14). In addition he prepared secure dwelling places for otherwise defenseless creatures (104:16–18). He also regulated times and seasons by the unending alternation of day and night (104:19). He stocked the land and sea with vast riches to which people are entitled to help themselves (104:28). But if He were to withdraw His gracious hand, all these things would cease and humanity would perish (104:29). Such a demonstration of power and goodness in nature left the psalmist with awestruck praise of the God who brought it all to pass (104:33).

PSALM 105

A. Introduction (105:1–6)
B. The Promise of the Lord (105:7–11)
C. The Protection of the Lord (105:12–15)
D. The Provision of the Lord (105:16–24)
E. The Power of the Lord (105:25–38)
F. The Possessions of the Lord (105:39–45)

A résumé of sacred history (see also Ps. 78), this theological interpretation of Israel's past is also one of four psalms that begin with a note of thanksgiving (see also Pss. 107, 118, 136). After a prelude exhorting all of God's glorious works in general to praise Him, the psalmist commenced his review by harking back to God's covenants with the patriarchs and Moses (105:9–10). God had promised them the land of Canaan, but even before the patriarchs could inherit it themselves they became the touchstone by which blessing was granted to or withheld from the pagans around them (105:14).

> The great events of God's redemptive grace cannot be fully understood apart from their historical context. For this reason alone it is important that they be recalled and recited regularly. Even Christians of a "noncreedal" tradition cannot afford to forget what God has done in history to bring about His magnificent plan of salvation.

The time came when Israel was forced to flee to Egypt for survival, and there God made them a great nation (105:23). The onslaught of Egyptian oppression next led to the Exodus deliverance (105:37). Israel then found herself in the harsh and merciless deserts of Sinai, but God found her even there and brought her safely through. At last He led them into Canaan and gave them that land as an arena where He might work out His gracious purposes for them (105:45). All this was done in fulfillment of the covenant pledges God had made to Abraham and his descendants (105:42).

PSALM 106

    A. Prelude (106:1–5)

    B. Redemption of the Lord (106:6–12)

    C. Rejection of the Lord (106:13–23)

    D. Rebellion against the Lord (106:24–33)

    E. Retribution by the Lord (106:34–43)

    F. Restoration through the Lord (106:44–46)

    G. Postlude (106:47–48)

Book IV ends with a communal lament just as it had begun in Psalm 90. This psalm is also the first in a series of "Hallel" (or Hallelujah) psalms, because they begin with this Hebrew word (as do Pss. 111–113, 117, 135, 146–150). The setting of this psalm seems to be the Babylonian exile (106:47). The combination of praise ("hallel") and lament is not unusual or paradoxical because psalms of this type always see a ray of hope in the Lord in the darkest of circumstances.

This is precisely the note on which the psalm begins (106:1, 5). It then proceeds to recount God's deliverance of His people in the Exodus even though they were undeserving (106:8). True to form, however, as soon as the crisis was over, they forgot the Lord, once again jeopardizing their standing as the elect nation (106:21, 23). Only Moses' intercession prevented the Lord from writing them off, but even this reprieve was only temporary. Again Israel commenced a pattern of rebellion and unbelief, a spirit that once more brought them to the brink of disaster (106:29). This time Phinehas and the Levites stood between Israel and the Lord and averted the judgment that should have fallen (106:30).

Things were no better in the eight hundred years of Israel's history in the Promised Land. The Israelites joined their Canaanite neighbors in idolatry (106:37–38), and as soon as the Lord punished and then rescued them they would take up these wicked practices again (106:43). Only the Lord's covenant commitment to them kept them from being eradicated (106:45). Now, in the most serious crisis yet—exile far from their homeland—the psalmist spoke on behalf of the community, imploring the Lord to end the captivity and allow them to return to their homes (106:47). His confidence that this will happen is reflected in the concluding doxology (106:48).

BOOK V: PSALMS 107–150

PSALM 107

    A. Introduction (107:1–3)
    B. Satisfaction in the Lord (107:4–9)
    C. Salvation through the Lord (107:10–16)
    D. Sacrifices to the Lord (107:17–22)
    E. Sovereignty of the Lord (107:23–32)
    F. Sustenance by the Lord (107:33–38)
    G. Support through the Lord (107:39–43)

This is a thanksgiving psalm (see also Ps. 105) by an individual who also was apparently writing in the exilic or postexilic period (107:3, 35). Speaking as a redeemed one (107:2), he rehearsed the wonderful preservation of post-Exodus Israel as analogous to his own experience (107:4, 8). He and his contemporaries had sinned and suffered the consequences (107:11–12), but God had now saved them, releasing them from Babylonian prison, as it were (107:16; see also Isa. 45:1–2). Such redemptive grace is more than adequate cause for praise (Ps. 107:21).

Beyond the immediate circumstance stands the Lord's sovereign majesty. In fact, it is precisely because He is the God of creation and nature that He is able to restore His chosen people (107:31). He manages the environment in which humans live and prosper (107:33–35), and thus He can meet the needs of each one. Those in most need of help—individuals who, like himself, are in the throes of affliction—find in such a great God all they need and can ever want (107:41).

PSALM 108

    A. Exaltation of the Lord (108:1–5)

    B. Exultation in the Lord (108:6–13)

This communal lament is a composite drawn from two others (compare Ps. 108:1–5, with 57:7–11; and 108:6–13 with 60:5–12). Why David combined these verses here in this psalm is not clear, but since he was the author of the other two psalms as well as this, one must conclude that apparently he felt the need to combine them in a new context. He praised God in the first part (108:1–5), and on the basis of this understanding of God, he spoke of the Lord's rule over Israel and all its neighbors. Clearly anticipating some kind of military encounter (108:13), David found comfort in the Lord of hosts, the One who leads the armies of heaven (108:11).

PSALM 109

    A. Rejection of the Psalmist (109:1–5)

    B. Response of the Psalmist (109:6–10)

    C. Request by the Psalmist (109:11–15)

    D. Reasoning of the Psalmist (109:16–20)

    E. Reproach of the Psalmist (109:21–25)

    F. Rejoicing of the Psalmist (109:26–31)

This psalm, an individual lament, shares sentiments, themes, and even wording with Psalm 69. The imprecations may be directed to Doeg, or Cush the Benjamite, or someone else associated with Saul's persecution of David (see 1 Sam. 22:11–19 and the title of Ps. 7). David began with a complaint about these adversaries who, he said, had repaid his good with evil (Ps. 109:5). They therefore deserved God's punishment. David urged the Lord to see to it that such sinners lose all that is near and dear, including their own lives (109:15). Grounds for this are the evil things such sinners have done toward others (109:16). Because of all David had suffered at the hands of others, he prayed that the Lord would extend special favor to him (109:21). When this was done, then others would recognize it as blessing from God (109:27). The wicked would become chagrined at what God can do in vindicating the cause of the righteous (109:29).

PSALM 110

    A. Messiah the King (110:1–2)

    B. Messiah the Priest (110:3–4)

    C. Messiah the Judge (110:5–7)

This royal psalm was one of the favorites of the early church because of its obvious messianic implications (Matt. 22:41–45; Acts 2:34–36; 1 Cor. 15:25–27; Heb. 1:13; 5:6, 10; 7:17, 21). While recognizing his own role as a messianic figure, David went far beyond anything that could possibly be attributed to him to speak of a coming figure who would be no less than divine. The New Testament identifies this One as Jesus Christ. David viewed Him as a triumphant Ruler sitting at God's right hand (Ps. 110:1) and also as a priest like Melchizedek, that is, non-Aaronic and interceding forever (110:4; see Heb. 6:20; 7:11–17). Also He will be Judge of all the nations, a role suitable for only God Himself (Ps. 110:6).

PSALM 111

    A. Prelude (111:1)

    B. The Greatness of God's Works (111:2)

    C. The Glory of God's Works (111:3–4)

    D. The Grace of God's Works (111:5–9)

    E. Postlude (111:10)

This is a Hallel hymn (see Ps. 106) created in an acrostic pattern in which each line begins with a letter of the Hebrew alphabet in sequence. The poet opened and closed the psalm with a reference to praise (111:1, 10), and in between he said the reason for his praise was God's mighty works. His works honor Him as Lord, and they provide everything needed for human life and happiness. Most marvelous of all, they flow from grace, the fruit of the covenant that He initiated with His people (111:5, 9).

PSALM 112

    A. The Blessings of the God-Fearer (112:1–4)

    B. The Benefits of the People-Lover (112:5–9)

    C. The Banishment of the Wicked (112:10)

Another acrostic, this poem is usually considered a wisdom psalm. The psalmist here connected blessing to covenant obedience (112:1), which involved not only worship of the Lord but also attention to the needs of those around him who were suffering deprivation and persecution (112:8–9). Such adherence to righteousness would have the effect of disheartening and even destroying the wicked who look on it (112:10).

PSALM 113

    A. Praise to the Lord (113:1–3)
    B. Position of the Lord (113:4–6)
    C. Prosperity through the Lord (113:7–9)

This Hallel psalm is connected to the Passover festival in Jewish tradition. It also draws language from the Song of Hannah (compare Ps. 113:7 with 1 Sam. 2:8; and Ps. 113:9 with 1 Sam. 2:5), and in turn the psalm is quoted by Mary in the Magnificat (Luke 1:46–55). After an exhortation to praise the Lord, the psalmist exalted Him to a place of glory above all other things (Ps. 113:4). But that same transcendent God, he wrote, is attentive to the lowliest and most needy of humanity, doing for them what they are powerless to do by themselves (113:7–9).

PSALM 114

    A. The Power of the Lord (114:1–4)
    B. The Presence of the Lord (114:5–8)

Sung on the eighth day of Passover week, this hymn reviews the history of the Exodus and the Conquest in terms that are almost taunting or teasing. Addressing the Red Sea, the Jordan River, and the mountains, the psalmist asked why they so easily yielded to the coming of the Lord in triumph.

PSALM 115

    A. The Sanctification of God (115:1–2)
    B. The Superiority of God (115:3–8)
    C. The Salvation of God (115:9–14)
    D. The Sovereignty of God (115:15–18)

This is generally identified as a communal psalm of confidence. The Septuagint, Vulgate, and other versions join it to Psalm 114, thus making it one long composition, which they number as Psalm 113. The subject matter of 114 and 115 is so different, however, that this combination seems unlikely.

The theme of this psalm is the vanity of idols and, conversely, the uniqueness and superiority of the Lord. The answer to pagan inquiries about the location of Israel's God is that He is in heaven (115:3). The idols on earth are earthly, impotent, lifeless, unreal. This being so, only the Lord should be trusted. He has proved Himself in the past (115:9–11) and is dependable for the future (115:12–14). For all these evidences of His sovereign power and grace, He is to be praised forever (115:18).

PSALM 116

A. Supplication to the Lord (116:1–4)
B. Salvation of the Lord (116:5–9)
C. Surrender to the Lord (116:10–14)
D. Sacrifice to the Lord (116:15–19)

This individual song of thanksgiving is divided in the Septuagint into two parts (vv. 1–9 and 10–19), forming Psalms 114 and 115 in that collection. Again, no clear reason exists for this partition, for the psalm makes good sense as a unified piece. After praising God for having delivered him from death (116:3), the unknown author generalized the truth that the Lord is a Savior, one whose grace should be repaid by obedient response (116:6, 9). This includes proper worship and fulfillment of any vows one makes to the Lord (116:14). Because God has not taken him in death— though that may be a precious thing in some respects (116:15)—the psalmist knew that God had spared him in order that he might praise Him in the land of the living (116:18).

PSALM 117

This brief hymn, the shortest chapter in the Bible, is an appeal to all the nations to recognize Yahweh as God and to praise him forever.

PSALM 118

A. Beginning the Procession (118:1–4)
B. Along the Way (118:5–18)
C. Entrance to the Temple (118:19)
D. Greeting the Procession (118:20–27)
E. Response of the Arrivals (118:28)
F. Common Doxology (118:29)

This psalm is presumably a psalm of communal thanksgiving in which the text was sung as Israelites proceeded to the temple. After an opening appeal to the covenant faithfulness of God (118:1; repeated at the end, 118:29), the poet described the obstacles and handicaps that must be overcome as one makes a pilgrimage to the temple (118:5–12). But God is always faithful to those who seek Him, and He will assist them in their pursuit (118:13–14). Arriving at the temple gate, the worshiper requested entrance (118:19). Those who opened to him extolled the name of the Lord (118:20–21) and expressed their praise that the place and occasion are indeed proper to the worship of God (118:22–26). The pilgrim added his assent (118:28), and he and all the others combined their voices in a final doxology (118:29).

PSALM 119

The acrostic structure and common theme of this lengthy wisdom psalm make it difficult to outline. It consists of twenty-two sections of eight verses each, with each verse in each section commencing with the same Hebrew letter and the eight-verse sections proceeding in the order of the Hebrew alphabet. The Word of God is alluded to in almost every one of the 176 verses by the words "law," "statutes," "ways," "precepts," "decrees," "commands," "word," and "promise." The lesson to be learned above all others is that knowledge and practical application of the Word will keep one from sin and thus enable him to know and serve God appropriately (119:9, 11, 92, 98, 105, 130, 133, 176). Of interest too are the many responses the psalmist expressed in response to the Word: to love, meditate on, hope in, obey, remember, delight in, and proclaim.

The Word of God is mentioned in all but three of the 176 verses of Psalm 119. The message is clear: God has revealed Himself in Scripture, and only in that revelation can one find forgiveness, life, and meaning.

PSALM 120

    A. Prayer of the Psalmist (120:1–4)

    B. Peril of the Psalmist (120:5–7)

This is an individual lament, the first of fifteen Songs of Ascent (Pss. 120–134). They bear this designation either because they were sung at various stages on the way to the temple heights at Jerusalem, or because they ascend to a theological or logical climax. Perhaps they find their setting in the thrice-annual festivals required of all adult Israelite males (Deut. 16:16). In this first of the series, the psalmist confessed his tendency to sin and asked divine power in overcoming it. He blamed his condition partly on his environment, living as he did among the ungodly (120:7).

PSALM 121

    A. The Power of the Lord (121:1–4)

    B. The Protection of the Lord (121:5–8)

A psalm of individual confidence, this favorite recognizes that help comes not from nature (121:1) but from the living God (121:2). He, the ever-vigilant One, keeps constant watch over His own (121:3–4), protecting them day and night (121:6) and in every activity of life (121:8).

PSALM 122

    A. Position of Jerusalem (122:1–3)

    B. Procession to Jerusalem (122:4–5)

    C. Peace of Jerusalem (122:6–9)

A song of Zion (see also Pss. 46 and 48), this psalm of ascent focuses on

Jerusalem as the pilgrim's destination. His heart is filled with joy at the very prospect of entering her gates (122:2). By divine choice this was the earthly setting of God's dwelling, symbolized by David's residence there (122:5; 2 Chron. 3:1). As long as it experienced peace, its people would also enjoy peace (Ps. 122:6). The appeal then was for prayer that the city would long enjoy the protection and blessing of the Lord.

PSALM 123

    A. Contemplation of the Psalmist (123:1–2)

    B. Contempt toward the Psalmist (123:3–4)

In this communal lament the psalmist asked the Lord to look with pity on His servant people. They were in some unnamed distress, the objects of contempt and vilification. They needed the Lord to show mercy by reversing their circumstances.

PSALM 124

    A. Peril of the Psalmist (124:1–5)

    B. Praise of the Psalmist (124:6–8)

The last of the psalms of communal thanksgiving (see Pss. 65–68, 118), this may be a response to the immediately preceding lament. David asserted that if the Lord had not intervened in a time of crisis, the nation would have drowned in a metaphorical flood (124:4–5). But He did intervene, and so David praised Him, the Maker of heaven and earth (124:8).

PSALM 125

    A. Presence of the Lord (125:1–2)

    B. Protection of the Lord (125:3)

    C. Preservation of the Lord (125:4–5)

This is a song of communal confidence in the Lord, evidenced by its reference to the temple and Jerusalem. It speaks of God's presence in relation to Jerusalem's security, hedged in as it is by surrounding hills (125:2). So long as the righteous trust the Lord, they too can be secure (125:3). To ensure that, the psalmist prays that God would bless the upright but also punish the wicked (125:4–5).

PSALM 126

    A. Joy at Restoration (126:1–3)

    B. Joy at Reaping (126:4–6)

This postexilic psalm of communal lament seems to reflect the discouragement of the Jews who had returned from captivity (126:1) to find their homeland in ruins and difficult to rebuild (see Ezra 3:12–13; Neh. 1:3; 2:17; Hag. 1:4–6; 2:3). They can only pray that God would give them success so that what had begun in such deep sorrow might end in triumphant joy (Ps. 126:5).

PSALM 127

    A. Possessions from the Lord (127:1–2)

    B. Progeny from the Lord (127:3–5)

A wisdom psalm, this composition is attributed to Solomon (as is Ps. 72), and it makes clear that anything attempted by human wisdom and labor alone is doomed to failure. Only God provides those things that have true value and durability, whether they are houses (127:1) or children (127:3). Those who have many of the latter may consider themselves blessed indeed (127:5).

PSALM 128

    A. Prosperity in the Family (128:1–3)

    B. Prosperity in the Future (128:4–6)

Another wisdom psalm, this one shares themes with the previous one such as a delight in children (128:2, 6). The poet declared that material and familial prosperity results from fearing the Lord. Those who thus revere and obey Him—all in connection with true worship at His dwelling place—can expect His favorable response (128:4–5).

PSALM 129

    A. Affliction of Zion (129:1–2)

    B. Assistance to Zion (129:3–5)

    C. Attitude of Zion (129:6–8)

Some difference of opinion exists as to the literary category of this psalm, but most likely it is a psalm of communal confidence. Written in the period of the exile, it consists largely of a prayer for restoration. The psalmist complained about Israel's affliction but admitted that it had never been fatal (129:2). God had always intervened, and the psalmist was sure God would do so again (129:4). He therefore condemned those who had mistreated Israel, comparing them to grain that will never mature and be harvested (129:6).

PSALM 130

    A. Forgiveness in the Lord (130:1–4)

    B. Favor from the Lord (130:5–8)

This song of ascent is also a psalm of individual lament. The anonymous author cried out to the Lord from the depths of his despair (130:1), pleading for God's forgiveness and grace (130:3), confident that God would grant his request (130:4). In the interim he can only wait patiently, and in his waiting he also encouraged Israel as a people to wait for God's deliverance. God would respond but only in His time and on His terms (130:7–8).

PSALM 131

    A. Testimony of the Psalmist (131:1)

    B. Temperament of the Psalmist (131:2)

    C. Trust of the Psalmist (131:3)

This psalm, the last of those categorized as a psalm of individual confidence, is attributed to David. Admitting his own limitations, he waited on the Lord to share with him all that he needed to know about divine matters. All he and his nation could do is hope in the Lord for such things both in the present and for all time to come.

PSALM 132

    A. Desire for the Temple (132:1–5)

    B. Devotion to the Temple (132:6–10)

    C. Destiny of the Temple (132:11–13)

    D. Dwelling in the Temple (132:14–18)

A royal psalm, this stirring composition may have originated when David placed the ark of the covenant in his newly built sanctuary on Mount Zion (132:8; see 1 Chron. 15:1–28; 2 Chron. 6:40–42). The psalm recounts David's desire to build a temple for the Lord (2 Sam. 7:1–2), and though that was not permitted he did construct a tabernacle into which the ark was eventually placed. The Lord then promised David that if he remained true to the terms of the covenant that the Lord made with him, his descendants would reign forever at Zion (Ps. 132:12–13; 2 Sam. 7:12–13). The Lord Himself would dwell there, blessing and prospering His priests and kings.

PSALM 133

    A. The Pleasantness of Unity (133:1)

    B. The Preciousness of Unity (133:2)

    C. The Permanence of Unity (133:3)

This wisdom psalm extols the virtue of brotherly love and unity. Such unity is as refreshing as the anointing oil that set Aaron apart to the priesthood (Exod. 29:7) or the heavy mountain dews that give life to the parched, barren ground. David appealed to Israel to be one people of the Lord, especially in their role as the covenant nation.

PSALM 134

    A. The Call (134:1–2)

    B. The Response (134:3)

This final psalm of ascent consists of a nighttime greeting to the priests and Levites who attended to the temple services. They were urged to praise the Lord and in turn offer their blessings to those who had finally arrived at the temple gates (see Num. 6:24–26; 1 Chron. 23:13).

PSALM 135

    A. The Person of the Lord (135:1–4)

    B. The Protection of the Lord (135:5–14)

    C. The Position of the Lord (135:15–18)

    D. The Praise of the Lord (135:19–21)

This hymn is one of the "Hallelujah" psalms (as are Pss. 146–150), a praise lifted up to the Lord because of His worth and works. He chose Israel as His own people, and for this He alone is deserving of praise (135:4). His works as Creator also speak of His glory, as does His miraculous deliverance of Israel from bondage and subsequent conquest of their enemies in Canaan (135:8–9, 12). In comparison to Him the gods of the nations are impotent; in fact, they are lifeless objects of human manufacture (135:15–18). No wonder all should praise the Lord—people and priests alike (135:19–20).

PSALM 136

    A. Creation by the Lord (136:1–9)

    B. Conquest through the Lord (136:10–22)

    C. Concern of the Lord (136:23–26)

The Jews refer to this hymn as the "Great Hallel" because of its appeal to thank God for a whole list of reasons relating to His attributes and deeds on Israel's behalf. First, He is the Creator of all things, an act, like everything else in the psalm, based on His covenant faithfulness. In other words, Creation itself was part of a plan whereby God would bless His people and bring glory to Himself. More immediately apparent to Israel was God's act in delivering His people from Egypt and then preserving them through the Red Sea and the wilderness. He smote their enemies (136:19–20) and brought them into the Promised Land (136:21–22). All these things He did because of His love and grace, attributes and actions certainly worthy of praise (136:23–26).

PSALM 137

    A. Remembrance of Zion (137:1–2)

    B. Relationship to Zion (137:3–6)

    C. Revenge of Zion (137:7–9)

This final communal lament was written in Babylon in the days of Judah's exile there. With great longing for their homeland, the Jews were unable to sing the joyful songs of Zion even when entreated to do so by their captors (137:3–4). They had not forgotten Jerusalem, however. In fact, they invoked curses on themselves if they should ever do so. Meanwhile in strong invective they pleaded with the Lord to do to their enemies what they had done to them, that is, to bring them to absolute ruin (137:9).

PSALM 138

    A. Praise to the Lord (138:1–2)

    B. Predominance of the Lord (138:3–6)

    C. Promise of the Lord (138:7–8)

An individual song of thanksgiving, this Davidic piece may relate to his desire to build a temple (2 Sam. 7:1–2). He first praised the Lord as a natural response to the covenant faithfulness with which God had blessed him. Especially precious are the promises of the Lord, which are as reliable as the very name of the Lord itself (Ps. 138:2). In David's distress God had heard him and now had elevated him to a position of prominence despite his lowly beginnings (138:6). Now he could know that what God had begun in his life He would complete, all his enemies notwithstanding (138:7–8).

PSALM 139

    A. The Presence of the Lord (139:1–12)

    B. The Power of the Lord (139:13–18)

    C. The Preservation of the Lord (139:19–24)

In this wisdom psalm David reflected on the mystery of his own creation and of God's gracious preservation of him. He marveled at divine omniscience, the fact that God knows all about him, even the secret things (139:2, 4). But God is also omnipresent. Were David to go anywhere in the universe God would also be there. Even more astounding, God knew about him before he was born. In fact, God had created him and even before he had achieved final form God knew how he would look and what would become of him (139:16). To David, such things were overwhelming in their implications. But God's care does not end in creation. God is not some distant deity who merely begins the life process and then lets it run on its own. He protects His own from harm and evil from without (139:19–20) and is also able to convict of evil within. David therefore prayed that God would probe deep within his heart, deal with the sin there, and then lead him into life everlasting (139:23–24).

> Among many precious jewels of truth in Psalm 139 is the unmistakable implication that the human person originates and begins development in his or her mother's womb. Anyone sympathetic to the cause of abortion must take full account of this and recognize, with Jesus Himself, the peril of doing harm to one of the least of these (Matt. 18:6).

PSALM 140

- A. Description of the Wicked (140:1–3)
- B. Design of the Wicked (140:4–5)
- C. Desire regarding the Wicked (140:6–8)
- D. Denunciation of the Wicked (140:9–11)
- E. Deliverance from the Wicked (140:12–13)

This psalm is the first of a series of four individual laments. A setting such as David's flight from his son Absalom is possible (2 Sam. 15:13–18), though we cannot be certain. David first portrayed his enemies as poisonous snakes (Ps. 140:3) and then wrote of their nefarious designs against him (140:5). He then prayed urgently that God would intervene and abort their schemes and visit them with the harm they intended for him (140:9). In any event, David was confident that everything would turn out well in the end, for God will never fail the righteous (140:13).

PSALM 141

    A. Desire for Sacrifice (141:1–2)

    B. Desire for Sanctification (141:3–4)

    C. Desire for Submission (141:5–7)

    D. Desire for Salvation (141:8–10)

The setting of this psalm of individual lament is unknown, though possibly it is David's escape and exile from Absalom. The king wanted to make sacrifice at the temple (141:2), something impossible to him because of his physical distance from it (2 Sam. 15:24–25). Even so, he prayed that God would keep him pure in speech and deed so that he would not imitate the evil of those who persecuted him (Ps. 141:4). In a remarkable statement David viewed the travail that had come on him as something positive. Even those things can teach a person something about God and His ways (141:5). But in the end sinners cannot prevail, so David prayed for his own deliverance and for the destruction of his enemies (141:9–10).

PSALM 142

    A. Petition of the Psalmist (142:1–3)

    B. Peril of the Psalmist (142:4–5)

    C. Prospects of the Psalmist (142:6–7)

According to its title this psalm of individual lament stems from David's experience in a cave when his life was in mortal peril. This was most likely in connection with Saul's attempts to destroy him (1 Sam. 22:1; 24:3). The poet cried out to Yahweh in great confidence (Ps. 142:3), grateful that He cared for him when no human being did (142:4). His plea was that he might escape and live, not just for his own sake but for the sake of others who will witness God's grace and find support in it (142:7).

PSALM 143

    A. Desire of the Psalmist (143:1–2)

    B. Desperation of the Psalmist (143:3–6)

    C. Dependence of the Psalmist (143:7–12)

This, the last of David's psalms of individual lament, lacks a clear historical setting, though his escape from Absalom is a possibility (143:6; see 2 Sam. 17:29). David appealed to God to intervene on his behalf, while confessing his own lack of moral perfection (Ps. 143:2). He saw himself in a hopeless situation from which he could not extricate himself (143:4). Only as David reflected on God's goodness in the past (143:5) did he have any hope at all for the present. With new confidence, then, he pleaded for God's gracious deliverance. More than that, he wanted to learn more about the will and ways of God (143:10) so that ultimately he would bring glory to God whereas his enemies would meet their deserved destruction (143:11–12).

PSALM 144

    A. God the Transcendent One (144:1–4)
    B. God the Terrible One (144:5–8)
    C. God the Triumphant One (144:9–11)
    D. God the Thankworthy One (144:12–15)

The final royal psalm of the Psalter, this appears to have been composed on the eve of a battle. David acknowledged that God is the One who fights from heaven, displaying His prowess in volcano and storm (144:5–6). It is He who gives victory in the final analysis (144:10), and for this and all the fruits of victory He is to be praised (144:15).

PSALM 145

    A. God's Greatness in the Past (145:1–7)
    B. God's Glory in the Future (145:8–13)
    C. God's Grace in the Present (145:14–21)

The Psalter concludes with six hymns, of which this is the first. This is the only one described by title as a "praise" (Hebrew, *t*^e*hillâ*, from *hillēl*, "to praise"), a term from which the entire Psalter derived its name *(t*^e*hillîm)*. Psalm 145 is also an alphabetic acrostic, with only one letter of the Hebrew alphabet missing.

    As David recollected the past, he was struck by the greatness of God

(145:3) displayed by His mighty acts of power and grace (145:7). All these are but portents of what He will do in days to come. His works then will cause the saints to thank and praise Him (145:10), to celebrate His glory (145:11), and to proclaim to all the world who He is and what He has done (145:12). And this will continue forever, because the kingdom to come is an everlasting one (145:13). Meanwhile the Lord is near to all who need Him (145:18). He saves those who love Him, but He must pour out His holy wrath on those who reject and disavow Him (145:20).

PSALM 146

    A. Praise to God (146:1–4)

    B. Power of God (146:5–6)

    C. Preservation by God (146:7–10)

This and the next four psalms are "Hallelujah" hymns, each of them beginning and ending with this appeal to praise God. The anonymous poet, in his ecstatic joy in the Lord, urged any who heard him to sing praise to the Lord alone, for human rulers, no matter how powerful, are mere mortals, unworthy of such adulation. Only God, the Creator of all things, gives hope and exercises righteous rule in the earth. Only He provides for the hungry, the confined, the blind, the oppressed, the righteous, the stranger, the orphan, and the widow. He also judges the evil one, an expression of His moral justice (146:9). All this He does in His role as sovereign God, the One who alone is praiseworthy (146:10).

PSALM 147

    A. Regathering of Israel (147:1–6)

    B. Refreshing of Israel (147:7–11)

    C. Restoration of Israel (147:12–20)

This hymn seems postexilic, perhaps composed in celebration of the restoration of Jerusalem and the rebuilding of its walls (147:12–13). The unknown poet exhorted his hearers to praise God simply because of His inherent worthiness (147:1). He then appealed to God's regathering of His people to Jerusalem as justification for praise (147:2). He could do all this, the psalmist wrote, because He is the omnipotent One, the Lord and Master of the heavenly hosts (147:4). He also showers His people with material provisions such as rain and fertility of soil. Nothing matches His faithfulness to His covenant promises, however. It is on the basis of these promises that He has regathered the nation to their homeland (147:19), an act unique in the history of the world (147:20a). Only Israel has received God's elective grace (147:20b), and for this reason Israel had the greatest motivation of all to sound out praises to her God (147:20c).

PSALM 148

    A. The World of the Heavens (148:1–6)
    B. The World of the Earth (148:7–10)
    C. The World of Humankind (148:11–14)

Here the psalmist addressed the whole universe by a figure of speech called an apostrophe. He called on all things to praise God, including angels, the sun, moon, and stars, and the waters above the firmament (148:4; see Gen. 1:7). All earthly creatures too must burst out in grand expressions of praise—living things, the hills and mountains, and the very elements of the weather. All can and must testify to the God of creation, for they are the products of His mind and will. Not least, human beings must praise Him, particularly His own elect people, Israel (148:14). Of all who have cause to celebrate who He is and what He has done, surely those whom He has called to Himself have most reason of all.

PSALM 149

    A. The Witness of the Saints (149:1–5)
    B. The Wrath of the Saints (149:6–9)

The narrowing focus of the previous psalm continues in this one, in which Israel is called on to praise the Lord. Of all the nations, God singled her out as the special object of His grace. The people of Israel should therefore celebrate this unspeakable favor by every possible means of expression. At the same time as they praise, however, they must be God's agents of vengeance (149:6–7). It is impossible for God to be glorified fully so long as there are sinful rebels who, by silencing his saints, mute their heartfelt songs of praise. God is praised ultimately only in the absence of evil.

PSALM 150

    A. The Unity of Praise (150:1–5)

    B. The Universality of Praise (150:6)

There could be no more fitting conclusion to the Psalms than this hymn, which thirteen times calls on God's saints to praise Him. It begins and ends with "Hallelujah" and never deviates from this theme. The poet urged that God be praised "in, for, and with." He must be praised *in* the sanctuary—indeed, in the heavens themselves (150:1)—and *for* the displays of His awesome power (150:2). Then, in addition to vocal praise there must be no limit to the means *with* which His servants magnify His name. Exhausting all vocabulary with which to press his case, the psalmist could only implore that all things living join their voices in a mighty chorus of praise to the Lord God (150:6).

PROVERBS
Practical Guide to Peaceful Living

AUTHOR

*T*hough commonly associated with Solomon, the Book of Proverbs in its present form is actually an anthology of wisdom texts ranging from the time of Solomon (971–931 B.C.) to at least as late as the time of King Hezekiah (729–686 B.C.). It is possible that parts of the book may be even later, though that is not possible to prove (see under "Date" on page 482). The title of the book, "Proverbs of Solomon," is responsible for the popular view that Solomon wrote—or at least provided the inspiration for—the entire composition. He clearly did contribute much of the material (chapters 1–9; 10:1–22:16; chapters 25–29), but other authors are Agur (chapter 30), Lemuel (31:1–9), and various anonymous sages (22:17–24:22; 24:23–34; 31:10–31).

UNITY

Proverbs is unified only in the sense of expressing common wisdom themes. The Solomonic material tends to be together, as does the last section (chapters 30–31), which is attributed by some scholars to non-Israelite sources.

DATE

The book itself attributes much of the material directly to Solomon (1:1; 10:1; 25:1), thus suggesting a date for those parts no later than 931 B.C. In the case of 25:1, however, reference is made to the "men [scribes] of Hezekiah" who "copied" some of Solomon's proverbs. This likely refers to copying them from older texts into the present collection. This would have occurred around 700 B.C. As for the rest of the material, no date can be assigned, since its various named and unnamed authors cannot be identified. Critical scholars appeal to such criteria as alleged Greek (8:22–31) influence and Aramaisms (10:1–22:16) to suggest that much of the book was written after the Babylonian exile, but such arguments are subjective. Most of the supposed indicators of a late date have now turned up in extrabiblical texts whose early dates are unassailable. In short, there is no reason to date the book as a whole later than 700 B.C.

ADDRESSEES

Much of the book is addressed to individuals such as "my son(s)" (for example, 1:8, 10; 2:1; 3:1), but a much broader audience is also in view. What is of practical benefit to the young man is likewise relevant to the population at large. On the other hand, the sages clearly had in mind the believing community—those who fear the Lord (1:7; 3:7; 8:13; 9:10; 10:27)—and not the world as a whole. The wisdom here is for God's people, Israel, to be sure, but it is also for believers today. The principles articulated throughout the book are as helpful for living the Christian life as they were for providing guidance to the ancient theocratic community of Israel.

PURPOSE

The stated purpose of the book appears at its very beginning: to provide instruction in wisdom, understanding, righteousness, justice, equity, prudence, knowledge, and discretion (1:2–4). In other words, Proverbs seeks to educate the people of the Lord in those principles and virtues that make life meaningful and productive (3:1–4, 13–18). On a larger theological plane, Proverbs is a handbook for believers to guide them in knowing how to live in relationship to the Lord and others. This is why the book insists on equating true wisdom with godliness (for example, 8:32–36) and, conversely, asserts that the person who has no time for God is an utter fool (for example, 1:7, 29–33). Only those related to the Lord can be wise, but they need instruction in order for their wisdom to be practical.

THEOLOGICAL EMPHASES

Proverbs focuses on three theological themes that may be formulated as a syllogism: (1) The secret of a happy, meaningful, and effective life is found in wisdom and the practical application of its principles; (2) wisdom comes only from knowing and confessing God as its source; therefore (3) a person must seek after God with all of his or her being in order to be wise and to enjoy wisdom's benefits.

OUTLINE

I. The Proverbs of Solomon, Son of David, King of Israel (chapters 1–9)
   A. The Prologue (1:1–7)
   B. Warning about Bad Company (1:8–19)
   C. Wisdom's Advice (1:20–33)
   D. First Warning about the Adulteress (chapter 2)
   E. Exhortation to Trust and Honor the Lord (3:1–12)
   F. The Infinite Value of Wisdom (3:13–18)
   G. The Infinite Power of Wisdom (3:19–26)
   H. Exhortation to Be Kind to Others (3:27–35)
   I. The Value of Family Instruction (4:1–9)
   J. Warning about Bad Company (4:10–19)
   K. Exhortation to Watch One's Step (4:20–27)
   L. A Second Warning about the Adulteress (chapter 5)
   M. Miscellaneous Advice (6:1–19)
   N. A Third Warning about the Adulteress (6:20–35)
   O. A Fourth Warning about the Adulteress (chapter 7)
   P. Contrasts between Wisdom and Folly (chapter 8–9)

II. The Proverbs of Solomon (10:1–22:16)

III. The Sayings of the Wise (22:17–24:22)

IV. Further Sayings of the Wise (24:23–34)

V. The Proverbs of Solomon Copied by Hezekiah's Scribes (chapters 25–29)

VI. The Words of Agur (chapter 30)

VII. The Words of Lemuel (31:1–9)

VIII. The Praise of the Good Wife (31:10–31)

I. THE PROVERBS OF SOLOMON, SON OF DAVID, KING OF ISRAEL (CHAPTERS 1–9)

The major motif of this section—one attributed to Solomon (1:1)—is the source and worth of wisdom. In it the wise king instructs his "son," and thus ultimately every young person, in the importance of knowing the Lord, for it is He who imparts wisdom sufficient for all the complexities and challenges of life.

A. The Prologue (1:1–7)

The Book of Proverbs opens by identifying the anthology as a whole as a composition by Solomon. Historical narratives about Solomon attest to his wisdom in general (1 Kings 3:11–12) and to his creation of proverbial sayings in particular (4:32–34). The prologue then articulates the purpose of the book: to impart to young men (and to all who are wise enough to listen) the principles by which life must be lived if it is to be successful (Prov. 1:2–5). This will be done, he said, through proverbs (Hebrew, māšāl, literally, "a comparison"), enigmas, and riddles. These common wisdom devices are effective because they are succinct, pithy, and universal in their meaning and application.

B. Warning about Bad Company (1:8–19)

Having made the point that reverential fear of Yahweh is the very essence of wisdom (1:7), a point often made in wisdom literature (9:10; 15:33;

Job 28:28; Ps. 111:10), Solomon urged his son to heed the teaching of his parents, teaching that is based on God's revealed truth (Prov. 1:8; see also 3:1; 4:1–2; 6:20–23). Contrariwise his son must reject the temptations of sinners who would cajole him into casting his lot with them (1:10–14). To yield to this will bring ruin, for though the way of evil looks safe, it has within it the seeds of its own imprisonment and death (1:15–19).

C. Wisdom's Advice (1:20–33)

Employing a figure of speech called personification, the author presented wisdom as a lady who takes on human attributes. She does her best to attract the attention of naive and foolish passersby (1:20–21), urging them to listen to her message (1:22–23). Her plea is in vain, however, so her message changes to a word of threat and a promise of taunting (1:24–27). The simpleminded will call for her too late, and wisdom will not respond (1:28). They have rejected knowledge (that is, the Lord Himself, 1:29), so they must now live with the consequences (1:30–32). Only those who heed wisdom's advice have assurance of a secure life (1:33).

D. First Warning about the Adulteress (chapter 2)

Wisdom was personified as a gracious lady (1:20–33), and folly is portrayed as a woman of the streets. Solomon most likely had in mind here both literal sexual indiscretion and spiritual deviance. He encouraged his son to seek wisdom wholeheartedly, for in doing so he would come to a knowledge of God (2:1–5). The point is that true wisdom is tantamount to intimate fellowship with God; wisdom is not just mere accumulation of information (2:6). When one knows God, he knows how to live in integrity and righteousness (2:7–11) and how to avoid the pitfalls of wickedness (2:12–15).

The epitome of evil is the adulteress who breaks her marriage vows and leaves her brokenhearted husband (2:16–17). She appeals to other men, who, if not careful, will follow her beguiling ways even to death (2:18–19). She must be avoided at all costs, for only those who see through her and commit themselves to uprightness have hope of life in the land (2:20–22).

E. Exhortation to Trust and Honor the Lord (3:1–12)

Solomon again turned to the need for the young man to learn from his instruction (3:1; see 2:1). Strict adherence to biblical truth will lead to a long, peaceful life (3:2), and a commitment to its principles (3:3; see Deut. 6:8; 11:18) will cause one to enjoy favor with both God and man (Prov. 3:4). It will make clear the path one is to follow in life (3:5–6). The youth should not follow his own inclinations, but rather he should submit to the Lord in reverential fear, an attitude that will ensure him the highest quality of life (3:7–8). Signs of true spiritual maturity are generous offerings made to the Lord—which God more than reciprocates (3:9–10)—and willingness to submit to divine discipline (3:11). Indeed, only those whom the Lord disciplines can be sure that they are His children (3:12; see Heb. 12:5–6).

F. The Infinite Value of Wisdom (3:13–18)

No one enjoyed more of this world's goods than Solomon (1 Kings 10:23–29), and no one realized more than he how empty they were in the final analysis. He was eminently well qualified to compare the matchless value of wisdom to the utter futility of materialism. Only wisdom brings long life characterized by respect and peace (Prov. 3:16–17). She is a veritable tree of life to those who partake of her (3:18).

G. The Infinite Power of Wisdom (3:19–26)

By a most bold image Solomon now said that wisdom was the tool by which God the Creator fashioned the universe (3:19; see also 8:22–31; Ps. 104:24). Though one should not read New Testament revelation back into the Old, it is striking that Jesus Christ, the living Word of God, is also identified as the very embodiment of wisdom and in a context of Creation (Col. 2:3; see also 1:15–17); John 1:1–3). As the agent of Creation, wisdom provides all the resources necessary for security in everyday life (Prov. 3:21–26).

H. Exhortation to Be Kind to Others (3:27–35)

A sure sign that one is wise in a godly way is his benevolent treatment of others. Those in need should not be turned aside (3:27–28; see Rom. 13:7), nor should one's neighbor be the object of abuse (Prov. 3:29–30). Such behavior is characteristic of the evil of the world, those whom the Lord calls fools (3:35) and whom He will bring into judgment (3:32–34).

I. The Value of Family Instruction (4:1–9)

Speaking more generally now to "sons" (4:1), Solomon related how profitable his father's instruction had been to him and why therefore his sons should give heed to his wisdom (4:2–3). It gives life and security (4:4–6) and is to be sought more than anything else (4:7). Those who find and elevate wisdom will in turn be elevated and made glorious in the eyes of the world (4:8–9).

J. Warning about Bad Company (4:10–19)

For a second time (see 1:8–19) the sage advised his young protégé to avoid destructive companionship (4:14). He should embrace wisdom, for wisdom is life itself (4:10–13). Sinners live only to cause harm to others (4:15–17). Their eyes are clouded over by their folly (4:19), a blindness in stark contrast to the brightly lighted pathway of the wise, that is, those who follow righteousness (4:18).

K. Exhortation to Watch One's Step (4:20–27)

A favorite Old Testament metaphor for life is the pathway or highway. Here Solomon reminded his son to hear and retain his instruction and to do so from deep within his heart. A person's conduct is only an indication of what he or she really is inwardly (4:20–23). Godly living is revealed by godly speech and godly behavior (4:24–25). It is like walking on a straight and level path (4:26–27).

L. A Second Warning about the Adulteress (chapter 5)

Because sexual immorality is so illustrative of spiritual infidelity, adultery and other such behavior occurs often in the Old Testament as a theological theme. The wise pursue the Lord as their true "Lover," but fools chase after harlots and adulteresses, symbolic of the evil course of this world. Solomon described the "adulteress" (that is, a harlot) as a person whose beauty is attractive but whose poison is lethal (5:3–6). One must avoid her place of business (5:7–8), for to yield to her allurements is to invite disgrace and destruction (5:9–11). All one will be able to do at the end of the road is to regret having pursued it in the first place (5:12–14).

> One reason the Old Testament underscores the awfulness of marital infidelity is that participation in or even toleration of adultery on the human level was a picture of covenant violation by Israel against the Lord. Such behavior was also symptomatic of apostasy, that is, of the rejection of the Lord as Israel's true Lover.

Rather than moving in that direction, the young man ought to drink from his "own well," that is, be satisfied with his wife alone (5:15–18). He should find sexual pleasure in her and have no need to look elsewhere (5:19–20). He may think he can get away with immorality, but God sees all and will bring about forces of retribution inherent in these wicked deeds (5:21–23).

M. Miscellaneous Advice (6:1–19)

This section consists of three subsections (6:1–5, 6–11, 12–19), the first of which is a warning against becoming surety for a stranger who is in financial difficulty—that is, against promising to pay the creditor in the event of the debtor's default. The sage advised one who has foolishly agreed to such an arrangement to go "with hat in hand," as it were, and try to be released from it.

The second counsel is to learn to be industrious and productive in life by observing the habits of the ant. Though irrational beings, they know enough to provide ahead for lean times (6:8). Solomon gained much wisdom from observation of nature (1 Kings 4:33), and here he passed on some of those insights.

In the third bit of counsel, Solomon addressed the troublemaker, the person who seeks by devious means to stir up strife and discord (Prov. 6:14). His mischief will not go on forever; in fact, he will be unexpectedly cut off (6:15). Such a person reminds the wise man of seven other sins (that is, a great many, symbolized by the number of completeness). Most of these have to do with disharmony in the community, a matter most detestable to the Lord (6:16).

N. A Third Warning about the Adulteress (6:20–35)

For a third time Solomon exhorted his son to keep the covenant Law assiduously so as to avoid the moral and spiritual pitfalls of life (6:20–23). This is particularly important in regard to sexual behavior because of its analogy to spiritual relationships (see 5:15–23). Sin in this area will leave one penniless and even dead (6:26). Just as surely as one is burned by touching hot coals, so the adulterer can expect to be seared by painful fires (6:27–29). A thief might be excused for stealing bread to stay alive, but there can be no sympathy for a man who "steals" his neighbor's wife (6:30, 32). He has every right to expect the vengeance of a jealous husband (6:33–35).

O. A Fourth Warning about the Adulteress (chapter 7)

The theme of sexual purity is so important to the sage that he spoke of it one more time, this time directly linking it to wisdom and folly. Once again he urged the young man to give strict heed to the father's teachings (7:1–3) and to embrace wisdom as a lover who can sustain him in the times of trouble that he will face (7:4). By embracing wisdom he is rejecting folly, personified here as a foreign woman (that is, a harlot; 7:5; see 5:3). Solomon was familiar with her wiles, having seen her from his window. With dismay he had also seen naive young men fall to her blandishments and, yielding to her seductions, follow her to her place of lovemaking (7:6–22). Under the pretense of religious devotion, she attempts to disguise her real character and probably makes an offer of food and drink that had not been fully given over to temple worship (7:14; see Lev. 7:11). She then adds that her husband is on a business trip, thus providing a safe and lengthy occasion for the tryst she has in mind (Prov. 7:18–20). Filled with passion, the youth submits like a dumb ox, not aware at all of the disaster to which he is headed. He will suffer mortal wounds and at last end up in folly's real house, the depths of Sheol (7:26–27).

P. Contrasts between Wisdom and Folly (chapters 8–9)

Proverbs 8 consists of the longest sustained personification in the Bible, an address in which lady wisdom is introduced (8:1–3) and does most of the speaking. She takes a highly visible position so as to garner the attention of as many people as possible (8:1–3; see 1:20–21). She describes her audience as fools (8:5), which, indeed, they are unless and until they heed her call. She will speak nothing but truth and righteousness, she says (8:7–8), virtues more rare and valuable than gold or precious gems (8:10–11).

She can do this because she is an extension of the Lord Himself, an instrument or influence by which He rules over all the earth through God-appointed leaders (8:12–16). Those who love her, that is, who listen to and follow her, will find that wisdom reciprocates. She will lavish her treasures on them, riches far superior to material things (8:17–21; see also 3:16, 24:4). Wisdom is such an expression of God that she was with Him at creation itself, an architect (8:30) assisting Him in the construction of the heavens and the earth (8:22–31; see 3:19–20). This bold figure does not mean that wisdom is an incarnation of God. It is a poetic way of teaching that God Himself is the very essence of wisdom. Those who know wisdom, then, know God and find life (8:35; see John 14:6), but those who despise wisdom will surely die (Prov. 8:36; see John 3:36).

Wisdom continues her appeal to the simple by describing the pleasantness and desirability of her surroundings (Prov. 9:1–2). Sinners are invited in to feast on all the dainties she provides (9:3–6). They seldom come, however, for the spiritually foolish are repelled by the reproof that often comes with truth and righteousness (9:7–8). Those whose hearts incline to wisdom will respond, for they are the God-fearers, ones who profit from the instruction of the sages (9:9). By their coming they enjoy the fruits of wisdom, especially length of days (9:10–11).

By contrast, folly, also personified as a woman, makes an appeal to partake of wickedness. Like the adulteress previously introduced, she sits in a public place inviting gullible passersby to sample her wares (9:14–15; see 7:12). The fool will do so because he erroneously concludes that what is gained surreptitiously tastes far better than what comes openly and legitimately (9:17). He also fails to learn that stolen sweets are laced with poisons that will carry him to the grave (9:18).

II. THE PROVERBS OF SOLOMON (10:1–22:16)

This section begins with a new heading that suggests Solomonic origin, and so it should be considered a collection separate from the previous one. The lack of longer literary units here also indicates a different collection. The proverbs that follow are more aphoristic or epigrammatic in form, truer, perhaps, to the usual definition of the term "proverb." The apparent randomness of the collection makes an outline of the whole virtually impossible. The following analysis then focuses on selective proverbs that are deemed particularly helpful or relevant.

Solomon first drew a contrast between wise and foolish sons, the former being promised prosperity and the latter poverty (10:1–5). He then compared their speech (10:6–11). Fools blabber nonsense and will finally fall into obscurity, whereas the wise achieve immortality through the truths and good sense of what they say. Seven proverbs follow (10:12–18), most, again, dealing with the benefits of wise speech. The theme continues by placing a high premium on the words of the righteous (10:20), whereas the prating of fools has little value (10:21). Behavior also comes in for attention. The lazy are soundly condemned (10:26), the righteous are offered hope (10:28), the godly are promised stability (10:30a), and the wicked are guaranteed no certain dwelling place (10:30b).

The bulk of chapter 11 concerns things that are abhorrent to the Lord

(11:1–21). These include unfair business practices (11:1), slanderous speech (11:9, 13), disrespect of others (11:12), cruelty (11:17), and perversity (11:20). On the other hand, the passage extols virtues such as discretion (11:22), liberality (11:25), and righteousness (11:31). In fact, true righteousness leads to life and encourages others to the same point of view (11:30).

Chapter 12 deals with such matters as the contrast between good and evil people and their respective outcomes (12:2, 7, 13), the use and misuse of words (12:17–19, 22), and the wholesome life (12:28). The awful power of the mouth receives continued attention in 13:1–5. One's speech will determine his outcome (13:2–3), and liars are reprehensible (13:5). Solomon addressed again the issue of materialism, pointing out the hollowness of riches as compared to righteousness (13:7–11). On the other hand, those who lack material goods can find comfort in the hope that in the end everything will turn out for their good (13:12–19). It is best to make companions with those who are wise in the Lord and to leave a legacy of godliness to one's children (13:20–24). Such relationships and behavior will result in true satisfaction (13:25).

Chapter 14 advises prudence in deed and speech (14:1–3). Those who plan well can expect abundance (14:4), and those who speak truth give evidence of real wisdom (14:5–7). They are able to assess correctly the great issue of life and death, whereas fools only think they can (14:8–15). At the end the wise receive a crown befitting their righteous character, but the foolish only bear a label attesting to their spiritual bankruptcy (14:24). The secret of success for any individual is the fear of the Lord (14:27). Likewise, the only true security for a nation is the righteousness of its citizens (14:28–35).

The influence of human speech dominates the content of chapter 15. Wise men and women know how to use their tongues skillfully, thus averting wrath (15:1), dispensing knowledge (15:7), and communicating joy (15:23). Fools can do nothing to please God. Their sacrifices are unacceptable (15:8), their deeds are despised (15:9, 26), and their prayers are unheeded (15:29). The Lord knows all things, not just what people speak with their lips but the very thoughts of their innermost being (15:11, 29). He responds to the prayers of His faithful ones (15:8, 29) but will judge and condemn those who rebel against Him (15:10, 25, 32).

A person's relationship to God has a direct bearing on how he or she impacts the lives of other people. Solomon taught that when one is living in such a way as to please God, even his enemies will be inclined to live in peace with him (16:7). The reason is that his opponents will have no real justification for their hostility. But a proud person, on the other hand, sets himself up for destruction (16:18), because he no longer depends on God but on his own resources. Only those who trust in God can find true happiness (16:20). The question, then, is whether to follow one's own devices or to seek after the Lord. The former may seem to be right but it inevitably leads to death (16:25).

One of the most difficult issues in life is how to respond to the failures of one's friends. To gloss over them as though they had not occurred suggests that all one is doing is seeking love at any cost. To harp on them constantly, on the other hand, is to risk losing a friendship (17:9). One can't justify the behavior of the wicked any more than he can condemn the behavior of the righteous (17:15). Both extremes are to be avoided. One must instead be a true friend through thick and thin (17:17), knowing when to be silent as well as when to speak (17:27–28).

Chapter 18 begins with the observation that the recluse who alienates himself from the community because of an antisocial disposition is unable to heed collective wisdom (18:1). Those who try to justify themselves are bound to be found out when more evidence is available (18:17). And when they alienate other people by their offensive behavior they find that it is nearly impossible to gain their confidence and friendship again (18:19). On the other hand, the person who tries to accumulate friends like so many possessions will discover that this leads to no friends at all. A few true friends will prove to be more loyal than one's own relatives (18:24).

An important virtue of the wise person is patience coupled with discernment. Those who understand the problems of others will not be as hasty in condemning them for their perceived shortcomings. In fact, they will ignore personal slights in such a case, for they will have already dealt with the mitigating circumstances (19:11). Such sensitivity is especially commendable when it affects the poor. To help the poor is like lending to the Lord, who will reward such helpers (19:17). Most important perhaps is the matter of respect for one's parents. Children who abuse their mothers and fathers bring on themselves the most profound shame (19:26).

Proper behavior in work and business is indicative of a wise spirit. Laziness is endemic to the human condition, but godly wisdom teaches that the indolent, who look for any excuse not to work, will come up empty in a time of need (20:4). Likewise, those who cheat others in the course of financial transactions are despicable in the eyes of the Lord (20:10). Even children know better (20:11) for God has given everyone a sense of right and wrong 20:12). Ill-gotten gain seems sweet at the time it is acquired, but eventually it comes back to haunt the cheat with bitter distaste (20:17). A tender conscience provides illumination to the person who wants to do right. It is God's way of giving moral direction (20:27).

Chapter 21 opens with a strong declaration of the sovereignty of God. Solomon, though himself a powerful monarch, realized that he was but an instrument of the omnipotent God who could and did employ him in any manner He saw fit (21:1). There is no room, then, for human pride at any level. Sneering arrogance on the part of a mere human being is sin against God (21:4). What really matters is to do righteousness, for God prizes that above anything else, even sacrifice (21:3). Samuel made this very point to Saul (1 Sam. 15:22), and Micah the prophet reaffirmed it later on (Mic. 6:7–8; see also Hos. 6:6).

The wise man or woman is blessed with God's grace and power to accomplish the otherwise impossible. Such resources enable one to overcome whole cities (Prov. 21:22) and to achieve victory in the day of conflict (21:31). To be wise, then, is to be mighty, for wisdom recognizes and is able to tap into the awesome power of Almighty God.

Of all the things one can possess in life, nothing is more valuable than a good reputation (22:1). One ought to be willing to part with everything else in order to achieve it. In its pursuit, the rich and poor are on the same level, for it is the Lord who has made all people and who bestows righteousness upon those who seek Him (22:2). The place to begin the pursuit of a good name is in the home. Children who are allowed to go their own way will develop into adults who manifest their childish inclinations. It follows, then, that parents who want their offspring to learn to fear and love the Lord must inculcate habits of character and conduct that will channel them into God-honoring maturity (22:6). Those who refuse to heed correction should not be ignored but should be disciplined firmly. Foolishness is indigenous to human nature, and only wise application of the biblical means of eradicating it will ensure that the young become responsible adults (22:15).

> *In our modern, hedonistic, pleasure-seeking culture, character and reputation have a way of being ignored if not actually denigrated. True value must be seen, however, not in what one has but in what he or she truly is. A good name is an asset whose currency is unaffected by the boom or bust of the material world.*

III. THE SAYINGS OF THE WISE (22:17–24:22)

This section, though located in the longer section traditionally attributed to Solomon (10:1–24:34), seems to have existed as an independent piece later attached to Solomonic material. This seems evident from the reference to "the wise" (22:17), a reference repeated in the next section as well (24:23). Most scholars have noted this, and many have gone beyond this observation to draw attention to similarities they perceive to exist between this composition and an Egyptian wisdom text known as "The Wisdom of Amenemope" (written around 1200 B.C.). The two works have a number of common themes and expressions. Also "Amenemope" consists of thirty chapters, and Proverbs 22:20 (NIV) asks, "Have I not written thirty sayings for you?"

The Book of Proverbs may have borrowed and adapted some of these sayings in Amenemope, or perhaps both Proverbs and Amenemope borrowed from some earlier writings. At any rate, this does not compromise the integrity of the biblical passage as the inspired word of God, for extracanonical and even non-Israelite writings are commonly cited by biblical authors (for example, Josh. 10:13; 2 Sam. 1:18; 1 Kings 11:41; Acts 17:28; Titus 1:12). Much of the wisdom of ancient Israelite teachers was common to the ancient Near Eastern world. The present text, then, may indeed consist of aphorisms known in Egypt as well. The Holy Spirit, however, guided in their being selected and included in the Scriptures.

This section opens with an appeal to the listener to heed the teachings of the wise (Prov. 22:17). The result will be a deeper trust in the Lord (22:19) and a responsibility to share them with others (22:21). The instructions include such matters as proper treatment of the oppressed (22:22), avoiding angry people (22:24), not standing surety when financially strapped (22:26), and protecting property rights (22:28). The wise also speak of proper protocol in the presence of royalty (23:1–2), the foolishness of envy and coveting (23:4–8), the need for strong discipline in the home (23:13–14), the dangers of intemperance (23:20–21, 29–35), and proper respect for one's parents (23:22–25). They also warn the young man to resist the allurements of the prostitute, for to yield to her is like falling into a deep ravine (23:26–28).

Once more the wise ones addressed the subject of envy, this time the envy of evildoers (24:1–2). They next extolled the virtues of wisdom, listing such benefits as a strong household (24:3), ability to overcome in strife (24:6a), and making good counsel available (24:6b). Fools do not appreciate such things, for wisdom is beyond their capacity (24:7). Only God can give the insight needed in times of stress and danger, so wisdom, like sweet honey, should be tasted as a means of gaining access to divine direction (24:13–14).

Turning to the sinner, the wise men counsel him not to waste time trying to subvert the righteous, for though they may temporarily be laid low they will rise again and again (24:15–16). One should not rejoice at the calamity of even his enemy, for the Lord might avert the judgment He had planned for him (24:17–18). On the other hand, one should not fear evildoers, for the Lord will take care of them in due time (24:19–20). All that is necessary is to give reverence to the Lord and human authorities, and God will see to matters of justice (24:21–22).

IV. FURTHER SAYINGS OF THE WISE (24:23–34)

The anonymous sages responsible for Proverbs 22:17–24:22 may also have composed this brief passage, the teachings of which are akin to those of that longer treatise. The wise men advise against showing partiality in judgment, for the one who does so will find himself condemned by everyone (24:23–25). Moreover, one should not bear false witness (24:28) or engage in retaliatory response when aggrieved (24:28–29). The lazy are rebuked, for he who does not work today to prepare for tomorrow will come to a ruinous end (24:30–34).

V. THE PROVERBS OF SOLOMON COPIED BY HEZEKIAH'S SCRIBES (CHAPTERS 25–29)

The title of this collection of proverbs (25:1) suggests that certain of Solomon's writings circulated in another form until they were incorporated into the Book of Proverbs by scribes employed by King Hezekiah of Judah. They may have been attached as an already completed text, or (more likely) they were transcribed onto a scroll that eventually included all of what is known now as the Book of Proverbs.

The subject matter is so varied that an outline is difficult if not impossible. However, certain themes can be isolated, many of which find expression elsewhere in the book. Not surprisingly, Solomon first deals with matters of kingship (25:2–7). He taught that kings—ideally, at least—should be wise and should not tolerate fools. As God's representatives they should be esteemed highly by their subjects and should be approached only as they give permission to "come up higher" (25:6–7; see Luke 14:7–11).

As for disputes among citizens, these should be resolved if possible without litigation (Prov. 25:8–10). This is to protect the reputation of everyone caught up in the conflict. Also one must use discretion in offering counsel, for a timely word on the appropriate occasion is a precious thing (25:11–12). Also commendable are reliable messengers (25:13), patience with authorities (25:15), and respect for privacy (25:17). One should avoid boasting (25:14), gluttony (25:16), false testimony (25:18), unreliability (25:19), and ill-timed efforts at bringing cheer (25:20). One should not do harm to an enemy but instead should do him good, a response that will produce surprisingly happy results (25:21–22; see Matt. 5:44; Rom. 12:20). On the other hand, a happy life is possible if one can avoid backbiting (Prov. 25:23), an argumentative wife (25:24), and attempts at self-exaltation (25:27).

Solomon provided a well-defined portrait of the fool. He does not know how to handle honor (26:1), he is unable to respond properly to correction (26:2–5), he is unreliable (26:6), he speaks nonsense (26:7), he is incompetent (26:10), and he never learns (26:11–12). The lazy person is no better. He finds any excuse not to work (26:13), lies in bed when he ought to be at work (26:14), and can hardly even feed himself (26:15). All the time, he justifies his indolence with remarkable logic (26:16).

The busybody also comes in for attention (26:17–22). He will suffer consequences for meddling in other people's affairs (26:17), will pay dearly for playing improper jokes on his friends (26:18–19), and stirs up trouble by constantly spreading rumors (26:20–22).

The liar does not escape Solomon's analytical description. He is a hypo-crite (26:23) whose words do not match the subtleties of his mind (26:24). He cannot be believed, no matter how pleasant his speech, for he has a hidden agenda (26:25–26). His dissimulations are painful to those whom he injures (26:28), but someday his lies will come back to crush him in retaliation (26:27).

Turning to the matter of personal responses to various life situations, Solomon counseled that one ought not fall victim to boasting but rather should let others praise him if such is appropriate (27:1–2). Fools and envious people are difficult to tolerate (27:3–4), but friends who honestly point out one's faults are indeed true friends (27:5–6). It is good to be appreciative of life's blessings (27:7), to delight in home (27:8) and friends (27:9–10). Wise men and women do not gossip (27:12), they seek justice (27:13), and they know how not to be offensive (27:14–16). In fact, they learn to cultivate good relationships, helping one another by constructive interaction (27:17–19). Greed is endemic to the human heart (27:20), and fools seem unable to be cured of it or of any other tendency to evil (27:21–22).

Planning ahead is a sure sign of wisdom. Solomon advocates that farm-ers should be constantly aware of the condition of their livestock and lands and should keep everything in good shape. They then can be as-sured that the harvests will be abundant and that their needs and the needs of their dependents will be well cared for (27:23–27).

Proverbs 28–29 consists of a great number of miscellaneous observa-tions and sayings. Solomon addressed such issues as the connection between sin in a nation and political stability (28:2), the lack of spiritual insight on the part of those who are ignorant of the Law (28:3–9), and the fate of those who attempt to conceal their wrongdoings (28:10–13). A people governed by wicked rulers are in constant chaos and fear, but those whose leadership is satisfied with what they have can enjoy a peaceful life (28:15–16). The wicked will eventually bring about their own ruin, whereas the righteous will be delivered (28:17–18).

A sign of wisdom is preparation for tomorrow. Those who plough today will reap tomorrow (28:19), and those who are faithful at the tasks of life will have abundant reward (28:20). One should not show partiality to gain some favor (28:21); indeed, more favor comes by rebuking those who need a word of reproof (28:23). Those who are so greedy as to steal from their own parents undermine the foundations of any society, for they cause all kinds of strife in the community (28:24–25). But the wise trust in the Lord and treat the poor with generosity. The foolish manifest their unrighteousness by walking according to their own standards. When they become powerful, they cause the righteous to go underground, but when they finally come to their inevitable ruin the righteous emerge and enjoy increase in every area of life (28:26–28).

Solomon observed that sinners who persist in rejecting godly reproof will meet a tragic and unexpected end (29:1). Some of the things of which they are guilty are oppressive rule, consorting with prostitutes, extortion, and flattery designed to manipulate (29:2–5). The righteous man, to the contrary, is joyful, sensitive to the poor, and inclined toward peace (29:6–8). His demeanor and behavior are not welcomed by sinners, however. He can never win a dispute with them (29:9) and is always the target of their persecution (29:10).

As a king, Solomon understood the problems and privilege of kingship in a unique way. He had learned by experience that rulers who care for the lowliest of their subjects have hope of a lasting reign (29:14). As a father, on the other hand, he saw the need for proper discipline of a child (29:15, 17). And then as an ordinary human being he recognized the disorientation of life apart from God's commands (29:18). The godly must be careful in speech (29:20) and must learn the value of true humility (29:23). Only when one is rightly related to the Lord is there security (29:25), justice (29:26), and a proper sense of the real wickedness of sin (29:27).

VI. THE WORDS OF AGUR (CHAPTER 30)

Agur, son of Jakeh, is not referred to elsewhere in the Old Testament. He clearly was a widely recognized and highly regarded sage, for otherwise his composition would not likely have become part of the Scriptures. The title (30:1) suggests that his address is a *maśśāʾ*, "an oracle," that is, literature akin to prophetic oracles (see Isa. 14:28; 17:1; 19:1; Jer. 23:33; Zech. 9:1; 12:1; Mal. 1:1). This oracle was addressed to Ithiel and Ucal (also otherwise unidentified), unless, as some scholars propose, the Hebrew should read "I have wearied myself, O God, I have wearied myself, O God, and am consumed." The text as it stands is preferable even without any further understanding of the addressees.

Agur first pointed out the limits of human understanding. In Job-like language he described himself especially as being deficient in the knowledge of the things of God (30:2–4; compare Job 26:8; 38:8–9). This being so, Agur warned against anyone having the arrogance to add to God's revelation (Prov. 30:5–6). He then implored the Lord to deliver him from falsehood and not to give him more than he needed. Otherwise he would have tended to become independent of God and to imagine that he could manage by his own skills (30:7–9).

The sage next spoke of proper respect for those in menial positions (30:10), but then he described truly "low -down" people—those who curse their parents, are puffed up with pride, and take advantage of the poor (30:11–14). These will meet a gruesome end, likened to an eye being plucked out and eaten by ravenous birds (30:17).

Agur then turned to listing various things that illustrate important moral and spiritual principles. He spoke first of covetousness, comparing human acquisitiveness to Sheol, the empty womb, the dry earth, and fire, none of which is satisfied until it is filled (30:15–16). He then confessed his ignorance of the lifestyle of the adulteress. How can she act out her sinful inclinations and then fail to see how wicked she is (30:20)? Such a mystery he likened to the marvels of an eagle's flight, a serpent's survival on rocky ground, a ship's ability to find its way in the midst of the sea, and the feelings that exist between lovers (30:18–19).

Four more realities confuse him as well, this time of a paradoxical nature. How can a servant become a king, how can a fool (that is, one who does not provide for himself) have plenty of food, how can a woman of unpleasant personality ever get married, and how can a maidservant become heir to her mistress's estate (30:21–23)? All these run contrary to the normal rules of life and to his own experience. Other anomalies follow: the wisdom of ants in preparing for the future, the wisdom of conies in finding secure dwelling places, the wisdom of locusts in organizing themselves into swarms, and the wisdom of lizards, which, though small and detestable, are able to take up residence in royal palaces (30:24–25). Finally, Agur listed four things—the lion, the rooster, the male goat, and the king—that are leaders in their own realms and that command respect among their own followings (30:29–31).

Agur's parting advice to his readers is to keep quiet about one's private sins, for to publicize such things can lead to no good result. In fact, it will only produce unnecessary strife (30:32–33).

VII. THE WORDS OF LEMUEL (31:1–9)

No individual by this name is otherwise attested to in the Old Testament, so it is not possible to identify him or even to be sure that Lemuel is a personal name. Some scholars suggest the word should be rendered "belonging to God" or something similar. The fact that his mother taught him the oracle (see 31:1) suggests that an actual king is in view, even if one cannot otherwise identify him. As to the extent of the oracle, there is general agreement that it does not include the description of the virtuous woman that commences in verse 10.

Lemuel's mother dealt with three matters that she believed were important to her son as a king. First, he must carefully avoid the pitfall of sexual appetite, for that would dissipate his capacity to reign (31:3). He should also abstain from intoxicating beverages. A drunken ruler loses the clarity of mind necessary to recollect and properly administer the Law (31:4–5). Being inebriated has value only for those who, about to die, want to forget their misery (31:6–7). This is no endorsement of insobriety but only an observation that strong drink has no value except in negative ways. The king's mother finally advised him to be a spokesman for the weak and disenfranchised who need an advocate. He should be willing to take his stand on their behalf (31:8–9).

VIII. THE PRAISE OF THE GOOD WIFE (31:10–31)

This anonymous poem, acrostically arranged (that is, with verses in an alphabetical order in the Hebrew), is one of the most beautiful in the Bible in both form and content. It describes the model wife and mother, suggesting in the process a measure of strength and independence ideally enjoyed by women in Old Testament Israel that can hardly be matched elsewhere in the ancient Near Eastern world. Yet she does not rule the family; in fact, she shows her greatest virtue in serving those she loves.

Her worth is incomparable, the poet began, and she is more to be treasured than anything material (31:10). She is absolutely reliable, meeting her husband's every need (31:11–12). She works day and night herself but also has the wisdom to delegate in efficient and productive ways (31:13–15). She is not confined to the four walls of her house. She is busy in the marketplace, buying and selling merchandise and creating goods to supply demand (31:16–19). All the while she is sensitive to the poor and to the needs of her own family, not neglecting them in order to pursue other interests (31:20–22). Her reputation is such that her husband's public image is also enhanced (31:23). Everyone seems to be aware of the wisdom of her deeds and speech (31:24–27). Little wonder that her children and husband praise her (31:28). It is obvious that she has native ability, and yet the secret of her great success is her reverent fear of the Lord (31:29–30). This more than anything else causes others to look on her with profound admiration (31:31).

In Christian marriages the husband, by biblical mandate, is the head of the wife and family. But many husbands, unfortunately, are unskilled at managing the affairs of family life. The "virtuous wife" of this passage provides the model of one who, though in godly submission, exercises her gifts and talents in such a way as to bless her husband and children.

ECCLESIASTES
The Man in the Street

$\mathcal{T}$he title of this wisdom treatise in the English Bible derives from the Septuagint, the Greek translation of the Old Testament. The Septuagint has *ekklēsiastēs,* "preacher." This in turn is a translation of *dibrê qōhelet,* "the words of the preacher." The term "preacher" in the Old Testament context has nothing to do with a pastor but simply suggests one who called or exhorted an assembly.

AUTHOR

The Hebrew Bible attributes the authorship of the book to an unnamed son of David ("Qohelet, son of David, king in Jerusalem"), a title further specified in the Septuagint as "Ecclesiastes, Solomon, king in Jerusalem." Internal references to wisdom (1:16) and great works (2:4–11) seem to support this identification. Arguments against it are (a) lack of mention of Solomon's name, (b) elements of background that seem not to be Solomonic (1:12–2:26; 3:1–15; 4:1–3; 5:7, 9–19; 7:1; 8:9). The last point is admittedly subjective, but on the whole it is difficult to establish with certainty that Solomon wrote the entire work, though it is certainly possible that he did so.

UNITY

Despite uncertainty about authorship there can be no question that the book as it stands is a unified, well-constructed text. One cannot detect a pattern of organization in the body proper, perhaps, for wisdom literature as a whole does not usually appear in clearly perceptible logical, chronological, or even theological sequences. Ecclesiastes does, however, consist of discrete topical units embraced by a prologue (1:2–11) and epilogue (11:9–12:14) that provide an instructive contrast.

DATE

Inasmuch as Solomonic authorship is inconclusive, it is impossible to assign a date to the book. Some scholars argue that the Aramaisms in it presuppose a postexilic date, whereas others point out that the alleged Aramaisms are questionable and that even if they do exist they prove nothing about date since Aramaisms are found also in early, preexilic literature. At present it is best to leave the matter unsettled.

AUDIENCE

The "assembly" presupposed by this being an address by the "preacher" is not to be taken in a literal and limited sense. It refers, rather, to the whole covenant community of Israel. By extension, it provides insight into the human condition that is pertinent also to the church and to the entire human race.

PURPOSE

The aim of the book, very succinctly, is to show the emptiness and meaninglessness of life without God as its controlling factor, and, on the other hand, the wisdom of knowing Him early in life so as to live out one's days with full satisfaction and fulfillment.

THEOLOGICAL EMPHASES

The unusually pessimistic statements in this book must be understood as the musings of a person attempting to think and live apart from divine revelation. That is, its conclusions in various matters must be taken with considerable caution, for as often as not the "man in the street" is wrong in his basic assumptions and therefore deviant in the theological assertions that derive from them.

On the other hand, the Fall has not obliterated all possibility of knowing truth and arriving at sensible interpretations of events and the created order. Ecclesiastes does display the positive fruits of unaided intuition and reasoning. In the final analysis, however, only a word from God is adequate to address the human situation. A major—if underlying—theme of the theology of the book is that God is not only necessary as Creator but also is essential to an understanding of creation and human life as its most fundamental expression.

OUTLINE

I. Title and Prologue (1:1–11)
II. Things That Are Vain (1:12–2:26)
III. The Futility of Human Effort (3:1–4:3)
IV. The Futility of Wealth (4:4–6:12)
V. Overcoming Life's Frustrations (7:1–8:15)
VI. Overcoming despite Powerlessness (8:16–11:8)
VII. Epilogue (11:9–12:14)

I. TITLE AND PROLOGUE (1:1–11)

After identifying himself as "the preacher, the son of David, king in Jerusalem" the author immediately launched into the main theme of the book, namely, that life "under the sun" is seemingly devoid of value and meaning. "Everything is meaningless," he said (1:2), a term figuratively reflecting the Hebrew word *hebel,* "unsubstantial, worthless." The phrase "under the sun" (1:3, 9) describes life and reality as perceived by mere human observation. It is a world-view devoid of special revelation.

Qoheleth (that is, the preacher) illustrated his premise by citing the birth and death of human generations (1:4); the regular, cyclical patterns of the sun, wind, and rivers (1:5–7); and the utter monotony and incomprehensibility of the human experience in general (1:8). Nothing is new, he said, for present events have also occurred in the past and will occur again in the future (1:9). Nothing is ever new, nor will future generations recall what presently exists (1:10–11).

II. THINGS THAT ARE VAIN (1:12–2:26)

Qohelet continued to make his case about life's meaninglessness by addressing a number of specific areas. First, he argued that human striving for wisdom is of no benefit (1:12–18). He himself had attempted to search out life's mysteries by applying more wisdom, but without success (1:12–14). Life's enigmas remained puzzles (1:15). Even the very pursuit of wisdom was fruitless, for the more he knew the more hopeless everything seemed to be (1:16–18).

Pleasure is also vain, he said (2:1–3), as are human accomplishments (2:4–11). Houses, gardens, reservoirs, a house full of servants, herds and flocks, silver and gold, professional musicians for his entertainment—all failed to yield satisfaction. His kingly office afforded him anything he wanted, but he always wanted more. He acknowledged that wisdom is better than folly (2:13), and yet both sage and fool die in time and become equally forgotten. How could he help but hate life when wisdom afforded him so little (2:17)?

Labor also has no reward for the person under the sun (2:18–23). What he accumulates he must bequeath at death to some successor, who may turn out to be a wasteful fool. Even in life one finds that his labor produces little reward, for life soon passes away and all its gains with it. What should a person do in light of all these vanities? The best he can do without God is to enjoy life's benefits as much as possible (2:24). The godly one, however, experiences true satisfaction and lasting reward (2:25–26).

III. THE FUTILITY OF HUMAN EFFORT (3:1–4:3)

Qoheleth viewed life under the sun almost fatalistically (3:1–15). In the span of eight verses he referred to "time" twenty-nine times, concluding that life is marked out by events over which people have no control (3:1–8). There is, therefore, no profit in human initiative, for though God has given people an intuitive sense of something eternal (3:11), they still see nothing better in life than to eat, drink, and be merry in the here and now (3:12–13). Qoheleth hoped, nonetheless, that the very patterns of life might be instructive to those open to divine sovereignty (3:14–15).

This is difficult, however, for life consists of moral anomalies (3:16–22). There seems to be a lack of justice (though Qoheleth hoped for a day of justice to come; 3:17), animals and human beings seem to be common in their mortality (3:18–21), and, in short, one should enjoy what he can now because he can't see beyond the grave (3:22). In fact, the dead seem to be better off than the living, and the unborn more fortunate than both (4:1–3; see also Job 3:16).

IV. THE FUTILITY OF WEALTH (4:4–6:12)

Turning next to material prosperity, Qoheleth observed that fools never have enough and that a person is better off having less with contentment than more with envy of others (4:4–6). Family and friends are also greater assets than riches, for life lived with companionship assures stability and strength in time of need (4:7–12). Then, possibly alluding to the story of David and Absalom, the author pointed out the great worth of sound counsel (4:13–16).

Another treasure is the wisdom to know when to speak and when to be silent (5:1–7). One should be especially careful in speaking to or about God. Only fools make rash vows, for they ignore the consequences of failing to follow through on their commitments. Indeed, it is better not to make such a vow to begin with. God is not to be trifled with, so silence before Him may be the wise course to follow. But God is concerned with foolish deeds as well as foolish words. One should not be surprised at evil, but he should also know that it will not go unpunished (5:8–9).

Riches not only are not satisfying but they have their own built-in liability (5:10–20). The wealthy fear robbery, and they can't take their assets with them when they die. One might as well enjoy them as much as he can in this life, for even apart from a hope of a better life to come such enjoyment can be seen as a sign of God's blessing (5:18–20). On the other hand, nothing is more frustrating and empty of value than to have amassed great riches only to have them confiscated by a foreigner before they can be enjoyed (6:1–2). Akin to this is the tragedy of long life and many children without inner contentment. Such a person would have been better off never having been born (6:3–6). The life of a person "under the sun" is like an unsatisfied appetite. The more he eats, the more he wants (6:7–9). Such a person is never able to discern what is truly worthwhile in life (6:10–12).

V. OVERCOMING LIFE'S FRUSTRATIONS (7:1–8:15)

The person "under the sun"—that is, all of us—faces problems of all kinds in life. Qoheleth identified many of them here, the first of which is suffering (7:1–10). Since suffering is inevitable, one must search for value in it. From one perspective, death is better than life and sorrow better than joy. Death precludes further suffering, and any alleviation of sorrow brings joy (7:1–4). Besides, the disciplines and sufferings of life are educational—they lead to a better end (7:5–10).

The wise man then extolled the value of wisdom (7:11–29), pointing out that it preserves one's life (7:12), provides strength to overcome (7:19), and makes clear that wickedness is folly (7:25). An example of such foolishness is capitulation to the seduction of an evil woman (7:26), a theme found frequently in the wisdom literature (for example, Prov. 2:16–19; 5:1–6; 6:20–25; 7:1–27). Wisdom sheds light on a number of other issues as well (Eccles. 8:1–15). It enables one to conduct himself properly before rulers (8:1–8); to understand that divine justice, though delayed, will eventually come to pass (8:9–13); and to see that though sometimes it seems that the evil prosper while the righteous suffer, this is illusory (8:14–15). The person "under the sun" therefore should not judge by appearance alone.

VI. OVERCOMING DESPITE POWERLESSNESS (8:16–11:8)

One thing all people share in common is their inability to comprehend God and His ways (8:16–9:1). A universal human condition causes them to see no apparent difference in the fate of the godly and the ungodly (9:2–3), to see no advantage to life over death (9:4–6), to live life as though there were no life to come (9:7–10), and to give up trying to make sense of any causal connection between natural gifts and ultimate consequences (9:11–12).

The application of wisdom to all these conundrums would, however, greatly clarify such perceptions (9:13–10:15). Wisdom is better than strength, though no one listens to it (9:13–16). On the other hand, a little folly undermines much good for it is likely to gain an audience (9:17–10:1). Like a ruler becoming a slave, so foolishness often dethrones wisdom (10:5–7). But wisdom must be used with skill lest it do more harm than good (10:8–11). One of wisdom's traits is its ability to be silent when circumstances warrant that course of action (10:12–15).

Nothing is more important to the powerless than good government (10:16–20). Qohelet pities those whose kings are like children rather than mature and seasoned (10:16–17). In any case the best policy is to honor human authority. To speak evil against them, even in privacy, is to invite disaster because rulers have a way of finding out. In a series of miscellaneous observations, Qohelet closes out the main body of the book (11:1–8).

VII. EPILOGUE (11:9–12:14)

Having addressed the woeful plight of the individual "under the sun," that is, the person without revelation from God, Qohelet offered counsel as to how to find joy and meaning in life. First, one must recognize that he or she is ultimately accountable to God (11:9–10). Next, early in life one should recognize the existence and claims of the Creator (12:1–8). In a brilliant metaphor describing the aging process (12:2–8), the sage suggested that one should not wait until his dotage before turning to the Lord. He should do so when young so as to live all of life with significance. Finally, Qohelet entreated the readers to revere the Lord. All his teachings have had this end in view (12:9–10). Wise instruction is worth far more than libraries of foolishness (12:11–12). The bottom line is to fear God and keep God's commands, for a day is coming when He will judge everyone and call them to account for all their works (12:13–14).

Jesus commanded His disciples to permit little children to come to Him (Matt. 19:14), for He understood the encroaching hardness of heart that often accompanies the onset of old age. Solomon also exhorted his hearers and readers to seek the Creator while in their youth, for if they waited too long they would lose their hunger and thirst for spiritual things. Surely this provides urgency to the ministry of reaching children with the message of salvation.

THE SONG OF SOLOMON
An Earthly Model of Heavenly Love

AUTHOR

The full title of the Hebrew composition may be rendered as "The Song of Songs pertaining to Solomon" or, more likely, "The Song of Songs by Solomon." In either case the book is closely related to Solomon by its own internal testimony. Other evidence to support this claim is more subjective, such as the author's obvious technical knowledge of flora and fauna, a knowledge attributed to Solomon elsewhere (for example, 1:14, 17; 2:2–3, 9, 12–13; 4:1–3; see 1 Kings 4:33).

UNITY

Despite disagreement about the identity (or even number) of the characters involved and, for that matter, the very outline of the narrative, consensus exists that the book is a beautifully crafted, well-integrated, and clearly unified composition.

DATE

Since the song is by Solomon, it could not have originated later than 931 B.C., the date of his death. The fact that the geographic references therein presuppose a united kingdom supports this early date. True, Persian (*pardēs*, "paradise, park"; 4:13) and Greek (*'appiryôn*, "portable bed"; 3:9) terms occur, but this no longer can prove lateness since Persian and Greek cultural influence is now attested from very ancient times.

ADDRESSEES

No addressees appear in the text, but in line with the wisdom literature in general it is safe to assume that all Israel (and later, the church) is the intended beneficiary.

PURPOSE

The purpose of the book—no matter its interpretation in detail—is to describe and extol human marital love. To have such a book in the Bible is not surprising, because God created man and woman (Gen. 1:27; 2:20–23) and established marriage (2:24). The love that exists between them also portrays love at a higher and more perfect level, that between God and the objects of His grace.

THEOLOGICAL EMPHASES

At first glance it would appear that the book offers little or no theological insight. Such a stance takes no account of the typical nature of its message or of the fact that pure human love is by itself a powerful statement of theological truth. The Song, then, teaches the love of God through human experience, much as does the Book of Hosea.

CHARACTERISTICS

Analyses of the Song of Solomon have ranged from its being a collection of love songs, an adaptation of a pagan liturgy, or a harem scene, to more exalted views such as its being a parable glorifying human and divine love, an Israelite allegory teaching God's love for Israel, or a Christian allegory revealing His love for the church. By form it is clearly a drama, and in terms of genre it is most likely an analogy. The human lovers provide a picture of the otherwise incomprehensible love of God for His people of all the ages.

OUTLINE

On the assumption that the piece is a dramatic composition, its outline may be viewed in terms of acts and scenes.

Act I: Mutual Affection of the Lovers (1:2–2:7)
    Scene 1: Expression by the Maiden (1:2–7)
    Scene 2: Expression to One Another (1:8–2:7)
Act II: Mutual Seeking and Finding of the Lovers (2:8–3:5)
    Scene 1: The Lover's Arrival (2:8–17)
    Scene 2: The Beloved's Search (3:1–5)
Act III: Consummation of the Relationship (3:6–5:1)
    Scene 1: The Wedding Procession (3:6–11)
    Scene 2: Lovemaking (4:1–5:1)
Act IV: First Conflict and Resolution (5:2–6:9)
    Scene 1: The Conflict: The Lover Is Gone (5:2–6:3)
    Scene 2: The Resolution: The Lover Returns (6:4–9)
Act V : Second Conflict and Resolution (6:10–8:4)
    Scene 1: The Conflict: The Maiden Is Gone (6:10–7:5)
    Scene 2: The Resolution: The Renewal of Love (7:6-8:4)
Act VI: Climax and Resolution (8:5–14)
    Scene 1: The Nature of True Love (8:5–7)
    Scene 2: The Attainment of True Love (8:8–14)

ACT I: MUTUAL AFFECTION OF THE LOVERS (1:1–2:7)

Scene 1: Expression by the Maiden (1:2–7)

After a brief introduction (1:1), an unnamed maiden expressed her longing for her lover, the king (1:2–4), a longing that she must admit may not find fulfillment because of her peasant social class (1:5–7).

Scene 2: Expression to One Another (1:8–2:7)

The lover spoke, calling the maiden the "most beautiful among women" (1:8), thus allaying her fears about acceptance. After elaborating on her beauty (1:9–11), the lover delighted in hearing her inviting response (1:12–14), a response that called for further words to her (1:15). After a series of such exchanges (the maiden, 1:16–2:1; the lover, 2:2; the maiden, 2:3–6), the maiden issued an appeal to her girlfriends not to get involved (v. 2:7).

ACT II: MUTUAL SEEKING AND FINDING OF THE LOVERS (2:8–3:5)

Scene 1: The Lover's Arrival (2:8–17)

Having been absent for some undisclosed reason, the lover returned to the maiden (2:8–9) and invited her to come with him (2:10–14), an invitation that she gladly accepted (2:15–17).

Scene 2: The Beloved's Search (3:1–5)

Before their wedding the maiden lay awake one night wondering about her lover's whereabouts. So distraught was she that she decided to search about until she had found him.

ACT III: CONSUMMATION OF THE RELATIONSHIP (3:6–5:1)

Scene 1: The Wedding Procession (3:6–11)

The next scene was viewed by the maiden's friends who, in a chorus, described the coming of Solomon, the lover, in regal splendor (3:6–10). They encourage each other to go and meet the entourage (3:11).

Scene 2: Lovemaking (4:1–5:1)

In a remarkably candid but beautiful recounting of sexual intimacy, the lover (4:1–5, 7–15) and the maiden (4:6, 16) expressed their mutual affection and admiration. The metaphors and similes, so foreign to a modern urban culture, communicate feelings and perspectives that literal language alone could not convey. After the wedding night was over, the lover invited his friends to celebrate with him and his bride (5:1).

> These bold but tender scenes from Song of Solomon point up a major difference between the world's concept of love to what was created and endorsed by God. In the former case the focus is on self-gratification. In the latter the emphasis is on the well-being of the loved one and the extolling of his or her virtues. No wonder Jewish and Christian interpreters alike have seen this kind of love as a type of God's great love for His own dear ones.

ACT IV: FIRST CONFLICT AND RESOLUTION (5:2–6:9)

Scene 1: The Conflict: The Lover Is Gone (5:2–6:3)

Sometime later the bride, sound asleep, dreamed that she heard her lover's voice, but when she stirred and opened the door to her chamber, he was nowhere to be found (5:2–8). Her friends wondered at her love for her husband (5:9), so she described his perfections to them (5:10–16). They then were moved to help her find him (6:1), looking, it seems, in one of his favorite haunts, a garden of spices (6:2–3).

Scene 2: The Resolution: The Lover Returns (6:4–9)

At last the lover came back, reassuring his bride as to his faithfulness and praising her for her many virtues.

ACT V: SECOND CONFLICT AND RESOLUTION (6:10–8:4)

Scene 1: The Conflict: The Maiden Is Gone (6:10–7:5)

After the maiden's friends described her beauty and the strength of her presence (6:10), she told them that she herself had gone away from her husband for a while (6:11–12). They then asked her to come nearer so that they might admire her, an overture she seemed to resist (6:13). They nonetheless burst out in effusive praise of all her charms (7:1–5).

Scene 2: The Resolution: The Renewal of Love (7:6–8:4)

The lover meanwhile found his bride and described her in most tender and adoring terms (7:6–9). She replied with equal passion, urging him to come away with her so that they might make love (7:10–13). Even as they made their way along, she expressed her impatience at the delay they were forced to endure (8:1–4).

ACT VI: CLIMAX AND RESOLUTION (8:5–14)

Scene 1: The Nature of True Love (8:5–7)

As the lovers proceeded in their walk together, the maiden's countrymen saw her and marveled at her now magnificent station in life (8:5a). The lover also reminded her that it was in this rustic place that he first found her (8:5b). The maiden then recommitted herself to her husband, commenting on the strength of love (8:6).

Scene 2: The Attainment of True Love (8:8–14)

It seems that the bride had a preadolescent sister whose future well-being was of concern to her (8:8). Her brothers promised to care for her (8:9) just as they had cared for the older sister who now stood before them as the wife of King Solomon himself (8:10–12). On that note, the maiden's friends from her home community entreated her to sing of her blessings and experience (8:13), a melody she eagerly directed to her beloved husband (8:14).

Introduction to the Prophets

WHY STUDY THE PROPHETS?

$\mathcal{W}$HY SHOULD WE STUDY the prophets? Three answers may be given. First, the Old Testament prophetic books—Isaiah through Malachi—are part of God's Word, and "all Scripture is God-breathed and is useful for teaching, rebuking, correcting and training in righteousness" (2 Tim. 3:16). The seventeen Old Testament prophetic books make up 40 percent of the Old Testament books, or 26 percent of the entire Bible. In volume, about a third of the Old Testament consists of the prophetic books. Thus to neglect the prophets is to neglect a large portion of God's Word.

Second, we need to study the prophets because they give us insight into the character and promises of God. For example, one discovers God's holiness by reading the prophet Isaiah, God's glory by reading Ezekiel, and God's justice by reading Amos. The prophets also describe in detail the "sufferings of Christ and the glories that would follow" (1 Pet. 1:11). Passages such as Isaiah 53 (the suffering servant), Daniel 9:24–27 (the time of the Messiah's arrival in Jerusalem), Micah 5:2 (the birth of the Messiah in Bethlehem), and Zechariah 9:9 (the entrance of the Messiah into Jerusalem on a donkey) are some of the many prophetic peaks that help us understand the life of Jesus Christ. Indeed, much of the New Testament would be incomprehensible without the words of the prophets.

Third, we need to study the prophets because they force us to consider *all* of God's Word. One cannot fully understand the Book of Isaiah without getting to know the Mosaic Covenant, the history of Israel from the time of Isaiah through the Babylonian Captivity, the ministry of Jesus Christ, and God's future plans for His creation. In one sense the prophets are like glue that connects the Old and New Testaments.

HOW ARE THE PROPHETS ORGANIZED?

One of the difficulties in studying the prophetic books is that they are not arranged chronologically or geographically. A basic knowledge of the chronological order—and geographical emphases—of these books can help us understand their individual messages. The following chart arranges the prophets chronologically in the left-hand column. The right-hand column lists the nation or nations that served as the main focus, or primary audience, for the prophets' messages.

The chart on the facing page illustrates the arrangement of the prophets.

WHO WERE THE PROPHETS?

Prophets ministered throughout much of Israel's history. The written messages of Isaiah through Malachi are only a small portion of the prophetic messages of the Old Testament. Non-Israelite prophets like Balaam (Num. 22–24)—and Israelite prophets like Nathan (2 Sam. 12:1–14), Elijah (1 Kings 17–2 Kings 2), and Elisha (2 Kings 2–8)—are examples of prophets who spoke God's word, even though separate collections of their messages were not included as part of the Bible.

The Bible uses several words to describe these unique men and women. The most common word was *prophet* (*nābî*), which suggests an authoritative spokesperson. It is used approximately three hundred times in the Old Testament. Early usage of the term suggests six elements essential to being a prophet.

The Hebrew words *rō'eh* and *ḥozēh* were both translated "seer." These synonyms came from verbs meaning "to see, look at, inspect, behold." The first word is used to refer to a prophet twelve times, and the second at

The Arrangement of the Prophets

Chronologically   *Geographically*

Preexilic Prophets

Ninth Century B.C.

1.	Obadiah	Edom
2.	Joel	Judah

Eighth Century B.C.

3.	Jonah	Nineveh
4.	Amos	Israel
5.	Hosea	Israel
6.	Isaiah	Judah
7.	Micah	Judah

Seventh Century B.C.

8.	Nahum	Nineveh
9.	Zephaniah	Judah
10.	Habakkuk	Judah
11.	Jeremiah	Judah

Exilic Prophets

Sixth Century B.C.

12.	Lamentations	Judah
13.	Daniel	Babylon
14.	Ezekiel	Babylon/Judah

Postexilic Prophets

15.	Haggai	Judah
16.	Zechariah	Judah

Fifth Century B.C.

17.	Malachi	Judah

least sixteen times. Both words focused on the manner in which the prophet received his or her message. Thus a "seer" was one who could "see" (through dreams or visions) the revealed will of God.

The Requirements of a Prophet

- A prophet was one who was authorized to speak for another (Exod. 6:28–30).
- A prophet received his or her message directly from God (Num. 12:1–2, 6).
- A prophet's message could be authenticated (Deut. 13:1–5; 18:15–22).
- The prophet's message had to conform to previous revelation (Deut. 13:1–5).
- The prophet had to speak in the Lord's name (18:18–20).
- The prophet's message was accompanied by authenticating signs (18:21–22; but see 13:1).

First Samuel 9:9 indicates the close relationship between a prophet and a seer. "Formerly in Israel, if a man went to inquire of God, he would say, 'Come, let us go to the seer,' because the prophet of today used to be called a seer." Evidently, during the period of the monarchy the word *prophet* replaced *seer* as the more common description of God's messengers.

The phrase "man of God" described prophets (as well as some others). It identified an individual who knew God and was sent by Him on a particular mission. It was used of Moses (1 Chron. 23:14), Samuel (1 Sam. 9:6, 8), Shemaiah (1 Kings 12:22), Elijah (17:18), Elisha (2 Kings 4:16), and two unnamed prophets (1 Kings 13:1; 2 Chron. 25:7).

The term "servant of the LORD" stressed the unique relationship that existed between God and His faithful messengers. It was used of Moses (Deut. 34:5), Ahijah (1 Kings 14:18), and the prophets in general (2 Kings 9:7; 17:13; Jer. 7:25; Ezek. 38:17; Zech. 1:6).

The term "messenger of the LORD" stressed the fact that a prophet was sent as God's messenger to deliver His word. It focused more on the mission and message than it did on the individual. This term was used of

Haggai (Hag. 1:13), John the Baptist (Mal. 3:1), and the prophets in general (2 Chron. 36:15–16; Isa. 44:26).

In conclusion, prophets were God's divinely appointed messengers, who received direct divine revelation from the Lord. While they sometimes predicted events that would take place in the future, most of their messages focused on the "here and now" of Israel's relationship to her God.

Two major themes dominated most of the messages of the writing prophets. First, they delivered God's pronouncement of *imminent judgment* because of Israel's failure to keep His covenant. Second, they announced God's *ultimate restoration* as they pictured God's final ingathering of His people in the future kingdom age. Both messages are consistent with the Mosaic Covenant, which pictured God's judgment on sin (Lev. 26; Deut. 28) and His ultimate restoration from captivity (Deut. 30).

ISAIAH

*Judgment and Deliverance from
the Holy One of Israel*

AUTHOR

ISAIAH, WHOSE NAME MEANS "the Lord is salvation," ministered in the Southern Kingdom of Judah after the Northern Kingdom of Israel had fallen to Assyria. Isaiah was married to a prophetess (8:3), and they had two children—Shear-Jashub ("A remnant will return," 7:3) and Maher-Shalal-Hash-Baz ("Swift is the booty, speedy is the prey," 8:3).

Isaiah's father was Amoz (stated thirteen times in the Old Testament). According to Jewish tradition Amoz was the brother of King Amaziah, who ruled Judah from 821 to 767 B.C. If this is true, then Isaiah would have been a cousin to King Uzziah (807–739 B.C.). This could explain why Isaiah was on such familiar terms with the royal court.

Isaiah served primarily as God's prophet to Judah (Isa. 6; see also 2 Chron. 26:22; John 12:38). Thus most of his book is prophetic in nature. However, he was also a historiographer who wrote a history of the lives of Uzziah (2 Chron. 26:22) and Hezekiah (32:32). He counseled Hezekiah regarding his policies toward Assyria (Isa. 37) and Babylon (Isa. 39).

Isaiah wrote that he prophesied through the reigns of several kings, concluding with Hezekiah (1:1), whose reign ended in 686 B.C. Nothing more is said in the Old Testament about Isaiah's later years, but Jewish tradition records that he was sawn in two in Manasseh's reign. The writer of Hebews may have alluded to Isaiah's martyrdom when he wrote, "They were sawed in two" (Heb. 11:37).

UNITY

Many scholars have questioned Isaiah's authorship of the book that bears his name. Some assign chapters 40–66 to the pen of another author or authors (often identified as "Deutero-Isaiah") who lived after the time of Judah's exile in Babylon. Those who see multiple authors for the Book of Isaiah give several reasons for their belief that the last half of the book was written by a different person or persons.

Three of the most common arguments are as follows. First, chapters 40–66 describe Judah's return from captivity in Babylon (Isa. 46:1–4) and even mention Israel's deliverer, Cyrus of Persia, by name (45:1–4). Thus these chapters could not have been composed, the critics argue, by Isaiah the son of Amoz, who lived two centuries before the events took place.

Second, stylistic and literary distinctions between the two sections point to different authors. For example, chapters 1–39 stress the nation Assyria, while chapters 40–66 stress Babylon. This points to different authors writing in different historical periods.

Third, different theological emphases between the two sections point to different authors. In chapters 1–39 the author stressed the majesty and judgment of God, whereas chapters 40–66 focus on God's uniqueness, eternality, and deliverance of His people.

These observations, however, do not automatically require multiple authors for the book. All these objections to the unity of Isaiah are based on the presupposition that predictive prophecy is not possible. Thus, the argument goes, no prophet living at the end of the eighth century B.C. could predict the rise and fall of Babylon in the sixth century B.C. Nor could that individual identify Cyrus by name two centuries before his reign.

However, if the possibility of predictive prophecy is accepted, these arguments vanish. Since God is the ultimate Author speaking through the prophet, can He not predict the future? It is no accident that in the very section where predictive prophecy is questioned by modern critics, God stated forcefully that He was predicting the future so that when the events took place He would receive the glory.

Does God Predict the Future?

Six times in nine chapters in Isaiah God claimed the ability to predict the future. Taken together, the passages make a bold statement about predictive prophecy. The verses from the New International Version are listed with the key statements in italics.

- "I am the LORD; that is my name! . . . See, the former things have taken place, and new things I declare; *before they spring into being I announce them to you*" (42:8–9).
- *"Who then is like me? Let him proclaim it. Let him declare and lay out before me what has happened since I established my ancient people, and what is yet to come—yes, let him foretell what will come. . . . Did I not proclaim this and foretell it long ago?"* (44:7–8).
- *"This is what the LORD says to his anointed, to Cyrus,* whose right hand I take hold of to subdue nations before him and to strip kings of their armor, to open doors before him so that gates will not be shut: . . . For the sake of Jacob my servant, of Israel my chosen, I summon you by name and bestow on you a title of honor, though you do not acknowledge me" (45:1, 4).
- *"Declare what is to be, present it—let them take counsel together. Who foretold this long ago, who declared it from the distant past? Was it not I, the LORD?"* (45:21).
- *"I make known the end from the beginning, from ancient times, what is still to come"* (46:10).
- *"I foretold the former things long ago, my mouth announced them and I made them known; then suddenly I acted, and they came to pass.* For I knew how stubborn you were; the sinews of your neck were iron, your forehead was bronze. Therefore I told you these things long ago; *before they happened I announced them to you* so that you could not say, 'My idols did them; my wooden image and metal god ordained them.' You have heard these things; look at them all. Will you not admit them? *From now on I will tell you of new things, of hidden things unknown to you"* (48:3–6).

In addition to the testimony of Scripture, five additional arguments for the unity of the book can be given. First, Babylon (which is said to be prominent only in "Deutero-Isaiah") actually plays a major role in *both* sections of the book (see 13:1–14:23; 21:1–10). Actually Babylon is mentioned more in chapters 1–39 than in 40–66.

Second, Christ attributed both sections of the book (6:9–10 and 53:1) to Isaiah the prophet (John 12:38–41).

Third, while there are some stylistic differences between Isaiah 1–39 and 40–66, a large number of stylistic similarities may also be noted. Some examples are "hands are full of/stained with blood" (1:15; 59:3); idolatrous worship among the "oaks" (1:29; 57:5); and Judah's lack of "justice" (10:1–2; 59:4–9).

Fourth, the title "the Holy One of Israel" expresses the central theology of the book and is equally divided between both sections. It occurs twelve times in chapters 1–39 and thirteen times in chapters 40–66.

Fifth, the scroll of Isaiah found at Qumran indicates that the Essene community made no division in the book. (Chapter 39 ends on the next to last line of a column, and chapter 40 begins on the very next line without any indication of a break.) Since this scroll is dated from the second century B.C., the unity of the book was established at least that early. This allows little time for a "Deutero-Isaiah" to arise and write (around 500 B.C.), be accepted as canonical, have his writings associated with (and then joined to) those of the original Isaiah, and then be forgotten.

DATE

Assuming the unity and individual authorship for the Book of Isaiah, Isaiah 1:1 gives the general chronological framework in which Isaiah prophesied. He served as a prophet during the reigns of four kings of Judah. The years overlap because of coregencies in which a son reigned for a while with his father.

- Uzziah (790–739 B.C.)
- Jotham (750–733 B.C.)
- Ahaz (735–715 B.C.)
- Hezekiah (729–686 B.C.)

"In the year that King Uzziah died" (Isa. 6:1) God called Isaiah to serve Him as His spokesman. That year was 739 B.C. If Isaiah prophesied through the reign of Hezekiah, his prophetic activity would have extended for at least fifty-three years—years of turmoil and trouble for the kingdom of Judah!

ADDRESSEES

Isaiah's message focused mainly on "Judah and Jerusalem" (1:1). However, he did direct some messages against the people of the Northern Kingdom (9:1, 8–12; 17:3–6). In chapters 13–23 he also spoke messages of judgment against a number of surrounding nations. Though the messages are directed *against* these other nations, the messages were likely spoken *to* the people of Judah.

PURPOSE

The purpose of the Book of Isaiah can be determined by examining some of the key themes in the book: God's holiness and glory, humanity's sinfulness, God's judgment, God's deliverance and blessing, and Israel's remnant. Stated briefly, the purpose of Isaiah is to display God's glory and holiness through His judgment of sin and His deliverance and blessing of a righteous remnant.

OUTLINE

I. Prophecies of Judgment (chapters 1–35)
  A. God's Judgment on Judah (chapters 1–12)
  B. God's Judgment on Surrounding Nations (chapters 13–23)
  C. God's Judgment on All the Earth (chapters 24–35)
II. Isaiah's Historical Bridge (chapters 36–39)
  A. A Look Back: Hezekiah and Assyria (chapters 36–37)
  B. A Look Forward: Hezekiah and Babylon (chapters 38–39)
III. Prohecies of Comfort (chapters 40–66)
  A. God's Deliverance (chapters 40–48)
  B. God's Deliverer (chapters 49–57)
  C. God's Delivered (chapters 58–66)

I. PROPHECIES OF JUDGMENT (CHAPTERS 1–35)

A. God's Judgment on Judah (chapters 1–12)

Focusing on God's judgment against Judah, chapters 1–12 weave together the themes of sin, judgment, and deliverance. In chapters 1–5 the prophet highlighted the sin of Judah against her Lord. God called Isaiah as a prophet to denounce Judah's sin (chapter 6), though He announced that Isaiah's message would fall on deaf ears. Judah would remain under judgment until the birth of a child who would lead the nation into blessing (chapters 7–12).

God's Indictment (chapter 1)

Isaiah began (1:1) by describing his prophecy's *what* (vision), *where* (Judah and Jerusalem), *who* (Isaiah son of Amoz), and *when* ("during the reigns of . . .").

    First charge: rebellion (1:2–9). God's basic indictment was that the children He had raised had "rebelled" against Him. More stubborn, stupid, and senseless than even an ox or donkey, the people of Judah had "turned their backs" on the Holy One of Israel. Their rebellion brought judgment that was tempered only by God's mercy in graciously leaving a remnant ("some survivors").

    Second charge: insincere worship (1:10–20). The people displayed their rebellion in their insincere worship. Rather than following God's command to "love the Lord your God with all your heart and with all your soul and with all your strength" (Deut. 6:5), the people sought to buy off God with their many sacrifices. God saw through their hypocritical worship. In a play on words Isaiah said that while their hands were red with the blood of all the sacrifices they had been offering, their hands were "full of blood" in the sense that they were guilty of sin.

    Third charge: injustice (1:21–31). A city once faithful to God had now prostituted itself for material gain. Murder, thievery, bribery, and injustice characterized ruler and subject alike. God vowed to avenge and purge the people as He promised one day to judge the rebels and restore His city to a place of righteousness.

Our heart attitude (whether obedience or rebellion) will display itself in how we relate to God and others.

The Coming of the "Last Days" (chapter 2)

Chapters 2–4 form a unit that bridges the gap from Isaiah's days of trouble to God's last days of ultimate victory. After painting a beautiful portrait of God's triumph in the "last days," Isaiah reminded his audience that God's victory would also spell defeat and judgment for those who continue in proud rebellion against the Lord. Occurring seven times in these chapters, the phrase "in that day" ties them together (2:11, 17, 20; 3:7, 18; 4:1–2).

God final plan for Jerusalem (2:1–5). Using the same imagery Micah later used (Mic. 4:1–3), Isaiah looked forward to the days when God's "mountain" (a figure of speech describing a kingdom; Dan. 2:35, 44–45) will rule over all other nations. The problems of Isaiah's day will vanish as *rebellion* is replaced with obedience ("we may walk in his paths"), *insincere worship* is replaced with a sincere desire to go "to the house of the God of Jacob," and *injustice* is replaced with God's judging between the nations. God's reign will bring universal peace as weapons of war are refashioned into agricultural implements.

God's impending judgment on the pride of Jerusalem (2:6–22). God's days of peace will be preceded by His birth pangs of judgment. The nation had turned from their true God to superstitious idolatry. As a result the last days will also reveal God's judgment on the proud, which will cause the people to abandon their worthless idols.

We cannot exalt God when we lift ourselves up in pride.

God's Judgment on the Pride of Jerusalem and Judah (chapter 3)

God's judgment on the pride of Jerusalem's men (3:1–15). God will judge Jerusalem's prideful men by removing His material blessings (3:1–2) and allowing the city to experience the consequences of ungodly, inexperienced, and foolish leaders (3:3–12). God said He would hold those leaders accountable for their actions (3:13–15).

God's judgment on the pride of Jerusalem's women (3:16–4:1). God will judge Jerusalem's prideful women by removing their beauty and outward adornment and replacing them with shameful loathing. Women who had everything will be reduced to begging a man to marry them, as their husbands and children will die in battle.

God's Promised Hope for the Remnant (chapter 4)

God's "Branch," who will bring blessing to the remnant (4:1–6). Isaiah reminded the people of God's ultimate plan. The day of trouble would end with the coming of "the Branch of the LORD," a messianic title describing Israel's future King, who will come from the line of David (see Isa. 11:1 and the chart near Zech. 6). This leader will gather the remnant who survived the time of persecution and who had been "cleansed" by God. This is the group who will experience God's presence and protection. Isaiah's reference to the "cloud of smoke by day and a glow of flaming fire by night" would remind the people of the Exodus from Egypt and God's guiding them in the wilderness (Exod. 13:21–22). The deliverance God began at that time will be completed in the "last days."

Isaiah's "Song of the Vineyard" (chapter 5)

The judgment of the worthless vineyard (5:1–7). Using a word picture perfectly suited to the terraced hillsides of Judah, the prophet sang of a vinedresser who did everything within his power to produce a productive vineyard. Yet, in spite of all God's gracious efforts, His "vineyard" (Israel and Judah) yielded only bad grapes. As a result, God threatened to destroy His worthless vineyard.

The six woes against the faithless followers (5:8–23). The prophet then announced six woes against the people of Israel and Judah. The specific judgments epitomize and summarize the sins of the people.

The condemnation against those who have sinned (5:24–30). Isaiah reminded the people that all sin and rebellion is ultimately against "the Holy One of Israel." (Isaiah used this or a similar title for God twenty-five times in his book.) Because God's holiness demands justice, He judges those who sin. The instrument God was going to use in Isaiah's time was "the distant nations," that is, Assyria and her allies.

Six Things the Lord Hates

Greed	Those who love possessions more than people (5:8)
Hedonism	Those who pursue pleasure more than God (5:11–13)
Rebellion	Those who choose to mock rather than submit (5:18–19)
Immorality	Those who love evil more than good (5:20)
Pride	Those who think they are wiser than God (5:21)
Injustice	Those who care for themselves while ignoring the rights of others (5:22–23)

God's Call of Isaiah (chapter 6)

Rather than recording his call to prophetic ministry in chapter 1, Isaiah inserted his divine call in chapter 6. While some consider this Isaiah's *recommissioning*, it seems more likely that this was his original call to prophetic ministry. Placing it here after the first five chapters served as a climax to the preceding five chapters and as a bridge to chapters 7–12. God called Isaiah to serve as His messenger because the nation stood on the brink of national calamity. His message was one of judgment—and hope. God would judge the nation for sin, and the judgment would continue until the coming of the Messiah.

The call of the prophet (6:1–8). Isaiah's call to prophetic ministry began with a vision of the awesome majesty and holiness of God. As the angels proclaimed God's absolute holiness, Isaiah realized his own sin as well as the sin of the nation. God forgave Isaiah and then asked for a willing messenger. In gratitude Isaiah stepped forward and responded, "Here I am. Send me!" This passage serves as a model for the way God calls others to serve Him.

The content of the message (6:9–13). Isaiah volunteered to be God's spokesman, but he was startled by the content of the message God asked him to deliver. The message would have no effect on the people. When

Isaiah spoke, it would be as if their hearts were calloused, their ears dulled, and their eyes blinded. Isaiah asked "how long" his message would go unheeded, and God said until the cities were destroyed and the people sent away in exile. This took place in 701 B.C. when Sennacherib of Assyria invaded Judah (36:1). If Isaiah began preaching in 739 B.C. ("the year King Uzziah died," 6:1), he preached for thirty-eight years before seeing true revival take hold on the nation.

A Model for God's Call to Service

Realize the awesome character of God (6:1–4)
Understand your sinfulness before God (6:5)
Recognize and accept God's forgiveness of your sin (6:6–7)
Serve God with a heart of gratitude (6:8)

The Sign of Immanuel (chapter 7)

Chapters 7–12 have been called "the Book of Immanuel." Many have debated whether the birth of the child predicted in 7:14 is a prophecy of a child in Isaiah's day or a prophecy of the virgin birth of Christ (or both). The specific interpretation does not affect the truth of the virgin birth of Jesus Christ because that is clearly taught in Luke 1:31–35. However, the larger context of Isaiah 7–12 can help interpret the specific prophecy of 7:14. This larger context is so specific in its identification of the child to be born that only the Messiah, Jesus Christ, matches all points.

The Prophecies of the Book of Immanuel

7:14	A young woman/virgin is to give birth to a son named "God with us."
8:3	As a "near sign" Isaiah's wife gives birth to another son named "Swift is the booty, speedy is the prey."
9:6–7	The child to be born is named "Wonderful Counselor, Mighty God, Everlasting Father, Prince of Peace," and will reign on David's throne forever.

11:1–9   The child, called "a shoot . . . from the stump of Jesse" and
           a "Branch," will reign with righteousness and justice and
           bring universal peace.
11:10–12 The "Root of Jesse" will rule over the nations and regather
           the people of Israel and Judah.

The historical background (7:1–12). Pekah, king of Israel, and Rezin, king of Aram, planned to attack Judah and Jerusalem about 734 B.C. Their goal was to depose Ahaz and set up a king (named Tabeel) who would join them in their revolt against Assyria. Isaiah went to see King Ahaz of Judah and gave him a *promise* (7:7–9a), a *warning* (7:9b), and permission to ask for a *sign* (7:10–11). Ahaz refused to ask for a sign because he had already decided to seek Assyria's aid rather than God's (7:12; see also 2 Kings 16:5–9).

The prophecy of Immanuel (7:13–25). God rebuked Ahaz for his unbelief and gave him a sign anyway: A virgin would conceive and give birth to a son who would be named Immanuel ("God with us"). Before the son would reach the age of accountability ("knows to reject the wrong and choose the right"), the land would be decimated by the very king whom Ahaz sought as his deliverer. The statement that all in the land would eat "curds and honey" indicates a time of hardship. "Curds and honey" are foods associated with a nomadic or nonagrarian lifestyle. They are to be eaten because the cultivated land will be devastated by war (7:22–25).

Immanuel was a sign of judgment to Ahaz. Ahaz's land would be destroyed, and he would be rejected as king because of his unbelief. Though the birth of the Child did not occur for another seven centuries (Matt. 1:22–23), it had meaning for Ahaz because it signaled his impending doom and because it had the *potential* to be fulfilled in his day. Like many other prophecies whose exact time of fulfillment was unknown, the concept of imminence meant it could happen at any time.

The Sign of Maher-Shalal-Hash-Baz (chapter 8)

The first part of chapter 8 is a "near sign" to validate the "far sign" of Immanuel just given in chapter 7. The two chapters are closely connected, but the children to be born are not the same. The latter part of chapter 8 returns to the subject of God's judgment on Judah until the coming of Immanuel.

Contrasts between the Children of Isaiah 7 and 8

Chapter 7	Chapter 8
Immanuel "God with us" (a name of blessing)	Maher-Shalal-Hash-Baz "Swift is the booty, speedy is the the prey" (a name of judgment)
Born to a virgin	Born to Isaiah's wife (this son was their second child; see 8:3)
"Before the boy knows enough to reject the wrong and choose the right" (about age twelve)	"Before the boy knows how to say 'My father' or 'My mother'" (about age one)
"The Lord will bring on you and your people and on the house of your father . . . the king of Assyria" (focus on Judah).	The "wealth of Damascus and plunder of Samaria will be carried off" (focus on Syria and Israel).

The birth of Maher-Shalal-Hash-Baz (8:1–4). Isaiah wrote out the words Maher-Shalal-Hash-Baz ("Swift is the booty, speedy is the prey") before reliable witnesses. When Isaiah's wife gave birth to a son, Isaiah named him the words he had written earlier on the scroll. He then predicted that before the child could say "dada" or "mama" the riches of Aram and Israel (represented by their capital cities Damascus and Samaria) would be plundered by Assyria's king. The events of 7:1–2 took place in 735–734 B.C., and the events of 8:1–4 probably happened about the same time. If Isaiah's wife became pregnant in 734 B.C. and gave birth in 733 B.C., then the message was that Damascus and Samaria would be laid waste before this new child would begin speaking. Both countries were plundered by Assyria in 732 B.C.!

The desolation of Judah (8:5–10). Having predicted the sure destruction of the two enemies feared by Ahaz, Isaiah returned to his message of judgment on Judah. Ahaz had rejected "the gently flowing waters of Shiloah," a reference to the waters of his own city, Jerusalem (and, by extension, to the God of Jerusalem who promised to sustain him). Therefore God would bring to Judah "the mighty floodwaters of the River—the king of Assyria." The Assyrians represented the Gentiles who would overrun the land until Immanuel (mentioned in 8:8, 10) would provide deliverance.

The folly of fear (8:11–17). God warned Isaiah not to follow after the people of Judah or to fear the physical enemies that caused the king and the people to make shortsighted, foolish decisions. Rather, Isaiah was to trust in God's awesome power and holiness and to fear Him, even during the time when He would bring judgment against Judah for unbelief.

The folly of spiritism (8:18–22). Isaiah reminded the people that he and his two sons were signs to the nation. One son (Shear-Jashub) was a sign of hope to those who trusted in God, while the other son (Maher-Shalal-Hash-Baz) was a sign of judgment to those who turned from God. Isaiah rebuked those who sought to learn the future by consulting the spirits of the dead rather than the Lord. Such individuals could only expect God's unrelenting judgment.

The Future Child and Impending Judgment (chapter 9)

God's light for Galilee (9:1–7). God promised, through the birth of a child, to shatter the darkness of gentile occupation experienced by the ten tribes of Israel. Four specific titles identify Him. "Wonderful Counselor" pictures His wise judgment. "Mighty God" stresses His divine power. "Everlasting Father" suggests His never-ending protection and support. "Prince of Peace" characterizes the type of kingdom He will rule. This Ruler, who will sit on David's throne, will bring lasting peace, justice, and righteousness to Israel.

God's fire against Israel (9:8–21). Though Israel's future hope would come only through the birth of the Child, many in Israel saw no need to wait on God. With "pride and arrogance of heart," they felt they could rebuild the ruined nation by their own strength. At the same time the rebellious Israelites had not sought the Lord. So God announced His continued judgment, four times repeating the theme, "Yet for all this, his anger is not turned away, his hand is still raised" (9:12, 17, 21; 10:4).

God's Judgment on Assyria (chapter 10)

God's woe against Israel (10:1–4). Structurally these verses relate to the preceding chapter. God announced woe against those leaders who passed unjust laws that took advantage of the weak and helpless (the "poor" and "oppressed"). God's judgment against these rich and powerful tyrants would match their crime. They would vainly try to seek help as their riches were stripped away, but the Lord would bring a "day of reckoning" against them.

God's woe against Assyria (10:5–11). Having announced the coming of an enemy who would despoil Israel, God then identified that nation and said He would judge her for her sin. Though Assyria was "the rod of my anger," she was still held accountable by God for her actions. Though He sent Assyria to loot Judah, the Assyrians went beyond what God permitted. Their king stepped over the line when he raised his hand against the God of Judah.

God's judgment on Assyria's pride (10:12–19). God said He would punish Assyria for her pride by sending "a wasting disease" on her soldiers. This occurred in 701 B.C. when Sennacherib was attacking Judah and "the angel of the Lord" put to death 185,000 Assyrian soldiers overnight (see 37:36–37).

God's deliverance of Jerusalem (10:20–34). A few would remain in Jerusalem to see God deliver the city. Though the Assyrian advance would destroy Israel and decimate Judah, God promised he would lift "their yoke from your neck." In dramatic fashion the prophet recorded the advance of the Assyrian army against Jerusalem from the north, halting at Nob (probably present-day Mount Scopus) on the northern edge of Jerusalem. Just when victory was seemingly in the Assyrians' grasp, God promised to "cut down" this nation that had grown so tall in pride.

The "Branch" and His Kingdom (chapter 11)

Gazing from one mountain peak to another, Isaiah moved from God's deliverance of Judah to His promised Messiah, who will bring about lasting peace. Though both events from Isaiah's perspective were future, the victory promised in chapter 10 took place shortly after his prediction, whereas the promised Child of chapter 11 did not come for seven centuries.

The Branch's character (11:1–5). The line of David was judged because of the sin of Ahaz (7:9, 13–17), but the arrival of the promised "shoot" from Jesse, David's father, will finally signal the end of cursing and the beginning of blessing. This Descendant, empowered by the Holy Spirit, will govern with righteousness and justice.

The Branch's peace (11:6–9). In a beautiful picture of peace Isaiah wrote that the Messiah's righteous influence will extend even to the animal kingdom. Even animals that have been natural enemies through the ages will dwell together peacefully. This theme of peace—and its association with the arrival of the Messiah and the establishment of God's kingdom—is echoed in other Old Testament prophets of this time (Hos. 2:16–20; Mic. 5:2–5a).

> *The world will come to know true peace only when the Prince of Peace is seated on His throne in Jerusalem.*

The Branch's people (11:10–16). The Branch will accomplish everything God has intended for His people. Standing as a "banner," or rallying point, for Israel, the Messiah will reclaim His remnant from wherever they might be scattered. Nations that have oppressed His people will be judged for their actions. In verses 14–18 Isaiah stated a series of opposites to show how thorough God's deliverance would be. The nations to the west (Philistia) and east (Edom, Moab, Ammon) that had oppressed Israel will now be plundered by God's people. Obstacles to the south (the Egyptian sea) and to the north (the Euphrates River) will be broken up so God's people can return.

Judah's Song of Salvation (chapter 12)

Two brief psalms of praise climax the transition from judgment to deliverance for Judah. Each of the psalms begins with the phrase, "In that day you will say" (12:1, 4). The "day" relates to the time of Israel's deliverance and redemption, brought about by her Messiah (also see 11:10–11).

Individual hymn of praise to God (12:1–3). The first hymn of praise to God was a psalm of thanksgiving for His deliverance from judgment. God had "turned away" His anger and brought about "salvation" (deliverance) for His people.

Corporate song of praise to the nations (12:4–6). While still thanking God for deliverance, the people sang the second hymn of praise, facing the nations of the world. Israel and Judah are to inform the nations what God had done for them. In doing so they will be fulfilling God's original plan for Abraham's descendants to be a "light for the Gentiles" (42:6) so that through them "all the peoples on earth will be blessed" (Gen. 12:3).

B. GOD'S JUDGMENT ON SURROUNDING NATIONS (CHAPTERS 13–23)

Having just announced judgment on surrounding nations (Isa. 11:14–16), the prophet now focused on this "rogues' gallery" of Israel's enemies, saying in effect, "If God didn't spare His people, what makes you think *you* will escape His judgment?" A list of the nations and cities included in this section is revealing.

God's Judgment against the Nations		
Nation	*Passage*	*Number of Verses*
Babylon	13:1–14:23	45
Assyria	14:24–27	4
Philistia	14:28–32	5
Moab	chapters 15–16	23
Damascus and Samaria	17:1–14	14
Cush and Egypt	chapters 18–20	38

Babylon	21:1–10	10
Edom	21:11–12	2
Arabia	21:13–17	5
Jerusalem	chapter 22	25
Tyre	chapter 23	18

Several observations should be noted about this list of nations. First, when the Bible presents a list of items, what is placed first or last is often of particular importance (in this case, Babylon and Tyre). Second, the items on which the writer spends the greatest amount of time could be of more importance (namely, Babylon and Cush/Egypt). Third, if any items are repeated in a list, this could indicate they are being emphasized by the author (Babylon). These three observations highlight Babylon's importance in Isaiah's message.

God's Judgment on Babylon (chapter 13)

Babylon stood at the top of God's list of "most wanted" nations. Though a relatively insignificant nation in Isaiah's day, Babylon was still the land that had spawned humanity's rebellion (Gen. 11). By describing God's judgment on Babylon in "the day of the LORD," Isaiah was also foreshadowing God's judgment on *all* nations.

God's call to battle against Babylon (Isa. 13:1–5). The banner God had raised to gather the nations against Judah (5:26) was now raised to gather nations against Babylon. God's army will come "from faraway lands," and their goal will be to destroy Babylon.

The Day of the Lord on Babylon (13:6–16). The Day of the Lord for Babylon is a time when God will judge the proud and ungodly. Isaiah described God's day of judgment for Babylon as a time of wrath and anger, with supernatural signs in the heavens (13:10), divine punishment for sin (13:11), and great loss of life (13:12). The entire population of Babylon will experience God's judgment.

The final destruction of Babylon (13:17–22). The army sent by God will wipe out the inhabitants of Babylon. When the attack is over, Babylon will be like Sodom and Gomorrah—a symbol of sudden, complete, and final destruction. People will not return later to rebuild the ruins or live in the city for extended periods ("generations"). Nor will they dwell there for short periods of time as nomadic visitors ("pitch his tent"). Nor will they even spend a single night ("rest his flocks"). After its final destruction the site will be suitable only for unclean animals and evil spirits.

God Restores Israel and Judges Others (chapter 14)

Israel's taunt against Babylon (14:1–23). When God judges Babylon, He will also "have compassion on Jacob." Babylon's fall signals the time when God will return His people to their land and allow them to rule over the nations who once oppressed them. At that time the people will take up a song against the former ruler of Babylon. While many have seen this as a reference to Satan, the taunt seems to be against the human ruler of Babylon. Though this ruler shares Satan's prideful boast of being equal to God, the text seems to point to a human ruler. This morning star claimed in his heart to be equal to God (14:13–14), he is identified as a "man" (14:16–17), and his body would not receive a proper burial (14:18–20).

God's judgment on Assyria (14:24–27). Having announced His judgment against "public enemy number one," God now turned to other nations that would feel the fury of His anger. Next on His list was Assyria, the most threatening power in Isaiah's day. God promised to "crush the Assyrian in my land." This prophecy, as noted earlier, was fulfilled in 701 B.C. when the angel of the Lord annihilated 185,000 Assyrian soldiers when they had surrounded Jerusalem (see 37:36–37).

God's judgment on Philistia (14:28–32). The Philistines saw a golden opportunity to return to greatness in 715 B.C. Ahaz, king of Judah, had died, and Sargon, king of Assyria, was fighting against other nations. The Philistines thought the "rod that struck" them (the Assyrians) was now "broken." But God said a "cloud of smoke" would come from the north, the direction from which the Assyrian army would march against the Philistines. Isaiah's prophecy of judgment against the Philistines was fulfilled a few years later when the Assyrians returned and destroyed the city of Ashdod (see 20:1).

God's Judgment on Moab (chapters 15–16)

Isaiah delivered this message of judgment against Moab sometime before 715 B.C. The Lord threatened to destroy the Moabites because of their pride.

Moab's wail of distress (15:1–9). When the Moabite cities fell, the people would weep and wail over their misfortune. Fugitives would flee toward the south, carrying their wealth as they desperately tried to escape from the invaders.

The plea of the refugees (16:1–5). The refugees of Moab would send tribute to Judah's king, asking him to take them in and "be their shelter from the destroyer." Moab would go to the king of the house of David and ask him to rule over them.

The destruction of Moab's pride (16:6–14). The pride of Moab, with her boasting over her abundant harvests, would cease as the invaders "trampled down" her land. Her prayers to her god for protection would go unanswered. Isaiah said this judgment on Moab would come "within three years" of his pronouncement. This was fulfilled precisely, for Assyria invaded Moab sometime between 715 and 713 B.C.

God's Judgment on Damascus and Samaria (chapter 17)

This chapter includes God's judgment against both Damascus and Samaria. In chapter 7 both nations were linked in a plot to attack Judah (7:1, 8–9), so it is fitting that both nations are linked together in judgment.

The destruction of Damascus (17:1–3). God announced the destruction of Damascus and Aram's other cities. The towns would be deserted when Aram's royal power was shattered. The prophet's linking the destruction of Damascus and Samaria in verse 3 is fitting, for in 732 B.C. the Assyrians captured Damascus along with several cities in Israel.

The destruction of Samaria (17:4–11). God's judgment on Damascus would continue until it reached Samaria. Though the nation would be "harvested" in judgment, God promised to preserve "some gleanings," that is, a righteous remnant. As cities were destroyed, people would be forced to look to the Lord rather than to the idols they had been worshiping.

The destruction of invading nations (17:12–14). God reminded His people that He would hold other nations accountable for their actions. Though these nations, including Assyria, might pour into Judah like a "raging sea," God said that when He rebuked them, these nations would "flee far away." The immediate application of this prophecy was the Assyrian invasion of Israel and Judah, which God stopped at the very gates of Jerusalem (see also 10:28–34; 14:25; 37:21–37).

God's Judgment on Cush and Egypt (chapters 18–20)

When Judah rebelled against Assyria, she relied on a military alliance with Cush and Egypt for protection. God announced that both Cush and Egypt would be humbled by His judgment. He spoke against Cush (chapter 18) and Egypt (chapter 19) individually, and then described the specific judgment He would bring on both nations together (chapter 20).

God's judgment on Cush (Chapter 18). Cush, immediately to the south of Egypt, was known for its inhabitants who were tall, smooth-skinned (with no facial hair like the Israelites and other Semitic peoples), and aggressive warriors. The Cushites came to Judah's aid when Assyria invaded Judah (see 37:9). God said He would wait quietly for them to come before destroying them. Like vine branches with ripening grapes being cut away by a farmer, the soldiers of Cush would be left on the mountains as food for the wild animals. Yet in a dramatic picture of the future, Isaiah described the time when Cushites will come to God's land bearing gifts for Him rather than brandishing weapons.

God's judgment on Egypt (chapter 19). Egypt, Israel's oppressor at the time of the Exodus, centuries later became her ally against Assyria. Isaiah prophesied that God would come in judgment against Egypt, bringing division and defeat. Egypt, with the life-giving Nile River, was a haven for others in times of drought. But "the waters of the river will dry up"—a picture of great calamity. But paralleling the previous message against Cush, the prophet moved from imminent destruction to future blessing for Egypt. He described a time (called "that day" in 19:16, 18, 19, 21, 23–24) when Egypt will acknowledge the Lord and will join with Israel in worshiping Him.

God's judgment on Egypt and Cush (chapter 20). In 711 B.C. Isaiah walked about barefoot and stripped of outer garments to deliver a dramatic message. Just as he stood humiliated before the people, so the armies of Egypt and Cush would be humiliated by the Assyrian army. At that time those in Judah who had put their hope in those nations would be afraid. This prophecy was fulfilled when Assyria defeated Egypt and Cush in 701 B.C.

God's Judgment on Babylon, Edom, and Arabia (chapter 21)

Judgment on Babylon (21:1–10). In describing a coming attack on the city of Babylon, Isaiah named two enemies—Elam and Media. He had in mind one of two possible attacks: the Assyrian's capture and destruction of Babylon in 686 B.C., or the Medo-Persians' capture of the city in 539 B.C. In both cases Elam and Media were allies with the principal invaders. The fact that the other messages in this section fit the Assyrian Empire in Isaiah's day, and the fact that Babylon was temporarily destroyed by the Assyrians in 686 B.C., make the attack in that day the more likely fulfillment of this prophecy. After the invasion the city was "fallen," with her idols demolished.

Judgment on Edom (21:11–12). In two terse verses Isaiah announced that the "night" of Assyrian occupation for Edom might eventually be followed by a "morning" of freedom. However, that short-lived time of freedom would be followed by another "night" of oppression, likely a veiled reference to the Babylonian occupation that followed that of Assyria.

Judgment on Arabia (21:13–17). Assyria's control extended into the Arabian Peninsula. Isaiah called on the caravans to bring food and water for the refugees who would flee from the battle. He then predicted that within a year God would destroy the glory of the Arabian city Kedar.

God's Judgment on Jerusalem (chapter 22)

Jerusalem's untimely rejoicing (22:1–4). The subject of this oracle is "the Valley of Vision," a reference either to Jerusalem as a valley or to one of two main valleys surrounding Jerusalem on the east (Kidron) or on the west and south (Hinnom). As Assyria approached, the city would be full of "tumult and revelry" rather than repentance. Conspiracy, intrigue, and treachery had stripped the city of leadership, so that those in charge fled before the enemy even approached.

Jerusalem's failure to seek God (22:5–14). When the enemy finally invaded Judah, they filled her valleys with their chariots. Judah looked everywhere for help except to God. She stockpiled her weapons, shored up her walls, and stored up her water. But the city failed to look to the Lord. As the enemy approached, the people hedonistically decided to "eat and drink" because they expected to die. God held the people accountable for their failure to acknowledge and return to Him.

What do you depend on to carry you through times of trouble?

Jerusalem's lackluster leaders (22:15–25). Instead of leading the people through perilous times, Shebna, who was in charge of the palace, was busy cutting out a grave intended to serve as a lasting memorial for himself. Shebna would be replaced by Eliakim, a more worthy leader for God's people. Isaiah's prophecy about these individuals seems to have been at least partially fulfilled by 701 B.C., because by that time Eliakim had been promoted while Shebna had been demoted (see 36:3). Interestingly, archaeologists have discovered remnants of the grave hewn by Shebna on the Mount of Olives east of Jerusalem.

God's Judgment on Tyre (chapter 23)

Isaiah reserved his final message of judgment for the city that most epitomized pride. While Tyre was judged by the Babylonians under Nebuchadnezzar and by the Greeks under Alexander the Great, Isaiah's message focused more on the judgment of this city by the Assyrians.

Tyre's fall (23:1–14). God called on the Mediterranean merchant ships to wail because the great seaport of Tyre would be destroyed. Everyone— from the coast of Tyre and Sidon on the east, to the Nile delta of Egypt in the south, to the far reaches of Tarshish in the west, and to the coast of Cyprus in the north—would know that God had made the kingdoms of the Mediterranean world "tremble." Assyria, the nation that had devastated Babylonia (see 21:1–10), would destroy Tyre.

Tyre's restoration (23:15–18). Tyre would be forgotten "for seventy years," probably 700–630 B.C., the time when the Assyrians restricted Tyre's ability to trade. However, after that time Tyre would resume her role as a commercial "prostitute"—plying her trade with the many nations throughout the Mediterranean world. Yet in a message that looked beyond Isaiah's day to the coming of Nebuchadnezzar, God vowed that the wealth of Tyre would ultimately be "set apart" for Him. This refers not to Tyre turning to the Lord and honoring Him, but to God taking the wealth of Tyre for Himself.

C. GOD'S JUDGMENT ON ALL THE EARTH (CHAPTERS 24–35)

In chapters 24–35 the prophet turned from the surrounding nations to state that God's judgment will extend to all the earth. This section moves from the immediate to the long-range, from the local to the universal, from the temporal to the eschatological. God is coming to judge the world for its sin and to reward those who trust in Him. In a number of ways this section parallels God's judgment against Judah in Isaiah 1–12.

Parallels between Isaiah 1–12 and 24–35		
	Isaiah 1–12	*Isaiah 24–35*
Messages of sin, judgment, and restoration "in that day"	chapters 1–4	chapters 24–27
A "song about his vineyard"	5:1–7	27:2–6
Six woes	5:8–30	chapters 28–33
Judgment on the gentile oppressors	chapter 10	chapter 34
Kingdom blessings for Israel	chapters 11–12	chapter 35

God's Universal Judgment (chapter 24)

The devastation by God (24:1–13). God, Isaiah wrote, was about to "lay waste the earth." The effects of God's judgment will be felt by all classes of people. The earth itself will be consumed, and all joy will turn to gloom. The results of God's judgment will be felt worldwide, "on the earth and among the nations."

The response of the believing remnant (24:14–16). God's intervention and judgment will not be dreaded by everyone. From the east to the west (and everywhere in between) a believing remnant will glorify God for His righteous actions. Those who had been persecuted and oppressed by the world will rejoice to see God's punishment of the wicked.

The terror of the earth's inhabitants (24:17–20). While the believing remnant will rejoice in God's vindication, all others will recoil in terror from His wrath. Vainly they will try to flee, but will be "caught in a snare." Like a dam unleashing the power of water it once held back, heaven will open the floodgates of divine wrath—and the earth will crumble as God's judgment sweeps through.

The reign of the Lord (24:21–23). God's judgment will have three effects. First, He "will punish the powers in the heavens above," a reference to Satan and his spiritual forces (see Eph. 6:11–12; Rev. 12:7–12). Second, He will punish "the kings on the earth below," that is, the wicked end-time rulers who will oppose the Lord and His people (see also Isa. 13:1–10; 16:12–14; 19:19–21). God will confine both groups "in prison" to be punished "after many days." (After Christ's one-thousand-year reign on earth [Rev. 20:4–6], Satan will be cast into the "lake of burning sulfur" [20:10] along with the wicked of all ages. This is called "the second death" [20:11–15].) Third, God will finally establish His reign over Israel "on Mount Zion and in Jerusalem." All the promises made to Abraham and his descendants will be fulfilled during the Messiah's reign.

Israel's Praise to the Lord (chapter 25)

Praise for God's judgment of the oppressors (25:1–5). Israel will respond in praise to God for judging her oppressors. God will destroy the "foreigners' stronghold" so that it "will never be rebuilt." In judging Israel's enemies the Lord will be a "refuge" for people in distress. Like a tree or cloud that blocks the harsh rays of the sun, God will intervene to protect His own.

Praise for God's blessings on His people (25:6–9). Having mentioned Mount Zion in 24:23, Isaiah recounted the blessings God will bring "on this mountain" (25:6–7, 10). God will hold a coronation feast on Mount Zion as He begins His reign. The imagery of a feast suggests great blessing associated with the King ascending His throne (see 1 Kings 1:25–27). God "will swallow up death forever." Sadness, sorrow, and separation will forever be replaced with joy and gladness.

Promise of Moab's destruction (25:10–12). Israel could look forward to God's promised blessings, but Moab could not. Instead, the prophet returned to his theme of judgment to show that Moab will be "trampled" by God. Moab's overwhelming pride (see 16:6) will lead to her judgment.

> *We can endure persecution if we realize God will someday reward our faithfulness and judge our oppressors.*

Judah's Song of Celebration and Reflection (chapter 26)

Events to Happen "in That Day" (Isa. 24–27)	
24:21–23	God will judge earthly and heavenly powers and rule in Jerusalem.
25:9	The people will praise and acknowledge God's protection.
26:1–6	Judah will sing a song of God's deliverance.
27:1	God will judge Leviathan, the serpent (Satan).
27:12	God will regather His people from all directions.
27:13	All Israel will return to worship the Lord.

Song of praise for the strong city (26:1–6). Isaiah predicted a day when the people of Judah will sing about Jerusalem as a "strong city" that will open its gates to the righteous. God will be known as the One who humbles the proud ("those who dwell on high") and levels their cities, allowing the oppressed to triumph over them.

Song of reflection on God's judgment (26:7–15). In times of difficulty the righteous are to walk in His ways as they wait for Him to act. Though God might delay judgment to show "grace . . . to the wicked," Isaiah reflected the nation's yearning for God's intervention. The righteous look forward to the time when God will establish peace, judge the wicked, and enlarge the nation.

Song of acknowledgment for the nation's failure (26:16–19). Isaiah recalled a time when the nation could "barely whisper a prayer" because of the distress they were experiencing at God's hands. They cried out in their pain like a woman in childbirth. But instead of being rewarded with life, their effort only "gave birth to wind." Because God had called Abraham and his descendants to be His channel of blessing to the nations ("all peoples on earth will be blessed through you," Gen. 12:3), Israel's God-given task was to be a "light for the Gentiles" (Isa. 42:6; 49:6). But sadly, the nation must now admit that it had failed in that task. And yet God promised that the nation will be resurrected and restored from the dead (see also Ezek. 37:11–14).

Song of exhortation to wait on the Lord (26:20–21). Isaiah ended this extended song by reminding the people of God's coming judgment. Israel was to hide until God's judgment had "passed by." God will judge people for shedding innocent blood (see Gen. 4:10).

God's Establishment of His Kingdom (chapter 27)

The phrase "in that day" divides this chapter into three sections, each of which develops the thought that God will establish His kingdom. He will judge His enemies (27:1), He will watch over—and purify—His people even during times of judgment (27:2–11), and He will finally regather His people to Himself (27:12–13).

The overthrow of Leviathan (27:1). In Canaanite mythology Leviathan was the "monster of the sea" associated with chaos. In borrowing this imagery, Isaiah was not condoning false religious beliefs. Instead, he was painting a graphic picture of God's destruction of His enemies. Isaiah may have had in mind the gentile nations that had persecuted the Lord's people. (The Bible uses similar imagery in Psalm 74:12–15 and Isaiah 51:9–10 to describe Israel's crossing of the Red Sea and in Ezekiel 29:2–5 to describe God's judgment on Egypt in Ezekiel's day.) However, Isaiah may also have been alluding to Satan, the ultimate "serpent" (Rev. 20:2). In either case, God will bring an end to those who rise up against Him.

God's watchcare over His vineyard (27:2–11). For a second time Isaiah compared Israel to a vineyard planted by God (see 5:1–7). Now, however, God is the jealous guardian of His vineyard, watching over it to keep anyone from harming it. Though the vineyard had undergone discipline because of disobedience, God promised that the nation will "take root," "bud and blossom," and eventually "fill all the world with fruit." While awaiting this promised blessing, the nation will suffer covenant curses (Lev. 26; Deut. 28) because of disobedience. These include war and exile. Yet His ultimate goal will be to bring about a time when Israel's sins will be forgiven.

God's regathering of His people (27:12–13). The phrase "in that day," used twice in these two verses, points to the physical and spiritual regathering of the Lord's people, in which He will "thresh" the land from east to west. Using imagery of the harvest (see also Matt. 13:24–30), God will regather His people "one by one." Those who are brought back into the land will also experience a spiritual renewal. When God sounds His trumpet, His people will return to worship Him "on the holy mountain in Jerusalem" (see also Isa. 2:2–5; 24:23).

God's Woes (chapters 28–33)

In chapters 28–33 the prophet announced six "woes" (denunciation messages) against the rulers of Israel and Judah, and against foreign powers who set themselves against God. Much as the six judgments in 5:8–23 summarized the sins of the people, these six woes epitomize and summarize the sins of the rulers.

Six Things the Lord Hates

Prideful scoffing by Samaria's and Jerusalem's leaders (chapter 28)

Religious hypocrisy in Jerusalem (29:1–14)

Deception by those who try to hide their actions from God (29:15–24)

Stubborn rebellion against God by seeking foreign alliances (chapter 30)

Lack of trust in God that is replaced by a dependence on
    military might (chapters 31–32)

Destructive opposition to God and His plans by Assyria (chapter 33)

God's Woe against Prideful Scoffing (chapter 28)

Woe to Samaria's prideful drunkenness (28:1–13). Isaiah first directed God's message of judgment against the city of Samaria which, like a "wreath" crowning a person's head, was situated "on the head of a fertile valley." The Israelites' heavy use of beer and wine caused the religious and civil leaders to "stagger when seeing visions, they stumble when rendering decisions." God threatened to bring "one who is powerful and strong" to destroy the city. After this judgment God will be the "beautiful wreath for the remnant of his people." Because the people refused to listen to God's word sent by His messengers, He would "speak" to them "with foreign lips and strange tongues"—a reference to the Assyrians sent by God to capture the people of Israel in 722 B.C.

Woe to Jerusalem's boastful scoffing (28:14–22). Scoffers of Jerusalem felt safe because they had "entered into a covenant with death," likely a reference to their trust in the supposed god of the underworld. The people of Jerusalem felt secure because, if the God of Israel failed them, they had an alliance with another god. God's response was to announce that there was only one "precious cornerstone for a sure foundation." Those who trust in Him and follow in His path will never be disappointed. But those trusting in other gods would not experience deliverance. "An overwhelming scourge" sweeping into the land would destroy those who had not trusted in God. This most likely refers to Assyria's invasion of Judah in 701 B.C. (Isa. 36–37).

God's grace in judgment (28:23–29). Isaiah ended the first woe with a hymn of praise to God for His grace in judgment. The hymn has two stanzas (28:23–26 and 28:27–29), both of which use imagery from planting and harvesting to show that (a) judgment is not forever and (b) judgment will be followed by blessing. In the first stanza the thought is that though the farmer plows, he does not do so "continually." Once the sharp edge of the plow has done its work of breaking and turning over the soil, the soil is ready to receive the seed of blessing. The idea in the second stanza is that though "grain must be ground to make bread," the crushing is appropriate to the grain and is not allowed to exceed certain boundaries.

God's Woe against Religious Hypocrisy and Deception (chapter 29)

God will bring a siege against Jerusalem for her religious hypocrisy (29:1–4). Isaiah identified Jerusalem ("the city where David settled") as "Ariel," a Hebrew word meaning "lion of God." While the people of Jerusalem scrupulously followed the annual festivals, their violence and bloodshed had made the city an "altar hearth"—a place where the blood of sacrifices was scattered. (For similar warnings by God see 1:11–15.) God threatened to "camp" against them and to "set up [His] siege works against" them. God did this when, as already noted, He brought the Assyrian army to Jerusalem in 701 B.C. (36:1–2).

God will destroy the enemy attacking Jerusalem (29:5–8). Though the Lord brought several nations against Jerusalem, He would also defeat them. The mighty enemies would "become like fine dust" because He would judge the invaders and rescue His city. Again, this was fulfilled in 701 B.C.

God will judge Jerusalem for her continued spiritual insensitivity (29:9–14). In spite of God's great victory over the army that surrounded Jerusalem, His people still failed to gain spiritual insight. Even the prophets and seers, who were spiritually blind and drunk, failed to grasp the true nature of their spiritual condition. The people seemed to be responding to God, for they honored Him "with their lips." Yet God, knowing everything, said, "their hearts are far from me." As a result, God would again judge His people. Possibly this message referred to the coming Babylonian captivity. God had spared Jerusalem from the Assyrians, but the city would fall to the Babylonians (see 39:5–7).

God will judge those who try to deceive Him (29:15–24). God's third woe would fall on those who try to "hide their plans from the LORD." In arrogance and pride these mere creatures sought to elevate themselves to the Creator's level. This was as if "the pot say[s] of the potter, 'He knows nothing.'" Looking ahead, Isaiah saw a day when God will rescue and reward the lowly (the "deaf ... blind ... humble ... and needy") and judge the wicked (the "ruthless . . . mockers . . . and all who have an eye for evil"). In that day the redeemed will come humbly to receive instruction from Him.

God's Woe against Stubborn Rebellion (chapter 30)

God denounced the proposed alliance with Egypt (30:1–5). Calling the people of Judah "obstinate children," God spoke against those who stubbornly sought to form an alliance with Egypt. God said these plans were not His. Evidently Judah sent delegates to Egypt to seek military help against Assyria. Egypt did come to rescue Judah during the Assyrian invasion (37:9), but the Assyrians defeated them (20:5–6). God announced in advance that they would be ashamed for going to Pharaoh for protection because the Egyptian army would be of no help. During the Assyrian attack against Judah, the Assyrian army commander described Judah's trust in Egypt as someone leaning on a "splintered reed of a staff" (36:6).

God will judge the nation because of her trust in Egypt (30:6–17). Isaiah spoke of donkeys and camels traveling through the Negev toward Egypt, loaded down with treasures to buy Egypt's protection. But Egypt's help would prove useless. Judah's main problem was her unwillingness to listen to the Lord. Refusing to hear God's word, the people preferred instead to have their prophets tell them "pleasant things." But in rejecting God's message, they had sealed their destruction. They would soon "break in pieces like pottery." Rather than trusting in God, they sought escape on swift horses. Yet only their pursuers would be swift.

God will be gracious to His people (30:18–33). Though the message in this chapter is one of judgment, Isaiah reminded the people that God longed to be gracious to them. If the people would turn to Him in repentance, He would respond by sending sound teachers to lead the people in His way of blessing (30:20–21) and to send them rain, sunshine, and plentiful harvests (30:23–26). God also vowed to "shatter Assyria," the nation that had been His instrument of destruction.

God's Woe against Those Who Refuse to Trust Him (chapters 31–32)

These two chapters, while containing a separate "woe," continue the theme of the previous chapter: Judah's depending on Egypt rather than God for protection. However, there are two important differences. First, this woe focuses more on Judah's *lack of trust in* God than on her *rebellion against* God. Second, this woe ends with a promise of the coming messianic King, who will deliver His people and bring peace.

God—not Egypt—will defend His people (31:1–5). Isaiah announced woe on those who go to Egypt for help. Their sin was trusting in Egypt's military might while refusing to seek help from the Lord. God responded by announcing He would oppose the wicked. The Egyptians and the Judeans would experience military defeat at God's hands. But then, with all human hope gone, God would intervene for His people and "shield" Jerusalem. Again, this was fulfilled in 701 B.C. (37:36–37).

God called on His people to return to Him (31:6–9). Isaiah called on the people to return to the Lord. In God's coming day of deliverance the remnant will reject the idols in which they had falsely trusted. Again God's power would be evident when "Assyria will fall by a sword that is not of man."

A king will reign in righteousness (32:1–8). Looking beyond the defeat of the Assyrians, God spoke of a time when He will send a King who will "reign in righteousness" (see 11:1–5). During that time Israelites will demonstrate love for each other, offering protection ("a shelter from the wind") and provision ("streams of water in the desert"). This will be a time when, spiritually, eyes will once again see and ears will hear (6:10; 35:5–6).

Blessing will follow judgment (32:9–20). The women of Jerusalem evidently thought the impending invasion would not come. But God said that

Judah would soon be judged. The fruitful land would become "overgrown with thorns and briers." Though not specifically stated, the larger context suggests that Isaiah was again predicting the coming Assyrian invasion that would decimate much of Judah (7:17–23). Moving from imminent judgment to ultimate restoration, the prophet announced that destruction would continue "till the Spirit is poured upon us from on high." This coming age of blessing will bring justice and righteousness to all Israel. As a result, the people will live in peace, security, and rest (see also 11:5–9).

God's Woe against Destructive Opposition (chapter 33)

God will judge the destroyer (33:1–12). Isaiah's final woe was directed against the "destroyer," a reference to Assyria. Verses 2–9 record a prayer to the Lord for Assyria's destruction. The people called on God to "be gracious" and to bring deliverance in their "time of distress" (33:2–4). Their prayer was based on the sure hope that God is exalted and would act on their behalf (33:5–6). Divine intervention was needed because the treaty was broken between Judah and Assyria and the Assyrian army was coming to attack (33:7–9). So God promised to come in response to His people's prayers.

God will deliver the righteous (33:13–24). God called on people everywhere ("far away" and "near") to acknowledge His power and to turn to Him. He promised that those who love Him and obey His commands will find protection and provision. Moving from the near to the far, Isaiah described a time when the righteous remnant "will see the king in his beauty." Past corruption and oppression will be only a distant memory. Instead, Jerusalem will enjoy peace and security. Jerusalem will be like a ship in safety that will not need to be prepared for war because "the LORD is our king; it is he who will save us." God will remove Jerusalem's physical and spiritual illnesses.

Judgment against the Nations (chapter 34)

This chapter serves as a fitting climax to the six woes. When God comes to rescue His people, He will judge all the nations who have opposed Him and oppressed His own. In the previous chapters the focus was specifically on Assyria. However, in this chapter Edom is the country epitomizing all nations who are the object of God's judgment (as in Obadiah).

God will judge all the nations (34:1–4). Angry with the nations, God will destroy them. Judgment will extend even to the heavens; the sky will be "rolled up like a scroll" and "all the starry hosts will fall." Neither sky nor earth will escape God's punishment.

God will judge Edom (34:5–17). From the earliest days Edom coveted Israel's land. Her destruction would serve as a reminder to all nations that God will hold them accountable for the way they have treated His people. God would bring on Edom "a year of retribution, to uphold Zion's cause." As Edom had done to Judah, so God would do to her. The land of Edom would become the domain of wild animals. Isaiah recorded this so future generations could "look in the scroll" and recognize that God is the One who had "given the order."

Blessing for the Redeemed (chapter 35)

God will bless the land (35:1–2). Though the land of Edom became desolate (34:9–13), the land of Israel will be blessed. God will turn the desert areas of Judah along the Dead Sea and south of the Negev into fertile country. They will bloom with the beauty and lushness normally reserved for the well-watered lands of Lebanon, Mount Carmel, and the plain of Sharon.

God will bless the people (35:3–7). God's presence will also bring a change to the hearts of His people. Those who are afraid will be strengthened as He comes to save them from their oppressors. This will be a time when, spiritually, eyes will once again see, ears will hear, and those who are lame will walk (see also 6:10; 32:3–4). Land that was once "wilderness" or "burning sand" will become springs and pools of water. Jesus may have had this passage in mind when He responded to a question from John the Baptist (Matt. 11:2–6). Jesus pointed to His miracles among the blind and the lame, perhaps alluding to this passage, to show He is indeed the Messiah, offering the kingdom to Israel.

God will bring His people back to the land (35:8–10). God will provide a roadway ("the Way of Holiness") for His people to return to the land. He will protect travelers from all dangers so the redeemed can return to Zion in safety and in joyful celebration as the sorrow of former times vanish.

II. ISAIAH'S HISTORICAL BRIDGE (CHAPTERS 36–39)

Chapters 36–39 shift from prophecy to history. These chapters function as a bridge that allows the reader to travel from the first half of the book to the second half. The material in these chapters is also found in 2 Kings 18–20 and in a more abbreviated fashion in 2 Chronicles 32. Isaiah 36–37 form a unit that looks back and concludes the first thirty-five chapters. Isaiah 38–39 form a unit that looks ahead and sets the stage for chapters 40–66.

Isaiah's Historical Bridge	
Isaiah 36–37	*Isaiah 38–39*
Assyria prominent	Babylon prominent
Judah's deliverance accomplished (Looks back to chapters 1–35)	Judah's captivity announced (Looks ahead to chapters 40–66)

A. A LOOK BACK: HEZEKIAH AND ASSYRIA (CHAPTERS 36–37)

Sennacherib's attack against Judah (36:1–3). All Isaiah's earlier predictions about Assyria came true in 701 B.C. when Sennacherib of Assyria attacked the cities of Judah and captured them. Jerusalem remained the ultimate goal of the Assyrian army, and so Sennacherib sent his field commander with a large army to Jerusalem to demand its surrender. Three of king Hezekiah's officials went out to meet with the commander.

The field commander's first address to Jerusalem (36:4–10). Sennacherib's commander attempted to demoralize Jerusalem's leaders by exposing the city's weakness in two ways. First, if Judah was "depending on Egypt," they would discover that Egypt was an unreliable ally. Second, if Judah

Archaeological Confirmation of Sennacherib's Attack on Judah

When Sennacherib became king of Assyria in 705 B.C., Hezekiah and several other nations used this opportunity to stop paying tribute to Assyria. Sennacherib first had to secure his throne at home, but in 701 b.c. he led his army west to attack the rebellious nations and bring them back under Assyrian control. This campaign is recorded on the Prism of Sennacherib (the so-called Taylor Prism). The attack is also recorded in 2 Kings 18:13–19:27; 2 Chronicles 32:1–23; Isaiah 10:5–34; 36:1–37:38; and Micah 1:8–16. Part of the inscription from the prism reads as follows:

> But as for Hezekiah, the Jew, who did not bow in submission to my yoke, forty-six of his strong walled towns and innumerable smaller villages in their neighborhood I besieged and conquered by stamping down earth-ramps and then by bringing up battering rams, by the assault of foot-soldiers, by breaches, tunneling and sapper-operations. I made to come out from them 200,150 people, young and old, male and female, innumerable horses, mules, donkeys, camels, large and small cattle; and counted them as the spoils of war. He himself I shut up like a bird in a cage within Jerusalem, his royal city. I put watch-posts strictly around it and turned back to his disaster any who went out of its city gate.

—TAYLOR PRISM (British Museum No. 91032)

was "depending on the LORD" (as the Assyrians understood the God of Judah), hadn't Hezekiah already offended his god when he removed "the high places and altars"? This refers to the religious reforms brought about by Hezekiah when he destroyed idols throughout Judah and restored the worship of God at the temple in Jerusalem (2 Chron. 29–31). Evidently the Assyrians (and some Israelites) saw these idols as part of the syncretistic worship of the God of Israel. From their pagan perspective, when Hezekiah destroyed the idols he "offended" this god who would therefore now refuse to aid Jerusalem. The envoy sent by Hezekiah asked the Assyrian commander to speak in Aramaic (the international language of the day, which these Judean leaders understood) rather than in Hebrew (which the common people of Jerusalem would have understood).

The field commander's second address to Jerusalem (36:11–22). The Assyrian commander, sensing an opportunity to provoke rebellion within the city, spoke directly to the men seated on the wall. Three times he called on them not to listen to their king. He said Hezekiah was powerless to deliver them, but the king of Assyria would treat them well in captivity if they would surrender. The commander also warned the people not to trust in the God of Israel because the gods of no other nation had been able to stop Assyria. "How then can the LORD deliver Jerusalem from my hand?" (36:20). The people did not respond to the Assyrian commander's speech because Hezekiah had ordered them to remain silent.

Hezekiah's request to God through Isaiah (37:1–7). In response to the Assyrian threat Hezekiah tore his clothes (a sign of deep emotion, mourning, and humility) and entered the temple. He also sent an envoy to Isaiah, asking him personally to pray for his people. Hezekiah recognized that God was the only hope for Jerusalem, and he also acknowledged Isaiah's role as the Lord's prophet. God responded dramatically and directly: "Do not be afraid of what you have heard." The Assyrian commander's words were blasphemous, and so God assured Isaiah that He would make the king of Assyria return to Assyria, where he would be assassinated.

Sennacherib's letter to Hezekiah (37:8–13). As Sennacherib continued his invasion of Judah, he heard that the Egyptian army was coming to Judah's aid. He responded by sending a messenger to Hezekiah, telling him not to take this as a sign of God's protection: "Do not let the god you depend on deceive you." Sennacherib reminded Hezekiah that Assyria had already destroyed other gods and defeated other kings.

Hezekiah's prayer to God in the temple (37:14–20). In a magnificent display of humble trust, Hezekiah took the letter from the king of Assyria and "spread it out before the LORD." As he acknowledged to the Lord that He alone is God, Hezekiah asked Him to look at "all the words Sennacherib has sent to insult" Him. Hezekiah acknowledged that the Assyrians had defeated and destroyed the gods of other nations, but this was possible because they were only idols made of wood and stone. He asked the Lord to deliver Jerusalem so that all nations would know that He alone is God.

God's response to Hezekiah (37:21–35). God sent Isaiah to deliver His answer to Hezekiah's prayer. God said He would put His "hook" in Sennacherib's nose and make him return to Assyria. To validate the message of deliverance, God gave a sign to Hezekiah. For that year and the next the people of Judah would struggle, being forced to "eat what grows by itself" rather than being able to plant and cultivate. But by the third year they would be able to "sow and reap." Since the nation was already in the first year of trouble, God was promising that the threat of Assyrian invasion would be completely eliminated within two years.

God's judgment on the Assyrian army (37:36–38). After the dramatic promises and threats in chapters 36–37, the section ends abruptly. "The angel of the Lord," the preincarnate Jesus Christ, put to death 185,000 Assyrian soldiers in a single night. The Assyrian army returned to Nineveh, and sometime later two of Sennacherib's sons assassinated him, fulfilling God's promise to Hezekiah.

B. A LOOK FORWARD: HEZEKIAH AND BABYLON (CHAPTERS 38–39)

The account of Hezekiah's illness (38:1–8). When Hezekiah became ill, God sent Isaiah to tell Hezekiah he would die. Hezekiah prayed, and in response God sent Isaiah back with the message, "I will add fifteen years to your life." While some see Hezekiah's prayer as a sign of weakness or lack of faith, this does not seem to be the case. Hezekiah fell ill during Sennacherib's attack. Had he died then, the nation, lacking another strong, godly leader, would likely have surrendered to the Assyrians. God had promised to "deliver you and this city from the hand of the king of Assyria" (38:6). Thus Hezekiah sought to live so he could continue to lead the nation back to God.

Hezekiah's song of thanksgiving to God (38:9–22). In the first stanza (38:10–14) of this song, Hezekiah complained about his illness. Death would deny him the opportunity to worship the Lord. Like a shepherd's tent being taken down or a rug being cut from the loom, he felt his life was being wrapped up before its time. Physically his pain felt as if a lion had broken all his bones. In the second stanza (38:15–20), Hezekiah praised God for His healing: "You restored me to health and let me live." Only the living can praise God, and Hezekiah vowed to "sing with stringed instruments."

Isaiah appended a brief historical notation to the end of the song. First, he recorded that he prescribed a medical treatment to help promote healing. Second, he recorded Hezekiah's request for a sign to confirm God's promise. Though not recorded in Isaiah, the promised sign is explained in 2 Kings 20:8–11 (see also 2 Chron. 32:24).

Isaiah's prediction of captivity (chapter 39). God's great victories over the Assyrian army and over Hezekiah's personal illness made the king vulnerable to pride (see 2 Chron. 32:25). Envoys arrived from Merodach-Baladan, king of Babylon, who had been forced off his throne by Sennacherib in 703 B.C. and who spent his remaining years trying to regain his throne. The envoys brought "letters and a gift" to Hezekiah. Probably these were intended to buy Hezekiah's aid in an alliance against the king of Assyria (Judah had sent gifts to Egypt for the same reason; Isa. 30:6–7). Fawning over Hezekiah's physical recovery and the supernatural sign that accompanied it (2 Chron. 32:24, 31), the envoys were shown all his treasures. Confronting Hezekiah over his rash, prideful act, Isaiah predicted that the Babylonians would carry off all the treasures Hezekiah had hoarded. Even some of Hezekiah's descendants would be taken captive to Babylon. Hezekiah was content with the message because it would not occur in his lifetime. By the end of the historical bridge (Isa. 36–39) the threat from Assyria was past, but future captivity in Babylon was assured.

We are often most vulnerable to temptation immediately after a period of great spiritual blessing.

III. PROPHECIES OF COMFORT (CHAPTERS 40–66)

Judah's captivity in Babylon (39:6–7) occurred a century after Isaiah delivered his message to King Hezekiah. Yet this captivity was so certain it formed the backdrop for the remainder of the book. Beginning in chapter 40 the prophet wrote to those who would be in captivity. The break is so dramatic that many believe the words are from the pen of someone other than Isaiah. Yet in this very section God emphasized that He *was* predicting future events so those in captivity would know He is God. (See the discussion under "Author" in the Introduction.) To say these chapters came from the pen of another individual writing after the rise of Cyrus and the fall of Babylon is to deny the very claims God was making in this section about His sovereign power and ability to predict the future.

The following chart shows some of the thematic differences between Isaiah 1–35 and 40–66.

Isaiah 1–35	Isaiah 40–66
Focus on Assyria	Focus on Babylon
Primary theme: Judgment	Primary theme: Deliverance
Historical details present	Historical details absent
Messiah as the "Shoot from Jesse"	Messiah as the "Servant of the LORD"
Life of Isaiah prominent	Life of Isaiah absent

In 40:1–2 Isaiah introduced the second half of his message to the people of Judah. The message was one of "comfort" for a coming remnant in captivity. God called on the prophet to proclaim a threefold message to His people, and the three clauses that follow form a fitting outline for the remainder of the book.

The Clauses in Isaiah 40:2	The Content	The Chapters
Her hard service has been completed.	Judah's captivity in Babylon will end (God's Deliverance).	40–48
Her sin has been paid for.	God will provide a sacrifice for sin (God's Deliverer).	49–57
She received from God a double [portion] in place of all her sins.	Israel will receive her promised kingdom blessings (God's Delivered).	58–66

A. GOD'S DELIVERANCE (CHAPTERS 40–48)

The first of the three clauses in 40:2 focuses on God's deliverance of His people from captivity in Babylon. In this section Isaiah highlighted God's sovereign majesty over any other supposed deities. The Lord is preeminent because of His ability to state the future before it occurs. And as the sovereign God, He controls the future. The highlight of this section is God's identification of the individual He will send to rescue His people from captivity in Babylon—made before the nation even went *into* Babylon!

Comfort from a Sovereign God (chapter 40)

The announcement of comfort and deliverance (40:1–11). God's theme of comfort is proclaimed immediately to His people. Like a messenger sent before a king to announce his arrival, a "voice of one calling" cries out, encouraging the people to "prepare the way for the LORD." This found fulfillment in the ministry of John the Baptist, who was sent to prepare the way for Jesus (see Matt. 3:1–3; Mark 1:2–4; Luke 3:2–6; John 1:19–23).

Though the nation had been destroyed and the people scattered, they could find hope in God's promises because His word "stands forever" (Isa. 40:8). The messenger pointed the people to God as he painted two portraits designed to give them hope. The first is a picture of their God as the "Sovereign Lord" who comes with "power" to reward those who have been faithful (40:10). The second portrait pictures God as a tender shepherd who carries His weary lambs "close to his heart" (40:11).

God has the sovereign power to do anything He desires, and what He desires most is to hold us in His loving arms.

The basis for comfort and deliverance (40:12–26). Isaiah's audience in captivity would struggle to believe God's announcement. Their nation had been shattered, their houses demolished, their temple looted. God's promises were wonderful, but did He have the power to make them come to pass? Isaiah addressed that very issue by asking and answering four questions. The questions were designed to make the people of Israel compare their God to the physical and spiritual forces of Babylon. Whether it was the nation of Babylon, the idols of Babylon, the king of Babylon, or the supposed gods who watched over Babylon, in every case their power paled before the power of God. After each question, Isaiah provided evidence to show God's superiority to any possible opposition.

God's Superiority to All Possible Opposition		
Argument	*Question(s)*	*Conclusion*
His superiority to the nations is shown by His creation of the earth.	40:12–14	40:15–17
His superiority to idols is seen in the fact that they are created by craftsmen.	40:18	40:19–20

His superiority to the rulers of the earth is seen in the fact that He is transcendent while they are temporary	40:21	40:22–24
His superiority over other "deities" is shown by His creation of the heavenly bodies.	40:25	40:26

The application to Judah (40:27–31). Because of God's sovereign wisdom and power, the people of Judah were to realize that He knew of their problems, cared for them deeply, and would continue to uphold them. Those who relied on their own physical strength would fail, but those who trusted in God would find their strength renewed by Him so they could "soar on wings like eagles."

God's Witness to His Control of History (chapter 41)

God's selection of a deliverer from the east (41:1–7). God challenged the nations to stand before Him if they wished to contest His power. His first question to the nations was, "Who has stirred up one from the east" and given him authority over the nations? Though the individual is not named here, Isaiah later identified him as Cyrus, king of the Medo-Persian Empire (45:1). God's dare to the nations matched His ability in "calling forth the generations from the beginning." In a satirical jab at the nations Isaiah recorded that their response to God's challenge was to make more idols— as though new "gods" could succeed where their old ones had failed (41:5–7).

God's announcement of Israel's final victory over her foes (41:8–20). For the first time in the Book of Isaiah God referred to the nation Israel as His "servant." Sometimes this term is used of the whole nation, and sometimes it is applied to an individual. Here it refers to the "descendants of Abraham." God promised Israel final victory over her two greatest foes throughout history: other nations (41:11–16) and the forces of nature in her own land (41:17–20). A time will come when Israel's enemies "will be as nothing at all." Using harvest imagery, Isaiah said the nation will thresh and winnow those who once opposed her. But God will also change the land from foe to friend, making "rivers flow on barren heights" and turning the "desert into pools of water."

God's reaffirmation of His sovereign control (41:21–29). Beginning another theme that threads its way through this section of the book, God challenged false idols to describe their earlier predictions ("tell us what the former things were") or to issue new predictions ("tell us what the future holds"). Of course, these supposed gods, which cannot control the future, "are less than nothing." To back up His claim of superiority, God again spoke of the coming of His deliverer for Israel. This one will come from the north and east ("from the rising sun"). The Medes were northeast of Babylon, while Persia was east of Babylon. Before conquering Babylon Cyrus captured several empires north of the Babylonians. God concluded His challenge by again reminding Israel that no one foretold this except Him.

The Introduction of God's Servant (chapter 42)

Having introduced "the Servant of the LORD" in chapter 41, Isaiah began developing that theme in chapter 42. While God originally intended Israel to be His "servant," the nation never met His expectations. Isaiah developed a profile of the "ideal" servant that soon narrowed to a single individual, who would die on behalf of all others (chapter 53).

Isaiah's References to the "Servant of the Lord"	
41:8–10	Nation ("descendants of Abraham")
42:1–7	Individual ("called . . . in righteousness"/"light for the Gentiles")
42:18–22	("blind"/"deaf")
43:10	Nation ("witnesses"/"so that you may know and believe me and understand")

44:1–5, 21–23	Nation ("offspring"/"descendants"/"your offenses")
45:4	Nation ("For the sake of Jacob my servant . . . I summon [Cyrus]")
49:1–7	Individual ("before I was born"/"gather Israel to himself"/"light for the Gentiles")
50:4–11	Individual ("I have not been rebellious"/"did not hide my face from mocking and spitting")
52:13–53:12	Individual ("a man of sorrows"/"the LORD has laid on him the iniquity of us all")

The work of the Servant (42:1–17). This is the first of the four individual "Servant Songs" that point toward Israel's Messiah (see Matt. 12:18–21). God identified this individual as "my servant . . . my chosen one." Empowered by God's Spirit, the Servant's task is to "bring justice to the nations" and to be "a light for the Gentiles." God's original plan for Abraham's descendants was that they be the conduit for His blessing to the nations (Gen. 12:3). The Servant will succeed where the nation had failed. A new song of praise will be sung to the Lord for the victory He will accomplish through His Servant.

The difficulties of the servant Israel (42:18–25). While God's Servant, the Messiah, will open the eyes of the blind (42:7), God chastised His servant Israel for being spiritually blind and deaf (42:18–19). They had been called to be His messengers, but their spiritual insensitivity brought them to ruin. The new "Servant" was necessary because the original "servant" had turned from the Lord and was under God's judgment.

God's Promised Redemption for Israel (chapter 43)

God's promised protection for His people (43:1–13). God promised to protect Israel, even in times of judgment, "since you are precious and honored in my sight, and because I love you." Using a figure of speech called a merism, God vowed to restore captives "from the east" and "from the west," indicating that from east to west (and everywhere in between) no

Israelite would be outside the boundaries of His deliverance. God challenged all the nations to consult their gods ("who have eyes but are blind") and see which of them foretold Israel's deliverance from captivity. In announcing Israel's coming deliverance from captivity, God could claim that "I, even I, am the LORD, and apart from me there is no savior."

God's deliverance and Israel's rebellion (43:14–28). Becoming more specific, God declared He would judge the Babylonians because they had oppressed His people. He promised to make "a way in the desert" to guide and sustain Israel as they traveled back from captivity. One would expect Israel to respond with gratitude for God's graciousness, but the nation did not. He had not imposed a heavy burden on her, but ironically they had burdened Him with their sins. Though the Lord was eager to forgive, the people were unwilling to repent. So God said He would "consign Jacob to destruction and Israel to scorn."

God, Not Idols, Will Deliver Israel (chapter 44)

God's outpouring of His Spirit on Israel (44:1–5). Calling Israel His servant, God assured them He would sustain them. Like streams of water giving new life to barren ground, God said He would "pour out my Spirit on your offspring" (see also Joel 2:28–32). At that time spiritual barrenness and deadness will give way to a new relationship with God so that "one will say, 'I belong to the LORD.' "

God's promise based on His superiority to idols (44:6–20). God could make such remarkable promises because, as He said, "I am the first and I am the last; apart from me there is no God." His awesome power is displayed in His ability to foretell the future because He controls it. In contrast, idols are only blocks of wood, fashioned by a craftsman (who used another part of the wood to cook a meal!). People who "bow down to a block of wood" are depending on a god that is unable to deliver.

God's promise to remember His people (44:21–28). While other people made their gods, God promised to remember His servant nation, Israel, because, as He said, "I have made you." The God who made Israel would also restore Jerusalem and the other towns of Judah (44:26), and cause Cyrus to permit Jerusalem and the temple to be rebuilt (44:28).

God Will Use Cyrus to Restore His People (chapter 45)

Having identified Cyrus as the individual whom He would use to rescue His people (44:28), God described in more detail His plan to deliver Israel through this Medo-Persian king. His selection of Cyrus demonstrates His control over all creation, and the nations will ultimately bow down, both to redeemed Israel and to Him.

God selected Cyrus to deliver His people (45:1–13). Both parts of this section begin with the phrase "This is what the LORD says" (45:1, 11). God said Cyrus, His "anointed," would "subdue nations" and provide deliverance for His people. God named Cyrus long before he was even born, and He gave Cyrus his exalted position "though you do not acknowledge me," implying that Cyrus never placed his trust in the Lord. But why make such a prediction? God vowed to do this so that "men may know that there is none besides me. I am the LORD, and there is no other." Just as clay has no right to question the work of a potter, so no human can question the sovereignty of "the Holy One of Israel, and its Maker."

In What Way Was Cyrus "Anointed"?

The word "anointed" in 45:1 can also be translated "Messiah." Israel's kings were all "messiahs" in the sense that they were anointed, or set apart, for their position (1 Sam. 10:1; 16:1, 13). Cyrus was anointed by God to accomplish a mission for His people, and in this sense he can also be viewed as a "messiah." However, the people of Israel looked for God's ultimate Messiah, the chosen One from the line of David who will rule over Israel forever (Isa. 9:7; see also Mic. 5:2; Dan. 9:25–26).

Gentile nations will bow down to redeemed Israel (45:14–25). Besides being restored from captivity, Israel will ultimately rule over her former enemies, including Egypt, Cush, and the Sabeans (see 43:3). These nations will bow down before her as they humbly admit, "Surely God is with you, and there is no other." Isaiah concluded with praise to the awesome, majestic God. Those who depend on idols "will be put to shame and disgraced," while God's people Israel "will never be put to shame or disgraced" again. God displayed His superiority over idol-worshipers by declaring the future. He encouraged the nations to turn to Him and be saved for, He said, "I am God, and there is no other."

God Will Judge Babylon (chapters 46–47)

The impotence of Babylon's gods (chapter 46). Bel and Nebo, Babylon's two chief deities, were bowed down as they were carried "by beasts of burden." The heavy, wooden gods were "a burden for the weary" as the Babylonians tried to carry their gods to safety during Cyrus's attack. But their efforts failed, and both the idols and those bearing them were taken captive. In contrast to Babylon's false gods, God reminded His people He had "upheld" them since conception and "carried" them since birth. Unlike false idols that must be crafted and carried, and are unable to save, the God of Israel confidently stated, "My purpose will stand, and I will do all that I please." To prove His point He again said that "from the east" He would summon a man to fulfill His purposes. Through this one (Cyrus) God would rescue His people from Babylon.

> *There are two kinds of gods in this world: the kind you carry and the One who can carry you.*

The dethronement of the "Virgin Daughter of Babylon" (chapter 47). Israel would experience God's "splendor" (46:13), but the city of Babylon, pictured here as a virgin, would mourn "in the dust (47:1)." The city would be forced to perform hard labor ("grind flour"), and the "queen of kingdoms" would be shamefully exposed and degraded. God's judgment against Babylon was harsh because of what she had done to Israel. When God had handed His people over to Babylon for judgment, Babylon "showed them no mercy." Though Babylon felt secure ("I am, and there is none besides me"), God announced that the city would face disaster. Babylon's astrologers and sorcerers would be unable to stop His judgment from coming.

Those who dabble in the occult or in astrology are misleading themselves and trusting in practices that lead to destruction.

God's Appeal to Stubborn Israel (chapter 48)

God's predictions to stubborn Israel (48:1–11). Though Israel took "oaths in the name of the LORD," they did not do so honestly. God had earlier predicted Judah's fall to Babylon because, He said, "I knew how stubborn you were." The people were so caught up in idolatry that, had the events taken place without being announced in advance, they would have claimed, "My idols did them." In the same way God announced He was predicting new and hidden things that had never been predicted before. These "new things" refer to the rise of Cyrus, Israel's release from Babylon, and Babylon's fall (see 48:14–15). God's purpose in making these predictions was to protect His own name and reputation: "I will not yield my glory to another."

God's deliverance of stubborn Israel (48:12–22). Having announced His prediction of "new things" (48:6–7), God summarized those predictions in verses 14–15. God's "chosen ally" will arise to accomplish "his purpose against Babylon." God predicted this event during the days of Isaiah (750–700 B.C.) so that when the events took place in 539 B.C. the people would realize "at the time it happens, I am there." As a result, the people would recognize that the Lord is God and would acknowledge that He "teaches you what is best for you." Had they paid attention in the past, the nation could have avoided much heartache. But in the day of Babylon's fall, they could recall His words and "leave Babylon." Just as in the first Exodus, the people would experience God's protection as they returned home from Babylon.

B. GOD'S DELIVERER (CHAPTERS 49–57)

Isaiah 49–57 develops the second of the three clauses in 40:2: "her sin has been paid for." These chapters focus on God's deliverance of His people from their sin. In this section Isaiah highlighted God's faithful "Servant," who will be everything God intended Israel to be. The climax of the section is God's identification of "the servant of the LORD" as the One who will die for the sins of the people (52:13–53:12). The Servant's substitutionary death will bring salvation to Israel (chapters 54–55) and the nations (chapters 56–57).

The Servant of the Lord Commissioned (chapter 49)

The Servant's task explained (49:1–13). The Servant announced to the world that God had called Him and prepared Him to do God's work. Being called "my servant Israel" identified this individual with Abraham's chosen seed and indicated He would succeed where the nation had failed. His task was twofold: to "gather Israel to himself" and to be a" light for the Gentiles." (This was applied to Jesus in Luke 2:32.) God would help the Servant be a "covenant for the people" (see Isa. 42:6), "restore the land," and bring back Israel's "captives." The Servant's mission would fulfill God's promise to comfort His people (49:13; also see 40:1).

Israel's doubts alleviated (49:14–26). Heaven and earth burst into song at the Servant's announcement, but "Zion"—a figure of speech for the ruined city of Jerusalem and the people of Israel who once dwelt there (40:9–11)—could not share in the joy. Instead the city felt forsaken by the Lord. God responded by declaring He had more compassion for Jerusalem than a mother could ever have for her own child. The plight of the city (and her inhabitants) was as visible to God as if the people were "engraved . . . on the palms" of His hands. The city will again be inhabited, lovingly exhibiting her people as "ornaments" the way a "bride" wears jewelry on her wedding day. The once "bereaved and barren" city will not have room enough to hold all her inhabitants. She will be exalted, while her former oppressors "will lick the dust at your feet."

When times of discouragement and doubt come, never forget that God still loves you.

The Servant of the Lord Contrasted with Disobedient Israel (chapter 50)

Israel's disobedience brought judgment (50:1–3). Two illustrations from daily life showed Israel that her disobedience was the cause for judgment. First, a husband could divorce his wife by issuing a "certificate of divorce" (Deut. 24:1–4), but God had issued no such decree to Israel. Israel was sent out of the land because of her transgression, but she still belonged to Him. Second, someone in debt could sell his children as slaves to satisfy his creditor (2 Kings 4:1; Neh. 5:4–5), but God was in debt to no one. Israel was in slavery because of her own sins. God can rescue His people, but they first need to turn to Him.

The Servant's obedience brought vindication (50:4–9). In contrast to Israel, the Servant was not rebellious. Even in times of persecution He willingly turned His "back to those who beat" Him. This beating, along with "mocking and spitting," vividly pictures the events leading up to Jesus' crucifixion (Matt. 27:26–31). The Servant remained resolute (He set His face "like flint") throughout the mistreatment. He could face His accusers because of His confidence in God's ultimate deliverance.

The Servant's exhortation to Israel to trust the Lord (50:10–11). The Servant called on those who "fear the LORD" to continue to trust God even in times of distress (pictured as walking "in the dark"). But He issued a warning to those who try to solve their problems by using their own effort (pictured as walking "in the light of" their own "fires"). Those who refuse to trust God and who rely instead on their own abilities will ultimately face torment.

God's Encouragement for Jerusalem (51:1–52:12)

God's command to listen (51:1–8). Three times God asked His followers to "listen to me." The first summons (51:1–3) was to listen and look *back* to gain hope from history. God directed their gaze to "the quarry from which [they] were hewn," a figurative reference to their ancestor Abraham. Abraham served as an example of faith, and Israel's future rested in the covenant that God made with Abraham. The second summons (51:4–6) was to listen and look *up* to gain hope from God's awesome character and mighty power. God promised that His "arm will bring justice to the nations." Israel was hoping just to hang on, but God was telling them they would be victorious! The third summons (51:7–8) was to listen and *not fear*. Knowing God's promises and power, Israel need not fear her enemies, for they will be destroyed, but God's righteousness will endure forever.

God's Three Calls to Listen	
51:1–3	Listen and look back (remember what God has done).
51:4–6	Listen and look up (remember who God is).
51:7–8	Listen and do not fear (remember what God has promised).

God's command to awaken (51:9–52:12). God also issued three calls to awaken. The first call (51:9–16) focused on the *power* of God. The people summoned God to "awake, as in days gone by." Using mythological imagery of the sea monster Rahab being cut in pieces to picture Israel's exodus from Egypt (see 27:1), the people asked the Lord again to display His awesome power to redeem His people. God responded by reminding the people of the power He displayed when He created the heavens and the earth. The second call (51:17–23) focused on the *purpose* of God. The nation had drunk "the cup of his wrath," but God now promised to take His cup of judgment out of their hand and to put it into the hands of their tormentors. The third call (52:1–12) focused on the *peace* of God. God promised Jerusalem that she will be "enthroned" and "redeemed." Runners will come to bring peace, deliverance, and comfort to Jerusalem as they announce, "Your God reigns!" (see also 40:3, 9–11). As the people return to Jerusalem from captivity, they will not be forced to leave quickly because God will protect them throughout their journey.

Isaiah's Three Wake-Up Calls	
51:9–16	Wake up to the power of God (His power has not changed).
51:17–23	Wake up to the purpose of God (He has a plan for your life).
52:1–12	Wake up to the peace of God (He will not abandon you).

The Suffering Servant of the Lord (52:13–53:12)

The fourth Servant song highlights the suffering of the Servant. The song has five "stanzas," with three verses each. The obedient Servant is rejected by the people and put to death. The people assume the Servant's death is God's judgment, but in reality the punishment suffered by the Servant is for the sins of the people—an atoning sacrifice that brings forgiveness. Though put to death, the Servant will ultimately be rewarded by God. In Acts 8:30–35 Philip explained that this passage refers to Jesus.

The Servant's triumph (52:13–15). The first stanza of the song begins with a promise of the Servant's ultimate triumph. Because of His wise actions He will be "highly exalted." Though many were initially amazed because "his appearance was so disfigured" through cruel treatment, His actions ultimately will bring cleansing ("sprinkling") to many people. Kings will stand in awe when they finally realize what the Servant had accomplished for them.

The Servant's rejection (53:1–3). The second stanza focuses on the rejection of the Servant by the people. The Servant grew up like a "tender shoot" (see 11:1), and His simple beginnings gave no one reason to pay any attention. There was nothing special in His "majesty" or His "appearance" that hinted at His true greatness. Instead He was hated and rejected even by those who claimed to be God's people.

The Servant's suffering (53:4–6). The third stanza highlights the suffering experienced by the Servant. When the Servant suffered, the people assumed He was being judged ("stricken by God") for His own sins. But the awesome truth was that the Servant was acting as an atoning sacrifice for the sins of the people. While they all went "astray . . . the LORD has laid on him the iniquity of us all." The Servant became the Sin-Bearer for the people.

The Servant's death (53:7–9). The fourth stanza describes the Servant's death. Like a sacrificial lamb being offered on the altar, "he did not open his mouth." The Servant not only experienced physical pain; He also experienced death. He was "cut off from the land of the living." The wages of sin is death (Gen. 2:17; Rom. 6:23), and the Servant had to die to pay the price due for others' sin. In an ironic twist the Servant is associated in death with both "the wicked" and "the rich." This predicted Jesus' crucifixion between two thieves (Matt. 27:38) and His burial in the tomb of Joseph of Arimathea (27:57–60).

The Servant's reward (53:10–12). The final stanza looks beyond the tragedy of the Servant's death to the triumph of His resurrection. Though the Servant gave His life as a "guilt offering" for the sin of others, God announced that the Servant would "see his offspring and prolong his days," that is, the Servant will be alive to see future generations. His suffering and death must precede His triumph, but after He had suffered He would "see the light of life." The Servant willingly gave His life for others, and God promised to reward Him by allowing Him to "divide the spoils," as a king divides the spoils of conquest.

New Testament References to Isaiah 53	
Matthew 8:17	Jesus healed the sick (Isa. 53:4).
Mark 15:28	Jesus was crucified between two thieves (Isa. 53:12).
Luke 22:37	Jesus predicted His coming arrest and crucifixion (Isa. 53:12).
John 12:38	Israel rejected Jesus (Isa. 53:1).
Acts 8:26–35	Philip taught the Ethiopian eunuch (Isa. 53:7–8).
Romans 10:15	Paul wrote of Israel's unbelief (Isa. 53:1).
1 Peter 2:22	Peter presented Christ as an example of how to live (Isa. 53:9).

God's Promised Restoration of Israel (chapter 54)

Israel will be restored to her divine Husband (54:1–10). Though Israel felt as rejected and alone as a "barren woman," she will be restored and blessed. The many descendants will "spread out" beyond the boundaries of Israel and "dispossess nations" that had once oppressed them. As their "husband" and "Redeemer," God will call them back into a personal relationship with Himself. Using an illustration from Noah, Isaiah said the Lord's judgment will be followed by a "covenant of peace" that will never be removed.

Jerusalem will be glorified and protected (54:11–17). Though Jerusalem felt like a ship "lashed by storms," she will be rebuilt and restored to a place of glory with physical beauty, spiritual insight, peace, and righteousness. These will supplant the former "terror" she experienced; it will be "far removed." In this future time of blessing, no nation will be permitted to attack His people.

God's Invitation for Salvation to Israel (chapter 55)

God's offer to those who repent (55:1–7). Using beautiful imagery of free food and water for the hungry and thirsty, God called on all who are needy to come to His place of blessing. The water of life is free, and the bread of life is "the richest of fare." They can come without cost, because God had paid the price. God offered to make an everlasting covenant with those who come to Him. This phrase looks back to the work of the Servant of the Lord who was a "covenant" to Israel and to the nations (42:6; 49:8). But it also identified the Servant as the Messiah (9:6–7; 11:1) since this "covenant" is associated with the Davidic Covenant ("my faithful love promised to David") that looked forward to the Messiah (2 Sam. 7:8–16; 1 Chron. 17:4–14).

God's awesome ways and effective Word (55:8–13). God's ability to forgive sin, offer blessing, and unite the work of the Servant with the messianic promises made to David are extraordinary. But this is exactly why His ways are higher than our ways. Only God can bring all these details together in such a way. Israel can depend on God's blessing because His words of promise will not return to Him "empty" but will accomplish what He desires. The people will experience God's blessing, and even the land will change from a place of judgment ("thornbush" and "briers"; see 5:6; 32:13) to a place of productive beauty.

God's Invitation for Salvation to the Nations (chapter 56)

God's promise to Israelites who hold fast (56:1–2). God encouraged His people to follow His standards of justice and to do "what is right." They could do so in confidence, knowing that His promised deliverance was "close at hand." The ones who by faith held fast would be "blessed."

God's promise to foreigners who hold fast (56:3–8). Though God's promises had been to Israel, no foreigner who trusted in Him should feel excluded. God promised all foreigners who bound themselves to Him that He would allow them to worship Him and He would "give them joy" in His temple. God promised to "gather still others" from among the nations to share His blessings with Israel.

God's judgment against foreigners who persecute Israel (56:9–12). Israelites and foreigners who turn to the Lord can expect His blessing. However, those who oppose God and persecute His people will be judged. God referred to them as "beasts of the field" who attacked Israel when she was led by blind "watchmen," "mute dogs," and selfish "shepherds"—pictures of Israel's ineffective leaders who brought destruction on the nation.

God's Condemnation of the Wicked (chapter 57)

God's judgment on the wicked (57:1–13). When the righteous died, it was God's way of sparing them from the horrors of the judgment He was about to bring on His people. But those who mocked God by committing spiritual adultery with idols (who "made a pact with those whose beds you love") would experience judgment. Since they continually searched for new gods, He threatened to expose their works.

God's mercy on the contrite (57:14–21). Though God is "high and lofty," He also promised to live with anyone "who is contrite and lowly in spirit." God had punished, but He also promised to "heal . . . guide . . . and restore comfort." Those who submit to God will find peace, but the wicked will have no peace.

C. GOD'S DELIVERED (CHAPTERS 58–66)

Isaiah 58–66 develops the third of the three clauses in Isaiah 40:2 ("received from the LORD's hand double for all her sins"). These chapters focus on God's blessings to be poured out on the righteous remnant. In this section Isaiah highlighted the kingdom blessings to be received by those who turn to the Lord. Some may question whether the third clause of Isaiah 40:2 actually refers to blessing. (At first glance it seems to say God will punish the people twice as much as they have sinned.) However, Isaiah used the phrase again in 61:7, where it clearly refers to the double portion (inheritance) to be received by God's people. "Instead of their shame my people will receive a double portion, and instead of disgrace they will rejoice in their inheritance; and so they will inherit a double portion in their land, and everlasting joy will be theirs."

From Guilt to Glory
Cycles of Redemption in Isaiah 58–66

First Cycle: The Cleansing of the Nations (58:1–63:6)

- Fact of Israel's sin (58:1–59:8)
- Confession of Israel's sin (59:9–15)
- Forgiveness and deliverance (59:16–21)
- Appearance of God's glory and blessing (60:1–63:6)

Second Cycle: The Response of the People (63:7–66:24)

- Confession of Israel's sin (63:7–64:12)
- Forgiveness and Deliverance (65:1–16)
- Appearance of God's glory and blessing (65:17–66:24)

Israel's Hypocritical Worship (58:1–59:8)

Israel's hypocritical fasting (58:1–12). When God ordered His messenger to rebuke the people for their rebellion, they seemed surprised. They publicly affirmed they were "eager for God to come near them," and they "fasted" and "humbled" themselves (perhaps through the wearing of sackcloth and through public prayer; see 2 Chron. 7:14; Joel 1:13–14; Jon. 3:5–9). But God saw their hearts and knew they were insincere. As they fasted, they continued to exploit their workers, and their fasts would often end in physical violence ("striking each other with wicked fists"). But change could be brought about by a true fast. Injustice, oppression, and the lack of care for the poor would disappear. "Then you will call, and the LORD will answer."

Israel's hypocritical Sabbath-keeping (58:13–14). Isaiah introduced a second illustration to show the insincerity of the people. Evidently the people chafed under God's Sabbath regulations and failed to follow His command. They were doing as they pleased and "going [their] own way." But if they would keep the Sabbath, they could then "feast on the inheritance" promised to their forefather Jacob.

Israel's violence and injustice (59:1–8). Israel's problems were *not* caused by God's inability to rescue them. His arm was not "too short" to reach out to them, nor were His ears "too dull" to hear their cries of distress. If God was not the problem, then who was? Isaiah answered in 59:2 with a scathing accusation against the people. One can almost feel the tip of his finger pressed against the people's chest as he pointed to them and said, in effect, the problem is *you!* Verses 2–3 repeatedly use the words "you" and "your." It was their sins that separated them from God and kept Him from responding to their pleas for help. With hands full of blood and mouths full of lies, "their thoughts are evil thoughts; ruin and destruction mark their way." In Romans 3:15–17 the apostle Paul quoted from this passage to stress God's condemnation of all humanity because of sin.

Israel's Confession and Forgiveness (59:9–21)

Israel's confession of her sin (59:9–15). Isaiah wrote the words the remnant of Israel will finally utter just before their Messiah returns. They are without justice and righteousness, and they stumble along as if they are blind. But instead of blaming God, the people will finally acknowledge that their problems have resulted from their own sin. "Our offenses are ever with us, and we acknowledge our iniquities." Isaiah wrote in the first person ("we," "us," "our") in verses 9–15 to make the repentance personal for the people.

God's forgiveness and deliverance (59:16–21). Once the people turn to God, He will forgive and deliver them. Since "there was no one to intervene," God Himself will come to rescue those who turn to Him. He will judge those who have persecuted His people, but He will come as the Redeemer to those who repent. The Lord will make a covenant with those He will rescue. His Spirit and the words He had imparted to them "will not depart from [their] mouth." This special indwelling of God's Holy Spirit and the writing of God's word on people's hearts (so they will know and do His will) are key parts of God's kingdom promises to Israel (44:3–5; Jer. 31:31–34; Ezek. 36:24–30; Joel 2:28–32). The prophet Jeremiah identified this as the "New Covenant."

The Appearance of God's Glory (chapter 60)

God's glory will come to Zion (60:1–2). God will call on Israel to stand up and "shine" because of His coming (see 59:20). God spoke of Himself as "light," perhaps a picture of the brightness of His glory (see also Ezek. 1:27–28). While other nations will feel the "darkness" of judgment, God's glory will be poured out on Israel.

The nations will come to Zion (60:3–14). God originally called Abraham and his descendants to be the channel for God's blessing to the world and a light to the Gentiles (Gen. 12:3; Isa. 42:6; 49:6). When Israel failed, God provided His "Servant" to fulfill that role. But in the future the "nations will come to your light," that is, Israel will ultimately become a light to the nations. These nations will bring their wealth to God's people, to help rebuild her walls and to "adorn" the temple.

God's blessings will come to Zion (60:15–22). Though Israel went through a period when she was "forsaken and hated," God promised that in this future era she will be enriched by the wealth of others. (She will "drink the milk of nations.") Violence and destruction will be replaced by peace and righteousness. Jerusalem will no longer need the sun or moon for light because the Lord will be her "everlasting light." Isaiah then announced two important promises from God. First, the "people will be righteous." The substitutionary death of the suffering Servant will be sufficient for the sins of the people (see 53:4–6). Second, Israel "will possess the land forever." God's promises to Abraham (Gen. 13:14–15) will find their ultimate fulfillment in the messianic kingdom.

The Coming of the Magi

"Magi from the east" came to worship the newborn King of the Jews and to bring presents of "gold and of incense and of myrrh" (Matt. 2:1–11). This event should have reminded Matthew's Jewish audience of Isaiah 60:6. When God's glory arrives for Israel, "all from Sheba will come, bearing gold and incense and proclaiming the praise of the Lord." The visit of the Magi should have alerted Israel to the identity of this child born in Bethlehem!

The Appearance of God's Messiah (chapter 61)

The coming of the Messiah (61:1–9). Speaking in the first person (see the Servant songs in 49:1–5; 50:4–9), God's Anointed One announced that "the Spirit of the Sovereign LORD is on me." The presence of God's Spirit was characteristic of the "Branch" from the line of David (11:2) and the "servant of the LORD" (42:19), pointing to the fact that both descriptions are of the same individual, Jesus Christ. After the Messenger's coming, God will "comfort all who mourn" and "rebuild the ancient ruins." The "shame" of their present oppression will be replaced by "a double portion"—a reference to the double share of the inheritance normally reserved for the firstborn (Deut. 21:17). God will remove their "disgrace" and give them instead "everlasting joy."

Jesus quoted Isaiah 61:1–2a when He spoke at the synagogue in Nazareth (Luke 4:16–19) and then proclaimed, "Today this scripture is fulfilled in your hearing" (4:21). The "good news" of redemption was fulfilled at Christ's first advent, but the "day of vengeance" (the point where Christ stopped reading) will be fulfilled at His second advent.

The response of the nation (61:10–11). Personified, the nation (or perhaps Jerusalem) will speak as a single voice in praising God for His blessing.

God will clothe the nation with "salvation" and "righteousness" in a manner befitting a bridegroom and bride at a wedding. Changing figures of speech, Isaiah said the nation will praise God for causing "righteousness and praise" to spring up in Israel like plants from the soil.

The Exaltation of Jerusalem (chapter 62)

God's delight in Jerusalem (62:1–5). God will not rest until all nations see Jerusalem's righteousness and change her name. Instead of "Deserted" or "Desolate" Jerusalem will be called "Hephzibah" ("My delight is in her"), and the land of Israel will be called "Beulah" ("married"). Both indicate the close, lasting relationship God will forge with His redeemed people.

God's restoration of Jerusalem (62:6–12). When Jerusalem is restored, it will become "the praise of the earth." God vowed on oath ("sworn by his right hand and by his mighty arm") that His redeemed city will never again be oppressed by "foreigners." Alluding back to 40:10, God called on His messenger to announce to Zion that her "Savior comes!" His arrival will bring God's promised blessing for the people and the city. The people will be known as "Holy People," and the city will be known as "Sought After, the City No Longer Deserted."

God's Judgment on Edom and Israel's Prayer (chapters 63–64)

A major break occurs in chapter 63. Verses 1–6 complete the theme of God's coming in glory in 60:1–63:6. While God's coming will bring deliverance for His people (60:1–62:12), it will also bring judgment on Israel's enemies (63:1–6). The remainder of this section focuses on the prayer of those awaiting God's deliverance.

God's judgment on Edom (63:1–6). Chapter 63 begins with a question: Isaiah asked the identity of the one he saw "coming from Edom." This individual came from battle ("garments [were] stained crimson"), he came in regal apparel ("robed in splendor"), and he came in mighty power ("striding . . . in the greatness of his strength"). The speaker identified Himself in a way that indicated He was the Lord. He spoke "in righteousness, mighty to save." The crimson on His robe was the "blood" of His enemies whom He had crushed. No one else had been able to help Israel (59:16), so God's "own arm worked salvation."

God's loyal love and the people's rebellion (63:7–10). In a dramatic break Isaiah moved from the subject of God's deliverance to Israel's prayer. The speaker—either Isaiah or Israel personified—began by recounting God's past kindness ("the deeds for which he is to be praised"). Likely the speaker had in mind God's redemption of Israel from Egypt when the people were in distress (Exod. 2:23–25) and God sent "the angel of his presence" to deliver them (12:1–30). However, after leaving Egypt the people "rebelled," and God had to judge them in the wilderness (He "fought against them").

Remembrance of God's past deliverance (63:11–14). The second stanza of this prayer of lament asked where God's gracious deliverance was that Israel experienced during the days of Moses. Twice the writer asked, "Where is he who . . . ?" The prayer focused on God's past display of power on behalf of His people, especially during the crossing of the Red Sea. God "brought them through the sea" and "led them through the depths." This mighty event gave the people "rest" from their oppression by Egypt. Sadly, the speaker reminded God that "this is how you guided your people" in the past.

Lament over their present suffering (63:15–19). Moving from the past to the present, the writer asked God to see the present plight of His people. Though God was still their "Father," the nation had strayed from His ways. The writer reminded the Lord that the nations had "trampled down [His] sanctuary," the temple.

Request for God to intervene in spite of their sin (64:1–7). Isaiah then called on God to act. His specific petition was that God would "rend the heavens and come down." The picture is of God splitting the sky and coming in awesome majesty to rescue His people. And yet the speaker asked a haunting question: Why should God come to rescue sinners? "All of us have become like one who is unclean." If no one calls on God, how can He come to rescue?

Request for God to intervene because of His covenant faithfulness (64:8–12). The final stanza of the prayer changed the focus from the people's sin to God's covenant faithfulness. In spite of their sin God was still their Father." He was the master "potter," and the people were "the work of

[His] hand." In a plea for mercy, the speaker asked God not to remember their sins. Specifically, he prayed for God's people who were oppressed, God's "cities" (especially Jerusalem) that were desolate, and God's temple that had been "burned with fire." (Daniel later voiced the same three requests in Dan. 9:15–19.)

God's Deliverance and Judgment (65:1–16)

Following the pattern of the first "Cycle of Redemption" (58:1–63:6), Israel's confession is followed by God's intervention to provide forgiveness and deliverance to the righteous remnant. In this section the focus alternates between judgment on those who have rejected God and deliverance for those who turn to Him.

Judgment and Deliverance	
65:1–7	God will judge idolators.
65:8–10	God will deliver the righteous remnant.
65:11–12	God will judge idolators.
65:13–16	Summary: The righteous "servants" will be blessed, while the unrighteous will be judged.

God will judge those who worship idols (65:1–7). God had "held out [His] hands to an obstinate people," but they provoked Him with their idolatrous practices (65:3–5). God said their offense against Him was like smoke in His nostrils. Because they chose to serve idols rather than God, He would require of them "full payment" for their sins.

God will bless the righteous remnant (65:8–10). A righteous remnant still remained in Israel. Like those who would spare a cluster of grapes because a bit of juice still remained, so God will spare His righteous "servants." This remnant will possess the land God promised to His people. From Sharon on the west to the Valley of Achor on the east, those who seek God will possess the land.

God will judge those who worship idols (65:11–12). Returning to those who choose to "forsake" the Lord to serve the gods of "Fortune" and "Destiny," God vowed to "destine" them for judgment because they ignored His appeals and chose instead to do "evil."

God will bless His righteous "servants" and curse the wicked (65:13–16). This section concludes with a series of contrasts between the righteous and the wicked. The righteous servants will eat and drink, while the wicked will go hungry. The righteous will rejoice and sing, but the wicked will be ashamed and cry out in anguish. The righteous will have a name associated with blessing, but the name of the wicked will be like a curse.

Appearance of God's Glory and Blessing (65:17–66:24)

As in the first "Cycle of Redemption" (58:1–63:6), God's intervention will be followed by the appearance of His glory and blessing. After announcing God's new creation, Isaiah gave a broad outline of events that will transpire at Christ's second coming. Though Isaiah recorded the message as one glorious event, later revelation provides greater details on the specific fulfillment of the individual parts of this prophecy.

God's new creation for His people (65:17–25). God promised to "create new heavens and a new earth." This prophecy ultimately looked beyond the millennial kingdom to the Lord's new creation (Rev. 20:4–6; 21:1). However, Isaiah stated it first because he wanted to focus on the "new" things that will come to pass (as in Isa. 41:22–23; 42:9; 48:6). Some of these "new" things will be prosperity, longevity, and peace. The messianic promises of peace in 11:6–9 ("wolf/lamb," "lion will eat straw," "neither harm nor destroy on all my holy mountain") are repeated here.

God's "New Things" for Jerusalem

- Joy will replace weeping and crying (65:18–19).

- Longevity will replace sorrow and death (65:20–23).

- Answered prayer will replace God's previous silence (65:24).

- Universal peace will replace violence (65:25).

God's judgment on wicked worshipers (66:1–4). God's awesome majesty exceeds heaven and earth, and His presence cannot be confined to a mere "house" built by humans. God will reward those who are "humble and contrite in spirit," but He will judge those whose view of Him is so small that they believe they can manipulate Him with mere sacrifices (see also 1:11–14). God will regard their sacrifices as if they were killing someone or sacrificing a dog or a pig—sacrifices considered an abomination by the Lord.

God's promise to His righteous remnant (66:5–6). God has a special "word" for those who trust in Him in spite of opposition. This righteous remnant will experience the hatred of those who discriminate against them and mock them. But the remnant's tormentors "will be put to shame." God will come to Jerusalem to repay His enemies.

God's "rebirth" of Israel and Jerusalem (66:7–17). Using the analogy of childbirth, God asked if anyone had ever heard of a woman delivering a baby "before the pains come upon her." God's point is that the process of birth is usually long and difficult, but it will not be so for Israel. It will be a country "born in a day." God will allow Jerusalem to "give birth to her children" in the sense that the righteous remnant will experience joy, comfort, and peace.

God's glory extended to the nations (66:18–21). God's coming will affect not only Israel. He also will "gather all nations" who will come to Jerusalem to "see [His] glory." Even distant nations who had not previously heard of Him will hear the message and travel to Jerusalem with Israel's remnant. God will choose some of them to be priests and Levites. This could refer to God's allowing Gentiles to serve as priests in His temple or, more likely, it refers to God's selecting as priests some of Israel's remnant whom the Gentiles are bringing back.

God's final destiny for the righteous and the wicked (66:22–24). The Book of Isaiah ends with reference to two destinies. Those who put their trust in God will experience His redemption and glory and will endure just as "the new heavens and the new earth that I make will endure." But those who reject the Lord and oppose His plans will experience enduring judgment: "their worm will not die, nor will their fire be quenched." The apostle John pictured the same two destinies in Revelation 20:4–6, 11–15.

Perhaps the most enduring lessons from the Book of Isaiah are the reminders that (a) there is a God, (b) He is coming back, and (c) our eternal destiny is determined by our response to Him in this life.

JEREMIAH
God's Judgment on Judah's Sin

AUTHOR

*J*EREMIAH BECAME the premier prophet of Judah during the dark days leading up to her destruction by Babylon. Though the light of other prophets, such as Habakkuk and Zephaniah, flickered in Judah at that time, Jeremiah was the blazing torch who, along with Ezekiel in Babylon, exposed the darkness of Judah's sin with the piercing brightness of God's Word. He faithfully served as a weeping prophet to a wayward people.

The author of the book is Jeremiah, a son of Hilkiah (1:1). Jeremiah's father was a priest who lived in Anathoth, a village about three miles northeast of Jerusalem. Thus like Ezekiel (Ezek. 1:3) and Zechariah (Zech. 1:1), Jeremiah was from the priestly line. However, he never entered the priesthood in Jerusalem.

DATE

Jeremiah's ministry as a prophet extended from "the thirteenth year of the reign of Josiah" (Jer. 1:2) until the time of the Exile (1:3). Thus he prophesied from 627 B.C. until 586 B.C. However, the events recorded in chapters 40–44 *after* Jerusalem's fall to Babylon indicate that Jeremiah's ministry continued on until at least 582 B.C.

ADDRESSEES

Jeremiah's primary audience was the people of Judah and Jerusalem (2:2; 3:17; 7:2; 18:11). However, he also spoke directly to Judah's kings (13:18; 21:3, 11; 22:1–2, 11, 18, 24), priests (20:1–3), and prophets (23:9; 28:15). In addition he served as God's prophet to the nations around Judah (1:5; 27:2–4; 46:1).

PURPOSE

Jeremiah arranged his message in a logical pattern in developing the theme of God's judgment. Chapters 2–45 focused on God's judgment on Judah, and chapters 46–51 focused on God's judgment on the gentile nations.

OUTLINE

   I. Introduction (chapter 1)
  II. Prophecies concerning Judah (chapters 2–45)
    A. Divine judgment on Judah (chapters 2–25)
    B. Personal conflict with Judah (chapters 26–29)
    C. Future comfort for Israel and Judah (chapters 30–33)
    D. Present catastrophe of Judah (chapters 34–45)
 III. Prophecies concerning the Nations (chapters 46–51)
    A. Prophecy against Egypt (chapter 46)
    B. Prophecy against Philistia (chapter 47)
    C. Prophecy against Moab (chapter 48)
    D. Prophecies against Other Nations (chapter 49)
    E. Prophecy against Babylon (chapters 50–51)
  IV. Conclusion (chapter 52)

I. INTRODUCTION (CHAPTER 1)

The Book of Jeremiah opens by introducing its readers to the reluctant prophet from Anathoth. Jeremiah's background and call to ministry set the stage for the rest of his book. The chapter highlights the autobiographical nature of much of the material found later in the book. We are introduced to God's word *and* God's messenger.

The prophet's background (1:1–3). Though Jeremiah was a priest from the line of Aaron, God called him to be a prophet in "the thirteenth year of the reign of Josiah," which was 627 B.C. Jeremiah continued as God's spokesman to Judah until the city was destroyed in July/August 586 B.C. Thus Jeremiah's ministry lasted at least forty-one years.

The prophet's call (1:4–10). God selected Jeremiah as a prophet before he was even formed in his mother's womb. He was appointed to be a prophet both to Judah and to the nations. Jeremiah objected to his appointment as a prophet by claiming a lack of eloquence (he said he did not know "how to speak") and experience (he said he was "only a child"), but God answered Jeremiah's objections. Jeremiah did not have to be an eloquent elder statesman—just a faithful messenger—who was to say whatever God told him to say. Then God showed Jeremiah a vision that pointed to the source of his message. The Lord reached out and touched Jeremiah's mouth. Jeremiah needn't worry about what to say, for God would provide the very words He wanted Jeremiah to speak.

God's Answers to Jeremiah's Objections

God graciously taught Jeremiah, and us, that He specializes in using "ordinary people" to accomplish His extraordinary work. He will use us if we:

- Trust Him in spite of our fears
- Obey Him in spite of our inexperience
- Proclaim His Word in spite of our feelings of inadequacy

The prophet's confirming visions (1:11–16). God confirmed Jeremiah's call by giving him two visions. The first (1:11–12) focused on the *nature* of the message Jeremiah would deliver. God used a play on words to associate an almond-tree branch with His activity. The word for "watching" is related to the Hebrew noun for almond tree. God was awake and "watching" over His word to make sure it came to pass. God's second vision pointed to the *content* of Jeremiah's ministry. Jeremiah saw a boiling pot spilling its contents toward the south. The pot represented invaders from the north (later identified as Babylon) whom the Lord was summoning to punish Judah. After the Babylonians captured Jerusalem, Jeremiah recorded the fulfillment of this prophecy in 39:2–3.

The prophet's challenge (1:17–19). After explaining the task, God charged Jeremiah to take up the challenge. God gave him the needed strength to stand against the people of Judah, strength that would be needed because the people would oppose his message. However, God also highlighted the fact that his enemies would not be able to overcome him. (God had to remind Jeremiah of this promise in 15:19-20!)

II. PROPHECIES CONCERNING JUDAH (CHAPTERS 2–45)

Jeremiah began by recording thirteen messages of divine judgment against Judah (chapters 2–25). These include nine general prophecies of judgment (chapters 2–20) and four specific ones (chapters 21–25). Personal conflicts followed as the people rejected his messages (chapters 26–29). Judah's fate was sealed; but before the judgment took place, Jeremiah inserted God's message of future comfort for Israel and Judah (chapters 30–33). After this message of future hope, Jeremiah recorded the fall of Judah to Babylon (chapters 34–45) in fulfillment of God's word of judgment.

A. DIVINE JUDGMENT ON JUDAH (CHAPTERS 2–25)

Jerusalem's Faithlessness (2:1–3:5)

In Jeremiah's first of nine general messages, he confronted Jerusalem with her waywardness. Using the bold images of apostasy and adultery, he contrasted Judah's former devotion to God with her present departure from God.

Judah's former devotion (2:1–3). At the time of the Exodus, Israel had loved God and followed Him through the desert. She had been set apart as holy to the Lord (Exod. 19:6; 22:31), and those who dared attack her were punished by God. He brought disaster on anyone who dared touch His beloved (see Gen. 12:3).

Judah's spiritual apostasy (2:4–19). Israel's faithfulness to God, however, did not last. Instead, the nation turned from God to follow "worthless idols," and they polluted the land with their idolatry (2:7). Jeremiah singled out three specific groups charged with leading the nation (priests, leaders, and prophets) and exposed their lack of obedience (2:8). He asked the people to contrast Judah's disobedience with the faithfulness of the Gentiles. From "the coasts of Kittim" (Cyprus) in the west to "Kedar" (north Arabian desert tribes) in the east, no pagan society had ever exchanged its gods for other gods. These nations were more faithful to their false gods than Israel had been to the true God of the universe. Specifically Israel was guilty of two sins: She had "forsaken" the true God and had replaced Him with false idols. Jeremiah compared the nation's actions to their abandoning a refreshing spring of "living [running] water" to seek satisfaction by drinking from "broken cisterns." In addition to forsaking the Lord for false gods, Judah had also forsaken the Lord for false alliances. The nation vainly went from Egypt to Assyria, trying to forge treaties that would guarantee her safety. But no alliance could protect Judah from the results of her sin.

> ### Water in Israel
>
> The people had three main sources of water in Israel. The most dependable, pure, and satisfying was a spring or stream of "living" (flowing) water. The second source was well water. Wells were also satisfactory, but they were difficult to dig, and sometimes could dry up or become filled in (Gen. 21:30–31; 26:18). The third source was the most common but least satisfying and most undependable. These were cisterns—pits dug into the rock to catch rainwater. The water was brackish, and the rains were not always reliable. To exhange a fountain of "living water" for a "broken cistern" was an act of lunacy!

Judah's spiritual adultery (2:20–28). Judah's spiritual apostasy was matched by her spiritual adultery. Jeremiah painted four verbal pictures of Judah that described her wayward condition. Judah was like (a) an animal that had broken the yoke that bound her to the Lord, (b) a vine planted and nurtured by God that had become incapable of producing any good fruit, (c) a stain that could not be washed off, and (d) a wild animal in heat (Judah could not be restrained in her lust for numerous foreign gods).

Judah's spiritual irresponsibility (2:29–37). Judah eventually became so spiritually irresponsible that God's judgment was necessary to curb their rebellion. Yet in spite of God's punishment, the people still refused to respond. They even killed God's messengers, the prophets. Judah's irresponsibility showed up most clearly in her forgetfulness of God's past goodness. A bride would never forget her "wedding ornaments" that identified her as a married woman, but Judah had forgotten her God who had given her great blessings.

Judah also displayed her irresponsibility by the shedding of innocent blood. Though her clothes were covered with the blood of the innocent, she continued to assert her innocence. In addition Judah followed a fickle foreign policy, constantly changing her ways in her dealings with other nations. But because the Lord had rejected these nations, Judah could not be helped by them.

Judah's spiritual harlotry (3:1–5). If a couple divorced and the wife married another man, she was prohibited by the Mosaic Law from ever being reunited with her first husband (Deut. 24:1–4). Yet Judah had separated from her Husband, the Lord, and had "lived as a prostitute with many lovers." It was almost impossible to find a place where Judah had not practiced her idolatry. Even after God judged Judah, she still refused to be ashamed and chose instead to continue on her evil way.

> *Persistent, habitual sin can desensitize an individual to the nagging of one's conscience, the convicting work of God's Spirit, or the direct rebuke of God's Word.*

Repentance in Light of Coming Judgment (3:6–6:30)

Jeremiah's second message is a series of prophecies given at different times from the first message. Yet the content of this section is logically related to 2:1–3:5 and forms a fitting conclusion.

The summons to repent (3:6–4:4). The Northern Kingdom of Israel "committed adultery," a reference to her turning from God to worship idols. When she refused to return to God, He gave her a "certificate of divorce" and sent her away (see 2 Kings 17:5–20). Unfortunately the Southern Kingdom of Judah did not learn from Israel's fall. Instead she also was guilty of spiritual adultery.

Jeremiah paused to offer a message of repentance and hope to Israel. If she would repent and return to God (Jer. 7:3; 26:13), He would halt His judgment. Looking to the future, God promised to gather a remnant and bring it to Jerusalem. Judah and Israel will be reunited as a nation (31:31–33) and will return from captivity to the land God promised them as their "inheritance." The fulfillment of this promise awaits the return of Christ.

Jeremiah then returned to the problems of his day. While God promised to respond if Israel and Judah would return to Him, their repentance had to be genuine. They had to remove their idols and stop pursuing false gods. Though circumcised physically, the men of Judah needed to circumcise their hearts so that their inward condition matched their outward profession. If Judah did not repent, God vowed that His wrath would "burn" against them.

> *Just as a farmer does not sow his seed on unplowed ground, so God does not sow His blessings in unrepentant hearts.*

The warning of coming judgment (4:5–31). Jeremiah described the coming judgment as the unleashing of Judah's enemies "from the north." Those living in the countryside would flee to Jerusalem to escape the destruction of the Babylonian invasion which would leave Judah in ruins and uninhabited. Babylon's army would be like an approaching windstorm that would sweep into Judah "like a whirlwind" 4:13). God again graciously encouraged the people to repent and announced that if they would, He would then deliver them from the impending doom. Otherwise, messengers from the northern part of Israel would soon appear in Jerusalem to announce that an army was coming against Judah's cities (4:14–17). Jeremiah responded to the news of the coming invasion by crying out as he pictured God's judgment as a cosmic catastrophe. God would make Judah "formless and empty" (4:23), a phrase used in Genesis 1:2 to describe the chaos that preceded God's works in Creation. As the armies approached, people would flee to avoid being killed (Jer. 4:29). Like a harlot, Jerusalem would try to lure the Babylonians away from their attack, but the ruse would not work because Jerusalem's former "lovers" would now seek her life (4:30).

The reasons for coming judgment (chapter 5). Judah was to be judged because of her corruption. God sent Jeremiah on a divine scavenger hunt in Jerusalem to find an honest person. If he could find just one, God would forgive the city. Unfortunately Jeremiah's search was less fruitful than Abraham's search at Sodom (Gen. 18:22–23). The people's faces were "harder than stone" (Jer. 5:3), indicating their refusal to repent. Even the leaders refused to serve God, so God said He would punish Judah for her idolatry and adultery (5:5–11). Yet the people still refused to believe God would ever destroy Jerusalem. God therefore told Jeremiah that His words would be like a fire that would consume the people (5:14). Jeremiah concluded by listing the people's sins to show that all elements of society preferred wickedness to righteousness (5:23–31).

The certainty of coming judgment (chapter 6). Jeremiah again announced Babylon's impending invasion. God threatened to destroy Jerusalem so completely that shepherds would "pitch their tents" and graze their herds on its site (6:3). Still, the people would not listen to Jeremiah as he tried to warn them of the coming calamity (6:10). This is the first of more than three dozen times when Jeremiah said the people did not listen to (that is, they disobeyed) God's words. God vowed that His wrath would be felt by all—from the children to the old—because Judah had strayed from the "ancient paths" of His righteousness (6:11–16). She rejected God's Law, thinking she could substitute rituals for obedience. God responded by showing His disdain for sacrifices and other rituals that were divorced from a genuine love for Him. Jeremiah concluded his second message by again pointing to the foe "from . . . the north" (6:22; see also 1:13–15; 4:5–6; 6:1). The coming army would "show no mercy" (6:23) to those it captured, an apt description of the Babylonians (Hab. 1:6–11). God's attempts to reform the nation had failed, so judgment was inevitable.

> *People often substitute religious ritual for the personal relationship God wants them to have with Him.*

False Religion and Its Punishment (chapters 7–10)

These chapters, often known as Jeremiah's temple address, focus on God's punishment of the people because of their false religion. The people believed God would never destroy Jerusalem or them because of the presence of the temple and because of their outward display of religion. Jeremiah destroyed this false hope and exposed the idolatry of the people. Chapter 26 probably indicates the people's response to this message.

The temple sermon and Judah's false worship (chapter 7). God summoned Jeremiah to go to the entrance of the temple and announce His message to those coming there to worship. The message was similar to that just recorded: The people had to "reform" if they wanted to continue living there.

The people believed "the temple of the LORD" (repeated three times to emphasize their belief) was a good-luck charm that could ward off any attack, but God did not value buildings over obedience. God's protection would remain only if the people would change their ways. Jeremiah asked them to remember what God did to Shiloh—where the tabernacle had first dwelt (Josh. 18:1; 1 Sam. 1:3; 4:3–4)—because of Israel's evil. If Judah did not change, God would destroy the temple just as He had destroyed His tabernacle at Shiloh (Jer. 7:12–15).

God told Jeremiah not to pray for Judah because He would not listen (7:16). Though the people claimed to worship the Lord, they also worshiped "the Queen of Heaven," the Assyrian goddess Ishtar (7:17–18). They had constructed idols in the temple itself, while outside the city they had built the "high places of Topheth" in the Hinnom Valley where they practiced child sacrifice (7:31). God vowed that the name of this valley would be changed to the "Valley of Slaughter" because of the great number of dead who would be buried there after the destruction of Jerusalem (7:32).

The "High Places of Topheth"

The Hinnom Valley extends along the southern and western edges of Jerusalem and was the natural garbage dump for the city. The gate on the southern end of the city leading into the valley was called the "Dung Gate" or "Refuse Gate" (Neh. 2:13; 3:14; 12:31). The Hinnom Valley is a steep, narrow valley and was described by Jeremiah as *gēy-Hinnōm* "the [steep] valley of Hinnom." Jeremiah identified a place in this valley where children were being sacrificed to Baal as "Topheth." The area was possibly referred to as *tāphteh* ("the place of burning") or as *ʾashpōt* ("place of refuse"). Jeremiah substituted the vocalization for the Hebrew word "shame" *(bōshet)*. Thus the "place of burning" or "place of refuse" was in reality a "place of shame."

During the intertestamental period the rabbis—noticing the continual burning and decay in the garbage dump and remembering the threats of judgment uttered against the valley—began equating the Hinnom Valley with the fiery judgments of hell. It was only a short step between associating the two concepts and making the names synonymous. Thus the "Valley of Hinnom" *(gēy-Hinnōm)* became the name for "hell" (Gehenna), the place "prepared for the devil and his angels," where there will be "weeping and gnashing of teeth" (Matt. 5:22; 13:42, 50; 25:41).

God's retribution on Jerusalem (chapter 8). God asked a series of questions to expose Judah's stubborn refusal to turn back to Him (8:4–5). Judah felt superior in her wisdom to other nations because she had the Mosaic Law. Unfortunately that Law was being "handled . . . falsely" by the scribes and by everyone else (8:8). Jeremiah pictured the panic that would ensue when God's judgment began. The people would "flee to the fortified cities" (8:14) when the terror of the Babylonians filled the land.

Responding to Judah's plight with a heartfelt cry to God, the prophet asked the Lord to listen to the cry of the people who had been deported to a faraway land (8:19). Those captured by the Babylonians wondered how their city could have fallen since God's temple was there. God responded by indicating that Jerusalem's destruction was brought about by their sin, not by His absence. God brought the army of Babylon because Judah's idolatry had angered Him. The "harvest," representing God's opportunities to repent, was "past" (8:20). By not taking advantage of God's provision for deliverance from judgment when it had been available, the people were now without hope ("we are not saved").

God's mercy is great, but it is not without limits. Those who willfully continue to rebel against God may reach a point where the opportunity to repent has passed.

Jeremiah's lament over Jerusalem (chapter 9). Jeremiah's grief caused him to wish his eyes were a "fountain of tears" so he could weep continually for those who had been slain. His heartfelt empathy with his people's suffering earned him the nickname "the weeping prophet" (13:17; 14:17).

Yet his empathy for their suffering was balanced by his revulsion at their sin. An isolated desert "lodging place" was preferable to living with the unfaithful people of Judah (9:1–2). Honesty was not being practiced, and so the very fabric of society unraveled (9:3–6). So God vowed to place Judah in the crucible of judgment and deal with her deceitfulness (9:7–9).

We must balance a love for sinners with a hatred for sin.

Jeremiah wept and wailed because the Babylonian invasion and deportation would make Judah a desolate "heap of ruins" inhabited only by wild animals (9:10–11). This destruction was certain because the people had turned from God's Law and had worshiped "Baals," various local idols representing the Phoenicians' false god Baal (9:12–16).

Jeremiah recorded three pronouncements from the Lord (9:17–21, 22, 23–26), each beginning with a similar phrase. In the first one God called for professional mourners ("wailing women") to lament for Jerusalem. Their funeral dirge was to be over the death of the children and the young men who would be killed when the Babylonians broke into the city. In the second section (9:22), God pictured the severity of the massacre by Babylon. The corpses would resemble the "cut grain" left after reapers had gone through a field. But no one would be left to gather this gruesome harvest. The third pronouncement (9:23–26) summarized the response God expected from the people. Instead of God's people boasting in their human wisdom, strength, or wealth, they were to boast only to the extent that they understood and knew God.

Coming exile because of idolatry (chapter 10). The first sixteen verses of chapter 10 are parenthetical. Before continuing his discussion of the coming exile (10:17–25), Jeremiah focused both on the nature of the God who would bring this judgment and on the foolishness of trying to replace God with idols.

Addressing the entire "house of Israel," which included the Northern Kingdom already in exile, the Lord explained the foolishness of idols. Israel was not to "learn the ways" of idolatry, nor was she to be frightened by "signs in the sky." Such idolatrous practices were worthless because the so-called gods being honored were mere creations of their worshipers. These idols were as lifeless as a "scarecrow in a melon patch" (10:5). Such idols had no power to hurt those who disregarded them, nor were they able to help those who followed them. In contrast, Israel's God is truly unique (10:6–7; see also Isa. 40:18, 25). The Lord is the genuine ("true") God in contrast to the false idols. He is alive, but they were lifeless; and He is "eternal," while they were carved by craftsmen and subject to decay (Jer. 10:9–16).

Jeremiah resumed his temple address by describing the coming destruction and exile. The people of Jerusalem were to gather their meager belongings to prepare for exile (10:17–18). Jerusalem responded in anguish to the thought of their captivity. The judgment she would suffer seemed almost "incurable" (10:19). Her children would be deported because the "shepherds" (leaders; see 2:8) had allowed them to be "scattered"

(10:21–22). In a prayer to the Lord, Jeremiah admitted that a person's life cannot be considered his or her own as though that individual is free to "direct" his own "steps" (10:23–25). God is in control, and only those who let Him direct their ways will be truly blessed.

The Broken Covenant (chapters 11–12)

Jeremiah's fourth message focused on Judah's broken covenant with her God. The message was probably spoken by Jeremiah in 621 B.C., six years after he began his ministry. That year the temple was being repaired as part of King Josiah's reforms, and a copy of the Law was discovered in the renovation (2 Chron. 34:14–33). Alluding to this discovery of God's Law and the realization of the broken covenant (Jer. 11:3–5), Jeremiah called on the people to heed the words of the covenant that King Josiah read to them (11:6; 2 Chron. 34:19–32).

The violation of the covenant (11:1–17). Jeremiah was told to share the words of God's "covenant" with the people. Though God had repeatedly warned the nation to obey Him, they refused to listen. Because of this, God vowed to bring on them "all the curses of the covenant." Josiah forced an outer conformity to the covenant, but his reform did not penetrate the hearts of the people in a lasting way. After Josiah died, the people returned to their idolatrous ways. Instead of heeding the warning of Jeremiah (11:2–8), they continued serving false gods, which assured their doom. As a result the nation would not be able to escape the coming "disaster."

The plot against Jeremiah (11:18–23). The people responded to Jeremiah's rebuke by trying to kill him. This is the first in a series of incidents in which the people actively opposed Jeremiah's ministry. When God revealed their plot to him, he asked God to judge these conspirators, and God said He would do so swiftly. The men of Jeremiah's own hometown, Anathoth, would suffer "disaster" because of their opposition to God's message and messenger.

Jeremiah's complaint to God (12:1–6). In view of the plot against his life, the prophet complained about the prosperity of the wicked. Though admitting that God was righteous, Jeremiah still questioned God about His "justice." Specifically he wanted to know why the wicked seemed to prosper if God was indeed angry with their sin. When Jeremiah asked God to judge the unrighteous, God's answer was something of a surprise. He warned Jeremiah of even greater difficulties. Jeremiah's future situation would be even worse.

> *We need to remember that living for God in this life will not always be easy. We must be prepared for obstacles and trials.*

The consequences of violating the covenant (12:7–17). Jeremiah continued God's message of judgment that was interrupted in 11:18–23. God would "forsake" the land of Judah, and turn the people over to their enemies. Jeremiah compared the coming devastation to a flock of sheep entering a vineyard and ruining it by trampling it down. Jeremiah closed this fourth message by citing God's threat to the surrounding nations: Those "wicked neighbors" who had seized Israel's inheritance (12:7–9) would themselves be uprooted. In contrast, God promised that someday He will bring the people of Judah back from those gentile nations where they had been scattered and will restore them to their land. This will happen when Christ returns to establish His millennial kingdom on earth.

The Linen Belt and the Wineskins (chapter 13)

The illustration of the linen belt (13:1–11). God told Jeremiah to purchase and wear a linen belt, a symbolic act that would pique the curiosity of his unresponsive audience. After wearing it for a time, he was to take it to Perath and hide it in a rock crevice. Sometime later, when Jeremiah dug up the sash, it had rotted. God said this belt represented Israel and Judah. When the prophet was wearing it, it was useful and attractive. However, when he removed it and buried it, it became "completely useless." Similarly Israel and Judah had become ruined by departing from their God to serve false gods.

Perath is usually translated Euphrates; and many have felt that Jeremiah walked to the Euphrates River, a round-trip journey of about seven hundred miles, to bury this sash. However, another possibility is that Jeremiah traveled to the Spring of Perath a few miles northeast of Anathoth. A location so close to home would have allowed the people to observe Jeremiah's symbolic actions, and the similarity of names would have reminded them of the army from the Euphrates that was coming to destroy them.

The parable of the wineskins (13:12–14). When Jeremiah declared, "Every wineskin should be filled with wine," the people scoffed at the prophet's silly saying. Of course every wineskin or wine jar should be filled with wine. Then Jeremiah explained the point of the parable. The empty jars, representing all who lived in the land, would be filled with drunkenness—a frequent symbol of judgment (Isa. 49:26; 63:6; Jer. 25:15–25; 51:7, 39). God threatened to "smash" the people like jars; nothing would stop Him from punishing them.

The message on sin and its results (13:15–27). Because of the approaching time of judgment, Jeremiah warned the people to acknowledge their sin and return to God. If they refused to listen, Jeremiah would "weep bitterly" (13:17) because they would surely become captives. He then turned to address the royal family. They are not identified here, but probably the king was Jehoiachin (also known as Jeconiah) and the queen mother was Nehushta—the widow of Jehoiakim (29:2; 2 Kings 24:8, 12, 15). They went into captivity in 597 B.C. after Jehoiachin had reigned just three months (24:8). Their deportation to Babylon was a foretaste of Judah's judgment because the whole nation would be exiled. If, when the judgment came, the people asked why, God let them know in advance that it was because of their many sins (Jer. 13:22). Using language to match Judah's lewd conduct, God declared that He would "pull up" her "skirts" to expose her to the nations (13:26). Judah's faithless acts of idolatry had been seen by God, and she would suffer the consequences.

The Drought and Prayer (chapters 14–15)

One of the covenant curses God threatened to send on the disobedient nation was drought (Lev. 26:18–19; Deut. 28:22–24). In his sixth message Jeremiah described such a drought and the response it produced in the people (Jer. 14). He then shared God's response to the words spoken by the people (Jer. 15).

The plight because of the drought (14:1–18). The drought's severity produced a cry of distress from Jerusalem (14:2). The rainfall had ceased, and the stored water was running out. Those who had rejected the Living Water of life for false cisterns (2:13) now found their physical water supply matching the spiritual water supply to which they had turned (14:3–4). While admitting their sins and their "backsliding," they asked God to intervene and supply rain (14:7–9). But amazingly, instead of accepting the people's confession, God upbraided them for their waywardness because He knew their confession was only superficial (14:11–12). They claimed God as their Lord, but they refused to "restrain their feet" from following evil (14:10) and they listened to false prophets (14:14–16). Jeremiah's sorrow burst forth at the thought of Jerusalem's judgment. His eyes welled up with tears as he cried yet again over Jerusalem's impending fall (14:17–18).

The "confession" and God's response (14:19–15:4). The people addressed God a second time and pleaded for His intervention. Though they longed for peace, they had experienced only "terror" (14:19). Their appeal for God's help was based on His personal character ("for the sake of your name"), His temple (His "glorious throne"), and His "covenant" (14:21). They finally admitted that the idols they had worshiped could not produce rain to quench the drought. The first four verses of chapter 15 are God's answer to this apparent "confession." The nation's sin was so ingrained that judgment was inevitable. Even the intercessory prayer of Moses or Samuel could not stop God's judgment. Judah had passed the point of no return in her dealings with God. That line was crossed through the actions of King Manasseh (2 Kings 21:1–18; 2 Chron. 33:1–20), who so polluted Jerusalem with idolatry that her destruction was inevitable.

The fate of Jerusalem (15:5–9). God asked the Jerusalemites, "Who will take pity on your city when you are judged?" The only One who had ever cared for her was God, but she had rejected Him. Therefore God vowed to destroy her without mercy. The awesome effects of judgment would touch all the people. Widows would become as plenteous as sand because the Babylonians would slaughter all the men. Even mothers would not escape.

Jeremiah's complaint (15:10–21). Jeremiah lamented his own condition in life as he pictured all the people being against him. God answered by assuring Jeremiah he would be vindicated. But Jeremiah wanted swift justice. He painfully lamented his pitiful condition and wondered if God, who claimed to be like a spring of living water (2:13), had become like a spring that "fails" (15:18). The disappointment of a dry wadi bed that held water only after a heavy rain was a depressing sight to those searching for water (see Job 6:15–20). Jeremiah hoped God would not disappoint him, but he was beginning to have doubts. Rebuking Jeremiah for his doubt and self-pity, God told him to remain steadfast. God then restated the promises He made when He commissioned Jeremiah as a prophet (15:20; see 1:18–19). Though opposition would come, God promised to keep Jeremiah safe from his enemies (15:21).

> *Sometimes God needs to take us "back to the basics" to remind us what He has promised and has not promised to His children.*

Jeremiah's Restrictions and Judah's Sin (chapters 16–17)

Judah's deep sin required dramatic action. God placed several restrictions on Jeremiah to make his entire life an object lesson to the people. Yet their sin was so deeply etched on their hearts that repentance was unlikely.

Jeremiah's restrictions (16:1–9). The first restriction on Jeremiah's personal life was the Lord's command that he not marry and raise a family. Why did God deny the prophet this relationship that was cherished by all Israelites? It was to demonstrate that the coming catastrophe would disrupt all normal relationships. The second restriction was that he not "mourn or show sympathy" when someone died. This was to show Judah that no one would console the survivors of Jerusalem over their loss. The third restriction was that he not enter a house where there was "feasting." This illustrated that times of feasting and happiness would soon cease.

Judah's stubborn heart (16:10–18). As Jeremiah explained his behavior to the people, they asked why God would plan such a great judgment against them. Naively they asked what sin they had done to deserve such harsh treatment (16:10). God's answer to these questions underscored the root problem throughout Israel's history. They were being stubborn and evil rather than obeying God (16:11–12). God vowed to hurl them out of the land because of their sin. But again He paused to remind them that this judgment was not permanent. After the coming captivity there would be a new exodus, in which God would again bring Israel back to her land. After assuring the nation of her final restoration, God continued describing her impending judgment. She would be restored in the future, "but now" (16:16) the people were facing deportation.

Jeremiah's trust (16:19–21). Jeremiah affirmed his trust in God as his Strength, Fortress, and Refuge, three words that emphasize the protection God gave him. Jeremiah looked ahead to the day when all the world will know God. Though Judah had turned to the false gods of the Gentiles, a time will come when the opposite will happen and the gentile nations will turn to the true God of Israel.

God's cursings and blessings (17:1–13). The people of Judah were so entrenched in idolatry that it was as if their sins were etched on their hearts with an "iron tool" or a "flint point." Because of the people's sin God said He would hand over Jerusalem and its wealth as plunder to the invaders. Jeremiah breathed back the thoughts of Psalm 1 as he contrasted the way of the wicked (17:5–6) with the way of the righteous (17:7–8). Judah had been turning to false gods and foreign alliances for protection, but a person who trusts in others instead of God for protection is "cursed." A righteous person, on the other hand, is "blessed" because his trust is in God. If the ways of blessing and cursing are so clear, why would anyone choose the path of sin? The answer lies in the fact that the heart is deceitful and seemingly no one can even understand it. But God said He can "search the heart and examine the mind" (17:9–10). Since He knows those innermost thoughts and motives that an individual might hide from others, He can justly render to each person what he deserves. Those who forsake the Lord, "the spring of living water," will be judged (17:13).

Jeremiah's plea for vindication (17:14–18). Again Jeremiah called on God to vindicate him. He contrasted his faithful devotion to God with the unbelief of those persecuting him. They scoffed at his predictions and demanded that his prophecies be fulfilled immediately if they were true. Yet in spite of this opposition Jeremiah had faithfully served as God's messenger. So he asked God to shame his persecutors by bringing on them the day of judgment which they deserved.

The keeping of the Sabbath (17:19–27). Jeremiah's previous messages dealt with the general rebellion of the people. In these verses, however, he focused on one specific command in the Mosaic Law, the Sabbath, to show how far the nation had departed from God. Standing at a gate of the temple, the prophet told the people to "keep the Sabbath day holy." If the people obeyed God's command, Jerusalem would remain inhabited. However, if they would not obey God's command to keep the Sabbath, He would bring judgment that would leave her defenseless.

The Potter and the Broken Jar (chapters 18–20)

Jeremiah's ninth message includes a parable of the potter (chapter 18), which demonstrated God's sovereign dealings with Judah, and the symbolic breaking of a potter's jar, which showed God's impending judgment (chapter 19). Chapter 20 serves as a pivot in the book. Connected chronologically with chapter 19, it also prepares the reader for the open opposition and specific prophecies of judgment that follow.

The message at the potter's house (chapter 18). As Jeremiah watched a potter mold clay into pots on his wheel, the prophet saw that the potter discovered a flaw in the pot as he was shaping it. The potter then pressed the clay into a lump and reformed it. The people of Judah were like clay in His hand (18:1–10). If Judah would "turn from her evil ways," God would revoke the judgment He threatened to send. However, the people refused to turn from idolatry to follow the Lord (18:13–17). Instead they rejected Jeremiah and his message (18:18–23).

The message of the broken jar (chapter 19). Jeremiah bought a clay jar, gathered a group of elders and priests, and walked to the Hinnom Valley (see 7:31). With the valley as a backdrop, Jeremiah delivered his message: God would judge Jerusalem because of her idolatry. The valley itself was a witness against the people because in it were "the high places of Baal," where people slaughtered and burned their sons as sacrificial offerings. Because of these wicked deeds God again vowed to rename the place the "Valley of Slaughter" as He destroyed the people there (see 7:32–33). To dramatize his message,

Jeremiah broke the jar he was carrying and announced that God would "smash" Judah and Jerusalem. Returning from the valley to the city, Jeremiah went directly to the temple and repeated his message to all the people.

The response of Pashhur (20:1–6). Jeremiah's message of judgment was rejected by Pashhur, the temple's "chief officer." He seized Jeremiah and had him flogged with forty lashes (see Deut. 25:2–3). Then he put Jeremiah in stocks for public ridicule. When Jeremiah was released, he refused to change his message. Instead he changed Pashhur's name. God's new name for Pashhur was "Magor-Missabib" ("terror on every side"). Because Pashhur refused to heed God's message and had "prophesied lies," he would see the outpouring of God's judgment.

The complaint of Jeremiah (20:7–18). In public Jeremiah was fearless, but in private he expressed the depth of his inner emotions to the Lord. He felt God had "deceived" him by letting him be "ridiculed" by the people for his message. He had faithfully warned them of God's coming judgment, but he was rewarded with insults. Discouraged, Jeremiah considered withholding God's word to avoid persecution. But when he did, the word flamed "like a fire" within him and he was unable to contain it (20:9). The message of "terror on every side" (20:10) that he was constantly proclaiming (6:25; 17:22; 20:3–4; 17:18; 46:5; 49:29; Lam. 2:22) was now being hurled back at him. Even his friends were watching for him to "slip" up, perhaps by uttering a wrong prediction, so they could take their revenge on him as a false prophet.

Jeremiah continued his prayer by expressing his trust in God and by calling on God to avenge him (see also Jer. 18:19–23). This assurance of vindication allowed Jeremiah to "sing" and "praise" God for His mighty acts. Then in a sudden change of emotion, Jeremiah again plunged from a height of confidence (20:11–13) to the depths of despair (20:14–18). Perhaps he realized that the vindication he sought could come only through the destruction of the city and nation he dearly loved. His agony made him wish he had never been born (see 15:10; Job 3:1–19).

The Rebuke of the Kings (chapters 21–22)

With the recording of Pashhur's response and the first physical attack on Jeremiah (chapter 20), Jeremiah's prophecies were now directed against specific individuals and groups, and Judah's hope of repentance was replaced with the certainty of God's judgment. The first group Jeremiah singled out was the kings—those appointed by God to be shepherds of the flock of Judah. Jeremiah rebuked the wicked kings who had ruled Judah. Jeremiah's messages to the kings were arranged in an unusual order. The first king listed was Zedekiah, who was the last king chronologically (21:1–22:9). The other kings were then arranged chronologically beginning with Shallum (also called Jehoahaz, 22:10–12), continuing with Jehoiakim (22:13–23), and ending with Coniah (also called Jehoiachin and Jeconiah, 22:24–30). By discussing Zedekiah at the beginning, Jeremiah was able to put the story of "Pashhur son of Malkijah" (21:1) next to the story of "Pashhur son of Immer" (20:1). The fact that these two individuals had the same name provided continuity. The vindication the prophet sought because of Pashhur son of Immer's ridicule (chapter 20) was realized when Pashhur son of Malkijah was sent to Jeremiah to inquire of the Lord (chapter 21). Jeremiah also arranged the kings in this order so that the striking prophecy against Coniah would climax God's judgments against the kings.

The message to Zedekiah (21:1–22:9). King Zedekiah sent several officials to Jeremiah to see what the Lord would say about Nebuchadnezzar's attack on Jerusalem. Unfortunately for Zedekiah, Jeremiah's message was one the king did *not* want to hear. Rather than being Jerusalem's Deliverer, God vowed to "fight against" her Himself (21:5). The people had two clear choices: "the way of life and the way of death" (21:8). Those who chose to remain in the city would die, but those who surrendered to the enemy besieging Jerusalem would live (21:9). Focusing specifically on the sin of Judah's royal line, Jeremiah said that because of the king's proud self-reliance and sinful disobedience, God would punish him and his people. The royal palace would become a "ruin" (22:5).

The message to Shallum (22:10–12). Shallum, another name for King Jehoahaz, was a son of Josiah who came to the throne in 609 B.C. after Josiah was killed by Pharaoh Neco (2 Kings 23:34). Jeremiah predicted that Shallum, who was taken captive to Egypt after reigning for just three months, would die there.

The message to Jehoiakim (22:13–23). After being appointed as king by Pharaoh Neco, Jehoiakim acted the part of a typical oriental despot. He was a corrupt, petty king who built a palace for himself at the expense of his subjects. They were forced to work without pay as Jehoiakim lavished money on cedar panels for the palace. As God's shepherd, Jehoiakim was expected to nurture the flock of Judah, not decimate it. However, he cared only for "dishonest gain," "oppression," and "extortion" (22:17). As a result, the people would not bemoan his demise. Instead, Jehoiakim would have the "burial of a donkey." Like an animal that dies in the city and is tossed outside the city gates, Jehoiakim would not be given a decent, royal burial (22:19).

The message to Jehoiachin (22:24–30). Jehoiachin followed his father, Jehoiakim, to the throne. After a three-month reign Jehoiachin surrendered to Nebuchadnezzar and was deported to Babylon. God indicated that even if Jehoiachin were as valuable to Him as a "signet ring," He would still pull him off His finger, as it were, because of his sins. A signet ring was highly valued because it was used to stamp its owner's seal on various documents. (For a reversal of this judgment, see the promise to Zerubbabel in Haggai, 2:21–23.) God vowed to hand Jehoiachin over to the Babylonians, and he and his mother would die in Babylon. This is Jeremiah's second prophecy of their deportation (see Jer. 13:18–19). By a series of questions, Jeremiah indicated that God was responsible for Jehoiachin's judgment (22:28–30).

The Curse of Jehoiachin's Line

Though King Jehoiachin (also called Coniah and Jeconiah) did have children (22:28; 1 Chron. 3:17), he was to be considered "childless" because none of his descendants would be allowed to "sit on the throne of David." This prophecy helps explain the genealogies of Christ in Matthew 1 and Luke 3. Matthew presented the legal line of Christ through His stepfather, Joseph. However, Joseph's line came through Shealtiel, a son of Jehoiachin (Matt. 1:12; 1 Chron. 3:17). Had Christ been a physical descendant of Joseph and not virgin-born, He would have been disqualified as Israel's King. Luke probably presented the physical line of Christ through Mary, who was descended from David through the line of his son Nathan (Luke 3:31). In that way Christ was not under the "curse" of Jehoiachin.

The Righteous Branch and the False Prophets (chapter 23)

The message concerning the righteous Branch (23:1–8). Judah's many unrighteous kings were like shepherds who had destroyed and scattered God's flock. They deserved punishment because of the evil they had done (see also Ezek. 34:1–10). But if God removed them, whom would He appoint to regather His sheep? Jeremiah gave a twofold answer. First, God Himself will "gather the remnant" of the people who were dispersed and will restore them. Second, God will raise up new shepherds who will care for the people the way God intended. The line of David through Jehoiachin had been cut off. However, God promised to raise up in David's line another King who would be "a righteous Branch," that is, another descendant of the Davidic line (see Isa. 11:1). Jesus Christ is the fulfillment of this prediction. As King, He will reign "wisely" and justly; and His name will be "the Lord Our Righteousness." His reign will bring about a new exodus when God will summon the Israelites out of all the countries where they have been scattered and restore them to their own land (see Jer. 16:14–15).

The rebuke of the false prophets (23:9–40). Jeremiah turned from addressing Judah's kings to deliver God's verbal broadside against the false prophets. These individuals opposed Jeremiah's declaration of doom and offered in its place a promise of peace. The basic flaw of all Judah's spiritual leaders ("both prophet and priest") was that they were "godless" (23:11). This Hebrew word means "to be polluted or profaned." These leaders had such a low view of God's holy character that they would even pollute His temple by committing adultery and supporting evildoers. Their conduct was so repulsive that both they and the Jerusalemites had become like Sodom and Gomorrah (23:14). God's only alternative was to judge them for their sin. The false prophets' message was of their own making, with visions coming "from their own minds" (23:16) instead of from God. God opposed these prophets vigorously because they were leading the people astray (23:30–32). When the people sought for a message from God, Jeremiah was to announce that there was none (23:25–38). It had already been given; and the word from God was that He would forsake them. God also said He would punish those who claimed that any other message was from Him. These false prophets faced disgrace and shame for their wicked words.

A prophet was God's spokesperson whose life and message reflected the One who sent him. Thus the false prophets were impugning God's name because they claimed that their message came from Him and that He had authorized them to speak.

The Two Baskets of Figs (chapter 24)

The vision of two baskets (24:1–3). A vision of two fig baskets came to Jeremiah after Jehoiachin and the other leaders of Jerusalem were carried into exile by the Babylonians. Thus this prophecy can be dated sometime in 597 B.C. at the beginning of the reign of Zedekiah.

The two baskets represented two groups of people—the exiles in Babylon and those still remaining in Judah. This vision called to mind the offering of the firstfruits in a basket before the Lord (see Deut. 26:10). In one of the baskets the good figs were "those that ripen early"—those firstfruits that were to be offered to God (see Deut. 14:22). The second basket contained "very poor figs" that had deteriorated to the point where they were inedible. Such offerings were unacceptable to the Lord.

The explanation of the good figs (24:4–7). The good figs, God explained, represented the people of Judah who had been carried away to Babylon. This was a surprising answer because the people of Jerusalem believed that those in captivity had been forsaken by the Lord. Yet God promised to "watch over" the remnant in captivity and restore them in their land. He also promised to give them a new heart so they would know Him and return to Him. Yet the people who returned to Palestine after the Babylonian captivity never experienced the full blessings of fellowship promised by God. This awaits a still-future fulfillment when God again will regather Israel at the beginning of Christ's millennial reign on earth (Matt. 24:29–31).

The explanation of the poor figs (Jer. 24:8–10). The poor figs represented Zedekiah and the other survivors (see 29:17–19), including those remaining in Israel as well as those who had fled to Egypt (see 43:4–7). They would be ridiculed and cursed wherever they went, and God would send His instruments of judgment ("sword, famine and plague") against them until they were all destroyed. These survivors had felt blessed of God, but in reality they were cursed.

Guard against evaluating someone's spiritual condition based solely on outward circumstances.

The Seventy-Year Captivity in Babylon (chapter 25)

Jeremiah's thirteen messages of judgment (chapters 2–25) were arranged topically, not chronologically. Chapter 25 was placed last because it served as the capstone for all Jeremiah's previous messages. Jeremiah predicted the final curse of God's covenant (captivity) would come on the people of Judah and Jerusalem.

Warnings ignored (25:1–7). Jeremiah's final message concerned "all the people of Judah." He had been prophesying for twenty-three years—a ministry that had spanned the reigns of three kings at the time of this prophecy. But though he had spoken to the people repeatedly, they had not listened to his warnings to repent. God had also sent other prophets, who warned the people to turn from their wicked ways, but the people had not responded to these messengers either.

Judgment described (25:8–14). Because the people had repeatedly re-jected God's warnings, He vowed to bring the Babylonians ("the peoples of the north") against them. Their leader, Nebuchadnezzar, was called God's "servant" in the sense that he would do God's bidding in coming to destroy Jerusalem. God said He would deport the people of Judah to Babylon for "seventy years" (25:11). After the seventy years were fulfilled, God would "punish" the Babylonians for their sin in mistreating the people of Judah.

Why a Seventy-Year Exile?

Why did God predict that the Babylonian Exile would last seventy years? Because this was the number of times the people had failed to observe God's law of a "Sabbath rest" for the land. God had decreed that every seventh year the land was to lie fallow (Lev. 25:3–5). If the people failed to follow this command, God would remove them from the land to enforce this "sabbath rest" (26:33–35). The writer of 2 Chronicles indicated that the seventy-year Babylonian captivity allowed the land to enjoy its "sabbath rests" (2 Chron. 36:20–21).

Wrath promised (25:15–29). Jeremiah had a vision of the Lord holding a cup in His hand filled with God's wrath. Jeremiah's task was to make the nations drink it. The first to drink were the towns of Judah. But other nations would follow Judah in judgment. If God would bring disaster on His own city (Jerusalem) because of its sin, how could these heathen nations hope to remain unpunished?

Universal judgment affirmed (25:30–38). Switching from prose to poetry, Jeremiah continued the theme of divine judgment on the nations. This judgment was pictured as a "mighty storm" that will envelop all nations. In its wake the slain will be scattered, their leaders (pictured as "shepherds") will mourn, and their lands will become desolate.

B. PERSONAL CONFLICT WITH JUDAH (CHAPTERS 26–29)

Though Jeremiah did record earlier opposition to his message (11:18–23; 15:10; 20:1–6), that was not his main focus in chapters 1–25. But beginning in chapter 26 Jeremiah focused on the people's response to his message. He and his message were rejected by the people in Judah and by those already in captivity in Babylon.

Conflict with the People (chapter 26)

Since this message was delivered early in the reign of King Jehoiakim, it should probably be associated with the temple address of chapter 7. In that chapter Jeremiah focused on the *content* of the message, whereas in this chapter he focused on the *response* to the message.

The content of Jeremiah's message was again one of judgment for disobedience (26:1–6). If the people refused to obey the Law or to respond to God's prophets, God would make the temple ("this house") as desolate as the tabernacle that once stood at Shiloh (see 7:14).

After "the priests, the prophets, and all the people" heard Jeremiah's message, they demanded that he be put to death. The mob dragged Jeremiah before the "officials" to be tried for treason. The religious leaders expected a swift trial and a certain execution (26:7–15).

After hearing the case, the officials along with the people sided with Jeremiah against the priests and false prophets. Their view that Jeremiah should not be put to death was supported by some "elders" who quoted from the prophet Micah (26:18–19, 24; see Mic. 3:12). Though Jeremiah was spared, other prophets were not so fortunate. Another prophet during this time was Uriah son of Shemaiah, who was convicted of treason and killed (Jer. 26:20–23).

> *Sometimes God delivers us from trials, while at other times He sustains us through trials. In both instances our response must remain the same: Trust and obey!*

Conflict with the False Prophets in Judah (chapters 27–28)

Jeremiah also experienced conflict with the false prophets of Jerusalem. The background for these chapters is a secret meeting of delegates in Jerusalem to discuss uniting in rebellion against Babylon. This event probably took place sometime after a failed coup attempt in Babylon against Nebuchadnezzar that occurred in December 595–January 594 B.C.

The message to the ambassadors (27:1–11). God told Jeremiah to make a yoke like those used to hitch together teams of oxen and to wear it on his neck. Then he sent word to the envoys who were in Jerusalem meeting with King Zedekiah to discuss a possible revolt against Babylon. Jeremiah's public pronouncement dashed any hope the delegates might have had of keeping their meeting secret. God's message was that the nations would "serve" Babylon, and so Jeremiah warned the ambassadors not to rebel. If a nation refused to submit to Babylon's yoke, it would be punished by "sword, famine and plague" from God. Jeremiah warned his audience not to listen to the false prophets who were lying when they promised a successful rebellion against Babylon.

The message to Zedekiah (27:12–15). Jeremiah delivered the same message to Judah's king, telling him to submit to Babylon's yoke and to continue to serve Babylon as a vassal king. He also warned Zedekiah not to trust the false prophets.

The message to the priests and people (27:16–22). Jeremiah modified his message to the priests and the masses, cautioning them not to listen to the prophets who were predicting that the "articles from the temple of the LORD" that had been taken to Babylon (2 Kings 24:13; Dan. 1:1–2) would soon be brought back.

Jeremiah's conflict with Hananiah (28:1–11). Chapter 28 continues chapter 27 and gives the exact month and year: the "fifth month" of the "fourth year" of King Zedekiah. A false prophet named Hananiah challenged Jeremiah's message, directly contradicting his prophecy. He stated that God promised to break the yoke of Babylonian oppression. Hananiah urged Judah and the nations to rebel against Babylon, promising that the rebellion would be followed by restoration. He said that within two years God would bring back to Judah all the temple articles along with King Jehoiachin and all the exiles. To convince the people he was right, Hananiah took the yoke off Jeremiah's neck and broke it, graphically visualizing his prediction that God would break the yoke of Nebuchadnezzar. Rather than opposing this open insult from Hananiah, Jeremiah left.

Jeremiah's message to Hananiah (28:12–17). Sometime later, God told Jeremiah that Hananiah had broken a wooden yoke, but that He would replace it with a "yoke of iron" that could not be broken. This iron yoke, figuratively speaking, would be fastened to the necks of all the nations who gathered in Jerusalem (27:3) to force them to serve Nebuchadnezzar. After answering Hananiah's predictions (28:12–14), Jeremiah attacked Hananiah's credentials as a prophet (28:15–16). God would bring about his death, and this would expose him as a false prophet. Less than two months after Jeremiah's prediction, Hananiah died—in fulfillment of God's word.

Conflict with the False Prophets in Exile (chapter 29)

Jeremiah's first letter to the exiles (29:1–23). To those who had been exiled from Jerusalem, Jeremiah sent a letter in which he told them to prepare for a long stay in Babylon. Instead of hoping for Babylon's quick destruction, they were to seek its peace and prosperity. The Lord would restore the exiles only when the seventy years of judgment that He had announced were completed (see 25:11–12).

However, the exiles did not believe Jeremiah's message because it contradicted what the false Jewish prophets in Babylon had been saying. Jeremiah singled out two men, "Ahab son of Kolaiah and Zedekiah son of Maaseiah," who were evidently the ringleaders of those false prophets. They were to be executed by burning, a specific form of punishment used by Nebuchadnezzar (see Dan. 3).

Jeremiah's second letter to the exiles (29:24–32). Evidently after Jeremiah's first letter to the exiles Shemaiah, another prophet in Babylon, wrote to the leaders in Jerusalem, urging them to punish Jeremiah (29:25–28). However, the letter was read to Jeremiah (29:29), who then wrote a second letter to the exiles. He quoted Shemaiah's letter (29:24–28) and said God would punish both "Shemaiah . . . and his descendants" (29:29–32). Shemaiah forfeited his right to take part in God's blessings because he had "preached rebellion" against the Lord.

C. FUTURE COMFORT FOR ISRAEL AND JUDAH (CHAPTERS 30–33)

God had threatened Judah with judgment for her disobedience, but the nation refused to mend her ways. The stage was set, and the curtain was about to rise on the final act of Judah's history as a nation. But before this sad scene of suffering started to unfold, Jeremiah inserted "The Book of Consolation," a collection of prophecies that offered hope in desperate times. These prophecies looked beyond Judah's imminent collapse and pointed to a new age when Israel and Judah will be returned to their land, reunited as a nation, and restored to their God.

The Restoration of Israel and Judah Declared (chapters 30–31)

Jeremiah looked beyond the imminent collapse of Judah to her time of future restoration. By announcing "the days are coming" (30:3; 31:27, 31, 38), "in that day" (30:8), "in days to come" (30:24), "at that time" (31:1), and "in those days" (31:29), Jeremiah pointed toward a time in the future when Israel will experience national and spiritual renewal.

The nation's physical deliverance (30:1–11). God told Jeremiah to write

His promises of comfort in a book so they would be available to the exiles after Jerusalem fell. This book would declare a note of hope that the "days are coming" when God will restore His people. However, this return will be preceded by a time of national distress. The coming calamity will be so awful that nothing will compare to it. Jeremiah called it "a time of trouble." When God comes to rescue the nation, He will break the yoke of bondage He had placed on her neck. Instead of serving foreign powers, the nation will once again serve the Lord and submit to the authority of "David their king," whom God "will raise up" for them. This could refer to Christ who is from the line of David, or it could refer literally to David, who will be resurrected as part of the future restoration of a united Israel (see Ezek. 34:23–24; 37:24–25; Hos. 3:5). When God brings His people back to their land, they will enjoy peace and security.

Jeremiah's "Time of Trouble"

To what "time of trouble" was Jeremiah referring? It is likely that he spoke of the still-future Tribulation period when the remnant of Israel and Judah will experience a time of unparalleled persecution (Dan. 9:27; 12:1; Matt. 24:15–22). The period will end when Christ returns to the earth to rescue His elect (Rom. 11:26) and establish His kingdom (Matt. 24:30–31; 25:31–46; Rev. 19:11–21; 20:4–6).

The nation's spiritual healing (30:12–17). Though Israel's sin had caused her present judgment, God vowed to reverse her misfortunes. Those who were devouring the nation would themselves be "devoured" by God. At the same time God promised to restore Israel, intervening on behalf of His people.

The nation's material blessing (30:18–22). God's restoration will involve a physical rebuilding of the city of Jerusalem. The festive sound of rejoicing that had been silenced by Babylon (7:34; 16:9; 25:10) will once again be heard. The nation will be reestablished, and God will punish anyone who tries to attack her. Her leader will again be an Israelite instead of some foreign despot. Israel will finally experience the relationship with God He always intended.

The judgment on the wicked (30:23–31:1). With minor variations, Jeremiah repeated the same words he had written in 23:19–20. Before God's blessing can be experienced, He must judge sin. Though the words in 23:19–20 applied to false prophets, Jeremiah used them here to refer to God's judgment on the wicked nations who opposed Israel. God's fierce anger that had been poured out on Judah would also be extended to other nations. When God judges the world for its sins, He will also restore Israel to Himself. "All the clans" of Israel, not just the tribe of Judah, will be known as God's people.

The national restoration of Israel (31:2–22). The long years of exile of the Northern Kingdom will cease when God intervenes to give them rest. He vowed to restore the Northern Kingdom because of His "everlasting love" and His "loving-kindness," and His restoration will be accompanied by songs of joy and deliverance. Jeremiah used the image of a father-son relationship to show God's deep love for His people (31:9). The nation's future hope will contrast sharply with her present misery. The cry from Ramah was one of "mourning and great weeping" as Jeremiah pictured the women of Judah sobbing as they watched their children being carried into exile. But God offered a word of comfort. There was hope because their children would return to their homeland. Jeremiah ended this section by recording Israel's cry of contrition which she will recite when she returns to the land. Though she had "strayed," she will repent and will be ashamed because of her sin. God in turn will express His great compassion for the wayward but returning nation.

The national restoration of Judah (31:23–26). God will also reverse the fortunes of Judah. Those in Judah will again invoke a blessing on Jerusalem (God's "righteous dwelling") and the temple area ("the sacred mountain"). The land itself will be repopulated, and God will meet every need.

The establishment of a new relationship with Israel and Judah (31:27–40). The words "Behold, days are coming" (31:27, 31, 38), which introduce the three sections of this unit, highlight three aspects of the Lord's new relationship with His people. First, God will provide a new beginning for His covenant people. He had judged Judah for her sin, but He will reverse that judgment. Second, He will "make a new covenant" with His people.

This New Covenant was expressly for the "house of Israel" (the Northern Kingdom) and the "house of Judah" (the Southern Kingdom). It will be unlike the covenant God had made with Israel at the time of the Exodus, because that covenant, the Mosaic Covenant, had been broken by the people. Third, God will establish a new city for His people. Jerusalem was destroyed by Babylon, but the city will be rebuilt and will be "holy to the Lord," never again to be destroyed. These promises await their future fulfillment in the Millennium.

The New Covenant

In God's New Covenant He will put His Law "in their minds" and "on their hearts," not just on tablets of stone (Exod. 34:1). This will give Israel the inner ability to obey His righteous standards (by means of the Holy Spirit; Ezek. 36:24–32).

The New Covenant will also provide for forgiveness of Israel's wickedness through the shedding of Jesus' blood (Matt. 26:27–28; Luke 22:20). Forgiveness of sin would be part of the new covenant only because God provided a Substitute to pay the penalty.

While the ultimate fulfillment of this covenant awaits the millennial reign of Christ, the church today participates in some of the benefits of that covenant. By her union with Christ, the church shares in many of the spiritual blessings promised to Israel (Rom. 11:11–27; Eph. 2:11–22), including the New Covenant (2 Cor. 3:6; Heb. 8:6–13; 9:15; 12:22–24).

But ultimately the New Covenant will be fulfilled when Israel is restored to her God in the future kingdom age (see also Zech. 12:10–13:1).

The Restoration of Israel and Judah Illustrated (chapter 32)

The illustration (32:1–12). Jeremiah was arrested and confined in the palace "courtyard of the guard," imprisoned by King Zedekiah for his prophecies. In this grim time God told Jeremiah that his cousin Hanamel would visit him in prison, asking him to purchase a field in Anathoth. The village of Anathoth, Jeremiah's hometown, was already under

Babylonian control, so this purchase would appear foolish. Who would buy a parcel of land that had already fallen into enemy hands? Yet under God's guidance Jeremiah bought the field, had two copies of the deed of purchase made, and gave both copies to Baruch, Jeremiah's scribe and friend (see 36:4, 8, 26).

The explanation (32:13–15). Jeremiah told Baruch to keep both documents in a clay jar. They had to "last a long time" because it would be many years before the people would be able to return from captivity and claim their land. Why did Jeremiah buy the lot and have the deeds preserved? To show that "houses, fields and vineyards" would "again be bought" by the people of Israel.

The prayer of Jeremiah (32:16–25). In this prayer Jeremiah began by focusing on the incomparable greatness and majesty of God's character, which were displayed in His deeds throughout Israel's history. From the time of the Exodus, God's "signs and wonders" had continued on Israel's behalf. But when Israel violated her covenant with Him, God was forced to display His power and justice as He brought the judgment of His curses on them (Lev. 26:14–39; Deut. 28:15–68). After speaking of God's mighty character and deeds, Jeremiah expressed his continued perplexity at the Lord's workings. The prophet was not doubting *if* God would accomplish the restoration of His people; he was bewildered over *how* He would do it.

The answer of the Lord (32:26–44). God answered Jeremiah by first reminding him of His character. As Jeremiah had said, nothing is "too hard" for God (see also 32:17). Jeremiah could depend on God's word even though he didn't understand how it would be fulfilled. Nebuchadnezzar would indeed destroy Jerusalem, setting it afire because of the people's sin. But that catastrophic event did not signal the end of God's covenant people. He promised to gather His people "from all the lands" where they had been taken in exile and to return them to the land of Israel where they will live in safety (31:1–17). He also promised an "everlasting covenant" (32:40), another term for the New Covenant (31:31–34). It was called "everlasting" because in the future Millennium God "will never stop doing good" to His people, and "they will never [again] turn away from" Him.

The Restoration of Israel and Judah Reaffirmed (chapter 33)

The coming judgment (33:1–5). Chapter 33, which concludes "The Book of Consolation," began with Jeremiah still being confined in the courtyard of the guard. Jeremiah did not understand how God could restore a nation that was destined for doom (32:24–25), so the Lord challenged the prophet to call to Him for understanding. God said He would then reveal "great and unsearchable things." Only God can unlock the secrets of the future, and He offered this knowledge to Jeremiah. The first revelation focused on Jerusalem's impending fall: Feeble attempts to shore up her defenses were futile. The partially dismantled houses would soon be filled with the dead bodies of those slain by the Babylonians. But why did Jerusalem have to be destroyed? Because of all her "wickedness."

> *God wants us to come to Him for understanding and insight. All true wisdom ultimately begins with Him (Prov. 1:7).*

The future restoration (33:6–13). God's message then moved from Judah's imminent judgment to her ultimate restoration. Someday the Lord will bring "health and healing" to His city and people. This blessing will involve a restoration to the land (33:6–7), to the Lord (33:8), and to a special place of honor among the nations (33:9). The contrast between Judah's present judgment and her future blessing was highlighted by two pictures of the changes that would come. Each picture began with the phrase "this is what the LORD [or LORD Almighty] says" (33:10, 12). The deserted streets of Jerusalem will again be filled with voices of joy and gladness, and the Judean towns destroyed by Babylon will experience peace and prosperity.

The covenants with David and the Levitical priests (33:14–18). The "righteous Branch," who will "sprout" from the line of David, will rule as King over the nation. This is a prophecy about Jesus Christ, who descended from the line of David and who will reign from David's throne (23:5–6; Luke 1:31–33). God also said He will restore Jerusalem as His dwelling place. The city that was about to be destroyed by Babylon will someday live in safety. It is significant that Jeremiah singled out the royal (33:15) and religious (33:16) aspects of God's restoration. Both were vital to Israel's existence as His covenant community. To emphasize the importance of both elements, God reiterated His covenants with the line of David and the Levitical priests. The first covenant mentioned was God's covenant with David (2 Sam. 7:8–16; 1 Chron. 17:4–14). God vowed, "David will never fail to have a man to sit on Israel's throne" (Jer. 33:17). That is, David's line would not fail before the righteous Branch came to claim His throne (Luke 1:31–33). The second covenant, which was with the Levitical priests, promised that they would never "fail to have a man to stand before" Him "to offer burnt offerings . . . grain offerings," and "sacrifices." That is, the Levitical priesthood would not be extinguished. God was referring back to the promise He made to Phinehas (Num. 25:12–13). In other words, neither the monarchy nor the priesthood would be abolished; in due time, when Christ reigns on the earth, they will be reestablished.

The confirmation of the covenants (33:19–26). Only if someone could "break" God's "covenant with the day and . . . the night" (Gen. 1:14–19), could that individual hope to break God's covenant with David or with the Levitical priests. These two covenants are as fixed as the natural order of the universe. The point God was making was that they could not be overthrown by mere mortals; the covenants were conditioned not on the people's obedience but on God's character. Only if the fixed laws of heaven and earth could be undone would God spurn Levi's and David's descendants.

D. *Present Catastrophe of Judah (chapters 34–45)*

After describing the future hope of Judah (chapters 30–33), Jeremiah returned to discuss its present judgment. The collapse of the kingdom that he had been predicting (chapters 2–29) would now come to pass. Chapters 34–36 continued the theme of rejection that began in chapters 26–29. Judah's judgment was certain because the people rejected God's word of warning. Chapters 37–45, arranged in chronological order, detail the events that occurred before, during, and after Jerusalem's fall to Babylon.

The Inconsistency of the People (chapter 34)

The warning to Zedekiah (34:1–7). When Nebuchadnezzar and the Babylonian army were attacking Jerusalem, God gave Jeremiah a message for King Zedekiah. This message was that Zedekiah's rebellion against Babylon would not succeed, and God would hand the city over to the Babylonians, who would burn it down. Though Zedekiah would try to flee, he would not be able to escape. Yet God did offer a message of hope. Zedekiah could have been executed, but God promised he would not die by the sword.

The warning to the people (34:8–22). Jeremiah exposed many social evils being practiced in his day, including the enslavement of Israelites by their own people, which violated God's Law (Exod. 21:2–11; Lev. 25:39–55; Deut. 15:12–18). In a desperate attempt to win God's favor, the king ordered everyone to free their Hebrew slaves. But their obedience to God did not last. The people "changed their minds . . . and enslaved them again." What caused this reversal? After the people had released the slaves, Babylon broke off its siege of Jerusalem to repel an attack by Egypt (see Jer. 37:4–13). The people hoped for an Egyptian victory, and so they reneged on their promise to God when it seemed life would return to normal. By doing so they "profaned" God's "name" (His reputation) because the covenant had been made before Him in the temple. God delivered punishment that matched their sin. Because the people had not given freedom to those Israelites wrongfully enslaved, He would give them "freedom" to die by "the sword, plague, and famine." Though the Babylonians had withdrawn from Jerusalem, God said He would order them to return.

The Consistency of the Recabites (chapter 35)

The fidelity of the Recabites (35:1–11). This prophecy was given during the reign of King Jehoiakim (609–598 B.C.), years before the events predicted in chapter 34. Jeremiah placed the chapter here to contrast the faithfulness of the Recabite family with the unfaithfulness of the people of Judah. When Jeremiah asked the Recabites to drink some wine, they refused because their forefather Jonadab had prohibited it. They had never "drunk wine or built houses to live in," nor had they ever cultivated "vineyard, fields or crops."

The Recabites were a nomadic clan (35:7–10) descended from "Jonadab [or Jehonadab] son of Recab" (35:6), who assisted Jehu in exterminating Baal worship from Israel (2 Kings 10:15–27). They were related to the Kenites (1 Chron. 2:54–55), who descended from Moses' father-in-law, Jethro (Judg. 1:16). Evidently Jonadab rejected a settled way of life for the life of a nomad, and his lifestyle became the norm for his clan (Jer. 35:6–10). They traveled in the wilderness of the Negev (Judg. 1:16; 1 Sam. 15:6), but were forced to move to Jerusalem when Nebuchadnezzar threatened Judah in 598 B.C. (Jer. 35:11).

The example of the Recabites (35:12–17). Why did Jeremiah bring the Recabites into the temple and offer them wine, when he knew they would refuse it? This was to teach Judah a lesson. In obeying their forefather's command, the Recabites stood in sharp contrast to the people of Judah who had consistently disobeyed the Lord. Judah deserved to be punished because, unlike the Recabites, she had not heeded God's words.

The reward of the Recabites (35:18–19). Because the Recabites were faithful to the command of their forefather, the Lord assured them they would always have descendants who would worship the Lord. The promise pointed to a continuing line, not a specific place of ministry.

> *God is always looking for individuals whose lives are characterized by faithfulness. Such individuals will experience God's blessing even in the midst of trials.*

Jehoiakim's Scroll Burning (chapter 36)

The writing of the scroll (36:1–7). The events of this chapter began in the fourth year of King Jehoiakim (605–604 B.C.; see 25:1). God told Jeremiah to write on a scroll all the prophecies God gave him, so that they could be read aloud to the people. If the people repented, God would forgive their wickedness. Jeremiah was barred from the temple—possibly because of his earlier unpopular addresses there (7:1–15; 26:1–19)—so the prophet told Baruch to go to the temple in his place. Jeremiah hoped that as Baruch read to the people from the scroll they would repent.

The reading of the scroll (36:8–19). Baruch went to the temple and read to the people gathered in the temple courtyard. Hearing these words, an individual named Micaiah reported the contents of the scroll to the officials in the royal palace. The officials summoned Baruch to appear before them and to read the scroll. The officials then looked at each other in fear, because they realized they must report what they heard to King Jehoiakim. They warned Baruch and Jeremiah to hide so the king could not find them.

The burning of the scroll (36:20–26). The officials went to the king and reported the incident to him. Jehudi read to the king as the officials watched. Being in his winter apartment, Jehoiakim had a fire burning in a brazier to provide warmth. Each time Jehudi read three or four columns, Jehoiakim interrupted him, cut those columns off the scroll with a knife, and threw them into the firepot. Showing no fear of God's judgment, the king burned the entire scroll, and then ordered the arrest of Baruch and Jeremiah. However, they were hidden by the Lord.

The rewriting of the scroll (36:27–32). Since Jehoiakim had destroyed the first scroll, Jeremiah wrote on "another scroll ... all the words" of the first one. He also included additional words for King Jehoiakim. Because the king had refused to believe God's warning about the king of Babylon, the Lord told Jehoiakim that no descendant of his would permanently sit on the throne of David, and that Jehoiakim would not receive a proper burial (see 22:18–19).

Jeremiah's Imprisonment (chapters 37–38)

Jeremiah's message to Zedekiah (37:1–10). The events in this section focused on Zedekiah, Judah's last king. Judah needed a strong, godly leader, but Zedekiah possessed neither quality. From the king to the common people, no one "paid any attention to the words of Jeremiah." But Zedekiah did send a delegation to Jeremiah, asking him to pray to the Lord for Jerusalem. Babylon had just lifted her siege against Jerusalem because the army of Egypt had marched to Jerusalem's aid. Zedekiah hoped Jeremiah's prayers would help the Egyptians force Babylon out of the land, but God's answer was not the one Zedekiah sought. Jeremiah announced that the Egyptian army that had marched out to support Judah would be crushed, and the Babylonian army would return and attack Jerusalem.

Jeremiah's arrest and confinement in a dungeon (37:11–16). The withdrawal of the Babylonian army brought a period of relative calm. Jeremiah planned to travel to Anathoth to take care of personal business, either to secure some land or to divide up some land to sell to others. But just as he started to leave Jerusalem, the guard's captain seized him and charged him with deserting to the enemy. Jeremiah was beaten and put in prison, where he was held for a long time.

Jeremiah's first meeting with Zedekiah (37:17–21). When Babylon returned to Jerusalem and renewed her siege of the city, Zedekiah secretly sent for Jeremiah and brought him to the palace to ask if he had a message from the Lord. The prophet said Jerusalem would fall and Zedekiah would be "handed over to the king of Babylon" (see also 21:3–7). Also Jeremiah affirmed his innocence and asked Zedekiah not to send him back to prison, because if he were taken back to that dungeon he might die there. Zedekiah ordered Jeremiah's transfer from the underground vaulted cistern to the courtyard of the guard in the royal palace (see 32:2). Zedekiah also arranged for Jeremiah to be given bread each day so he would not starve. This continued until "all the bread in the city was gone" (see also 52:6).

> *By being imprisoned in the royal palace, Jeremiah was assured a steady supply of food while many others in Jerusalem died of starvation during the siege. This is an example of how "in all things God works for the good of those who love him" (Rom. 8:28).*

Jeremiah's confinement in a cistern (38:1–6). While in the guard's courtyard, Jeremiah had some freedom to meet with people and to deliver God's message to any who would listen. Four powerful officials heard Jeremiah speaking to the people, and they went to Zedekiah and demanded that Jeremiah be put to death, because his words were "discouraging" the soldiers and the people. Though earlier the king had agreed to protect Jeremiah (37:18–21), Zedekiah now handed him over to those who sought his life. The officials took Jeremiah and threw him into a cistern, where he "sank down into the mud" at the bottom of the pit.

Jeremiah's rescue from the cistern (38:7–13). Many wanted Jeremiah killed. The only official who cared enough to help him was Ebed-Melech (whose name means "servant of the king"), a Cushite from the area of upper Egypt. Ebed-Melech went to the king and reported that the other officials had "acted wickedly" by throwing Jeremiah into the cistern. Zedekiah had either not known the officials' specific plan to kill Jeremiah or had not believed they would carry it out. But now, knowing Jeremiah's life was in danger, the king ordered Ebed-Melech to take thirty soldiers and rescue Jeremiah from the cistern. Jeremiah was then pulled from the cistern with the ropes and was again put in the courtyard of the guard.

Jeremiah's second meeting with Zedekiah (38:14–28). Zedekiah sent for the prophet again because he had a question, and he told the prophet not to hide anything from him. Jeremiah's message remained the same as before. If Zedekiah would surrender to the Babylonians, his life would be spared, his family would not be harmed, and the city would not be burned. Zedekiah refused to heed Jeremiah's advice because he was afraid of the Jews who had already surrendered to the Babylonians. He felt they might mistreat him for his past acts of cruelty to them. Jeremiah tried to assure Zedekiah that this would not happen, but the king refused to heed Jeremiah's advice. Instead he warned Jeremiah not to tell anyone about their conversation. Jeremiah remained in the courtyard as a political prisoner until Nebuchadnezzar captured Jerusalem.

Jerusalem's Destruction (chapter 39)

The fate of the Jews (39:1–10). In one sense chapter 39 is a climax to God's message of judgment against Jerusalem. Jeremiah provided a detailed account of how Jerusalem was taken. The entire siege lasted just over thirty months, from January 15, 588, to July 18, 586 B.C. When the Babylonians finally broke through the city wall, their officials entered the city and "took seats in the Middle Gate" to establish their control over the city and to judge those taken captive. In a desperate bid to escape, Zedekiah and his soldiers fled from the city at night. The army "headed toward the Arabah," probably hoping to cross the Jordan River and escape to the capital of their allies, the Ammonites. But the Babylonians overtook them on the broad plains of Jericho just before the Jordan River. Zedekiah was captured and taken to Nebuchadnezzar, who "pronounced sentence" on him for rebelling against Babylon. Jerusalem, too, suffered the ignominious fate predicted by Jeremiah. The Babylonians set fire to the city and tore down the walls so the city would remain defenseless. Most of the people remaining alive were taken away as captives. But Babylon left behind a remnant of the extremely poor people.

The fate of Jeremiah (39:11–18). Nebuchadnezzar issued orders through Nebuzaradan for his soldiers to take Jeremiah and look after him. Jeremiah was released from the courtyard of the guard and turned over to Gedaliah, who was appointed governor of those who remained in the land.

Jeremiah's Ministry to the Remnant Who Remained (chapters 40–42)

One would think Jerusalem's fall would have taught Judah a lesson she would never forget. However, by recording the events that happened *after* the fall of the city, Jeremiah demonstrated that the basic character of the people who remained in the land was unchanged. They still refused to trust in God or to submit to Babylon.

The governorship of Gedaliah (40:1–12). Jeremiah was released in Ramah, where he had been taken "bound in chains" with the other captives. He was free to go to Babylon with the other captives or to stay in Judah with Gedaliah. Jeremiah chose to stay at Mizpah with Gedaliah. When Judah's remaining soldiers heard that Gedaliah was now governor, they went to him at Mizpah where he encouraged them to "settle down in the land and serve . . . Babylon." He promised they would be free to live in the towns they had taken over.

The assassination of Gedaliah (40:13–41:15). Peace and stability were returning to the land, but forces of intrigue and rebellion still churned and bubbled. A report reached Gedaliah that the king of the Ammonites had sent Ishmael son of Nethaniah to assassinate him. As Ishmael and Gedaliah ate together, Ishmael and his cohorts killed the governor. They also killed all the Jews (probably those attending the banquet) as well as the Babylonian soldiers stationed there. Ishmael and his band of cutthroats also slaughtered seventy of eighty pilgrims who happened by the next day. Ishmael took as captives all the rest of those living at Mizpah, including Jeremiah. The group set out from Mizpah to go to Ammon, but a band of Israelite soldiers led by a man named Johanan caught up with the slower group of captives "near the great pool in Gibeon" (see 2 Sam. 2:12–16). The captives fled from Ishmael, while Ishmael along with eight of his men escaped and fled home to Ammon.

The leadership of Johanan (41:16–42:22). Johanan fled southward with all the survivors who had been rescued from Ishmael. This group included "soldiers, women, children, and court officials." But instead of returning to Mizpah, the group started on its way to Egypt to escape from the Babylonians. They were afraid Babylon would retaliate for the death of Gedaliah. Before continuing, everyone decided to seek God's guidance. They asked Jeremiah to pray to the Lord on their behalf. The people promised to obey whatever God commanded, whether it was "favorable or unfavorable." Ten days later God answered, and Jeremiah called together the group. He told them to stay in the land and not be afraid of the Babylonians because God would deliver them from any harm. Much like the blessings and cursings of Deuteronomy 28, Jeremiah followed his list of blessings for obedience with a list of judgments for disobedience. Jeremiah concluded his message by repeating God's command that they not go to Egypt because, if they went there, they would die by the "sword, famine and plague."

Jeremiah's Ministry to the Remnant in Egypt (chapters 43–44)

The true character of the remnant surfaced in their response to Jeremiah's message. In spite of his previous vindication as God's prophet, they still refused to believe him. Their solution was to seek protection in Egypt. However, Jeremiah's message to these rebels was that God's judgment would follow them to Egypt.

The remnant's flight to Egypt (43:1–7). After Jeremiah told the people God's answer to their request, the leaders said he was lying, and they accused Baruch of inciting Jeremiah to hand them over to the Babylonians, who would then kill them or carry them into exile. The leaders also forced Jeremiah and Baruch to go along with them as they made their way to

Egypt where they settled in Tahpanhes, a fortress city on the border of Lower (northern) Egypt.

In spite of all God had done to vindicate Jeremiah, the people still refused to believe him. The issue was not one of divine miracles or messages, but a question of faith. "And without faith it is impossible to please God" (Heb. 11:6).

The prophecy of Nebuchadnezzar's invasion (43:8–13). As the Jews in Egypt watched, Jeremiah gathered some large stones and buried them under the "brick pavement" that covered the large courtyard at the entrance to Pharaoh's palace. The purpose of the stones was to mark the spot where Nebuchadnezzar would place his throne when God brought him to Egypt. The specters of death, captivity, and the sword, which these exiles were fleeing (see 42:13–17), would follow them into Egypt. Nebuchadnezzar's attack on Egypt probably occurred sometime between 571 and 567 B.C.

The warning of God's judgment (chapter 44). God gave Jeremiah a message for the Jews living in Egypt. Reminding them of the calamity He had brought against Jerusalem and all Judah's towns, Jeremiah applied this history lesson to the Jews in Egypt. Instead of realizing the folly of idolatry, they were burning incense to Egyptian gods. As a result, God said He would bring disaster on the remnant in Egypt for their sin just as He had on the nation of Judah.

Unfortunately those listening to the prophet's message still refused to repent. Instead, they planned to continue doing everything just as they had in the past, including burning incense to the Queen of Heaven (the Babylonian goddess Ishtar). God took a solemn oath affirming that His judgment would pursue them until all were destroyed. Only a few would survive to return to Judah. God then gave a sign to validate the truth of His prophecy: Pharaoh Hophra would be handed over to his enemies just as Zedekiah had been handed over to Nebuchadnezzar.

Jeremiah's Ministry to Baruch (chapter 45)

Chapter 45 serves as the final pivotal point in the Book of Jeremiah. Jeremiah's message to Baruch became God's word to all righteous Jews scattered among the Gentiles because of Israel's sin. In one sense this chapter concludes the first forty-four chapters by picturing the Jews experiencing the final curse of God's covenant—exile. But by mentioning the nations, the chapter also looks ahead to chapters 46–51. God had judged His people, but His judgment on the nations was yet to come.

Baruch's discouragement (45:1–3). This chapter was written in the fourth year of Jehoiakim (605–604 B.C.), after Baruch had recorded the message Jeremiah dictated to him. The specific event in view was probably that recorded in 36:1–8. Evidently Baruch was discouraged because of the message. He felt God had "added sorrow to [his] pain." Much like Jeremiah earlier (8:21–9:2; 14:17–18; 15:10, 15–18), Baruch was discouraged and could "find no rest."

God's encouragement (45:4–5). God's message to Baruch was intended to evoke a response of faith in the midst of judgment. God would indeed "overthrow" what He had built and "uproot" what He had planted, as stated earlier in 1:10. Baruch's discouragement came because the realities of judgment clashed with his personal aspirations of greatness. But rather than being sad because God did not provide all he wanted, Baruch should have been thankful that God spared him, despite the calamities happening all around him. Jeremiah placed this chapter last in his prophecies to Judah (chaps. 2–45) to emphasize the response God wanted from godly Jews during the Exile.

We can choose to be bitter because God has withheld what we desire, or we can choose to be thankful because God has supplied what we need.

III. PROPHECIES CONCERNING THE NATIONS (CHAPTERS 46–51)

Jeremiah had been commissioned as a prophet to the nations (1:5; 46:1). He grouped his prophecies concerning the nation of Judah first (chapters 2–45) because Judah was God's covenant nation and because she consumed the largest amount of Jeremiah's prophetic activity. Yet other nations did not escape his prophetic eye. If God would judge His own covenant people for their sin, how could the heathen nations around Judah hope to escape when their sin was even more pronounced?

A. Prophecy against Egypt (chapter 46)

Egypt to Be Defeated at Carchemish (46:1–12)

Egypt had encouraged Judah's revolt against Babylon; but when it came time for Egypt to protect her partner in rebellion, she proved incapable of meeting her commitments (see 37:4–10; Ezek. 29:6–7). Jeremiah spoke against Pharaoh Neco's army, and he penned his prophecy after the army was defeated at Carchemish in 605 B.C. God sarcastically summoned the Egyptian army to march out for battle against the Babylonians. But the battle did not go Egypt's way because Babylon's swift attack defeated the Egyptians. The panic-stricken soldiers fled in haste, but the Babylonians overtook them and killed them. Egypt was trying to rise "like the Nile" and "cover the earth" with her conquests, but God vowed to bring vengeance on Egypt until she was destroyed. As God destroyed the Egyptians at Carchemish by the Euphrates River, He compared this slaughter to the offering of a sacrifice.

Egypt to Be Invaded and Exiled (46:13–26)

Nebuchadnezzar defeated the Egyptians at Carchemish in 605 B.C., but he did not invade Egypt until sometime between 571 and 567 B.C. Jeremiah asked why Egypt's warriors would be "laid low" (46:15), and then he answered his own question. The warriors could not stand because God had pushed them down. God was sending to Egypt someone (that is,

Nebuchadnezzar) who towered above all others as Mount Tabor stands out among Israel's mountains. The Egyptians were to pack their belongings for exile because Nebuchadnezzar would attack Memphis and leave it "in ruins without inhabitant." God's judgment would come against Pharaoh, all Egypt's gods, and all the people who relied on Pharaoh. However, God graciously promised that Egypt's destruction would not be permanent.

Israel to Be Regathered (46:27–28)

In contrast with Egypt, who would be taken into exile, Israel was not to fear or be dismayed. Israel could look forward to a time when she would enjoy "peace and security." A remnant would survive to receive again God's blessings.

B. Prophecy against Philistia (chapter 47)

Babylon's Armies Coming like a Flood (47:1–4)

The Babylonians were about to become an "overflowing torrent" that would sweep away the Philistines. Jeremiah identified the Philistines as the "remnant from the coasts of Caphtor," that is, Crete (Amos 9:7; Zeph. 2:5). They were one of the groups of Sea Peoples who had made their way to the coast of Canaan. Philistia had been a thorn in Israel's side throughout much of her history. Jeremiah delivered this message "before Pharaoh attacked Gaza."

God's Judgment Coming like a Sword (47:5–7)

Gaza and Ashkelon, two of the five most important Philistine cities (Josh. 13:3; 1 Sam. 6:4, 18), were singled out for special mention. Gaza was attacked by the Egyptians (Jer. 47:1), and Ashkelon was later destroyed by Nebuchadnezzar. God predicted that the Philistines would be caught in the middle of the struggle between Babylon and Egypt and would be destroyed. God's sword of judgment would not rest till it had attacked Ashkelon and the seacoast and destroyed them.

C. Prophecy against Moab (chapter 48)

Moab's Land to Be Destroyed (48:1–10)

Located east of the Dead Sea, Moab was separated from Edom on the south by the Zered River and from Ammon on the north by the Arnon River. Jeremiah listed many of the Moabite cities that God would destroy. Much of the imagery used by Jeremiah was borrowed from Isaiah 16:6–12.

Jeremiah first identified several cities inhabited by the tribe of Reuben (see Num. 32:37–38; Josh. 13:19) that were later captured by Moab. God was now predicting that they would be captured from Moab by others. Because Moab had trusted in her "deeds and riches," she would be judged by being taken captive. Her national god, Chemosh (1 Kings 11:7), would not be able to rescue her. God was so determined to destroy Moab that He threatened to curse those nations appointed to destroy Moab who were "lax" in doing His work.

Moab's Complacency to Be Shattered (48:11–17)

Moab's history was one of relative peace, for she had never felt the harsh reality of exile. Times were coming, however, when God would send soldiers to pour her out like wine that was no longer fit to drink. Even her valiant warriors would not be able to prevent her destruction.

Moab's Cities to Experience Catastrophe (48:18–28)

Jeremiah listed the cities of Transjordania that would be destroyed. Though the locations of some are not certain, he seemed to follow a general movement from north to south. Jeremiah used two symbols to show that Moab's power would be shattered: Moab's "horn" would be cut off, and her "arm" would be broken. Moab's impending doom would be like someone becoming drunk who would be forced to wallow in his own vomit and be ridiculed by others.

Moab's Pride to Cease (48:29–39)

Moab's chief problem was her pride, because of her physical security and relative peace. Moab was known for its vineyards, and so Jeremiah pictured Moab as a vineyard whose branches had extended to the Dead Sea. But now the "destroyer" had come to trample down her ripened fruit and grapes. From north to south the land would be devastated. God would put an end to idolatrous practices at Moab's many high places where offerings were being made to false gods. The once-proud country would become ridiculed.

Moab's Destruction to Be Complete (48:40–47)

Like an eagle Moab's enemies would swoop down and seize her in its claws. Lest Moab think her captivity was just accidental, God reminded her that her destruction would come because she defied Him. God would make sure that everyone living in Moab would feel the effects of her punishment. Yet God still offered hope to Moab. He promised to "restore the fortunes of Moab in days to come," that is, during the millennial reign of Christ.

D. *Prophecies against Other Nations (chapter 49)*

Prophecy against Ammon (49:1–6).
Located east of the Jordan River and north of Moab, the Ammonites were allied with Judah against Babylon during Judah's final revolt, but they provoked the assassination of Gedaliah. God announced that days were coming when an enemy would attack Rabbah, Ammon's capital city. The people of Rabbah would mourn (see also 48:37) because their god Molech would go into exile. Ammon's problem, like that of Moab, was pride (see 48:29). She trusted in her wealth, but God's judgment would shatter her complacency. Yet in His grace God vowed that afterward He would restore their fortunes.

Prophecy against Edom (49:7–22)

Edom was east of the Dead Sea and south of Moab. It had a history of conflict with Judah and came to symbolize all the heathen nations that sought Judah's harm (Ezek. 35; 36:5; Obad. 15–16). Those living in Edom were warned to turn and flee from the disaster God was about to bring. Edom had to be judged because of her many crimes. If nations not closely related to Judah were to be punished for their mistreatment of her, then nations with close family ties to Judah (like Edom) deserved even greater condemnation. Jeremiah pictured God sending an envoy to His allies among the nations, asking them to assemble for an attack on Edom. As God reduced her prestige and power, Edom would become "small among the nations" and "despised." The "young of the flock," probably her young men, would be exiled. Unlike Jeremiah's messages to Egypt, Moab, and Ammon, Edom was given no promise of future restoration. This prophecy was fulfilled in the intertestamental period when desert tribesmen drove the Edomites from their land. The Edomites migrated into southern Judah where they were subjugated and made to accept Judaism.

Prophecy against Damascus (49:23–27)

The major cities of Syria were alarmed because of the news of Babylon's advance. Damascus's pain was like that of a woman in labor. After Nebuchadnezzar's attack the soldiers of Damascus would be "silenced" (killed) and the fortifications of Ben-Hadad would be burned. Ben-Hadad (literally, "son of [the god] Hadad") was the name of the dynasty that ruled in Damascus in the ninth and eighth centuries B.C.

Prophecy against Kedar and Hazor (49:28–33)

Kedar was a nomadic tribe of Ishmaelites (see Gen. 25:13) in the Arabian desert, and Hazor, too, was in that desert. God summoned Nebuchadnezzar to destroy Kedar's black, goat-hair tents (Song of Sol. 1:5) and seize their flocks along with their "goods and camels." The people of Hazor were urged to flee and hide because Nebuchadnezzar planned to go against them in battle. These Arabian people felt so secure in their remote desert location that they did not even have city gates or bars to protect themselves against attack. Nebuchadnezzar would take their camels and other animals as booty, the inhabitants would be scattered, and the city itself would become a "haunt of jackals."

Prophecy against Elam (49:34–39)

"Elam" was east of Babylon in what is today northern Iran. God promised to "break the bow of Elam" which He called the "mainstay of their might." This is significant because the Elamites were known for their archery skills (see Isa. 22:6). Though Nebuchadnezzar defeated the Elamites about 596 B.C., his subjugation at that time did not fulfill this message. Jeremiah's statement about Elam's destruction seems to take on eschatological dimensions as God said He would set His throne in Elam to supervise her destruction. Yet Elam's destruction will not be total because God will restore her fortunes in days to come.

E. Prophecy against Babylon (chapters 50–51)

Jeremiah's longest message against the nations focused on Babylonia. Content wise, almost half of Jeremiah's messages against the nations were directed against this one nation.

The Announcement of Judgment (50:1–10)

Jeremiah announced to the nations the public humiliation of Babylon. She would be captured and her gods would be put to shame. Jeremiah's prophecy looked beyond the fall of Babylon to Cyrus in 539 B.C. to describe an eschatological destruction that will reverse the fortunes of Israel and Judah. The destruction of Babylon will be the climax of God's judgment on the gentile powers that have oppressed His people and will open the way for the fulfillment of His promises to Israel. Other portions of Scripture also point to this still-future destruction of Babylon and rebuilding of Israel (Isa. 13–14; Zech. 5:5–11; Rev. 17–18).

The Fall of Babylon (50:11–16)

Babylon sinned in proudly destroying Judah. God vowed to judge any nation that can rejoice and be glad as it pillages His inheritance. He will disgrace Babylon by making it an uninhabited desert. The once-great city will be so thoroughly destroyed that people will be amazed at her condition. Jeremiah graphically portrayed the battle as he described the enemy surrounding the city and shooting arrows at her defenders. When the city finally surrenders, God's "vengeance" will be poured out on those who remain. God warned any foreigners living in Babylon to "flee to their own land." This was not fulfilled when Cyrus attacked Babylon in 539 B.C. It awaits a future fulfillment.

The Restoration of Israel (50:17–20)

The people of Israel had become like scattered sheep. The Northern Kingdom had been conquered by Assyria in 722 B.C., and the Southern Kingdom was crushed by Babylon in 586 B.C. God will "punish" the kings for attacking His people, and He will also restore Israel to her land. In those days He will also bring about a spiritual renewal within His people. Though some will seek to point out the nation's sins, they will not find any because God will forgive His "remnant."

The Attack on Babylon (50:21–40)

Babylon's enemies will come from great distances to break her open as one would break open grain silos. The bodies of her slain will be piled up "like heaps of grain." The bustling metropolis of Babylon will become a deserted wilderness where only wild desert creatures will live. After this destruction Babylon will "never again be inhabited." Her desolation will be as complete as that of Sodom and Gomorrah (see Isa. 13:19). This prediction has not yet been fulfilled. Babylon has been inhabited throughout her history, and the government of Iraq has begun restoring the ancient city. The prophecy about Babylon's complete ruin awaits fulfillment during the future Tribulation period.

The Anguish of Babylon (50:41–46)

The army attacking Babylon will come "from the ends of the earth . . . armed with bows and spears." This invading army will be cruel and will show no mercy. Reports about this approaching army will bring terror to Babylon's king; he will be as fearful as a "woman in labor." When God attacks Babylon, the rest of the world will "tremble" at His judgment.

God's Vengeance against Babylon (51:1–14)

This enemy will destroy Babylon so that Israel and Judah will be free to return home (see also 50:33–34). The judgment is so certain that God called on His people to flee from Babylon to avoid being destroyed (see Rev. 18:4). The remnant who escape and return to Israel will sing praises to God in the temple.

God's Sovereignty over Babylon (51:15–26)

Using language that is virtually synonymous with 10:12–16, Jeremiah stressed God's sovereignty and power in guaranteeing Babylon's fall. Babylon had been a "war club" God used to shatter other nations. Now, however, He will repay Babylon for the evil she had done to Jerusalem. The judgment will be so complete that people will not even search the ruins to find a "cornerstone" or a "stone for a foundation" to rebuild elsewhere. Instead, the city will lie desolate forever.

The Summons to the Nations against Babylon (51:27–33)

For the third time God summoned the nations to lift up their banners and rally their troops against Babylon (see also 50:2; 51:12). God will send these invaders against Babylon, to destroy the land and to kill its people. The invaders will press their attack by setting Babylon's dwellings on fire. Messengers will rush from the various quarters of the city to announce to the leader that the "entire city is captured." Babylon will be like a threshing floor that has been swept clean. When Babylon will be trampled down by these invaders, the people will know that God's harvest of judgment has arrived.

God's Revenge on Babylon (51:34–44)

In 586 B.C. Babylon had "devoured" the Jews and "swallowed" Judah whole. But God said that Babylon would release the exiles from captivity. The Jews had called on God to avenge the violence done to them, and God said He would answer their request. He promised to make Babylon a "heap of ruins" and a "place where no one lives" (see 50:3). Babylon will drink from His cup of judgment and will never recover (see also 51:57).

The Warning to the Remnant in Babylon (51:45–48)

God ordered His people to run for their lives from Babylon to escape His anger. They were not to be afraid of the many rumors of victory or violence floating through the land. Instead they were to remain confident that God will judge Babylon and that eventually "heaven and earth . . . will shout for joy" over His victory (see Rev. 18:20).

The Certainty of Babylon's Fall (51:49–53)

God has ordained that Babylon must fall because she is responsible for killing many Israelites. Babylon's destruction will be the catalyst God uses to bring the Jews home. The remnant still in exile were disgraced because they remembered that foreigners had "entered the holy places" of the temple and desecrated it. As a result, God will send destroyers against Babylon who will wipe her out, while the people of Israel are restored.

God's Repayment of Babylon (51:54–58)

Jeremiah announced that a sound of destruction will be heard from Babylon as "waves" of enemy soldiers come to attack the city. These invaders will capture Babylon's army, thus destroying her military power. Jeremiah ended this message about Babylon's destruction by quoting a proverb to show the futility of Babylon's attempts to resist God's judgment. Since God had already announced that "Babylon's . . . wall will be leveled and her . . . gates set on fire" (50:15; 51:30), any labor expended to prevent His judgment and shore up the defenses will only provide more fuel to feed the flames when the enemy finally arrives.

Seraiah's Symbolic Mission (51:59–64)

The capstone of Jeremiah's oracle against Babylon was a message he gave to Seraiah, a staff officer to the king of Judah. Compiling all his prophecies about Babylon, Jeremiah gave the scroll to Seraiah and told him to read the words aloud when he got to Babylon. After affirming God's intention to destroy that place, Seraiah was to "tie a stone" to the scroll and "throw it into the Euphrates." As the scroll and stone sank beneath the water, Seraiah was to announce that Babylon, like the scroll, would "sink to rise no more" (also see Rev. 18:21).

IV. CONCLUSION (CHAPTER 52)

Chapter 52 is nearly identical to 2 Kings 24:18–25:30 and was written sometime after 561 B.C. when King Jehoiachin was released from prison in Babylon (Jer. 52:31). Much of the material is parallel to information recorded by Jeremiah in chapter 39. Why, then, was this chapter added to Jeremiah's prophecies? Most likely it was added to show that the prophet's words of judgment against Jerusalem had been fulfilled and that his words about Judah's release from the exile were about to be fulfilled. This final chapter served to vindicate the prophet and encourage the remnant still in captivity.

The Fall of Zedekiah (52:1–11)

The history of Judah's final king is again summarized (see also 39:1–7). Zedekiah rebelled against Nebuchadnezzar, and on January 15, 588 B.C., Nebuchadnezzar began the final siege of Jerusalem. On July 18, 586 B.C., the famine in the besieged city had become so severe that the food ran out. All resistance was gone, and on that day the Babylonians made a breach in the city wall. Zedekiah and his soldiers tried to flee, but they were captured. Zedekiah was taken to Nebuchadnezzar, was forced to watch the execution of his sons, was blinded, bound with chains, and taken to Babylon, where he remained imprisoned until he died.

The Destruction of the City and the Temple (51:12–23)

Jerusalem fared no better than her king. By August 17, 586 B.C., the city had been cleared of rebels, sacked, and put to the torch. Every major building was burned down. Those who survived the siege were taken into exile to Babylon, and only the poorest people were left behind. Just as Jeremiah had predicted (27:19–22), the furnishings still remaining in the temple were taken to Babylon (51:17–23). The "bronze pillars, the movable stands," and the other furnishings named by Jeremiah were carried off to Babylon. This was such an extensive undertaking that the prophet paused to explain the size of the bronze pillars that were removed (52:21).

The Fate of Those in the City during Its Fall (52:24–27)

All the city's leaders, including the chief priest and several other key temple officials, were rounded up by the Babylonians. Also captured were the "officer in charge of the fighting men" (secretary of defense), seven royal advisers, and the officer who was in "charge of conscripting the people" along with several of his men. These were taken to Nebuchadnezzar and executed.

The Fate of the Exiles (52:28–30)

This section is not included in 2 Kings 25. The author added it to show that other groups of exiles were taken to Babylon. The two deportations mentioned in Jer. 52:28–29 are secondary deportations. Jeremiah mentioned them here (along with a third minor deportation, 52:30) to show the full extent of Babylon's destruction of Judah.

The Blessing of Jehoiachin (52:31–34)

Jehoiachin became the firstfruits of those in captivity in Babylon. In 561–560 B.C., the thirty-seventh year of Jehoiachin's exile, Evil-Merodach became king of Babylon. As part of the festivities at the end of his accession year he "released Jehoiachin . . . from prison" on March 21, 560 B.C. and allowed him to eat "regularly at the king's table." Just as Jeremiah's prophecies of destruction had come true, so now his prophecies of future blessing were beginning. Jehoiachin's favor gave hope to the exiles that God's promise of restoration would come.

> *God will do exactly what He has promised. If we believe this, our lives will exhibit a sense of obedience and expectancy.*

LAMENTATIONS
The Sorrow of Sin

*L*AMENTATIONS IS a mournful postscript to the Book of Jeremiah. In five dirges, or funeral laments, the prophet Jeremiah grieves over the fate of Jerusalem because of her sin. But the Book of Lamentations contains more than just the sad reflections of a vindicated but mournful prophet. It is a reminder that sin carries with it the consequences of sorrow, grief, misery, and pain.

AUTHOR

The book does not specifically name its author, but Jewish tradition unanimously attributes the work to the prophet Jeremiah. The Septuagint translation added the following words as an introduction to the book: "And it came to pass, after Israel was taken captive, and Jerusalem made desolate, that Jeremiah sat weeping, and lamented with this lamentation over Jerusalem, and he said . . ." In both Jeremiah and Lamentations the writer said his eyes flowed with tears (Jer. 9:1, 18; Lam. 1:16; 2:11); and in both books the writer said he was an eyewitness of Jerusalem's fall to Babylon. Also both books report the atrocities that befell Jerusalem in her final days (Jer. 19:9; Lam. 2:20; 4:10).

DATE

Assuming Jeremiah was the author of Lamentations, the book must have been composed within a brief period of time. Jeremiah would have composed it after Jerusalem fell to Babylon in 586 B.C. (1:1–11) but before he was taken to Egypt (583–582 B.C.; see Jer. 43:1–7). The vivid descriptions and deep emotions argue for a composition shortly after the events occurred, possibly in late 586 B.C. or early 585 B.C.

ADDRESSEES

Jeremiah directed this message to the people of Judah still alive after the destruction of Jerusalem. This would have included those taken into captivity to Babylon, those who remained in the land of Judah, and those who had fled to Egypt. All these individuals were now experiencing the Lord's ongoing judgment because of their sin. They needed to read—and heed—the lessons found in this book.

PURPOSE

All the heartaches and hardships experienced by Jerusalem, as recorded in Lamentations, had been predicted almost nine hundred years earlier in Leviticus 26 and Deuteronomy 28. God had warned of the fearful consequences of disobedience, and, as Jeremiah carefully noted, God carried out those curses. Yet this characteristic makes the Book of Lamentations a book of hope for Israel. God was *faithful* in discharging every aspect of the covenant He had made. Israel was punished for disobedience, but she was not consumed because God's covenant was still in force. The same covenant that promised judgment for disobedience also promised restoration for repentance (Deut. 30:1–10). Jeremiah's message to Judah was for the nation to turn back to the Lord.

STRUCTURE

The Book of Lamentations has three structural distinctives. First, the book is written as a series of five laments. A lament was a funeral poem or song written and recited for someone who had just died (see, for example, 2 Sam. 1:17–27). Jeremiah used this literary form to convey the feelings of sadness and loss being experienced by the survivors. Second, each of chapters 1–4 has an acrostic arrangement, a form in which the first word of each line or sentence, when taken in order, follows the sequence of the letters of the Hebrew alphabet. Third, the book has a definite structural balance. Chapters 1 and 5 parallel each other and focus on the people, and chapters 2 and 4 are parallel and focus on the Lord. Chapter 3 provides the pivot for the book, pointing to Jeremiah's response in the midst of affliction.

OUTLINE

I. First Dirge: Jerusalem's Desolation because of Her Sin (chapter 1)
  A. Jeremiah's Lament over Jerusalem's Desolation (1:1–11)
  B. Jerusalem's Plea for Mercy (1:12–19)
  C. Jerusalem's Prayer to God (1:20–22)

II. Second Dirge: God's Punishment of Jerusalem's Sin (chapter 2)
  A. God's Anger (2:1–10)
  B. Jeremiah's Grief (2:11–19)
  C. Jerusalem's Plea (2:20–22)

III. Third Dirge: Jeremiah's Response (chapter 3)
  A. Jeremiah's Afflictions (3:1–18)
  B. Jeremiah's Hope (3:19–40)
  C. Jeremiah's Prayer (3:41–66)

IV. Fourth Dirge: The Lord's Anger (chapter 4)
  A. Contrasts before and after the Siege (4:1–11)
  B. Causes of the Siege (4:12–20)
  C. Call for Vindication (4:21–22)

V. Fifth Dirge: The Remnant's Response (chapter 5)
  A. The Remnant's Prayer for Remembrance (5:1–18)
  B. The Remnant's Prayer for Restoration (5:19–22)

I. FIRST DIRGE: JERUSALEM'S DESOLATION BECAUSE OF HER SIN (CHAPTER 1)

Jeremiah's first dirge established the book's theme—the sorrow of sin. Jerusalem had turned from the protective care of her God to pursue foreign alliances and lifeless idols; and now she found herself alone, destitute, and defenseless.

A. Jeremiah's Lament over Jerusalem's Desolation (1:1–11)

Jeremiah described the ways in which Jerusalem had changed. Her population had been decimated, and the city was deserted. Economically the city was reduced to the status of a "widow." All this took place because Jerusalem had forsaken her true Lover and Friend, the Lord, for false gods and foreign alliances. When she turned from God to pursue her own idolatrous ways, Jerusalem "did not consider her future." Because of her sin Jerusalem saw her temple become desecrated as pagans entered her sanctuary. Jerusalem also experienced famine. People were forced to "barter their treasures for food to keep themselves alive" (see also 1:19; 2:20; 4:10).

> *As is true of many individuals, Jerusalem did not seem to realize that sin, though it might promise temporary pleasure, leads only to death and destruction (Ezek. 18:4; Rom. 6:23).*

B. Jerusalem's Plea for Mercy (1:12–19)

Jeremiah pictured Jerusalem as if she were a person calling out to those passing by to stop and take note of her condition. Her destruction was not a chance occurrence; it was a direct result of God's judgment. The attack was like fire sent into Jerusalem's "bones," like a hunter spreading a net for Jerusalem's feet, like binding her sins into a yoke to be placed on her neck, and like the treading of grapes in a winepress as God trampled her. In a scene of touching sadness, Jeremiah pictured Jerusalem as a broken, weeping widow (see also 1:1), stretching out her hands to seek some condolence and aid but finding no one to give her comfort. The city admitted that her judgment was caused by a righteous God. "The LORD is righteous, yet I rebelled against his command."

C. Jerusalem's Prayer to God (1:20–22)

Jerusalem had called to those passing by (1:12–19), but now she turned to cry out to God. Baring her soul to the Lord, Jerusalem called on Him to notice her plight. Those who tried to escape by breaking through Babylon's siege were cut down by swords, and those who remained in the city died of starvation and plague. Jerusalem also called on God to extend His judgment to her enemies and to bring "the day" He had announced. The "day" was the Day of the Lord, the time when God's judgment would extend to all the earth to avenge injustice and bring about the age of righteousness He had promised. Jerusalem wanted God to judge the sins of her enemies as He had judged her sins.

II. SECOND DIRGE: GOD'S PUNISHMENT OF JERUSALEM'S SIN (CHAPTER 2)

The focus of Jeremiah's attention moved from the personified city of Jerusalem to the punishment inflicted by God. The first ten verses depict God's anger against the city. Verses 11–19 include Jeremiah's anguished cry as he wept over the destruction of the city and called on the people to cry out to God. Verses 20–22 give the people's response, in which the Jerusalemites again cried out for the Lord to see their plight.

A. God's Anger (2:1–10)

This second dirge began by focusing on the real cause for Jerusalem's calamity. God was the One who destroyed the city and its people. Jeremiah hammered home the reality of God's judgment on Jerusalem because of her sin. In His anger God removed all those to whom the people looked for guidance and leadership. God seemed to Judah like "a flaming fire" (2:3–4) and "an enemy" (2:4–5), as He systematically dismantled everything in which they trusted. God also directed His anger against the temple which He "laid waste . . . like a garden," that is, He was like a farmer tearing down a temporary booth that provided shade during a harvest. Every group charged by God to lead the people—the king, the priests, and the prophets—was affected by Jerusalem's fall. In response to their loss of leadership, the people mourned, sprinkling dust on their heads and wearing sackcloth, both signs of sorrow and anguish (see Gen. 37:34; Job 2:12–13; Neh. 9:1).

B. Jeremiah's Grief (2:11–19)

Jeremiah cried out in anguish at the scene he had been surveying. Five portraits of Jerusalem's condition prompted his cry. The first sketch highlighted the starvation that had haunted Jerusalem during the siege (2:11–12). Jeremiah wept as he described children calling out for food as their lives ebbed away in their mothers' arms. His second sketch was of a man trying desperately to offer comfort to a grieving friend (2:13). The third sketch was of false prophets hastening rather than hindering Jerusalem's downfall as they encouraged the people to believe their misleading lies (2:14). The fourth sketch pictured the victorious enemy mocking the vanquished people (2:15–17). The once-majestic and secure city of Jerusalem was now the object of scoffing and derision. Jeremiah reminded the Jews again that the destruction was the work of God: "He has let the enemy gloat over you, he has exalted the horn of your foes." Jeremiah's fifth sketch pictured the remnant ceaselessly wailing to God in despair because of their calamity (2:18–19). The people were to unleash their innermost thoughts and emotions and share them with God: "pour out your heart like water."

C. Jerusalem's Plea (2:20–22)

In a cry of pain and horror the city called on God to "look" and think about her calamity. The siege was so severe that some parents became cannibals and ate their own children (see Lev. 26:27–29; Deut. 28:53–57). The slaughter also encompassed the religious leaders and people of all ages. Priests and prophets alike were slain inside the temple precincts, while the bodies of young and old littered the streets. Lest anyone forget the ultimate Judge, Jeremiah again (see Lam. 2:17) reminded the people that God was the One wielding the sword of punishment. Those whom He had loved were now destroyed.

> Some people view sin as a "victimless crime" that affects only the one who is sinning. But the horror of sin is that its consequences often reach beyond the sinner to touch those who are otherwise "innocent." For example, drunken drivers kill innocent victims.

III.   THIRD DIRGE: JEREMIAH'S RESPONSE (CHAPTER 3)

Chapter 3 is the heart of Lamentations and gives the book a positive framework around which the other chapters revolve. The black velvet of sin and suffering in chapters 1–2 and 4–5 serves as a fitting backdrop to display the sparkling brilliance of God's loyal love in chapter 3. The chapter itself differs from the first two. Instead of twenty-two verses it has sixty-six—three verses for each letter of the Hebrew alphabet. In a first-person narrative the writer described his personal reaction to the suffering he had experienced. Jeremiah detailed his afflictions during the time of Jerusalem's fall (3:1–18). But his knowledge of God's ways in the midst of his affliction produced hope, not despair (3:19–40). So Jeremiah could lead Israel in prayer to God for deliverance, restoration, and vindication (3:41–66).

A. Jeremiah's Afflictions (3:1–18)

In a long list of metaphors Jeremiah enumerated the many afflictions that he, as Judah's representative, suffered at the hand of God's wrath. Instead of walking in the "light" of God's guidance, he had been forced to stumble in "darkness" as God turned against him. God's afflictions had taken their toll on Jeremiah's body and spirit. God refused to acknowledge his prayers, and all avenues of escape seemed to be blocked. Jeremiah felt as if God was taking target practice at him. He was mocked and laughed at by his compatriots, filled with bitterness, trampled underfoot, deprived of peace and prosperity, and in despair.

B. Jeremiah's Hope (3:19–40)

Jeremiah's condition paralleled that of Judah. His outer and inner turmoil pushed him toward despair ("my soul is downcast"). But one thought crowded out the hopelessness threatening to overwhelm him: "Because of the LORD's great love we are not consumed, for his compassions never fail" (3:22). God was punishing Judah for her sin, but He had not rejected her as His covenant people. His "loving-kindnesses" (NASB) "are new every morning." Much like the manna in the wilderness, God's loyal love could not be exhausted. This truth caused Jeremiah to call out in praise, "Great is your faithfulness." He would wait for God to bring about restoration and blessing because he now understood how inexhaustible was the Lord's supply of loyal love. Jeremiah placed his (and Judah's) affliction in proper perspective by remembering how it related to God's character and His covenant with His people. Judah's afflictions were not cruel acts of a capricious God, who delighted in inflicting pain on helpless people. Rather the afflictions came from a compassionate God, who was being faithful to His covenant. Jeremiah ended this section by exhorting the people, "Let us examine our ways . . . let us return to the LORD." God's affliction was designed as a corrective measure to restore His wayward people.

> Focusing on our problems can make us discouraged. But focusing on God's never-ending faithfulness gives us hope. Think on the words of the great hymn "Great Is Thy Faithfulness," written by Thomas O. Chisholm.

C. Jeremiah's Prayer (3:41–66)

The prophet exhorted the people to confess their sins to God (3:41–47). This section was written in the plural ("we," "us," "our"), showing that Jeremiah was identifying with the people. When Judah would recognize the awful consequences of her sin, she would finally admit her guilt. In verses 48–66 Jeremiah recalled God's personal deliverance after his cry. This section was written in the singular ("I," "me," "my"); Jeremiah was a representative of Judah and a model for her. As God rescued Jeremiah and judged his enemies, so God would rescue Judah and judge her enemies, if she would call on Him. In Judah's final days Jeremiah faced many enemies. He cried to God for deliverance from the "pit" where he was facing certain death, and God answered (see Jer. 38:7–13) and "came near" him. Also the prophet called on God to vindicate him before his enemies. This was fulfilled historically when his enemies were punished by Babylon. The parallel to Jerusalem was obvious. She too was persecuted by her enemies (Lam. 3:46–47), but she could be confident that God would vindicate her before her enemies if she would turn to Him.

IV. FOURTH DIRGE: THE LORD'S ANGER (CHAPTER 4)

Chapter 4 parallels the judgment discussed in chapter 2. After describing the response of an individual in the midst of judgment (chap. 3), Jeremiah again surveyed the scene of calamity in Jerusalem.

A. Contrasts before and after the Siege (4:1–11)

The stark reality of Jerusalem's judgment was brought into sharp focus by comparing her present condition with that before the fall. In their former glory the inhabitants of Jerusalem had been as precious as "gold," but they were now like "pots of clay." The treatment of children by their mothers during the siege was worse than that expected of loathsome animals. Jackals nourished their offspring, while the cries of the children of Jerusalem for food and water went unheeded by their parents. The city leaders suffered the same fate as everyone else. They too saw their skin darken (it became "blacker than soot") and shrivel as their bodies became emaciated.

Jeremiah again pointed to the Lord as the source of Zion's punishment. Jerusalem was experiencing God's wrath and anger for her sin.

B. Causes of the Siege (4:12–20)

One cause of Jerusalem's siege and fall was the sins of her prophets and priests. Instead of promoting righteousness and stressing faithfulness to God's covenant, these leaders had killed innocent people. A second cause of Jerusalem's siege was the faithlessness shown in her search for foreign alliances. Instead of trusting in God, Jerusalem had turned to Egypt for protection from Babylon, but this was of no avail. A third cause of Jerusalem's siege and fall was King Zedekiah, "the LORD's anointed." The leader Jerusalem looked to for security (her "very life breath" and her "shadow") was powerless to protect her.

> God holds Christian leaders responsible to promote and display righteousness and faithfulness.

C. Call for Vindication (4:21–22)

These two verses draw a contrast between Israel and her gentile enemy, Edom. Though Edom rejoiced over Jerusalem's calamity, the bitter "cup" would someday be passed to her. Drinking from a cup pictured being forced to undergo judgment (Jer. 25:15–28). God was judging Jerusalem for her sin, but He would also judge Edom (and, by extension, all gentile nations) for their sins. Jerusalem could look forward to restoration, but Edom could expect only judgment.

V. FIFTH DIRGE: THE REMNANT'S RESPONSE (CHAPTER 5)

The prophet's final lament breaks the pattern established in his earlier laments, for the acrostic pattern is not followed in this chapter. In fact the entire chapter is more properly a prayer than a lament. Chapters 1–3 each closes with a prayer to the Lord (1:20–22; 2:20–22; 3:55–66), but no prayer is included in chapter 4. Therefore it is possible to see chapter 5 functioning as the prayer following chapter 4. The remnant called on God to restore both the land of Israel and the blessings of the covenant (Deut. 30:1–10).

A. The Remnant's Prayer for Remembrance (5:1–18)

The remnant cried to God to remember the indignities they had suffered and to note their present disgrace and to do something about it. Their new taskmasters were cruel despots who cared little for them. Persecution and fear dogged the Jews' every footstep. The sin of Judah's past leaders (their "fathers") resulted in the survivors bearing the punishment due their ancestors. The present generation was not claiming to be suffering unjustly, but they saw their punishment as a logical conclusion to their ancestors' folly. Their forefathers' willing submission to godless nations was now bearing bitter fruit. After speaking of their general conditions of suffering (5:2–10), the people described the effects of God's judgment on different groups of individuals (5:11–18). No element of society escaped the ravages of judgment. Women were assaulted, and princes were "hung up by their hands." A veil of gloom hung over Jerusalem as the once-thriving city had become ruins inhabited only by wild animals.

B. The Remnant's Prayer for Restoration (5:19–22)

After describing her condition, Judah concluded her prayer by calling on God to act. The basis for this call was God's eternal sovereignty: "You, O LORD, reign forever." The knowledge of God's ability to restore the nation prompted the people to ask God why He had abandoned them. They prayed, "Restore us to yourself . . . that we may return." Their ultimate hope for restoration was God's faithfulness to His covenant promises. Unless God had totally rejected the nation (which He had vowed never to do; Lev. 26:44; Jer. 31:31–37), the people could depend on Him to answer their request.

The Book of Lamentations ends on a note of hope. In spite of severe suffering because of her sin, Judah had not been abandoned as a nation.

EZEKIEL
The Glory of the Lord

$\mathcal{F}$OR THE AVERAGE READER of the Bible, the Book of Ezekiel is a mystifying maze of symbols and visions—a kaleidoscope of whirling wheels and dry bones that defy interpretation. This impression often causes readers to shy away from studying the book and to miss one of the great literary and spiritual masterpieces of the Old Testament.

AUTHOR

The author of this book is identified as "Ezekiel the priest, the son of Buzi" (1:3). Like Jeremiah (Jer. 1:1) and Zechariah (Zech. 1:1; see also Neh. 12:4, 16), Ezekiel was a priest from the line of Aaron (Ezek. 1:3). All three of these prophet/priests ministered during the exilic or postexilic periods. Ezekiel's priestly background explains in part his emphasis on the temple in Jerusalem, the glory of the Lord, the actions of Jerusalem's priests, and God's future temple.

DATE

The date for Ezekiel's ministry can be determined by noting the specific chronological markers within the book (1:2; 8:1; 20:1; 24:1; 29:1, 17; 30:20; 31:1; 32:1, 17; 33:21; 40:1). All of his prophecies are arranged chronologically except those introduced in 29:1, 17. These two variations may be explained by the fact that the specific messages are grouped topically as part of the prophecies against Egypt in chapters 29–32.

Ezekiel's ministry began on July 31, 593 B.C. (1:1–2). The last dated prophecy identified by Ezekiel came on March 26, 571 B.C. (29:17). Therefore his prophetic activity spanned at least twenty-two years (593–571 B.C.). He began his prophetic ministry at the age of thirty (cf. 1:1), so he would have been fifty-two years old at the time of his last dated prophecy.

ADDRESSEES

Ezekiel ministered to Israelites in captivity in Babylon. He was taken into captivity as part of the second deportation in 597 B.C. when Nebuchadnezzar "carried into exile all Jerusalem: all the officers and fighting men, and all the craftsmen and artisans—a total of ten thousand" (2 Kings 24:14). Ezekiel's ministry paralleled that of Jeremiah who prophesied in Jerusalem. The content was much the same, but their audiences differed.

PURPOSE

God called Ezekiel as a prophet to predict the coming collapse of Judah and Jerusalem by the Babylonians. Ezekiel's message fell on deaf ears until word of the city's destruction finally reached the exiles in Babylon. The fall of the city prompted a change in Ezekiel's prophetic message. Before the siege of Jerusalem began, Ezekiel's message focused on Judah's coming destruction because of her sin. After Jerusalem's fall, his message centered on Judah's future restoration. Between these two great themes, he also announced God's judgment on the Gentiles.

OUTLINE

I. Judgment on Judah (chapters 1–24)
   A. Ezekiel's Preparation (chapters 1–3)
   B. Ezekiel's Prophecies against Judah and Jerusalem (chapters 4–24)

II. Judgment on Gentile Nations (chapters 25–32)
   A. Judgment to the East and West (chapter 25)
   B. Judgment to the North (chapters 26–28)
   C. Judgment to the South (chapters 29–32)
III. Blessings on Israel (chapters 33–48)
   A. Ezekiel Reappointed as a Watchman (chapter 33)
   B. The Present False Shepherds Contrasted with the Future True Shepherd (chapter 34)
   C. The Enemy (Edom) Destroyed (chapter 35)
   D. The People Blessed (chapter 36)
   E. The Nation Restored (chapter 37)
   F. The Attack by Gog Repulsed (chapters 38–39)
   G. A New Temple (chapters 40–43)
   H. A New Service of Worship (chapters 44–46)
   I. A New Land (chapters 47–48)

I. JUDGMENT ON JUDAH (CHAPTERS 1–24)

The first half of the Book of Ezekiel focuses on God's coming judgment of Judah. God was about to attack Jerusalem, and He commissioned Ezekiel to announce to those already in captivity what God's judgment entailed and why it was coming.

A. Ezekiel's Preparation (chapters 1–3)

God's commissioning of Ezekiel is the longest such call to prophetic ministry in the Bible. Like Isaiah and Jeremiah (see Isa. 6; Jer. 1), Ezekiel was prepared for his ministry by receiving a vision of God's glory and majesty before he was called to serve the Lord.

Introduction (1:1–3). In the first few verses Ezekiel stated three phrases that outline the content of the Lord's appearance. "I saw visions of God" was Ezekiel's summary of the visions he then described in detail in 1:4–2:7. "The word of the LORD" pointed to the source of Ezekiel's message (2:8–3:11). Ezekiel was to receive the message *God* wanted him to deliver. "The hand of the LORD" described Ezekiel's mandate for his ministry. He was not acting on his own initiative but was constrained by God to minister (3:12–27).

The Outline of Ezekiel's Call to Ministry

1. "Visions of God" (1:1b)—expanded in 1:4–2:7
2. "The Word of the LORD" (1:3a)—expanded in 2:8–3:11
3. "The hand of the LORD" (1:3b)—expanded in 3:12–27

The four living beings (1:4–14). Ezekiel noticed an approaching storm with flashing lightning. But as the cloud approached, Ezekiel spotted "four living creatures" in the midst of the fire. These beings are identified in chapter 10 as cherubim, a special order of angelic beings. In general they looked like men. However, they could not be mistaken for humans, for each had four faces and four wings. The cherubim always moved straight ahead, but with faces on all sides they could go in any direction without turning. And they were directed in their motion by "the spirit," probably God's Spirit.

The four wheels (1:15–21). Beside each cherub Ezekiel saw a wheel, which had an unusual shape. One wheel intersected another wheel at right angles. Thus the wheels could roll in four directions without being turned and could move with the cherubim. The wheel rims were "full of eyes." This unusual feature probably pictures divine omniscience (2 Chron. 16:9; Prov. 15:3), the eyes representing the all-seeing nature of the One who rides on this throne-chariot.

Ezekiel envisioned the God of the universe on a mobile platform— His personal throne-chariot. As God directed the cherubim, the wheels responded and the chariot was propelled on its way. Though unusual to us, this is a common biblical picture of God's presence. For other allusions to the throne-chariot of God see Exodus 25:10–22 (compare Heb. 8:5); 1 Chronicles 28:18; Psalm 18:9–12; Daniel 7:9; and Revelation 4.

The expanse (1:22–24). The outstretched wings of the cherubim joined together. The area above their wings looked to Ezekiel like a brilliant expanse, reminding Ezekiel of ice crystals sparkling in the light of the sun. The apostle John also described the expanse around God's throne as being "clear as crystal" (Rev. 4:6).

The throne (1:25–28). Ezekiel heard a "voice from above the expanse" over the angels. This was the voice of God seated on His throne. As the prophet instinctively glanced upward in the direction of the voice, he saw Someone whose glory was so bright that he could see only His form before he was forced to look down. Ezekiel then noticed a multisplendored rainbow with colors refracting from the blazing light of God's glory. John described the same beauty in his vision of God's throne in heaven (Rev. 4:3). Ezekiel explained that what he saw was "the appearance of the likeness of the glory of the LORD." God had appeared to Ezekiel in a visionary form; and by using the terms "appearance" and "likeness" Ezekiel was indicating that he had not seen God directly. That would have caused immediate death (Exod. 33:18–23; John 1:18). The prophet responded in humble submission; falling prostrate on his face.

> *The effectiveness of our ministry for God is directly related to the depth of our understanding of God. Knowing Him precedes serving Him.*

The task for Ezekiel (2:1–7). God told Ezekiel to rise and receive His message. Used here for the first time, the title "son of man" occurs ninety-three times in the Book of Ezekiel to refer to the prophet. It emphasized his humanity before God, stressing the distance that separates humans from God. God told Ezekiel his task was to declare God's word to a "rebellious nation." Whether they responded was their own responsibility. But when the events announced by Ezekiel finally took place, the people would "know that a prophet" had been in their midst. Three times in 2:6 God told Ezekiel, "Do not be afraid." Ezekiel needed this encouragement because the task ahead was difficult and dangerous. Ezekiel was to communicate God's word.

The reception of God's word (2:8–3:3). Israel had rebelled against God and His word, but Ezekiel was to eat what God gave him, that is, he was to be receptive and responsive to God's words. God showed Ezekiel a scroll that had writing on both sides, words of "lament and mourning and woe." This accurately summarizes the contents of Ezekiel 4–32. It does not, however, reflect the latter part of the book, in which the prophet spoke of Israel's restoration. This could explain, in part, why Ezekiel was recommissioned (chapter 33)—the content of his message was substantially changed after his message of woe was fulfilled. As Ezekiel ate the scroll, it tasted like honey. That is, though his message was one of judgment, it was still God's word. The sweetness came from the source of the words (God) rather than the content of the words (judgment).

God's word must be "taken in" before it can be "given out."

The delivery of God's Word (3:4–11). After receiving God's word, Ezekiel was told to proclaim it to Israel. His message was not for some distant land with an "obscure speech and difficult language"; it was for his own countrymen. Had Ezekiel gone to another nation, they would have responded to his message. Amazingly, those who knew nothing of the true God of the universe would have been more responsive than those who claimed His name. Israel would not respond to Ezekiel because they were "not willing to listen" to God. God encouraged Ezekiel by offering him the needed strength. God's making Ezekiel's "forehead like the hardest stone" means Ezekiel would not waver when beset by opposition. To be an accurate channel of God's revelation Ezekiel was to "listen carefully and take to heart" God's word.

We are responsible to proclaim God's word accurately— regardless of the response.

The leading of the Spirit (3:12–15). After seeing this vision of God, Ezekiel was bitter and angry. Associating himself with God, Ezekiel felt the same emotions toward Israel's sin as God did. The prophet was guided by the "strong hand of the LORD," that is, by God's power or authority. Ezekiel returned to his fellow exiles and sat with them a week—"overwhelmed." The character of the vision he had just seen and the awesomeness of the task before him left the prophet stunned. He needed time to collect his thoughts and prepare himself for his ministry.

The appointment as a watchman (3:16–21). A week later God appointed

Ezekiel as a "watchman" for Israel. In this role he was responsible for warning Israel of impending judgment. He was to warn both the wicked (3:18–19) and the righteous (3:20–21). If Ezekiel did not warn the people, he would be held as responsible for their murder as if he had killed them himself. However, if he fulfilled his assignment, then he would have delivered himself from any responsibility for the coming calamity. People who refused to heed his warning had only themselves to blame.

The physical restraints of the Lord (3:22–27). Ezekiel was called "out to the plain" to meet with God. When he saw the glory of the Lord for the second time, his response was again one of humble submission—he fell prostrate on the ground (see 1:28). God then placed several restraints on the prophet. Ezekiel was not to move about among the people; he was confined to his house because of their opposition to his message. This God-imposed restraint would demonstrate to the people their rebellion. Ezekiel also experienced temporary dumbness so that he could not speak to the people (the Spirit made his tongue stick "to the roof" of his mouth). This dumbness, however, was not continuous (3:27) or permanent (33:22). Ezekiel spoke only when God told him to. God said, "But when I speak to you I will open your mouth." When Ezekiel was silent, it was because God had not spoken. When he spoke, it was because God had given him a message. As a watchman, he was to open his mouth and say, "This is what the Sovereign LORD says."

B. Ezekiel's Prophecies against Judah and Jerusalem (chapters 4–24)

These chapters include Ezekiel's sounding of an alarm as God's watchman. In chapters 4–11 Ezekiel focused on the need for judgment because of the people's disobedience. The prophet then attacked the futility of false optimism (chapters 12–19). Then he placed the nation's present disobedience and impending judgment in perspective by reviewing the history of Judah's corruption (chapters 20–24).

Four Signs of Coming Judgment (chapters 4–5)

Though Ezekiel was confined to his home (3:24), God still expected him to deliver His message of judgment. To arouse interest Ezekiel used objects and actions, possibly in his courtyard or at the entrance to his house. These were signs about the coming siege against Jerusalem.

The sign of the brick (4:1–3). On a clay tablet (likely a brick) Ezekiel sketched an outline of Jerusalem. God then told Ezekiel to "lay siege" to the brick. Because Jerusalem was a well-fortified city, it would take Babylon months to capture it. The purpose of a siege was to starve out one's enemy—to wear them down by halting their flow of food, supplies, and weapons. As Nebuchadnezzar's siege tightened its grip around Jerusalem, the people called to God for deliverance. Ezekiel pictured the futility of the people's cries by putting an "iron pan" like a wall between him and the city. The pan represented an impregnable barrier between God and Jerusalem because of her sin. As the siege progressed, Jerusalem would cry out for deliverance, but God would not answer her prayers.

The sign of Ezekiel's lying on his sides (4:4–8). God told Ezekiel to lie first on his left side for 390 days, and then on his right side for forty days. This sign referred in some way to the Babylonian siege of Jerusalem, since the 430 days are called the "days of your siege" (4:8). Babylon would lay siege to Jerusalem, and in some way the length of the siege would correspond to the past years of Israel's and Judah's sin.

The sign of the unclean food (4:9–17). Ezekiel's third sign emphasized the severity of the siege of Jerusalem. God told him to take wheat, barley, beans, lentils, millet, and spelt and to put them together to make bread. Normally each of these foods was found in abundance. During the siege, however, supplies were so scarce that several foods had to be combined to provide enough for a meal. The purpose of his eating and drinking these meager rations was to show the scarcity of food and water in Jerusalem during the siege (4:16–17). This sign also showed the pollution and defilement the people would experience at that time.

The sign of the shaved head and divided hair (chapter 5). This fourth sign visualized Jerusalem's fate. The sign was given in 5:1–4 and explained in 5:5–17. God told Ezekiel to shave his head and beard and then weigh his hair in three equal piles with a few strands left over. Later, Ezekiel carried a third of his hair to the middle of the city and burned it. The purpose of this action, explained in verse 12, was to illustrate that a third of Jerusalem's inhabitants would die by the plague or by famine. Those who survived the famine had to face the sword. After burning the first third of his hair, Ezekiel went through the city with another third and chopped it with his sword to show that a third of the Jerusalemites would die by the sword. The remaining third of Jerusalem's inhabitants (those who had survived the plague or famine and the sword) would still be in jeopardy. This was illustrated by the prophet's scattering a third of his hair "to the wind." Those who weathered Jerusalem's fall to Babylon would be taken away in captivity and would live in fear. After Ezekiel had burned, chopped, and scattered his hair, God told him to tuck the few remaining strands in his clothing to represent God's preserving a remnant in the midst of judgment.

Even in times of judgment God shows mercy.

Two Messages of Coming Judgment (chapters 6–7)

After giving his four dramatic signs, Ezekiel delivered two sermons, each beginning with the words, "The word of the LORD came to me" (6:1; 7:1). The first message (chapter 6) focused on Israel's idolatry, the cause for judgment, and the second message (chapter 7) depicted the nature of the judgment.

Message on the cause of judgment (chapter 6). Israel was supposed to worship only the God of heaven in His temple in Jerusalem, but the people had set up shrines to false gods throughout the land, in mountains, ravines, and valleys. Both the false places of worship—and those who built them and worshiped at them—would be destroyed by God's sword. Yet in the midst of judgment, God in His mercy promised to "spare some." The impending defeat of Judah by Babylon did not signal the end of God's covenant promise to Israel. God was not turning away from His promises. Three times in this chapter Ezekiel stated that as a result of the judgment Israel would come to "know" that God is "the LORD" (6:7, 10, 14), that is, to acknowledge His supreme authority.

Message on the nature of judgment (chapter 7). Ezekiel's second message was that God's judgment would extend to the "four corners of the land," that is, throughout Judah. The doom about to come on Jerusalem had no historical parallel. Those who had been at ease in their idolatry on the high places would be thrown into a state of apprehension when overtaken in judgment. God's judgment would also have economic consequences. When disaster struck, everything valuable would be destroyed. Even those who would try to escape outside Jerusalem's walls would be hunted down and murdered by Babylon's army.

Those who sought protection within the city walls faced plague and famine. The majority of the people would die, and even those who survived would pay a price. The pitiful wail of those hiding in the mountains, who were weeping over their sins and material losses, would sound like the mournful cooing of doves. Israel's pride and religious prostitution would be crushed under Babylon's heavy boot. Judah's desperate search for deliverance and peace would be in vain as God vowed to bring calamity after calamity. Their punishment would be "according to their conduct," a standard mentioned five times in this chapter (7:3–4, 8–9, 27).

A Vision of Coming Judgment (chapters 8–11)

In this vision God took Ezekiel back to Jerusalem to show him the people's wickedness. The vision contains four sections, one recorded in each chapter.

The wickedness in the temple (chapter 8). Ezekiel saw in Jerusalem "the idol that provokes to jealousy" (8:3). This idol violated the second of the Ten Commandments (Exod. 20:4; Deut. 4:23–24). God was provoked because a foreign god was standing in the temple and receiving the worship that should have been His alone. As Ezekiel stared at this idol, beside him "was the glory of the God of Israel." God's moral outrage was expressed in His rhetorical question to Ezekiel: "Do you see what they are doing . . . detestable things . . . that will drive me far from my sanctuary?" If the idol inhabited the temple, God would leave.

Then God led Ezekiel through the gateway to a secret chamber in the temple. As Ezekiel looked around, he saw on the walls all sorts of idols. Worshiping there were seventy elders, leading men of Jerusalem. They sought to justify their sin by claiming God had forsaken them. Next God took Ezekiel to the northern entrance of the temple where he saw women mourning for Tammuz, a Sumerian god whose worship involved cultic prostitution.

Worship of the true Giver of rain had been supplanted by the debased adoration of a pagan deity. Then God led Ezekiel near the temple entrance, where he saw twenty-five men, probably priests, who were bowing toward the east to worship the sun. God's response was decisive: "I will deal with them in anger" and "not . . . with pity." God would not allow such open rebellion to continue. The stage was set for judgment.

The slaughter in Jerusalem (chapter 9). God summoned His angelic "guards of the city . . . each with a weapon in his hand." With the six guards was a seventh individual dressed in linen and carrying a "writing kit." God told this angelic scribe to go throughout Jerusalem and "put a mark on the foreheads" of everyone who grieved over the sin being committed in the city. Knowing those who had remained faithful to Him, God would spare them in His judgment (see also Rev. 7:3–4). God then told the guards to follow the scribe through the city and "kill, without showing pity." Those not receiving the mark were to be destroyed, beginning at the sanctuary. The fulfillment of this judgment is recorded in 2 Chronicles 36:17–19.

The departure of God's glory from the temple (chapter 10). Still standing beside the altar, Ezekiel looked at the sanctuary and saw God's throne above the cherubim. From the throne God ordered the angelic scribe to scatter "burning coals" over the city. Like a fire, God's judgment was to be scattered on Jerusalem. It was now time for God's glory to depart, and so His throne-chariot ascended into the air. God's glory mounted His throne-chariot to ride out of His temple and city (10:18). The throne-chariot began moving toward the east; but as the cherubim approached the edge of the temple precincts, they paused when they reached the east gate of the temple. Before God left the temple and the city, there was one final stop. As if to delay the final departure of God's glory, Ezekiel inserted the story of twenty-five wicked rulers (chapter 11).

Once God passed from the gate, the name Ichabod ("the glory has departed") could have been applied to Jerusalem just as it had been applied earlier to Shiloh (1 Sam. 4:21–22).

The judgment on Jerusalem's rulers (chapter 11). This fourth portion of Ezekiel's vision completed his "tour" of the temple area in Jerusalem. Before God's glory departed from the city, it stopped at the eastern gate and gave Ezekiel another glimpse of the sin of Jerusalem's inhabitants. Standing at the gate were twenty-five men, probably the elders who sat to administer justice and oversee legal matters. These men were "plotting evil and giving wicked advice" by encouraging the Jerusalemites to forget the various predictions of the coming Babylonian invasion. Instead they urged the people to "build houses," a sign of peace and safety. God told Ezekiel to tell them that He would hand them over to foreigners. As Ezekiel prophesied against the elders and the city, one of the elders died. This was a confirmation of Ezekiel's message and foreshadowed the judgment that would soon destroy all of Jerusalem's wicked leaders. God assured the prophet that He would preserve a remnant, but it would be comprised of those in captivity, not those in Jerusalem (11:13–15). As a sign of His faithfulness, God promised to restore a remnant to the land (11:16–21). His glory then continued its departure as it "went up from within the city and stopped above the mountain east of it," that is, the Mount of Olives.

Thus the city would be devoid of God's blessing until His glory will return to the Mount of Olives (see 43:1–3). It is no coincidence that Christ ascended to heaven from the Mount of Olives (Acts 1:9–12) and promised to return to the same place (1:11; see Zech. 14:4).

The Futility of False Optimism (chapters 12–19)

Ezekiel had shown the necessity of Jerusalem's judgment because of her disobedience. He demonstrated the fact of the siege throughout a series of signs (chapters 4–5), and then he explained the reason for the siege through two messages (chapters 6–7) and an extended vision (chapters 8–11). However, the people still did not believe Jerusalem would fall. Therefore Ezekiel gave a new series of signs and messages. Any optimism would be futile, for Jerusalem's fate had been sealed. Ezekiel used the clause, "The word of the LORD came to me," in introducing ten of the eleven signs, sermons, and proverbs in chapters 12–19. The only variation is the final section (19:1), but this is a lament which seems to sum up the entire section's theme.

> *The Futility of False Optimism in Ezekiel 12–19*
>
> - They trusted in the remnant in Jerusalem (12:1–20).
> - They trusted in parables (12:21–28).
> - They trusted in other prophets (chapter 13).
> - They trusted in idols (14:1–11).
> - They trusted in righteous intercessors (14:12–23).
> - They trusted in their position as God's vine (chapter 15).
> - They trusted in the holy city of Jerusalem (chapter 16).
> - They trusted in Zedekiah (chapter 17).
> - They trusted in God's justice (chapter 18).
> - Conclusion: Lament for the princes of Israel (chapter 19).

Two signs about impending captivity (12:1-20). In the first of two action-signs Ezekiel packed his belongings and went to "another place" as the exiles watched him. This first daytime action was followed by a second action in the evening. While the people watched, Ezekiel dug through the mud-brick wall of his house to drag out his belongings. As Ezekiel pantomimed this escape attempt, he was also to hide his face so that he could not "see the land." This showed the inevitability of the exile ("they will go into exile as captives") and Zedekiah's failed escape attempt. All this was dramatically and accurately fulfilled in 586 B.C.

Ezekiel's second sign was briefer than the first, but it also conveyed a message about those "living in Jerusalem and in the land of Israel" (12:19). Ezekiel was to "tremble" as he ate and "shudder" as he drank (12:18). Ezekiel's actions represented the terror the people of Israel would experience as they watched God's judgment on their country.

The message against the proverbs (12:21-28). Following Ezekiel's two signs (12:1–20), the prophet delivered a series of five messages (12:21–25; 12:26–28; chapter 13; 14:1–11; 14:12–23) to destroy the people's false optimism and to show the certainty of judgment. The first message began with God asking Ezekiel about the proverb, "The days go by and every vision comes to nothing." The point of this proverb was the belief that Ezekiel's (and other prophets') predictions of doom would not take place. God said He would keep the people from quoting that proverb any longer.

The people's smug assurance would end when the judgments arrived. God would remove "false visions" and "flattering divinations" with His impending judgment. The second proverb expressed the people's doubts about the *imminency* of God's judgment. Even those who believed Ezekiel was a prophet of God doubted the soon fulfillment of his oracles: "He prophesies about the distant future." If God does act, they reasoned, it will not be soon. But Ezekiel said the judgment was near.

The message against false prophets (chapter 13). Ezekiel's third message was directed against Israel's false prophets and prophetesses who were leading the nation astray. The message of the false prophets came from "their own imagination," not from God. Besides being untrue, their message was also dangerous. Israel's moral walls were ready to collapse, but the false prophets did nothing to fix them. Their deceptive ministry was like using whitewash to cover a "flimsy wall." They were compounding Israel's difficulties by hiding problems that needed to be exposed. Ezekiel turned from the false prophets (13:1–16) to address the false prophetesses who spoke "out of their own imagination," women who sewed "magic charms" and who used mysterious veils to appeal to the gullible. Because these prophetesses were lying, God said He would judge them and would deliver His people from them.

> *Anyone can claim to speak for God. But those whose lives and messages do not reflect the truth of God's written word are not His spokespersons.*

The messages against the elders (chapter 14). In his fourth message (14:1–11) Ezekiel condemned the idolatry of some of the elders. These hypocritical elders came to the true God for answers while secretly harboring a love for false gods. God asked Ezekiel, "Should I let them inquire of me at all?" The Lord then informed the elders that if any Israelite harbored idolatry in his heart, God would judge him. The urgent message was, "Repent! Turn from your idols and renounce all your detestable practices!"

In his fifth message (14:12–23) Ezekiel gave four examples of judgment. God could use any of these four means to punish the land and kill its people. But could God's judgment be avoided in response to the prayers of His righteous remnant? For example, would He send such judgment if three of the most righteous men who ever lived—Noah, Daniel, and Job—inhabited this land? He answered that it would make no difference. Noah, Daniel, and Job were each men of righteousness and men who overcame adversity. Even if these three pillars of past righteousness prayed together for mercy in a land under judgment, their praying for others in that case would be of no avail; they could save only themselves. Applying this truth to Jerusalem, Ezekiel said it would be worse for Jerusalem because she did not have three giants of righteousness to intercede for her. If those righteous leaders could not save a wicked land, how could Jerusalem hope to escape with her paucity of righteous individuals?

The parable of the fruitless vine (chapter 15). In chapters 15–17 Ezekiel recorded three parables that illustrated certain judgment. God posed a parable to Ezekiel: "Son of man, how is the wood of a vine better than that of a branch on any of the trees in the forest?" The obvious answer is that apart from its ability to bear fruit the wood of a tangled vine is inferior to the wood of a tree. The wood of grapevines is useless as a building material. Its twisting, gnarled branches cannot even be fashioned into stout pegs for hanging objects. If the vine by itself was nearly useless, it would even be less useful after it had been through the fire. God then applied this parable to Jerusalem. She was a vine branch; but since she had stopped bearing the fruit of righteousness, she was useless. The only use for worthless vine branches was as "fuel for the fire"—and that is the way God said He would treat His people in Jerusalem.

Believers are also "branches" connected to the "vine," Jesus Christ, and we are to bear fruit (John 15:5—8).

The parable of the adulterous wife (chapter 16). In this parable on Jerusalem's unfaithfulness, Ezekiel pictured Jerusalem as an unwanted child of a mixed union. Jerusalem moved from rags to riches, only to be returned to rags in judgment because of her unfaithfulness. The early beginnings of Jerusalem were like those of an unwanted child, thrown out into an open field (16:5). The cruel practice of infanticide was prevalent in the ancient world. Unwanted and deformed children were cast out at birth and left to die. God came to Jerusalem's aid and ordained her survival: "I said to you, Live!" (16:6). As time went by, this baby grew into a young woman. When she was "old enough for love" (16:8), that is, of marriageable age, God pledged His fidelity to Jerusalem and took her as His own wife, clothing her in splendor befitting a queen (16:9–14). Under God's blessing Jerusalem became a magnificent city.

Ezekiel added a bizarre twist to his story as he pictured the unfaithfulness of this woman who was made a queen (16:15–52). Jerusalem forgot the One who had supplied her with her wealth and turned away from Him. Instead she basked in her beauty and prostituted herself to other gods. Ezekiel used vivid imagery to drive home the truth of the vileness of Jerusalem's sin. In her pride she forgot who had saved her from her destitute state as a neglected newborn and had elevated her to her exalted position. Jerusalem degenerated from a queen to a tramp. Her beauty was gone, so she used her few remaining resources to try to bribe others into illicit relationships (16:33–34). God tried to stop her mad rush to destruction, but she refused to listen. It was now time for Him to judge. God said He would punish Jerusalem as women were punished "who commit adultery and who shed blood" (16:38).

The first part of Ezekiel's parable (16:15–43) was an analogy between Jerusalem and an adulterous wife. The second part of the parable (16:44–52) was an analogy between Jerusalem and her "sisters" Samaria and Sodom. If Jerusalem's wicked sisters received judgment for their sin, how could Jerusalem, who was even more depraved, hope to escape?

Having announced Jerusalem's sin and her judgment, Ezekiel then offered consoling words for her. All three "sisters" would be restored. "I will restore the fortunes of Sodom . . . and of Samaria . . . and your fortunes along with them" (16:53). If God would restore Jerusalem, could He do any less for her more righteous sisters? Ezekiel was speaking of the restoration of these cities in the future kingdom age. He stressed that God will not abandon His people forever. God had entered into a binding covenant with His people, and He would keep it. This "everlasting covenant" is the New Covenant spoken of by Jeremiah (Jer. 31:31–34).

The parable of the two eagles (chapter 17). This parable about two eagles pictures Zedekiah's rebellion against the king of Babylon and the judgment that would result. Ezekiel's riddle or parable was stated in 17:3–10 and explained in 17:11–21. The first "eagle" symbolized Nebuchadnezzar, and "Lebanon" stood for Jerusalem. Nebuchadnezzar weakened Jerusalem, but he did not destroy it. Instead he set up Zedekiah as a vassal king. Jerusalem's military might was gone; but as long as she remained faithful to Nebuchadnezzar, her people could continue to live in peace. Though Judah was brought low, weakened and humiliated, she could survive if she kept the treaty with Nebuchadnezzar.

However, a new "eagle," representing Egypt, influenced Zedekiah to rebel against Babylon. When Ezekiel penned this prophecy, Zedekiah's final revolt had not yet happened. Ezekiel predicted the revolt about three years before it took place. The results for Jerusalem would be disastrous. Nebuchadnezzar would not spare the city. As Ezekiel explained, this revolt meant that Zedekiah would "die in Babylon."

Ezekiel then added an addendum to his prophecy against Jerusalem. Though not specifically calling God an eagle, Ezekiel compared God's future actions to those of the two eagles (Babylon and Egypt) already mentioned. Neither of those eagles had been able to provide the security and prosperity Israel desperately longed for, but God would succeed where they had failed.

The message on individual responsibility (chapter 18). God asked Ezekiel about a proverb being circulated. This proverb—"The fathers eat sour grapes, and the children's teeth are set on edge"—must have been well known in Israel because Jeremiah also quoted it (Jer. 31:29–30). The proverb's point was that children were suffering because of their parents' sins. By blaming God for their misfortunes, the people were denying their own guilt. This was wrong because every individual is personally responsible to God. The people of Israel could not rightly charge God with injustice.

Ezekiel then presented three "cases" to prove the principle of individual responsibility (18:5–20). Each hypothetical situation begins with "Suppose" (18:5, 10, 14). The cases are those of a righteous man who does right (18:5–9), a violent son of a righteous father (18:10–13), and a righteous son of a violent father (18:14–18). In each case Ezekiel described the individual's actions and God's response. God's conclusion is obvious: In each case the individual would not die for another person's sins. A righteous person will not be punished for another's evil deeds. But an evil person "will die for his own sin." The popular proverb (18:2) was incorrect. When the people were judged, it was not for the sins of someone in a former generation. It was for their own sins! Only those who remained faithful to God would be delivered (18:19).

Escape from judgment was possible (18:21–32). Sinners could avoid judgment if they repented by turning from their sins (see Prov. 28:13) and kept God's commands. Ezekiel was not teaching salvation by works; his point was that these righteous works would spring only from "a new heart and a new spirit" (Ezek. 18:31). Why would God allow a sinner who repented to avoid judgment? The answer lies in God's character. He takes no "pleasure in the death" of the wicked (18:32). As a God of grace He longs for people to forsake their wickedness and turn to His righteous ways. Though God forgives the sins of those who turn to righteousness, He does not excuse the sins of someone who has been walking in righteousness and then turns to wickedness. Ezekiel reminded Israel of the responsibility for sin borne by each member of the nation. "I will judge you, each one according to his ways." The life or death of the people depended on their individual responses to God.

> *Good works result from a changed heart; they do not bring about such a change.*

Ezekiel's lament over Israel's princes (chapter 19). Ezekiel concluded this section on the futility of false optimism (chapters 12–19) with a lament or dirge for Israel and her leaders. This is the first of five laments in the book (see 26:17–18; chapter 27; 28:12–19; 32:1–16). A lament was a funeral song usually sung in honor of a dead person. The song generally stressed the good qualities of the departed and the tragedy or loss engendered by his death (see, for example, 2 Sam. 1:17–27).

This lament was for Israel's "princes." Ezekiel was taking up a funeral dirge even though the city's destruction was still future. Jerusalem's fall was so certain that Ezekiel considered it inevitable. Part of this dirge traces the fate of Jehoahaz and Jehoiachin—two of the three kings who preceded Zedekiah. In Ezekiel's lament he recalled with fondness the "lioness" (Israel) who had produced the fallen lions. She was the one who set up her kings but saw them destroyed, and she was the one who would go into captivity. The first "lion" was King Jehoahaz, who came to the throne after Josiah's untimely death. After a reign of only three months he was deposed by Pharaoh Neco II, who took him to Egypt, where he died. Skipping over Jehoiakim, Ezekiel's next "lion" was King Jehoiachin. Though a strong lion, he reigned for only three months before he was deposed by Nebuchadnezzar, who imprisoned him in Babylon because of the revolt of his father, Jehoiakim.

Ezekiel also compared Israel to a vine that had prospered under the blessing of God and produced many rulers (Ezek. 19:10–14). "Its branches were strong, fit for a ruler's scepter." However, in Ezekiel's day the vine had been "uprooted" (the nation was deported) because it forgot that God was her source of blessing. God's judgment also affected the royal line: "No strong branch is left on it fit for a ruler's scepter." The nation that had produced mighty rulers in the past would now have no king. After Zedekiah was overthrown by Babylon, no king from the Davidic dynasty replaced him.

> Not until Christ returns will a "ruler's scepter" again arise in the line of David and reign as Israel's king.

The History of Judah's Corruption (chapters 20–24)

These prophecies against Judah and Jerusalem focus on Judah's history. Ezekiel had presented that history in a parable (chapter 16), but in this section he gave a more direct presentation, especially in chapters 20 and 23.

Chiasm in Ezekiel 20–24

Ezekiel 20–24 is structured as an extended chiasm with the prediction of God's coming judgment serving as brackets to highlight the Lord's indictment against Jerusalem.

A. History of Israel's rebellion: Judgment is coming! (20:1–44)
  B. Parable of the forest fire (20:45–49)
    C. Messages of the sword (chapter 21)
      D. Indictment against Jerusalem (chapter 22)
    C.' Oholah and Oholibah slain by the sword (chapter 23)
  B.' Parable of the boiling pot (24:1–14)
A.' Death of Ezekiel's wife: Judgment is coming! (24:15–27)

The message of Israel's past rebellion and restoration (chapter 20). This chapter traces the checkered past of Israel. From Egypt, through the wilderness, and into the Promised Land, Israel had been unfaithful. Yet God promised to keep Israel from becoming just like its neighbors.

As in chapters 8 and 14, this message was given to Ezekiel when some of Israel's elders "came to inquire of the LORD." Their question is not recorded, but it must have been inappropriate because God refused to respond: "I will not let you inquire of me." God then gave a review of their history. To find an answer, the people needed simply to look into their past. When God sovereignly selected Israel to be His people, He bound Himself to them as their Lord and Protector. He revealed Himself to them in Egypt, promising deliverance from bondage and provision for blessing. He assured Israel He would take her "into a land . . . flowing with milk and honey." God asked the nation only to be faithful to Him and to turn from the idolatry of Egypt. But because Israel refused to heed this command, God was ready to pour out His wrath on the Israelites in Egypt. Yet the wrath did not come; Israel was spared because of His grace and mercy, "for the sake of [His] name."

Israel's wilderness experience began with another outpouring of God's grace, by which He led them out of Egypt. But instead of responding in obedience to His gracious provision, the nation rebelled against His rule, choosing to remain in idolatry (20:10–26). God's response was the same as His response in Egypt. The people deserved to die, but because of His name (that is, reputation) He spared them.

Israel's new location in the land of promise did not change her sinful actions. In the land the people offered sacrifices to idols on hills and under trees, using the Promised Land as the setting for their idolatry (20:27–31). Israel's rebellion continued all the way up to Ezekiel's day. The nation was still involved in idolatry and child sacrifice. Therefore God refused to let them inquire of Him (see 20:3).

After recounting Israel's past history of rebellion, God told of her future restoration (20:32–44). The people wanted to imitate their idolatrous neighbors, but God would not let them. "What you have in mind will never happen." Much as the Exodus brought Israel out of bondage into the wilderness, so God's new "exodus" will restore Israel from the countries where she had been scattered. God will again bring Israel into a covenant relationship with Him—but this covenant will be permanent. God's ideal for Israel will finally be realized in the future messianic kingdom. She will serve the Lord, knowing that He is sovereign, and she will repent of her past evil.

God told Ezekiel to preach against the "southland" (this word can also be translated *Negev*, the name of the southern portion of Israel near her border with Edom). God said He would burn the trees of that area (20:45–49). The Negev is a semi-arid region, and Ezekiel's reference to the Negev "forest" must have been startling. The people heard Ezekiel's message but did not understand. They thought he was "just telling parables."

The four messages of the sword (chapter 21). Since the people refused to understand Ezekiel's message about the fire on the southland (20:45–49), he gave four messages to expand his parable's meaning. In these messages Ezekiel changed the "fire" to a sword and the "Negev" to Judah and Jerusalem.

In his first message about the sword (21:1–7) Ezekiel was to preach against the sanctuary and to prophesy against Israel. The object of God's judgment was His land, His holy city, and His dwelling place. By a sword God would destroy both the righteous and the wicked. This seems to contradict Ezekiel's earlier prophecy (18:1–24) that only the wicked would die and the righteous would live. One possible solution is that the righteous and the wicked may be viewed from the people's perspective. As far as the people could tell, the judgment was indiscriminate. It affected those who were in open idolatry as well as those who claimed to be followers of God. Yet in God's eyes only the wicked were being punished since He had promised to deliver those who were truly righteous.

Ezekiel's second message about the sword was a poetic song of judgment (21:8–17). Its theme was that God's sword was ready "for the slaughter." Much like a soldier preparing for battle, God had honed His weapon so it would be effective. The sword was coming against God's people and all of Israel's leaders, who had rejected God's advice.

God told Ezekiel to "mark out two roads for the sword of the king of Babylon to take." When Nebuchadnezzar led his forces from Babylon, he had to decide which nation he would attack first. His choice then was whether to travel along the international highway and attack Judah and Jerusalem or to head down the Transjordanian highway and attack Ammon and its capital, Rabbah. Nebuchadnezzar used three means to determine his course of action: casting lots with arrows, consulting his idols, and examining an animal's liver. The practices by themselves could do nothing, but God worked through them to accomplish His judgment. When Nebuchadnezzar reached into his quiver to select one of the marked arrows, he would pick the lot for Jerusalem. God then pronounced judgment on the people (21:24) and the prince (21:25–27). Because of their rebellion, Jerusalem would be taken into captivity.

The sword that had been "polished" for Jerusalem (21:9, 11) would also reach Ammon (21:28–32). The Ammonites, east of Judah, thought they had escaped Nebuchadnezzar's judgment, but Ezekiel announced that they would be punished. In God's wrath He would hand Ammon over to "brutal men." The fire of judgment directed against Judah (see 20:45–49) would also consume Ammon.

Three messages on the defilement and judgment of Jerusalem (chapter 22). In this chapter Ezekiel discussed the causes of Jerusalem's judgment (22:1–16), the means of her judgment (22:17–22), and the recipients of that judgment (22:23–31).

God gave Ezekiel two charges to present against Jerusalem: shedding blood and making idols. Ezekiel mentioned blood or bloodshed seven times in this message in order to drive home the city's sin of extreme violence. These two sins opposed the Mosaic Law's standards for Israel's relationships with God and her fellow Israelites (see Matt. 22:34–40). Rather than loving God she had turned to idolatry, and her love for her fellow Israelites had been replaced by treachery. The proud and insolent people who treated God's commands lightly would not be able to avoid His judgment. Moses had warned Israel that national disobedience would eventually lead to dispersion (Lev. 26:27–39; Deut. 28:64–68). Because Israel had defiled God's Law, she would now be "defiled in the eyes of the nations."

Jerusalem would become a furnace of affliction—a smelting furnace of judgment that would melt those who remained in it (Ezek. 22:17–22). To God, Israel was like dross—worthless because of her sin. Much as metals are melted in a furnace, so God would gather the people of Jerusalem and "melt" them. This thought is stated three times. In other words, the city became a crucible as God's fiery blasts of judgment blew on the people.

In discussing the recipients of judgment (22:23–31), Ezekiel first addressed the sins of Jerusalem's princes. They were probably the royal family, including King Zedekiah, who had used their power for material gain, ravaging the people like a lion. The religious leaders were no better than the princes. The priests were not instructing the people in the ways of God or enforcing the Law's statutes. Other government leaders besides those in the royal family were also guilty of "unjust gain." The prophets should have denounced these wicked deeds, but the prophets (except for a few like Ezekiel and Jeremiah) ignored those sins and gave the people false messages. Then Ezekiel denounced the people, commoners who followed their leaders' example. The populace was also involved in oppressing the poor people. The corruption was so complete that when God searched for someone to stem the tide of national destruction (to "stand . . . in the gap"), none was available.

The parable of the two adulterous sisters (chapter 23). Ezekiel presented another parable to illustrate Judah's unfaithfulness and the certainty of her punishment. In one sense chapter 23 seems to be a restatement of the parable in chapter 16, since both chapters deal with Judah's unfaithfulness to God. However, in chapter 16 Ezekiel focused on Judah's idolatry, whereas in chapter 23 he stressed Judah's illicit foreign alliances in addition to her idolatry. In chapter 16 her trust was in other gods; in chapter 23 it was in other nations.

In the parable two sisters shared the same moral degradation; from their youth they had been "prostitutes in Egypt." Ezekiel's reference to Egypt would call to mind the origins of the nation Israel in Egyptian bondage. The older sister was Oholah (Hebrew for "her tent"), and her younger sister was Oholibah ("my tent is in her.") Ohola represented the people of Samaria, the capital of Israel, and Oholibah represented Jerusalem, Judah's capital. The sin of Oholah, the older sister, was her association with the Assyrians, an alliance that ultimately led to Israel's doom. While this should have been a warning to the younger sister, Oholibah (Jerusalem), she failed to heed the warning. In fact Jerusalem was "more depraved than her sister." Jerusalem followed the immoral course charted by her sister in also desiring help from the Assyrians.

Jerusalem's political intrigues, however, did not stop there; she "carried her prostitution still further" by appealing next to Babylon. But when Babylon came, Jerusalem found Babylon to be a harsher taskmaster than either Assyria or Egypt. Jerusalem then sought to escape Babylon's dominance; but while Jerusalem turned from Babylon, God turned from her. Yet instead of repenting of her sin, she sought additional human help, becoming "more and more promiscuous." Her cycle of sin brought her back to the very nation with which she had originally been defiled and which had enslaved her, namely, Egypt (22:3, 19, 21).

In 23:22–35 Ezekiel gave four oracles, each beginning with the words, "This is what the Sovereign LORD says" (23:22, 28, 32, 35). The oracles all focused on Jerusalem's judgment. Those whom Jerusalem despised (the Babylonians) would be the ones who would punish her. The punishment God would inflict on her in His anger through Babylon would be like the punishment of physical mutilation. Jerusalem would be rendered unattractive to any other potential lovers. When the Babylonians were done, Jerusalem would be left "naked and bare." Jerusalem's illicit "affairs" with other nations came after she forgot her source of protection and openly rejected God. Because of this rejection she would suffer the consequences of her spiritual-political "lewdness."

Idolatry, though not the subject of 23:1–35, was common to Israel and Judah. The apex of their spiritual adultery was child sacrifice: "they even sacrificed their children, whom they bore to me" (23:37). This detestable practice of the Canaanite religion had infiltrated both Israel and Judah. The spiritual adultery of the two nations was matched only by their political adultery. Both countries enticed foreign nations into illicit alliances. The sisters used their charms to gain others' favors, so God reduced them to the status of prostitutes (23:44; see 23:3). This appropriately pictures Israel and Judah turning to pagan nations for help and being molested by them.

The climax of God's judgment on Judah (chapter 24). This chapter concludes the third series of judgments on Judah (chapters 4–11, 12–19, 20–24).

Ezekiel's final prophecies of doom against Jerusalem came on January 15, 588 B.C.—a day of national calamity for Jerusalem. On that very day, when Babylon's king began his siege of Jerusalem, Ezekiel told Israel a parable about a pot of boiling meat (24:1–14). Ezekiel said Jerusalem was like a "pot now encrusted, whose deposit will not go away!" In the fire of God's judgment Jerusalem's "impurities" floated to the surface. Her corruption could not be hidden. She was as unappealing as rusty scum floating on the surface of a meal being cooked. The meal was ruined by the rusty scum, so the contents of the pot were dumped. The meat in the pot was to be cooked well done, picturing the slaughter of the Jerusalemites by Babylon. The "empty pot" (Jerusalem without its inhabitants) was to be "set . . . on the coals" until its rust was burned away. The city itself had to be destroyed to remove its spiritual impurities.

> God's mercy prompts Him to withhold judgment as long as possible to enable people to repent (2 Pet. 3:8–10), but He does not wait indefinitely. A time comes when God punishes wickedness.

Through the heartbreaking experience of his wife's death, Ezekiel acted out the inner pain about to be felt by Judahites already in captivity (24:15–27). God told Ezekiel about the tragic death of his wife and commanded Ezekiel not to bemoan or grieve over her death. He had to keep his personal feelings of loss bottled up inside. The exiles realized that the prophet's action had some national significance, so they asked him to tell them what it meant. He explained that the death of his wife symbolized the destruction of God's temple and the slaughter of the people of Jerusalem—people loved by those in exile. Ezekiel had lost the "delight" of his "eyes" (24:16), and the exiles would lose Jerusalem, the "delight" of their "eyes." The tragedy would be so awesome that any public expression of grief would seem insignificant. They would simply "waste away" because of their sins, while groaning among themselves. The catastrophe would send all the exiles into a state of shock and would force them to acknowledge their Lord: "When this happens, you will know that I am the Sovereign LORD" (24:24).

> Sometimes God uses personal tragedy to accomplish His larger purposes.

II. JUDGMENT ON GENTILE NATIONS (CHAPTERS 25–32)

Babylon's siege of Jerusalem had begun; its destruction would soon be complete. So Ezekiel turned from Jerusalem to speak against those nations surrounding it. If God would not spare His own people because of their sin, how could the nations around her hope to escape His judgment? The first three—Ammon, Moab, Edom—formed the eastern boundary of Judah; the fourth nation, Philistia, was on her western boundary. Tyre and Sidon, cities of Phoenicia, were the principal powers north of Judah, and Egypt was the major power to the southwest. God's judgment would extend out from Judah in all directions.

A. Judgment to the East and West (chapter 25)

In this chapter Ezekiel used a "Because . . . therefore . . . then you will know" formula to describe God's judgment against four nations.

Judgment on Ammon (25:1–7). Ammon and Israel had been in conflict since the time of the judges (Judg. 10:6–11:33). But in Ezekiel's day

Ammon united with Judah and Tyre against Babylon, a common foe. Yet instead of coming to Judah's aid when Babylon attacked, Ammon rejoiced over Judah's misfortune, hoping to profit territorially from Judah's destruction. So God said His judgment would fit Ammon's sin. Since Ammon rejoiced over Judah's downfall, Ammon would fall. God would send them to "the people of the East," possibly nomadic desert tribesmen, "as a possession." Because of Ammon's malice against Israel, Ammon would be plundered by other nations and destroyed.

Judgment on Moab (25:8–11). The hostility between Moab and Israel reached back to the time of the Exodus (Num. 22–24). Moab held God's people in contempt, saying, "Look, the house of Judah has become like all the other nations." As a result God vowed to expose Moab's northern border to attack. In addition to losing her defenses Moab would also lose her freedom. God would "give [Moab] . . . to the people of the East," the same fate as that of Ammon (Ezek. 25:4).

Judgment on Edom (25:12–14). Edom too was involved in a long series of conflicts with Israel. The strife actually began when Edom refused to let Israel cross her territory at the time of the wilderness wanderings (Num. 20:14–21). Ezekiel said Edom's sin was that she "took revenge on the house of Judah." Because Edom had aided in Judah's destruction, God would aid in Edom's destruction, killing Edom's "men and their animals . . . from Teman to Dedan."

Judgment on Philistia (25:15–17). The Philistines had been Israel's enemy from the time of the Conquest (Judg. 3:14). Because Philistia had tried to destroy Judah, God would destroy those "along the seacoast." During the intertestamental period, the Philistines disappeared as a nation. This nation that had tried to usurp God's people discovered His true character (they "will know that I am the LORD," Ezek. 25:7, 11) when He judged them for their sin.

B. Judgment to the North (chapters 26–28)

Ezekiel delivered a long prophecy against the cities of Tyre and Sidon to Israel's north. This section is actually five separate oracles, each beginning with "The word of the LORD came to me" (26:1; 27:1; 28:1, 11, 20). The first oracle (26:2–21) was a direct prophecy of Tyre's destruction; the second prophecy (chapter 27) is a lament or funeral dirge for the fallen city. The third and fourth messages were directed against the ruler of Tyre (28:1–10) and the king of Tyre (28:11–19). The final message focused on God's destruction of Sidon (28:20–26).

Destruction of Tyre (chapter 26). In 26:1–6 Ezekiel followed the "Because/therefore/then you will know" format he used in chapter 25. Tyre's sin was her greedy rejoicing over Jerusalem's fall. Without Jerusalem being able to secure the overland caravan routes, more products would be shipped by sea. God's judgment against Tyre fit her crime as He vowed to bring many nations against her "like the sea casting up its waves." Tyre would be so devastated that the once-bustling city would be barren enough to use as a drying place for "fishnets." Nebuchadnezzar besieged Tyre for thirteen years (585–572 B.C.) until all "settlements on the mainland" were destroyed. As Tyre's allies came to sit and mourn her passing, they also sang a funeral lament, contrasting her present condition with her former glory. Ezekiel said Tyre's fate was like a ship caught in a storm and lost at sea, a fitting illustration for the seafaring Phoenicians.

Dirge over Tyre (chapter 27). This second message against Tyre could be called "The Sinking of Tyre's Ship of State." The first section (27:1–9), written in poetry, pictured Tyre's former glory by describing her, appropriately, as a beautiful ship. The second section (27:10–25), in both poetry and prose, enumerated Tyre's many trading partners. The third section (27:26–36), again in poetry, described Tyre's catastrophic shipwreck. The violent storm from the "east" refers to Babylon, east of Tyre. Tyre's ship of state was about to go down, with the loss of her people and her wealth.

Downfall of the ruler of Tyre (28:1–10). Ezekiel's third message against Tyre was directed specifically to the ruler of Tyre. The underlying sin of Tyre's king was his pride, which prompted him to view himself as a god. Yet God said he was only a "man and not a god" (28:2). God would not let the pride of Tyre's ruler go unchallenged. This king who claimed to be a god would suffer an ignoble death at the hand of the Babylonians.

Pride distorts a person's view of God—and of his or her relationship to God.

Downfall of the king of Tyre (28:11–19). Ezekiel's fourth prophecy was a lament concerning the king of Tyre. The use of "king" instead of "ruler" (as in 28:2) is significant. In 28:1–10 Ezekiel rebuked the *ruler* for claiming to be a god, though he was just a man. But in 28:11–19 Ezekiel described the *king* in terms that could not apply to a mere person. This "king" had appeared in the Garden of Eden, had been a guardian cherub, had possessed free access to God's holy mountain, and had been sinless from the time he was "created" (28:13–15). Ezekiel was describing Satan, who was the true "king" of Tyre, the one motivating the human "ruler." God had originally appointed Satan as a "guardian cherub" (28:14), part of the inner circle of angels who had the closest access to God. As originally created by God, Satan was "blameless . . . till wickedness was found" in him (28:15). Satan's pride led to his fall and judgment. This shows that spiritual forces of darkness are often at work behind kings and nations.

Judgment on Sidon (28:20–26). Ezekiel's fifth message in this series was directed against Sidon, a Phoenician city so closely allied with Tyre that Ezekiel felt it unnecessary to cite the same sins. She had violated God's holy character, and He would not allow her sin to remain unpunished. As God would reveal His holiness by destroying Sidon (28:22), so He also said He would reveal His holiness by rescuing Israel. This promise, made through Ezekiel, has never been literally fulfilled; it awaits fulfillment in the millennial kingdom.

> *The sinful practices of Baal worship had entered Israel through "Jezebel daughter of Ethbaal king of the Sidonians" (1 Kings 16:31).*

C. Judgment to the South (chapters 29–32)

The seventh and final nation against which Ezekiel prophesied was Egypt. This prophecy was actually a series of seven oracles directed against Egypt and its Pharaoh. Each oracle is introduced by the clause, "The word of the LORD came to me" (29:1, 17; 30:1, 20; 31:1; 32:1, 17).

The sin of Egypt (29:1–16). This prophecy includes three sections, each of which closes with the words seen so often in Ezekiel, "then [they] . . .

will know that I am the LORD" (29:6, 9, 16). Ezekiel compared Pharaoh to a "great monster" in the Nile River. Pharaoh would learn he was no match for the true God when God would drag Egypt away from her place of protection in the Nile River and leave her in the desert. Israel leaned on Egypt for support in her revolt against Babylon, but Egypt's support was as fragile as the reeds that grew along the Nile's shores. When the pressure came, the reed snapped and Israel found herself unable to stand. God's judgment on Egypt would extend from "Migdol to Aswan" (from north to south) and would last for forty years. Though God would let the Egyptians return to their land after this captivity, Egypt would not regain the place of power she once held.

The defeat of Egypt by Babylon (29:17–21). Ezekiel's second prophecy against Egypt was written shortly after Tyre's surrender to Babylon. When Tyre fell to Babylon after Nebuchadnezzar's thirteen-year siege, there were no vast spoils of war to distribute as booty to his army. Evidently Tyre shipped off her wealth before she surrendered. Nebuchadnezzar needed money to pay his soldiers for their labor, so he attacked Egypt and plundered its wealth.

The destruction of Egypt and her allies (30:1–19). Ezekiel's third message against Egypt stressed Babylon's judgment on Egypt and her allies. It has four sections, each beginning with "This is what the sovereign LORD says" (30:2, 6, 10, 13). Egypt had many mercenary soldiers in her army. God announced that these allies would be crushed, and the cities where they had settled would be ruined. Babylon would be God's tool to accomplish His purpose. By naming Egypt's major cities God was saying that the strength of the entire nation would be ended, like breaking a yoke.

The scattering of Egypt (30:20–26). Ezekiel's fourth of seven prophecies against Egypt was given after the Babylonians defeated Egypt when Egypt came to rescue Judah. The theme of the prophecy was Egypt's defeat by God. Nebuchadnezzar broke the "arm" of Egypt so she was unable to defend Judah, and the damage was irreparable. God said He would totally wipe out Egypt's strength. Ezekiel contrasted the recent defeat suffered by Egypt (her one "broken arm") with the still greater defeat she would suffer when she would follow Judah into exile.

The similarity of Egypt and Assyria (chapter 31). Ezekiel's fifth prophecy against Egypt was an allegory on Pharaoh's fall. Ezekiel called on Egypt to compare herself to Assyria. In Assyria's former exalted position, she had been like a "cedar in Lebanon" that had attained power and influence far above that of Egypt. Assyria was the perfect example to show Egypt the effects of God's judgment. Assyria's fall was an object lesson to other nations, including Egypt. Egypt's desire to become a lasting great power in the Middle East was destined to failure. If the strong "cedar" (Assyria) could fall, then how could any lesser "trees" (like Egypt) hope to remain standing?

The lament for Pharaoh (32:1–16). Ezekiel's sixth prophecy against Egypt was a lament concerning Pharaoh, who was like a lion or a sea monster. The monster could refer to a crocodile, as Ezekiel said Pharaoh was churning up the international scene. But if Pharaoh were a crocodile, God vowed to lead Pharaoh's enemies on a crocodile hunt. Pharaoh's power would be broken and his people scattered. Ezekiel described this destruction in terms that conjured up images of Egypt's judgment at the time of the Exodus. Egypt's judgment would have a profound effect on other nations. If mighty Egypt could be destroyed, so could they.

The descent of Egypt into Sheol (32:17–32). Ezekiel's last of seven prophecies against Egypt consigned the hosts of Egypt to Sheol. God's word of judgment was so sure that Egypt's appointment with the grave was already made. Egypt's pride would be shattered when her people were destroyed. The descent of Egypt's defeated army and her allies into Sheol would be derided by those already there. The fate of these other nations was an object lesson to Egypt. Like those once-powerful nations that were now in the grave, Pharaoh and his army could expect the same fate.

III. BLESSINGS ON ISRAEL (CHAPTERS 33–48)

This last major division of the book focuses on the restoration of Israel's blessings. Israel would be judged for her sin (chapters 1–24), as would the surrounding nations (chapters 25–32). But Israel will not remain under judgment forever. God has set her apart as His special people, and He will fulfill His promises to her. The first step in Israel's restoration will be national renewal (chapters 33–39), and the final step will be the establishment of a new order (chapters 40–48).

A. Ezekiel Reappointed as a Watchman (chapter 33)

Ezekiel's duties as a watchman (33:1–20). Now that Ezekiel's original ministry of judgment was completed, God appointed him as a "watchman" for a second time. His message still stressed individual accountability and responsibility, but the focus was now on the Lord's restoration of Israel.

The opening of Ezekiel's mouth (33:21–33). Ezekiel's new ministry began when news of Jerusalem's fall reached the captives in Babylon. Now that Ezekiel's message was confirmed, there was no need for him to be silent. So his "mouth was opened" (33:22) the night before the messenger arrived. Ezekiel then rebuked two groups of people: the Israelites who remained in the land, expecting a quick end to the Babylonian captivity (33:23–29) and those who gathered to hear him in Babylon (33:30–33). Each person would be held accountable for his or her actions and responses to God's word.

B. The Present False Shepherds Contrasted with the Future True Shepherd (chapter 34)

The present false shepherds (34:1–10). Rulers were often called shepherds (Ps. 78:70–72; Isa. 44:28; 63:11; Jer. 23:1–4; 25:34–38) and were to be strong, caring leaders who guarded their nation like a flock. But Israel's leaders had put their own interests above those of the people. They had ruled "harshly and brutally" and allowed the sheep to become scattered. So God said He would judge the rulers and remove them from their positions of power.

The future true Shepherd (34:11–31). What the false shepherds failed to accomplish, God will bring to pass because He will intervene personally on Israel's behalf. His first action will be to restore Israel to her land. In exercising His justice God will begin by judging between the individual Israelites. God will also appoint a new "shepherd" to tend His sheep. God's care and protection will result in peace for His people. This "covenant of peace" (34:25) looks forward to the blessings Israel will experience in the coming messianic kingdom.

The world will experience true peace only when the Prince of Peace takes His place on David's throne.

C. The Enemy (Edom) Destroyed (chapter 35)

Ezekiel devoted a second prophecy to Edom (see 25:12–14) to represent the judgment God will inflict on all nations who oppose Israel. Edom was the prototype of all Israel's later foes. The destruction of Edom would signal the beginning of God's judgment on the whole earth based on that nation's treatment of Israel (Gen. 12:3). The prophecy against Edom is in three parts, each ending with Ezekiel's common expression, "Then you/they will know that I am the LORD" (Ezek. 35:4, 9, 15).

In a direct statement of judgment on Edom, God said He was against Mount Seir. Seir, Edom's geographical name, was the mountain range east of the Arabah south of the Dead Sea. This was the mountainous homeland where the Edomites lived. God would make that people as desolate as their land.

Because Edom had assisted in Israel's slaughter (35:5), God would assist in her slaughter. Edom would suffer the same fate she had tried to inflict on Israel. Edom had tried to possess Israel's land (35:10), so she would now experience the consequences as God vowed to make her desolate.

D. The People Blessed (chapter 36)

Chapter 36 stands in antithesis to chapter 35. When God intervenes on Israel's behalf, the mountains of Israel's enemies will be judged (35:1–3, 8), but the mountains of Israel (35:12) will be blessed (36:1, 8).

Ezekiel contrasted Israel's present humiliation before her enemies with her future glorification. God promised to punish Israel's enemies for their sin. In contrast, God will renew Israel's land so that it can provide for the restored remnant. Once Israel is restored to the land, her inheritance will be secure. The land will never again deprive Israel of her "children." This will take place during Christ's millennial reign.

Before highlighting Israel's future cleansing, Ezekiel reminded the exiles of their past sin which resulted in judgment (36:16–21). He then discussed the nation's future restoration in three parts, each beginning with "This is what the Sovereign LORD says" (36:22, 33, 37). God had shown His justice when He punished Israel for her sin; He will show His grace and faithfulness when He restores the nation physically and spiritually and gives them a new heart and a new spirit. God will also restore the land and cause the nation to increase numerically.

Ezekiel 36 parallels the New Covenant God promised to Israel and Judah in Jeremiah 31. This covenant includes at least three specific elements: (a) restoration to the land (Ezek. 36:24; Jer. 31:27–29), (b) forgiveness of sin (Ezek. 36:25; Jer. 31:34), and (c) the indwelling presence of God's Holy Spirit (Ezek. 36:26–27; Jer. 31:33).

E. The Nation Restored (chapter 37)

Chapter 37 vividly illustrates the promise of chapter 36. God had just announced that Israel will be restored to her land and be under the leadership of David her king. However, this seemed remote in light of Israel's present condition. She was "dead" as a nation—deprived of her land, her king, and her temple. She had been divided and dispersed for so long that unification and restoration seemed impossible. So God gave a vision (37:1–14) and a sign (37:15–28) to illustrate the fact of restoration and confirm the promises just made.

The vision of the dry bones revived (37:1–14). God transported Ezekiel to a valley "filled with bones" that were bleached under the hot sun. God told Ezekiel to prophesy to them. As he did, God gave life to the bones. This reviving of the dry bones pictures Israel's future national restoration. The vision showed that Israel's new life depended on God's power. God will restore Israel nationally and spiritually.

The sign of the two sticks united (37:15–28). God then told Ezekiel to take two sticks of wood and to write on one the name "Judah" (the Southern Kingdom) and on the other the name "Joseph" (representing the Northern Kingdom). He was then to hold them together, which pictured God's restoring and reuniting His people in the land as a single nation. The visible reminder of God's presence will be His temple. These promises anticipate the detailed plans for God's new sanctuary given later in chapters 40–43.

Ezekiel's "New" Exodus

In Ezekiel 38–48 the prophet used parallels from Israel's first Exodus to describe God's "new" exodus preceding the kingdom era. All that God intended for Israel during the first Exodus will be accomplished in this "new" one.

- Destruction of Gentile oppressors (Exod. 5–12; Ezek. 38–39)
- Plans for building God's house (Exod. 20–40; Ezek. 40–43)
- Climax: God's glory enters His house (Exod. 40:35; Ezek. 43:5)
- Instructions for worship (Leviticus; Ezek. 43–46)
- Land boundaries for Israel (Num. 34; Ezek. 47)
- Division of land among the tribes (Josh. 14–21; Ezek. 48)

F. The Attack by Gog Repulsed (chapters 38–39)

Israel had been trampled underfoot by her enemies, but God will intervene in the future to insure her safety. He will defend His people and judge her enemies in distant countries. Ezekiel described a battle that will involve Israel's remotest neighbors. They will sense their opportunity to attack when Israel feels secure under the false protection of her covenant with the Antichrist sometime at the beginning of the seven-year Tribulation period. The nations involved in the attack will include portions of present-day Russia, Turkey, Iran, Sudan, Ethiopia, and Libya.

The invasion by Gog (38:1–16). The attack on Israel will actually be orchestrated by God. God will use "Gog" (an individual) and all his allies as pawns in His larger plans for Israel. Gog and his allies will attack in massive strength. Their intended purpose will be to plunder and loot unwalled and unsuspecting Israel. Because of Israel's importance geographically, politically, and economically, she will be a strategic target for any power wanting to control commerce between Asia and Africa. The attack will come from all sides. Gog will come from the "far north." With him will come his allies from the east (Persia = Iran), the south (Cush = Sudan, southern Egypt, and northern Ethiopia), and the west (Put = Libya). This army will overrun all obstacles as effortlessly as a "cloud covering the land."

The defeat of Gog (38:17–39:8). Gog's attack will be crushed by God Himself. When the armies reach Israel, a massive earthquake will interrupt Gog's invasion plans and spread fear and confusion throughout the invading forces. In the pandemonium the armies will begin attacking each other. The slaughter of the armies will be aided by additional natural catastrophes, including "torrents of rain, hailstones and burning sulfur" (38:22). The invading armies will be totally destroyed by God, and He will also punish their homelands. Through all this God will teach Israel and the nations that He is the Holy One in Israel.

The aftermath of the battle (39:9–20). Those who will come to plunder Israel will themselves be plundered. Israelites will use the fallen soldiers' weapons as fuel for seven years. After the battle Israel will also bury Gog's dead. The number of soldiers killed will be so great that Israel will be burying them for seven months.

The effects of the battle on Israel (39:21–29). The defeat of Gog will hasten God's plans to restore the Israelites from other nations. God will "bring Jacob back from captivity" and pour out His Spirit on the house of Israel. The ultimate result of the battle with Gog will be Israel's national repentance and spiritual restoration. This will be fulfilled at the beginning of the millennial kingdom.

Israel's New Order

Chapters 33–39 dealt with the new life Israel will experience when she is gathered back into her land and restored to fellowship with God. The last nine chapters of the book explain how Israel's new order will be established. A new temple will be built as a sign of God's presence among His people (chapters 40–43), and a new service of worship will be established so the people will have access to their God (chapters 44–46). Then a new division of the land will be made for the people (chapters 47–48).

G. A New Temple (chapters 40–43)

God had promised to rebuild His sanctuary among His people (37:26–28). Chapters 40–43 give the plans for the temple that is to be rebuilt. Ezekiel described the millennial temple in great detail because it will be the visible symbol of God's presence among His people. The prelude to Israel's judgment began when God's glory departed from Solomon's temple in Jerusalem (chapters 8–11). The climax to her restoration as a nation will come when God's glory reenters the new temple in Jerusalem (43:1–5). The new temple will also become the visible reminder of Israel's relationship to God through His New Covenant.

Introduction (40:1–4). The vision of the new temple came to Ezekiel sometime in 573 B.C. The phrase "the beginning of the year" could refer to the first month of Israel's religious new year (April–May) or the first month of her civil new year (October–November). God took Ezekiel back to Jerusalem in a vision and led him on a tour of the future temple. This tour was given by an individual who was probably an angel.

The outer court (40:5–27). The angelic being with Ezekiel had a measuring rod about 10 ½ feet in length. The wall surrounding the temple was 10 ½ feet high. Entering the outer court, Ezekiel saw a pavement all around the court with 30 rooms along the sides, probably spaced in even numbers along the north, east, and south walls of the outer court. These rooms may be storage rooms or meeting rooms for the people when they celebrate their feasts.

The inner court (40:28–47). After measuring the outer court the angel measured the "inner court." At the sides of the inner gates, tables were set up for slaughtering the sacrifices. The sacrifices would then be offered on the altar in the inner court. Ezekiel also noticed two rooms, one by the north gate and one by the south gate of the inner courts, which probably will serve as utility rooms and rest areas for the priests on duty.

The temple building (40:48–41:26). Standing in the inner court, Ezekiel's gaze shifted to the temple building itself. Ezekiel climbed the stairs and entered through the vestibule into the outer sanctuary. However, only the angel went into the inner sanctuary to measure it. Surrounding the temple were thirty side rooms on three levels. These rooms are probably storerooms for the temple equipment and storage chambers for the people's tithes and offerings (see Mal. 3:8–10).

The chambers in the inner court (42:1–14). Leaving the temple proper, Ezekiel then described several adjacent structures for use by the priests. In those rooms the priests will eat the offerings and store their clothes. According to the Mosaic Law the priests received a portion of some offerings (Lev. 2:3, 10; 6:16, 26–30; 7:7–10). A similar provision will be made for the millennial priests.

The outer walls of the temple (42:15–20). After the angel measured everything within the temple complex, he led Ezekiel outside to record the external dimensions of the temple. The complex was a square measuring 875 feet ("five hundred cubits") on each side.

The return of the Lord's glory (43:1–12). In a dramatic reversal of the departure of the Lord's glory (chapters 10–11) Ezekiel saw God's glory returning from the east to dwell once again in His temple. God said the new temple will be the place where He will "live among the Israelites forever." It will serve as God's permanent dwelling place among His people.

The altar of burnt offering (43:13–27). When the millennial temple is established and God is enthroned in it, daily services will begin. Ezekiel was given a description of the altar (43:13–17) and regulations for consecrating it (43:18–27). The height of the altar above the ground will be 17 ½ feet. The "altar hearth," 21 feet square, was reached by a flight of steps facing east. A seven-day consecration service will mark the full resumption of God's fellowship with His people. These sacrifices will point Israelites to Christ, who will have given them access to God the Father (Heb. 10:19–25).

H. A New Service of Worship (chapters 44–46)

After the temple was described, its daily operation was explained to Ezekiel. A new way of life and worship will be practiced by the people during the Millennium. Yet in describing the holy standards of Israel's future, Ezekiel asked the people of his day to reevaluate their present practices. He explained the duties of the temple ministers (chapter 44), described the allocation of land for the temple priests (45:1–12), and then spoke of the offerings to be made to the Lord (45:13–46:24).

The temple ministers (chapter 44). The duties of the Levites for the new temple were explained to Ezekiel. Because of their sinful practices before Israel's fall to Babylon, their position will be downgraded in the new temple from ministers to servants. Then Ezekiel discussed the duties of the priests of Zadok. The line of Zadok was one branch of the priestly line, a limited group of Levites. Though the people had sinned, the priests in Zadok's line had remained faithful to God. So they will be restored to their position of honor. Several Mosaic laws governing the priests were repeated by the Lord. These actions, designed to promote holiness, will help the people see the difference between the holy and the common. To emphasize the priests' position as the Lord's ministers, God will not let them possess land in Israel outside the allotment surrounding the temple (see 45:4).

God wants His servants to reflect His holy character.

The land of the temple priests (45:1–12). Because Ezekiel had been speaking extensively about the priests and Levites (44:10–31), he then included their inheritance in the land (see also 48:9–12). They will not have inheritances as will people in the other tribes (44:28). In the division of the land, Israel is to give a portion of the land as a sacred district. This district will be about 8.3 miles long and about 6.6 miles wide. Within this land area will be the temple complex Ezekiel had just described (chapters 40–43). This land rectangle will be divided into two equal portions, one for the priests and the other for the Levites. The rectangle formed by the priests' and Levites' portions was converted into a square with the addition of land for the city of Jerusalem itself. The city is to cover an area about 1.7 miles wide and about 8.3 miles long, adjoining the sacred portion. Ezekiel then used the reality of God's promised future blessings as a springboard to exhort the princes in his day to repentance.

The offerings (45:13–46:24). Having just chastised the princes of Israel for using unjust weights, Ezekiel returned to discussing the Millennium, in which the future prince will use just weights to receive and offer gifts to God (45:13–17). This mention of offerings caused the prophet to describe briefly the future sacrificial system (45:18–46:24) before returning to the subject of the division of the land. Ezekiel listed specific amounts of produce the people will give the prince. The festivals where offerings will be given will include the New Year's feast (45:18–20), the Passover/Unleavened Bread feast (45:21–24), and the seven-day Feast of Tabernacles (45:25). After speaking of selected feasts in Israel's religious year, Ezekiel included information on the daily aspects of Israel's worship. He gave regulations for the Sabbath and New Moon sacrifices (46:1–10), the conduct and offerings of the people in the temple (46:11–15), freewill gifts in the Year of Jubilee (46:16–18), and the consuming of sacrifices by the priests and the people (46:19–24).

Who Is the "Prince"?

Ezekiel 45–46 describes specific duties to be performed by the "prince." While many have felt the "prince" is the glorified Jesus Christ, this seems unlikely because the prince is commanded to "provide a bull as a sin offering for himself" as well as for the people (45:22). Jesus would never need to offer a sin offering for Himself, for He is the "spotless lamb of God" who "knew no sin." Since Jesus will reign as *King* over the whole earth during this future age, the *prince* is likely a human ruler (possibly David) under Jesus who will rule over Israel.

I. A New Land (chapters 47–48)

The river from the temple (47:1–12). One new feature in this future kingdom age will be a life-giving river flowing from the temple. Joel had mentioned this river before Ezekiel's time (Joel 3:18), and Zechariah spoke of it after Israel returned from the Babylonian captivity (Zech. 14:8). In the Millennium this river will be another visible reminder of God's presence and blessing. The stream of water, flowing out from God's temple, will flow eastward and go down into the Jordan Valley and the Dead Sea. The Dead Sea, now some six times saltier than the oceans, will become "fresh" and all kinds of fish will live there. Another way God will provide for Israel is by the trees on the riverbanks that will bear fruit year-round. God will use these trees to meet people's physical needs.

> *The Dead Sea today is a symbol of barren desolation. This future change is a visible reminder that God can turn death to life. Our God specializes in changing the unchangeable!*

The boundaries of the land (47:13–23). God promised Abraham and his descendants the land of Israel, and that promise has never been rescinded. When God inaugurates His New Covenant with Israel in the future, she will be restored to her place of blessing in the land (chapters 36–37). To prepare the people for this new occupation, God defined the boundaries of the country. Israel's borders during the Millennium will be identical to those promised her originally during the time of Moses (Num. 34:1–12).

The division of the land (48:1–29). In dividing the millennial land among the people, God will give seven tribes portions in the northern part of the land. Proceeding from north to south these tribes will be Dan, Asher, Naphtali, Manasseh, Ephraim, Reuben, and Judah (48:1–7). The central band of land was allotted to the prince, the priests, and the Levites and will include the city of Jerusalem and its suburbs. The lower part of the land will be allotted to the five remaining tribes: Benjamin, Simeon, Issachar, Zebulun, and Gad (48:23–27). The locations of all twelve tribes differ somewhat from their original allocations during Joshua's time (Josh. 13–19).

The gates of the city (48:30–35). In describing the gates of the new city of Jerusalem, Ezekiel brought the city "full circle" from what it was at the beginning of his book. The city doomed for destruction will be restored to glory. The new city of Jerusalem will have twelve gates, three on each side. But its most remarkable aspect will be the presence of the Lord. God's glory had departed from the city as a prelude to its judgment (chapters 10–11), and His return will signal Jerusalem's blessing. This fact so impressed Ezekiel that he wrote that the city will be given a new name: "The LORD is there."

As the prophet Ezekiel had stated repeatedly, God will return to dwell with His people. No longer worshiping lifeless idols and engaged in detestable practices, the nation Israel will enjoy the Lord's holy presence in the future millennial kingdom. Her future is guaranteed by God.

DANIEL
God's Kingdom and the Times of the Gentiles

AUTHOR

$\mathcal{T}$HE NAME "Daniel" means "God [is] my Judge." Daniel was deported to Babylon by Nebuchadnezzar in 605 B.C. It is possible that Daniel was a member of Judah's royal family (1:3; see Isa. 39:6–7). Daniel's ministry was that of a statesman in Babylon. Thus his book is listed in the Hebrew Bible among the "Writings" rather than the "Prophets."

DATE

The date this book was written can be determined through some internal chronological markers. Daniel was taken to Babylon in 605 B.C. (Dan. 1:1), and his rise to prominence came in 603 B.C. (2:1). The latest dated prophecy in the book was "in the third year of Cyrus" (10:1) which was 536 B.C. Thus Daniel's ministry spanned a period of about sixty-nine years (605–536 B.C.).

Some scholars have objected to such an early date for the writing of the book, arguing instead that the book was composed almost four centuries later. Their objections (and a conservative response to those objections) follow:

    A.   "The Book of Daniel is included in the Writings instead of among the Prophets in the Hebrew Bible, thus suggesting a late date." However, the book is placed among the Writings because of

Daniel's office as a statesman in Babylon, not because of a later date of composition.

B.   "Several historical inaccuracies in the book indicate that the writer was unfamiliar with the historical situation and thus must have composed the book sometime after the time period in question." However, the suppposed "historical inaccuracies" have been refuted by archaeology. For example, in Daniel 5 King Belshazzar of Babylon offered Daniel the position of "third highest ruler in the kingdom" (5:16). Belshazzar could offer nothing higher because he reigned as coregent with his father Nabonidus. The record of Belshazzar's coregency had been lost by the time of Heroditus (around 450 B.C.) and was not discovered until recently. Thus Daniel must have been composed *before* 450 B.C., while knowledge of this fact was still available.

C.   "The Book of Daniel uses several Greek loan words, which points to a composition after 330 B.C. when the Greek language spread throughout the Middle East." However, the Greek words can be explained by their function. The Greek words found in Daniel describe musical instruments (3:5), and it is well known that musical instruments crossed national boundaries. Also records indicate that Greeks were sold into slavery in Babylon and Persia as early as 700 B.C.

D.   "The book records the rise of the Greek Empire, which took place about 330 B.C." This argument assumes that predictive prophecy is not possible. If one allows God to foretell the rise of Persia, Greece, and Rome, then there is no problem with Daniel predicting these nations even though he lived during the kingdom of Babylon. God specifically claimed to be revealing "what will happen in days to come" (2:28). The final vision of the book contains detailed predictions of events that occured hundreds of years after Daniel. The vision was introduced by God's angelic messenger, who announced that "the vision concerns a time yet to come" (10:14).

BACKGROUND

Events recorded in the Book of Daniel occurred in "the times of the Gentiles." Daniel and his three friends were taken into captivity in 605 B.C. as part of Nebuchadnezzar's first deportation of Jews from Jerusalem (1:1–7). Daniel assumed that "the times of the Gentiles" had begun (Nebuchadnezzar himself was the "head of gold" that began the statue of Gentile kingdoms; chapter 2), and Daniel did not record any information about the final days of Judah such as Jerusalem's destruction in 586 B.C.

ADDRESSEES

Daniel wrote to the Jews in captivity during "the times of the Gentiles." These Jews were under gentile domination and influence and without a king from David's line. Daniel's message was a message of hope to all Jews awaiting the Messiah and God's kingdom on earth.

PURPOSE

Daniel's purpose in writing blended the two themes of prophecy and piety. He wrote first to show God's *future* program for the nation of Israel (in light of her fall) during and after "the times of the Gentiles." Second, he wrote to show what the believers' *present* response should be as they await the coming kingdom of God. Daniel encouraged his readers to remain faithful to God in a hostile society while they waited for God's promised kingdom.

OUTLINE

I. Daniel's Dedication (Hebrew Section; chapter 1)
   A. Captivity of the Jews (1:1–2)
   B. Selection of the Young Men (1:3–7)
   C. Commitment of the Young Men (1:8–16)
   D. Superiority of the Young Men (1:17–21)

II. The Future of the Nations (Aramaic Section; chapters 2–7)
   A. Nebuchadnezzar's Dream (chapter 2)
   B. The Fiery Furnace (chapter 3)
   C. Nebuchadnezzar's Insanity (chapter 4)
   D. Belshazzar's Feast (chapter 5)
   E. Daniel in the Den of Lions (chapter 6)
   F. The Four Beasts (chapter 7)
III. The Future of Israel (Hebrew Section; chapters 8–12)
   A. The Two Beasts (chapter 8)
   B. The Seventy "Weeks" (chapter 9)
   C. The Future Panorama (chapters 10–12)

I. DANIEL'S DEDICATION
(HEBREW SECTION; CHAPTER 1)

Chapter 1 sets the stage for the remainder of the book. The Gentiles gained control of Jerusalem, and the Jews were taken into captivity. Even though this was only the first of three invasions and deportations by Babylon, Daniel assumed it began the time of the Jewish Diaspora among the Gentiles. Daniel and his three friends became models of how Jews were to remain faithful to God while under gentile dominion.

A. Captivity of the Jews (1:1–2)

Daniel briefly described Nebuchadnezzar's siege and capture of Jerusalem. Nebuchadnezzar captured King Jehoiakim and took the temple treasures to Babylon. God allowed this gentile ruler to despoil the city, capture the king from the line of David, and take the treasures of Solomon's temple. This foreshadowed the complete destruction of all three during the final fall of Jerusalem in 586 B.C.

B. Selection of the Young Men (1:3–7)

Nebuchadnezzar also ordered his chief court official to select some Jewish men of royal descent—the best of Israelite society physically, mentally, and socially—and teach them "the language and literature of the Babylonians" so they could eventually serve him. Part of the assimilation process was to give them Babylonian names to help in their cultural transformation. The goal was to make these future leaders thoroughly Babylonian in their thoughts and actions.

C. Commitment of the Young Men (1:8–16)

Changing names and learning a new language did not violate God's Word, but the royal food offered to them had been dedicated to idols and was ceremonially unclean. Daniel and his friends decided not to eat that food because it would violate God's dietary laws. Exercising great wisdom, Daniel offered a creative compromise as he urged the official to let him and his friends have only vegetables and water for ten days. God honored Daniel's faithfulness, and at the end of the test the four young men were "healthier and better nourished" than the others.

> ### Daniel's Principles for Handling Tests
>
> In times of testing believers need to remain faithful to God. Sometimes this will require:
> - *Wisdom* to seek a creative compromise that enables the believer to meet society's expectations without violating his or her beliefs (1:8–14).
> - *Courage* to be willing to stand up for one's beliefs when no compromise is possible (3:15–18).
> - *Personal discipline* to develop a lifestyle of faithfulness so the right response to a test will come "naturally" (6:10).

D. Superiority of the Young Men (1:17–21)

The insight of Daniel and his three friends surpassed that of all their fellow students. God also gave Daniel the ability to understand visions. In Nebuchadnezzar's own personal examination he found that their wisdom was "ten times better" (that is, fully superior) to that of the magicians and enchanters, who were expected to be the wisest of all the king's advisers (see 2:2).

II. THE FUTURE OF THE NATIONS
(ARAMAIC SECTION; CHAPTERS 2–7)

Chapters 2–7 offered encouragement and hope to the Jews during the times of the Gentiles. Beginning in 2:4 Daniel switched from Hebrew (the language of Israel) to Aramaic (the "international" language of the day). This change in language highlights Daniel's focus on "the times of the Gentiles" that would exist from his day until God establishes His messianic kingdom. Chapters 2 and 7 explain the succession of four gentile empires that would exert control over Jerusalem and the Jews until God's kingdom is established. Chapters 3 and 6 warned the Jews of the persecution they would face during this period and exhorted them to remain faithful to God. Chapters 4 and 5 encouraged the Jewish remnant by reminding them that a time would come when even the gentile rulers would acknowledge that the God of Israel rules over the nations.

The Structure of Chapters 2–7

Chapters 2–7 are set in a chiastic (reverse-order) arrangement:
A.   Prophecy concerning Gentile Nations (chapter 2)
    B.   Supernatural Persecution and Deliverance (chapter 3)
        C.   God's Revelation to a Gentile King (chapter 4)
        C.' God's Revelation to a Gentile King (chapter 5)
    B.' Supernatural Persecution and Deliverance (chapter 6)
A.' Prophecy concerning Gentile Nations (chapter 7)

A. Nebuchadnezzar's Dream (chapter 2)

The setting (2:1–30). Soon after graduating from his three-year program of study, Daniel entered the king's service. This was still Nebuchadnezzar's "second year" since, in the Babylonian calendar, a portion of his first year was considered his accession year. Nebuchadnezzar had a dream that disturbed him, and he summoned his key advisers. Daniel and his friends were excluded; they would have been among the lower echelon of royal advisers because of their young age. To test the accuracy of their interpretation, Nebuchadnezzar asked his advisers to state the dream and interpret it. Some feel Nebuchadnezzar had forgotten his dream, but this is probably not correct. What had "gone from" Nebuchadnezzar (2:5, KJV) was not the dream, but his command that the advisers tell him both the dream and its interpretation. Their failure to do so almost cost them their lives, but Daniel heard of the problem and offered to seek God's help. God revealed the dream and its interpretation to Daniel at night, and Daniel went to the king with the information.

The dream (2:31–35). Daniel said the dream pertained to "what will happen in days to come." He then described a large statue, with a head of gold, chest and arms of silver, a bronze belly and thighs, iron legs, and feet of iron and clay. Then a large rock struck the statue at its feet and destroyed it, and the rock grew into a large mountain that "filled the whole earth."

The interpretation (2:36–45). Daniel told Nebuchadnezzar, "You are that head of gold." The second part of the statue was not another king but instead another kingdom that would rise up after Babylon. The bronze part of the statue was a third kingdom that would replace the second. The feet of iron represented a fourth kingdom, and the feet of iron and clay indicated this kingdom would be formed by various groups of people who "will be a mixture and will not remain united." The rock that smashed the statue and became a mountain symbolized the messianic kingdom to be set up by the God of heaven.

Who Are the Nations of Daniel 2?

The nations of the statue can be identified as follows:

Gold	Nebuchadnezzar (and the Babylonian Empire)
Silver	Medo-Persian Empire
Bronze	Greek Empire
Iron	Roman Empire (at Christ's first coming)
Iron and clay	Revived Roman Empire (at Christ's second coming)
Rock	Messianic kingdom of Jesus Christ

The results (2:46–49). Nebuchadnezzar responded to Daniel's interpretation by prostrating himself before him and honoring him. He also
announced that Daniel's God was a "God of gods" (that is, superior to
other gods). This is the first step in Nebuchadnezzar's journey of faith
through the book. The king also promoted Daniel and his friends, putting Daniel in charge of the province of Babylon and placing him over its
wise men. Daniel's three friends were given lesser positions as administrators. They ruled throughout the district, while Daniel remained "at the
royal court." This helped set the stage for the next chapter.

B. The Fiery Furnace (chapter 3)

The likely background for the events of chapter 3 was a coup attempt
against Nebuchadnezzar that occurred in December 595–January 594 B.C.
This event was significant enough to have been recorded in the Babylonian
Chronicle. After the coup attempt failed, Nebuchadnezzar presumably
summoned all his provincial rulers and vassal kings back to Babylon for a
loyalty oath. Those who had proven themselves loyal at the royal court in
Babylon would have been exempt from the ceremony. Thus Daniel did
not have to appear at the gathering because he had been with
Nebuchadnezzar at the royal court. Daniel's three friends, however, were
summoned with the other officials because they had been serving as administrators in the province of Babylon (2:49).

The setting (3:1–7). Perhaps reflecting on his earlier vision,
Nebuchadnezzar constructed an "image of gold" (probably a gold-plated
statue of the Babylonian deity Nabu) that stood ninety feet high and nine
feet wide. Nebuchadnezzar then summoned seven groups of governmental
officials and ordered them to pledge loyalty to him by bowing down before the gold image. The penalty for disobedience was severe: All who
refused would be tossed alive into a furnace.

The accusation (3:8–18). As the orchestra played, all the participants
worshiped the image except for Daniel's three friends. Some astrologers
accused the three, who were then summoned before Nebuchadnezzar.
The king, furious that they had refused to bow down, gave them another
chance to submit. He must have had some indication that they refused to

bow on religious grounds because he added, "Then what god will be able to rescue you from my hand?" Shadrach, Meshach, and Abednego answered the king by asserting that God was able to deliver them. But even if God allowed them to die, they said they would worship neither the king's gods nor his image.

> *Our ability to stand against temptation is directly proportional to our trust in God's ability to deliver us (1 Cor. 10:13).*

The test (3:19–27). Nebuchadnezzar was furious and ordered the furnace (likely a brick kiln) to be heated "seven times hotter" to make the heat as intense as possible. The fire was so hot that it killed the soldiers who carried the bound victims to the entrance of the kiln to throw them in. But when Nebuchadnezzar gazed into the mouth of the furnace, he saw four men in it. These were the three Israelites and one who looked like "a son of the gods." Astonished, Nebuchadnezzar called on the men to come out. When they did, he discovered the fire had not touched them. They didn't even smell smoky!

While it is possible that the fourth individual in the fire was a revelation of the preincarnate Jesus Christ, this is not required by the text. Nebuchadnezzar did not recognize the "Son of God," but rather he saw a supernatural individual whom he identified as a "son of the gods." This could have been an angel sent by God to protect the three friends (see also 3:28; 6:22).

The results (3:28–30). Responding with praise to God, Nebuchadnezzar prohibited anyone from saying "anything against" the God of the three men. While not yet acknowledging the supreme sovereignty of the true God, Nebuchadnezzar still realized that "no other god can save in this way." The three friends who stood true to the Lord were rewarded by the king, who "promoted" them to higher positions.

C. Nebuchadnezzar's Insanity (chapter 4)

Though no date is recorded for the events of this chapter, they likely took place toward the end of Nebuchadnezzar's forty-three-year reign, when his kingdom was at peace and he had finished rebuilding much of Babylon.

The summary (4:1–3). Nebuchadnezzar addressed a document to those who "live in all the world," not just to those in Babylon. The purpose of the document was to report on the signs and wonders he had experienced at the hand of "the Most High God." Nebuchadnezzar then praised the Ruler of heaven as he acknowledged that "His kingdom is an eternal kingdom."

> *Eventually all rulers on earth will acknowledge the ultimate rule of God through His Son, Jesus Christ (Phil. 2:10–11).*

The dream (4:4–18). For the second time in the book, Nebuchadnezzar had a dream that could not be interpreted by his advisers (see 2:1–2). He then told Daniel, whom the king called Belteshazzar, that in the dream he saw a large tree that provided food and shelter for many birds and animals. An angel was told to cut the tree down but to preserve its stump and roots. The stump, symbolic of a person, was to be given "the mind of an animal." This would continue "till seven times pass by for him." The angelic messenger announced that all this would happen so the living would know that "the Most High is sovereign."

The interpretation (4:19–27). Daniel wished the dream applied to Nebuchadnezzar's enemies, but unfortunately the tree was Nebuchadnezzar. Cutting down the tree symbolized a time of insanity for Nebuchadnezzar when he would be isolated and would live with wild animals. This would continue for "seven times" (probably seven years) until his sanity would return and he would "acknowledge that Heaven rules." Daniel then urged the king to turn from his sins and do what was right so the dream would not be fulfilled.

The fulfillment (4:28–37). Perhaps Nebuchadnezzar listened for a while, but a year later his pride brought judgment. As he looked over the city of Babylon, he boasted, "Is not this the great Babylon I have built . . . by my mighty power and for the glory of my majesty?" Immediately a voice from heaven announced that his authority had been taken away. During his insanity, his throne was occupied by another (possibly the heir apparent). At the end of that time Nebuchadnezzar "praised the Most High," thus acknowledging the sovereignty of the "King of heaven."

Will We See Nebuchadnezzar in Heaven?

While the Book of Daniel does not specifically state Nebuchadnezzar's spiritual condition, it does present a progression in this king's understanding of God. After forty-three years of observing Daniel's faith, Nebuchadnezzar must have learned much about the God of Israel. His final declaration implies that the king came to know Daniel's God in a personal way.

"Surely your God is the God of gods and the Lord of kings" (2:47).
"No other god can save in this way" (3:29).
"I praised the Most High; I honored and glorified him who lives forever" (4:34).

D. Belshazzar's Feast (chapter 5)

The center of Daniel's Aramaic section moves from the first king of Babylon (chapter 4) to the last king of Babylon (chapter 5). The events of Daniel 5 took place on October 12, 539 B.C. The Babylonians were waiting inside Babylon for an expected attack by the Medo-Persian army. Though Nabonidus was king of Babylon, his son, Belshazzar, was ruling as coregent. The Medo-Persian soldiers diverted the water of the Euphrates River, and as the water level lowered, they crept along the walls of the city to gain entry. At the very moment Daniel was interpreting the handwriting on the wall inside the palace, the water level of the Euphrates was dropping just outside the palace!

The setting (5:1–4). In preparation for the expected battle with the Medo-Persian army, King Belshazzar hosted a banquet for a thousand of his nobles. Perhaps to bolster the spirits of the leaders, Belshazzar had them drink from the goblets stolen from the Jerusalem temple. As they drank, they praised the gods whom they supposed had given them victory in the past.

The revelation (5:5–12). Suddenly human fingers wrote on the wall. When Belshazzar saw the mysterious hand, his "face turned pale," his "knees knocked together," and his "legs gave way." The king summoned all his wise men to interpret the writing, offering to make the one who could read the writing "third highest ruler in the kingdom." However, all were "baffled" by the writing until the queen entered and suggested that Belshazzar summon Daniel.

Why did Belshazzar offer the one who could interpret the writing the position of "third highest ruler" rather than second highest? Because that was the highest position next to his own. King Nabonidus was still alive and was officially first. As a result, Belshazzar was only the second highest ruler.

The interpretation (5:13–28). Summoning Daniel, the king promised him great rewards if he could interpret the writing. Daniel told the king he didn't want his gifts but he would read the writing. However, Daniel first reminded the king of the events that happened to his "father" (that is, his ancestor) Nebuchadnezzar. After summarizing the events of Daniel 4, the prophet rebuked Belshazzar. "But you . . . have not humbled yourself, though you knew all this" (5:22). The writing was God's message of judgment to a proud king who had refused to "honor the God who holds in his hand your life." The four-word wall message was that God had "numbered" the days of Belshazzar's reign because he had been "weighed" on God's scales of justice. His kingdom was to be "divided" and given to another nation.

The Message on the Wall

Měnē: "To number" repeated twice
(related to the Hebrew word *maneh*)
Teqel: "To weigh, to be found light"
(related to the Hebrew word *šeqel*)
Uparsîn: A combination of "and" (*u*) and the word *pāras*,
"to divide"
The message read, "Numbered, numbered, weighed, and divided."

The results (5:29–31). Belshazzar honored Daniel for his interpretation, but the honor did not last long, for that very night Belshazzar was killed, and Babylon fell to the Medo-Persian Empire.

E. Daniel in the Den of Lions (chapter 6)

Daniel 6 took place at the beginning of the Medo-Persian rule over Babylon. Structurally, Daniel 6 is parallel to Daniel 3 in the Aramaic portion of the book. God had shown His superiority to the gentile rulers (chapters 4–5), and He had promised that His kingdom would come after a succession of four gentile powers (chapters 2 and 7). However, while awaiting God's final victory, His believers would experience persecution and must remain faithful (chapters 3 and 6).

The setting (6:1–5). Daniel became one of three administrators who watched over a group of 120 satraps or regional rulers. In fact, he was so successful that the king planned to appoint him over the whole kingdom. The other rulers were jealous and looked for a way to charge him with misconduct. But since Daniel was a man of integrity, they could find no area in which he was vulnerable.

> As Christians living in a pagan society, our lives need to be beacons of light. To maintain a consistent witness for our God, we must guard against corruption (sins of commission) and neglect (sins of omission).

The accusation (6:6–15). The leaders hatched a plot against Daniel. They persuaded the king to issue an edict prohibiting prayer to any god or man except the king. All violators would be thrown into the lions' den. When Daniel learned of the decree, his response was automatic. Just as before, he opened his window toward Jerusalem and "got down on his knees and prayed, giving thanks to his God." The leaders knew where to wait, and they caught Daniel in this act of disobedience. Returning to the king, they made him enforce the law that he now regretted.

The Administrators' Conspiracy

The sense of conspiracy against Daniel is heightened by the use of the same phrase three times.

They "went as a group" to get the king to pass the edict (6:6).

They "went as a group" to watch Daniel pray in his window (6:11).

They "went as a group" to make the king enforce his edict (6:15).

The test (6:16–22). Soldiers threw Daniel into the lions' den and sealed the den. The king went to his palace to spend a sleepless night in anguish, worried because he had been trapped into executing his top administrator. Early in the morning he returned and called to Daniel. Daniel responded and announced that God had "sent his angel" to protect him because of his innocence.

The results (6:23–28). The king had Daniel lifted from the lions' den, and then he ordered those who had falsely accused Daniel to be thrown into the den. The officials and their families were killed, and the king then sent a decree to all nations ordering his subjects to "fear and reverence the God of Daniel."

F. The Four Beasts (chapter 7)

Chapter 7 is the final chapter in the Aramaic section of Daniel's book. Instead of interpreting dreams for others, Daniel now had an angel interpret his dream of four beasts. The four beasts parallel the four parts of the statue in chapter 2. In chapter 7 Daniel provided additional information about the fourth world empire.

The setting (7:1). Daniel's dream came in the first year of Belshazzar, probably 553 B.C. Belshazzar is the final king in the first of the four gentile powers described in Daniel 2.

The vision (7:2–14). In Daniel's dream he saw four beasts coming up out of the sea, with the fourth beast having ten horns plus a smaller eleventh horn. This little horn uprooted three of the first ones and began to boast until he was destroyed. Then "one like a son of man" approached the "Ancient of Days" (God the Father) and received an everlasting kingdom.

The Four Beasts of Daniel 7	
Description	Interpretation
Lion with eagle's wings	Babylon
Wings are plucked off	Leaders were humbled (chapters 4–5)
Bear raised up on one side	Medo-Persia (Persia dominated)
Three ribs in teeth	Conquered Lybia, Babylon, and Egypt
Leopard with four wings	Greece (swift conquest by Alexander)
Four heads	Empire divided into four parts after Alexander's death
Frightening beast	Rome
Ten horns and a little horn	Revived Roman Empire and the Antichrist (see Rev. 13:1–10)
Son of Man and the kingdom	Christ's future millennial kingdom

The interpretation (7:15–27). When Daniel asked what this dream meant, God's messenger told him the four beasts represented four coming kingdoms. Keenly interested in the fourth beast, Daniel inquired especially about the ten horns and the little horn that came up later. God told him that the beast is a fourth kingdom that will appear, and that the ten horns represent ten kings in this kingdom. The other horn was another king who will "speak against the Most High" and will trouble God's people. He will appear to succeed for "a time, times, and half a time" (that is, three and a half years; see also 9:27; Rev. 13:5). However, God vowed that He will ultimately take away the power of this horn and establish His kingdom in its place.

The results (7:28). At the end of the divine interpretation Daniel was deeply disturbed. The picture of evil, though temporary, still caused Daniel's face to turn pale.

III. THE FUTURE OF ISRAEL
(HEBREW SECTION; CHAPTERS 8–12)

In the final chapters of Daniel, the prophet returned to writing in Hebrew. These five chapters present three specific visions regarding the future of Israel and the Jewish people, especially in their relationships with the Gentiles. Each vision presents gentile oppression against Israel and God's ultimate deliverance.

A. The Two Beasts (chapter 8)

In this vision God presented Daniel with a brief overview of the Medo-Persian and Greek empires. These were the second and third empires in Daniel's history of "the times of the Gentiles." He traced prophetically the history of Medo-Persia and Greece until the reign of Antiochus Epiphanes. At that point God gave numerous details, because this little horn (Antiochus Epiphanes) was the mirror image of the still-future little horn of chapter 7 (the Antichrist).

The setting (8:1–2). The vision occurred in Belshazzar's third year (551–550 B.C.). Though still in Babylon physically, Daniel was transported in a vision over two hundred miles to the east to Susa. Susa had been the capital of Elam, but in Daniel's day it was part of the Medo-Persian Empire.

The vision (8:3–14). Daniel's vision had three sections. In the first (8:3–4), a two-horned ram appeared at Susa and charged toward the west, north, and south. In the second part of the vision (8:5–8), a goat with a large horn charged at the ram from the west. The goat shattered the ram, but the goat's large horn was broken, and four other horns grew in its place. In the third part of the vision (8:9–14), a small horn grew out of one of the four horns. It started very insignificantly but grew in prominence until it tried to make itself "as great as the Prince of the host" (that is, God). It took away the daily sacrifices in the temple, which would remain desolate, God said, for 2,300 evenings and mornings (that is, 1,150 days).

The interpretation (8:15–26). Daniel was perplexed until the angel Gabriel explained the vision. The two-horned ram represented the kings of Media and Persia (the Medo-Persian Empire). The goat with the prominent horn was the king of Greece (Alexander the Great), and the four horns that arose after the prominent horn was broken represented the four nations that would come from the Greek Empire following Alexander's death. The little horn was a king who would rise from part of Alexander's empire, bringing devastation to Israel and persecuting the Jews. This pictured the rise of Antiochus IV (Epiphanes), who rose to power through deceit and who desecrated the Jerusalem temple between 168 B.C. and 165 B.C. (1,150 days).

The results (8:27). The vision caused Daniel to be exhausted and ill for several days. He was frightened by the vision though he could not fully understand it. To Daniel—writing before the events took place—the vision was "beyond understanding."

B. The Seventy "Weeks" (chapter 9)

Daniel 9 presents God's chronological timetable for the people of Israel. Their assigned time in Babylon was almost over, but God announced that an additional period of time must take place before His people would be delivered and His kingdom established on earth.

The setting (9:1–2). This vision occurred in the first year of the Medo-Persian rule over Babylon. Daniel studied the Book of Jeremiah and realized that Jerusalem's desolation was to last seventy years. God's prophetic time of judgment was almost over, because Daniel had been in captivity for at least sixty-eight years.

Daniel's prayer (9:3–19). The background to Daniel's prayer was the covenant curses in Leviticus 26 and Deuteronomy 28 and the promises in Deuteronomy 30. Having torn His people from the land and cast them into captivity (the final curse of the covenant), God also promised He would restore His people when they turned to Him in prayerful confession. Daniel knew the time for restoration was close, so he began to confess the sin of the people (9:3–10). He acknowledged that the nation had been wicked, and he admitted that their exile in Babylon resulted from their being unfaithful to Him. Daniel carefully acknowledged God's righteous judgment (9:11–14), for He had brought on Israel the curses and judgments written in the Mosaic Law, just as He had threatened. Daniel concluded his prayer by requesting divine mercy (9:15–19). Twice Daniel moved from the past to the present by asking God to act "now" (9:15, 17). Daniel prayed specifically for two things: (a) God's city, "Jerusalem" (especially His "sanctuary," the temple, within the city), and (b) God's people ("your people"). Both the city and the people were said to bear God's name (9:18–19).

God's answer (9:20–27). Gabriel, whom God sent to Daniel, declared that seventy "sevens" were decreed for Daniel's people (the Jews) and for the holy city (Jerusalem). The word "seven" can refer to seven days (as in Gen. 29:27–28) or seven years (as in Lev. 25:3–5). In Daniel 9, God's message seems to refer to seventy groups of seven years—a period of 490 years. This time period, God said, would be divided into two sections. The first extended from the issuing of a decree to restore and rebuild Jerusalem (Neh. 2:2–8) until "the Anointed One, the ruler," and would be seven "sevens" and sixty-two "sevens" long (7+62=69; 69x7 years = 483 prophetic years). Many believe this time period ended on the very day Jesus rode into Jerusalem as Israel's Messiah (Matt. 21:1–11). God then inserted a time gap in His calendar after this first period. During this gap three things would happen: (a) the "Anointed One" (Christ) would be "cut off" (crucified), (b) Jerusalem and the newly rebuilt temple would be destroyed by the "people of the ruler who will come" (fulfilled when the Romans destroyed Jerusalem in A.D. 70), and (c) the Jewish people would again experience "desolations" (ongoing fulfillment since A.D. 70).

The final part of God's prophetic timetable will begin when a certain ruler will make a covenant with Israel for one "seven." The fact that the ruler will come from the "people" who destroyed Jerusalem in A.D. 70 allows us to identify him as the future Antichrist of the revived Roman Empire (see also Dan. 2:40–43; 7:19–25). He will make a seven-year agreement with the people of Israel, but in the "middle" of that seven-year period he will break the agreement and end the Jewish temple sacrifices.

After setting up "an abomination that causes desolation" (perhaps an image of himself) in the temple, he will persecute Israel for the remaining three and a half years until the "end" finally comes for him (see also 7:25–26; Matt. 24:15–22; Rev. 13:5).

Chart of Daniel's Seventy "Sevens"*

69 "sevens"	444	B.C.			
x 7 years	+ A.D. 33				
483 years	477	years			
	−1	(1 B.C. to A.D. 1 = 1 year, not 2)			
	476	years			
	x 365	days			
	173,740	days			
	+ 25	Nisan 1,444 B.C.	=	March	5
		Passover, A.D. 33	=	March	30
					25

x 360	days (prophetic years)	+ 115	days for leap years	
173,880	days	173,880	days	

*Adopted from *Chronological Aspects of the Life of Christ*, by Harold W. Hoehner (Grand Rapids: Zondervan, 1977), 139.

Rationale for 360-Day Years

Daniel 9:27	"middle of the 'seven'"
Daniel 7:25; 12:7	"time, times, and half a time"
Revelation 12:14	"time, times, and half a time"
Revelation 11:3; 12:6	"1,260 days"
Revelation 11:2; 13:5	"42 months"

These parallel passages imply that a prophetic year was composed of twelve months with thirty days each. A "time" was parallel to a year; and a "time" (1), "times" (2), and "half a time" ($1/2$) were equivalent to three and a half years, or the "middle of the 'seven.'"

C. The Future Panorama (chapters 10–12)

The final vision is a grand prophetic panorama of events from the time of Cyrus to the final establishment of God's kingdom on the earth. Chapter 10 records the arrival of God's angelic messenger and provides a glimpse of the spiritual forces swirling just out of sight. In chapter 11 the messenger predicted God's sweep of history from Medo-Persia through Greece to Antiochus Epiphanes and ultimately to the still-future Antichrist. Chapter 12 describes the end times for the Jewish people, focusing especially on their final persecution by the Antichrist.

> Daniel 10–12 contains some of the most intricate prophetic details recorded in the Bible, and shows how specific God can be in describing future events. The passage also serves as a rebuke to those who try to interpret all the details of future events. Many specific prophetic details will make sense only when they are fulfilled.

The setting (10:1–3). Daniel's final vision—in 536 B.C. in Cyrus's third year— concerned a "great war." Daniel's response to the vision was to fast and mourn for three weeks as he sought God's interpretation.

The arrival of the heavenly messenger (10:4–21). After three weeks an angel finally came to Daniel. He had been sent to Daniel on the first day Daniel started praying, but the demonic prince of the Persian kingdom had delayed him until Michael, Israel's angelic guardian, came to the aid of this spiritual messenger. Daniel was overcome by the awesomeness of this heavenly visitor and had to be strengthened by him. The messenger promised to explain the vision, and he warned Daniel that the angelic "prince of Greece" would also come to oppose the Jews.

> *Spiritual forces are at work behind the scenes in personal, national, and international affairs. Christians need to realize that our struggles are ultimately with "spiritual forces of evil in the heavenly realms" (Eph. 6:12). At the same time believers must also realize that "the one who is in you is greater than the one who is in the world" (1 John 4:4).*

Prophecies concerning Medo-Persia and Greece (11:1–20). The messenger first explained to Daniel the remaining history of the Medo-Persian Empire (11:2), announcing that three more kings would appear in Persia (Cambyses, Pseudo-Smerdis, and Darius I). They in turn would be followed by a fourth king (Xerxes) who would invade Greece. Having mentioned Greece, the angel then shifted forward to describe the future of that kingdom as it related to the Jews (11:3–20). A "mighty king" (Alexander) would appear in Greece. After his death his empire would be divided four ways. Daniel focused especially on two of these four remnants of Alexander's empire. The "king of the South" (11:5) refers to Ptolemy I and the Ptolemaic Empire that ruled in Egypt. The "king of the North" (11:6) refers to Antiochus and the Seleucid Empire that ruled in Syria and Mesopotamia. In 11:5–20 Daniel traced the interaction between these two empires.

Prophecies concerning Antiochus Epiphanes (11:21–35). Daniel's brief history of conflict slowed dramatically when he came to Antiochus Epiphanes, whom he described as a "contemptible person" who seized power "through intrigue" (see also 8:23–25). Antiochus would invade Egypt (the "king of the South") twice, but during the second invasion ships from the west would oppose him. Roman ships commanded by Popilius Laenas threatened Antiochus and forced him to leave Egypt. Angry, and determined to unify what remained of his empire, Antiochus went to Judea and desecrated the temple, abolishing the daily sacrifices. He converted God's temple into a pagan shrine and set up "the abomination that causes desolation."

Has the "Abomination of Desolation" Already Been Fulfilled?

The "abomination of desolation" set up by Antiochus is *not* the ultimate fulfillment of Daniel 9:27 because (a) Antiochus does not fit the time sequence given in that verse, and (b) long after the time of Antiochus, Jesus said Daniel's prophecy of the abomination of desolation was *still* future (Matt. 24:15–16).

Prophecies concerning the Antichrist (11:36–45). Antiochus Epiphanes was the historical figure most closely parallel to the future Antichrist. As a result,

Daniel's prophecy jumped directly from Antiochus to this still-future world leader. Unlike Antiochus, who promoted the gods of Greece, this future leader will "show no regard for the gods of his fathers." Instead, he will exalt himself. He will also honor a "god of fortresses," which could refer to military might or possibly to Satan himself (see Rev. 13:1–4). This leader will invade several countries including Israel, here called the "Beautiful Land." Daniel described the battles that will lead up to his final campaign against Jerusalem in which he will pitch his tents between the Dead Sea and the Mediterranean Sea as he attacks "the beautiful holy mountain," Jerusalem. With victory seemingly in his grasp "he will come to his end." Jesus will return to earth to fight against the Antichrist and to rescue His people (Zech. 14:2–5; Rev. 19:11–21).

Prophecies concerning the Jews (chapter 12). The messenger then explained to Daniel what these final events meant for the Jews. Michael, the angelic prince, will arise to protect Daniel's people. Michael will be needed because the days of this last evil ruler will be a time of distress that will exceed any previous period of suffering for Israel. Yet God promised that believers—those whose names are recorded in God's book of life—will be rescued. Some will have been delivered *from* death, but others will be delivered *through* death. God will resurrect those who have died. Some will be raised to everlasting life, but the unbelieving will receive "everlasting contempt." The angel then told Daniel to seal his prophetic message until the end times. As the time gets closer, people will search Daniel's prophecies to increase their understanding of these events.

Daniel ended by recording three specific time references for these prophecies. First, the time of distress will last "for a time, times, and half a time" (7:25; see 9:27). Second, the time when "the daily sacrifice is abolished" and the "abomination that causes desolation" is set up to the time when the temple will be cleansed and reopened for use will be "1,290 days." This will be three and a half years (1,260 days; see Rev. 11:3; 12:6) plus an additional thirty days to cleanse the temple. Then Daniel was told that anyone who "reaches the end of the 1,335 days" will be blessed. This will be the three and a half years (1,260 days) of the Great Tribulation plus an additional seventy-five days for God to gather the nations and judge those who remain on the earth (Matt. 25:31–46). Those who come to the Lord in the Tribulation and survive it and the time of judgment will be truly "blessed" because they will remain alive to enter God's promised kingdom.

HOSEA
God's Love for His Adulterous Wife

AUTHOR

 $\mathscr{H}$ OSEA'S NAME means "salvation." All we know about Hosea is what he recorded about himself in the first three chapters of the book. Apart from the name of his father (Beeri, 1:1), nothing is known about Hosea's ancestry. Hosea also recorded the name of his wife and her father (Gomer daughter of Diblaim, 1:3) and the names of the children born to Gomer (Jezreel, 1:4; Lo-Ruhamah, 1:6; and Lo-Ammi, 1:9). Hosea's occupation is not recorded.

DATE

Hosea 1:1 gives the general chronological framework in which Hosea prophesied. He listed four kings of Judah (whose dates overlap because of their coregencies) and one king of Israel.

Judah	*Israel*
Uzziah (790–739 B.C.)	Jeroboam II (793–753 B.C.)
Jotham (750–731 B.C.)	
Ahaz (735–715 B.C.)	
Hezekiah (729–686 B.C.)	

Though Hosea mentioned only Jeroboam II as a king in Israel, the fact that he also listed Jotham, Ahaz, and Hezekiah of Judah indicates he continued prophesying *after* the time of Jeroboam II. Why, then, did he not mention Israel's later kings who reigned at the same time as Jotham, Ahaz, and Hezekiah (namely, Zechariah, Shallum, Menahem, Pekahiah, Pekah, and Hoshea)? Possibly because Jeroboam II was the last king by divine appointment who reigned for any significant period of time. God promised Jehu that his descendants would sit on the throne of Israel "to the fourth generation" (2 Kings 10:30; 15:12). This included Jehoahaz, Jehoash, Jeroboam II, and Zechariah. However, Zechariah reigned for only six months before he was assassinated (15:8–10). The five kings after Zechariah were all usurpers. Hosea indirectly referred to these later kings in 8:4 ("they set up kings without my consent").

Hosea prophesied for nearly forty years (around 760–722 B.C.). His contemporaries were Isaiah, Amos, and Micah. He began his prophetic ministry during the later part of the reign of Israel's greatest king (Jeroboam II) and continued until Israel fell to the Assyrians in 722 B.C.

BACKGROUND

The period during which Hosea prophesied is recorded in 2 Kings 14:23–17:41. During this time Israel fell from being a major political power to being a vassal of Assyria (15:19). Eventually she was completely destroyed by Assyria (17:5–6). While Jeroboam's reign brought much prosperity to Israel, it was also a time of idolatry and carnal luxury (as noted in the Book of Amos). Following Jeroboam II's death, the nation entered a period of political upheaval and rapid decline. Jeroboam II had reigned for forty years, but in the next thirty years six kings ascended Israel's throne. Four of these six were assassinated (Zechariah, 15:10; Shallum, 15:14; Pekahiah, 15:25; and Pekah, 15:30). Hosea referred to this political intrigue in 7:6–7: "they devour their rulers. All their kings fall."

The religious leaders in Israel were illegitimate. They were not members of the levitical priesthood but were part of the line of priests appointed by Jeroboam I to officiate at his rival religious centers in Israel (1 Kings 12:31). The priests were hypocritical leaders who were involved in everything from robbery and murder (Hos. 6:9) to idolatry (10:5).

ADDRESSEES

Though Hosea did include Judah within his prophecies (Hos. 1:7; 5:10–14; 6:4, 11), the main thrust of his activity was directed toward the Northern Kingdom of Israel (1:4–6; 4:1; 5:1; 7:1; 11:1; 12:1; 13:1; 14:1). Possibly Hosea was from the Northern Kingdom. (In 7:5 he referred to the king of the Northern Kingdom as "our king.") If so, he and Jonah were the only two writing prophets from Israel. Hosea called the Northern Kingdom by the name "Ephraim" thirty-seven times. This could be because Ephraim was the strongest and most influential tribe, or because the first king of Israel, Jeroboam I, was an Ephraimite (1 Kings 11:26).

PURPOSE

Through the personal tragedy of unfaithfulness in his own marriage, Hosea was allowed to experience something of the heartache God Himself felt for His bride, Israel. Hosea pictured God's love for His adulterous wife. In the second major part of the book (chapters 4–13) God "took Israel to court" to prove His charges that Israel had no faithfulness, no loyal love, and no knowledge of God.

Characteristics of the Book of Hosea

- Hosea is the longest of the Minor Prophets.
- Hosea is mentioned nowhere else in the Old Testament and is mentioned only once by name in the New Testament (Rom. 9:25). However, the book is referred to directly or indirectly thirty times in the New Testament.
- Hosea employed a cyclical pattern of sin, judgment, and restoration.
  Cycle 1: Hosea 1:1–2:1
  Cycle 2: Hosea 2:2–23
  Cycle 3: Hosea 3
  Cycle 4: Hosea 4–14

OUTLINE

I. Hosea's Marriage: The Wayward Spouse (chapters 1–3)
   A. The First Cycle: Hosea's Family (1:1–2:1)
   B. The Second Cycle: Hosea's Divorce (2:2–23)
   C. The Third Cycle: Hosea's Reconciliation (chapter 3)
II. Hosea's Message: The Wayward Nation (chapters 4–13)
   A. The First Charge: No Acknowledgment of God (chapters 4–5)
   B. The Second Charge: No Loyal Love toward God (6:1–11:11)
   C. The Third Charge: No Faithfulness to God (11:12–13:16)
III. Israel's Future Restoration (chapter 14)

I. HOSEA'S MARRIAGE: THE WAYWARD SPOUSE (CHAPTERS 1–3)

In Hosea 1–3 God's message to Israel is based on Hosea's relationship with his wife. Hosea's marriage to a woman of flawed character paralleled God's relationship to Israel. Gomer's unfaithfulness and adultery pictured Israel's rejection of God to pursue idolatry. The three chapters present three separate cycles of sin, judgment, and restoration.

A. The First Cycle: Hosea's Family (1:1–2:1)

Introduction (1:1). This verse supplies the basic historical pegs on which to hang Hosea's ministry. He prophesied from approximately 760 to 722 B.C.—four decades in which the Northern Kingdom slid into oblivion.

Hosea's wife (1:2–3). Writing after the fact, Hosea recorded that God told him to take "an adulterous wife and children of unfaithfulness." God could have directed Hosea to marry a morally impure woman, just as He permitted the nation of Israel to allow Rahab the harlot to join them and to became an ancestor of David and Jesus (Josh. 6:25; Matt. 1:5–6). However, four key points in the text seem to indicate that Gomer's adulterous acts took place *after* the marriage instead of before.

When Did Gomer Become an Adulterous Woman?

1. The word "adulterous" is plural in Hebrew, indicating character more than specific acts. (God had Hosea marry "a wife of adulterous character.") Her character may have been present at the time of marriage, but the adulterous acts were not necessarily already committed.

2. Hosea was to take an adulterous wife "and children of unfaithfulness." He then named the children . . . and they were born *after* his marriage to Gomer (1:3–9).

3. The first child is specifically said to belong to Hosea (1:3, "she . . . bore him a son"), but the next two children are not, indicating Gomer's unfaithfulness began after the birth of the first child.

4. Hosea 2:4–5 says Gomer's children were "children of adultery" from a woman who had "been unfaithful" and "conceived them in disgrace." Again, the "children of adultery" are those children conceived *after* Hosea married Gomer.

Hosea's children (1:4–9). Gomer bore three children, but apparently Hosea was the father of only one. God had Hosea give each child a name that symbolized His judgment on Israel. Hosea named his first child "Jezreel," which means "God scatters" or "God sows." Hosea used the name in four different ways: (a) the agricultural metaphor of *scattering seed* to picture God's scattering of Israel (1:4); (b) the agricultural metaphor of *sowing seed* to picture God's ultimate planting of Israel back in the land (1:11; 2:22–23); (c) the *Valley of Jezreel* in northern Israel where the Assyrians defeated the army of Israel (1:5); and (d) the *city of Jezreel* where Jehu slaughtered many innocent people following his rise to power (1:4; 2 Kings 9:23–33; 10:6–11). Hosea named the second child "Lo-Ruhamah," which means "no compassion" or "no love." God would "no longer show love to the house of Israel" but would allow them to fall to the Assyrians. Hosea named the third child Lo-Ammi, which means "not my people." God announced that Israel was "not my people, and I am not your God."

Hosea's Children		
Name	Meaning	Purpose
Jezreel	God scatters	God will scatter His people.
Lo-Ruhamah	No compassion	God will no longer show compassion by rescuing Israel from destruction.
Lo-Ammi	Not my people	God will sever His relationship because of their disobedience.

Israel's future restoration (1:10–2:1). Having just announced that Israel was no longer His people, God quickly announced that His judgment was temporary, not permanent. The change from judgment to blessing is so dramatic that 1:10 in the Hebrew Bible is 2:1 and chapter 2 has twenty-five (not twenty-three) verses. Each child's name was reversed to show God's ultimate blessing on His people. In that day those once called "Not my people" (Lo-Ammi) will be called "Sons of the living God." That great time of blessing will be known as the "day of Jezreel" ("God sows") because God will again sow His people back in the land of promise. And those once called Lo-Ruhamah ("Not loved") will be called "My loved one" (Ruhamah). Hosea listed four specific characteristics of this future time of blessing:

1. The decimated population will again "be like the sand of the seashore" (1:10).
2. The people of Judah and the people of Israel will be reunited into a single kingdom (1:11).
3. The reunited nation will appoint one leader to rule over it (1:11).
4. The remnant "will come up out of the land" where they had been exiled to the land God promised to them (1:11).

Even in times of judgment, God wants His people to remember His promises of hope for the future.

B. *The Second Cycle: Hosea's Divorce (2:2–23)*

Hosea's complaint (2:2–5). Hosea called on his children to "rebuke" their mother. The word can have the idea of lodging a complaint or bringing a charge in court. The charge was that "she is not my wife and I am not her husband." Gomer's unfaithfulness had shattered their marriage relationship. Yet Hosea still wanted reconciliation. He urged his faithless wife to "remove the adulterous look" and return to her husband. If she refused, she would suffer the shameful judgment of a prostitute: stripped naked and exposed in her sin (see also Ezek. 16:35–41; 23:29–30). Even her children would not experience compassion, because "they are the children of adultery."

Israel's judgment (2:6–13). Hosea introduced each of God's two judgments on His faithless wife with the word "therefore" (2:6, 9). In verse 8 it becomes obvious that Hosea was describing *both* his wife Gomer ("she," "her") and faithless Israel ("which *they* used for Baal"). The first judgment was her loss of satisfaction (2:6–8). She might "chase after her lovers" but she would "not catch them." God vowed that neither Gomer nor Israel would find the lasting satisfaction they sought in their pursuit of sin. Eventually a sadder but wiser nation would seek to return to her first love and admit that "then I was better off than now." The second judgment was her loss of material support (2:9–13). God said He would judge those who rebel against Him and would take away grain, wine, wool, and linen, and punish the nation for its sin.

"You will never find in sin what you go into sin to find."
—Doug Cecil

Israel's future restoration (2:14–23). For a third time (2:14) Hosea introduced the results of God's actions with the word "therefore." However, this time the word introduced God's promised restoration of His wayward nation. Using imagery from Israel's Exodus, God announced that He would lead Israel "into the desert," where He would "speak tenderly to her." Like a gentle husband wooing back a wayward wife, God said He would "give her back her vineyards" that had been taken in judgment. Three specific blessings will occur "in that day" when God restores His people.

First, there will be a *new relationship* (2:16–17). The people will call God "my husband," not "my master" (literally, "my Baal"), because the word "Baal" will be distasteful to them, even when used of the true God.

Second, there will be a *new covenant* (2:18–20). God will institute a new covenant with His people that will bring universal peace. This peace will extend to "the beasts of the field and the birds of the air" (see also Isa. 11:6–9; 65:25) and to all humanity. God will abolish all fighting and allow all Israel to live safely. Such peace is possible because God will "betroth" Israel to Himself, and the people will return to the Lord.

Third, there will be a *new blessing* (2:21–23). God's promised blessings and fruitfulness will be poured out on the people. Rain will come and will produce crops. Hosea again reversed the original names of his children to emphasize God's promised blessing. The productivity will respond to Jezreel because God vowed to "plant" her in the land. He also vowed to show His love (Ruhamah) to the one He had earlier called "Not my loved one" (Lo-Ruhamah). And He announced that the one who used to be called "Not my people" (Lo-Ammi) will one day be told "You are my people" (Ammi).

C. The Third Cycle: Hosea's Reconciliation (chapter 3)

Hosea's love (3:1–3). God commanded Hosea to "go show [his] love" to his wife. Though the New International Version suggests that three individuals were involved in the scene (Hosea, Gomer, and her lover), the one who still loved Gomer is Hosea, not some other man. The New American Standard Bible perhaps translates it better when it records that God ordered Hosea to "Go again, love a woman who is loved by her husband [Hosea], yet an adulteress." To picture the compassionate heart of God, Hosea was asked to "love her as the LORD loves the Israelites." Finding Gomer living as a slave, Hosea purchased her for fifteen shekels of silver and about ten bushels of barley. The normal price for a female slave was thirty shekels of silver (Exod. 21:7–8, 32), so Hosea paid half in silver and the other half in produce. Gomer came home, but she was not immediately restored as Hosea's wife. Instead, he ordered her, as his servant, to "not be a prostitute or be intimate with any man." This relationship would continue for "many days."

> *Forgiveness from the guilt of sin does not always bring freedom from the consequences of sin. Those consequences can often be painful and long-lasting.*

God's love (3:4–5). Hosea's actions paralleled God's plan for Israel. God would rescue Israel from slavery, but the people would not immediately be restored to a place of complete fellowship with Him. Instead they would live "many days without king or prince, without sacrifice or sacred stones, without ephod or idol." They would return from their ruinous relationship with idols, but they would not have the restored Davidic monarchy or temple sacrifices. But in "the last days" Israel will finally "seek the LORD their God and David their king." Hosea's reference to David could point either to the resurrection of the literal King David or to the future messianic King who was to come from the line of David (Jer. 30:9; Ezek. 34:23–24). In either case Hosea was looking forward to Israel's complete restoration to God in the future kingdom age.

II. HOSEA'S MESSAGE: THE WAYWARD NATION (CHAPTERS 4–14)

In Hosea 4–14 the prophet dropped all allusions to his family and focused instead on God's "lawsuit" against His people. God took Israel to court and charged the nation with three sins. Hosea stated the charges in 4:1 and then developed the charges through the rest of the book. Two key points must be made to understand the remainder of Hosea. First, Hosea presented the material in a chiastic structure. That is, having stated charges A, B, and C, Hosea then developed the charges in reverse order (C, B, then A). Second, each charge is an incomplete cycle that focused only on sin and judgment. Hosea did not complete the cycle until chapter 14, where he finally announced Israel's future restoration.

God's Lawsuit against Israel	
The Charges Stated	*The Charges Developed*
(4:1–3)	*(4:4–13:16)*
No faithfulness (trustworthiness)	11:12–13:16
No love (loyal love)	6:1–11:11
No acknowledgment of God	4:4–5:15

A. The First Charge: No Acknowledgment of God (chapters 4–5)

Introduction (4:1–3). Hosea called on Israel to hear God's legal "charge" against them. He stated three specific indictments against the nation: "no faithfulness, no love, no acknowledgment of God." Hosea named five of the Ten Commandments (Exod. 20:13–16) to demonstrate how Israel had broken their covenant with the Lord. With "all bounds" broken, God's ensuing judgment would cause even the land to mourn.

Israel's sin in refusing to acknowledge God (4:4–19). The first charge developed by God was that the people of Israel were being destroyed because of a "lack of knowledge." Speaking first to the false priests of Israel (4:4–9), Hosea charged them with having "rejected knowledge." As a result God would punish both the priests and the people for their sin. In rejecting the knowledge of God, the people turned to spiritual "prostitution" (4:10–19). They thought their spiritual and physical adultery would bring prosperity and fertility, but it only led to ruin. God sadly concluded that "Ephraim is joined to idols." Because of this refusal to acknowledge God, their sacrifices would bring them only shame.

Israel's judgment for refusing to acknowledge God (chapter 5). To the priests, all Israelites, and the royal house God announced, "This judgment is against you." Because Israel was like a prostitute, she was unwilling to "acknowledge the LORD." So God's only recourse was to punish her. While focusing primarily on the Northern Kingdom, Hosea also announced that God would extend His wrath on Judah as well. Like a lion,

He would "tear them to pieces" in judgment until they were willing to "admit their guilt" and seek God's face.

B. The Second Charge: No Loyal Love toward God (6:1–11:11)

Hosea's second charge focused on Israel's lack of loyal love (*hesed*) toward God and toward others. The word *hesed* is sometimes translated "mercy" or "love," but it has the idea of covenant loyalty. After exposing Israel's false confession in chapter 6, Hosea revealed in chapters 7–9 the specific ways Israel had demonstrated a lack of loyal love. Then in 10:1–11:11, he described God's judgment on Israel for that lack.

Israel's false plea of repentance (chapter 6). The people of Israel responded to Hosea's charge that they failed to acknowledge God. Though they admitted that God had torn them "to pieces" (see 5:14), they firmly believed His judgment would last for only a short time. Thinking that God would restore them in two or three days, they optimistically affirmed that they would "press on to acknowledge him"—parroting back the words they felt God wanted them to say. God's rejoinder must have jarred the people. Their flippant response only highlighted God's second indictment: "Your love [*hesed*] is like the morning mist, like the early dew that disappears," that is, it was only temporary. Hoping to win God's favor, they offered sacrifices, but their commitment was only temporal and fleeting. Once the trouble vanished, so did their commitment to God. Like Adam, they had "broken the covenant" and proven themselves unfaithful to God.

Israel's overt acts of disloyalty to others (chapter 7). Israel's lack of loyal love could be seen in the common people (7:1–2), the rulers (7:3–7), and Israel's relationships with other nations (7:8–16). Thieves broke into homes while others robbed in the streets. But God told these robbers He would "remember" their sinful actions. Kings and other leaders engaged in illicit adultery as their lust smoldered. Palace intrigue was rampant as secret alliances and plots swirled through the royal court. The people devoured their rulers, perhaps an allusion to the fact that four of Israel's last six kings were assassinated. On the international scene, Israel tried to manipulate the major powers to the east and west. Turning first to Egypt and then to Assyria, Israel sought alliances with these nations for protection.

But because Israel did not turn to the Lord, her lack of loyal love would result in judgment.

Israel's overt acts of disloyalty to God (chapter 8). The Israelites also chose to ignore their covenant with God. They appointed kings without God's consent, and they made idols and altars in disobedience to God's Law. Using a proverb to make his point, Hosea said the people had sown "the wind" and would now "reap the whirlwind." They chose to forget their Maker and to trust instead in well-fortified palaces and towns. So their fortresses would be destroyed because of their disloyalty.

Israel's barren harvest (chapter 9). Possibly this message was delivered at harvest time when the people felt rich, rewarded, and content. Hosea warned them not to rejoice, because they had been unfaithful to the Lord. Their harvest was like "the wages of a prostitute." When God first "found Israel," it was "like finding grapes in the desert." The nation was cherished and prized. But before they could even enter the Promised Land, the people chose to worship an idol at Baal Peor. Hosea was referring to the incident of sexual immorality and idolatry described in Numbers 25. As a result of their continued immorality and idolatry, God would remove the nation's fertility and replace it with barrenness—"no birth, no pregnancy, no conception."

God's judgment on Israel's wickedness (chapter 10). When Israel prospered, the people built idols instead of acknowledging the One who had blessed them. So now they had to suffer the consequences. The calf idol of Beth Aven (another name for Bethel) would be taken to Assyria. Because Israel depended on its own strength, their fortresses would be destroyed and the king of Israel killed.

Beth Aven, "house of wickedness," is a play on words. The calf idol was one of two such idols that had been set up by Jeroboam I at Dan and Bethel (1 Kings 12:28–30). The people went to worship at Bethel ("house of God"), but in reality they were going to Beth Aven ("house of wickedness").

God's judgment on His disobedient son (11:1–11). Israel's lack of loyal love was even more shocking in light of God's great faithfulness. God's calling of Israel out of Egypt is clearly a reference to the Exodus, over seven hundred years earlier. In Hosea's indictment, Israel was the *disobedient* son who departed from God to serve idols. Then in 11:5 Hosea completed his word picture by announcing that Assyria would rule over Israel because of its disobedience. Yet because of His love, God would not destroy Israel completely. He would again return its people to their land.

Hosea 11:1 and Matthew 2:15

While Hosea 11:1 clearly points to the time of the Exodus, some see in these verses a veiled prophecy of Christ's flight to Egypt as a young baby. This is because Matthew quoted this verse in Matthew 2:15. But God's call of His "son" Israel out of Egypt in Hosea 11 is clearly historical, not prophetic. Hosea was looking back seven hundred years to the first Exodus from Egypt, not to Christ's return from Egypt following the death of Herod.

How then was Matthew using Hosea 11:1? Matthew wrote to the Jews, and much of his Gospel was devoted to proving to his Jewish readers that Jesus Christ is indeed their Messiah. In the first part of the book Matthew drew a series of parallels between Jesus and the nation Israel. In effect, Matthew sought to prove that Jesus is the Messiah because He is the embodiment of all that Israel as God's "son" should have been. Jesus succeeded where the nation as a whole had failed. The parallels can be charted as follows:

Israel's History	Point of Comparison Christ's Life	Point of Contrast
Israel was called from Egypt as a "child" (Hos. 11:1).	Christ was called from Egypt as a child (Matt. 2:15).	Israel was a disobedient child; Christ was not (Hos. 11:2–5).
Israel was "baptized" as a nation in the Red Sea (Exod. 14; 1 Cor. 10:1–2).	Christ was baptized by John the Baptist in the Jordan River (Matt. 3).	Israel disobeyed God within three days after the Red Sea baptism (Exod. 15:22–26); Christ was "my Son, whom I love; with him I am well pleased" (Matt. 3:17).

Israel went into the wilderness where she was tempted for forty years (Exod.–Num.).	Christ went into the wilderness where He was tempted for forty days (Matt. 4:1–10).	Israel failed her temptations and incurred God's wrath; Christ successfully passed every temptation.
Israel went to Mount Sinai to receive God's Law (Exod. 19–20).	Christ "went up on a mountainside" and explained the Law (Matt. 5–7).	Israel broke God's Law before Moses could carry the tablets down from the mountain (Exod. 32); Christ said, "Do not think that I have come to abolish the Law or the Prophets; I have not come to abolish them but to fulfill them" (Matt. 5:17).

C. The Third Charge: No Faithfulness to God (11:12–13:16)

Hosea's third charge focused on Israel's lack of faithfulness. The transition to this third point is in 11:12. God announced that Israel was guilty of lying and deception, in contrast to God, who is faithful. In Hosea 12 the prophet highlighted Israel's history of faithlessness, and in chapter 13 he pictured God's judgment because of the nation's lack of faithfulness.

Israel's history of faithlessness (11:12–12:14). Hosea stressed Israel's history of faithlessness in her dealings with other nations. She lied when she made a treaty with Assyria and then bribed Egypt for protection. The patriarch Jacob, from whom the nation of Israel has descended, had "struggled with God" until he finally "found him at Bethel" (Gen. 28:10–22; 35:1–7). In the same way Israel needed to return to her God. In their faithlessness in commerce, merchants defrauded others. So God sent prophets to give Israel His message, as He had done from the very beginning when He used Moses. God would "repay" Israel for its contempt.

God's judgment of Israel's faithlessness (chapter 13). The sin of the Israelites grew ever worse. They worshiped Baal and even sacrificed humans. God had cared for them in the desert, but when they were satisfied, they forgot Him. Though God would attack them as a wild animal tears apart its prey, He said He would "redeem them from death." He was referring to a national redemption from the death of exile, but Paul applied the passage to personal resurrection (1 Cor. 15:55). Yet this future hope cannot erase the penalty for sin. "The people of Samaria must bear their guilt, because they have rebelled against their God" (Hos. 13:16).

III. ISRAEL'S FUTURE RESTORATION (CHAPTER 14)

The requirements for restoration (14:1–3). God summoned the prophet of Israel, ruined by sin, to come humbly to Him and ask Him to forgive them. They needed to confess that neither foreign alliances nor foreign gods ("what our own hands have made") could save them. Only in God could they find compassion.

The benefits of restoration (14:4–8). The genuine repentance of the people of Israel will allow God to show His grace and mercy, to "heal their waywardness and love them freely." He will also bless them and allow them to flourish. Hosea used imagery of several flowers, plants, and trees to picture Israel's future blessing. In a play on words God reminded Ephraim (which means "fruitful;" see Gen. 41:52) that her fruitfulness comes from Him.

The conclusion (14:9). Hosea ended his book by applying his message to each reader. Those who were wise would realize the truth of his words and the rightness of the path established by God. The righteous will follow God's path, but the "rebellious" will "stumble" because of their disobedience.

JOEL
The Coming Day of the Lord

AUTHOR

$\mathcal{T}$HE NAME JOEL means "Yahweh is God." Apart from the name of Joel's father, Pethuel, nothing else is known about this prophet. Eleven other individuals in the Old Testament are named Joel (1 Sam. 8:2; 1 Chron. 4:35; 5:4; 7:3; 11:38; 15:7; 26:22; 27:20; 2 Chron. 29:12; Ezra 10:43; Neh. 11:9).

DATE

Joel did not give any specific chronological markers to help date his book, so the date of writing must be assigned on the basis of internal evidence. Scholars have proposed preexilic (around 835–830 B.C.), exilic (around 609–580 B.C.), and postexilic (around 400 B.C.) dates for the book. While the evidence is divided, it seems best to accept the early date.

BACKGROUND

If the events described by Joel occurred about 835–830 B.C., the book would have been written in the early part of King Joash's reign. After Jehu killed King Ahaziah in 841 B.C. (2 Kings 9:27–29), Ahaziah's mother, Athaliah, seized the throne in Jerusalem. She was the daughter of King Ahab of

Israel (2 Kings 8:18, 26; 2 Chron. 21:6) and was not from the line of David. Knowing she was not legally entitled to the throne of Judah, she tried to have all the legitimate heirs killed (2 Kings 11:1). However, Ahaziah's son, Joash, who was only a baby, was rescued and hidden in the temple for six years (11:2–3). In 835 B.C., when Joash was seven, the high priest, Jehoiada, masterminded a palace coup that killed Athaliah and placed Joash on the throne (11:4–12:1).

Athaliah, as the daughter of Ahab, had attempted to promote Baal worship in Judah. After her death the high priest, Jehoiada, led the people in a revival of sorts and tried to purge the land of Baal worship (2 Chron. 23:16–17). In the early years of Joash's reign the king was under the tutelage of Jehoiada, who continued to exert major influence in the country (2 Kings 11:15–12:3; 2 Chron. 23:9–24:3). Only after the death of Jehoiada did Joash assume sole authority as king in Jerusalem. The extent of the power and influence of Jehoiada the high priest during those years can be seen in the honor bestowed on him at the time of his death: "He was buried with the kings in the City of David" (24:16).

ADDRESSEES

Joel wrote to the people of Judah, addressing the elders (1:2, 14; 2:16), the entire populace (1:2; 2:1), farmers (1:11), and priests (1:13; 2:17). Notable by its absence is any mention of the king, which implies that Joel wrote at a time when a king was not on the throne or, as in the case of young King Joash, was not old enough to rule independently.

PURPOSE

Using a recent locust plague as an object lesson, Joel wrote of a future invasion in the Day of the Lord and of the blessing that would follow when Israel would repent and be restored by God.

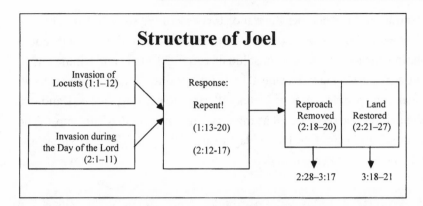

OUTLINE

I. Judgment of Israel in the Day of the Lord (1:1–2:17)
   A. The First Locust Plague in Joel's Day (chapter 1)
   B. The Future Locust like Plague in the Day of the Lord (2:1–17)
II. Deliverance of Israel in the Day of the Lord (2:18–3:21)
   A. The Restoration of Israel in Joel's Day (2:18–27)
   B. The Restoration of Israel in the Day of the Lord (2:28–3:21)

I. JUDGMENT OF ISRAEL IN THE DAY OF THE LORD (1:1–2:17)

The Book of Joel pivots around the prophet's two calls for Israel to repent. In 1:1–12 Joel described a series of locust plagues that had devastated the land. These plagues, a symbol of God's covenant curses (Deut. 28:38), were intended to force the people to repent and return to the Lord (Joel 1:13–20). But as severe as the locust plague in Joel's day was, it paled in comparison to God's threatened invasion in the Day of the Lord (2:1–11). Yet as the people looked ahead to that imminent attack, Joel again announced that "even now" they still had an opportunity to repent (2:12–27).

A. The First Locust Plague in Joel's Day (chapter 1)

The devastating invasion of locusts (1:1–12). Joel began by reporting that the current locust invasion was unique because of the extent of its devastation.

No one could remember their ancestors describing such destruction, and they would be talking about it with their own children. Like an invading nation, the locusts came against Judah, ruining the land and wiping out all the agriculture. Fig trees, wheat, barley, grapevines, and olive trees were all eaten. The people therefore had no offerings to bring to the Lord, and this denied them access to God at the very time they needed Him most. The depressing effects of the locust plague caused the people's joy to wither, just like the locust-eaten crops.

The Identification of the Locusts in Joel 1:4

The four types of locusts identified by Joel are apparently four successive stages in the development of the swarming desert locust. Joel 1:4 records the order in which the locusts appeared in the land, while 2:25 presents the logical order in which the locust develops (starting with the adult and then showing the development of their offspring). The order found in Joel 1:4 is as follows:

1. "Locust swarm" (NIV)/"Gnawing locust" (NASB) = young locusts
2. "Great locusts" (NIV)/"Swarming locust" (NASB) = mature locusts
3. "Young locusts" (NIV)/"Creeping locust" (NASB) = newly hatched locusts
4. "Other locusts" (NIV)/"Stripping locust" (NASB) = younger locusts

From John A. Thompson, "Translation of the Words for Locust," *Bible Translator* 25 (October 1974): 405–11.

The call to repentance (1:13–20). Joel called on his audience to wear sackcloth (garments made of a coarse cloth) and to fast, symbols of national repentance and humility before God. The priests, elders, and all the people were urged to pray for forgiveness and deliverance. Such drastic action was needed because of impending famine. The land had dried up, and the famine was felt by the cattle and even by the sheep (who can normally graze on land unsuitable for agriculture or herds of cattle). The locust plague had devastated the land like a fire. Probably a drought accompanied the plagues of locust, for even the streams of water were dry. The locusts had destroyed all the plants, and a continuing drought made replanting impossible.

B. The Future Locust like Plague in the Day of the Lord (2:1–17)

The report of a future invasion (2:1–11). The devastation of chapter 1 was still fresh in the people's minds when Joel called on the watchman to sound an alarm on his trumpet. The impending doom of the Day of the Lord was "close at hand." Joel described the invaders in language that brought back vivid memories of the past locust invasion. The soldiers, Joel said, will devour the land like a fire, come with a great noise, scale walls, and climb into houses without breaking ranks—just as locusts do! Even the sun and moon will be darkened at the approach of this army sent from God. Yet Joel also distinguished this invading horde from any previous army (including the swarms of locusts in chapter 1). No past or future army will match this one in its devastating effects. In chapter 3 Joel dropped the locust like language and stated clearly that the future invasion is an army of humans, not locusts.

The Day of the Lord was "close at hand" for Joel's readers in the same sense that the coming of Christ is "near" for believers in this age (Rev. 3:11; 22:7, 12, 20). Joel's point was *not* that the Day of the Lord had, in fact, arrived but that it was *near* in the sense that it was imminent and could come at anytime.

The call to repentance (2:12–17). Though the threatened invasion was near, God's people still had opportunity to return to Him. But God wanted genuine repentance ("rend your heart"), rather than a mere outward demonstration of humility ("not your garments"). The people could turn back to God because He was by His very nature "gracious and compassionate, slow to anger and abounding in love." Because of God's character, Joel urged everyone to fast and to assemble before God as the priests prayed for deliverance.

> *Sometimes God brings problems and difficulties into our lives to "get our attention" and to prod us to turn back to Him. We can return to the Lord with the assurance that He will hear— and forgive—if we willingly confess our sin (1 John 1:9).*

II. DELIVERANCE OF ISRAEL IN THE DAY OF THE LORD (2:18–3:21)

A. The Restoration of Israel in Joel's Day (2:18–27)

Joel's description of the nation's genuine heartfelt cry to God is the pivot on which the book turns. After the nation repents, "then the LORD will be jealous for his land and take pity on his people." Joel first pictured God removing the people's reproach by driving the invading locusts from the land. Some would be pushed into "the eastern sea" (the Dead Sea) and others into "the western sea" (the Mediterranean). God also promised to restore the land by providing autumn and spring rains. The rainy season in Israel normally extends from late November through early March. These rains are signs of God's blessing. Removing the locusts (a sign of His curse on Israel), God will replace them with the early and latter rains (a sign of His blessing on Israel).

From Judgment to Blessing

Beginning in Joel 2:18, Israel ceases to be the object of God's judgment and becomes instead the object of His blessing. In a similar reversal the hordes (locust and human) cease to be the instruments of God's judgment on Israel and become instead the objects of God's judgment. This reversal was originally foretold by God through Moses in Deuteronomy 30:1–9.

B. The Restoration of Israel in the Day of the Lord (2:28–3:21)

Beginning in 2:28 (3:1 in the Hebrew Bible) Joel moved from discussing the physical restoration of the land in his day to the subject of the spiritual restoration of the people in the Day of the Lord. God promised to pour out His Spirit on all the people. Throughout the Old Testament the Holy Spirit was given only to select individuals for special tasks. God put His Spirit on skilled craftsmen (Exod. 31:1–5), prophets (Mic. 3:8), and kings (1 Sam. 10:9–10; 16:13). God's Spirit could also leave individuals (1 Sam. 16:14; Ps. 51:11). But Joel pictured a day when "all people" would receive God's Spirit.

"Your sons and daughters" suggests no gender distinction, "your old men [and] your young men" suggest no age distinction, and "my servants" suggests no social distinction. This will happen in the Day of the Lord when God's supernatural signs fill the heavens (2:30; 3:14–16), and "everyone who calls on the name of the LORD will be saved." Peter quoted this passage in Acts 2 because (a) it related to the outpouring of God's Spirit (2:4, 15–16), (b) it stressed his theme of repentance (2:21, 37–39), and (c) it fit with his understanding that the Jews were about to enter the Day of the Lord, leading up to the return of Israel's Messiah, Jesus (1:6–8; 2:36; 3:19–21).

Judgment of the nations (3:1–17). When God restores Judah and Jerusalem, He will also judge those nations that have persecuted His people. Joel specifically mentioned Tyre and Sidon (chief cities of Phoenicia) and Philistia (3:4) as well as Egypt and Edom (3:19). The chief antagonists against Judah in the ninth century B.C., these nations represent all nations whom God will judge in this end-time event. Having announced *what* He will do (3:1–8), God then explained *how* He will accomplish it (3:9–17). The nations will prepare for battle ("beat your plowshares into swords") in the Valley of Jehoshaphat. This can be translated "the valley where the LORD judges" and is often associated with the Kidron Valley just to the east of Jerusalem. Just as the nations reach their military objective, with victory seemingly in sight, God will intervene to punish these invaders. Joel pictured God's judgment as a great harvest. The supernatural signs of that day will herald God's promised return to be a Refuge for His people.

The Final Battle against Jerusalem

The second coming of Jesus Christ will take place as the nations of the world gather to attack Jerusalem.

Daniel 11:45	The Antichrist will "come to his end" with his army camped "between the seas" (the Dead Sea and the Mediterranean Sea) "at the beautiful holy mountain" (Mount Zion).
Joel 3:10–14	The final battle will occur in "in the Valley of Jehoshaphat" as God intervenes to judge the nations who have gathered against Jerusalem.
Zechariah 14:2–8	When He returns, the Messiah will stand on the Mount of Olives, and He will help His people who are fighting against the armies gathered at Jerusalem.

The physical restoration of Israel (3:18–21). God's return in power and blessing will transform the land and the people. Dry wadis will be filled with water, and a unique fountain of water "will flow out of the LORD's house" to water the Judean wilderness. This living water, symbolizing the life-giving blessing and fertility that comes from the presence of God, is also described by two later prophets (Ezek. 47:1–12; Zech. 14:8). The land God had promised to His people "will be inhabited forever," fulfilling His promise to Abraham (Gen. 15:17–21). God also will forgive their sins. Joel began and ended this final section with a message of hope. Restoration and blessing will come when God "dwells in Zion" among His people (Joel 3:17, 21).

Forgiveness of sin and the indwelling of the Holy Spirit are two key benefits of the New Covenant (Jer. 31:31–34; Ezek. 36:24–30).

AMOS
Prepare to Meet Your God

AUTHOR

*T*HE AUTHOR OF THIS BOOK is simply named Amos, which
probably means "burden-bearer." Amos's hometown was Tekoa, a
city five miles southeast of Bethlehem on the edge of the Judean wilderness (1:1). Tekoa is situated in a marginally dry area to the east of the
central mountain ridge running north to south through Judah. However,
it was located along a relatively important road to Jerusalem from the
Dead Sea. Therefore King Rehoboam of Judah, who followed Solomon to
the throne, established Tekoa as a fortified city (2 Chron. 11:5–12).

Amos provided some biographical information about himself. He said
he was a shepherd (1:1) and a herdsman (7:14, NASB). Both cattle and
sheep would be common in the grazing land near Tekoa. Amos also said
he was a grower of sycamore figs (7:14, NASB). The word for grower should
more accurately be rendered "nipper." Sycamore figs are not true figs but
are a tree of the mulberry family, which produces figlike fruit. Each fruit
must be scratched or pierced to let the juice flow out so the "fig" can
ripen. Sycamore fig trees need a lot of water and do not grow in the region of Tekoa. They do grow, however, in the Shephelah (the coastal plain)
and the Jordan Valley. So Amos traveled to one of these locations, possibly Jericho, to carry on this sideline occupation.

Amos affirmed that he was "neither a prophet nor a prophet's son" (7:14). The terms "son of a prophet" and "sons of the prophets" were used at that time to identify a group of disciples or followers who were attached to a prophet (2 Kings 2:3; 4:1, 38; 5:22). Rather than being a professional prophet or a member of the prophetic guild who earned his living through prophesying, Amos was a "layman" called by God to deliver His message to the people of Israel.

DATE

Amos said that he received his message "two years before the earthquake, when Uzziah was king of Judah and Jeroboam son of Jehoash was king of Israel" (1:1). Uzziah reigned in Judah 790–739 B.C., and Jeroboam II ruled Israel 793–755 B.C. Thus Amos's prophecy can be dated between 790 and 755 B.C. The earthquake mentioned by Amos was evidently so severe it could be used as a chronological marker. Zechariah mentioned the same earthquake two hundred years later (Zech. 14:5). Archaeologists have found evidence of a major earthquake about 760–755 B.C. It is reasonable to date Amos's prophetic activity about the same time. Since Amos stated that his prophecy was received (and delivered) two years *before* the earthquake, one can assume he recorded his message sometime *after* the earthquake.

BACKGROUND

Amos delivered his message at a time when the Northern Kingdom of Israel was strong militarily and economically. Jeroboam II ruled for almost four decades, an unprecedented period of stability and prosperity. Unfortunately he also presided over a time of unparalleled greed, immorality, and idolatry. The wealthy preyed on the poor, and injustice abounded. God sent Amos from Judah to deliver His message of judgment to a nation that seemed invincible but was rotting spiritually.

ADDRESSEES

Amos's primary audience was Israel (1:1; 2:6), the ten tribes of the Northern Kingdom. He addressed specific messages of judgment to the women of Samaria (4:1) and the "Israelites," literally, the "sons of Israel" (4:5). He also prophesied against Jeroboam's family (7:9) and against Amaziah, the priest at Bethel (7:14–17).

Amos also delivered God's message of judgment against surrounding gentile nations, including Damascus, Gaza, Tyre, Edom, Ammon, and Moab (1:3–2:3). However, while Amos's messages were spoken *against* these nations, he spoke the words *to* the people of Israel. They were still his primary audience.

Amos also spoke against the Southern Kingdom of Judah (2:4–5). He delivered a message of woe to those who were "complacent in Zion," that is, in Jerusalem. And at the end of the book Amos gave a message of hope, announcing that God would someday "restore David's fallen tent." His image is of the Davidic monarchy, torn apart after the death of Solomon, again being repaired and reunited as a single kingdom in the coming messianic age.

PURPOSE

Amos's purpose in writing was to pronounce God's judgment on Israel's sin. Through a series of messages and visions Amos exposed the social and moral degeneration of Israel, and he warned of the impending judgment God was about to bring. The Israelites needed to prepare to meet their God, who was coming to judge the nation. Amos 5:24 expresses the central theme of the book—God was looking for *justice* (our relationship to each other) and *righteousness* (our relationship to God).

OUTLINE

I. Eight Prophecies of Judgment (chapters 1–2)
   A. Introduction (1:1–2)
   B. Judgment on Damascus (1:3–5)

C. Judgment on Philistia (1:6–8)

D. Judgment on Phoenicia (1:9–10)

E. Judgment on Edom (1:11–12)

F. Judgment on Ammon (1:13–15)

G. Judgment on Moab (2:1–3)

H. Judgment on Judah (2:4–5)

I. Judgment on Israel (2:6–16)

II. Three Messages of Judgment (chapters 3–6)

A. Destruction of Israel (chapter 3)

B. Depravity of Israel (chapter 4)

C. Dirge over Israel and Woe against Apostasy (chapter 5)

D. Woe against Complacency (chapter 6)

III. Five Visions of Judgment on Israel (chapters 7–9)

A. Visions of Locusts, Fire, and a Plumb Line (chapter 7)

B. Vision of the Basket of Ripe Fruit (chapter 8)

C. Vision of God's Coming and Israel's Future Restoration (chapter 9)

I. EIGHT PROPHECIES OF JUDGMENT (CHAPTERS 1–2)

How does one go about delivering an unpopular message to a hostile audience? Amos solved this problem by beginning with a series of messages describing God's judgment on Israel's *enemies*. As God judged each nation for the "three sins . . . even for four" (a poetic way to describe their "many" sins), the people of Israel must have applauded Amos and acknowledged him as a true prophet from God. Once he had their full attention, Amos thrust home the dagger of God's judgment as he announced that God would also judge *Israel* for "three sins . . . even for four."

Amos's Use of Repetition in Chapters 1–2

- Introduction to each message:
  "For three sins . . . even for four, I will not turn back my wrath."
- Reason for God's judgment:
  "Because they ______, I will _____."
- Imagery of God's judgment:
  "I will send fire upon _____."

Amos's Pattern of Judgment against the Nations (1:3–15)

DAMASCUS	Threshed Gilead	To be exiled				
PHILISTIA		Exiled an entire population	Exiled an entire population to Edom			
PHOENICIA			Exiled an entire population to Edom	Broke a covenant of brotherhood		
EDOM					Pursued his brother	Used the sword (against his brother)
AMMON						Used the sword against pregnant women of Gilead

A. Introduction (1:1–2)

Amos, a shepherd and cattleman from Tekoa, faithfully delivered God's message two years before the earthquake that occurred during the reign of King Uzziah (see also Zech. 14:5). Much like the "roar" heard from a lion before it pounces on his prey, God was speaking through His prophet before descending in judgment on Israel. But when God's judgment came, it would be felt by all—from the weak and lowly ("pastures of the shepherds") to the strong and proud ("the top of Carmel").

B. Judgment on Damascus (1:3–5)

Amos's first message of judgment was against Damascus, northeast of Israel. Though Damascus had committed multiple offenses ("for three sins . . . even for four"), God singled out her attack against the land of Gilead east of the Jordan River. Like the sharp, iron teeth of a threshing sledge slicing through thin stalks of grain, Damascus had "threshed Gilead." So God would send the people of Damascus into exile for their sin against Israel.

C. Judgment on Philistia (1:6–8)

Amos's second message was against Gaza and the coastal land of the Philistines, southwest of Israel. The Philistines had captured entire communities of Israelites and sold them as slaves to Edom. Amos prophesied that God would fight against Philistia until all the Philistines were killed. Amos specifically named four of the five major cities in Philistia. Only Gath was unnamed, perhaps because the city had already fallen to Judah.

D. Judgment on Phoenicia (1:9–10)

Amos directed his third message of judgment against Tyre (chief city of Phoenicia), northwest of Israel. Like the Philistines, the people of Tyre had "sold whole communities of captives to Edom." In doing so they had ignored "a covenant of brotherhood (NASB)" between Israel and Phoenicia.

So the Phoenicians would be destroyed for breaking this pact of friend-ship. The "covenant of brotherhood" could refer to a treaty made between Solomon and Hiram, king of Tyre: "There were peaceful relations be-tween Hiram and Solomon, and the two of them made a treaty" (1 Kings 5:12). Or it could refer to a treaty between Israel and Phoenicia that had been sealed with the marriage of Jezebel daughter of Ethbaal king of the Sidonians to King Ahab of Israel (16:30–31).

E. Judgment on Edom (1:11–12)

The fourth message focused on the sin of Edom located to Israel's south-east. By purchasing Israelite slaves from the Philistines and the Phoenicians (1:6, 9), the Edomites had "pursued [their] brother with a sword." (Israel and Edom were "brother" nations in the sense that they were both de-scendants of Isaac; Gen. 25:22–34). Moses had told Israel not to despise an Edomite because "he is your brother" (Deut. 23:7). "Stifling all com-passion," Edom went after Israel, seeking to harm the people of God for their own material gain. Edom would be destroyed, God said, because of her evil deeds against Israel (see also the Book of Obadiah).

F. Judgment on Ammon (1:13–15)

Like the people of Damascus, the Ammonites also coveted the rich land of Gilead east of the Jordan River. To extend their territory, the soldiers of Ammon engaged in brutal slaughter and even "ripped open the pregnant women of Gilead." God promised to destroy Rabbah, Ammon's capital (which is modern-day Amman, Jordan), and to send her king and offi-cials into exile.

G. Judgment on Moab (2:1–3)

The prophet's sixth message singled out the country of Moab along the eastern edge of the Dead Sea. This section would be judged because they had "burned, as if to lime, the bones of Edom's king." To desecrate a tomb was a heinous crime that affected the deceased and his entire family. Moab showed wanton disregard for this most basic standard of civility; and in violating the honor of Edom's king they had also offended Israel, Edom's "brother." God threatened to judge Moab's ruler and her officials with him for their sin.

H. Judgment on Judah (2:4–5)

God judged all the previous nations based on their treatment of others, especially His people. But God held Judah to a higher standard because they had His Word. He would judge Judah "because they have rejected the law of the LORD." By turning to idols they violated His law. As a result God would destroy the fortresses of Jerusalem. This, of course, was fulfilled two hundred years later when Nebuchadnezzar conquered Jerusalem in 586 B.C.

I. Judgment on Israel (2:6–16)

Having begun with Israel's enemies, Amos circled the land until his coil of condemnation finally arrived at Israel. Israel was guilty of social injustice (they "deny justice to the oppressed"), sexual immorality ("father and son use the same girl"), and religious hypocrisy (they "lie down beside every altar on garments taken in pledge"; see Exod. 22:26–27). They had also forgotten God's past deeds on their behalf as He led them out of Egypt and gave them Canaan, "the land of the Amorites." When God sent prophets or Nazirites to be His witness, Israel tried to corrupt the Nazirites by making them drink wine (see Num. 6:1–4), and they ordered the prophets to quit prophesying. Because of their persistent pattern of sin, God affirmed His plan to crush them "as a wagon is weighted down when filled with sheaves" (Amos 2:13, NASB).

II. THREE MESSAGES OF JUDGMENT (CHAPTERS 3–6)

After his initial messages Amos spoke directly to the people of Israel. In a series of three sermons he stressed their coming judgment because of sin. Each message begins with the phrase "Hear this word" (3:1; 4:1; 5:1), as he challenged the people to listen to the Lord's words. Midway through each message he stressed the consequences of their sin. Beginning with "Therefore," God announced what He would do because of their behavior. Amos ended this section by pronouncing two woes on the people. The first was directed at those who naively longed for the Day of the Lord, not realizing that it would bring them judgment rather than deliverance. The second woe was directed at complacent people in Zion who allowed their material wealth to blind them to the desperate needs of the nation.

A. Destruction of Israel (chapter 3)

The nation's sin (3:1–10). Israel's sin was heightened because of her position before God. God had specifically chosen Israel, and with that privilege came great responsibility. Amos asked a series of questions designed to remind his audience that all effects must have a cause. Just as a bird does not go into a trap when no snare has been set, even so "when disaster comes to a city, has not the LORD caused it?" God does not bring such calamity "without revealing his plan to his servants the prophets" (like Amos). His main points are (a) Amos *is* a prophet, (b) God *has* spoken, and (c) God *will* bring His judgment against Israel. All this would come to pass because the people did "not know how to do right."

> *To whom much is given, much is required (Luke 12:48).*

The nation's judgment (3:11–15). Amos's message was direct and detailed: An enemy would invade the land, and only a few people would remain. It would be as if a lion had attacked a sheep, and the shepherd was able to save only the sheep's "two leg bones or a piece of an ear." God would destroy Israel's religious shrines, including the sanctuary at Bethel (see 1 Kings 12:28–29) as well as the magnificent "houses adorned with ivory" built by the wealthy of Samaria.

B. Depravity of Israel (chapter 4)

Amos's second message focused on the stubborn sinfulness of the people. The women cared only for their material needs, and the men boasted about their spirituality while refusing to submit to God.

Depravity of the women (4:1–3). Amos compared the women of Samaria to cattle grazing in the region of Bashan. Bashan was the fertile highlands northeast of Gilead known for its fat, well-fed cattle (see Ps. 22:12, "strong bulls of Bashan"). These women were willing to oppress poor and needy fellow Israelites to satisfy their own material greed. As a result they would be taken away into captivity with "hooks." These wealthy women acted like fat cows, and so that was how they would be treated by their captors, who would lead them into exile.

Carved reliefs have been discovered that show Assyrians leading captives by a rope attached to a hook placed through their jaw or lip.

Depravity of the men (4:4–11). Amos then addressed Israelite men and chastised them for their religious apostasy and hypocrisy. Bethel and Gilgal were religious centers. In an ironic twist Amos called on the men of Israel to go to Bethel and "sin" or to go to Gilgal and "sin yet more." What they boasted about as religious devotion, God saw as sin. Their zealous so-called worship masked an underlying spiritual insensitivity. Though God repeatedly sent His threatened judgments to prompt them to repent, they refused to do so.

The Covenant Curses and Israel's Response

God's covenant curses on Israel:

- Amos 4:6   Famine (Deut. 28:17–18)
- Amos 4:7–8   Drought (Deut. 28:23–24)
- Amos 4:9   Wind, mildew, caterpillar (locust) (Deut. 28:38–39, 42)

- Amos 4:10   Plague and warfare (Deut. 28:25–27, 60–61)
- Amos 4:11   Near destruction (Deut. 28:62)

Israel's response:
- "'Yet you have not returned to me,' declares the LORD" (Amos 4:6, 8–11).

God's coming in judgment (4:12–13). The consequences of Israel's disobedience were catastrophic. The people had rejected God's ever-increasing warnings. Now they would face God Himself: "Prepare to meet your God, O Israel." When God came in judgment, the people would finally understand that He is "the LORD God Almighty." From this point on, Amos stressed two key themes: the coming of God in judgment and the covenant name of God (namely, "LORD," or Yahweh). The LORD was coming to bring the final curse of the covenant (expulsion from the land) because Israel had refused to respond to His earlier warnings.

C. Dirge over Israel and Woe against Apostasy (chapter 5)

God's coming in judgment was so certain that Amos could sing a "lament" for Israel. A lament was a funeral poem or song written and recited for someone who had just died (see 2 Sam. 1:17–27). The song usually emphasized the good qualities of the departed and the loss felt by those mourning his or her death. Israel's "death" was so certain that Amos could already compose the nation's funeral dirge. The entire song was arranged by Amos as an extended chiasm, a pattern of Hebrew parallelism in which the first and last statements are similar, the second and next-to-last statements are similar, and so on throughout the work. At the end of the song Amos began the first of his two woes (pronouncements of judgment) against the people, focusing first on their religious apostasy (Amos 5:18–27).

Chiasm in Amos's Lament over Israel (Amos 5:1–17)

Amos composed his funeral lament for Israel as an extended chiasm. The center of the chiasm pointed Israel to the Lord, who had just announced He was coming in judgment (4:12–13).

   A. Mourning because of God's judgment (5:1–3)
      B. Seek the Lord (5:4–6)
         C. Justice is perverted (5:7)
            D. God acts in judgment over nature (5:8a–c)
               E. "The Lord is his name" (5:8d)
            D.' God acts in judgment over man (5:9)
         C.' Justice is perverted (5:10–13)
      B.' Seek good, not evil (5:14–15)
   A.' Mourning because of God's judgment (5:16–17)

Mourning over Israel's fall (5:1–17). Amos began and ended his lament with a statement of mourning because of God's impending judgment. He pictured Israel as a "fallen . . . virgin," and he foresaw the people's anguish when God would judge them. Israel needed to "seek the Lord and live"; its only hope was to turn to Him. Amos emphasized this by using another chiasm (see next page). Repentance was necessary because in their willingness to receive bribes the powerful had deprived the poor of justice in the courts. God displayed His power in creating the Pleiades and Orion (two bright constellations in the winter sky) and in bringing rainstorms. He now threatened to use that same power to destroy Israel.

Chiasm in Amos's Call to Seek the Lord (Amos 5:4–6)

In this chiasm the focus is on the beginning and end rather than on the center. Amos called on the people of Israel to seek God, not idols, if they hoped to be delivered from judgment.

  A. Seek Me and live;
      B. Do not seek Bethel,
          C. Do not go to Gilgal,
              D. Do not journey to Beersheba.
          C.' For Gilgal will surely go into exile,
      B.' And Bethel will be reduced to nothing.
  A.' Seek the Lord and live.

Woe against apostasy (5:18–27). Amos directed the first of his two woes against those in Israel who wanted the Day of the Lord to come. These people mistakenly thought the Day of the Lord was only a time when God would bless Israel and judge her enemies. However, the Day of the Lord was any day when God would come to settle accounts, and Israel was on the wrong side of God's ledger of justice. When God would bring His day of reckoning against Israel, it would be a time of darkness. It would be like someone running from a lion and being met by a bear. If by some miracle he escaped again and made it to his house, he would be bitten by a snake there. Their religious feasts were filled with sacrifices but were devoid of true worship. What God really wanted was justice and righteousness.

Justice relates to our treatment of each other, while righteousness focuses on our walk before God. These two concepts summarize the Mosaic Law (Matt. 22:34–40).

D. Woe against Complacency (chapter 6)

The complacency of the people (6:1–7). Amos pronounced his second woe against those who were "complacent in Zion" and those "who feel secure on Mount Samaria." In both capital cities were leaders to whom others came for advice. Yet these men failed to heed the lessons of other cities and countries God had allowed to fall. Instead, these leaders reclined on "beds inlaid with ivory," dined "on choice lambs," played on their "harps like David," and drank "wine by the bowlful." These were all outward signs of great wealth and luxury, and yet God did not condemn them for having material possessions. However, He did condemn them for being consumed with their own personal wealth while much of the nation suffered great poverty and hardship because of injustice and corruption. These individuals were so absorbed in their own luxury that they did not grieve over "the ruin of Joseph" (that is, Israel's impending social, moral, and politican collapse). Therefore these men of luxury would be "among the first to go into exile."

Material possessions by themselves are not evil, but the love of money is the root of all kinds of evil (see 1 Tim. 6:9–10; James 5:1–6).

The judgment of God (6:8–14). Identifying Israel's underlying sin as pride, God said that He abhorred and detested her arrogance. He pictured a coming time of judgment when the few remaining survivors would be afraid even to mention the Lord's name because of His wrath. One does not run "horses . . . on the rocky crags" or "plow there with oxen," because to do so would destroy both the horse and the plow. But the people of Israel "turned justice into poison" and yet somehow thought they could avoid God's judgment. In their deluded pride they rejoiced in the conquest of Lo Debar, which in Hebrew literally means "no word, nothing." The name of the city was probably Debir (Josh. 13:26; 2 Sam. 17:27). They also claimed to have captured Karnaim by their own strength. Karnaim comes from the Hebrew *qeren,* which means an animal horn. A horn was a symbol of power and strength. The play on words is as follows: "By our own strength we have taken the city of strength." God responded to this foolish pride by announcing He would have a nation attack and oppress all of Israel.

III. FIVE VISIONS OF JUDGMENT (CHAPTERS 7–9)

A. Visions of Locusts, Fire, and a Plumb Line (chapter 7)

Overview. The first two visions focus more on Amos than on the people of Israel. This "stern" prophet had a tender heart as he pleaded with the Lord on behalf of Israel. God twice spared the people in response to Amos's prayers, but in the third vision God reminded Amos that mercy had to be balanced with justice. If the people refused to repent, God could no longer withhold His judgment. As if to illustrate Israel's lack of repentance, Amos inserted his encounter with Amaziah, the head priest at Bethel. Through this conflict Amos realized that the leaders (and the people) would not repent.

Vision of the locusts (7:1–3). In the first vision Amos saw the Lord preparing swarms of locusts to send against the land of Israel (see also Joel 1:6–12) "just as the second crop was coming up." The king had taken his share of the crop, but the people had not yet gathered the grain needed to sustain them through the next year. Amos fervently prayed that the Lord would forgive Israel. God responded to Amos's intercession and promised, "This will not happen."

> *The fervent prayers of a righteous individual can alter the events of history (James 5:16—18).*

Vision of the fire (7:4–6). The second vision was similar to the first in that Amos saw the Lord preparing to send judgment on Israel. This time God planned to send judgment by fire. While fire was used as a symbol of military conquest (1:4, 7, 10, 12, 14; 2:2, 5), in this specific passage it seems best to take the message literally. God threatened to bring a great drought and subsequent fire that would burn its way across the land (see also Joel 1:19–20). Amos again called on the Lord to withhold His judgment. God again "relented" in response to Amos's prayer, and Israel was spared from this devastating fire.

Vision of the plumb line (7:7–9). The third vision did not directly picture God's threatened judgment. Instead, God had Amos take note of a plumb line, which is used to determine if a wall is truly vertical. It set the standard against which a wall or other vertical structure was measured. God's plumb line was composed of the righteous standards of His Law. They were the absolutes by which the nation was to be measured. And if the nation was "out of plumb," the religious establishment ("high places" and "sanctuaries") and the civil government ("the house of Jeroboam") would be judged.

Opposition of Amaziah (7:10–17). Amos inserted here the account of Amaziah's opposition in the middle of his five visions. The account was placed here to illustrate the truth of the third vision. How far "out of plumb" was the nation of Israel? The actions of Amaziah showed how evil Israel had become. Amaziah urged Jeroboam to silence Amos. He misquoted Amos by saying the prophet predicted the death of Jeroboam "by the sword" (see 7:9 and 7:11). Amaziah also tried to intimidate Amos into leaving Israel and returning to Judah: "Get out, you seer! Go back to the land of Judah." Defending his call from God, Amos delivered a message from the Lord to Amaziah. Because Amaziah actively opposed the word of the Lord, he would live to see his wife become a prostitute, his children killed by the sword, and his land divided up. Amaziah himself would be taken into exile, where he would die. Amos finally grasped the severity of Israel's sin, because instead of pleading for God's mercy, he acknowledged that Israel would certainly go into exile.

B. Vision of the Basket of Ripe Fruit (chapter 8)

Amos's fourth vision stressed the imminence of God's judgment on Israel. The time for mercy was past; the time for judgment had arrived.

Judgment on the people (8:1–10). God showed Amos a basket of ripe fruit. The word for ripe fruit is *qāyis*, which means "ripened fruit" or summer fruit. The word is related to the Hebrew word *qēs* which can be translated "ripe" or "end." In this play on words Amos saw "ripe" fruit because the time was ripe for God to judge His people. Just as the final fruit of the summer signaled the end of the harvest season, so God's "end" for Israel was now at hand. God would judge the religious hypocrisy and greed of the people. "I will never forget anything they have done."

Nothing New under the Sun!

Amos's description of the merchant's greed and deception is as current as today's business environment. Then, as now, the watchword was "Buyer, beware!"

Phrase	Meaning
"Skimping the measure"	Making the container smaller to hold less wheat
"Boosting the price"	Making the shekel weight larger so that the buyer had to pay more
"Cheating with dishonest scales"	Modifying the scales to trick the buyer into paying more
"Selling even the sweepings with the wheat"	Including chaff with wheat to give the buyer less for his or her money

Famine of God's word (8:11–14). A famine would occur—but it would not be a physical famine of food or lack of water. Instead it would be a famine "of hearing the words of the LORD." Israel rejected God's message spoken through Amos, but in the coming day of distress the people would wander through the land, "searching for the word of the LORD." However, their search would be in vain, because God would not send them a prophetic word in that time of calamity. Those who depended on the false gods of Israel rather than listening to the word of the Lord would fall.

C. Vision of God's Coming and Israel's Future Restoration (chapter 9)

God's arrival to judge His people (9:1–10). As the final vision began, Amos saw the LORD standing by the altar, probably the altar at Bethel (3:14; 7:9–13). As God stood before the worshipers, the temple thresholds shook, and the temple roof collapsed. This was fulfilled two years later when the great earthquake in the days of Uzziah took place (1:1). But the earthquake was only the beginning of the series of judgments God would bring on His people (see 5:18–20). Using a series of opposites, God showed the impossibility of escape. The grave was not deep enough, nor was heaven high enough to escape. They could find no hiding place on the rugged heights of Mount Carmel, nor could they hide from God at the ocean bottom. God threatened to search out and destroy all His enemies, no matter where they tried to hide. And when they finally came face to face with God, the people would realize "the LORD is his name" (see also 4:12–13; 5:8, 17, 27). God would "shake the house of Israel among the nations," picturing the final curse of the covenant—national exile (Lev. 26:33; Deut. 28:64).

Imagery of the Earthquake in Amos	
1:1	Amos delivered his message "two years before the earthquake."
6:11	The Lord "will smash the great house into pieces and the small house into bits."
7:9	The "high places . . . will be destroyed and the sanctuaries . . . will be ruined."
8:3	"Many, many bodies—flung everywhere! Silence!"
8:7–8	The land will "rise" and "sink" like the Nile.
9:1	"Strike the tops of the pillars so that the thresholds shake. Bring them down on the heads of all the people."
9:5	The land will "rise" and "sink" like the Nile.

God's promise to restore His people (9:11–15). Virtually all of Amos is a message of judgment. Yet Amos, like the other prophets, did look forward to a time of national blessing when God will one day fulfill His covenant promises with Israel. God's restoring "David's fallen tent" is an allusion to His restoration of a united kingdom of Israel under the rule of David's descendant, the Messiah (see also Jer. 30:3, 9; Ezek. 34:24; 37:21–25; Hos. 3:5). God said this will be a time of unparalleled prosperity and peace. The grain harvest will be so abundant that the reaper will be overtaken by the plowman. That is, it will be time to plant before the workers can finish harvesting all of last year's crop! God will restore the exiles to "rebuild" their cities and "plant" their crops. God then gave a dramatic announcement: During this messianic age He will "plant Israel in their own land," and they will "never again . . . be uprooted." That is when all His promises to Israel will be fulfilled.

> God's promises for the future are anchor points to keep us stable, and to give us hope in times of personal distress and difficulty. The more we understand what God has promised for the future, the more we can endure our problems today.

OBADIAH
God's Judgment on the Pride of Edom

AUTHOR

$\mathcal{T}$HE NAME OBADIAH, which means "Servant of Yahweh," was common in Old Testament times and is used in the Bible of about a dozen individuals (1 Kings 18:3–16; 1 Chron. 3:21; 7:3; 8:38; 9:16; 12:9; 27:19; 2 Chron. 17:7; 34:12; Ezra 8:9; Neh. 10:5; 12:25). Thus there is no compelling reason to understand Obadiah as anything other than the prophet's personal name. Apart from his name, nothing is known about this prophet except for the fact that he seems to be associated with the kingdom of Judah (Obad. 11–12, 17, 20–21).

DATE

Two major dates have been advanced for the writing of the Book of Obadiah. The first is about 845 B.C. during the reign of King Jehoram, and the second is sometime after 586 B.C., following Jerusalem's fall to Babylon. While the evidence is divided, the early date seems more consistent with the internal evidence of the book. If this is the case, Obadiah was a contemporary of the prophets Elijah and Elisha, who were prophesying in Israel about that time.

Four facts point to the early date. First, the events described by Obadiah fit more naturally with the revolt of Edom against Judah and the Philistine and Arabian attack against Judah and Jerusalem in King Jehoram's day (2 Kings 8:20–22; 2 Chron. 21:8–17). Judah's enemies in the book are Edom and the Philistines (Obad. 19), not Babylon. Second, Jeremiah may have borrowed from Obadiah's prophecy (see Jer. 49:7–22), suggesting that Obadiah would have been written before the time of Jeremiah's prophecy. Third, in 586 B.C. the Jews were deported to Babylon. But Obadiah 20 speaks of the exiles' deportation to Zerephath and Sepharad (Sardis) to the west, not Babylon to the east. Fourth, the words "as the LORD has said" in Joel 2:32 strongly suggest that Joel was quoting from Obadiah.

BACKGROUND

Jehoram reigned over Judah from 853 to 841 B.C. The attack that prompted Obadiah's prophecy was the Philistine/Arab sack of Jerusalem, which occurred shortly after Edom revolted against Judah (2 Chron. 21:8–10, 16–17). Second Chronicles also states that *after* this attack Jehoram was inflicted with a two-year illness, which ultimately led to his death (21:18–19). Thus the Philistine/Arab attack occurred sometime between 848 and 843 B.C. Jehoram "walked in the ways of the kings of Israel, as the house of Ahab had done. . . . He did evil in the eyes of the LORD" (2 Kings 8:18). He was influenced by his wife, a daughter of Ahab and Jezebel (8:18, 27). He promoted idolatry in Judah and tried to import Baal worship into the Southern Kingdom (2 Chron. 18:11–13). Elijah and Elisha were ministering in Israel during his reign, and Elijah wrote a letter to Jehoram, denouncing his sin (21:12–15).

ADDRESSEES

Obadiah wrote his prophecy *about* Edom, but he wrote and delivered the message *to* Judah. Though his words speak of judgment on Edom, the prophecy was intended as a message of hope to the beleaguered nation of Judah.

PURPOSE

The purpose of the Book of Obadiah was to announce the destruction of Edom because of her pride and sin against Judah. The prophet also sought to comfort Judah by announcing Edom's destruction and Judah's restoration and deliverance in the Day of the Lord. Edom symbolized all the nations that opposed God's plans and oppressed God's people.

History of Conflict between Edom and Israel during the Monarchy

- Edom was captured by David, who stationed a garrison there and made it a vassal state (1 Chron. 18:12–13).
- Solomon developed the port of Elath (1 Kings 9:26–28).
- Opposition to Solomon arose in Edom. Hadad, of the royal family of Edom, set up a "government in exile" in Egypt (11:14–17).
- Judah still controlled the land at the time of King Jehoshaphat, who had a governor posted there (22:47–48).
- Edom gained her freedom from Judah about 845 B.C. by rebelling against Jehoram, son of Jehoshaphat (2 Kings 8:20–22; 2 Chron. 21:8–10, 16–17).
- Edom was partially recaptured by King Amaziah of Judah between 790 and 770 B.C. (2 Kings 14:7).
- The port of Elath was recaptured by Uzziah, also known as Azariah (14:21–22).
- Elath was later taken from Judah by Aram (Syria) (16:5–6).
- In the reign of King Ahaz the Edomites revolted and attacked Judah a second time (2 Chron. 28:17).
- The Edomites aided the Babylonians' assaults on Judah (Ps. 137:7; Jer. 49:7–22; Ezek. 25:12–14; 35:1–15).

OUTLINE

I. The Destruction of Edom (vv. 1–14)
  A. The Inevitability of Destruction (vv. 1–9)
  B. The Reasons for Destruction (vv. 10–14)
II. The Day of the Lord (vv. 15–21)
  A. God's Judgment on the Nations (vv. 15–16)
  B. God's Deliverance of Israel (vv. 17–21)

I. THE DESTRUCTION OF EDOM (VV. 1–14)

Obadiah stood among Jerusalem's ragged remnant following its defeat and humiliation at the hand of foreigners. The prophet encouraged those survivors by announcing that God would judge the nation that caused such misery. God stated that He was already at work summoning His army for an attack against Edom. In the first half of the book (vv. 1–14) Obadiah stressed the what and the why of Edom's destruction. *What:* God vowed He would destroy the Edomites. *Why:* He would bring this destruction because of Edom's mistreatment of the people of Judah and Jerusalem.

A. *The Inevitability of Destruction (vv. 1–9)*

With the nation securely protected (by living "in the clefts of the rocks"), the people of Edom felt invincible. They boasted, "Who can bring me down to the ground?" God announced that He would be the One who would destroy them. His judgment would be more complete than robbers and more thorough than grape pickers during harvest. Ironically the "wise men of Edom" would be deceived by those they considered "allies" and "friends."

Pride deceives and leads to sin.

B. *The Reasons for Destruction (vv. 10–14)*

God said He would judge Edom because of her violence against her "brother Jacob." The Edomites were descendants of Esau and were a "brother" nation to the Israelites who descended from Esau's brother, Jacob. Obadiah identified four ways Edom had sinned against Judah: (a) They had "stood aloof" and refused to help when Judah was attacked (v. 11), (b) they gloated over Judah's misfortune ("look down on your brother") and boasted over Jerusalem's troubles (v. 12), (c) like vicious looters they came through the gates to seize the people's wealth (v. 13), and (d) waiting "at the crossroads" for Judah's refugees, they killed ("cut down") some and handed over others—probably to be sold into slavery (v. 14). Ten times in verses 11–14 Obadiah used the word "day" to stress Judah's time of troubles when Edom caused such grief and heartache.

> *Sin against a "brother" was a heinous crime as old as Abel (Gen. 4:1–12). In Deuteronomy 23:7 God told Israel, "You shall not detest an Edomite, for he is your brother" (NASB).*

II. THE DAY OF THE LORD (VV. 15–21)

Obadiah developed and expanded three key themes from the first 14 verses. God's judgment against Edom was expanded to God's judgment against "all nations" (v. 15); Judah's day of trouble (vv. 11–14) now became the universal "day of the LORD"; and God's judgment against Judah in the first half of the book is replaced with God's deliverance and restoration of Judah in the last half. The fortunes of Judah—and the gentile nations—will be reversed in the coming Day of the Lord.

A. God's Judgment on the Nations (vv. 15–16)

Edom symbolized all nations that had attacked and persecuted the people of Israel. God announced to those nations: "As you have done, it will be done to you" (v. 15). Their treatment of God's people would determine how He would treat them. Just as these enemies "drank on my holy hill" (profaning God's temple), so God said He would make them "drink continually" from His cup of judgment.

> *God's standard of judgment for the nations is ultimately based on His original promise to Abraham: "I will bless those who bless you, and whoever curses you I will curse" (Gen. 12:3).*

B. God's Deliverance of Israel (vv. 17–21)

While the nations could expect only judgment for their wicked deeds, the people of Judah could look forward to God's deliverance. The temple mount will again be holy, and the nation of Israel will once more possess its land. God's people will experience deliverance and blessing, whereas no Edomite will survive. Edom had forced Judah from the Negev, so God said that Judah will "occupy the mountain of Esau." The Philistines had pushed Judah from the foothills, so God said that Judah will "possess the land of the Philistines." Those taken from the land as exiles will return and again worship the Lord on Mount Zion. Obadiah concluded with God's promised outcome for His people. All He has promised will be fulfilled because "the kingdom will be the LORD's."

> *God's goal in history is the establishment of His kingdom. For Israel this will include the return of the people, the possession of the land, the judgment on Israel's enemies, and the restoration of the kingdom in holiness.*

JONAH
God's Concern for the Gentiles

AUTHOR

*T*HE BOOK OF JONAH is named for its author and principal character—Jonah son of Amittai (Jon. 1:1). Jonah recorded little about himself in the book except the name of his father. However, a reference to Jonah in 2 Kings 14:25 provides additional information. Jonah was from the village of Gath Hepher, a small town in the Northern Kingdom of Israel, just north of Nazareth. Jonah lived and prophesied during the reign of Jeroboam II, who ruled in Israel from 793 to 753 B.C.

DATE

The book does not provide a specific chronological indicator apart from stating that the events took place in Jonah's lifetime. Many critical scholars have dated the Book of Jonah to the postexilic period because of the ministry to Gentiles presented in the book. However, there is no compelling evidence for this position. It is better to accept the historical tradition that Jonah himself was the author and that he wrote the book sometime after the events actually took place. A date of sometime between 770 and 750 B.C. would not be too far from wrong.

BACKGROUND

The city of Nineveh was founded by Nimrod, who built it after the Lord scattered all humanity at the Tower of Babel (Gen. 10:8–11; 11:5–9). At the time of Jonah, the city of Nineveh was not yet the capital of the Assyrian Empire. However, it was still considered one of the most significant Assyrian cities. In the reign of Sargon II (721–705 B.C.) it became one of the capitals of Assyria; and by the time of his son, Sennacherib (705–681 B.C.), it was the sole capital. Sennacherib was murdered in Nineveh by his sons (2 Kings 19:36–37; Isa. 37:37–38).

The Northern Kingdom saw the threat posed by Assyria long before the time of Jonah. In 853 B.C. King Ahab of Israel joined in an alliance of twelve kings, who fought against Shalmaneser I of Assyria at the battle of Qarqar. This, though not mentioned in the Bible, temporarily blunted the Assyrian advance.

Just over seventy-five years later, several events heightened Assyria's threat to Israel. In 782 B.C. Jeroboam II became sole ruler in Israel. (He had reigned as coruler with his father, Jehoash, from 793 to 782.) Jeroboam led Israel in a series of military victories that expanded the nation's borders. He eventually took control of Syria, Moab, and Ammon. He was helped in part by the Assyrians, who had weakened the Syrians by attacking Damascus in 773 and 772 B.C. Under Jeroboam II Israel became a recognized power in the Middle East, and the northeastern edge of the empire now rubbed against the western edge of the Assyrian Empire. Conflict was inevitable.

ADDRESSEES

Jonah's audience for his initial prophetic message was the people of Nineveh: "Go to the great city of Nineveh and preach against it." However, the written message was for Israel and Judah, not Nineveh. That is, the readers of the book were Israelites who, in their nationalistic zeal, forgot that God had called them to be His conduit of blessing to the Gentiles (see Gen. 12:3; Isa. 42:6; 49:6).

PURPOSE

Jonah's purpose in writing was to show Israel God's concern for the nations of the world. Israel was to be God's light to the world and the mediator of God's blessing to the Gentiles. The lessons the Lord taught Jonah needed to be heard by all Israel.

OUTLINE

I. Jonah's Disobedience: Jonah in the Boat (chapter 1)
    A. God's Command (1:1–2)
    B. Jonah's Response (1:3)
    C. God's Judgment (1:4–17)
II. Jonah's Prayer: Jonah in the Fish (chapter 2)
    A. Jonah's Lament (2:1–9)
    B. God's Response (2:10)
III. Jonah's Ministry in Nineveh: Jonah in the City (chapter 3)
    A. God's Command (3:1–2)
    B. Jonah's Response (3:3)
    C. Jonah's Message of Impending Judgment (3:4)
    D. Nineveh's Response and God's Mercy (3:5–10)
IV. Jonah's Anger at God: Jonah under the Plant (chapter 4)
    A. Jonah's Complaint (4:1–3)
    B. God's Response (4:4–11)

I. JONAH'S DISOBEDIENCE: JONAH IN THE BOAT (CHAPTER 1)

In chapter 1 God had to deal with Jonah's disobedient actions. Jonah put selfish, nationalistic interests above obedience to God, and the gentile sailors were more responsive to the true God of heaven than was Jonah.

A. God's Command (1:1–2)

Like the cities of Sodom and Gomorrah (Gen. 18:20–21) Nineveh had reached a depth of evil God could no longer ignore. So He commanded Jonah to go to Nineveh and preach against its great wickedness.

B. Jonah's Response (1:3)

God told Jonah to head northeast toward Nineveh, but he went in the opposite direction—southwest to the Jewish seaport of Joppa. His ultimate goal was Tarshish, possibly the city of Tartessus in southwest Spain. Jonah was trying to "run away from the LORD."

C. God's Judgment (1:4–17)

God responded to Jonah's rebellion by sending a wind that threatened to destroy the ship. As Jonah slept, the sailors fought desperately to keep the ship from sinking in the storm. After Jonah was discovered, the sailors urged him to call on his God to "take notice" so they wouldn't perish. When all their efforts failed, the superstitious sailors finally decided to cast lots to see who was responsible for the calamity, and the lot fell on Jonah. Jonah explained his attempt to flee from God, and he urged them to throw him into the sea. When they did so, the storm stopped. Jonah's actions had two effects: these gentile sailors came to know the true God of Israel (1:16), and God "provided a great fish" to spare Jonah from drowning in the sea (1:17). This is one of several things God "provided" in the Book of Jonah: a great wind (1:4), a great fish (1:17), a vine (4:6), a worm (4:7), and a scorching east wind (4:8).

II. JONAH'S PRAYER: JONAH IN THE FISH (CHAPTER 2)

A. Jonah's Lament (2:1–9)

Jonah's prayer traced his response to God's judgment on his disobedience. The opening verse summarizes the content of the psalm ("I called . . . he answered"). Jonah then pictured the awful conditions he experienced in "the deep" as he realized he might never live again to worship God. In his extreme distress he prayed to the Lord, vowing to offer a sacrifice to Him in thanksgiving for His deliverance.

B. God's Response (2:10)

God responded by commanding the fish to vomit Jonah onto dry land. God had now dealt with Jonah's disobedient actions. The next time God called, Jonah would obey.

> *Even in the midst of judgment, God still extends mercy to His children.*

III. JONAH'S MINISTRY IN NINEVEH: JONAH IN THE CITY (CHAPTER 3)

Chapter 3 is somewhat parallel to chapter 1. It reflects what Jonah should have done in response to God's command in 1:2. This chapter contains the only "prophetic" words spoken by Jonah in the book.

A. God's Command (3:1–2)

Again God told Jonah to go to Nineveh and proclaim His message. God did not repeat the explanatory phrase ("because its wickedness has come up before me"). There was no need to repeat it because nothing had changed about Nineveh.

B. Jonah's Response (3:3)

This time Jonah obeyed. His actions now conformed to God's expectations. Because Nineveh was an important city, Jonah's visit would require three days. This could mean that it took Jonah three days to wander through all the streets of Nineveh, or it could mean that Jonah visited both Nineveh and the surrounding cities and towns that stretched for a distance along the Tigris River.

C. Jonah's Message of Impending Judgment (3:4)

Jonah's message to Nineveh was simple and direct: "Forty more days and Nineveh will be overturned." Though Jonah did not offer any hope of a reprieve, such hope is implied in God's gracious provision of a forty-day warning and in Jonah's response to Nineveh's repentance.

Conditional Fulfillment

Sometimes God's fulfillment of an event is conditioned on the response of the people even if no specific condition is stated. God's promise (or threat) will occur as announced unless the people change in response to the message. A clear explanation of this principle is seen in Jeremiah 18:7–10. While it seems from our perspective as though God "changed His mind," His actions always remain consistent with His character. The real change took place in the hearts of the people of Nineveh.

D. Nineveh's Response and God's Mercy (3:5–10)

Nineveh responded to Jonah's message and "believed God." All Nineveh ("from the greatest to the least") put on sackcloth as an outward expression of their humility before God. When Nineveh's king heard about Jonah's message, he too repented, and he proclaimed a time of fasting and prayer. He also urged the people to "turn from their evil, violent ways." The people were to throw themselves on God's compassion in the hope that He might spare the city.

IV. JONAH'S ANGER AT GOD: JONAH UNDER THE PLANT (CHAPTER 4)

Jonah had accomplished what God commanded (3:2–3), but his heart was not in it. Once Jonah revealed his disappointment, God began to deal with his selfish attitude.

A. Jonah's Complaint (4:1–3)

Watching an entire city turn to the Lord should make an individual joyful, but Jonah was very annoyed. His response indicated that he knew God's word would bring about a change of heart in Nineveh. Jonah finally admitted that he fled toward Tarshish because he realized God was a gracious and compassionate and "slow to anger and abounding in love." Faced with Nineveh's repentance (and expected deliverance) Jonah asked God to take his life. This prophet preferred to die rather than live to see the enemies of his own country spared.

B. God's Response (4:4–11)

God responded by asking Jonah if he had any right to be angry. When Jonah said he did, God used three object lessons to teach Jonah about His heart of compassion. As Jonah sat outside Nineveh to see what would happen, God had a vine shade him from the hot sun. Jonah appreciated the vine, but then God had a worm gnaw at the vine so that it withered. Then came a scorching wind to add to Jonah's discomfort. For a second time God asked Jonah if he had any right to be angry. His point was that if Jonah had a right to be concerned about a vine over which he had little control, shouldn't God have a right to be "concerned" about the city of Nineveh with its more than 120,000 people, plus many animals?

Our care for objects of little significance should remind us of God's great care for things of infinite worth.

MICAH
A Just God Requires a Just People

AUTHOR

$\mathcal{T}$HE AUTHOR of the book is Micah of Moresheth (Mic. 1:1), whose name means "Who is like Yahweh?" Micah's hometown of Moresheth should probably be identified with Moresheth Gath in the foothills of western Judah. This village was one of many that Sennacherib of Assyria captured in his attack on Judah in 701 B.C. (1:14). Moresheth was an important city that guarded a key route into the hill country of Judah south of Jerusalem. Because of its importance it was fortified by Solomon's son, Rehoboam, as a defensive center (2 Chron. 11:5–12). Nothing else is known about the prophet Micah.

DATE

Micah's prophecies occurred "during the reigns of Jotham, Ahaz and Hezekiah" (Mic. 1:1), kings of Judah. Jotham began a coregency with his father Uzziah (Azariah) in 750 B.C., and he assumed sole authority when his father died in 739 B.C. (the year Isaiah was called as a prophet; Isa. 6:1). Hezekiah began ruling with his father, Ahaz, in 735 B.C.; he assumed sole authority when Ahaz died in 715 B.C. Hezekiah continued his reign until 686 B.C. Thus Micah's ministry was between 750 and 686 B.C.

The time frame for Micah's message can be narrowed more because of internal chronological markers. First, the fact that Micah did not mention Uzziah would imply Uzziah had already died and Jotham was ruling alone as king. This would place Micah after 739 B.C. Second, Micah began prophesying before the fall of Samaria in 722 B.C., because he announced the city's still-future fall (Mic. 1:6–7). Third, Micah's prophecies extended to Assyria's invasion of Judah in 701 B.C., because he recorded the distress accompanying that invasion (1:10–16; 5:6). Fourth, Micah also intimated that Judah would go into exile in Babylon, possibly echoing Isaiah's message after Hezekiah's reception of the envoy of Merodach-Baladan in 701 B.C. (4:10; Isa. 39:1–8). Thus Micah's ministry could be assigned generally to a time between 735 and 700 B.C.

BACKGROUND

Micah prophesied during a period of upheaval and crisis. The reign of Ahaz brought spiritual lethargy, apostasy, and hypocrisy. The people still worshiped God, but their ritual had no life-changing reality. Their treatment of fellow Israelites violated the basic tenets of the Mosaic Covenant as they failed to practice justice or covenant loyalty love; and their pursuit of idolatry revealed their failure to walk humbly before God (Mic. 6:8).

Ahaz's reign also brought subjection to Assyria, the rising power in the east. To protect himself against the combined attack of the Israelites and the Arameans, Ahaz entered into a treaty with Assyria and made Judah a vassal to the Assyrians (2 Kings 16:5–9). Hezekiah inherited these political realities from his father when Ahaz died, and Assyria's hold on Judah was strengthened when it conquered Aram and Israel.

When Sennacherib became king of Assyria in 705 B.C., Hezekiah and a number of other vassal states tried to break away from the yoke of Assyrian bondage. After securing his throne at home, Sennacherib subdued the rebellious states to his south and north. In 701 B.C. he marched west to attack Judah and other nations that had tried to break free from Assyria's grip. Judah was decimated as Sennacherib captured—according to his own record—"forty-six of his [i.e., Hezekiah's] strong cities, walled forts and ... countless small villages in their vicinity." He also captured "200,150 people, young and old, male and female, horses, mules, donkeys, camels, big and small cattle beyond counting." Sennacherib's two-pronged attack against Judah and Jerusalem focused on the two strategic approaches into the hill country of Judah and its capital. The first prong attacked the cities on the Central Benjamin Plateau north of Jerusalem—the main entry to Jerusalem from the north (Isa. 10:28–32). The second prong swept through the western foothills of Judah, capturing the approaches into the hill country to the south of Jerusalem (Mic. 1:10–15). The chief city in the foothills was Lachish, a city second in importance only to Jerusalem in the kingdom of Judah. Sennacherib captured Lachish; this event was so significant to him that he commissioned a relief to be made of the battle to adorn the walls of a room in his palace in Nineveh. Micah's hometown of Moresheth was also destroyed by Sennacherib at this time, and its people were killed or deported as slaves.

ADDRESSEES

Micah and Isaiah were contemporaries, and their books are parallel in several ways. One possible difference (apart from the geographical and social background of each prophet) is the general emphasis in each book. Isaiah's prophecies were directed more to the royal household and the people of Jerusalem, whereas Micah's prophecies were directed more to the "common people" of the land, especially those living in the western foothills of Judah.

Similarities between Micah and Isaiah	
"In the last days the mountain of the LORD's temple will be established" (Mic. 4:1).	"In the last days the mountain of the LORD's temple will be established" (Isa. 2:2–4).
"You will go to Babylon" (Mic. 4:10).	"Everything . . . will be carried off to Babylon" (Isa. 39:6).
A child will be born "who will be ruler over Israel" (Mic. 5:2–3).	A child will be born who "will reign on David's throne" (Isa. 9:6–7).

God will deliver Judah "from the Assyrian when he invades our land" (Mic. 5:6).	God will "crush the Assyrian in [his] land" (Isa. 14:25).
God will restore His people to the land "from Assyria and the cities of Egypt" (Mic. 7:12).	God will "reclaim the remnant . . . from Assyria, from Lower Egypt, from Upper Egypt" (Isa. 11:11).

PURPOSE

Micah's purpose in writing was to show Judah that her covenant relationship to God was to result in justice and holiness. His focus on God's justice was to remind the people that God would judge them for their sin and disobedience (chapters 1–3), but that He will ultimately establish a kingdom whose King will reign in righteousness (chapters 4–5). Micah repeated this cycle of imminent judgment and ultimate restoration as God "took Judah to court" for its violation of His covenant (chapters 6–7).

OUTLINE

I. Imminent Judgment on God's People (chapters 1–3)
  A. The Coming of the Lord to Condemn (1:1–5)
  B. The Condemnation of the Lord (1:6–16)
  C. God's Judgment on the Greedy (chapter 2)
  D. God's Judgment on the Mighty (chapter 3)
II. Ultimate Blessing for God's People (chapters 4–5)
  A. The Coming Kingdom (4:1–5:6)
  B. The Characteristics of the Coming Kingdom (5:7–15)
III. Present Response of God's People (chapters 6–7)
  A. God's "Lawsuit" against Israel (chapter 6)
  B. Israel's Judgment and Restoration (chapter 7)

I. IMMINENT JUDGMENT ON GOD'S PEOPLE (CHAPTERS 1–3)

In Micah 1 the prophet pictured God coming in judgment against His people. The judgment would be felt first by Samaria (1:6–7). However, it would extend into Judah and even reach to Jerusalem itself (1:8–16).

A. The Coming of the Lord to Condemn (1:1–5)

Micah began by providing a brief summary of his message. *What?* The message was the word of the Lord. *Who?* The message came to Micah of Moresheth, a prophet from a small town in the western foothills of Judah, southwest of Jerusalem. *When?* Micah spoke God's message during the reigns of three kings in Judah: Jotham, Ahaz, and Hezekiah. *Where?* Micah's message focused on Samaria and Jerusalem, two capital cities.

Micah then called on the people of the earth to listen to God's witness against them. God first announced this judgment from heaven. Then Micah pictured God coming from heaven to earth to execute His judgment. As God's feet touch the earth, the mountains would "melt" and the valleys would "split apart." God's presence signaled judgment, and He had arrived to judge "the sins of both Judah and Israel." Micah traced the source of sin to the two capital cities, Samaria and Jerusalem.

B. The Condemnation of the Lord (1:6–16)

The Northern Kingdom of Israel was at the top of God's list for destruction. God said He would make Samaria "a heap of rubble" by allowing the invaders to "lay bare her foundations." This happened in 722 B.C. when the Assyrian army captured and destroyed Samaria (2 Kings 17:5–6). The Assyrians broke apart the idols and temple objects, burning the wood and carrying off the precious metals. Ironically the wealth that Samaria claimed to have received as "wages" from her worship of false idols would be used by the Assyrian soldiers as the "wages of prostitutes" whom they would pay for sexual favors. In other words wealth gained through illicit spiritual prostitution by Israel would be used by pagans for physical prostitution.

Micah wept at the coming destruction, because the "incurable" wound of sin that brought about Samaria's destruction did not stop at her border. Instead it would come to Judah and even to Jerusalem. Just twenty-one years after Samaria's destruction the Assyrian army poured into the land of Judah. In a series of wordplays, Micah pictured the destruction of several cities in the foothills of Judah, including his own hometown. Individuals from Micah's own village, perhaps even members of his own family, would have been among the many hapless victims deported as slaves to Assyria.

Wordplays in Micah 1:10–15

Name	Hebrew Word	Meaning
Gath	"wine/olive press" (proverb from the time of David)	Don't tell the enemy of our misfortune (2 Sam. 1:20).
Beth Ophrah	"house of dust"	In the "house of dust" roll yourself in the dust.
Shaphir	"to be beautiful or pleasant"	The inhabitants of the "pleasant" town will go away in shameful nakedness.
Zaanan	"to go out"	The inhabitants of the "going out" town will not get away.
Beth Ezel	"house of proximity conjunction"	The inhabitants of the "foundation house" will lose their support.

Maroth	"bitter"	The inhabitants of the "bitter" town will wait in vain for a change of fortune.
Lachish	sounds like "[team of] steeds, horses"	The inhabitants of the "team-of-horses" town will hitch up their team of horses to retreat.
Moresheth Gath	sounds like "betrothed," so "wine press of the "betrothed"	The inhabitants of the "betrothed" town will be departing to live under their new jurisdiction.
Aczib	"lie, falsehood"	The inhabitants of the "deceit" town will prove deceitful to those in Israel who depend on her.
Mareshah	from "possession"	The inhabitants of the "possessor" town will be possessed by the king of Assyria.
Adullam	cave known from the time of David	The nobles of Israel will retreat to the town known for its caves (so they can hide; 1 Sam. 22:1).

C. God's Judgment on the Greedy (chapter 2)

In chapter 2 Micah continued announcing Judah's destruction. However, in this chapter he moved from the *where* to the *why*. God's judgment was coming to Judah (chapter 1), and the reason it was coming was because of the people's greediness and covetousness. Only a "remnant" would finally experience God's still-future restoration.

God will judge the greedy (2:1–5). Micah announced a "woe" against those who would lie awake at night, thinking up ways to sin. As soon as morning came, these individuals would rush off to put their evil plans into action. Ignoring God's prohibition against covetousness (Exod. 20:17), they would "covet fields and seize them." In a direct challenge to God's commands on the sanctity of the land (Lev. 25:10–17), they would even steal a fellow Israelite's home and posessions. So God's punishment would fit their crime. Soon the Assyrians would make fun of the people, scornfully mimicking their cry, "My people's possession is divided up. He takes it from me!"

God will judge corrupt prophets (2:6–11). Micah turned to face the false prophets who opposed his message. They urged Micah not to prophesy as they confidently predicted, "Disgrace will not overtake us." But Micah reminded the prophets that God's words benefit those whose ways are upright. These people were abusing and attacking the most helpless members of society: foreigners ("those who pass by"), the physically handicapped (wounded soldiers), and the helpless (women and children). As a result, God's word—in contrast to the false message of the prophets—was that the land was "defiled" and would be "ruined." Unfortunately the people wanted to listen only to prophets who predicted "plenty of wine and beer."

> *A true prophet tells people what they need to hear. A false prophet tells people what they want to hear.*

God will ultimately deliver His remnant (2:12–13). Micah had twice announced that the people would be taken from the land into exile (1:16; 2:10). But he ended chapter 2 by sharing a message of hope about their future restoration. God promised to bring together a remnant. Micah's message looked beyond his day and focused on the still-future kingdom period for Israel. In that day Israel will be led by the One who "will go up before them." Micah then referred to this future leader as "breaker"(NASB) (who will remove all obstacles), King (who will rule from David's throne), and Lord (who is divine).

D. God's Judgment on the Mighty (chapter 3)

God will judge the civil leaders (3:1–4). Micah focused first on the leaders of the land. They were expected to "know justice" (Exod. 23:6–8; Deut. 16:18–20), but instead they hated good and loved evil. These harsh, callously indifferent rulers crushed those under their jurisdiction (tearing their skin and breaking their bones). God's punishment was appropriate. When the enemy finally invaded the land, these rulers would seek the Lord's help, but He would not answer them. God would be as indifferent to their cries of distress as they had been to the cries of others.

God will judge the false prophets (3:5–7). Micah again turned to address the false prophets, who led the people astray. In an arrogant use of their power, the prophets thought they could move the hand of God. Pay them enough money and they would "proclaim 'peace.'" But fail to pay and they would "prepare to wage war." God's judgment again fit their sin. Night and darkness would descend on the prophets, meaning that in the coming time of judgment these prophets would turn to God for His message, only to discover that "there is no answer from God." God would refuse to speak to these prophets at a time when they would most want Him to answer.

> *Be very wary of anyone who claims to speak exclusively for God . . . or who suggests that he or she can move the hand of God.*

Conclusion: The contrast between Micah and the leaders (3:8–12). Judah's leadership was corrupt. Civil and religious leaders alike were "in it for the money," as they looked out only for themselves. This could have been a time of great discouragement, but Micah saw it as an opportunity to take a bold stand for the Lord. In one of the most remarkable contrasts in the entire book, Micah began verse 8 by stating, "But as for me. . . ." Others may have thrown in the towel, but Micah stood firm. He was filled with God's "power" that came from the "Spirit of the LORD." He was also filled with "justice and might." Turning to Judah's leaders, he boldly spoke of their sin and judgment. The leaders, the priests, and the prophets had all perverted what was right for material gain. As a result of their corrupt leadership, Jerusalem would "become a heap of rubble."

Can One Person Make a Difference?

A century after Micah, Jeremiah the prophet stood alone against Judah. On one occasion he delivered an impassioned message. When he finished, a crowd seized him and screamed, "You must die!" (Jer. 26:8). But some leaders stepped forward to defend Jeremiah. They compared his words to those of Micah. After quoting Micah's prophecy of judgment (Mic. 3:12), the elders reminded the mob of the impact of Micah's message. "Did Hezekiah king of Judah or anyone else in Judah put him to death? Did not Hezekiah fear the LORD and seek his favor? And did not the LORD relent, so that he did not bring the disaster he pronounced against them? We are about to bring a terrible disaster on ourselves!" (Jer. 26:19). Micah's willingness to stand for what was right changed an entire generation. God held back His judgment because a nation repented in response to Micah's words and deeds. One person can make a difference!

II. ULTIMATE BLESSING FOR GOD'S PEOPLE (CHAPTERS 4–5)

In Micah 4–5 the prophet shifted from Judah's imminent judgment to her ultimate restoration "in the last days." Having just announced that the temple hill would become a "mound overgrown with thickets," Micah then described a time when the "mountain of the LORD's temple will be established" and have a place of supremacy among the nations. Micah stated this pattern of imminent judgment/ultimate restoration four times within these two chapters (though the pattern is not so clear in the New International Version).

Fourfold Pattern of Judah's Distress and Deliverance (Mic. 3:9–5:6)

I. Judah's Temple (3:9–4:8)
   A. Introduction ("Hear this")
   B. Destruction of the temple because of injustice and greed (3:9–12)
   C. Restoration of the temple when God brings justice and peace "in the last days" (4:1–8)
II. Judah's Captivity (4:9–10)
   A. Introduction ("Now")
   B. Coming captivity in Babylon (4:9–10a)
   C. Future redemption of the Lord (4:10b)
III. Judah's Enemies (4:11–13)
   A. Introduction ("And now")
   B. Present gloating of Judah's enemies (4:11)
   C. Future defeat of Judah's enemies (4:12–13)
IV. Judah's Leadership (5:1–6)
   A. Introduction ("And now")
   B. Present subjection of Judah's king (5:1)
   C. Future deliverance of Judah's king (5:2–6)

A. The Coming Kingdom (4:1–5:6)

God's final plan for Jerusalem (4:1–8). Using the same word pictures as Isaiah 2:1–5, Micah looked forward to the last days when God's "mountain" (a figure of speech describing a kingdom; Dan. 2:35, 44–45) will rule over all other nations. The problems in Micah's day (Mic. 3:9–12) will vanish as rebellion is replaced with obedience ("we may walk in his paths") and injustice is replaced with God's judging the nations justly.

God's reign will bring universal peace as weapons of war are refashioned into agricultural implements. In that day the remnant will submit to God's rule in Mount Zion, and Jerusalem will be prominent again when the Messiah from the line of David comes.

God's restoration from captivity (4:9–10). In the first of three additional cycles Micah took his readers from the glorious future back to their present problems. In Hebrew, 4:9 begins with the word "now" to point up the transition. Micah pictured a time in Jerusalem's near future when the people would moan at the loss of their king. They would be in agony because the nation would be taken to Babylon as exiles (see Isa. 39:6). But Micah completed his cycle by announcing that the Lord would restore these exiles from their Babylonian enemy.

God's defeat of Judah's enemies (4:11–13). Micah began the next cycle by using the phrase "but now" to call their attention back to their imminent judgment. Micah saw a time in Judah's near future when many nations would gather against her and gloat over her destruction. Micah then moved from that time of imminent judgment to Judah's glorious future when Jerusalem will "break to pieces many nations." In this time of future greatness, the people will take the wealth of the nations and give it to the Lord.

God's restoration of Judah's leadership (5:1–6). Micah began the fourth cycle with the same Hebrew phrase ("And now"). Once again Micah returned to the subject of Judah's imminent judgment. He pictured a time when Jerusalem would be placed under siege. The enemy would prevail and "strike Israel's ruler" in the face with a rod. This ruler was likely Zedekiah, Judah's last king, who was captured, blinded, and shackled by Nebuchadnezzar (Jer. 39:5–7). Though this king would be humbled by the nations, another King will arise. This new King was to be born in Bethlehem and will be ruler over Israel. He was in existence before the time of His human birth because His "origins are from of old, from ancient times." This new King will be the one who will finally bring peace to Israel. Jesus fulfilled the first part of this prophecy when He was born in Bethlehem (Matt. 2:1–12).

B. *The Characteristics of the Coming Kingdom (5:7–15)*

When God restores His people in the last days, He will deliver them from their enemies and give them a place of blessing (like dew and rain showers) as well as a place of respect ("like a young lion among flocks of sheep") among the nations of the world. God will also eliminate all the sinful practices Israel had relied on for protection, including horses and chariots, strongholds, witchcraft, carved images, sacred stones, and Asherah poles. God alone will be their protection.

> *What are you trusting in right now for your personal security? Trusting in anything other than the Lord is idolatry.*

III. PRESENT RESPONSE OF GOD'S PEOPLE (CHAPTERS 6–7)

Micah, along with other prophets of the eighth and seventh centuries B.C., used the imagery of a lawsuit to rebuke Israel and Judah for their sin. God took Judah to court for breach of contract because the nation had violated the Mosaic Covenant, which God had made with them. Structured as a "treaty" between God and Israel, Deuteronomy contains a list of blessings for obedience and curses for disobedience. In Micah's "lawsuit" God demonstrated that He had faithfully kept His obligations to the covenant but that Judah had not. Thus God was just in judging Judah for disobedience.

A. *God's "Lawsuit" against Israel (chapter 6)*

Opening appeal (6:1–3). Micah introduced God's lawsuit against Israel by using legal terms like "case," "accusation," and "lodging a charge." In ancient Israel one would gather together the judge or "elders" to decide a legal case (Deut. 25:1, 7; Ruth 4:3). God summoned the mountains, hills, and the whole earth to serve as the "elders" for His lawsuit. Figuratively speaking, the mountains of Israel could function as the impartial judge or jury because they had observed the actions of both God and the people. God asked the people to produce evidence that He had "burdened" them. But the people had no answer.

Specific evidence (6:4–8). Then God presented the evidence for His faithfulness to the covenant. He had "redeemed" the nation from Egypt, provided competent leadership throughout Israel's time in the wilderness, refused to allow Balaam to curse them (Num. 23:13–20), and blocked the Jordan River so the people could walk into the Promised Land ("from Shittim to Gilgal") on dry land (Josh. 3:1; 4:19). From Egypt to the land of Israel the people had seen "the righteous acts of the LORD." God had been absolutely faithful to His promises, and Israel had no excuse for their flagrant disobedience.

Their response was to try to buy off God with more sacrifices. Somehow they thought that more offerings—or possibly even a human sacrifice of their firstborn—would be sufficient to appease God. But the Lord's response must have startled them. He wanted covenant obedience shown in justice, loyal love, and humility—three characteristics lacking among the people (Mic. 3:1–3, 5, 9–11).

What Does the Lord Require?

Micah summarized the entire Mosaic Law in three terse statements.

"To act justly" — Justice focuses on our relationship to each other.

"To love mercy" — Mercy (*hesed,* loyal love) focuses on our relationship to each other as well as our relationship to the Lord.

"To walk humbly" — A humble walk focuses on our relationship to the Lord.

In the New Testament Jesus summarized the Mosaic Law in a similar fashion. "'Love the Lord your God with all your heart and with all your soul and with all your mind.' This is the first and greatest commandment. And the second is like it: 'Love your neighbor as yourself.' All the Law and the Prophets hang on these two commandments" (Matt. 22:37–40).

Declaration of guilt and judgment (6:9–16). Micah called on Jerusalem to heed God's judgment. Common business practices in Judah included reducing the size of the ephah (so people received less than they paid for), and employing inaccurate scales and "false weights" (so people would be forced to pay more), but God knew their wickedness. As a result He had already begun to punish Judah because of their sins. In 6:14–15 Micah summarized some of the curses of the Mosaic Covenant God would bring on His people (see Deut. 28:38–40).

B. Israel's Judgment and Restoration (chapter 7)

In his final chapter Micah traveled the spectrum from gloom to glory. After lamenting Judah's certain destruction because of her disobedience, Micah determined to wait for God's future restoration. He then described that future time when God will restore His people, rebuild His cities, and reclaim His inheritance.

Micah's lament over Israel's sin (7:1–6). Micah was miserable as he faced Judah's certain judgment. Like someone searching for the gleaning after the harvest, he searched in vain for the godly—only to discover that he couldn't find even one godly person! Most people favor one hand over the other, but the people of Judah were ambidexterous in doing evil. Even the best people were "worse than a thorn hedge." Sin had unraveled the very fabric of society so that even family members were considered enemies.

Micah's hope for Israel's future deliverance (7:7–13). In the darkness of Judah's sin Micah's faithfulness shone all the more brightly. For the second time in the book, Micah decided to walk a different path and proclaimed, "But as for me" (see also 3:8). Micah had given up on the people of Judah, but he could still "watch in hope for the LORD" because he knew God would answer his prayers. Speaking on behalf of all the nation, the prophet boldly announced that though he had to face the impending time of judgment, there would come a time when God would bring him back into the light. In that future time Judah's enemies will be ashamed, while Judah will be rebuilding her cities.

Micah's prayer for God's intervention (7:14–20). Micah concluded by asking God once again to "shepherd" His people as He had done previously. Micah was thinking specifically of the Exodus, and he could make his bold request because of two attributes of God. The first was God's *mercy*. Micah exclaimed, "Who is a God like you, who pardons sin and forgives the transgression of the remnant of his inheritance?" Only God had the power to "tread" the people's sins "underfoot." The second attribute was God's covenant *faithfulness*. God, Micah confidently announced, will be "true to Jacob" and will "show mercy to Abraham." Micah had in mind God's covenant promises made to these two patriarchs (in Gen. 12:1–3; 13:14–17; 15:17–21; 28:13–14; 35:11–13). Micah was absolutely confident that God had a future for Israel because of the Abrahamic Covenant ("oath") He pledged with their forefathers. God was faithful, and He would fulfill the promises He made to Abraham and Jacob. Micah then fell silent, knowing Israel's future rested securely in the hands of God, who keeps His Word.

How much confidence do you have in God's Word? As the prophet Balaam discovered long ago, "God is not a man, that he should lie, nor a son of man, that he should change his mind. Does he speak and then not act? Does he promise and not fulfill?" (Num. 23:19). If God said it, you can believe it—just as Micah did!

NAHUM
God's Destruction of Nineveh

AUTHOR

*T*HE NAME "NAHUM" means "comfort" or "consolation." Nahum's message of Nineveh's destruction comforted those whom the Assyrians had oppressed. The only bit of information recorded about Nahum personally is found in Nahum 1:1, where he is called an "Elkoshite." The location of Elkosh is uncertain, since it is not mentioned anywhere else in the Old Testament. Some have suggested that Elkosh was situated by the Sea of Galilee. They find support for this in the New Testament town of Capernaum. "Capernaum" is the transliteration of the Hebrew words *kāpār nahûm*, "village of Nahum." However, there is no evidence that the "village of Nahum" (Capernaum) was actually named after the prophet Nahum. Most likely Elkosh was located somewhere in Judah, but the specific site is unknown.

DATE

While an exact date for the Book of Nahum cannot be determined with certainty, some parameters can be established. The earliest and latest possible dates can be determined through specific events mentioned in the book itself. The most prominent event described in the Book of Nahum is the still-future destruction of Nineveh prophesied by Nahum. Since the book predicted the coming destruction of Nineveh because of her sin, the book must have been written *before* 612 B.C., for that is the year Nineveh fell to the Babylonians.

The second event in the Book of Nahum that helps determine the date of writing is the destruction of the city of Thebes (No Amon) mentioned in 3:8–10. Nahum compared the coming destruction of Nineveh to the past destruction of Thebes. Thebes, the capital of Upper (southern) Egypt, was ransacked by the Assyrians in 663 B.C. Thus Nahum must have penned his prophecy after 663 B.C. (since Thebes was already destroyed) but before 612 B.C. (since Nineveh had not yet been destroyed). A date of about 650–640 B.C. is a good approximation.

BACKGROUND

Like the prophet Jonah, who ministered nearly one hundred and fifty years earlier, Nahum directed his message against the city of Nineveh. Having been founded by Nimrod (Gen. 10:8–12), Nineveh had a long history. It was located on the east bank of the Tigris River, which formed the western and southern boundaries of the city. A wall extended for eight miles around the northern and eastern boundaries. The section of the city within the walls was nearly three miles in diameter at its greatest width, and it held a population that has been estimated to have been as high as 150,000. The three days' walk required to traverse Nineveh (see comments on Jon. 3:3) is no exaggeration.

Nineveh was destroyed by the combined armies of the Babylonians, Medes, and Scythians in 612 B.C. The city was destroyed so completely that the site was not even positively identified as Nineveh until the excavations of Botta and Layard in the mid 1800s. The fact that Nineveh was never rebuilt after her destruction seems to confirm Nahum's prediction in 1:9 ("distress will not rise up twice," NASB).

ADDRESSEES

Though Nahum addressed his message of judgment *against* Nineveh, he delivered the message *to* Judah. The prophecy was intended as a message of comfort to Judah, which was still struggling under the harsh yoke of Assyrian domination and cruelty.

PURPOSE

The purpose of the book was to bring comfort to Judah by announcing the coming destruction of Nineveh. That destruction was coming because of God's justice and because of Nineveh's sin.

OUTLINE

I. Nineveh's Doom Declared (chapter 1)
   A. Introduction (1:1)
   B. Nineveh's Doom Declared because of God's Character (1:2–8)
   C. Nineveh's Doom Declared because of Her Sin (1:9–15)
II. Nineveh's Doom Described (chapter 2)
   A. The Coming of Nineveh's Enemies (2:1–2)
   B. The Attack on Nineveh's Defenses (2:3–10)
   C. The Destruction of Nineveh's "Lair" (2:11–13)
III. Nineveh's Doom Deserved (chapter 3)
   A. Nineveh's Doom Deserved because of Her Promiscuity (3:1–7)
   B. Nineveh's Doom Deserved because of Her Cruelties (3:8–11)
   C. Nineveh's Doom Deserved because of Her False Security (3:12–19)

I. NINEVEH'S DOOM DECLARED (CHAPTER 1)

A. Introduction (1:1)

This verse served as a brief byline for the prophet and his message. The book is an oracle or message of doom, and the object of the message is Nineveh, the capital of the Assyrian Empire. The author of the message is the prophet Nahum, an inhabitant of an otherwise unknown village named Elkosh.

B. Nineveh's Doom Declared because of God's Character (1:2–8)

Nahum focused on three unique aspects of God's character. First, God would destroy Nineveh because of His *justice*. He does "not leave the guilty unpunished." Second, God would destroy Nineveh because of His *omnipotence*. God displayed His power in drying up the waters of the Red Sea and the Jordan River. Even the imposing heights of Bashan, Carmel, and Lebanon withered at His rebuke. Third, God would destroy Nineveh because of His *goodness*. He is a refuge for those who look to Him for help in times of trouble. His compassion for the people of Judah caused Him to oppose those who oppressed His people. So God would "make an end of Nineveh."

> *In times of trouble and difficulty, we need to focus anew on God's justice, power, and mercy.*

C. Nineveh's Doom Declared because of Her Sin (1:9–15)

Nahum then turned the spotlight on Nineveh's wickedness. Nineveh's king (possibly Ashurbanipal, who reigned 669–627 B.C.) plotted against the Lord and encouraged people to be wicked. In spite of Nineveh's apparent power and great strength, God announced He would "prepare your grave for you are vile." Nahum said a messenger would one day arrive in Judah to announce Nineveh's destruction.

II. NINEVEH'S DOOM DESCRIBED (CHAPTER 2)

A. The Coming of Nineveh's Enemies (2:1–2)

In staccato bursts Nahum summarized the events leading up to Nineveh's destruction. He first announced the approach of "an attacker," probably referring to Nabopolassar, king of Babylon. Nineveh's response was to prepare itself for battle. Pulling back the veil, Nahum revealed God's hand behind the attack. God's purpose in bringing these invaders against Nineveh was to "restore the splendor of Jacob."

B. The Attack on Nineveh's Defenses (2:3–10)

The shields of the Babylonians coming to attack Nineveh were red, the polished metal of the chariots flashed in the sunlight, and the soldiers brandished their spears as they prepared to attack. Inside Nineveh, pandemonium reigned as chariots raced through the streets and soldiers stumbled as they ran to the walls to take up positions for the expected battle. But instead of describing an epic battle, Nahum announced the city's sudden fall. The river gates were thrown open and the palace collapsed as a flood apparently washed away part of Nineveh's defenses. In panic the defending troops fled like water draining from a pool. The invading army entered Nineveh with one main goal: to plunder the city's silver and gold. The faces of those unable to flee grew pale as they watched the invaders begin to pillage and plunder this once-great city.

C. The Destruction of Nineveh's "Lair" (2:11–13)

Nahum then asked, "Where now is the lions' den?" as he compared Nineveh to a pride of vicious lions that had filled their lairs with the kill. Now God would devour her young lions, that is, her soldiers. Nahum predicted that the voices of messengers sent by Nineveh to terrorize the nations would be silenced. Her destruction would be complete.

III. NINEVEH'S DOOM DESERVED (CHAPTER 3)

God's judgment was harsh because Nineveh's sin was heinous. God's radical judgment was necessary because of Nineveh's deep rebellion. Nahum singled out two specific sins. First, Nineveh had prostituted all that was good and right for the sake of material gain. Second, Nineveh had displayed unusual cruelty in her harsh treatment of other nations.

A. Nineveh's Doom Deserved because of Her Promiscuity (3:1–7)

Nineveh was a city of blood that was "full of plunder" and "never without victims." Nineveh's great wealth came at the expense of her slaughtering many people. Possessing the "wanton lust of a harlot," Nineveh had corrupted all that was good, right, and proper for the sake of material gain. So God would judge her the way a common prostitute was judged in the ancient Near East: He would expose her nakedness and treat her with contempt (see Jer. 13:22; Ezek. 16:38–41). When Nineveh fell, no one would mourn for her because she had been so vile.

B. Nineveh's Doom Deserved because of Her Cruelties (3:8–11)

Nahum compared Nineveh to the Egyptian city of Thebes (or No Amon, which means "city of the god Amun"). The cities shared much in common. Since Nineveh had destroyed the city of Thebes in 663 B.C., she should have realized that natural defenses and extensive allies did not always offer protection against attack. Thebes had been conquered, and her little children had been dashed to pieces by Nineveh's cruel army. Nahum ended his comparison by reminding Nineveh that she, too, would "seek refuge from the enemy." As they had done to others, God would do to them.

Comparison between Thebes and Nineveh		
	Thebes	*Nineveh*
Both were protected by water	Nile River	Tigris River
Both had several allies	Cush, Put, Libya	Babylon, Medes
Both were destroyed	By Assyria	By Babylon

C. Nineveh's Doom Deserved because of Her False Security (3:12–19)

Though the city's fortifications hung like ripe fruit on a fig tree, they would fall just as figs fall from trees "when they are shaken." Nahum likened Nineveh's troops to women of the ancient Near East who were not trained for battle. Nineveh's many merchants were as numerous as locusts, but like insects they would strip the land and then fly away. Nahum also compared Nineveh's guards and officials to locusts "that settle in the walls on a cold day." When the sun appears (that is, when things really get "hot"), they fly away. Nineveh's leaders were also like slumbering shepherds who allowed the people to become scattered. As a result, Nahum concluded that "nothing can heal your wound." Nineveh's doom was inescapable, and her fall would not be mourned by others because they had all experienced her terrible cruelties.

> God will hold nations and individuals accountable for their treatment of others. We may not know when God will act, because He is "slow to anger." But we can trust in His justice, because He "will not leave the guilty unpunished" (Nah. 1:3).

HABAKKUK
A Life of Trust in Troubling Times

AUTHOR

$\mathcal{T}$HE BOOK OF HABAKKUK is named for its author; but apart from his name and ministry ("Habakkuk the prophet"), nothing else is known about this individual. However, the book presents Habakkuk as an individual of faith who grieved over the sin he saw in the land of Judah.

DATE

Habakkuk gave no specific chronological markers in his book, but two internal characteristics help date his ministry. First, the prophecy was evidently written shortly before the Babylonian invasion of Judah in 605 B.C. because God announced that He was raising up the Chaldeans to punish Judah (1:5–11). Second, Habakkuk's description of Judah's social conditions—justice was ignored and wickedness abounded (1:2–4)—seems less likely to apply to the latter part of the reign of Josiah (640–609 B.C.) when Judah experienced a brief period of national reform (2 Chron. 34:1–35:19). Therefore the most likely time for the book to have been written would seem to be immediately after the death of Josiah, when a series of wicked kings ruled Judah and led the nation toward destruction. This would date the book sometime between 609 and 605 B.C.

BACKGROUND

King Josiah (640–609 B.C.) was the last godly king of Judah. In 622 B.C. the "Book of the Law" was rediscovered while repairs were being made to the temple (2 Kings 22:3–10). This book (either the Book of Deuteronomy or the entire Mosaic Law) was likely lost in the dark days of idolatry during Manasseh's reign (697–642 B.C.).

After hearing the words in the book, Josiah called the people together in a sacred assembly and "read in their hearing all the words of the Book of the Covenant." Josiah and all the people pledged themselves to keep the covenant (2 Kings 23:1–3). The spiritual renewal that followed was significant, but it was not permanent. The people followed the king's orders to tear down the high places, destroy the pagan altars, and follow the laws established by God (23:4–25). However, as soon as Josiah was killed by the Egyptians in 609 B.C., they rebuilt the altars, renewed their idolatrous practices, and forgot God's laws.

ADDRESSEES

Habakkuk did not directly prophesy against the people of Judah. Instead, he recorded a "conversation" between himself and the Lord. His readers were the righteous remnant of Judah who needed to be encouraged to live by faith in the dark days ahead.

PURPOSE

Habakkuk's purpose in writing was to show the problems faced by the righteous when confronted with the realities of sin and to show the means God used to punish sin. Habakkuk wrote to show how the righteous should live by faith in unsettling times.

OUTLINE

I. Habakkuk's Dialogue with God (chapters 1–2)
    A. How Can God Permit Wickedness to Continue? (1:1–11)
    B. How Can God Use the Wicked to Punish Judah? (1:12–2:20)
II. Habakkuk's Response to God (chapter 3)
    A. His Prayer to God (3:1–15)
    B. His Resolve to Wait on God (3:16–19)

I. HABAKKUK'S DIALOGUE WITH GOD (CHAPTERS 1–2)

A. How Can God Permit Wickedness to Continue? (1:1–11)

In a dialogue between the prophet and the Lord, Habakkuk first asked why God allowed violence and injustice in Judah to go unpunished. Habakkuk saw God as the One ultimately responsible for permitting evil to continue, since He seemed willing to tolerate sin. God responded by announcing He would use the Babylonians as His instruments of judgment on Judah. This "ruthless" nation would descend on Judah "like a vulture swooping to devour."

B. How Can God Use the Wicked to Punish Judah? (1:12–2:20)

God's answer caused even more confusion for Habakkuk. In astonishment he asked how a God who "cannot tolerate wrong" could use people as wicked as the Babylonians to judge people who were "more righteous than themselves." Habakkuk then waited to see how God would answer (2:1). God responded by showing Habakkuk that Babylon was merely an instrument used by Him, and that she would also be judged for her actions. He reminded Habakkuk that, in spite of outward circumstances, "the righteous will live by his faith" (2:4), realizing that God is at work. Evil may seem to triumph for a little while, but "the LORD is in his holy temple" (2:20) and will ultimately make all things right.

God sometimes uses evil people to accomplish His larger purpose in life. But He never condones evil, and those who do evil He holds accountable for their actions.

II. HABAKKUK'S RESPONSE TO GOD (CHAPTER 3)

A. *His Prayer to God (3:1–15)*

Habakkuk responded to God's answer by asking Him to intervene in history to accomplish His will. This prayer is in the form of a psalm, complete with musical notations (3:1, 19b). He intended his prayer to be remembered—and used—by the remnant in captivity. Habakkuk asked God once again to perform saving deeds, as He had done for Israel in the past. Though God's judgment on Judah was certain, Habakkuk asked that even during the coming time of wrath God might graciously "remember mercy." This would come about when God would finally intervene to rescue His people and crush "the leader of the land of wickedness."

B. *His Resolve to Wait on God (3:16–19)*

Habakkuk's personal response was to trust in God (he would "wait patiently") in spite of the judgment facing Judah. In doing so, he could rejoice in God even in a time of hardship and difficulty because God would supply the strength and stability needed to endure the uncertain days ahead.

"In all things God works for the good of those who love him" (Rom. 8:28), even though all things we face in life are not good. We will not always understand why evil seems to triumph, but we can rest in the truth that God is in control and will someday make all things right.

ZEPHANIAH
The Day of the Lord for Jerusalem

AUTHOR

$\mathcal{T}$HE NAME ZEPHANIAH means "the Lord hides." The genealogical background of the prophet is given in Zephaniah 1:1 and is far more extensive than what is normally listed for a prophet. He listed four generations of ancestors from his father, Cushi, to his great-great-grandfather, Hezekiah. If this Hezekiah was Judah's king, this would place Zephaniah in David's royal line. Zephaniah's interest in and knowledge of Jerusalem (1:4, 10–11) points to that city as his primary residence.

DATE

The latest possible date for the writing of Zephaniah's book must be before the fall of Nineveh in 612 B.C., because Zephaniah 2:13 indicates that Nineveh's destruction was still future. The earliest possible date is more difficult to determine. Since Zephaniah prophesied "during the reign of Josiah" (1:1), he could not have begun his ministry before 640 B.C. Assuming that Zephaniah was the great-great-grandson of King Hezekiah (715–686 B.C.) and assuming that he did not begin his prophetic ministry until he was at least twenty years old, then the earliest date for his ministry would be about 630–620 B.C. Thus the prophecy should probably be dated sometime between 630 and 612 B.C., in the latter part of King Josiah's reign. Possibly Zephaniah's ministry coincided with Josiah's reforms in 622 B.C.

BACKGROUND

When Zephaniah prophesied, the international scene was in a state of flux. The power of Assyria was on the wane, and the capital of Nineveh was destroyed during the latter part of Josiah's reign. Babylon was on the rise in the east and was attempting to establish an empire at Assyria's expense. Egypt seized the opportunity to try to reestablish her influence in the west. To do this she supported the crumbling Assyrian Empire to act as a buffer state between her and the Babylonians. During this period of shifting alliances and empires, Judah enjoyed a brief period of national independence.

However, Judah was in a tenuous position spiritually. For nearly fifty years (686–640 B.C.) the nation had been ruled by evil kings. Manasseh reinstituted many of the idolatrous practices that had been repressed by Hezekiah (2 Kings 21:2–7). Manasseh's reign was so evil it brought an announcement of impending judgment from the Lord (21:11–15). Finally Josiah became king, and during his reign—beginning in 622 B.C.—there was a spiritual revival (22:3–23:27; 2 Chron. 34:1–35:19). However, the nation had progressed so far in sin that the revival could not prevent God's coming judgment—it could only postpone it (2 Kings 23:4–8, 10–14; 2 Chron. 34:23–28). The temporary revival of Josiah did not grip the hearts of the people in a permanent way, because after he died the kings and the people returned to their evil ways (2 Kings 23:37; Ezek. 8:1–8).

ADDRESSEES

Zephaniah wrote to the people of Judah and Jerusalem at the end of the Judean monarchy. Though he also prophesied against several nations surrounding Judah (2:4–15), the messages were spoken to the people of Judah.

PURPOSE

The Book of Zephaniah serves as a bridge between eras. The threat of Assyria had passed, but the threat of Babylon was looming just over the horizon. The reign of Manasseh had sealed Judah's fate. Understanding that fact, Zephaniah's purpose was to announce coming judgment on Judah in the Day of the Lord. However, he said that judgment would extend to all the nations of the earth, indicating that the Day of the Lord would also bring deliverance for Israel and the Gentiles.

OUTLINE

I. Judgment in the Day of the Lord (1:1–3:8)
   A. Introduction (1:1–3)
   B. Judgment on Judah (1:4–13)
   C. Judgment on the Whole World (1:14–18)
   D. God's Call to Repent (2:1–3)
   E. God's Judgment on the Nations (2:4–15)
   F. God's Judgment on Jerusalem (3:1–8)
II. Salvation in the Day of the Lord (3:9–20)
   A. The Nations Will Be Purified (3:9–13)
   B. Jerusalem Will Rejoice (3:14–17)
   C. God Will Restore (3:18–20)

I. JUDGMENT IN THE DAY OF THE LORD (1–3:8)

Those in Judah who had rebelled against the Lord and turned to idolatry would be judged in the Day of the Lord. But the imminent "day of the Lord" for Judah (1:4–13) foreshadowed the eschatological Day of the Lord which God will bring on the whole world (1:14–18). Having pictured the coming day of judgment, Zephaniah urged his readers to repent so they might be spared during this time of wrath (2:1–3). Zephaniah then returned to his theme of judgment. God's wrath would be felt by nations all around Judah (2:4–15). But sadly, the judgment would also be felt by those in Jerusalem because they refused to heed his call to repent (3:1–8).

A. Introduction (1:1–3)

Zephaniah identified himself as the great-great-grandson of Hezekiah and noted that God's word came to him during Josiah's reign. The remainder of the introduction summarized the message that was to follow: God would come in judgment to "sweep away everything" from the earth.

B. Judgment on Judah (1:4–13)

God's judgment would begin in Judah because they had turned from the true God to worship idols. Four times Zephaniah identified this coming judgment as the Day of the Lord (1:7–10), and he pictured it as a time when God would punish priests, princes, and all others engaged in pagan practices. He vividly pictured the fall of Jerusalem as the Babylonians entered in the north and fought their way across the Western Hill and into the Central Valley (1:10–11). When the battle was over, the people's possessions would be plundered by these invaders.

C. Judgment on the Whole World (1:14–18)

Like Obadiah and Joel, Zephaniah used the term "the Day of the Lord" for Judah as a springboard to discuss the "great day of the Lord" coming on all the earth. In this time of wrath, darkness will cover the whole earth. It will be a time when God will make a sudden end of all who live in the earth, that is, all evildoers.

D. God's Call to Repent (2:1–3)

Before the time of judgment arrived, Zephaniah urged the people of Judah to humble themselves and seek God and His righteousness. If they did, God would shelter them during His coming time of anger against Judah.

E. God's Judgment on the Nations (2:4–15)

Zephaniah paused in his message to Judah to focus on those nations around her. If God was about to judge His people for their sin, how could these nations ever hope to escape? As the following chart indicates, Zephaniah arranged the nations in a specific order to make his point. God would judge nations west and east, north and south of Judah (and everywhere in between). He would also judge nations that were near as well as nations that were far away. Those near would be plundered and possessed by Judah. Those far away would simply be destroyed by the Lord.

Judgment on the Nations in Zephaniah 2

Nation(s)	Direction from Judah	Proximity to Judah	Fate	Effect on Judah
Philistia (2:4–7)	West	Near	Destroyed	Given to the remnant
Moab and Ammon (2:8–11)	East	Near	Destroyed	Plundered by the remnant
Cush (2:12)	South	Far	Destroyed	None stated
Assyria (2:13–15)	North	Far	Destroyed	None stated

F. God's Judgment on Jerusalem (3:1–8)

Zephaniah began and ended this section (2:1–3:8) by focusing on Jerusalem, the city that deserved God's judgment. All the politial and religious leaders arrogantly disobeyed God, profaned His sanctuary, and mistreated His people. Though God had always remained righteous, "yet the unrighteous know no shame." God called on the city to await His "day" of judgment because it was certain to come.

II. SALVATION IN THE DAY OF THE LORD (3:9–20)

A. The Nations Will Be Purified (3:9–13)

God will use the coming Day of the Lord to "purify the lips of the peoples" (see also Isa. 6:5–7), that is, He will cleanse and forgive those nations that had been judged. These peoples will go from being enemies to becoming worshipers. At the same time the remnant in Jerusalem "will speak no lies" as they rest under God's protection.

B. Jerusalem Will Rejoice (3:14–17)

Jerusalem will burst into a song of thanksgiving at God's presence ("the LORD . . . is with you," 3:15, 17). He will bring forgiveness (by taking away her punishment) and deliverance ("he is mighty to save"). God's wrath will be replaced with His "delight" and His "love."

> We can find hope in times of difficulty if we focus on God's power, God's deliverance, and God's love. He is our King (3:15), our Savior (3:16–17a), and our Beloved (3:17b).

C. God Will Restore (3:18–20)

In the future the Lord will make all things right for His people. He will deal with those who have oppressed the people of Judah, and He will re-gather the dispersed Jews. Their shame will be replaced with "honor and praise" because God will bring them to their rightful place of blessing.

> God will someday make all things right for His people (Rev. 21:3–5). We can trust the Lord of the universe to keep His promises.

HAGGAI
Rebuilding God's House

AUTHOR

$\mathcal{T}$HE NAME HAGGAI is derived from the Hebrew word for festival and can be translated "festal" or "my feast." Nothing is known about Haggai's family or his background. Haggai's ministry in the postexilic period is corroborated by Ezra (see Ezra 5:1; 6:14).

Because of Haggai's reference to those "who saw this house in its former glory" (Hag. 2:3), some feel that Haggai was alive when the first temple of Solomon was still standing—prior to the Babylonian captivity. If so, then Haggai would have been in his seventies or eighties at the time he announced the words contained in his book. However, it is not at all certain that 2:3 points to Haggai's being alive and in Judah before the destruction of the temple in 586 B.C.

DATE

Haggai delivered four prophecies within four months. His first prophecy came "in the second year of King Darius, on the first day of the sixth month" (1:1). This was August 29, 520 B.C. His second message was delivered "on the twenty-first day of the seventh month" (2:1), which was October 17, 520 B.C., the last day of the Feast of Tabernacles. The third and fourth messages were delivered "on the twenty-fourth day of the ninth month, in the second year of Darius" (2:10, 20). This was December 18,

520 B.C. Thus Haggai's prophetic ministry recorded in his book took place between August 29 and December 18, 520 B.C.

BACKGROUND

On October 12, 539 B.C., the city of Babylon fell to the forces of Medo-Persia, ruled by King Cyrus. In 538 B.C. Cyrus issued a decree allowing the Jews to return from Babylon to Jerusalem and to rebuild the temple (Ezra 1:2–4; 6:3–5). Approximately fifty thousand Jews under the leadership of Zerubbabel, grandson of King Jehoiachin (1 Chron. 3:17–19), made the long trek back to Jerusalem from Babylon. It would have taken several months to make preparations for the journey and several months to travel from Babylon to Jerusalem with the elderly and the young. The next time reference is in Ezra 3:1, where Ezra recorded that "when the seventh month came" the Israelites who had already arrived in Jerusalem and settled in their towns (see 2:68–70) came to Jerusalem to build the altar and celebrate the Feast of Tabernacles. This could not have been the seventh month in 538 B.C. because that would not leave enough time for the Israelites to hear the command, make preparations to return, make the journey, and settle in their homes. Most likely, the people gathered in Jerusalem to begin rebuilding in the seventh month of 537 B.C. That month began on September 6, 537 B.C. They had completed the altar by the beginning of the Feast of Tabernacles, which began on September 20, 537 B.C. (3:3–4).

Work on the temple proper started "in the second month of the second year after their arrival at the house of God in Jerusalem" (3:8). That month began on April 29, 536 B.C. and was the same month Solomon had begun building his temple 430 years earlier (1 Kings 6:1). Two thoughts must have been uppermost in the minds of those who had returned. First, they were excited about starting to rebuild God's house in Jerusalem. Second, they must have remembered the promises God gave through Moses (Deut. 30) and the prophets. Both Moses and the prophets had foreseen a time when the people would be regathered to the land of Israel and when the restored kingdom would finally experience all its promised blessings. Was their return to the land and their rebuilding of the temple the beginning of God's restoration of His kingdom on earth?

The hope of those who had returned from Babylon soon turned into confusion. Work on the temple slowed and then stopped as opposition grew from "the enemies of Judah and Benjamin" (Ezra 4:1). The temple foundation stood idle and neglected for almost sixteen years until God raised up the prophets Haggai and Zechariah to urge the people to begin anew the project to rebuild (5:1–2). The hope of promised blessing and peace was lost amid the difficulties confronting those in the land. They faced opposition from their enemies (4:4–5), and they faced a land that seemed cursed rather than blessed (Hag. 2:15–19). If their return was to be the beginning of the golden era of Israel's kingdom under the rule of her Messiah, why was everything going so wrong? Those were the issues Haggai addressed.

ADDRESSES

Haggai named three specific individuals or groups as his audience: Zerubbabel, who ruled as governor; Joshua, who served as high priest; and the people who had returned to Judah from captivity in Babylon. Ezra identified Haggai's audience: "Haggai the prophet . . . prophesied to the Jews in Judah and Jerusalem" (Ezra 5:1).

PURPOSE

Haggai's primary purpose in writing was to encourage the people who returned to Israel to continue the task of rebuilding the temple after a sixteen-year hiatus. However, he also wrote to give the people hope by announcing that God's program of blessing would come "in a little while" (Hag. 2:6) when God would again "shake the heavens and the earth" (2:6, 21).

OUTLINE

I. First Message: The Call to Rebuild the Temple (chapter 1)
   A. Rebuke to the Nation (1:1–11)
   B. Obedience of the Nation (1:12–15)
II. Second Message: Announcement of Future Blessing (2:1–9)
III. Third Message: Call to Moral Purity (2:10–19)
IV. Fourth Message: Prediction of the Future for Zerubbabel (2:20–23)

I. FIRST MESSAGE: THE CALL TO REBUILD THE TEMPLE (CHAPTER 1)

A. *Rebuke to the Nation (1:1–11)*

On August 29, 520 B.C., Haggai the prophet stood up and rebuked the people of Judah for their laxness toward God. This message was delivered near the end of the summer harvest season. The people assumed "the time [had] not yet come for the LORD's house to be built," though they had begun the project sixteen years earlier (Ezra 3:6–10; 4:4–5, 24). God's house remained in ruins while the people were "living in paneled houses," so God withheld blessing. For years their thorough planting had resulted in only small harvests. Their problem was misplaced priorities—they put their interests above honoring the Lord. Haggai's solution was simple: The people were to get right with the Lord and get back to constructing the temple.

> *Those who plan to give to God "once they have enough for themselves" will never have enough for themselves!*

B. *Obedience of the Nation (1:12–15)*

The leaders and the people responded positively to Haggai's message and "feared the LORD." Under the prophet's encouragement, the people began working on the temple on September 21, 520 B.C.—about three weeks after Haggai began prophesying.

II. SECOND MESSAGE: ANNOUNCEMENT OF FUTURE BLESSING (2:1–9)

Haggai's second message was a call to take courage in light of God's future blessings for Israel (2:1–9). The message was delivered on October 17, 520 B.C., which was significant for two reasons. First, the people had begun rebuilding only three weeks earlier. Second, this was the last day of the Feast of Tabernacles, which celebrated the summer harvest (Lev. 23:33–43). Some of the remnant were old enough to remember Solomon's temple, though it had been destroyed sixty-six years earlier. Those who remembered the temple "in its former glory" now saw the results of their few weeks of labor, and to their discouraged eyes it looked "like nothing." Haggai encouraged the people to look *up* to the Lord or *ahead* to the future rather than *back* to the past. He urged them to work because God promised He was with them, and that He would make this temple greater than the glory of Solomon's temple ("the former house"). How could their temple be greater than Solomon's? First, because this temple was later modified and enlarged by Herod the Great and exceeded Solomon's temple in size and splendor. And second, in this temple the incarnate Son of God later stood and taught, whereas in Solomon's temple God's glory was hidden behind a veil in the Most Holy Place.

III. THIRD MESSAGE: CALL TO MORAL PURITY (2:10–19)

Haggai spoke his third message on December 18, 520 B.C. Work on the temple was well underway, but the winter rains (a sign of God's blessing) had not yet begun. The people were perplexed because they felt God should be blessing them since they were doing His work. Haggai asked the priests for two rulings to show that holiness could not be transmitted by contact, but that defilement could. He then applied this principle to the people (2:14). They were contaminated by sin so that "whatever they do" (building the temple) and "whatever they offer there" (sacrifices) were "defiled" because the people had touched them. Merely doing God's work wasn't enough to make the people right with God. Before they began building the temple they had not experienced God's blessing (2:15–17), and since they began building they still had not seen God's blessing (2:18–19a). But now that they were willing to purify themselves, they would be blessed.

> *Haggai's two questions can be better understood today if they are put in a context we can relate to more readily. Imagine Haggai asking, "Could giving a pint of hepatitis-free blood to someone with hepatitis cure him or her?" No. "Could giving a pint of hepatitis-infected blood to someone without hepatitis infect him or her?" Yes. Purity cannot be transmitted through contact, but impurity can.*

IV. FOURTH MESSAGE: PREDICTION OF THE FUTURE FOR ZERUBBABEL (2:20–23)

Haggai's final message, also delivered on December 18, 520 B.C., was for Zerubbabel, Judah's governor. Zerubbabel was discouraged because his grandfather, King Jehoiachin, had been cursed by God for disobedience. God had told Jehoiachin that He would remove him as the "signet ring on my right hand" and would never allow any of his offspring to "sit on the throne of David" (Jer. 22:24–30). What hope could Zerubbabel have in the future since his line was cursed? God assured Zerubbabel that the time will come someday when He will "shake the heavens and the earth" and "shatter the power of foreign kingdoms" to establish His kingdom. And in that day He will make Zerubbabel "like my signet ring." Zerubbabel would receive a place of blessing and honor because he had been faithful to God, in spite of his background.

> *We cannot undo our past, but God can bless us in spite of our past if we are faithful to Him.*

818

ZECHARIAH
The Lord Remembers

AUTHOR

ZECHARIAH gave his genealogy as the "son of Berekiah, the son of Iddo" (Zech. 1:1). Iddo was one of the priests who returned to Jerusalem with Zerubbabel (Neh. 12:4). In the Book of Ezra, Zechariah is referred to as "a descendant of Iddo" (Ezra 5:1; 6:14), possibly indicating that Berekiah was already dead or that Iddo was the better known person with whom Zechariah was associated. Zechariah was referred to as a "child" or " youth" (Zech. 2:4), which indicates he was probably a young man during the time of his ministry.

DATE

God raised up the prophets Haggai and Zechariah to promote the rebuilding of the temple in Jerusalem (Ezra 5:1; 6:14). Zechariah's first prophecy came "in the eighth month of the second year of Darius" (1:1), which was October/November 520 B.C. The visions pictured by Zechariah came a few months later—"on the twenty-fourth day of the eleventh month . . . in the second year of Darius" (1:7). This was February 15, 519 B.C. The final date given by Zechariah was "the fourth year of King Darius . . . on the fourth day of the ninth month" (7:1), which was December 7, 518 B.C. Thus Zechariah's ministry stretched from at least October/November 520 B.C. to December 7, 518 B.C.—a two-year period of prophetic activity. The final chapters of Zechariah are not dated but may have been recorded after the temple was rebuilt.

Some have raised questions about the unity of the Book of Zechariah, charging that chapters 9–14 were written *before* the Babylonian exile. Linguistic differences do occur between the two sections of the book, and, as noted, chapters 9–14 are not dated. However, the linguistic differences can just as easily be explained by the different subject matter in the chapters and a different time of writing by the same author.

BACKGROUND

Like Haggai, Zechariah was called by God to encourage the remnant who had returned from Babylonian captivity to finish rebuilding God's temple. Work on the temple had begun "in the second month of the second year after their arrival at the house of God in Jerusalem" (Ezra 3:8). But work slowed and then stopped as opposition grew from "the enemies of Judah and Benjamin" (4:1). The temple foundation stood idle and neglected for almost sixteen years until God raised up Haggai and Zechariah to urge the people to begin to rebuild the temple (5:1–2). The hope of promised blessing and peace was lost amid the difficulties facing those in the land. Zechariah reminded the people that the Lord "remembered" them and would bring His plan of blessing to completion. This message would have impact because Zechariah's name means "the Lord remembers."

ADDRESSEES

Zechariah named three individuals or groups as those to whom he addressed his messages. He delivered God's word to Zerubbabel, who ruled as governor (Zech. 4:6–9), to Joshua, who served as high priest (3:1–10; 6:9–15), and to all the people who had returned to Judah from captivity in Babylon (7:4–7). Ezra wrote that "Zechariah the prophet, a descendant of Iddo, prophesied to the Jews in Judah and Jerusalem" (Ezra 5:1).

PURPOSE

While Zechariah joined with Haggai in promoting the rebuilding of the temple, Zechariah's message extended beyond that specific event. Zechariah's larger purpose was to provide a message of hope to those Jews who had returned to Israel. God would preserve His remnant from the gentile threat and would ultimately restore Israel's kingdom by sending the Messiah.

OUTLINE

I. The Eight Night Visions of Zechariah (1:1–6:8)
   A. The Riders and the Horses (1:1–17)
   B. The Four Horns and the Four Craftsmen (1:18–21)
   C. The Man with the Measuring Line (chapter 2)
   D. The Cleansing of Joshua (chapter 3)
   E. The Lampstand and the Olive Trees (chapter 4)
   F. The Flying Scroll (5:1–4)
   G. The Woman in the Basket (5:5–11)
   H. The Four Chariots (6:1–8)
II. The Crowning of Joshua (6:9–15)
III. The Question concerning Fasting (chapters 7–8)
IV. The Two Burdens of Zechariah (chapters 9–14)
   A. The First Burden (chapters 9–11)
   B. The Second Burden (chapters 12–14)

I. THE EIGHT NIGHT VISIONS OF ZECHARIAH (1:1–6:8)

After an initial call to repentance, which was probably associated with the summons to rebuild the temple (1:1–6), Zechariah delivered a series of eight night visions showing God's work on behalf of His people (1:7–6:8). These visions are arranged in a chiastic structure that begins and ends with God's intervention in the world on behalf of His people. The heart of the structure focuses on God's restoration of His people, symbolized by the cleansing of the high priest (chapter 3) and the promise to restore the temple by His Holy Spirit (chapter 4).

The Chiasm of Zechariah's Eight Night Visions

A. The riders and the horses among the myrtle trees (1:7–17)
  B. The four horns and the four craftsmen (1:18–21)
    C. The man with the measuring line (2:1–13)
      D. The cleansing of Joshua the high priest (chapter 3)
      D.' The lampstand and the olive tree (chapter 4)
    C.' The flying scroll (5:1–4)
  B.' The woman in the basket (5:5–11)
A.' The four chariots (6:1–8)

A. The Riders and the Horses (1:1–17)

Zechariah began his ministry in October/November 520 B.C. ("the eighth month of the second year" of the reign of Darius), about the time Haggai was delivering his prophetic message (see Hag. 2:1, 10; Ezra 5:1–2). Zechariah's initial message focused on the remnant's need to return to the Lord. Like Haggai, the prophet reported that the people repented in response to his message. This likely refers to their decision to rebuild the temple.

The first vision—that of the riders and the horses—indicated that God was intervening in the world to bring peace to His people. Two supernatural beings were highlighted. The first was an interpreting angel who appeared eleven times in chapters 1–6 to interpret the night visions (1:9, 13–14, 19, 21; 4:1, 4–5; 5:5, 10; 6:4). The second was the man among the myrtle trees (1:8, 10), who in 1:11 is identified as the angel of the Lord, a preincarnate appearance of Jesus Christ. The angelic riders had been sent by God to report on what was happening on the earth. Their report was that the world was at peace except for Jerusalem and other towns of Judah. God promised to rebuild Jerusalem and the temple, along with the other cities of Judah.

B. The Four Horns and the Four Craftsmen (1:18–21)

Zechariah's second vision pictured four horns and four craftsmen. The horns (a symbol of strength) represented those nations that had scattered God's people. The craftsmen represented the nations sent by God to destroy the nations that had tried to destroy Judah. Zechariah's four horns are probably parallel to the four nations described in Daniel 2 and 7, and can be interpreted as follows.

The Four Horns   *The Four Craftsmen*

Babylon ←——destroyed—— Medo-Persia

Medo-Persia ←——destroyed—— Greece

Greece ←——destroyed—— Rome

Rome ←——will destroy—— God's messianic kingdom

God will hold accountable those who seek to harm His people.

C. The Man with the Measuring Line (chapter 2)

In his third vision Zechariah asked a man with a measuring line where he was going, and he answered that he was on his way to "measure Jerusalem." Then the angel explained the meaning of the vision: Jerusalem will again be rebuilt and will overflow with people. Physical walls will be unnecessary because God will be "a wall of fire around it." The heavenly being urged those Jews still living in the "land of the north" to flee and return to Zion. They should do so because God will judge those nations that have persecuted His people, and because God will again live among His people in the Promised Land.

D. The Cleansing of Joshua (chapter 3)

The fourth vision pictured a three-stage change in the status of Joshua the high priest. At the beginning of the vision Joshua was in God's presence with Satan accusing him. In the second stage Satan was eliminated, but Joshua still stood before the Lord in filthy clothes. In the final stage a cleansed Joshua was given a clean turban and clothing while the angel of the Lord stood by watching. Joshua was "symbolic of things to come." His cleansing pictured God's ultimate restoration and cleansing of the nation Israel, and Joshua himself also symbolized God's Servant, "the Branch," the future messianic King/Priest. Through Jesus Christ, God will ultimately "remove the sin of this land in a single day."

> Satan is always looking for opportunities to "accuse" believers before God (Job 1:6–12; 2:1–7; Rev. 12:10). However, we can defeat this accuser through (a) the finished redemptive work of Jesus Christ, (b) the Word of God, and (c) our willingness to give our lives in service for Jesus Christ.

E. The Lampstand and the Olive Trees (chapter 4)

The angel awakened Zechariah to introduce the fifth night vision, in which he saw a gold lampstand, possibly shaped like the menorah that provided light in the temple. Above the lamp was a bowl that served as a reservoir for the olive oil used as fuel in the seven lights at the top of each branch. Individual channels led from the bowl to the lights, providing a constant source of fuel to keep the lamp burning. Beside the reservoir were two olive trees that provided olive oil to keep the reservoir filled. In effect, Zechariah saw a lamp that would never go out because it had a constant supply of oil. The point of the vision was that God would enable Israel's leaders to accomplish His work. The never-failing supply of oil pictures the power of the Holy Spirit. Zerubbabel would "bring out the capstone" to complete the temple he had just begun. No opposition was too great for God. In another twist the two olive trees represented Joshua and Zerubbabel, who were anointed to serve God. But in a larger sense they also looked forward to Jesus Christ, the ultimate Anointed One, who will fill the dual roles of Priest and King.

No task is too difficult—nor is any opposition too great—if God is on our side. "The one who is in you [Jesus Christ] is greater than the one who is in the world [Satan]" (1 John 4:4).

F. The Flying Scroll (5:1–4)

The sixth vision revealed that God would judge evildoers and purge sin from His land. The scroll symbolized the righteous standards God would use to judge the wicked. Like the original tablets of the Law (Exod. 32:15), the scroll was written on both sides. One side condemned "every thief" (the eighth commandment; 20:15), while the other side condemned "everyone who swears falsely" by my name (the third commandment; 20:7). Those who refuse to turn from such wickedness will not experience God's blessings.

G. The Woman in the Basket (5:5–11)

The seventh vision, the woman in the "measuring basket," indicated that Babylon would again be the center of worldwide evil. This is parallel to the second vision (four horns and four craftsmen) in the sense that both picture the gentile powers that oppose God's people. (Babylon and the final gentile power appear together in Revelation 17.) The woman in Zechariah's vision represented "iniquity" and "wickedness." The cover holding the woman captive pictured God's restraint of evil. As bad as things were in Zechariah's day, things could have been worse if God had not been restraining evil (see also 2 Thess. 2:7). The basket was taken away to Babylonia, where a "house" would again be prepared for wickedness to dwell. The Babylonian Empire had fallen, but evil will again reside in that region of the world. (See comments on Isaiah 13–14 and Jeremiah 50–51.)

H. The Four Chariots (6:1–8)

The eighth vision showed that God would send His judgment on all the nations because of the way they treated Israel. The chariots represented the "four spirits of heaven" God had sent out into the world. As they went out, God indicated that the one who went toward the north had given God's Spirit "rest" there. From Zechariah's perspective the "north" probably pictured Babylon (see Jer. 1:14–15; 4:6; 6:1, 22; 25:9). This "rest" could picture the fall of the Babylonian Empire (the first of the "horns" in the second night vision), which had occurred by the time of this vision.

II. THE CROWNING OF JOSHUA (6:9–15)

Zechariah placed a crown on the head of Joshua the high priest to foreshadow the "Branch," who, as the future King/Priest, will build the Lord's temple. This prophetic action ultimately pointed to Jesus Christ, who will be both King, from the line of David (Matt. 1:1), and Priest, from the order of Melchizedek (Heb. 7). For more on the "Branch" as the Messiah see Isaiah 4:2; 11:1; Jeremiah 23:5–6; 33:15–16; Zechariah 3:8.

III. THE QUESTION CONCERNING FASTING (CHAPTERS 7–8)

Now that a new temple was being constructed, the people of Bethel asked whether they should continue to "mourn and fast" during the fifth month (August/September) to commemorate the destruction of the first temple (Jer. 52:12–13).

God's answer through Zechariah was divided into four sections, each of which begins with the phrase "the word of the LORD Almighty came to me" (7:4, 8:1, 18, see 7:8). God rebuked the false ritualism of the people for the past seventy years (7:4–7). Zechariah reminded them of their past failures that had prompted God to scatter them and make the land "desolate"

(7:8–14). Now, however, the rebuilding of the temple symbolized God's renewed blessing for His people (8:1–17). So instead of fasting, the people should hold joyous festivals as they celebrated God's work on behalf of His people (8:18–23).

Of interest is the fact that ten times in chapter 8 Zechariah wrote, "This is what the LORD [or LORD Almighty] says" (8:2–4, 6–7, 9, 14, 19–20, 23). Each clause introduces a promise of future blessing for Israel.

IV. THE TWO BURDENS OF ZECHARIAH (CHAPTERS 9–14)

These final chapters in Zechariah's prophecy are undated and could have been composed after the temple was completed. Zechariah had two burdens about Israel's future, in which he traced key prophetic events related to the Messiah's first and second comings.

The two burdens form a chiastic structure, with the one focusing on the rejection of the Messiah at His first coming and the second one focusing on the acceptance and triumph of the Messiah at His second coming.

> *Chiasm of Zechariah 9–14*
>
> A. God comes to protect and bless (chapters 9–10)
> > B. The people reject God's shepherd (11:1–14)
> > > C. The worthless shepherd hurts the flock (11:15–17)
> > > C.' The nations come to destroy Jerusalem (12:1–9)
> > B.' The people repent and turn to God (12:10–13:6)
> A. 'God comes to protect and bless (13:7–14:21)

A. The First Burden (chapters 9–11)

By tracing God's work on behalf of His people from the conquests of Alexander the Great to the arrival of the Messiah, Zechariah highlighted God's promises to protect and bless Israel. One would expect God's work to result in the final establishment of God's kingdom, but it didn't take place because the people rejected God's shepherd.

God's judgment on the nations (9:1–8). Zechariah described God's judgment on several nations that had oppressed the people of Israel. Moving generally from north to south, Zechariah foretold the conquests of Alexander the Great against these nations. God's judgment on them would come because of His promise to "defend" His people "against marauding forces."

The cities named by Zechariah were captured by Alexander the Great during his conquests in 333 B.C. From north to south the cities named include Hadrach (a district of Syria located north of Hamath), Damascus (the capital of the Aramean, or Syrian, Empire), Hamath (an important city on the major route going north from Damascus), Tyre and Sidon (major trading ports on the Mediterranean in the region of Phoenicia), and the cities of the Philistines (Zechariah mentions four of the five cities that were part of the Philistine pentapolis—Ashkelon, Ashdod, Ekron, and Gaza—omitting Gath).

The coming of Israel's Messiah (9:9–10). Zechariah encouraged Jerusalem to "shout" in triumph over God's victories because they heralded the arrival of the messianic King. This righteous King would arrive in Jerusalem "riding on a donkey, on a colt, the foal of a donkey." He will establish peace in the world and will rule worldwide.

The first part of this prophecy was fulfilled when Jesus made His triumphal entry into Jerusalem (Matt. 21:1–7). The people recognized the significance of Jesus' actions as they shouted, "Hosanna to the Son of David" (acknowledging His messianic heritage). The final part of the prophecy awaits His return when "He will rule [the nations] with an iron scepter" (Rev. 19:15).

God's promise to defend His people (9:11–17). After explaining the successful mission of the Messiah, Zechariah again addressed the people of Judah ("As for you . . ."). Though coming *after* the announcement about the Messiah, these verses actually describe events that occurred *before* the advent of Christ. Because of God's "covenant" with His people (likely, both the Abrahamic and Mosaic covenants; Lev. 26:40–45; Deut. 30:1–10), He would free them from captivity and enable them to return to their land. He would also give them victory over Greece. These verses possibly picture the victory of the Maccabees over the Seleucid dynasty in the second century B.C. (Dan. 8:21–25; 11:29–35).

The Good Shepherd (10:1–11:14). Chapter 10 focuses on the blessings that Judah should expect when the Messiah comes. At that time, God would bless His people and punish wicked leaders who had persecuted His people and promoted idolatry. God would also fulfill His promise to "care for his flock." These blessings would come when the Ruler of the tribe of Judah arrives.

Yet the blessings did not materialize. Chapter 11 explains why: The blessings were delayed because the people rejected the Messiah. Zechariah acted out a parable to show how the people refused to follow the Messiah, whom he pictured as a shepherd. Zechariah took two staffs labeled "Favor" (picturing God's blessing) and "Union" (picturing the unity of the Jewish nation) and symbolically "pastured the flock." But the flock detested this shepherd and called for His dismissal. The price at which the shepherd was valued was thirty pieces of silver, which were then thrown into the temple for the potter. Then Zechariah broke the second staff, "Union," symbolizing the disunity that would result between the Jews.

The payment of thirty pieces of silver—and its being cast into the temple for the potter—are graphic symbols of the Messiah's rejection and were literally fulfilled at Jesus' betrayal. Judas received thirty silver coins for betraying Jesus (Matt. 26:14–16). After Jesus' arrest Judas threw the money into the temple, where it was then used to buy a potter's field (27:3–10).

The foolish shepherd (11:15–17). With the good shepherd rejected, Zechariah acted out another prophetic parable. This time he spoke of a "foolish shepherd." This individual—likely the future Antichrist—will abuse and oppress the sheep of Israel. The sword will "strike his arm and his right eye," symbolic of God's making him powerless and foolish, or of physical harm that will come to him (see Rev. 13:3, 12).

When individuals resist God's will for their lives, they often receive exactly what they wanted, only to find out too late that the results bring misery instead of happiness.

B. The Second Burden (chapters 12–14)

Zechariah's second burden focused on events related primarily to the Messiah's second coming, which pictured a threat to Jerusalem from the nations (12:1–9) that will force the people to turn to God (12:10–14). Once the people repent, God will be free to intervene to protect and bless them (chapters 13–14). The very thing God set out to do at the beginning of the first burden will finally be achieved.

In these three chapters Zechariah emphasized the future time element by using the phrase "on that day" fifteen times (12:3–4, 6, 8–9, 11; 13:1–2, 4; 14:4, 6, 8–9, 13, 20).

The nations come to destroy Jerusalem (12:1–9). As the end approaches, God will make Jerusalem a "cup" that will cause nations to reel. Jerusalem also will be a rock on which nations will "injure themselves" as they try to move it. Jerusalem will take center stage as Israel secures its control over the city while other nations try to "attack" it.

> *As the end times approach, Jerusalem will become the focal point of the world's attacks against Israel. This city will take center stage when the curtain rises on God's end-time activities.*

The people repent and turn to God (12:10–13:6). One effect of the sustained pressure put on Jerusalem is that it will force the people of Israel to look on Christ, "the one they have pierced." The people will mourn over their wickedness as they turn from their sin to accept this One whom they had previously rejected. At that time God will cleanse the people of their sin. All idolatry and every false prophet will be removed from the land as God provides for the spiritual cleansing of His people.

The remarkable prophecy about the One Israel pierced (12:10) looks toward a time when Israel will recognize and accept Jesus Christ as its Messiah. In the present age "Israel has experienced a hardening in part until the full number of the Gentiles has come in" (Rom. 11:25). But a time will come when the Jews will realize—and acknowledge—that the Messiah they have long awaited has already come and was "pierced" when He died to pay for their sins (Ps. 22:16; Isa. 53:5). This realization will bring about a national repentance so that "all Israel will be saved" (Rom. 11:26). All this will take place at the second coming of Jesus Christ when "the deliverer will come from Zion" (11:26).

The coming of the Lord to protect and bless Jerusalem (13:7–14:21). Having pictured the repentance of the people, Zechariah then described the events in Jerusalem that will lead up to that repentance. After the true shepherd was struck (probably a reference to Christ's crucifixion; Matt. 26:31), the sheep (Israel) were scattered. Their period of struggle continues now until the end times.

Zechariah again returned to his theme of nations coming to fight against Jerusalem (see 12:2–3). The nations will capture the city; but just when it looks as though final victory is in their grasp, God will oppose them. The climactic moment will occur when the Messiah "will stand on the Mount of Olives." The mountain will split apart to form a "valley" through which the remnant can escape as God and "all the holy ones" (angels) come from heaven to fight against the nations (see Rev. 19:11–21). Zechariah said little about the battle itself, perhaps highlighting the fact that no one can oppose God. Instead, he focused on the results. When God will come to protect and defend His people, "living water" will flow from Jerusalem (see also Ezek. 47:1–12; Joel 3:18) and the Messiah will assume His rightful place as the world Ruler.

After picturing the physical changes that will take place in Jerusalem and the surrounding area (Zech. 14:10–11), Zechariah pictured the specific judgment God will bring on those who will try to attack the holy city (14:12–15). From that time on, those who have survived among the nations will return to Jerusalem yearly to worship the King. The spiritual changes in Jerusalem will be so great that even bells on horses and common cooking pots in the temple will be inscribed with the words "HOLY TO THE LORD," symbolizing God's complete restoration of His people.

God's plans never fail. He will complete what He has set out to do. This is a great message of hope to all who have put their trust in Jesus Christ (Rom. 8:28–31).

MALACHI
God's Messenger

AUTHOR

SOME HAVE QUESTIONED whether the word "Malachi" in Malachi 1:1 should be understood as a personal name or translated from the Hebrew as simply "my messenger" (as in 3:1). While both options are possible, on the whole it seems better to take "Malachi" as a proper name in 1:1. All the other prophetic Old Testament books name their authors, and so one would expect "Malachi" to be understood as a proper name. Nothing else is known about this individual.

DATE

Several pieces of internal evidence help date the book. First, Malachi 1:7–10 and 3:8 indicate that the temple was already rebuilt and that sacrifices were being offered. This would place the book in the postexilic period sometime *after* 516 B.C. Second, in 1:8 the leader of the land was referred to as a "governor," which also points to the postexilic period (see Neh. 5:14; Hag. 1:1). Third, the conditions described by Malachi are similar to those that developed in Judah between Nehemiah's two governorships. For example, both Malachi and Nehemiah had to deal with priestly laxity (Mal. 1:6; Neh. 13:4–9), neglect of tithes (Mal. 3:7–12; Neh. 13:10–13), and intermarriage between Israelites and foreigners (Mal. 2:10–16; Neh. 13:23–28). Therefore a date of 435–430 B.C. is a good estimate for the date of the writing of the Book of Malachi.

BACKGROUND

In 537 B.C. the remnant of Judah returned to the land, and in 516 B.C. they rebuilt the temple under the leadership of Zerubbabel the governor and Joshua the high priest. During the intervening years the remnants' initial attitude of excitement and anticipation gradually gave way to a sense of lethargy and apathy. Both Ezra (458 B.C.) and Nehemiah (444 B.C.) brought temporary renewal when they arrived back in Judah to help the people refocus on God's Law and rebuild Jerusalem's walls. Still, the people kept slipping back into their old patterns of laxness, patterns that had led to their original judgment and deportation a century and a half earlier.

The people needed to be reminded of how far they had slipped from the Lord. They also had to be reminded of God's future plans for His people and of their need to be watchful as they waited for God's promised deliverance. Serving as a bridge between the Old and New Testaments, Malachi exhorted the people to remain faithful to God's past covenant as they looked ahead to future redemption.

ADDRESSEES

Malachi addressed the Jewish remnant that had returned to the land after the Babylonian captivity. While some portions of the book are addressed specifically to the priests (1:6; 2:1), most of Malachi's message was addressed to all of Judah. Malachi recorded a number of rhetorical questions that highlighted the people's sin—and cynicism. These questions serve as the broad outline for his message.

Malachi's Use of Rhetorical Questions to Judah

God rebuked Judah in doubting His love for them (1:2–5).
"'I have loved you,' says the LORD. But you ask, 'How have you loved us?'" (1:2).

God rebuked the priests for their faithlessness (1:6–2:9).
"It is you, O priests, who show contempt for my name. But you ask, 'How have we shown contempt for your name?' You place defiled food on my altar. But you ask, 'How have we defiled you?'" (1:6b–7a).

God rebuked the people for their faithlessness (2:10–16).
"Have we not all one Father? Did not one God create us? Why do we profane the covenant of our fathers by breaking faith with one another?" (2:10).

God rebuked Judah for their lack of trust in His promised justice and redemption (2:17–3:7).
"You have wearied the LORD with your words. 'How have we wearied him?' you ask" (2:17).
"'Return to me, and I will return to you,' says the LORD Almighty. But you ask, 'How are we to return?'" (3:7).

God rebuked Judah for robbing Him of His tithes and offerings (3:8–12).
"Will a man rob God? Yet you rob me. But you ask, 'How do we rob you?'" (3:8).

God rebuked Judah for doubting His promises and discouraging others from remaining faithful (3:13–4:6).
"'You have said harsh things against me,' says the LORD. Yet you ask, 'What have we said against you?'" (3:13).

PURPOSE

Malachi's purpose in writing was to rebuke Judah for her sin and to exhort her to be faithful to the Lord as she awaited God's messenger, who would herald the coming day of the Lord.

OUTLINE

   I. God's Compassion for Israel (1:1–5)
  II. God's Complaint against the Priests (1:6–2:9)
    A. Cheating God (1:6–14)
    B. Violating God's Covenant (2:1–9)
 III. God's Complaint against the People (2:10–3:15)
    A. Mixed Marriages (2:10–12)
    B. Divorce (2:13–16)
    C. Condoning Evil (2:17–3:7)
    D. Robbery (3:8–12)
    E. Arrogance (3:13–18)
  IV. God's Exhortation to Israel (chapter 4)
    A. God's Announcement That His "Day" Is Coming (4:1–3)
    B. God's Promise to Send Elijah (4:4–6)

I. GOD'S COMPASSION FOR ISRAEL (1:1–5)

After a brief introduction, Malachi's word from God was "I have loved you." The people responded by asking, "How have you loved us?" They saw their present, pitiful condition as proof of God's displeasure—not His love. God's response took the nation back to its roots. Though Esau was the oldest of Isaac's twin sons (and should have received the inheritance of the firstborn), God declared that He had "loved" Jacob and "hated" Esau. The words "love" and "hate" picture His selection of Jacob over Esau. (For similar uses of "love" and "hate," see Gen. 29:30–33; Deut. 21:15–17; and Luke 14:26.) God's selection of Jacob and rejection of Esau also guaranteed the ongoing desolation of Edom, whose people descended from Esau. Though Edom boasted of a time when they would rebuild their nation, God said He would "demolish" whatever they built.

God "loved"—and selected—Jacob. He has done the same for believers. "In love he predestined us to be adopted as his sons through Jesus Christ" (Eph. 1:4–5).

II. GOD'S COMPLAINT AGAINST THE PRIESTS (1:6–2:9)

God's second rebuke was directed against the priests because of their lack of faithfulness. They were not honoring and repecting the Lord, and their lack of respect had led to their misuse of God's word.

A. Cheating God (1:6–14)

God asked the priests why they refused to show Him the honor due a father or the respect shown a master. The priests responded, "How have we shown contempt for your name?" God's answer revealed their actions ("You place defiled food on my altar") and their attitude ("saying that the LORD's table is contemptible"). They were offering blind, crippled, and diseased animals as sacrifices to God—even though they would never think of giving such poor offerings to the governor. Any individual who would dare treat the divine King of Israel that way was cursed.

God deserves our best. Are we giving God what He deserves, or are we guilty of offering Him our "leftovers"?

B. Violating God's Covenant (2:1–9)

The underlying sin of the priests was their failure to honor the Lord. So God would send a curse on them. Former priests had honored God, and so they walked with Him "in peace and uprightness" and had taught the people properly. But the priests in Malachi's day ignored their mandate to be faithful teachers of God's word. Instead, they were sharing false teaching that caused Israel to "stumble."

Our true heart attitude toward God is demonstrated by our personal response to His word.

III. GOD'S COMPLAINT AGAINST THE PEOPLE (2:10–3:15)

Here Malachi rebuked Israel for "breaking faith" (2:10–11, 14–16) with the Lord in committing several sins.

A. Mixed Marriages (2:10–12)

Malachi rebuked the people for disregarding the covenant that bound them together as a nation. They shared a common "Father" (God, or possibly Abraham), but they broke the covenant established between God and their ancestors. The specific act Malachi singled out was the desecration of God's temple by idolatry ("marrying the daughter of a foreign god"). Such an individual was to be punished by death.

Mixed Marriages

Mixed marriages were expressly forbidden in the Mosaic Law. Invariably they led to apostasy and ultimately idolatry (Exod. 34:15–16; Deut. 7:1–4).

- The prophet Balaam, who was prohibited from cursing Israel (Num. 22:12), still brought God's judgment on Israel by encouraging the Moabite and Midianite women to entice Israel into idolatry through sexual immorality (Num. 25:1–18). His wicked advice was later called the "teaching of Balaam" (Rev. 2:14).
- After the Conquest, Joshua warned Israel not to intermarry with pagans who remained in the land, because it would ultimately bring God's judgment (Josh. 23:12–13).
- King Solomon "loved many foreign women," and they "turned his heart after other gods," bringing God's judgment on him and his kingdom (1 Kings 11:1–5, 9–12).
- Ezra rebuked the people for intermarrying with their pagan neighbors. He forced them to "send away" the foreign spouses (Ezra 9:1–10:17).

• Twenty-five years after Ezra's reforms Nehemiah reacted violently to news that the remnant were again intermarrying with their pagan neighbors (Neh. 13:23–27).

B. Divorce (2:13–16)

Malachi addressed divorce, a second example of Israel's "broken faith." Weeping before the altar, the people asked why God no longer accepted their offerings. God answered that He was displeased because they had violated the "marriage covenant" with their spouses. Quoting Genesis 2:24, Malachi reminded the people that in marriage the husband and wife are "one." Lest the people miss the point, God stated directly, "I hate divorce." Their callous disregard of the marriage covenant, established by God at creation, was a severe offense.

Malachi 2:10–16 is one unit—though the passage addressed two seemingly unrelated issues (mixed marriages and divorce). However, it is possible that the two issues are closely related. Perhaps the Israelite men were divorcing their Israelite wives to marry pagan women, using such marriages to advance politically, economically, or socially among the powerful local population. Such actions violated their covenant obligations to God and their fellow Israelites.

C. Condoning Evil (2:17–3:7)

Malachi's third rebuke of the people focused on their lack of trust in His promised justice and redemption. They cynically felt that people who sin are acceptable to the Lord. They doubted God's threat to hold people accountable for their actions. Their lack of trust also showed up in their question, "Where is the God of justice?" God said He would send His "messenger" who would "prepare the way" before Him. Unfortunately, when God would come near "for judgment," He would testify against those who committed a number of specific sins (3:5). Likely the people were guilty of many, if not most, of these transgressions. Malachi then exhorted the people to return to the Lord to find forgiveness for their sins.

My Messenger

The words "my messenger" (3:1) translate the Hebrew word *mal'ākî*, which is the name of the author of the book! In a sense, Malachi himself had the potential to fill this role. However, the prophet was probably reminding the people of the promise in Isaiah 40:3–5 that God would send a herald who would "prepare the way for the LORD." The ultimate fulfillment of this messenger was John the Baptist (Matt. 3:1–3; 11:7–11).

D. Robbery (3:8–12)

In his fourth charge against the people Malachi asked, "Will a man rob God?" The answer should have been no, but God added that they were indeed robbing Him by refusing to pay their "tithes and offerings." Borrowing imagery from Leviticus 26 and Deuteronomy 28, God said the people were under a "curse" for their disobedience. He added that they could be blessed if they would obey His commands.

God will honor and bless those who put Him first in their lives.

E. Arrogance (3:13–18)

God's final rebuke began with a statement that the people had said "harsh things" against Him. In response to their demand to know what they had said against God, the Lord quoted them: "It is futile to serve God. What did we gain by carrying out his requirements?" The people had begun questioning God's goodness, and they were starting to call the arrogant, who exalted themselves against God, "blessed." Those still faithful to the Lord decided to prepare a scroll that would record the names of those who feared Him and honored His name.

How to Remain Faithful to God

How can an individual remain faithful to God in a faithless world? Malachi gave three tips for developing a lifestyle of faithfulness.

- Vow to be faithful to God, even if those around you are not. Consider writing your own "scroll of remembrance."
- Surround yourself with a group of likeminded individuals for encouragement. This group "talked with each other" (Mal. 3:16) as they encouraged each other to remain faithful (see Heb. 10:25).
- Remember that God's day of reckoning will come someday. Keep a long-range perspective (1 Cor. 3:12–15).

IV. GOD'S EXHORTATION TO ISRAEL (CHAPTER 4)

Malachi returned to his earlier theme of God's imminent return to His people. He urged the remnant to remember God's Law as they awaited the arrival of "Elijah," who would come before the Day of the Lord.

A. *God's Announcement That His "Day" Is Coming (4:1–3)*

Malachi had already announced God's coming day of judgment (3:2–5) and deliverance (3:17–18). Now in chapter 4 he returned to this theme of the Day of the Lord. (The word "day" is used four times in this chapter: 4:1 [twice], 3, 5.) He first pictured a day that will "burn like a furnace," as God returns to judge the wicked. But for those who know the Lord, the same day will bring deliverance and blessing as His "sun of righteousness" will rise with "healing" for those who are broken. In that day the righteous remnant "will trample down the wicked."

B. *God's Promise to Send Elijah (4:4–6)*

Malachi reminded the people of two individuals. First, they were to obey the law given through Moses. Second, they were to look forward to the arrival of Elijah, who would return before that time of trouble to bring about a national renewal. As the Old Testament fell silent, the last words in the ears of the people were to look back to Moses for stability and guidance and to look ahead to Elijah for hope.

Moses and Elijah, perhaps the greatest of the Old Testament prophets, appeared together with Christ at the Transfiguration (Matt. 17:3). John the Baptist is identified with Elijah (11:11–14), but his ministry also had associations with Moses (John 1:21; see Deut 18:15–18). In the period leading up to the second coming of Christ, two prophets will appear whose ministries will also parallel those of Moses and Elijah (Rev. 11:3–6).

BIBLIOGRAPHY

Genesis

Hamilton, Victor P. *The Book of Genesis*. 2 vols. Grand Rapids: Wm. B. Eerdmans Publishing Co., 1990, 1995.

Kidner, Derek. *Genesis*. Downers Grove, Ill.: InterVarsity Press, 1967.

Leupold, H. C. *Exposition of Genesis*. Grand Rapids: Baker Book House, 1942.

Mathews, Kenneth A. *Genesis 1–11:26*. Nashville: Broadman & Holman Publishers, 1996.

Ross, Allen P. *Creation and Blessing*. Grand Rapids: Baker Book House, 1988.

———. "Genesis." In *The Bible Knowledge Commentary, Old Testament*. Edited by John F. Walvoord and Roy B. Zuck. Wheaton, Ill.: Victor Books, 1985.

Sailhamer, John H. "Genesis." In *The Expositor's Bible Commentary*, vol. 2. Grand Rapids: Zondervan Publishing House, 1990.

Exodus

Archer, Gleason L. *Exodus*. Springfield, Mo.: World Library Press, 1996.

Cassuto, Umberto. *A Commentary on the Book of Exodus*. Jerusalem: Magnes Press, 1967.

Cole, R. A. *Exodus*. Downers Grove, Ill.: InterVarsity Press, 1973.

Kaiser, Walter C. "Exodus." In *The Expositor's Bible Commentary*, vol. 2. Grand Rapids: Zondervan Publishing House, 1990.

Youngblood, Ronald F. *Exodus*. Chicago: Moody Press, 1983.

Leviticus

Harris, R. Laird. "Leviticus." In *The Expositor's Bible Commentary*, vol. 2. Grand Rapids: Zondervan Publishing House, 1990.

Harrison, R. K. *Leviticus*. Downers Grove, Ill.: InterVarsity Press, 1980.

Hartley, John E. *Leviticus*. Dallas: Word Books, 1992.

Lindsey, F. Duane. "Leviticus." In *The Bible Knowledge Commentary, Old Testament*. Edited by John F. Walvoord and Roy B. Zuck. Wheaton, Ill.: Victor Books, 1985.

Wenham, Gordon J. *The Book of Leviticus*. Grand Rapids: Wm. B. Eerdmans Publishing Co., 1979.

Numbers

Allen, Ronald B. "Numbers." In *The Expositor's Bible Commentary*, vol. 2. Grand Rapids: Zondervan Publishing House, 1990.

Ashley, Timothy R. *The Book of Numbers*. Grand Rapids: Wm. B. Eerdmans Publishing Co., 1993.

Harrison, R. K. *Numbers*. Chicago: Moody Press, 1990.

Merrill, Eugene H. "Numbers." In *The Bible Knowledge Commentary, Old*

Testament. Edited by John F. Walvoord and Roy B. Zuck. Wheaton, Ill.: Victor Books, 1985.

Noordtzij, A. *Numbers.* Grand Rapids: Zondervan Publishing House, 1983.

Wenham, Gordon J. *Numbers.* Downers Grove, Ill.: InterVarsity Press, 1981.

Deuteronomy

Craigie, Peter C. *The Book of Deuteronomy.* Grand Rapids: Wm. B. Eerdmans Publishing Co., 1976.

Kalland, Earl S. "Deuteronomy." In *The Expositor's Bible Commentary*, vol. 3. Grand Rapids: Zondervan Publishing House, 1992.

Merrill, Eugene H. *Deuteronomy.* Nashville: Broadman & Holman Publishers, 1994.

Ridderbos, J. *Deuteronomy.* Grand Rapids: Zondervan Publishing House, 1984.

Schultz, Samuel J. *Deuteronomy: The Gospel of Love.* Chicago: Moody Press, 1971.

Thompson, J. A. *Deuteronomy.* Downers Grove, Ill.: InterVarsity Press, 1974.

Joshua

Butler, Trent C. *Joshua.* Waco, Tex.: Word Books, 1983.

Hess, Richard S. *Joshua.* Downers Grove, Ill.: InterVarsity Press, 1996.

Howard, David M. Jr. *Joshua.* New American Commentary. Nashville: Broadman & Holman Publishers, 1998.

Madvig, Donald H. "Joshua." In *The Expositor's Bible Commentary*, vol. 3. Grand Rapids: Zondervan Publishing House, 1992.

Woudstra, Marten H. *The Book of Joshua.* Grand Rapids: Wm. B. Eerdmans Publishing Co., 1981.

Judges

Block, Daniel I. *Judges, Ruth.* Nashville: Broadman & Holman Publishers, 1999.

Cundall, Arthur E., and Leon Morris. *Judges, Ruth.* Downers Grove, Ill.: InterVarsity Press, 1968.

Davis, John J. *Conquest and Crisis: Studies in Joshua, Judges, and Ruth.* Grand Rapids: Baker Book House, 1969.

Wolf, Herbert. "Judges." In *The Expositor's Bible Commentary*, vol. 3. Grand Rapids: Zondervan Publishing House, 1992.

Wood, Leon J. *Distressing Days of the Judges.* Grand Rapids: Zondervan Publishing House, 1975.

Ruth

Campbell, Edward F. Jr. *Ruth.* Garden City, N.Y.: Doubleday & Co., 1975.

Cundall, Arthur E., and Leon Morris. *Judges, Ruth.* Downers Grove, Ill.: InterVarsity Press, 1968.

Hubbard, Robert L. *The Book of Ruth.* Grand Rapids: Wm. B. Eerdmans Publishing Co., 1988.

Huey, F. B. Jr. "Ruth." In *The Expositor's Bible Commentary*, vol. 3. Grand Rapids: Zondervan Publishing House, 1992.

1 and 2 Samuel

Anderson, A. A. *2 Samuel.* Dallas: Word Books, 1989.

Baldwin, Joyce G. *1 & 2 Samuel.* Downers Grove, Ill.: InterVarsity Press, 1988.

Bergen, Robert D. *1, 2 Samuel.* Nashville: Broadman & Holman Publishers, 1996.

Gordon, Robert P. *I and II Samuel: A Commentary*. Grand Rapids: Zondervan Publishing House, 1986.

Klein, Ralph W. *1 Samuel*. Waco, Tex.: Word Books, 1983.

Youngblood, Ronald F. "1, 2 Samuel." In *The Expositor's Bible Commentary*, vol. 3. Grand Rapids: Zondervan Publishing House, 1992.

1 and 2 Kings

DeVries, Simon J. *1 Kings*. Waco, Tex.: Word Books, 1985.

Hobbs, T. R. *2 Kings*. Waco, Tex.: Word Books, 1985.

House, Paul R. *1, 2 Kings*. Nashville: Broadman & Holman Publishers, 1995.

Patterson, Richard D., and Hermann J. Austel. "1, 2 Kings." In *The Expositor's Bible Commentary*, vol. 4. Grand Rapids: Zondervan Publishing House, 1988.

Wiseman, Donald J. *1 & 2 Kings*. Downers Grove, Ill.: InterVarsity Press, 1993.

1 and 2 Chronicles

Braun, Roddy. *1 Chronicles*. Waco, Tex.: Word Books, 1986.

Dillard, Raymond B. *2 Chronicles*. Downers Grove, Ill.: InterVarsity Press, 1994.

Merrill, Eugene H. *1, 2 Chronicles*. Grand Rapids: Zondervan Publishing House, 1988.

Payne, J. Barton. "1, 2 Chronicles." In *The Expositor's Bible Commentary*, vol. 4. Grand Rapids: Zondervan Publishing House, 1988.

Selman, Martin J. *1 Chronicles*. Downers Grove, Ill.: InterVarsity Press, 1994.

————. *2 Chronicles*. Downers Grove, Ill.: InterVarsity Press, 1994.

Thompson, J. A. *1, 2 Chronicles*. Nashville: Broadman & Holman Publishers, 1994.

Ezra and Nehemiah

Breneman, Mervin. *Ezra, Nehemiah, Esther*. Nashville: Broadman & Holman Publishers, 1993.

Fensham, F. Charles. *The Books of Ezra and Nehemiah*. Grand Rapids: Wm. B. Eerdmans Publishing Co., 1982.

Kidner, Derek. *Ezra and Nehemiah*. Downers Grove, Ill.: InterVarsity Press, 1979.

Williamson, H. G. M. *Ezra, Nehemiah*. Waco, Tex.: Word Books, 1985.

Yamauchi, Edwin M. "Ezra–Nehemiah." In *The Expositor's Bible Commentary*, vol. 4. Grand Rapids: Zondervan Publishing House, 1988.

Esther

Baldwin, Joyce. *Esther*. Downers Grove, Ill.: InterVarsity Press, 1984.

Breneman, Mervin. *Ezra, Nehemiah, Esther*. Nashville: Broadman & Holman Publishers, 1993.

Bush, Frederic W. *Ruth, Esther*. Dallas: Word Publishing, 1996.

Huey, F. B. Jr. "Esther." In *The Expositor's Bible Commentary*, vol. 4. Grand Rapids: Zondervan Publishing House, 1988.

Job

Alden, Robert. L. *Job*. Nashville: Broadman & Holman Publishers, 1994.

Andersen, Francis I. *Job*. Downers Grove, Ill.: InterVarsity Press, 1976.

Clines, David J. A. *Job 1–20*. Dallas: Word Publishing, 1989.

———. *Job 21–42*. Dallas: Word Publishing, 1998.

Hartley, John E. *The Book of Job*. Grand Rapids: Wm. B. Eerdmans Publishing Co., 1988.

Smick, Elmer B. "Job." In *The Expositor's Bible Commentary*, vol. 4. Grand Rapids; Zondervan Publishing House, 1988.

Zuck, Roy B. "Job." In *The Bible Knowledge Commentary, Old Testament*. Edited by John F. Walvoord and Roy B. Zuck. Wheaton, Ill.: Victor Books, 1985.

———. *Job*. Everyman's Bible Commentary. Chicago: Moody Press, 1978.

———, ed. *Sitting with Job*. Grand Rapids: Baker Book House, 1992.

Psalms

Allen, Leslie C. *Psalms 101–150*. Waco, Tex.: Word Books, 1983.

Craigie, Peter C. *Psalms 1–50*. Waco, Tex.: Word Books, 1983.

Kidner, Derek. *Psalms*. 2 vols. Downers Grove, Ill.: InterVarsity Press, 1973.

Leupold, H. C. *Exposition of Psalms*. Grand Rapids: Baker Book House, 1952.

Ross, Allen P. "Psalms." In *The Bible Knowledge Commentary, Old Testament*. Edited by John F. Walvoord and Roy B. Zuck. Wheaton, Ill.: Victor Books, 1985.

Sabourin, Leopold. *The Psalms: Their Origin and Meaning*. New York: Alba House, 1974.

Tate, Marvin E. *Psalms 51–100*. Dallas: Word Publishing, 1990.

VanGemeren, Willem A. "Psalms." In *The Expositor's Bible Commentary*, vol. 5. Grand Rapids: Zondervan, 1991.

Proverbs

Alden, Robert L. *Proverbs: A Commentary on an Ancient Book of Timeless Advice*. Grand Rapids: Baker Book House, 1984.

Buzzell, Sid S. "Proverbs." In *The Bible Knowledge Commentary, Old Testament*. Edited by John F. Walvoord and Roy B. Zuck. Wheaton, Ill.: Victor Books, 1985.

Garrett, Duane A. *Proverbs, Ecclesiastes, Song of Songs*. Nashville: Broadman & Holman Publishers, 1993.

Kidner, Derek. *Proverbs*. Downers Grove, Ill.: InterVarsity Press, 1964.

Ross, Allen P. "Proverbs." In *The Expositor's Bible Commentary*, vol. 5. Grand Rapids: Zondervan Publishing House, 1991.

Zuck, Roy B., ed. *Learning from the Sages*. Grand Rapids: Baker Book House, 1995.

Ecclesiastes

Eaton, Michael A. *Ecclesiastes*. Downers Grove, Ill.: InterVarsity Press, 1964.

Garrett, Duane A. *Proverbs, Ecclesiastes, Song of Songs* Nashville: Broadman & Holman Publishers, 1993.

Glenn, Donald R. "Ecclesiastes." In *The Bible Knowledge Commentary, Old Testament*. Edited by John F. Walvoord and Roy B. Zuck. Wheaton, Ill.: Victor Books, 1985.

Longman, Tremper III. *The Book of Ecclesiastes*. Grand Rapids: Wm. B. Eerdmans Publishing Co., 1997.

Murphy, Roland E. *Ecclesiastes*. Dallas: Word Books, 1992.

Wright, J. Stafford. "Ecclesiastes." In *The Expositor's Bible Commentary*, vol. 5. Grand Rapids: Zondervan Publishing House, 1991.

Zuck, Roy B., ed. *Reflecting with Solomon*. Grand Rapids: Baker Book House, 1994.

Song of Solomon

Carr, G. Lloyd. *The Song of Solomon*. Downers Grove, Ill.: InterVarsity Press, 1984.

Deere, Jack S. "Song of Songs." In *The Bible Knowledge Commentary, Old Testament*. Edited by John F. Walvoord and Roy B. Zuck. Wheaton, Ill.: Victor Books, 1985.

Garrett, Duane A. *Proverbs, Ecclesiastes, Song of Songs*. Nashville: Broadman & Holman Publishers, 1993.

Glickman, S. Craig. *A Song for Lovers*. Downers Grove, Ill.: InterVarsity Press, 1976.

Kinlaw, Dennis F. "Song of Songs." In *The Expositor's Bible Commentary*, vol. 5. Grand Rapids: Zondervan Publishing House, 1991.

Prophetic Books

Bullock, C. Hassell. *An Introduction to the Old Testament Prophetic Books*. Chicago: Moody Press, 1986.

Chisholm, Robert B. *Interpreting the Minor Prophets*. Grand Rapids: Zondervan Publishing House, 1990.

Freeman, Hobart E. *An Introduction to the Old Testament Prophets*. Chicago: Moody Press, 1968.

McComisky, Thomas E. *The Minor Prophets: An Exegetical and Expository Commentary*. 3 vols. Grand Rapids: Baker Book House, 1992, 1993, 1998.

Wood, Leon J. *The Prophets of Israel*. Grand Rapids: Baker Book House, 1979.

Young, Edward J. *My Servants the Prophets*. Grand Rapids: Wm. B. Eerdmans Publishing Co., 1952.

Isaiah

Alexander, Joseph Addison. *Commentary on the Prophecies of Isaiah.* Reprint, Grand Rapids: Zondervan Publishing House, 1953.

Bultema, Harry. *Commentary on Isaiah.* Translated by Cornelius Lambregtse. Grand Rapids: Kregel Publications, 1981.

Garland, D. David. *Isaiah.* Grand Rapids: Zondervan Publishing House, 1968.

Lindsey, F. Duane. *The Servant Songs.* Chicago: Moody Press, 1985.

Martin, Alfred, and John Martin. *Isaiah: The Glory of the Messiah.* Chicago: Moody Press, 1983.

Motyer, J. A. *The Prophecy of Isaiah.* Downers Grove, Ill.: InterVarsity Press, 1993.

Oswalt, John N. *The Book of Isaiah, Chapters 1–39.* Grand Rapids: Wm. B. Eerdmans Publishing Co., 1987.

_____. *The Book of Isaiah, Chapters 40–66.* Grand Rapids: Wm. B. Eerdmans Publishing Co., 1998.

Young, Edward J. *The Book of Isaiah.* Grand Rapids: Wm. B. Eerdmans Publishing Co., 1965.

Jeremiah

Bright, John. *Jeremiah.* Garden City, N.Y.: Doubleday & Co., 1965.

Dyer, Charles H. "Jeremiah." In *The Bible Knowledge Commentary, Old Testament.* Edited by John F. Walvoord and Roy B. Zuck. Wheaton, Ill.: Victor Books, 1985.

Feinberg, Charles L. *Jeremiah: A Commentary.* Grand Rapids: Zondervan Publishing House, 1982.

Harrison, R. K. *Jeremiah and Lamentations.* Downers Grove, Ill.: InterVarsity Press, 1973.

Huey, F. B., Jr. *Jeremiah, Lamentations*. Nashville: Broadman Press, 1993.

Jensen, Irving L. *Jeremiah and Lamentations*. Chicago: Moody Press, 1966.

Morgan, G. Campbell. *Studies in the Prophecy of Jeremiah*. Westwood, N.J.: Fleming H. Revell Co., 1955.

Thompson, J. A. *The Book of Jeremiah*. Grand Rapids: Wm. B. Eerdmans Publishing Co., 1980.

Von Orelli, C. *The Prophecies of Jeremiah*. Translated by J. S. Banks. Reprint, Minneapolis: Klock & Klock Christian Publishers, 1977.

Lamentations

Dyer, Charles H. "Lamentations." In *The Bible Knowledge Commentary, Old Testament*. Edited by John F. Walvoord and Roy B. Zuck. Wheaton, Ill.: Victor Books, 1985.

Gottwald, N. K. *Studies in the Book of Lamentations*. London: SCM Press, 1962.

Harrison, R. K. *Jeremiah and Lamentations*. Downers Grove, Ill.: InterVarsity Press, 1973.

Hillers, D. R. *Lamentations*. Garden City, N.Y.: Doubleday & Co, 1973.

Huey, F. B., Jr. *Jeremiah, Lamentations*. Nashville: Broadman Press, 1993.

Jensen, Irving L. *Jeremiah and Lamentations*. Chicago: Moody Press, 1966.

Kaiser, Walter C., Jr. *A Biblical Approach to Personal Suffering*. Chicago: Moody Press, 1982.

Swindoll, Charles R. *Bible Study Guide: The Lamentations of Jeremiah*. Anaheim, Calif: Insight for Living, 1977.

Ezekiel

Alexander, Ralph. *Ezekiel*. Chicago: Moody Press, 1976.

Allen, Leslie C. *Ezekiel 1–19*. Dallas: Word Books, 1994.

———. *Ezekiel 20–48*. Dallas: Word Books, 1994.

Block, Daniel I. *The Book of Ezekiel*. 2 vols. Grand Rapids: Wm. B. Eerdmans Publishing Co., 1997, 1998.

Cooper, Lamar Eugene. *Ezekiel*. Nashville: Broadman Press, 1994.

Dyer, Charles H. "Ezekiel." In *The Bible Knowledge Commentary, Old Testament*. Edited by John F. Walvoord and Roy B. Zuck. Wheaton, Ill.: Victor Books, 1985.

Fairbairn, Patrick. *An Exposition of Ezekiel*. Reprint, Minneapolis: Klock & Klock Christian Publishers, 1979.

Feinberg, Charles Lee. *The Prophecy of Ezekiel: The Glory of the Lord*. Chicago: Moody Press, 1969.

Taylor, John B. *Ezekiel: An Introduction and Commentary*. Downers Grove, Ill.: InterVarsity Press, 1969.

Zimmerli, Walther. *Ezekiel*. 2 vols. Philadelphia: Fortress Press, 1979, 1983.

Daniel

Anderson, Robert A. *Daniel: Signs and Wonders*. Grand Rapids: Wm. B. Eerdmans Publishing Co., 1984.

Baldwin, Joyce G. *Daniel: An Introduction and Commentary*. Downers Grove, Ill.: InterVarsity Press, 1978.

Lang, G. H. *The Histories and Prophecies of Daniel*. Reprint, Grand Rapids: Kregel Publications, 1973.

McDowell, Josh. *Daniel in the Critics' Den*. San Bernardino, Calif.: Campus Crusade for Christ, 1979.

Pentecost, J. Dwight. "Daniel." in *The Bible Knowledge Commentary, Old Testament*. Edited by John F. Walvoord and Roy B. Zuck. Wheaton, Ill.: Victor Books, 1985.

Price, Walter K. *In the Final Days.* Chicago: Moody Press, 1977.

Walvoord, John F. *Daniel: The Key to Prophetic Revelation.* Chicago: Moody Press, 1971.

Whitcomb, John C. *Darius the Mede.* Phillipsburg, N.J.: Presbyterian and Reformed Publishing Co., 1959.

Wood, Leon J. *A Commentary on Daniel.* Grand Rapids: Zondervan Publishing House, 1973.

Hosea

Andersen, Francis I., and David N. Freedman. *Hosea.* Garden City, N.Y.: Doubleday & Co., 1980.

Chisholm, Robert B., Jr. "Hosea." In *The Bible Knowledge Commentary, Old Testament.* Edited by John F. Walvoord and Roy B. Zuck. Wheaton, Ill.: Victor Books, 1985.

Cohen, Gary G., and H. Ronald Vandermey. *Hosea/Amos.* Chicago: Moody Press, 1981.

Garrett, Duane A. *Hosea, Joel.* Nashville: Broadman & Holman Publishers, 1997.

Mays, James Luther. *Hosea: A Commentary.* Philadelphia: Westminster Press, 1969.

Riggs, Jack R. *Hosea's Heartbreak.* Neptune, N.J.: Loizeaux Brothers, 1983.

Joel

Allen, Leslie C. *The Books of Joel, Obadiah, Jonah, and Micah.* Grand Rapids: Wm. B. Eerdmans Publishing Co., 1976.

Finley, Thomas J. *Joel, Amos, Obadiah.* Chicago: Moody Press, 1990.

Garrett, Duane A. *Hosea, Joel.* Nashville: Broadman & Holman Publishers, 1997.

Hubbard, David Allan. *Joel and Amos*. Downers Grove, Ill.: InterVarsity Press, 1989.

Price, Walter K. *The Prophet Joel and the Day of the Lord*. Chicago: Moody Press, 1976.

Wolff, Hans Walter. *Joel and Amos*. Philadelphia: Fortress Press, 1977.

Amos

Cohen, Gary G., and H. Ronald Vandermey. *Hosea/Amos*. Chicago: Moody Press, 1981.

Coote, Robert B. *Amos among the Prophets: Composition and Theology*. Philadelphia: Fortress Press, 1981.

Finley, Thomas J. *Joel, Amos, Obadiah*. Chicago: Moody Press, 1990.

Garland, D. David. *Amos*. Grand Rapids: Zondervan Publishing House, 1966.

Hubbard, David Allan. *Joel and Amos*. Downers Grove, Ill.: InterVarsity Press, 1989.

Martin-Achard, Robert, and S. Paul Re'emi. *Amos and Lamentations: God's People in Crisis*. Grand Rapids: Wm. B. Eerdmans Publishing Co., 1984.

Mays, James Luther. *Amos: A Commentary*. Philadelphia: Westminster Press, 1969.

Smith, Bailey K., and Frank S. Page. *Amos, Obadiah, Jonah*. Nashville: Broadman Press, 1995.

Wolff, Hans Walter. *Joel and Amos*. Philadelphia: Fortress Press, 1977.

Obadiah

Allen, Leslie C. *The Books of Joel, Obadiah, Jonah, and Micah*. Grand Rapids: Wm. B. Eerdmans Publishing Co., 1976.

Finley, Thomas J. *Joel, Amos, Obadiah*. Chicago: Moody Press, 1990.

Gaebelein, Frank E. *Four Minor Prophets (Obadiah, Jonah, Habakkuk, and Haggai)*. Grand Rapids: Baker Book House, 1968.

Marbury, Edward. *Obadiah and Habakkuk*. Reprint, Minneapolis: Klock and Klock Christian Publishers, 1979.

Smith, Bailey K., and Frank S. Page. *Amos, Obadiah, Jonah*. Nashville: Broadman Press, 1995.

Watts, J. D. *Obadiah: A Critical and Exegetical Commentary*. Grand Rapids: Wm. B. Eerdmans Publishing Co., 1967.

Wolff, Hans Walter. *Obadiah and Jonah: A Commentary*. Translated by Margaret Kohl. Minneapolis: Augsburg Publishing House, 1986.

Jonah

Allen, Leslie C. *The Books of Joel, Obadiah, Jonah, and Micah*. Grand Rapids: Wm. B. Eerdmans Publishing Co., 1976.

Fairbairn, Patrick. *Jonah: His Life, Character, and Mission*. Reprint, Grand Rapids: Kregel Publications, 1964.

Gaebelein, Frank E. *Four Minor Prophets (Obadiah, Jonah, Habakkuk, and Haggai)*. Grand Rapids: Baker Book House, 1968.

Smith, Bailey K., and Frank S. Page. *Amos, Obadiah, Jonah*. Nashville: Broadman Press, 1995.

Wolff, Hans Walter. *Obadiah and Jonah: A Commentary*. Translated by Margaret Kohl. Minneapolis: Augsburg Publishing House, 1986.

Micah

Allen, Leslie C. *The Books of Joel, Obadiah, Jonah, and Micah*. Grand Rapids: Wm. B. Eerdmans Publishing Co., 1976.

Barker, Kenneth L., and Waylon Bailey. *Micah, Nahum, Habakkuk, Zephaniah*. Nashville: Broadman & Holman Publishers, 1998.

Bennett, T. Miles. *The Book of Micah*. Grand Rapids: Baker Book House, 1968.

Copass, B. A., and E. L. Carlson. *A Study of the Prophet Micah*. Grand Rapids: Baker Book House, 1950.

Mays, James Luther. *Micah: A Commentary.* Philadelphia: Westminster Press, 1976.

Smith, Ralph L. *Micah–Malachi*. Waco, Tex.: Word Books, 1984.

Wolff, Hans Walter. *Micah the Prophet*. Translated by Ralph D. Gehrke. Philadelphia: Fortress Press, 1981.

Nahum

Barker, Kenneth L., and Waylon Bailey. *Micah, Nahum, Habakkuk, Zephaniah*. Nashville: Broadman & Holman Publishers, 1998.

Bennett, T. Miles. *The Book of Nahum and Zephaniah*. Grand Rapids: Baker Book House, 1968.

Freeman, Hobart E. *Nahum, Zephaniah, Habakkuk: Minor Prophets of the Seventh Century B.C.* Chicago: Moody Press, 1973.

Maier, Walter A. *The Book of Nahum*. Reprint, Grand Rapids: Baker Book House, 1980.

Robertson, O. Palmer. *The Books of Nahum, Habakkuk, and Zephaniah*. Grand Rapids: Wm. B. Eerdmans Publishing Co., 1990.

Smith, Ralph L. *Micah–Malachi*. Word Biblical Commentary. Waco, Tex.: Word Books, 1984.

Habakkuk

Armerding, Carl E. "Habakkuk." In *The Expositor's Bible Commentary*, vol. 7. Grand Rapids: Zondervan Publishing House, 1985.

Barker, Kenneth L., and Waylon Bailey. *Micah, Nahum, Habakkuk, Zephaniah*. Nashville: Broadman & Holman Publishers, 1998.

Freeman, Hobart E. *Nahum, Zephaniah, Habakkuk: Minor Prophets of the Seventh Century B.C.* Chicago: Moody Press, 1973.

Gaebelein, Frank E. *Four Minor Prophets (Obadiah, Jonah, Habakkuk, and Haggai)*. Grand Rapids: Baker Book House, 1968.

Lloyd-Jones, David Martin. *From Fear to Faith*. Downers Grove, Ill.: InterVarsity Press, 1970.

Marbury, Edward. *Obadiah and Habakkuk*. Reprint, Minneapolis: Klock and Klock Christian Publishers, 1979.

Robertson, O. Palmer. *The Books of Nahum, Habakkuk, and Zephaniah*. Grand Rapids: Wm. B. Eerdmans Publishing Co., 1990.

Smith, Ralph L. *Micah–Malachi*. Word Biblical Commentary. Waco, Tex.: Word Books, 1984.

Zephaniah

Barker, Kenneth L., and Waylon Bailey. *Micah, Nahum, Habakkuk, and Zephaniah*. Nashville: Broadman & Holman Publishers, 1998.

Freeman, Hobart E. *Nahum, Zephaniah, Habakkuk: Minor Prophets of the Seventh Century B.C.* Chicago: Moody Press, 1973.

Kleinert, Paul. *The Book of Zephaniah*. Translated by Charles Elliott. Grand Rapids: Zondervan Publishing House, 1960.

Robertson, O. Palmer. *The Books of Nahum, Habakkuk, and Zephaniah*. Grand Rapids: Wm. B. Eerdmans Publishing Co., 1990.

Smith, Ralph L. *Micah–Malachi*. Waco, Tex: Word Books, 1984.

Haggai

Baldwin, Joyce G. *Haggai, Zechariah, Malachi: An Introduction and Commentary*. Downers Grove, Ill: InterVarsity Press, 1972.

Gaebelein, Frank E. *Four Minor Prophets (Obadiah, Jonah, Habakkuk, and Haggai)*. Grand Rapids: Baker Book House, 1968.

Merrill, Eugene H. *Haggai, Zechariah, Malachi*. Chicago: Moody Press, 1994.

Moore, T. V. *A Commentary on Haggai and Malachi*. London: Banner of Truth Trust, 1960.

Smith, Ralph L. *Micah–Malachi*. Waco, Tex.: Word Books, 1984.

Wolff, Richard. *The Book of Haggai*. Grand Rapids: Baker Book House, 1967.

Zechariah

Baldwin, Joyce G. *Haggai, Zechariah, Malachi: An Introduction and Commentary*. Downers Grove, Ill.: InterVarsity Press, 1972.

Baron, David. *The Visions and Prophecies of Zechariah*. London: Marshall, Morgan & Scott, 1919.

Feinberg, Charles L. *God Remembers: A Study of the Book of Zechariah*. Portland, Oreg.: Multnomah Press, 1965.

Merrill, Eugene H. *Haggai, Zechariah, Malachi*. Chicago: Moody Press, 1994.

Smith, Ralph L. *Micah–Malachi*. Word Biblical Commentary. Waco, Tex.: Word Books, 1984.

Unger, Merrill F. *Zechariah: Prophet of Messiah's Glory* Grand Rapids: Zondervan Publishing House, 1963.

Malachi

Alden, Robert L. "Malachi." In *The Expositor's Bible Commentary*, vol. 7. Grand Rapids: Zondervan Publishing House, 1985.

Baldwin, Joyce G. *Haggai, Zechariah, Malachi: An Introduction and Commentary*. Downers Grove, Ill.: InterVarsity Press, 1972.

Kaiser, Walter C., Jr. *Malachi: God's Unchanging Love*. Grand Rapids: Baker Book House, 1984.

Merrill, Eugene H. *Haggai, Zechariah, Malachi*. Chicago: Moody Press, 1994.

Smith, Ralph L. *Micah–Malachi*. Waco, Tex.: Word Books, 1984.

Verhoef, Pieter A. *The Books of Haggai and Malachi*. Grand Rapids: Wm. B. Eerdmans Publishing Co., 1987.

The
Swindoll Leadership Library

ANGELS, SATAN AND DEMONS
Dr. Robert Lightner

The supernatural world gets a lot of attention these days in books, movies, and television series, but what does the Bible say about these other-worldly beings? Dr. Robert Lightner answers these questions with an in-depth look at the world of the "invisible" as expressed in Scripture.

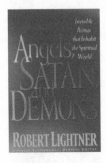

BIBLICAL COUNSELING FOR TODAY
Dr. Jeffrey Watson

Written by veteran counselor Dr. Jeffrey Watson, this handbook explores counseling from a biblical perspective—how to use Scripture to help others work through issues, choose healthy goals, and work toward those goals for a healthier, more spiritually grounded life. In *Biblical Counseling for Today,* both professional and lay counselors will find insightful, relevant answers to strengthen their ministries.

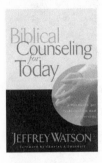

THE CHURCH
Dr. Ed Hayes

In this indispensable guide, Dr. Ed Hayes explores the labyrinths of the church, delving into her history, doctrines, rituals, and resources to find out what it means to be the Body of Christ on earth. Both passionate and precise, this essential volume offers solid insights on worship, persecution, missions, and morality: a bold call to unity and renewal.

COACHING MINISTRY TEAMS
Dr. Kenn Gangel

When it comes to effective discipleship, it takes a discipler, a coach, who is capable of not only leading by example, but also empowering his "players" to stay the course. In fifteen practical chapters, Christian education expert Kenn Gangel examines, among other topics, the attitudes in "The Heart of a Champion," leadership modeling in "Setting the Standard for the Team," and strategic planning in "Looking Down the Field."

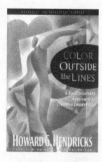

COLOR OUTSIDE THE LINES
Dr. Howard G. Hendricks

Just as the apostle Paul prodded early Christians "not to be conformed" to the world, Dr. Howard Hendricks vividly—and unexpectedly—extends that biblical theme and charges us to learn the art of living creatively, reflecting the image of the Creator rather than the culture.

EFFECTIVE CHURCH GROWTH STRATEGIES
Dr. Joseph Wall and Dr. Gene Getz

Effective Church Growth Strategies outlines the biblical foundations necessary for raising healthy churches. Wall and Getz examine the groundwork essential for church growth, qualities of biblically healthy churches, methods for planting a new church, and steps for numerical and spiritual growth. The authors' study of Scripture, history, and culture will spark a new vision for today's church leaders.

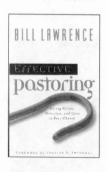

EFFECTIVE PASTORING
Dr. Bill Lawrence

In *Effective Pastoring,* Dr. Bill Lawrence examines what it means to be a pastor in the 21st century. Lawrence discusses often overlooked issues, writing transparently about the struggles of the pastor, the purpose and practice of servant leadership, and the roles and relationships crucial to pastoring. In doing so, he offers a revealing look beneath the "how to" to the "how to be" for pastors.

EMPOWERED LEADERS
Dr. Hans Finzel

What is leadership really about? The rewards, excitement, and exhilaration? Or the responsibilities, frustrations, and exhausting nights? Dr. Hans Finzel takes readers on a journey into the lives of the Bible's great leaders, unearthing powerful principles for effective leadership in any situation.

END TIMES
Dr. John F. Walvoord

Long regarded as one of the top prophecy experts, Dr. John F. Walvoord now explores world events in light of biblical prophecy. By examining all of the prophetic passages in the Bible, Walvoord clearly explains the mystery behind confusing verses and conflicting viewpoints. This is the definitive work on prophecy for Bible students.

THE FORGOTTEN BLESSING
Dr. Henry Holloman

For many Christians, the gift of God's grace is central to their faith. But another gift—sanctification—is often overlooked. *The Forgotten Blessing* clarifies this essential doctrine, showing us what it means to be set apart, and how the process of sanctification can forever change our relationship with God.

GOD
Dr. J. Carl Laney

With tenacity and clarity, Dr. J. Carl Laney makes it plain: it's not enough to know *about* God. We can know *God* better. This book presents a practical path to life-changing encounters with the goodness, greatness, and glory of our Creator.

THE HOLY SPIRIT
Dr. Robert Gromacki

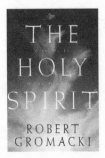

In *The Holy Spirit*, Dr. Robert Gromacki examines the personality, deity, symbols, and gifts of the Holy Spirit, while recapping the ministry of the Spirit throughout the Old Testament, the Gospel Era, the life of Christ, the Book of Acts, and the lives of believers.

HUMANITY AND SIN
Dr. Robert A. Pyne

Sin may seem like an outdated concept these days, but its consequences remain as destructive as ever. Dr. Robert A. Pyne takes a close look at humankind through the pages of Scripture and the lens of modern culture. As never before, readers will understand sin's overarching effect on creation and our world today.

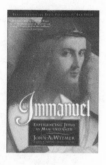

IMMANUEL
Dr. John A. Witmer

Dr. John A. Witmer presents the almighty Son of God as a living, breathing, incarnate man. He shows us a full picture of the Christ in four distinct phases: the Son of God before He became man, the divine suffering man on Earth, the glorified and ascended Christ, and the reigning King today.

A LIFE OF PRAYER
Dr. Paul Cedar

Dr. Paul Cedar explores prayer through three primary concepts, showing us how to consider, cultivate, and continue a lifestyle of prayer. This volume helps readers recognize the unlimited potential and the awesome purpose of prayer.

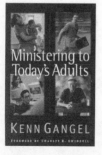

MINISTERING TO TODAY'S ADULTS
Dr. Kenn Gangel

After 40 years of research and experience, Dr. Kenn Gangel knows what it takes to reach adults. In an easy-to-grasp, easy-to-apply style, Gangel offers proven systematic strategies for building dynamic adult ministries.

Moral Dilemmas
J. Kerby Anderson

Should biblically informed Christians be for or against capital punishment? How should we as Christians view abortion, euthanasia, genetic engineering, divorce, and technology? In this comprehensive, cutting-edge book, J. Kerby Anderson challenges us to thoughtfully analyze the dividing issues facing our age, while equipping believers to maneuver through the ethical and moral land mines of our times.

The New Testament Explorer
Mark Bailey and Tom Constable

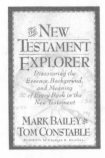

The New Testament Explorer provides a concise, on-target map for traveling through the New Testament. Mark Bailey and Tom Constable guide the reader paragraph by paragraph through the New Testament, providing an up-close-and-to-the-point examination of the leaders behind the page and the theological implications of the truths revealed. A great tool for teachers and pastors alike, this exploration tool comes equipped with outlines for further study, narrative discussion, and applicable truths for teaching and for living.

Salvation
Earl D. Radmacher

God's ultimate gift to His children is salvation. In this volume, Earl Radmacher offers an in-depth look at the most fundamental element of the Christian faith. From defining the essentials of salvation to explaining the result of Christ's sacrifice, this book walks readers through the spiritual meaning, motives, application, and eternal result of God's work of salvation in our lives.

Spirit-Filled Teaching
Dr. Roy B. Zuck

Whether you teach a small Sunday school class or a standing-room-only crowd at a major university, the process of teaching can be demanding and draining. This lively book brings a new understanding of the Holy Spirit's essential role in teaching.

TALE OF THE TARDY OXCART AND 1501 OTHER STORIES
Dr. Charles R. Swindoll

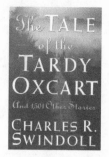

In this rich volume, you'll have access to resourcing Dr. Charles Swindoll's favorite anecdotes on prayer or quotations for grief. In *The Tale of the Tardy Oxcart*, thousands of illustrations are arranged by subjects alphabetically for quick-and-easy access. A perfect resource for all pastors and speakers.

THE THEOLOGICAL WORDBOOK
Campbell, Johnston, Walvoord, Witmer

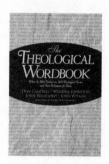

Compiled by four of today's best theological minds, *The Theological Wordbook* is a valuable, accessible reference guide to the most important theological terms. Definitions, scriptural references, engaging explanations—all in one easy-to-find, applicable resource—for both the lay person and serious Bible student.

WOMEN AND THE CHURCH
Dr. Lucy Mabery–Foster

Women and the Church provides an overview of the historical, biblical, and cultural perspectives on the unique roles and gifts women bring to the church, while exploring what it takes to minister to women today. Important insight for any leader seeking to understand how to more effectively minister to women and build women's ministries in the local church.